Tides from the West
A Chinese Autobiography

西　潮

蒋梦麟 著

外语教学与研究出版社
FOREIGN LANGUAGE TEACHING AND RESEARCH PRESS
北京 BEIJING

图书在版编目(CIP)数据

西潮 = Tides from the West: A Chinese Autobiography: 英汉对照/ 蒋梦麟著. — 北京:外语教学与研究出版社,2012.7
ISBN 978-7-5135-2265-6

Ⅰ.①西… Ⅱ.①蒋… Ⅲ.①蒋梦麟(1886~1964)—回忆录—英、汉 Ⅳ.①K825.46

中国版本图书馆 CIP 数据核字(2012)第 168212 号

出 版 人:蔡剑峰
系列策划:吴 浩
责任编辑:易 璐 刘 佳
装帧设计:视觉共振设计工作室
出版发行:外语教学与研究出版社
社 址:北京市西三环北路 19 号(100089)
网 址:http://www.fltrp.com
印 刷:中国农业出版社印刷厂
开 本:650×980 1/16
印 张:33.5
版 次:2012 年 11 月第 1 版 2012 年 11 月第 1 次印刷
书 号:ISBN 978-7-5135-2265-6
定 价:72.00 元
* * *
购书咨询:(010)88819929 电子邮箱:club@fltrp.com
如有印刷、装订质量问题,请与出版社联系
联系电话:(010)61207896 电子邮箱:zhijian@fltrp.com
制售盗版必究 举报查实奖励
版权保护办公室举报电话:(010)88817519
物料号:222650001

"博雅双语名家名作"出版说明

　　1840 年鸦片战争以降，在深重的民族危机面前，中华民族精英"放眼看世界"，向世界寻求古老中国走向现代、走向世界的灵丹妙药，涌现出一大批中国主题的经典著述。我们今天阅读这些中文著述的时候，仍然深为字里行间所蕴藏的缜密的考据、深刻的学理、世界的视野和济世的情怀所感动，但往往会忽略：这些著述最初是用英文写就，我们耳熟能详的中文文本是原初英文文本的译本，这些英文作品在海外学术界和文化界同样享有崇高的声誉。

　　比如，林语堂的 *My Country and My People*（《吾国与吾民》）以幽默风趣的笔调和睿智流畅的语言，将中国人的道德精神、生活情趣和中国社会文化的方方面面娓娓道来，在美国引起巨大反响——林语堂也以其中国主题系列作品赢得世界文坛的尊重，并获得诺贝尔文学奖的提名。再比如，梁思成在抗战的烽火中写就的英文版《图像中国建筑史》文稿（*A Pictorial History of Chinese Architecture*），经其挚友费慰梅女士（Wilma C. Fairbank）等人多年的奔走和努力，于 1984 年由麻省理工学院出版社（MIT Press）出版，并获得美国出版联合会颁发的"专业暨学术书籍金奖"。又比如，1939 年，费孝通在伦敦政治经济学院的博士论文以 *Peasant Life in China—A Field Study of Country Life in the Yangtze Valley* 为名在英国劳特利奇书局（Routledge）出版，后以《江村经济》作为中译本书名——《江村经济》使得靠桑蚕为生的"开弦弓村"获得了世界性的声誉，成为国际社会学界研究中国农村的首选之地。

　　此外，一些中国主题的经典人文社科作品经海外汉学家和中国学者的如椽译笔，在英语世界也深受读者喜爱。比如，艾恺（Guy S. Alitto）将他 1980 年用中文访问梁漱溟的《这个世界会好吗——梁漱溟晚年口述》一书译成英文（*Has Man a Future? —Dialogues with the Last Confucian*），备受海内外读者关注；

此类作品还有徐中约英译的梁启超著作《清代学术概论》(*Intellectual Trends in the Ch'ing Period*)、狄百瑞(W. T. de Bary)英译的黄宗羲著作《明夷待访录》(*Waiting for the Dawn: A Plan for the Prince*),等等。

有鉴于此,外语教学与研究出版社推出"博雅双语名家名作"系列。

博雅,乃是该系列的出版立意。博雅教育(Liberal Education)早在古希腊时代就得以提倡,旨在培养具有广博知识和优雅气质的人,提高人文素质,培养健康人格,中国儒家六艺"礼、乐、射、御、书、数"亦有此功用。

双语,乃是该系列的出版形式。英汉双语对照的形式,既同时满足了英语学习者和汉语学习者通过阅读中国主题博雅读物提高英语和汉语能力的需求,又以中英双语思维、构架和写作的形式予后世学人以启迪——维特根斯坦有云:"语言的边界,乃是世界的边界",诚哉斯言。

名家,乃是该系列的作者群体。涵盖文学、史学、哲学、政治学、经济学、考古学、人类学、建筑学等领域,皆海内外名家一时之选。

名作,乃是该系列的入选标准。系列中的各部作品都是经过时间的积淀、市场的检验和读者的鉴别而呈现的经典,正如卡尔维诺对"经典"的定义:经典并非你正在读的书,而是你正在重读的书。

胡适在《新思潮的意义》(1919 年 12 月 1 日,《新青年》第 7 卷第 1 号)一文中提出了"研究问题、输入学理、整理国故、再造文明"的范式。秉着"记载人类文明、沟通世界文化"的出版理念,我们推出"博雅双语名家名作"系列,既希望能够在中国人创作的和以中国为主题的博雅英文文献领域"整理国故",亦希望在和平发展、改革开放的新时代为"再造文明"、为"向世界说明中国"略尽绵薄之力。

外语教学与研究出版社

人文社科出版分社

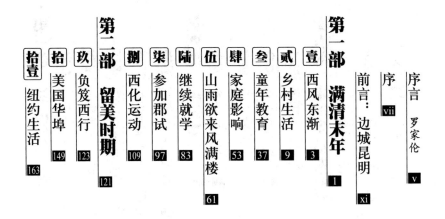

序　言

　　这是一本充满了智慧的书。这里面所包含的晶莹智慧，不只是从学问的研究得来，更是从生活的体验得来。

　　读这本书好像是泛舟在时间的洪流之中，一重一重世间的层峦叠嶂、激湍奔涛，都在我们民族和个人的生命中经过。而且这段时间乃是历史上一个极不平凡时代的新序幕，举凡人类中各个集团的冲突，乃至东西文化的磨荡，都集中在这风云际会。

　　时代的转变愈快，被人们忽略的史实愈多。若当时的人不予以记载，则后起的人更无从知道，无从了解。这种忽略和遗忘都是人类很大的损失，因为在不断的历史的过程中间，以往的经验，正是后来的教训。

　　了解这种意义，才能认识蒋梦麟先生这本书所蕴藏的价值。他生长在这极不平凡时代已经过了七十年了。他从中国学究的私塾到西洋自由的学府，从古老的农村社会到近代的都市文明，从身经满清专制的皇朝到接受革命思想的洗礼，他多年生活在广大的外国人群里面，更不断生活在广大中国人群尤其是知识青年群众里面。他置身于中西文化思想交流的漩涡，同时也看遍了覆雨翻云、沧海桑田的世局。经过了七十华年，正是他智慧结晶的时候，到此时而写他富有哲学内涵和人生风趣的回忆，其所反映的决不是他的一生，而是他一生所经历的时代。

　　《西潮》这本书里面每一片段都含有对于社会和人生的透视。古人所谓"小中见大"正可于此中求之。其将东西文化相提并论之处，尤其可以发人深省。著者好举平凡的故事，间杂以微妙而不伤人的讽刺，真使我们感到一股敦厚淳朴的风味。这种风味在当今是不容易尝到的了。至于其中的妙语妙喻，不断的流露，正像珍珠泉的泉水，有如粒粒的明珠，连串的喷了上来。

　　这本书最难达到的境界，就是著者讲这个极不平凡时代的事实，而以极平易近人的口吻写出来，这正像孟邻先生做人处世的态度。若不是具备高度文化的修养，真是望尘莫及的。我何敢序孟邻先生的大著，只能引王荆公两句诗以形容他的写作和生平。诗云：

　　"看似平常最奇绝，成如容易却艰难。"

罗家伦

1959 年 12 月 6 日

PREFACE

This volume will try to tell the story of what has happened in China during the last hundred years, from the cession of Hongkong in 1842[1] to the blitzkrieg of Pearl Harbor in 1941, with emphasis on the latter half of that period. A century is a long time, but of China's more than four thousand years of history it is but a small fraction, less than one fortieth. Yet the change China has gone through in that brief span is unprecedented in her long life. And now more rapid changes on a still larger scale are about to take place.

Since the first exchange of gunfire at Marco Polo Bridge the attention of the world has been drawn to China. The heroic resistance at Shanghai, Taierchuan, and Changsha has evoked sympathy and admiration in the hearts of millions of China's friends throughout the world. The part China is destined to play in the affairs of nations will be of great interest to the world in the period before us. She has been appraised somewhat too high by her well-wishers and somewhat too low by those who do not know her. In either case the interest is there and the fact remains that she has fought almost singlehanded, for eight long, suffering years, a strong enemy sustained by religious-patriotic fanaticism, superior weapons, and efficient organization.

Neither by her friends nor by her own efforts could China be lifted overnight to the level of modern industrialized democracies; nor could she be exterminated by her enemies in a few years or even a few centuries. In the time ahead of us she will become a focus of attention for the world, since future peace—at least one of the major factors of peace—will depend much on a prosperous and strong China.

How is this great country to be made prosperous and strong? The problem must be solved by herself alone. Effective co-operation of friendly Powers will accelerate her success, but she alone must bear the responsibility of making herself worthy to be a leading partner of peace in the world.

China is a nation neither of angels nor of incompetents; she is a nation of common mortals with feelings, ideas, love and hate, hopes and despair, beauty and ugliness, accomplishments and failings, virtues and vices. It is hoped that the world will not expect from her people more than it does from other ordinary human beings. She has no panacea for all her troubles, nor any magic box by aid of which she can transform herself at will into what she desires to be. Whatever success she has achieved has been paid for with sweat in time of peace and with blood in time of war.

序

《西潮》里所谈的是中国过去一百年间所发生的故事，从一八四二年香港割让起到一九四一年珍珠港事变止，尤其着重后五十年间的事。一个世纪是相当长的一段时间，但是在四千多年的中国历史里，却只是短暂的一个片段，几乎不到四十分之一。不过中国在这段短短的时间内所经历的变迁，在她悠久的生命史上却是空前的，而且更大规模的变化还正在酝酿中。

自从芦沟桥的枪声划破长空，中国的局势已经引起全世界人士的注意。国军在淞沪、台儿庄以及长沙的英勇战绩，已经赢得全球中国友人的同情与钦敬。在未来的岁月中，中国势将在国际舞台上担任众所瞩目的角色。这些年来，爱护中国的人士未免把她估计得太高，不了解中国的人士则又把她估计得太低。无论估计过高或过低，对中国的关切是一致的；而她几乎孤立无援地苦战八年之久，也是无可否认的事实。在这漫长痛苦的八年中，她与具有优越的武器、严密的组织以及宗教的爱国狂热的强敌相周旋，愈战愈奋，始终不屈。

不论是本身的努力，或者友邦的援助，都不能使中国在旦夕之间达到现代工业化民主国家的水准；但是她的敌人也不可能在几年之内，甚至几百年之内，灭亡她。在未来的岁月中，中国将是举世人士注意力的焦点，因为未来的和平与中国之能否臻于富强是息息相关的。

中国怎样才能臻于富强呢？这个问题必须由她自己单独来解决。友邦的密切合作固然可以加速她的成功，但是她必须独立担负起使自己成为世界和平支柱的责任。

中国既不是一个天神般万能的国家，也不是一个低能的毫无作为的国家。她是一群有感情、有思想的凡人结合而成的国家。他们有爱、有恨；有美、有丑；有善、有恶；有成就、有失败；有时充满希望，有时陷于绝望。他们只是一群平平常常的人，世界人士不能对他们有分外的要求和期望。中国没有解决一切困难的万应灵丹，也没有随心所欲脱胎换骨的魔术。如果她已经有所成就的话，那也是平时以汗，战时以血换来的。

To the question "What is the trouble with China?" the author can only answer that there are a number of troubles waiting for solution in that vast country of teeming millions, more than she will be able to solve in any limited span of time. Some were created by enemies who tried to conquer her, others by herself during the time of metamorphosis; still others have been imposed on her by force of circumstance or as legacies of the past. Some of the more difficult problems have been solved or partially solved during recent years before the war; many others remain to be dealt with in due course of time.

Looking back over the last fifty years which he has personally experienced—over the past hundred years with which he is familiar, and even farther, down the long reaches of China's history which he has been taught—the author has traced to the best of his knowledge the threads of a number of problems, some lying deep in her past, others arising from the rapid changes which caught her unprepared. He has tried to tell, within the limits of discretion, what has happened in China, especially during the last fifty years. For those friends who desire to co-operate with her, with a view to solving some of the difficult problems of a more enduring peace, this moderate volume may be helpful in giving an insight into the life and problems of the Chinese people. For co-operation cannot possibly proceed without mutual understanding. To understand what is actually the background—the mental, emotional, and moral constitution—of the country, is essential for a lasting co-operation.

With the above ideas in mind the author has described ordinary happenings in some detail so as to acquaint the reader in some measure of intimacy with the mental, emotional, and moral make-up of the Chinese people as revealed through their life in peace and war. As small things often reflect major developments in a country, it is hoped that some sense of the meaning of greater events may be gathered from these apparent trifles of daily life.

CHIANG MONLIN

如果有人问："中国的问题究竟在哪里？"作者只能答复：中国正有无数的问题等待四亿五千万人民去解决，而且不是任何短时间内所能解决。有些问题是企图征服她的敌人造成的，有些则是蜕变过程中她本身所制造的；另有一些问题是客观环境引起的，也有一些问题则是历史的包袱，有一些比较困难的问题已经在战前几年内解决，或者局部解决，更有许多问题则尚待分别缓急，逐一解决。

回顾作者身经目睹的过去五十年，以及作者所熟悉的过去一百年，甚至追溯到作者所研习过的中国的悠久历史，作者已经就其所知探求出若干问题的线索，有些问题深深植根于过去，有些则由急剧的变化所引起。作者已经力求平直客观地陈述中国过去所发生的变迁，尤其是过去五十年内所发生的事情。对于愿意与中国合作，共同解决妨碍持久和平的若干问题的国际友人，本书或可提供一点资料，帮助他们了解中国人民的生活与问题。合作是勉强不来的，必须彼此相互了解，然后才能合作。欲谋持久的合作，必须先对一国的真实背景有所了解，包括心理、情感，以及道德等各方面。

因此，作者对于日常琐事也往往不厌其详地加以描写，希望藉此使读者对中国人民在战时与平时所反映的心理、情感和道德等，能有比较亲切的认识，日常琐事往往可以反映一个国家的重大变迁，希望读者多少能从作者所记述的身边琐事中，发现重大史实的意义。

蒋梦麟

1943 年于重庆

PROLOGUE: FRONTIER CITY

During a world upheaval with bombs dropping from the sky and bursting all around, one is apt to wonder what caused these terrible things to happen.

What has happened in the world in the last decade is not something that merely dropped from the sky. Events have their causes. In the last years of the war, as I cast my mental view beyond the horizons of Kunming, where most of this volume was written, I saw how one event had led to another, with consequent social and political changes. Musing over the past in that scenic city on the Burma[1] Road overlooking tranquil, historic Kunming Lake, with bomb-shattered houses standing around me like the remnants of Pompeii, the scenes of what had happened during my lifetime unfolded themselves like a dream clearly and vividly before me; and I set pen to paper to put down what I had seen with my own eyes during the last half century of rapid change in the life of my country.

As I began to write we were in the midst of heavy munitions traffic coming in by truck from Burma. The fighting planes of the American Volunteer Group known as the "Flying Tigers" droned over our heads. War profiteers and truck drivers roamed the streets by hundreds and thousands with their pockets full of bank notes, while the price of commodities soared sky-high.

A British friend remarked to a professor of our university that we ought to have controlled prices at the beginning of the war. "Well," said the professor with a tinge of humor, "we will know better in the next war." He went on to remark that if he had had the capital he might have followed the example of the Greek philosopher who cornered olives in ancient Greece in anticipation of a poor olive crop. When the crop failed, he was rich. But the professor had no capital and too little of that sort of foresight, and in addition, too much of patriotism in his way.

After Pearl Harbor came waves of bad news of the Allies. Hongkong, the Malay States, and Singapore fell one after the other. The enemy headed for Burma. China rushed troops there; they retreated, after a stubborn resistance, through the mountains and swamps of Upper Burma, living on banana roots. They were greatly annoyed by the leeches that dropped on their heads from trees, suckers that hooked onto you and

前言：边城昆明

炸弹像冰雹一样从天空掉下，在我们周围爆炸，处身在这样的一次世界大动乱中，我们不禁要问：这些可怕的事情究竟为什么会发生呢？

过去几十年内世界上所发生的事情自然不是从天上掉下来的。任何事情有它的起因。本书的大部分是二次大战将结束时在昆明写的，当我们暂时忘掉现实环境而陷入沉思时，我常常发现一件事情如何导致另一件事情，以及相伴而生的政治、社会变化。昆明是滇缅公路的终点，俯瞰着平静的昆明湖，城中到处是敌机轰炸后的断垣残壁，很像庞贝古城的遗迹。我在这边城里冥想过去的一切，生平所经历的事情像梦境一样一幕一幕地展现在眼前；于是我捡出纸笔，记下了过去半世纪中我亲眼目睹的祖国生活中的急剧变化。

当我开始写《西潮》的故事时，载运军火的卡车正从缅甸源源驶抵昆明，以"飞虎队"闻名于世的美国志愿航空队战斗机在我们头上轧轧掠过。发国难财的商人和以"带黄鱼"起家的卡车司机倘徉街头，口袋里装满了钞票。物价则一日三跳，有如脱缰的野马。

一位英国朋友对西南联大的一位教授说，我们应该在战事初起就好好控制物价。这位教授带点幽默地回答说："是呀！等下一次战争时，我们大概就不会这样笨了。"这位教授说：如果他有资本，他或许早已学一位古希腊哲学家的榜样了。据说那位希腊哲学家预料橄榄将欠收而囤积了一大批橄榄。后来橄榄果然收成不好，这位哲学家也就发了大财。可惜我们的教授没有资本，也没有那种未卜先知的本领，而且他的爱国心也不容许他干损人利己的勾当。

珍珠港事变以后，同盟国家节节失利。香港、马来联邦和新加坡相继陷落，敌军继续向缅甸推进。中国赶派军队驰援印缅战区，经激战后撤至缅北的丛林泽地，有时还不得不靠香蕉树根充饥。尤其使他们寝食难安的是从树上落到他们身上的水蛭，这些吸血鬼钻到

drank your blood. If you tried to tear one off, it carried away in its mouth a piece of your flesh. The best way of getting rid of these nasty parasites was to rub salt on them, but salt there was none. The next best way, in the circumstances, was to slap at them until they gave you up.

Chinese nationals in Burma left by tens of thousands, and made their way back to China by the Burma Road. Enemy planes bombed and machine-gunned them. Three thousand people, men and women, young and old, died on the way. A torrent of refugees flowed along the road into Kunming. Streets were crowded with thousands of distressed people and public buildings were set aside for their temporary lodging. After two or three months they gradually melted into the neighboring provinces; many went back to their native provinces of Fukien and Kwangtung.

The Burma Road, built in eight months by the hands of some eighty thousand farmers, men, women, and children, was now cut at the other end and rendered useless. Kunming, once on the high-way of international traffic, was now an isolated city, and only by air could one travel to India. The Yunnan-Burma Railway, under construction by 250,000 men, was to be finished within twelve months; it was partially built, then suspended. China was cut off from the world, with the enemy on three sides and only the faintest trickle of supplies remaining. In this isolation she held out, fighting for her national existence every inch of the way, until the end of the war.

Let us forget recent history for the moment and look back to the past to see what we can learn from it.

你的皮下，不动声色地吸走了你的血液。你如果想用力把它拉出来，它就老实不客气连肉带血衔走一口。对付这些吸血鬼最好的办法是在它们身上擦盐，但是在丛林里却又找不到盐。在这种环境下，唯一的办法是用手死劲去拍，拍得它们放口为止。

成千成万的缅甸华侨沿着滇缅公路撤退回中国。敌机沿途轰炸他们，用机枪扫射他们，三千妇孺老幼就这样惨死在途中。难民像潮水一样沿滇缅公路涌入昆明。街头拥满了家破人亡的苦难人民，许多公共建筑被指定为临时收容所。经过两三个月以后，他们才逐渐疏散到邻近省份；许多人则直接回到福建和广东老家。

八万左右农民以及男女老幼胼手胝足建筑成功的滇缅公路现在已经因另一端被切断而告瘫痪。一度曾为国际交通孔道的昆明现在也成为孤城，旅客只有坐飞机才能去印度。二十五万人加工赶筑的滇缅铁路，原来预定十二个月内完成，但是部分筑成以后也因战局逆转而中止了。中国已与世界各地隔绝，敌人从三方包围着她，只有涓涓滴滴的外来补给靠越世界驼峰的空运在维持。中国就在这种孤立无援的窘境中坚持到底，寸土必争，直到战事结束为止。

我们且把近代历史暂时搁在一边，让我们回顾一下过去，看看能否从历史中找出一点教训。

（原载《传记文学》第十七卷第六期）

PART ONE

第一部　满清末年

IN AN OLD EMPIRE

CHAPTER 1   HOW EAST AND WEST MET

Centuries ago certain wise men from the East, following a star, traveled to the land where a religion was born destined in centuries to come to play a great part in the life of Western nations. A religion based upon meekness was adopted in the course of time by these peoples of extreme vigor. This religion of meekness, which teaches "whosoever shall smite thee on the right cheek, turn to him the other also," won its way through the West slowly but persistently by braving Roman lions and enduring hardships, suffering, and persecution. A few centuries later it began to trickle into China with the same meekness.

The Nestorians came to China during the Tang Dynasty (618-905 A.D.)[1], and the Tang emperors built churches for them. But they did not find China a fertile soil for their religion. Another few centuries passed; the Jesuits found their way into the court of the Ming Dynasty (1368-1643 A.D.)[2]. They brought with them Western astronomy, which caught the fancy of the Ming emperors.

The Western peoples, meanwhile, with vigorous blood in their veins, not only absorbed the new religion but also created science and made inventions which led to an industrial revolution in recent centuries. As a result they amassed an immense amount of capital, which had to find an outlet in other countries not as yet industrialized. It flowed to the East, first in a trickle, then in torrents, and finally in tides which flooded the Orient and almost swept China off her feet.

China had no trouble with Christianity, nor with any other religion. Only when it was coupled with commercialism supported by gunboats in the middle of the nineteenth century was the religion of meekness seen through Chinese eyes as that of an aggressor. For a religion seen arm in arm with force changes its color, and the Chinese were unable to dissociate the two. This naturally gave rise to the impression that while Buddha came to China on white elephants, Christ was borne on cannon balls.

Since we were knocked out by cannon balls, naturally we became interested in them, thinking that by learning to make them we could strike back. We could forget for the time being in whose name they had come, since for us common mortals to save our lives was more important than to save our souls.

壹 西风东渐

差不多两千年以前，几位东方的智者，循着天空一颗巨星的指示，追寻到一个新宗教的诞生地。这个宗教便是基督教。基督教后来在西方国家的生活中占着极其重要的地位。基督教以和平仁爱为宗旨，要求教徒们遇到"有人掌掴你的右颊时，你就把左颊也凑过去"。基督教的教徒经过不断的磨难和挫折，不顾罗马猛狮的威胁和异教徒的摧残迫害，逆来顺受，终于在罗马帝国各民族之间传播开来了。几百年之后，它以同样坚忍的精神慢慢地流传到中国。

景教徒在唐朝（公元六一八——九〇五）时来到中国，唐室君主曾为他们建造了景教寺，但是景教徒的传教成绩却很有限，再过了几百年，在十七世纪中叶，耶稣会教士带着西方的天文学来到中国，终于得到明朝（公元一三六八——一六四三）皇帝的垂青。

在这同时，活力旺盛的西方民族，不但接受了新兴的基督教，而且发展了科学，完成了许许多多的发明，为近代的工业革命奠立了基础。科学和发明渐渐流传到东方，先是涓涓滴滴地流注，接着汇为川流江涛，最后成为排山倒海的狂潮巨浪，泛滥整个东方，而且几乎把中国冲塌了。

中国人与基督教或任何其他宗教一向没有什么纠纷，不过到了十九世纪中叶，基督教与以兵舰做靠山的商业行为结了伙，因而在中国人的心目中，这个宣扬爱人如己的宗教也就成为侵略者的工具了。人们发现一种宗教与武力形影不离时，对这种宗教的印象自然就不同了。而且中国人也实在无法不把基督教和武力胁迫相提并论。慢慢地人们产生了一种印象，认为如来佛是骑着白象到中国的，耶稣基督却是骑在炮弹上飞过来的。

我们吃过炮弹的苦头，因而也就对炮弹发生兴趣。一旦我们学会制造炮弹，报仇雪耻的机会就来了。我们可以暂时不管这些炮弹是怎么来，因为对我们这些凡夫俗子而言，保全性命究竟比拯救灵魂来得重要。

But history seems to move through very curious ways. From studying cannon balls we came to mechanical inventions, which in turn led us to political reforms; from political reforms we began to see political theories, which led us again to the philosophies of the West. On the other hand, through mechanical inventions we saw science, from which we came to understand scientific method and the scientific mind. Step by step we were led farther and farther away from the cannon ball—yet we came nearer and nearer to it.

The story is a long one, but it all happened in the short span of a hundred years, the dramatic part of it in not more than half a century. I say a hundred years because in 1942 Hongkong was to celebrate its centenary as a British possession,[3] and it was a coincidence that Japan, Britain's former ally, had snatched it from British hands in the previous year by lightning attack. I mention Hongkong without the least intention of rubbing an old sore, only because it will serve as a convenient landmark for the earlier part of China's westernization. As everyone will remember, this group of hilly islands—situated in the south sea not far from Canton, and nests for pirates a century ago—was ceded to Britain in 1842 at China's defeat in the so-called "Opium War." What actually happened was that China, having forbidden the importation of opium, Britain's principal export from India to that country, burned British opium at Canton. Britain retaliated with cannon balls and China lost the war.

Torrents of Western manufactures began to pour in through the subsequent opening, also stipulated under the treaty, of five coastal cities as commercial ports. These cities lay scattered at fairly regular intervals along the coast of the prosperous southern half of the country. Thus new frontiers were formed; China's frontiers had lain hitherto solely inland, to the north and northwest. This change in China's map was the turning point in her history.

These five seaports—Canton, Amoy[4], Foochow, Ningpo, and Shanghai—running from south to north in a chain, served as depots for Western manufactured goods which flowed thence into the richest and most populous parts of the country, the Pearl and Yangtze Valleys. Supported by gunboats the Western merchants squatted like octopuses in the ports, sending their tentacles into the interior of the rich provinces. China, an enormous country larger than the United States, was herself unaware of the penetration and blind to what was bound to happen

　　历史的发展真是离奇莫测。我们从研究炮弹而研究到机械发明；机械发明而导致政治改革；由于政治改革的需要，我们开始研究政治理论；政治理论又使我们再度接触西方的哲学。在另一方面，我们从机械发明而发现科学，由科学进而了解科学方法和科学思想。一步一步地我们离炮弹越来越远了，但是从另一角度来看，也可以说离炮弹越来越近了。

　　故事说来很长，但是都是在短短一百年之内发生的，而且紧张热烈的部分还不过五十年的样子。我说一百年，因为香港本来可以在一九四二年"庆祝"香港成为"英国领土"的一百周年纪念，但是这也是历史上偶然的一件事，英国的旧盟邦日本却在前一年以闪击方式把香港抢走了。我提到香港，决不是有意挖旧疮疤，而是因为香港在中国欧化的早期历史上，恰恰是现成的纪念碑。大家都知道，香港这群小岛是中国在所谓"鸦片战争"中失败以后在一八四二年割让给英国的。这次战争的起因是中国继禁止鸦片进口之后，又在广州焚毁大批鸦片。鸦片是英国由印度输出的主要货物，于是英国就以炮弹回敬中国，中国被击败了。

　　一八四二年的中英条约同时规定中国的五个沿海城市开放为商埠。这就是所谓"五口通商"。大批西方商品随着潮涌而至。这五个商埠以差不多相似的距离散布在比较繁盛的中国南半部，为中国造成了与外来势力接触的新边疆。过去中国只有北方和西北那样的内陆边疆，现在中国的地图起了变化，这转变正是中国历史的转折点。

　　这五个商埠——广州、厦门、福州、宁波和上海——由南向北互相衔接，成为西方货物的集散地，舶来品由这五个口岸转销中国最富的珠江流域和长江流域各地。

　　西方商人在兵舰支持之下像章鱼一样盘踞着这些口岸，同时把触须伸展到内地的富庶省份。中国本身对于这些渗透并不自觉，对于

later on. The life of her millions went its leisurely and contented way from the cradle to the grave without making the least effort toward modernization, while a section of the people began casually to pick up foreign manufactures, whether for use, for pleasure, or out of curiosity.

The gunboat policy of the Western Powers, however, carried with it not only manufactured goods and opium but also the healthy seeds of Western science and culture, which we did not see at the time but which were to germinate years later to the benefit of China—one of the ironies of history.

Meanwhile the westernization of Japan went on by leaps and bounds. Again, China was unaware of it. Half a century later, by 1894, the little Island Empire suddenly loomed large over the horizon of the China Sea, sprang a surprise attack upon the sleeping giant, and bit off a mouthful. The next to go after Hongkong was Formosa[5], an island province near the east coast hundreds of times larger than Hongkong. China now began to feel the pinch and rub her eyes in wonder. What was it that was disturbing her sweet dreams?

My original plan was just to write out what I know and feel about my own country. As I have let these mental pictures run their course, one after another, they have developed into a volume something like autobiography, something like reminiscences or contemporary history. Whatever it may be, it is all from the indelible images that unrolled in my mind as clearly and vividly as if they had been printed there only yesterday. In the rapid march of events I felt myself a tiny cog on the vast whirling wheel.

必然产生的后果更茫无所知。亿万人民依旧悠然自得地过着日子，像过去一样过他们从摇篮到坟墓的生活，从没有想到在现代化的工作上下工夫。一部分人则毫不经心地开始采用外国货，有的是为了实用，有的为了享受，另一些人则纯然为了好奇。

但是，西方列强的兵舰政策不但带来了货品和鸦片，同时也带来了西方科学文化的种子。这在当时是看不出来的，但是后来这些种子终于发芽滋长，使中国厚蒙其利——这也是历史上的一大讽刺。

这时候，日本也正以一日千里之势向欧化的途程迈进，中国对此却毫无所觉。半世纪以后，这个蕞尔岛国突然在东海里摇身一变，形成了一个硕大的怪物，并且在一八九四年出其不意地咬了东亚睡狮一大口。中国继香港之后又丢了台湾。这只东亚睡狮这时可真有点感到疼痛了，茫茫然揉着惺忪的睡眼，不知道究竟是什么扰了它的清梦？

我原先的计划只是想写下我对祖国的所见所感，但是当我让这些心目中的景象一一展布在纸上时，我所写下的可就有点像自传，有点像回忆录，也有点像近代史。不管它像什么，它记录了我心目中不可磨灭的景象，这些景象历历如绘地浮现在我的脑际，一如隔昨才发生的经历。在急遽递嬗的历史中，我自觉只是时代巨轮上一颗小轮齿而已。

CHAPTER 2   VILLAGE LIFE

I came into the world as the youngest of five children, four boys and a girl, in a well-to-do family in a small village. The night before I was born my father dreamed of a bear coming to our house, the sign of a male baby. The next day the good omen came true: the spirits of our forefathers in heaven presented another son to the family.

Before my eldest brother was born, Father had dreamed of receiving a bouquet of orchids. So the child was named Orchid. My second brother was named Peach for the same reason. Naturally I was called Bear. As for my sister and third brother, Father had no dreams. My name was afterward changed from Bear to Unicorn when I registered at Chekiang College, because of events in the schools.

I was born a war baby, for the year in which I came into the world saw Britain cut off Burma from Chinese control; and the Sino-French War had just ended the previous year, by which China lost her suzerainty over Indo-China[1] to France. The peeling of dependencies off China was a prelude to further invasion by foreign Powers. For China kept dependencies to serve as buffer states, not for exploitation. She never interfered with their internal administration.

When the peel was gone, germs began to make inroads into the orange. However, people in China were not aware of it. These wars on the southwest frontiers were far away and mere ripples on her vast ocean. The villagers were the least concerned—in their profound isolation they gave less attention to such news than they would to ghost stories. Yet China drew a part of her defense forces from among just such villages, not interested in war.

When I came to know the little world around me I noticed that people spoke more realistically of the Taiping Rebellion, which had destroyed a part of the village some thirty years before. The chief of the elders of the Chiang clan, a carpenter by trade, had once joined the rebels. He told us many stories of pillage and atrocities committed by the Taipings,[2] of which he himself had been guilty. To listen to these horrors often made a chill run all over my body. Yet of the international wars of recent years people talked only casually, utterly unconcerned.

贰 乡村生活

我出生在一个小村庄里的小康之家。兄弟姊妹五人，我是最小的一个，三位哥哥，一位姊姊。我出生的前夕，我父亲梦到一只熊到家里来，据说那是生男孩的征兆。第二天，这个吉兆应验了，托庇祖先在天之灵，我们家又添了一个儿子。

我大哥出生时，父亲曾经梦到收到一束兰花，因此我大哥就取名梦兰。我二哥也以同样的原因取名为梦桃。不用说，我自然取名为梦熊了。姊姊和三哥诞生时，父亲却没有梦到什么。后来在我进浙江高等学堂时，为了先前的学校里闹了事，梦熊这个名字入了黑名单，于是就改为梦麟了。

我出生在战乱频仍的时代里。我出生的那一年，英国从中国拿走了对缅甸的宗主权；出生的前一年恰恰是中法战争结束的一年，中国对越南的宗主权就在那一年让渡给法国。中国把宗主权一再割让，正是外国列强进一步侵略中国本土的序幕，因为中国之保有属国，完全是拿它们当缓冲地带，而不是为了剥削他们。中国从来不干涉这些边缘国家的内政。

这情形很像一只桔子，桔皮被剥去以后，微生物就开始往桔子内部侵蚀了。但是中国百姓却懵然不觉，西南边疆的战争隔得太远了，它们不过是浩瀚的海洋上的一阵泡沫。乡村里的人更毫不关心，他们一向与外界隔绝，谈狐说鬼的故事比这些军国大事更能引起他们的兴趣。但是中国的国防军力的一部分却就是从这些对战争不感兴趣的乡村征募而来的。

我慢慢懂得一些人情世故之后，我注意到村里的人讲起太平天国革命的故事时，却比谈当前国家大事起劲多了。我们乡间呼太平军为长毛，因为他们蓄发不剃头。凡听到有变乱的事，一概称之为长毛造反。大约在我出生的三十年前，我们村庄的一角曾经被太平军破坏。一位木匠出身的蒋氏族长就参加过太平军。人们说他当过长毛的，他自己也直认不讳。他告诉我们许多太平军掳掠杀戮煮吃人肉的故事，许多还是他自己亲身参加的。我看他的双目发出一种怪光，我父亲说，这是因为吃了人肉的缘故。我听了这些恐怖的故事，常常为之毛骨悚然。这位族长说，太平军里每天要做祷告感谢天父天兄（上帝和耶稣）。有一天做祷告以后，想要讨好一位老长毛，就说了几句"天父夹天兄，长毛夺咸丰"一套吉利话。老长毛点头

There were fabulous stories of victory—simply amusing, in a sense tragic, as one thinks of them in after years. For the fact was that while Chinese troops made a good showing in some engagements, the conclusion was complete defeat.

The spearhead of modern invention had not yet penetrated to the villages and they lay there, secret, primitive, and calm, as our ancestors had founded them some five hundred years before. Yet the people were not idle. The farmers had to plow, sow, and reap; the fishermen to cast their nets in the canals; the women to spin, weave, sew; the traders to buy and sell; the craftsmen to make their beautiful articles; the scholars to read aloud, memorize the Confucian classics, and take civil examinations.

There were hundreds of thousands of such villages in China, varying only in size and mode of life according to topographical and climatic differences. The traditions, family ties, and trades which held them together were more or less the same. A common written language, common ideals of life, a common culture and system of civil examinations bound the whole country into a single nation known as the Chinese Empire.

Together with the large cities and centers of trade, these hundreds of thousands of villages in China kept the country supplied with food, goods, scholars, soldiers, and the rank and file of officials of the government. So long as they remained untouched by modernization, China would remain the same; if she could have built fences round the treaty ports they might have remained the same for centuries to come. But the tide of westernization refused to be contained within the treaty ports. It made itself felt in the immediate surroundings, extending gradually along waterways and highways. Villages and towns near the five invaded cities or along communication lines were the first to succumb. Like transplanted trees feeding on China's rich soil, branching off and multiplying fast, the modern influence extended in the course of some fifty years far into the interior.

The village of the Chiangs was one among many spread—with intervening spaces of one or two miles of luxuriant rice fields—over the alluvial plain formed by the Chien-tang River. This is well known for its scenery, both in the upper part and in the lower section near the mouth where the famous bores of Chien-tang make their impressive seasonal

称许他。他抖了，就继续念道："天下打不通，仍旧还咸丰。""妈"的一声，刀光一闪，从他头上掠过。从此以后，他不敢再和老长毛开玩笑了。

这样关于长毛的故事，大家都欢喜讲，欢喜听。但是村里的人只有偶然才提到近年来的国际战争，而且漠不关心。其间还有些怪诞不经的胜利，后来想起来可怜亦复可笑。事实上，中国军队固然在某些战役上有过良好的表现，结果却总是一败涂地的。

现代发明的锋芒还没有到达乡村，因而这些乡村也就像五百年前一样地保守、原始、宁静。但是乡下人却并不闲，农人忙着耕耘、播种、收获；渔人得在运河里撒网捕鱼；女人得纺织缝补；商人忙着买卖；工匠忙着制作精巧的成品；读书人则高声朗诵，默记四书五经，然后参加科举。

中国有成千上万这样的村落，因为地形或气候的关系，村庄大小和生活习惯可能稍有不同，但是使他们聚居一起的传统、家族关系和行业却大致相同。共同的文字、共同的生活理想、共同的文化和共同的科举制度则使整个国家结为一体而成为大家所知道的中华帝国。（我们现在称中华民国，在辛亥革命以前，欧美人称我们为中华帝国。）

以上所说的那些成千成万的村庄，加上大城市和商业中心，使全国所需要的粮食、货品、学人、士兵，以及政府的大小官吏供应无缺。只要这些村镇城市不接触现代文明，中国就可以一直原封不动，如果中国能在通商口岸四周筑起高墙，中国也可能再经几百年而一成不变。但是西洋潮流却不肯限于几个通商口岸里。这潮流先冲激着附近的地区，然后循着河道和公路向外伸展。五个商埠附近的，以及交通线附近的村镇首先被冲倒。现代文明像是移植过来的树木，很快地就在肥沃的中国土壤上发芽滋长，在短短五十年之内就深入中国内地了。

蒋村是散布在钱塘江沿岸冲积平原上的许多村庄之一，村与村之间常是绵延一两里的繁茂的稻田，钱塘江以风景优美闻名于世，上游有富春江的景色，江口有著名的钱塘江大潮。几百年来，江水

sweep in from the sea. The high, abrupt front of the tidal bore is of a grandeur to over-shadow Niagara Falls. Down the valley, through the centuries, the river slowly laid its rich earth, building its shores farther and farther into Hangchow Bay. On the newly formed shores people erected temporary enclosures to hold the brine from which common salt is made. A large quantity of salt was produced every year, supplying the needs of many millions.

After a number of years, as the shores were further extended, the salt would begin to exhaust itself and dikes would be built along the drying land at some distance from the water. The embanked land was now ready for pasturing. After a long period it was capable of growing cotton to feed the domestic looms, or mulberry trees to nourish silkworms. It was probably still another half century before it could be turned into rice fields. For plenty of water is needed for growing rice, and it takes time to build reservoirs and a network of canals for irrigation. And the land takes time to mature.

The village of the Chiangs, by the time I came to it, was situated about twenty miles from Hangchow Bay. Around it were endless chains of villages, large and small, running in all directions—southward to the mountains, northward to the sea, and east and west to towns and cities all connected by miles of footways or canals. The genealogy of the Chiangs tells us that our first ancestors immigrated to the Yuyao district from Hueichow, a mountainous region where the famous river finds its source. They came presumably to reclaim the then newly formed land. In my own time an ancient embankment was still visible in front of our clan temple, the Temple of the Four No's, popularly known as the "Temple Facing the Embankment."

Perhaps the reader would like to know what is meant by the "Four No's." They mean to see no evil, hear no evil, speak no evil, do no evil. The sets of three monkeys with hands covering their eyes, ears, and mouth, respectively, that one finds in Oriental bazaars exemplify them—the fourth being left out for obvious reasons. These moral precepts came from the Confucian classics. Moral ideas were driven into the people by every possible means—temples, theatres, homes, toys, proverbs, schools, history, and stories—until they became habits in daily life. This was one of the ways by which China attained social stability: governing the life of the people by moral bonds.

　　沿岸积留下肥沃的泥土，使两岸逐步向杭州湾扩伸。居民就在江边新生地上筑起临时的围堤截留海水晒盐。每年的盐产量相当可观，足以供应几百万人的需要。

　　经过若干年代以后，江岸再度向前伸展，原来晒盐的地方盐分渐渐消失净尽，于是居民就在离江相当远的地方筑起堤防，保护渐趋干燥的土地，准备在上面蓄草放牧。再过一段长时期以后，这块土地上面就可以植棉或种桑了。要把这种土地改为稻田，也许要再过五十年。因为种稻需要大量的水，而挖池塘筑圳渠来灌溉稻田是需要相当时间的，同时土地本身也需要相当时间才能慢慢变为沃土。

　　我童年时代的蒋村，离杭州湾约有二十里之遥。围绕着它的还有无数的村庄。大大小小，四面八方都有，往南一直到山麓，往北到海边，往东往西则有较大的城镇和都市，中间有旱道或河汊相通。蒋氏族谱告诉我们，我们的祖先是从徽州迁到奉化暂驻，又从奉化迁到余姚。徽州是钱塘江的发源地，我们的祖先到余姚来，可能就是为了开垦江边新生地。在我幼年时，我们蒋氏家庙的前面还有古堤岸的遗迹，那家庙叫做"四勿祠"，奉祠宋朝当过御史的一位祖先，他是奉化人，名叫蒋岘。然而一般人却惯叫"陂塘庙"，因为几百年前，庙前横着一条堤塘。

　　读者或许要问：什么叫"四勿"呢？那就是《论语》里的非礼勿视、非礼勿听、非礼勿言、非礼勿动四句话。我们玩具店里所看到的三只猴子分别蒙起眼睛、耳朵、嘴巴，就是指这回事。至于为什么没有第四只猴子，因为那三只猴子坐着不动，就可以代表了。但是我们那位御史公却把这四勿改为勿欺心、勿负主、勿求田、勿问舍，人称之为四勿先生。这些自古流传下来的处世格言是很多的。我们利用一切可能的方法，诸如寺庙、戏院、家庭、玩具、格言、学校、历史、故事等等，来灌输道德观念，使这些观念成为日常生活中的习惯。以道德规范约束人民生活是中国社会得以稳定的理由之一。

During the long centuries of history the population of China had expanded from its northern beginnings to the south, first to the Yangtze Valley, then to the Pearl River Valley, and finally to the mountainous regions of the southwest. The fertile soil of the south and the devastation caused by flood from the incorrigible Yellow River, as well as by invasions of warlike tribes from outside the Great Wall, together with the natural expansion of the race, all contributed to cause repeated southward movements of the Chinese people. It was following in the wake of such a movement that my ancestors came to stay here on the shores of Hang-chow Bay.

Our family tree owes its existence to a sprout of a royal family planted in consequence of a feud somewhere in the lower Yellow River Valley some three thousand years ago. That tract of land was called "Chiang," the ancient name for a species of aquatic grass (*Hydropyrum Latifolium*). The modern name of this plant is *Chiao-pei*; used as a vegetable it tastes somewhat like bamboo shoots. The country was probably so called because of the luxuriant growth of the plant in those regions. My first ancestor in the Chiang line was made the first feudal lord to rule over that land toward the end of the twelfth century B.C. He was Pei-ling, third son of Prince Regent Chow-kung of the Chow Dynasty, and his descendants took Chiang as their family name.

In the third century A.D., during the period of the Three Kingdoms, one of our ancestors appears in history. His name was Chiang Wen and he lived in the Yangtze Valley. This shows that the Chiangs living south of the Yangtze had already migrated from the Yellow River region by the third century. From our first ancestor down to the present day all the names in the direct line have been recorded in our genealogy. How authentic they are I cannot tell, for their lives were so obscure that verification is not easy, but this much we can say: all the Chiangs settled in the areas south of the Yangtze are of the same origin. How far we can trace back accurately to this origin we don't know, but it is certain that all the Chiangs living in the province of Chekiang find their common ancestral tree in Hueichow.

I am of the seventeenth generation in the ancestral line. The first settlement of our village by the Chiangs, more than five hundred years ago, came toward the end of the Yuan or Mongol Dynasty. During these five centuries, under two foreign dynasties[3] and one Chinese, the Chiangs saw the fall of the Mongols, the rise and fall of the Mings and the Manchus, and the Taiping Rebellion which almost overthrew the latter.

几千年以来，中国的人口从北方渐渐扩展到南方，先到长江流域，继至珠江流域，最后到了西南山区。中华民族一再南迁的理由很多，南方土地肥沃、塞外好战部落入侵，以及人口的自然繁殖都有关系，且从宋朝以后，黄河一再泛滥，更使人们想念江南乐土。我的祖先在早期就由北而南，由南而东，最后终于在杭州湾沿岸定居下来。

蒋姓的始祖是三千多年前受封的一位公子王孙。他的名字叫做百龄，是代周成王摄政的周公的第三个儿子。他在纪元[4]前十二世纪末期被封在黄河流域下游的一块小地方，他的封地叫做"蒋"，他的子孙也就以蒋为氏了。蒋是茭白古名。那块封地之所以定名为蒋，可能是那一带地方茭白生长得特别繁茂的缘故。

在三国时代，也就是公元第三世纪，我们的一位祖先曾在历史上露了脸。他的名字叫蒋琬，住在长江流域南部的湘乡，从蜀先主入蜀。诸葛亮称他是社稷之才。这证明住在长江以南的蒋姓子孙，在第三世纪以前就从黄河流域南迁了。从我们的始祖起到现在，所有嫡系子孙的名字，在我们的族谱上都有纪录可考。至于确实到什么程度，我却不敢说，因为他们的生平事迹很少有人知道，考证起来是很困难的。但相传江南无二蒋，所以我们至少可以说一句：住在长江以南所有姓蒋的都是同宗同支。究竟可以正确地追溯到多远，我们可不知道了。不过我们确切知道：住在浙江省境的蒋姓子弟，都在徽州找到了共同的宗脉。

我在宗谱中从迁余姚的始祖传到我为第十七世。蒋姓首先定居在我们村里的是五百多年前来的，那是元朝末年的事。这五百多年之中，两个朝代是外来民族建立的，一个是汉族自己的王朝，蒋姓一族曾经看到元朝的没落、明朝和满清的兴衰，以及几乎推翻满清的

During these changes they lived, worked, and retired to their graves in the same manner and in the same village. Dynasties came and went, but the village of the Chiangs remained the same.

During the Taiping Rebellion a few houses were burned by the rebels. The people ran into the mountains, but as soon as peace was restored they all came home like bees to the hive. In my childhood some of the ruins still stood to tell the story of the war.

When the Ming Dynasty fell at the hands of the Manchus, I was told by the villagers, people were not aware of it until the edicts of the new regime reached the villages. There was a play going on in one of the near-by village theatres when they were informed that they lived under a new dynasty. Perhaps the only forcible change in the life of my clansmen was the edict ordering the people to wear a queue and forbidding the male population to dress in the Ming style. Resentment was so great that men wore the Ming costume, to their graves; it was a common saying of our clan that "men surrendered but women did not; the living did, but the dead did not." The practice persisted in some cases until the downfall of the Manchu Dynasty[5] in 1911, when the Republic was established—a period of two centuries and a half.

Our village consisted of only some sixty households, with a population of about three hundred. It was one of the smallest among many villages, surrounded by a canal on three sides. On the south side a footway paved with granite slabs ran along it, leading across bridges to neighboring villages and towns. The canal was but part of a network connecting with large rivers which in turn led to such far-flung cities as Hangchow, Soochow, and Shanghai.

Although the village was small, it commanded easy communication by both land and water. Bridges spanned the canals and weeping willows grew luxuriantly on the banks. Fish, shrimps, eels, and turtles were abundant. Here and there one would find anglers taking their ease in the shade of the willows. Oxen could be seen walking in leisurely fashion round the water wheels to propel the chain of paddles which brought fresh water through a long trough to the fields. Miles of wheat fields in the spring and rice fields in summer gave one the feeling of living in a land of perpetual verdure. Swallows shuttled back and forth in the blue sky above a sea of rippling green, while eagles floated high above, circling around the village in search of little chicks.

太平天国。朝代更换了，蒋村却依然故我，人们还是照常地过活、做工，最后入土长眠。

太平军到了村子里，村中曾经有几所房子焚毁，留在村子里的老弱有被活活烧死的，有一处大门口残存的石阶上留有红斑，据传说是某位老太婆在此烧死时所流的血。大多数的老百姓都逃到山里躲起来，但是战事一平定，大家又像蜜蜂回巢一样回到村里。在我童年时代，村里还可以看到兵燹以后留下来的残垣断瓦。

村里的人告诉我，满洲人推翻明朝的消息，一直到新朝廷的圣旨到了村里时，大家才知道。清帝圣旨到达村里时，邻村还正在演社戏呢！改朝换代以后，族人生活上的唯一改变是强迫留辫子，同时圣旨严禁男人再穿明朝式样的衣服。大家敢怒不敢言，但是死后入殓时，男人还是穿明朝衣冠。因此我们族中流行着一句话："男投（降）女不投，活投死不投。"就是说男人投降，女人却不投降，活人投降，死人却不投降。一些人一直维持这个办法到一九一一年清室覆亡、民国建立为止，中间经过两百五十年之久。

我们村上只有六十来户人家，人口约三百人，是个很小的村庄。它的三面环绕着河汉，南面是一条石板路，通往邻近的村庄和城镇。小河汉可以通到大河，再由大河可以到达杭州、苏州和上海等大城市。

蒋村虽然小，水陆交通却很便利。河汉上随处是石桥，河的两岸则满是绿柳垂杨。河中盛产鱼、虾、鳝、鳗、龟、鳖。柳荫之下，常有人悠闲地在垂钓。耕牛慢慢地踱着方步，绕着转动牛车，把河水汲到水槽再送到田里。冬天是连阡穿陌的麦穗，夏天是一片稻海，使人生四季长青之感，麦穗和稻穗随着微风的吹拂，漾起一片涟漪，燕子就在绿波之上的蓝空中穿梭翱翔。老鹰忽高忽低地绕村回旋着，乘老母鸡不备的时候就俯冲而下，攫走小鸡。

Such was the background of my childhood and the environment of my clansmen. They lived there for more than five centuries with little change in life. Nature was kind to them. The land was fertile. Floods and droughts were not frequent. Rebellions or wars in the country at large did not disturb them more than once or twice during those long centuries; they lived in peace and contentment in a world by themselves, with little distinction between the very rich and the very poor. Sufficient rice, cotton, silk, fish, meat, bamboo shoots, and vegetables kept the people warm and well fed.

Morals, beliefs, and customs remained unchanged in Chinese villages through centuries of dynastic changes, in peace or war. For the villagers the world was good enough and no improvement was needed. Life alone was unstable, but consolation could be found in the transmigration of the soul. At death the soul was said to leave the body and enter that of a baby then being born. Indeed, in my own time I have seen convicts on the way to execution who shouted to the spectators that after eighteen years they would be young men again. What a consolation!

Our villagers said that a bad or sinful man's soul would be degraded to become a poor man, a horse, or a pig, or even split into minute parts to be insects or worms, according to the degrees of sins he had committed. The soul of a good or virtuous man would be promoted to a higher station in the next life.

What was sinful or virtuous had of course its accepted standards. The highest of all virtues was filial piety; the greatest of all sins was adultery. Filial piety kept the Chinese family intact and chastity kept the Chinese race pure. Respect for the elders, faithfulness to friends, loyalty to the sovereign, honesty in word and deed; kindliness and sympathy to the poor, the infirm or sick, all were regarded as virtuous behavior. Usury, treachery, lying, cheating, and the like were among sinful acts. Denunciation of a person whose conduct one disapproved often took the form of telling him that he would become a dog or a pig in his next life.

In business dealings verbal promises were as good as gold. On the whole, people were honest and trustworthy. Any person found to cheat would be surely tabooed by the whole community.

Marriages were not the business of the parties concerned; the parents of both parties made the match. As a rule, men married at twenty and women at eighteen. The men usually remarried if their wives died, while women of well-to-do families generally remained widows if they survived

这就是我童年时代的背景，也是我家族的环境。他们安定地在那里生活了五百多年，他们很少碰到水灾或旱灾，在这漫长的几百年中也不过遇上一两次的变乱和战争。他们和平而满足地生活在他们自己的世界里，贫富之间也没有太大的差别。富饶的稻谷、棉花、蚕丝、鱼虾、鸡鸭、蔬菜使人民丰衣足食。

几百年来，不论朝代如何更换，不论是太平盛世或战祸频仍，中国乡村里的道德、信仰和风俗习惯却始终不变。乡下人觉得这个世界已经很不错，不必再求进步。生命本身也许很短暂，但是投胎转世时可能有更大的幸福。人死以后，据说灵魂就离开肉体，转投到初生的婴儿身上。我自己就亲眼看到过绑赴刑场处决的罪犯，对围观的群众高喊："十八年之后又是一条好汉！" 这是何等的达观！

我们村子里的人说：一个坏人或作孽多端的人，死后要转世为穷人，或者变马变猪，甚至灵魂支离割裂，变为蚊蝇小虫。好人善士的灵魂转世时则可以享更高的福禄。这些都是随佛教而来的印度传说而被中国道教所采用的。佛教本身，倒不大理会这些事。

善恶当然有公认的标准。"万恶淫为首，百善孝为先。"孝道使中国家庭制度维系不堕；贞操则使中国种族保持纯净。敬老怜贫、忠信笃敬也被认为善行。重利盘剥、奸诈谎骗则列为罪行。斥责恶行时常骂人来生变猪变犬。

商业往来讲究一诺千金。一般而论，大家都忠实可靠。欺诈的人必然受亲朋戚友一致的唾弃。

婚姻是由媒妁之言、父母之命决定的。通例是男子二十而娶，女子十八而嫁。妻子死了，丈夫大概都要续弦，中上之家的女人如果死了丈夫，却照例要守寡。守寡的可怜人算是最贞节的，

their husbands. These unfortunates were regarded as most virtuous—Imperial posthumous honors were conferred upon them.

The local government of the village was a fully self-governing body without outside interference. It was a government by elders of the clan with the Ancestral Hall as its seat. "Elders" does not mean elderly men. They might be young but represented the oldest living generations in the ancestral line. They were obligated to see that the ceremonies of ancestral worship were properly performed and were entrusted with the duties of arbitration in case of dispute among the clansmen. No one was allowed to go to law without first going through arbitration. To "open the gate of the Ancestral Hall" meant to summon an arbitration court of the elders. Anyone in the village could go there to observe the proceedings. Candles and incense burned before the tablets of the ancestors and everyone felt that their spirits watched invisibly from the ethereal realm. Before these ancestral spirits the parties concerned must speak the truth, nothing but the truth. Generally they did.

For the arbitrators, fairness was the motto. Public opinion in the village was also a very important factor, of which all parties concerned were conscious, and there was also the public opinion of neighboring villages. No elders would dare to defame the Ancestral Hall with unfair judgments. Thus disputes were usually fairly settled in this way. No lawsuit was necessary.

There were, in fact, few cases of dispute which needed arbitration by "opening the gate of the Ancestral Hall," for people regarded this as a matter of weight, to be resorted to only in a case of grave importance. Disputes were usually settled by informal arbitration before the gate of the hall.

Scholars and the gentry had a strong voice in the local government. They also participated in cases of arbitration and the making of rules and regulations for the village. They formed inter-village committees to settle disputes and look after the common welfare of neighboring villages.

Land taxes were brought by owners of land to the district or hsien treasury, about twenty miles from the village. No tax collectors ever visited us. People never felt the influence of the state—it was a common saying that "Heaven is high above and the Emperor is far away."

Public worship other than ancestral, such as worship in Buddhist temples or temples of deified persons, national heroes, or local gods that had grown out of legends, was a matter of individual concern. Anyone might worship in any or all of these places; there was no

死后皇帝还要给她们建贞节牌坊。这种牌坊在乡间到处可以看见的。

村里的事全由族长来处理，不待外界的干涉。祠堂就是衙门。"族长"不一定是老头子，也可能是代表族中辈份最高一代的年轻人。族长们有责任监督敬先祭祖的礼仪遵奉不渝，族人中起了争执时，他们还须负责加以评断。没有经过族长评理以前，任何人不许打官司。族长升堂审判叫做"开祠堂门"，全村的人都可以来参观。祖宗牌位前面点起香烛，使得每个人都觉得祖先在天之灵就在冥冥之中监视似的，在祖先的面前，当事的两边不能有半句谎话。一般而论，说老实话的居多。

仲裁者力求做得公平。自然，村中的舆论也是重要的因素，还有，邻村的舆论也得考虑。族长们如果评断不公，就会玷污了祠堂的名誉。因此，争执多半在祠堂里得到公平的解决，大家用不到上衙门打官司。

实际上真需要"开祠堂门"来解决的事情并不多，因为大家认为"开祠堂门"是件大事，只有特别严重的案子才需要这样做。一般的纠纷只是在祠堂前评个理就解决了。

读书人和绅士在地方上的权威很大。他们参加排难解纷，也参加制定村里的规矩，他们还与邻村的士绅成立组织，共同解决纠纷，照顾邻近村庄的共同福利。

田赋由地主送到离村约二十里的县库去，粮吏从来不必到村里来。老百姓根本不理会官府的存在，这就是所谓"天高皇帝远"。

除了崇拜祖先之外，大家要信什么就信什么。上佛寺、拜神仙、供关公、祭土地，悉听尊便。没有宗教限制，也没有宗教

religious restriction or persecution. Your gods are as good as mine. If the Christians had allowed their Christ to sit beside Chinese gods in Chinese temples, I am sure that the villagers would have worshiped Him just as reverently as they did other gods.

Superstition grows out of the credulity of simple folk—it rolls like a snowball growing as it rolls along. Thus it is that superstitions gather through centuries of accumulation.

As I have said, the villagers believed in the transmigration of the soul. This does not seem to reconcile with the idea that there are spirits traveling about with lightning speed in the ethereal realm. Soul and spirit, however, were two different things: the soul transmigrated, but the spirit remained in space. The spirit of a great man lives eternally in the invisible realm, while that of a common man evaporates and dwindles, disappearing entirely with the course of time, or rather when it is entirely forgotten. The spirit moves with instant speed anywhere it wills. It may live in the Ancestral Hall or in its grave as it chooses. This is perhaps one reason why the Chinese are always willing to spend large sums on elaborate tombs and palatial ancestral halls.

My people always see things in relation to man. If spirits and gods wandered about in an unseen world without relation to, or contact with, living man, people would not see any use for them and would hardly believe they existed. Yes, they have images and tablets sitting in the shrines. But these sacred things, however awe-inspiring, do not step down and talk to them except in dreams. There must be something more active or lively. This was found in mediums, in automatic writing, or in the interpreting of dreams.

If someone was thinking of a departed friend or a dead relative, he could invoke the spirit to come to him through a medium, who was always a woman from some far-distant place. When the spirit called for approached, she would contract her ears three times as the signal of arrival of the invisible guest. This contraction of the involuntary muscles of the ear was something ordinary people could not do and this made them believe in the medium much more. She usually spoke through her throat like a cat's purr, so that the words uttered could be interpreted to suit the wishes of the listeners. When she had traced out something more

迫害。你信你的神，我拜我的佛，各不相涉，并且还有把各式各样的神拼在一起大家来拜。这就是通常所称的"道教"。如果基督徒肯让基督与中国神祇并供在中国庙宇里，我相信村里人一定会像崇拜其他神佛一样虔敬崇拜基督。

　　一般老百姓都是很老实的，人家说什么，他们就相信。迷信就是在这种背景下产生的，而且像滚雪球一样越滚越大，几百年积聚下来的迷信，当然是非常可观了。

　　我提到过村里的人相信灵魂轮回之说。这似乎与散鬼游魂之说互相矛盾的。不过，凡关于鬼神的事，我们本来是不甚深究的，几种矛盾的说法，可以同时平行。据说灵魂与鬼是两回事。灵魂转入轮回，鬼则飘游宇宙之间。伟人圣哲的鬼就成了神，永远存在于冥冥之中，凡夫俗子的鬼则逐渐飘散消逝，最后化为乌有。鬼能够随心所欲，随时随地出现。它可以住在祠堂里，也可以住在坟墓里，高兴怎么样就怎么样。我国不惜巨资建造富丽堂皇的坟墓和宫殿式的祠堂，大概和这些信仰不是没有关系的。这种鬼话各地皆有，虽各有不同，但大体是一致的。

　　中国人对一切事物的看法都不脱人本位的色彩。如果鬼神与活人之间毫无关系或毫无接触，那末大家就不会觉得鬼神有什么用处，或许根本就不会相信它们真的存在。寺庙祠堂里固然有神佛的塑像，也有祖宗的灵牌，但是这些偶像或木主虽然令人望之生畏，却不能走出神龛直接与生人交谈，除非在梦中出现。人们需要更具体、更实际的表现，因此就有了巫婆、扶乩和解梦。

　　如果一个人怀念作古了的朋友或去世的亲戚，他可以请一位巫婆把鬼魂召了来。当巫婆的多半是远地来的女人。被召的鬼魂来时，巫婆的耳朵就会连续抽搐三次。普通人是不能控制耳朵的肌肉的，巫婆的耳朵能够自己动，使得大家相信它的确有鬼神附体。她说话时，压着喉咙像猫叫，因此她讲的话可以由听的人随意附会。

definite in the course of conversation, she would purr more distinctly, to the amazement of the audience.

False or true, it served as a comfort to the hearts of living relatives. I still remember how thrilling it was when my dead mother conversed with me through a medium half a century ago.

Automatic writing is of a higher order. It was generally practiced by the educated class. Two persons were needed to hold the ends of a horizontal bar with a long wooden pin attached at the middle, which wrote on a tray of sand. A god or the spirit of some famous personage, it was believed, could be invoked to write. The device—not unlike a Ouija board—could be asked to predict future events. It might foretell a bumper crop in the coming year, or an impending famine, or peace, or war. One could ask almost any question. Poems were written by operators who did not know how to compose a poem; names of persons present unknown to the writers might be written out on the sand. It was all done through the subconscious as any person who knows about psychology can explain.

Mediums invoked only spirits of departed relatives or friends; automatic writing might invoke the gods as well. In dreams both might come voluntarily, uninvited. I heard numerous interpretations of dreams which I do not remember now, except for one instance. One of my great-granduncles went to Hangchow to take the civil examinations for the second degree. In his examination cell (where candidates remained for many hours) he saw in a dream a hand of enormous size stretch into the room through the window. This was interpreted to mean that, since it was the greatest hand he had ever seen, he was to head the list of successful candidates. And the good omen came true when the results of the examination were made known.

Gods, dead friends, relatives, or spirits might enter one's dreams to convey their wishes, requests, or warnings. A dead mother might request her son to repair her tomb. A dead father might demand paper money from his son. A good imitation of paper money was always burned at funerals; it was supposed to accompany the dead for use in the world to which they go.

A tragic coincidence happened in our village about which people talked for years after. Ah Yi, a young farmer, was to take his rice by boat to a neighboring town. Early in the morning he was found sitting on a bench in a somber mood, very rare for a farmer. To inquiry he replied

如果巫婆在谈话中摸清了对方的心思，她的话也就说得更清楚点，往往使听的人心悦诚服。

真也好，假也好，这办法至少使活着的亲戚朋友心里得点安慰。五十年前，我自己就曾经透过巫婆与我故世的母亲谈过话，那种惊心动魄的经验至今还不能忘记。

扶乩可比较高级了，扶乩的人多半是有知识的。两个人分执一根横木条的两端，木条的中央接着一根木棒，木棒就在沙盘里写字。神佛或者名人的鬼魂可以被请降坛，写字赐教。扶乩可以预言未来，可以预言来年的收成，也可以预告饥荒，甚至和平或战乱，几乎什么问题都可以问。完全不会作诗的也能写出诗来。写的人也能写出素昧平生的人的名字。懂一点心理学的人大概都能解释，这是一种潜意识的作用。但是有好几位外国留学的博士学士，到如今还是相信扶乩。有一位哈佛大学毕业生，于抗战期间任盐务某要职，扶乩报告预言，推测战局，终被政府革职。

巫婆只能召至去世的亲戚朋友的鬼魂，扶乩却能召唤神佛。在做梦时，鬼魂和神佛都能自动地来托梦。我听过许多关于做梦应验的事，但是多半不记得了。我记得一个圆梦的例子是这样的：我的一位曾叔祖到杭州去应乡试，俗称考举人，他在考棚里梦到一只硕大无比的手伸进窗子。因为他从来没有见过这样大的手，这个梦就被解释为他将独占鳌头的征兆。放榜时我的曾叔祖居然中试第一名，俗称解元。

神佛、死去的亲戚朋友或者精灵鬼怪可能由托梦提出希望、请求或者警告。一位死了的母亲可能要求她儿子给她修葺坟墓。死了的父亲可能向儿子讨纸钱。死人下葬时总要烧点纸钱，以备阴间使用。

我们村里发生过一件事，好几年以后，大家谈起来还是娓娓不倦。一位叫阿义的青年农夫预备用船载谷子进城市。那天早上，他坐在家里发呆，人家问他为什么，他说前一晚他死去的母亲来托梦，

that in his dreams the previous night his dead mother had warned him not to go near water. What could it mean? He was a good swimmer.

At dusk he brought his junk home and shoved the boat toward the landing with his bamboo pole. He joked with his friends on the bank that his danger was over, and laughed heartily. Suddenly his feet slipped and he plunged into the canal, where he struggled for a moment but went under. Friends dived for him but could not find him. After half an hour he was pulled out, cold and stiff, from the entangling roots of an aged willow tree that grew by the water.

People said it was the water ghost that hid him there. Perhaps it was a water monkey that nested in the roots. Several good swimmers drowned near that spot. Often the villagers saw the "water ghost" sitting on the bridge near by in the moonlight, staring at the moon. It plunged into the water as soon as it saw people approaching.

Illusions, hallucinations, dreams, nightmares, imaginings, wishful thinking, coincidence, rumors—every kind of inexplicable phenomenon of mind or nature, all contributed to swell the snowball. And time kept it rolling.

Medicine in the village was, of course, primitive. We had to go miles to see herb doctors in the bigger towns. For ordinary illness or certain more serious cases Chinese medicine is very effective. But in many serious ailments the old medicine is useless or even dangerous.

I myself have been twice at the point of death and was in each case saved by herb medicine, without which I would not be here writing these chapters. On one occasion I had been ill for many months and was reduced to emaciation. A famous herb doctor specializing in children's diseases saved me. On another occasion I contracted diphtheria and was treated by a Chinese throat specialist. He pricked my throat with a needle all over the affected part and then sprayed it with some kind of white powder. I do not know what it was, but my throat felt cool and soothed as after smoking a mentholated cigarette.

That part of my throat was relieved, but the case developed other complications. My tonsils swelled to the size of goose eggs, my cheeks puffed up like a balloon, and I could hardly swallow even liquid food. My nose kept bleeding as if I should bleed to death. Finally I could barely breathe and only a faint hope was left. While my life hung by a thread my

警告他不要走近水边。他的游泳技术很高明，他猜不透这个梦究竟是什么意思。

黄昏时，他安然划着船回到家，用竹篙把船拢了岸。他对站在岸上的朋友开玩笑，说他自己的危险总算过去了，说罢还哈哈大笑。突然间他足下一滑就跌进河里去了。挣扎了一阵子，他就沉入水底。朋友们赶紧潜水去救，但是到处找不到。半小时后他被拖上来了，但是已经手足冰冷，一命呜呼。原来他跌入河中以后，手足就被水边的一棵陈年老柳的盘根缠住了。

大家说他是被水鬼抓下去的，或许那是一只以柳树根作窝的水猴子。好几个游泳技术很好的人都在那个地方淹死。村里的人常常看到那个"水鬼"在月光下坐在附近的桥上赏月。它一看到有人走近就扑通一声钻到水里去。

各式各样无法解释的现象都使迷信的雪球越滚越大，错觉、幻象、梦魇、想像、巧合、谣言都是因素。时间更使迷信愈积愈多。

村中的医药当然也很原始。我们得走好几里路才能在大镇里找到草药医生，俗称"草头郎中"。对于通常的病痛或者某些特殊的病症，中国药是很有效的。但是对于许多严重的病症，草药不但无效而且危险。

我自己曾经两次病得奄奄一息，结果却都给草药救起了。有一次病了好几个月，瘦得只剩皮包骨，结果是一位专精儿科的草药医生救了我的命。另一次我染了白喉，请了一位中国的喉科专家来医治。他用一根细针在我喉头附近刺了一遍，然后敷上一些白粉。我不知道那是什么东西，只觉得喉头凉爽舒服，很像抽过一支薄荷烟的感觉。

喉头是舒服一点了，病状却起了变化。我的扁桃腺肿得像鹅蛋那末大，两颊鼓起像气球，我甚至连流质的食物都无法下咽。鼻子一直出血不止，最后连呼吸也感到困难了。正在奄奄一息的时候，

father said that he would try to "treat a dead horse like a live one." This was a Chinese proverb meaning that if the horse is ready to die anyway, it is worth trying the most extreme methods to save it. He dug into old medicine books, in which he found a prescription for a case showing similar symptoms. Several heavy doses were taken. The first brought immediate relief; in an hour or two I felt much better. By the next morning my tonsils had dwindled, and after a week or so I could take regular meals.

I have seen with my own eyes broken legs healed by ancient methods, while colds, sore eyes, coughs, and rheumatism were effectively cured by herbs.

Chinese doctors discovered long ago an antismallpox "vaccine" taken from the human body. They used a kind of herb that had once been inserted into the nostrils of an affected child. Putting it into the nose of a normal child gave the latter what was usually a very much milder form of the disease. There were some cases of mortality among the hundreds thus "vaccinated," for I often heard of a death here and there. My father preferred modern vaccination to the old Chinese method. All the children in our family and many of our relatives were vaccinated by the modern method without a mishap.

We did not know how to cure malaria in our village. We let it run for some weeks or even months until it stopped of itself. There were no malignant cases in our locality and while it might sap the energy of the affected person it was not fatal. When quinine powder was brought in by missionaries or merchants from Shanghai, people found great relief in Western medicine.

Some of our clansmen believed in the healing power of the supernatural. They prayed in a temple and took a pinch of ashes from the incense burner as a panacea for all diseases. It was a sort of psychological treatment and did cure in some cases where psychology could play its part.

In the gardens of our house each month of the year was presided over by the chief flower of that month. Camellias were for the First Moon— first month of the year in the lunar calendar, corresponding approximately to the Western late January and early February. In the Second Moon almond blossoms took over the reins of government in the flowery kingdom. Peach blossoms were for the Third Moon, roses for the Fourth, pomegranates for the Fifth, lotus for the Sixth, *Feng-hsian (Impatiens balsamina)* for the Seventh, *Kwei-hua (Osmanthus fragrans)* for the

我父亲认为只有"死马当作活马医"了。于是他就在古老的医书里翻寻秘方，结果真地找到一剂主治类似症候的方子。我吃了好几服重药。头一剂药就发生验效，一两个小时之后，病势居然大有起色。第二天早晨我的扁桃腺肿消了许多，个把星期以后饮食也恢复正常。

我曾经亲眼目睹跌断的腿用老法子治好，伤风咳嗽、风湿和眼睛红肿被草药治好的例子更是多不胜举。

中医很早以前就发现可以从人体采取一种预防天花的"瘊苗"，他们用一种草药塞到病婴的鼻孔里，再把这种草药塞到正常儿童的鼻孔里时，就可以引起一种比较温和的病症。这样"种了痘"的孩子自然不免有死亡，因此我父亲宁愿让孩子按现代方法种牛痘。我们兄弟姊妹以及许多亲戚的子弟都用现代方法种痘，而且从来没有出过毛病。

我们村子里的人不知道怎样治疗疟疾。我们只好听它自生自灭地流行几个礼拜，甚至好几个月。我们村子附近总算没有发现恶性疟疾，患了病的人虽然伤了元气，倒还没有人因此致命。后来传教士和商人从上海带来奎宁粉，叫做金鸡纳霜，吃了很有效，于是大家才发现了西药的妙用。

村里有些人相信神力可以治病。他们到寺庙里焚香祝祷，然后在香炉里取了一撮香灰作为治疗百病的万应灵丹。这是一种心理治疗，在心理学应用得上的时候，也的确能医好一些病。

我家的花园里，每月有每月当令的花，阴历正月是茶花，二月是杏花，三月桃花，四月蔷薇，五月石榴，六月荷花，七月凤仙，

Eighth, chrysanthemums for the Ninth, *Fu-yung* (*Hibiscus mutabilis*) for the Tenth, *Shuei-hsian* (*Narcissus tazetta*) for the Eleventh, and *La-mei* (*Chimonanthus fragrans*) for the Twelfth, the last month of the year. Each plant was represented by a particular goddess whom we all loved dearly.

The most popular seasonal flowers were the peach blossoms of spring, lotus in the summer, and osmanthus and chrysanthemums in autumn. In season, the villagers all joined in admiring these beauties of nature.

Festivals brought much enjoyment to both children and grownups alike. The most important was the New Year Festival which began near the end of the old year—on the twenty-third of the Twelfth Moon—when the Kitchen God took leave and went to heaven to report to the Supreme God the year's happenings in the household.

The Chinese believed in polytheism. But above all deities was the Supreme God who controlled them all. It was an anthropomorphic idea that He reigned over the ethereal realm like the Emperor of China. Other gods were his ministers, governors, and magistrates.

The Kitchen God was entrusted by the Supreme God with charge of the household. Naturally he had to report to Him at the end of the year. The Kitchen God was a vegetarian and was therefore treated with a vegetarian dinner before leaving for heaven. Everybody had to be very careful during the year in word and deed, since bad as well as good things were reported. Both the sending-off and the welcome-home ceremonies consisted of dinners for the family, burning of paper money, and firecrackers.

New Year's Eve was celebrated by a family banquet in which every member must participate. If some member was absent, he or she would be assigned a seat *in absentia*. Candles burned all night until the next morning and most of the grownups sat up through the night to watch the coming of the New Year. Next morning, on the first day of the year, the family worshiped Heaven and Earth. Candles, incense, paper money, and firecrackers were necessary parts of the ceremony.

The Lantern Festival, part of the New Year celebration, began on the thirteenth and ended on the eighteenth of the First Moon, which was also the end of the New Year Festival. Artistic lanterns—horses, rabbits, butterflies, dragonflies, mantis, cicada, lotus, anything one could think of—adorned the houses and the streets of the towns. We used to go to large towns to see the lantern parade; their streets were thronged with merrymakers.

八月桂花，九月菊花，十月芙蓉，十一月水仙，十二月腊梅。每种花都有特别的花仙做代表。

最受欢迎的季节花是春天的桃花、夏天的荷花，秋天的桂花和菊花。季节到来时，村里的人就成群结队出来赏花。

过年过节时，无论男女老幼都可以高兴一阵子。最重要的年节，通常从十二月二十三日开始。灶神就在这一天上天报告这一家一年来的家庭琐事。

中国人都相信多神主义的，在道教里，众神之主是玉皇大帝。据说玉皇大帝也有公卿大臣和州官吏卒，和中国的皇帝完全一样。玉皇大帝派灶神监视家庭事务，因此灶神必须在年终岁尾提出报告。灶神是吃素的，因此在它启程上天时，大家就预备素斋来祭送。灶神对好事坏事都要报告，因此大家一年到头都谨言慎行。送灶神和迎灶神时都要设家宴、烧纸钱、放鞭炮。

除夕时，家家都大鸡大肉地庆祝，叫做吃年夜饭。吃年夜饭时，家庭的每一个分子都得参加。如果有人远行未归，也得留个空座位给他。红烛高烧到天明，多数的大人还得"守岁"，要坐到子夜以后才睡。第二天早晨，也就是正月初一早晨，一家人都参加拜天地。祭拜时自然又免不了点香烛、焚纸钱和放鞭炮。

新年的庆祝节目之一是灯节，从正月十三开始，一直到正月十八，十八以后年节也就算结束了。灯节时家家户户和大街小巷到处张灯结彩。花灯的式样很多，马、兔、蝴蝶、蜻蜓、螳螂、蝉、莲花，应有尽有。我们常常到大城市去看迎灯赛会，街上总是人山人海。

There were other important festivals, such as the Dragon Festival in the Fifth Moon, the Moon Festival in the Eighth Moon, and the like. The Dragon Festival was celebrated by a boat race with all the boats decorated to look like dragons. The Moon Festival was enjoyed quietly and poetically—after a banquet we took a walk in the bright night and looked at the rabbit on the full, silvery autumn moon in a starless, moonlit sky.

Parades were popular, with hundreds of people participating and thousands watching. They were always religious in character: some god was to make an inspection trip around the villages. An image of the deity was carried in a carved, artistically decorated sedan chain, preceded by pennants, flags, floats, bands of music, monster dragons, men on stilts, and so forth.

Dragon dances were performed in the public squares of every village as the parade passed by. The men on stilts danced in theatrical roles in the crowded streets. Monstrous flags with fantastic designs of the dragon, tiger, or lion, each carried by dozens of people and supported by lines of rope in front and rear, were indeed a great sight. They moved up the highway among the fields like the sails of the Spanish Armada on a sea of rippling green. It was said that the idea originated during the old days when pirates from the Japan Sea wrought havoc among the people.

Traveling theatres made visits to the villages during festivals or birthday celebrations of deities, or on other important occasions. Each performance started about three o'clock in the afternoon and continued until the next morning with an intermission for supper. A frantic sounding of the gong served as a prelude to let country folk know that the play was starting. Plays were mostly based on historical episodes; the people learned history from the theatre. At the end of each play the moral lesson was invariably brought out. So it served a triple purpose: to teach history and morals as well as to entertain.

The roles of women were played by men, as in Shakespearean times in England. The actors painted their faces in fantastic designs of various colors to differentiate symbolically among virtuous and vile, honest and sneaky, the great and the mean, the stern and the kind. Thus one whose nose was painted white was either treacherous, cunning, mean, or clownish. In daily life we referred to such a person as "white-nosed." A red face suggested a character which was candid or virtuous in some way, but always kind. The "black face" was generally severe and stern. We often called a man who behaved sternly "black-faced," while "red-faced" meant a man who acted kindly or generously. The tradition of symbolic face painting still persists to the present day in Chinese classical dramas.

五月里的端午节和八月里的中秋节也是重要的节日。端午节有龙舟比赛。庆祝中秋节却比较安静，也比较富于诗意——吃过晚饭后我们就在月色下散步，欣赏团圆满月中的玉兔在月桂下捣药。

迎神赛会很普遍，普通有好几百人参加，沿途围观的则有几千人。这些场合通常总带点宗教色彩，有时是一位神佛出巡各村庄。神像坐在一乘木雕的装饰华丽的轿子里，前面由旌旗华盖、猛龙怪兽、吹鼓手、踩高跷的人等等开道前导。

迎神行列经过时，掉狮舞龙就在各村的广场上举行。踩高跷的人，在街头扮演戏剧中的各种脚色。一面一面绣着龙虎狮子的巨幅旗帜，由十来个人扛着游行，前前后后则由绳索围起来。这样的行列在旷野的大路上移动时，看来真好威风呀！这种举大旗游行的起源，据说是明代倭寇入侵时老百姓以此向他们示威的。

碰到过年过节，或者庆祝神佛生日，或者其他重要时节，活动的戏班子就到村庄上来表演。戏通常在下午三点钟左右开始，一直演到第二天早晨，中间有一段休息的时间，以便大家吃晚饭。开演时总是锣鼓喧天，告诉大家戏正在开始。演的戏多半是根据历史故事编的，人民也就从戏里学习历史。每一出戏都包括一点道德上的教训，因此演戏可以同时达到三重目的：教授历史、灌输道德、供给娱乐。

女角是由男人扮演的，这是和莎士比亚时代的英国一样。演员涂抹形形色色的脸谱象征忠奸善恶。白鼻子代表奸诈、狡猾、卑鄙或小丑。在日常生活中我们也常常指这一类人为白鼻子。红脸代表正直、忠耿等等，但是红脸的人心地总是很厚道的。黑脸象征铁面无私。这种象征性的脸谱一直到现在还被各地国剧所采用。

Such was the world of my childhood. It has been passing rapidly into history. The intrusion of foreign manufactures began the process; invasion from the West, whether by ideas or gunboats, hastened it; modern science, invention, and industry are to give the finishing touch.

这就是我的童年的环境。这种环境已经很快地成为历史陈迹。这个转变首由外国品的输入启其端，继由西方思想和兵舰的入侵加速其进程；终将由现代的科学、发明和工业化，完毕其全程。

CHAPTER 3 / EARLY SCHOOLING

Education was a family affair. Boys were prepared for the Imperial civil examinations, or for business, in the family school. Girls were tutored separately. Children of poorer families which could not support a teacher were destined to be illiterate.

There was generally one teacher to a dozen pupils, taught individually. There were no blackboards or classes in the school. The teacher was usually serene, sitting the whole day at his desk from early in the morning to sunset. The pupils did likewise. As clocks were very rare then, there was none in the school. In winter, when the day was short, lessons after dark were given by the dim light of a vegetable-oil lamp. Time was measured by a sun dial. On a cloudy or rainy day you had to guess your time. Often you missed the mark by an hour or two, but it did not matter much, for the lessons were given individually.

I was sent to school at the age of six, the traditional school age. But my actual years were only five and a month or so, since with us your age is called "one"—that is, you are in your first year—when you are born. The ordinary desk was a bit too high for me, so that my chair had to be raised by a wooden stand to bring me level with the desk. My tiny feet were thus left dangling from the seat.

I was given a textbook: *San-tze-ching*, or the "Classics of Three Characters." It is so named because each sentence contains three words, and it was rhymed so as to be easier for children to remember. After fifty-odd years I am still able to recite a great part of it. It starts with the following passage—I give a literal translation:

Man is originally

Endowed with a nature which is all-good.

And therefore by nature people are all alike.

It is practice that makes the divergence.

If they are not properly taught,

Their nature will be thwarted.

The all-good in human nature is the starting point of the Confucian philosophy of life and education, which exercised a strong influence upon the French Encyclopedists of the eighteenth century.

I understand what it means now, but of course I didn't then.

I must tell how I hated the school! After a short time, noticing that the attention of the teacher was not on me, I climbed down quickly from the chair and ran like a dog that has broken from its chain back home to my mother's lap.

叁 童年教育

在我的童年时代，没有学校，只有家塾。男孩子在家塾里准备功课应付科举或者学点实用的知识以便经商，女孩子不能和男孩子一道上学，要读书就得另请先生，穷苦人家的子弟请不起先生，因此也就注定了当文盲的命运。

一位先生通常教数十位学生，都是分别教授的。家塾里没有黑板，也不分班级。先生从清晨到薄暮都端端正正地坐在那里，学生们自然也就不敢乱蹦乱跳。那时候时钟是很难见到的。家塾里当然没有钟。冬天白昼比较短。天黑后我们就点起菜油灯，在昏暗的灯光下念书，时间是靠日晷来计算的。碰到阴天或下雨，那就只好乱猜了。猜错一两个小时是常事，好在书是个别教授的，猜错一把钟头也无所谓。

我在六岁时进家塾，一般小孩子差不多都在这个年岁"启蒙"的。事实上我那时才五岁零一个月的样子，因为照我家乡的算法，一个人生下来就算一岁了。家塾里的书桌太高，我的椅子下面必须垫上一个木架子之后我才够得上书桌，因此我坐到椅子上时，两只脚总是悬空的。

我最先念的书叫《三字经》，每句三个字，而且是押韵的，因此小孩子记起来比较容易。事隔六十多年，我现在还能背出一大半，开头几句是："人之初，性本善。性相近，习相远。苟不教，性乃迁。"性善论是儒家人生哲学和教育原理的出发点，这种看法曾对十八世纪的大光明时代的法国学派产生过重大的影响。

虽然我现在已经懂得什么叫"性本善"，在当时却真莫名其妙。

我恨透了家塾里的生活。有一天，我乘先生不注意我的时候，偷偷地爬下椅子，像一只挣脱锁链的小狗，一溜烟逃回家中，躲到母亲的怀里。

"Why do you come home, my child?" asked my mother in surprise.

"The school is no good, the teacher is no good, and the book is no good," I replied.

"Aren't you afraid of your teacher? He may come and get you," said my mother kindly.

"I'll kill the teacher! I'll burn the school!"

My mother didn't send me back to school that day, nor did the teacher come.

Early the next morning my nurse woke me, spoke many kind words to me, and persuaded me to go to school again. From childhood I responded to kind words only; no coercion ever did any good. It was the gentle reasonableness of my nurse that made me go back voluntarily.

I took to school my own rattan chair, which was very light. A servant followed me and put it on the stand to match the height of the desk. The teacher made no remark and acted as if nothing had happened, but I noticed several schoolmates making faces at me. I hated them but pretended not to see them. I climbed up on the chair and sat there without resting place for my poor feet. More lessons were given, in the same book. I read very loud, as was required in the old type of school, repeating the meaningless text again and again till every word was learned by heart. When the sun shone directly above our heads it was midday. The teacher ordered me to go home for lunch. Immediately after lunch I went back to school and kept on learning the same thing till sunset.

Day in and day out, there was no change in the curriculum. When I finished one textbook another meaningless one came in turn. It was memory and patience that we were training.

We were taught the "three P's" in reading: presence of mind, presence of eye, and the presence of lips. The first means concentration, a requisite for doing any work well. The second is important because by it one gets a clear impression of the ideographic letters, with the various arrangements of fine and intricate strokes in each letter. The third is attained by reading a passage aloud several hundred times; the words then fall from the lips fluently, thus relieving the burden of the memory. We were warned not to commit words to memory by artificial means, because then we would not retain them. If we stumbled in reciting a passage we were ordered to read it over again one or two hundred times more—if the teacher was not in

母亲自然很感意外，但是她只是慈祥地问我："你怎么跑回家来了，孩子？"

我答道："家塾不好，先生不好，书本不好。"

"你不怕先生吗？他也许会到家里来找你呢！"母亲笑着说。

"先生，我要杀他！家塾，我要放把火烧了它！"我急着说。

母亲并没有把我送回家塾，那位先生也没有找上门来。

第二天早上，奶妈喊醒了我，对我说了许多好话，总算把我劝回家塾。从童年时代起我就吃软不吃硬。好好劝我，要我干什么都行，高压手段可没有用。经过奶妈一阵委婉的劝谏，我终于自动地重新去上学了。

我带着一张自备的竹椅子，家里一位佣人跟着我到了家塾，把竹椅子放到木架上，使我刚好够得着书桌。先生没有出声，装作不知道我曾经逃过学，但是我注意到好几位同学对着我装鬼脸。我讨厌他们，但是装作没有看见。我爬上椅子坐在那里，两只脚却悬空挂着，没有休息的地方。我的课也上了，书却仍旧是那本《三字经》。我高声朗诵着不知所云的课文，一遍又一遍地念得烂熟。等到太阳不偏不倚地照到我们的头上时，我们知道那是正午了。先生让我们回家吃午饭，吃过饭我马上回到家塾继续念那课同样的书，一直到日落山才散学。

一日又一日地过去，课程却一成不变。一本书念完了之后，接着又是一本不知所云的书。接受训练的只是记忆力和耐心。

念书时先生要我们做到"三到"，那就是心到、眼到、口到。所谓心到就是注意力集中，不但读书如此，做任何事情都得如此。眼到对学习中国文字特别重要，因为中国字的笔划错综复杂，稍一不慎就可能读别字。所谓口到就是把一段书高声朗诵几百遍，使得句子脱口而出，这样可以减轻记忆力的负担。先生警告我们，念书不能取巧强记，因为勉强记住的字句很容易忘记。如果我们背书时有些疙瘩，先生就会要我们一遍又一遍地再念，甚至念上一两百遍。碰上先生心情不好，

a good humor you would probably receive in addition, without warning, a crack on the skull. Often when the day was over some boys left school with lumps on their scalps.

Discipline and obedience were aimed at without regard for the interest of the pupil. Sundays were unknown. We had half holidays in the afternoon on the first and fifteenth day of each lunar month. In addition, we had during the year several full holidays on festival days, such as the Dragon Festival and the Moon Festival. A comparatively long vacation came about New Year's time. It started on the twentieth[1] day of the Twelfth Moon and lasted till the same day of the First Moon of the new year, and was called the New Year vacation.

As several years went by, I grew older and learned by heart quite a number of characters. My teacher then began to explain the meaning of the text and studying grew to be less drudgery. From the Confucian classics I began to understand a little of the way to be a righteous man. It began with the culture of the person, then went on to the fulfillment of duties to the family, to the state, and finally the world. I did not appreciate its full significance until much later.

In the earliest years school was indeed a prison to me. The difference was that in a real prison the inmates have little hope, while in school the pupils had hopes for a bright future. Had not all the famous scholars and statesmen gone through years of suffering in schools? It was through suffering that men became great, we were told to believe. The path was difficult but it was the only road to success.

"If you have tasted the bitterest of the bitter you will become the greatest of the great."

"The Son of Heaven[2] honors the scholar. While everything else is of a lower order, learning is the highest of all."

"Do not envy others who possess the sword; you have a pen that is mightier."

These common sayings spurred me on the road of learning as the odors of an early spring in the air spur a sluggish horse to green pastures. Otherwise I should have dropped my schooling and taken to business in Shanghai. Ideals, hopes, and will power are the most important factors in shaping one's life. If education fails in these, the emphasis in modern methods upon the interest of the pupil is but a trifling thing. Interest is an important factor in education only when it is subordinated to inculcation of ideals.

脑袋上就会吃栗子。天黑放学时，常常有些学生头皮上带着几个大疙瘩回家。

不管学生愿意不愿意，他们必须守规矩，而且要绝对服从。我们根本不知道什么叫礼拜天。每逢阴历初一、十五，我们就有半天假。碰到节庆，倒也全天放假，例如端午节和中秋节。新年的假期比较长，从十二月二十一一直到正月二十。

在家塾里念了几年之后，我渐渐长大了，也记得不少的字。这时先生才开始把课文的意思解释给我听，因此念起书来也不再像以前那样吃力了。从四书五经里，我开始慢慢了解做人的道理。按照儒家的理想，做人要先从修身着手，其次齐家，然后治国、平天下。其中深义到后来我才完全体会。

在最初几年，家塾生活对我而言简直像监狱，唯一的区别是：真正监狱里的犯人没有希望，而家塾的学生们都有着前程无限的憧憬。所有的学者名流、达官贵人不是都经过寒窗苦读的煎熬吗？

"吃得苦中苦，方为人上人。"

"天子重英豪，文章教尔曹。万般皆下品，惟有读书高。"

"别人怀宝剑，我有笔如刀。"

这些成语驱策着我向学问之途迈进，正如初春空气中的芳香吸引着一匹慵懒的马儿步向碧绿的草原，否则我恐怕早已丢下书本跑到上海做生意去了。理想、希望和意志可说是决定一生荣枯的最重要的因素。教育如果不能启发一个人的理想、希望和意志，单单强调学生的兴趣，那是舍本逐末的办法。只有以启发理想为主、培养兴趣为辅时，兴趣才能成为教育上的一个重要因素。

It seemed tedious and foolish in the old Chinese schools to commit the classics to memory. But there was the advantage that in later years one could go to memory to find ready references for the conduct of life. In a static society where the world moved very slowly and the rules of conduct would need little modification, it seems to me that the old Chinese method of teaching and learning was quite adequate for the needs it filled. Only, in a country school like mine it ran to the extreme, giving unnecessary hardship to the pupils. I wonder how many promising boys were scared away before they began to realize the importance of learning.

There were no sports or physical exercises in any form in my school. The boys were forbidden to run fast; they must walk slowly and be dignified. Right after lunch we were required to practise calligraphy. Young life seemed to be practically squeezed out of us.

Nevertheless, the boys found their own way to satisfy their play instincts. When the teacher was absent we would take over control of the school. Sometimes desks were taken to form a platform on which a play could be staged. Chairs and stools would be used as stage properties. Sometimes we played blindman's buff. On one occasion, while I was serving as the "blind," the teacher returned and all the others slipped away. As I caught an easy prey I felt something strange—it was the teacher. The shock was so terrifying that as I write it reels in my senses as vividly as if it had happened yesterday.

In the spring, when school was over in the afternoon, we flew kites. We made our own. Some took the form of a monster centipede, others a gigantic butterfly. At night we would send into the sky along the kite string a chain of lanterns, numbering usually five, seven, or nine. The smaller boys played with smaller kites, generally in the shape of a dragonfly, a swallow, or an eagle. The "swallows" were the most ingenious; they usually went by pairs, tied to the two ends of a slip of bamboo balanced on the kite string, and danced up and down in the currents of air like a pair of feathered playmates. Once I saw several swallows darting around such a pair, seeking their company.

In summer we played with other boys in the village during the starry evenings. The fireflies in the air looked like moving stars. Some of us preferred to listen to the stories told by some elder of the village. With a big palm-leaf fan in his hands to chase away annoying mosquitoes, and a teapot by his side, the elder would give his account of historical personages, dynastic changes, and past happenings in the village.

在老式私塾里死背古书似乎乏味又愚蠢，但是背古书倒也有背古书的好处。一个人到了成年时，常常可以从背的古书里找到立身处事的指南针。在一个安定的社会里，一切守旧成风，行为的准则也很少变化。因此我觉得我国的老式教学方法似乎已足以应付当时的实际需要。自然，像我家乡的那个私塾当然是个极端的例子，那只有给小孩子添些无谓的苦难。我怕许多有前途的孩子，在未发现学问的重要以前就给吓跑了。

在我的家塾里，课程里根本没有运动或体育这个项目。小孩子们不许拔步飞跑，他们必须保持"体统"一步一步慢慢地走。吃过中饭以后，我们得马上练字。我们简直被磨得毫无朝气。

话虽如此，小孩子还是能够自行设法来满足他们嬉戏的本能。如果先生不在，家塾可就是我们的天下了。有时候我们把书桌搬在一起，拼成一个戏台在上面演戏，椅子板凳就成了舞台上的道具。有时候我们就玩捉迷藏。有一次，我被蒙上眼睛当瞎子，刚巧先生回来了，其余的孩子都偷偷地溜了，我轻而易举地就抓到一个人——我的先生。当我发现闯了祸时，我简直吓昏了。到现在想起这件事尚有余悸。

春天来时，放了学我们就去放风筝，风筝都是我们自己做的。风筝的形式不一，有的像蜈蚣，有的像蝴蝶。夜晚时，我们把一串灯笼随着风筝送到天空，灯笼的数目通常是五个、七个或九个。比较小的孩子就玩小风筝，式样通常是蜻蜓、燕子或老鹰。"燕子"风筝设计得最妙，通常是成对的，一根细竹片的两端各扎一只"燕子"，然后把竹片摆平在风筝绳子上。送上天空以后，一对对的"燕子"随风摆动，活像比翼双飞的真燕子。有一次，我还看到好几只真的燕子在一只"燕子"风筝附近盘旋，大概是在找伴儿。

满天星斗的夏夜，村子里的小孩子们就捉萤火虫玩儿。有些小孩子则宁愿听大人们讲故事。讲故事的大人，手中总是摇着一柄大蒲扇，一方面为了驱暑，一方面也是为了驱逐纠缠不清的蚊子。口中衔旱烟杆，旁边放着小茶壶，慢条斯理地叙述历史人物的故事、改朝换代的情形，以及村中的掌故。

About two hundred and fifty years ago [he would begin], when the Ming Dynasty was overthrown by the Manchus, the whole country was in turmoil, but our forefathers living in this village still enjoyed peace. Later on, the Imperial Edict reached our village ordering all male persons to cut their hair according to the Tartar fashion and to wear a queue.[2] Men were terrified and women wept. Barbers came to the village to enforce the order. They had Imperial sanction, if anyone should disobey, to punish the culprit by cutting off his head instead of his hair. No one preferred his hair to his head. Since a man could not retain both his head and his hair, he would stretch his head and let the barber do his job of haircutting and queue braiding. We have got used to it now, but my! it must have looked funny then...

This was a bit of history we learned outside of school.

Again, a bit of local anthropology:

Tens of thousands of years ago our far-distant ancestors had tails like the monkey. The man-monkey's tail gradually turned yellow as he grew older. When nine out of the ten segments of his tail had turned yellow, he knew he was about to die. Then he would crawl into his cave and die there. As years went by, his tail dropped. This is why we have no tails now. But you can find at the end of your backbone where it was broken off.

Here is a story about pugilism:

In front of a rice shop a small boy was stationed to sell rice. He amused himself by picking up pinches of it and throwing them swiftly back into the basket. On one occasion a monk came to beg for rice. Instead of giving him some, the boy threw a few grains of it right in his face. To his surprise he saw that the grains had pierced the man's skin. The monk made a polite bow with his hands pressed together palm to palm, saying "Namo Amita Buddha" [Hail, Great Buddha!], and went his way.

Seven days later a pugilist came to the town. By now the boy was looking rather pale. "What's the matter with you, my boy?" asked the pugilist. When he was told the story of the monk he said, "Ah, that monk is the most famous pugilist of our time. You have insulted him. You have received from his bow the terrible internal wounds which will bring you to death in forty-nine days. I have medicine for your cure, but you must

　　大人告诉我们，大约二百五十年前，清兵入关推翻了明朝，盗贼蜂起，天下大乱，但是我们村中却安谧如恒。后来圣旨到了村里，命令所有的男人按照满洲鞑子的发式，剃去头顶前面的头发，而在后脑勺上留起辫子。男子听了如同晴天霹雳，女人们则急得哭了，剃头匠奉派到村子里强制执行，他们是奉旨行事，如果有人抗旨不肯剃头，就有杀头的危险。留头究竟比留发重要，二者既然不可兼得，大家也就只好乖乖地伸出脖子，任由剃头匠剃发编辫了。当然，后来大家看惯了，也就觉得无所谓，但是初次剃发留辫子的时候，那样子看起来一定是很滑稽的。……

　　从这位讲故事的长者口中，我们总算学到了一点历史，那是在家塾中学不到的。此外，我们还得到一点关于人类学的传说。故事是这样的：

　　几万年以前，我们的祖先也像猴子一样长着尾巴。那时的人可说介于人与猿之间。人猿年岁长大以后，他的尾巴就渐渐变为黄色。人猿的尾巴共有十节，十节中如有九节变黄，他就知道自己快要死了。于是他就爬到窑洞里深居简出，结果就死在窑洞里面。再经过几千年以后，人的尾巴掉了，所以现在的人都没有尾巴，但是尾巴的痕迹仍旧存在。不信，你可以顺着背脊骨往下摸，尾巴根儿还是可以摸得到的。

　　下面是一则关于技击的故事：

　　一位学徒在一家米店前卖米。在没有生意的时候，这位学徒就抓着米粒玩儿，他一把一把地把米抓起来，然后又一把一把地把米掷回米筐里。有一天，一位和尚来化米，那位学徒不但没有拿米给和尚，反而抓了几颗米掷到和尚脸上。想不到那几颗米竟然颗颗深陷到和尚的皮肉里面去了。和尚似乎不生气，反而向那位学徒深深一鞠躬，双手合什，念了一声"南无阿弥陀佛"就走了。

　　七天之后，一位拳师经过村里，他看到米店学徒脸色苍白，就问学徒究竟是怎么回事。学徒把和尚化米的事说了，拳师听了不禁摇头叹息："啊呀，你怎么可得罪他呢？他是当今武林首屈一指的人物呀！他在向你鞠躬的时候，你已经受了致命的内伤，不出七七四十九天，你就活不成了！幸好我还有药可以给你医治，不过你要赶快躲开，永远不要再撞上

run away and not meet him again. He will come again after forty-nine days. Get a coffin, put some bricks in it, and pretend that you have died."

The monk did come, and asked for the boy. When he was told of his death, he sighed and said, "What a pity!" At his request he was led to see the coffin. Running his fingers over the top of it, he muttered, "Namo Amita Buddha." After he had gone the coffin was opened and it was found that all the bricks in it were cracked.

We boys pricked up our ears and listened attentively to these stories; they were one of the sources of my extracurricular education. I could retell many like them if space would allow.

I had several teachers, one after another, in my school. One of them was a kindly rustic scholar who had failed to pass the Imperial civil examinations for the First Degree, despite many attempts, and had to content himself with teaching in a family school. He had a round, moonlike face, was short and stout, and his bespectacled eyes looked habitually over the heavy brass rims of his glasses. His grey mustache hung bristling from his upper lip and he wore no beard. After he had taken egg soup at dinner, yellow particles would be seen adhering to the tips of his unclipped mustache. He was an encyclopedia of endless stories. But his literary style was rather poor; this is why, I presume, he failed repeatedly in the examinations; though he was an endless fountain of witticism. I think his memory in certain respects must have been bad, for he always forgot to carry with him either his umbrella or towel or fan when going back to the school after paying a visit to his friends. Necessity taught him finally to make an inventory of the articles he brought with him: pipe, umbrella, towel, and fan. When about to leave he would repeat, "Pipe, umbrella, towel, and fan." Even in winter, when no fan was needed, he would continue to mention it in his list, sometimes realizing that he had brought no fan with him, but at other times trying to find it, to the great amusement of both friends and pupils.

My mental scope was thus limited to what I learned from the Confucian classics and what the teachers and elders told me. I memorized quite a few of the classics and also had a rich store of stories. My early education, therefore, consisted chiefly of memory work. Yet I was fortunate to have been born and to live in the country, where nature offered plenty of instruction. Once I noticed that some beetles

这位和尚。四十九天之后他还会再来的。赶快备口棺木，放几块砖头在棺材里，假装你已经死了入殓待葬就是了。"

四十九天之后，和尚果然又来找学徒了。人们告诉他学徒已经死了。和尚叹口气说："可怜！可怜！"和尚要看看棺材，大家就带他去看，他用手轻轻地把棺盖从头至尾抚摸一遍，念了一声"南无阿弥陀佛"就走了。和尚走了之后，大家打开棺盖一看，里面的砖头已经全部粉碎。

小孩子们全都竖起耳朵听这些故事，这些故事就是我们课外知识的主要来源之一。

我们家塾里的先生，前前后后换了好几个。其中之一是位心地仁厚然而土头土脑的老学究。他的命运多舛，屡次参加府试都没有考上秀才，最后只好死心塌地教私塾。他的脸团团如满月，身材矮胖，一副铜框眼镜老是低低地滑到鼻梁上，两只眼睛就打从眼镜上面看人。他没有留须，鼻子下面却养着一撮蓬松的灰色胡子。碰到喝蛋花汤的日子，他的胡子上常常挂着几片黄蛋花。他的故事多得说不尽，简直是一部活的百科全书。但是他的文才很差，我想这或许就是他屡试不中的缘故。不过人很风趣，善于笑谑。他在有些事情上非常健忘，看过朋友回到家塾时，不是忘了雨伞，就是丢了扇子。老是这样丢三落四究竟不是事，于是他就把他出门时必带的东西开了个清单：烟管、雨伞、毛巾、扇。每当他告辞回家时，他就念一遍："烟管、雨伞、毛巾、扇。"冬天不需要带扇子的时候，他也照样要按清单念扇子。有时候他也记得根本没有带扇子出门，有时却仍然到处找扇子，他的朋友和学生就在暗中窃笑。

我童年时的知识范围，可以说只局限于四书五经，以及私塾先生和村中长辈所告诉我的事。我背得出不少的古书，也记得很多的故事，因此我的童年教育可以说主要的是记忆工作。幸而我生长在乡村，可以从大自然获得不少的知识和启发。有一次，我注意到

which lived on a large soap tree—so named because we used its nuts for soap—had on their heads horns like those of a deer. These looked exactly like the thorns that grew at the tips of the twigs of the tree. The beetles, I was told, were born of the tree and therefore looked like their mother. Somehow I felt suspicious. I reasoned that if a tree was capable of giving birth to beetles, they would in turn be capable of laying eggs that would be the seeds for the tree. That not being the case, I felt there must be some other reason for the remarkable likeness. I found it when I saw a bird feeding on insects in the tree without noticing the deer-horned beetles near by. The horns were therefore imitations of the thorns of the tree, for protection from the birds.

On the banks of the canal there grew candle trees, so called because the oil from the nuts is good for making candles. In the winter months the farmer would tie a few straws around the trunk of the tree, which he took off in the spring and burned. It was a common belief that by virtue of this act a magic force would kill the parasites. The fact was that if you tied enough straw around the trunk the parasites laid their eggs in the straw, and by burning it you destroyed the eggs, thus preventing them from propagating. It was no magic.

There were many such instances of naïve nature study in my childhood. The two above mentioned are, I think, enough for illustration.

Thus there were three sources of the education I received in my childhood. The first was the study in school of the Confucian classics, which served as guidance to moral conduct as well as a foundation to the future study of modern social sciences. The second was the storytelling which was to prepare the way for an appreciation of modern literature. The last was the innocent nature study which later served as a stem on which the buds of modern science could be grafted. Had I been born in a crowded city, resembling—on a smaller scale, minus electricity and wide streets—the East Side of New York or London, I would have missed the all-important training of nature. The whole course of my life might have been different. For the natural endowment of sense perception, observation, curiosity, and reasoning that are in every child and indispensable to life in a modern world might have been altogether smothered by the all-memory traditional training of my early youth.

生长的皂荚树上的甲虫头上长着鹿角一样的角，这些角和枝上的刺长得一模一样，人家告诉我，这些甲虫是树上长出来的，因此也就和母体长得很像。不过我总觉得有点相信不过。我心里想，如果一棵树真能生下甲虫，那末甲虫产下的卵也就应该可以作皂荚树的种籽了。甲虫卵既然种不出皂荚树，那么甲虫的角和皂荚树的刺这样相像一定另有原因。后来我看到一只鸟在皂荚树上啄虫吃，但是这只鸟对于身旁长着鹿角的甲虫却视而不见。于是我恍然大悟，原来甲虫的角是摹拟着刺而生的，目的是保护自己以免被鸟儿啄死。

河汉的两岸长着许多柏树，柏子可以榨油制蜡烛，因此柏树的土名就叫蜡烛树。冬天里农夫们用稻草把树干裹起来，春天到了，就把稻草取下烧掉。一般人相信，这种办法可以产生一种神秘的力量杀死寄生虫。事实上这件事毫无神奇之处，只要我们在树干上扎上足够的稻草，寄生虫就只好在稻草上产卵，烧掉稻草等于毁掉虫卵，寄生虫也就无法繁殖了。

在我童年时代里，这类对自然的粗浅研究的例子很多，举了前面的两个例子，我想也就够了。

由此可见我的童年教育共有三个来源。第一是在私塾里念的古书，来自古书的知识，一方面是立身处世的指针，另一方面也成为后来研究现代社会科学的基础。第二个知识来源是听故事，这使我在欣赏现代文学方面奠立了基础。第三个知识来源是对自然的粗浅研究，不过在这种粗浅研究的根基上却可以移接现代科学的幼苗。如果我生长在草木稀少的大城市里，那我势将失去非常重要的自然训练的机会，我的一生可能完全改观。每一个小孩子所具备的感受力、观察力、好奇心和理解力等等天赋，都可能被我童年所受的全凭记忆的传统训练所窒息。

I must confess that I did not apply myself to study as earnestly as some of my schoolmates, for I did not like to memorize but to see, touch, and reason. My teachers took this as a misfortune or curse of my disposition.

I loved to play and listen to storytelling. I liked to inquire into things to a degree disgusting to the elders. I took delight in watching frogs catch locusts in the rice fields and geese and ducks swimming in the canal. I enjoyed seeing the bamboos grow and flowers blooming, and loved to make kites and fly them. All these propensities were regarded by my teachers as a curse and I myself believed it must be so. But it is an irony of fate that the curse happened to turn out a blessing to me in later years, and the blessings my teachers bestowed upon some of my schoolmates have turned out to be curses. For some have died of consumption and others became bookish scholars, incapable of adjusting themselves to a changing environment when the tides of westernization swept over China.

我得承认，我并没有像某些同学那样用功读书，因为我不喜欢死记，我愿意观察、触摸、理解。我的先生们认为这是我的不幸、我的个性上的祸根。

　　我喜欢玩，喜欢听故事。我喜欢打破砂锅问到底，使大人感到讨厌。我喜欢看着稻田里的青蛙捉蚱蜢，或者鹅鸭在河里戏水。我欣赏新篁解箨。我的先生认为这些癖好都是祸根。我自己也相信将来不会有出息。但是命运是不可捉摸的，我的这些祸根后来竟成为福因，而先生们认定的某些同学的福因结果都证明是祸根。那些好学生后来有的死于肺痨，有的成为书呆，在西化潮流横扫中国时无法适应日新月异的环境而落伍了。

CHAPTER 4   FAMILY INFLUENCE

During the plastic years of childhood and adolescence, family influence upon youth is indeed formative. Bad as well as good habits acquired during this period are difficult to eradicate in later years. On the whole the influence exercised upon me by my family was good and wholesome.

My father was a small landowner and a shareholder in some native banks in Shanghai. My grandfather had left him fairly well off and his mode of living was always simple so that the family never had uneasiness about financial matters. Father was an honest and generous man, respected by the people of the village in particular and surrounding districts generally. He was frugal in private life but very generous toward public affairs, contributing liberally to benevolent organizations.

He would not say anything with intent to deceive and his words were accordingly trusted by those who came in contact with him. He believed in *feng-shui*, the spirits of wind and water, and in fortunetelling and therefore—with a sort of fatalism—that a man's life was predetermined by supernatural forces. However, he also believed that by virtuous conduct and clean thinking one could make these forces respond by bestowing blessings upon oneself as well as one's family; thus the predetermined course of life would gradually shift its ground to a better course. His moral influence upon me was really great. The only regret I have is that I have fallen far short of his good example.

My mother was a cultured and beautiful woman. My childhood memories of her have become somewhat vague. I recall that she could play the harp and sing to it—one of the songs she loved most still lives in my memory. It was about a buried harp whose owner had deserted her. Clink, clink, clink, the harp sang to herself that her lover had not yet kept his promises to come back to her. She waited and waited in vain. She remembered how happy they had been when they sang together. Now she was buried on the shady side of crumbling walls. The autumn wind was blowing, the grass fading, and the white clouds deepening. A nearby stream flowed under a broken bridge and no one ever passed by that place. Only gloom and loneliness reigned.

Someone remarked that it was an ill omen that such a beautiful young lady as my mother should like to sing such a sad song.

肆 家庭影响

童年时代和青春时代的可塑性最大，因而家庭影响往往有决定性的作用。这时期中所养成的习惯，不论好坏，将来都很难根除。大致说来，我所受到的家庭影响是良好而且健全的。

我的父亲是位小地主，而且是上海当地几家钱庄的股东。祖父留给父亲的遗产相当可观，同时父亲生活俭朴，因此一家人一向用不着为银钱操心。父亲为人忠厚而慷慨，蒋村的人非常敬重他，同时也受到邻村人士的普遍崇敬。他自奉俭约，对公益事业却很慷慨，常常大量捐款给慈善机构。

他从来没有说过一句存心骗人的话，因此与他交往的人全都信任他的话。他相信风水和算命。同时他又相信行善积德可以感召神明，使行善者添福增寿，因此前生注定的命运也可以因善行而改变。我父亲的道德人品对我的影响的确很大，我唯一的遗憾是没有好好学到父亲的榜样。

我的母亲是位很有教养而且姿容美丽的女人。我童年时对她的印象已经有点模糊了。我记得她能够弹七弦古琴，而且能够抚琴幽歌。她最喜欢唱的一支歌，叫做"古琴引"，词为：音音音，尔负心。真负心，辜负我，到如今。记得当年低低唱，千千斟，一曲值千金。如今放我枯墙阴，秋风芳草白云深，断桥流水过故人。……切切，冷冷清清，……切切，冷冷清清。

有人说：像我母亲那样青春美貌的妇人唱这样悲切的歌，是不吉利的。

The drawing room where she played her harp looked out under a giant camphor tree. A canal wound its way around the other side of the bamboo grove which served as a fence. A crêpe myrtle, an osmanthus, and an orange tree struggled for such sunlight as the wide spread of the aged camphor could spare. There she could hear birds singing and fish splashing. At sunset the level beams pierced through the grove and cast the shadows of bamboo leaves dancing on the window screens. The walls were hung with landscape paintings and works of well-known calligraphers. Her lacquered harp, inlaid with jade, lay on a long redwood stand with legs carved in the phoenix motif.

The drawing room was kept as it was for many years after her death. A painted likeness of her hung in the middle of the wall. But Mother was no more! The harp, veiled in dark satin velvet, lay alone on the same stand in the same room. How could I help feeling that I was like that buried harp whose song she used to teach me to sing?

My mother died young. I saw her in her coffin in a beautiful embroidered jacket and skirt, wrapped in a long scarlet satin cape down to her feet. There was a hood attached to the cape. Her face alone was exposed. A large pearl shone on her forehead against the red background of the hood.

My stepmother was a very able woman and she was kind to people, but my relation with her was rather unhappy. She did not live long, and Father never married again.

My grandfather had been the manager of a Shanghai bank. During the time of the Taiping Rebellion (1851-1864) he put up a money stand in the native city of Shanghai. This grew later into a small money exchange shop which in turn developed into a native bank—a concern with unlimited liability, making loans on credit. When Mexican silver dollars were introduced into China as auxiliary currency to taels, the foreign money gained popularity among the people. Counterfeit pesos increased in proportion to the widening circulation of the money. By clinking two dollars on their fingers the bankers could tell the bad from the good. But Grandfather beat them all; he could tell by merely glancing at them.

Unfortunately in the prime of life he suffered a leg injury; the leg had to be amputated and he died of blood poisoning. To my father, at the age of twelve or thereabouts, he left some seven thousand taels, at that time

母亲弹琴的书斋，屋后长着一棵几丈高的大樟树。离樟树不远的地方种着一排竹子，这排竹子也就成为我家的篱笆。竹丛的外面围绕着一条小河。大樟树的树荫下长着一棵紫荆花和一棵香团树，但是这两棵树只能在大樟树扶疏的枝叶之间争取些微的阳光。母亲坐在客厅里，可以谛听小鸟的啁唱，也可以听到鱼儿戏水的声音。太阳下山时，平射过来的阳光穿过竹丛把竹影子投映在窗帘上，随风飘动。书斋的墙上满是名家书画。她的嵌着白玉的古琴则安放在长长的红木琴几上，琴几的四足则雕着凤凰。

她去世以后，客厅的布置一直保留了好几年没有变动。她的一张画像高悬在墙的中央。但是母亲已经不在了！她用过的古琴用一块软缎盖着，仍旧放在红木琴几上。我有时不禁要想像自己就是那个饮泣孤塚幽幽低诉的古琴。

我母亲去世时还很年轻。我看到母亲穿着华丽的绣花裙袄躺在棺里，裙袄外面罩一个长长的红绸披风，一直盖到足踝，披风上缀着大红的头兜，只有她的脸露在外面，一颗很大的珍珠衬着红头兜在她额头发出闪闪的亮光。

我的继母是位治家很能干的主妇，待人也很和气，但不久也去世，此后父亲也就不再续弦了。

我的祖父当过上海某银庄的经理。太平天国时（一八五一——一八六四）祖父在上海旧城设了一个小钱摊，后来钱摊发展为小钱庄，进而成为头等钱庄。这种钱庄是无限责任的机构，做些信用贷款的生意。墨西哥鹰洋传到中国成为银两的辅币以后，洋钱渐渐受到国人的欢迎。后来流通渐广，假币也跟着比例增加，但是钱庄里的人只要在指尖上轻轻地把两块银元敲敲，他们就能够辨别那个是真，那个是假，我祖父的本领更使一般钱庄老板佩服，他一眼就能看出哪个是真的，哪个是假。

不幸他在盛年时伤了一条腿，后来严重到必须切去，祖父也就因为血液中毒辞世。父亲当时还只有十二岁左右，祖父给他留下了七千两银子，

considered a big fortune. This helpless orphan was looked after by his future father-in-law, who was a local scholar. By sound investment and careful economy the property grew, in the course of some thirty years, to the value of seventy thousand taels.

This bit of family history will show the reader that some Western influence must in early days have crept into the family.

Father had an inventive mind. He loved to make plans or designs and direct carpenters, blacksmiths, coppersmiths, farmers and basket makers to carry them out according to specifications. He built houses, made experiments in raising silkworms and planting mulberry trees, manufactured guns (of a type already obsolete in the West), and made many other things according to his fancy. Finally he conceived the bright idea of building a "steamboat" without steam. Father occasionally went to Shanghai to look over his business. He took a rowboat from the village to Ningpo, where he boarded a paddle-wheeled steamer for Shanghai. "It took us three days and two nights to Ningpo in a rowboat," he would say, "and only one night from there to Shanghai by the steamer, while the distance is ten times farther." So he made a sketch of how a miniature paddle-wheel boat might be made.

Carpenters and boatbuilders came. The carpenters were instructed to make paddle wheels, the boatbuilders to build a boat according to my father's plan. A month passed and the boat began to take shape. On the day when the tiny "steamer" was to be launched many visitors came and their mouths gaped in admiration for the wonderful invention. Now the boat was on the canal near our house. Two husky fellows were employed to turn the wheels by a wooden handle. The watching crowd stirred with excitement as the boat started to plow slowly through the water. Presently it began to gather momentum and went faster. When it reached approximately the speed of a rowboat, it refused to accelerate further despite the efforts of the crew. The passengers gesticulated as if helping the boat to go faster. Some even lent their arms to the handle and helped to turn the wheels. But the boat was very stubborn and held to the same speed.

Father made several modifications in the paddle wheels, hoping to increase the speed. All attempts failed. The worst of it was that when the boat went for some distance, weeds and water plants gathered on the wheels and at length even the handle refused to pump. "We have to give all credit to the foreigners who made steamboats," said Father with a sigh.

在当时说起来，这已经是一笔相当大的遗产了。父亲成了无告的孤儿，就归他未来的丈人照顾。由于投资得当，调度谨慎，这笔财产逐渐增加，三十年之后，已经到七万两银子。

从上面这一点家庭历史里，读者不难想像我的家庭一定在早年就已受到西方的影响。

父亲很有点发明的头脑。他喜欢自己设计，或者画出图样来，然后指示木匠、铁匠、铜匠、农夫或篾匠按照尺寸照样打造。他自己设计过造房子，也实验过养蚕、植桑、造枪（照着西方一种过时了的式样），而且按着他的想像制造过许多别的东西。最后他想出一个打造"轮船"的聪明办法，但是他的"轮船"却是不利用蒸汽的。父亲为了视察业务，常常需要到上海去。他先坐桨划的木船到宁波，然后从宁波趁轮船到上海。他常说："坐木船从蒋村到宁波要花三天两夜，但是坐轮船从宁波到上海，路虽然远十倍，一夜之间就到了。"因此他就画了一个蓝图，预备建造一艘具体而微的轮船。

木匠和造船匠都被找来了。木匠奉命制造水轮，造船匠则按照我父亲的计划造船，隔了一个月，船已经造得差不多。小"轮船"下水的那一天，许多人跑来参观，大家看了这艘新奇的"轮船"都赞不绝口。"轮船"停靠在我家附近的小河里，父亲雇了两位彪形大汉分执木柄的两端来推动水轮。"轮船"慢慢开始在水中移动时，岸上围观的人不禁欢呼起来。不久这只船的速度也逐渐增加。但是到了速度差不多和桨划的船相等时，水手们再怎样出力，船的速度也不增加了。乘客们指手划脚，巴不得能使船驶得快一点，有几位甚至亲自动手帮着转水轮。但是这只船似乎很顽固，始终保持原来的速度不增加。

父亲把水轮修改了好几次，希望使速度增加。但是一切努力终归白费。更糟的是船行相当距离以后，水草慢慢缠到水轮上，而且愈积愈多，最后甚至连转都转不动了。父亲叹口气说："唉！究竟还是造轮船的洋人有办法。"

The "steamer" finally reverted to a rowboat. But it was too heavy to row. Years after, we found it rotting on the banks of the canal, the green moss growing thick on its hull. Even when it failed, however, Father never gave up the idea of making a further attempt until he was told the story of Watt and his boiling kettle. Then he began to see that there was something deeper than appeared in the thing itself. From that time on he was heart and soul for giving his boys a modern education which would some day enable them to learn the foreigners' "tricks" in making wonderful things.

This is an example of how China began to venture on the road to westernization. However, in human relations Father never seriously advocated the foreigners' ways. "The foreigners are as honest, reasonable, and hard working as we Chinese," he would say. He never saw anything beyond that. Neither did he see any objection to his boys learning their ways and manners.

My teacher, on the other hand, was opposed to Father's ideas. "The artifice in making clever things," he would say, "would have a degrading influence on morals. Haven't our sages told us so?" He believed that good morals could only be kept on a high level by living a simple life. Uncle King, my mother's brother, held the same view. He wrote his ideals of life on a piece of red paper which he posted on the wall near his desk: "Burn a stick of incense early in the morning. Be thankful to Heaven, Earth, the Sun, the Moon, and Stars. There shall be no traitors to usurp the power of the ruling dynasty, nor disobedient sons to worry their parents. Everywhere there shall be bumper crops of rice. Then why shall I worry even if I am poor?"

Uncle King was an old scholar. He had passed the civil examinations for the First Degree in his early years. He always carried a long pipe, longer than a walking stick, and one heard him constantly knocking its brass bowl on the brick floor. There were no wrinkles on his forehead in his old age, an indication of peace, health, and contentment. He was so gentle that I never saw him in a temper. He spoke slowly but distinctly and never let unkind words cross his lips.

那条"轮船"最后改为普通桨划的船。但是船身太重，划也划不动。几年之后，我们发现那条船已经弃置在岸上朽烂腐败，船底长了厚厚的一层青苔。固然这次尝试是失败了，父亲却一直想再来试一下，后来有人告诉他瓦特和蒸汽机的故事，他才放弃了造船的雄心。他发现除了轮船的外表之外，还有更深奥的原理存在。从这时候起，他就一心一意要让他的儿子受现代教育，希望他们将来能有一天学会洋人制造神奇东西的"秘诀"。

这个造轮船的故事也正是中国如何开始向西化的途程探索前进的实例。不过，在人伦道德上父亲却一直不大赞成外国人的办法。固然也认为"外国人倒也同我们中国人一样地忠实、讲理、勤劳"，但是除此之外，他并不觉得外国人有什么可取的地方。话虽如此，他却也不反对他的孩子们学习外国人的生活方式和习惯。

我的先生却反对我父亲的看法。他说："'奇技淫巧'是要伤风败俗的。先圣以前不就是这样说过吗？"他认为只有朴素的生活才能保持高度的道德水准。我的舅父也持同样的看法。他用一张红纸写下他的人生观，又把红纸贴在书桌近旁的墙上："每日清晨一支香，谢天谢地谢三光。国有忠臣护社稷，家无逆子闹爷娘，……但愿处处田稻好，我虽贫时也不妨。"

我的舅父是位秀才，他总是携带着一根长长的旱烟杆，比普通的手杖还长。他经常用烟管的铜斗敲着砖地。他在老年时额头也不显皱纹，足见他心境宁静，身体健康，而且心满意足。他斯文有礼，我从来没有看到他发脾气。他说话很慢，但是很清楚，也从来不骂人。

CHAPTER 5   TROUBLE BREWING

It was customary during the New Year days for vendors to come to the village to sell pictures, some depicting important or thrilling happenings in the country, others showing theatrical performances. During one New Year vacation the attention of the children was drawn to a set of pictures which were rather novel to them. The multicolored scenes showed the Sino-Japanese War of 1894. One was of a naval battle in the north China Sea. One of the Japanese battleships had struck several large pottery jugs filled with gunpowder, which exploded and set the ship on fire, and it was sinking. There were in the picture hundreds of such jugs floating on the sea. In another picture Japanese prisoners of war were seen locked in chains, and some kept in cages. A great victory for China! It existed only on paper, but we children believed it. As I grew older I began to understand that China had been defeated, that we had lost Formosa, that our navy had been destroyed by the Japanese, and Korea torn away. Within a short span of nine years China had lost three dependencies: first Indo-China, then Burma, and now Korea.

One summer day as the sun was setting a farm helper was seen running breathlessly out of my father's study. He had heard a bell ring there without seeing anyone to cause the sound. To him it must be a ghost. But it was the clock striking seven in the evening.

From time immemorial the villagers had been getting their fire by striking a steel blade on flint. Someone brought a few boxes of matches from Shanghai. The grownups were delighted with this easy method. The children loved the firefly glow obtained by scratching a match on the palm in dark corners. It was called "self-coming light" or "ocean light" because it came from across the sea.

Clocks were unnecessary—for what is the use of keeping exact time in a village? What difference would it make to be two or three hours too late or too early? The country folk counted their time in days and months, not in minutes or hours. Matches were a luxury—had we not got along nicely with our steel blades and flints? But when we came to kerosene it was a different proposition. This made night as brilliant as day. There was a world of difference between this and the dim light of a vegetable-oil lamp.

伍 山雨欲来风满楼

新年里常常有些小贩到村子里卖画片，有些画的是国家大事，有的则是戏中情节。有一年新春假期里，有一套新鲜的图画引起小孩子们的浓厚兴趣。这套五彩图画绘的是一八九四年（甲午年）中日战争的故事。其中有一张画的是渤海上的海战场面[1]，日本舰队中的一艘军舰已被几罐装满火药的大瓦罐击中起火，军舰正在下沉。图中还画着几百个同样的大瓦罐在海上漂浮。这种瓦罐，就是当时民间所通用的夜壶，夜间小便时使用的。另一幅画中则画着一群带了铐链的日本俘虏，有的则关在笼子里。中国打了大胜仗了！自然，那只是纸上的胜仗，但是我们小孩子们却深信不疑。后来我年纪大一点以后，我才知道我国实际上是被日本打败了，而且割让了台湾，我们的海军被日本消灭，高丽也被日本抢走了。短短九年之内，中国已经相继丧失了三个承认中国宗主权的外围国，最先是越南，继之是缅甸，现在又丢了高丽。

一个夏天的傍晚，一位临时雇工气喘如牛地从我父亲的书房里跑了出来。他说在书房里听到一阵叮当的声音，但是房里找不到人影。他说那一定是鬼在作怪。后来一追究，原来是时钟在报时。

从无可稽考的年代起，乡下人一直利用刀片敲击火石来取火，现在忽然有人从上海带来了几盒火柴。大人们对这种简便的取火方法非常高兴。小孩们也很开心，在黑暗的角落，手上火柴一擦，就可以发出萤火虫一样的光亮。火柴在当时叫"自来火"，因为一擦就着；也叫"洋火"，因为它是从外洋运进来的。

时钟实际上并无必要，因为在乡村里，时间算得再准也没有用处。早二三个钟头，迟二三个钟头又有什么关系？乡下人计时间是以天和月做单位的，并不以分成小时来计算。火柴其实也是奢侈品——用刀片火石不也是一直过得很好吗？至于煤油，那可又当别论了，煤油灯可以把黑夜照得如同白昼，这与菜油灯的昏暗灯光比起来真有天渊之别。

The Standard Oil Company, known as Meifoo, was the torchbearer that was leading China out of the "dark ages" to modernization. People kept matches and clocks as curiosities but kerosene as a necessity. But if kerosene was a necessity, wasn't the telegraph a necessity to take the place of a foot messenger, and steamboats to take the place of rowboats or sailboats? And so it went.

Few could grasp the significance of one tiny segment of the vast circle. While we played innocently with clocks and matches and enjoyed our kerosene lamps, we never realized that we were toying with a fire that would some day set all China aflame. These were the signs of an impending volcanic eruption which destroyed peace and order first in my village and others like it and eventually in the whole country.

Christian missionaries played their part in introducing foreign manufactures into the interior. Braving hardship, disease, and personal danger, they went to almost every hamlet in the land to save the souls of the heathen Chinese. As a matter of course they took kerosene, cloth, clocks, soap, etc., with them into the interior. People in general were more interested in these things than in the gospel; they opened up a new horizon of wants for the Chinese people. A market for foreign goods was thus created unintentionally by missionaries whose real purpose was to preach the gospel of Christ.

I do not mean that the missionaries were chiefly responsible for the growth of modern commercialism in China. But they played their part—a considerable part, for they penetrated the vast country to every corner. The major role, of course, was played by the merchant ships and gunboats of the Western Powers. It was the Christian missions coupled with gunboats that forced the old literary and agricultural China on the road to modern industrial and commercial life.

With my own eyes I saw the growth of a new class of compradors— middlemen between the Chinese and foreign merchants—and their satellites, and the dying of the old class of literati which I was about to join and from which I eventually sneaked away. The foreign merchants brought their goods to seaports such as Shanghai, Tientsin, and others. Through Chinese compradors they were distributed to cities in the interior and from there to the towns and villages. People were attracted by the easier and larger sums of money they could make. The more

美孚洋行是把中国从"黑暗时代"导引到现代文明的执炬者。大家买火柴、时钟是出于好奇,买煤油却由于生活上的必要。但事情并不到此为止。煤油既然成为必需品,那末,取代信差的电报以及取代舢舨和帆船的轮船又何尝不是必需品呢?依此类推,必需的东西也就愈来愈多。

很少人能够在整体上发现细微末节的重要性。当我们毫不在意地玩着火柴或享受煤油灯的时候,谁也想不到是在玩火,这点星星之火终于使全中国烈焰烛天。火柴和煤油是火山爆发前的迹象,这个"火山"爆发以后,先是破坏了蒋村以及其他村庄的和平和安宁,最后终于震撼了全中国。

基督教传教士曾在无意中把外国货品介绍到中国内地。传教士们不顾艰难险阻、瘴疠瘟疫甚至生命危险,遍历穷乡僻壤,去拯救不相信上帝的中国人的灵魂。他们足迹所至,随身携带的煤油、洋布、钟表、肥皂等等也就到了内地。一般老百姓似乎对这些东西比对福音更感兴趣。这些舶来品开拓了中国老百姓的眼界,同时也激起了国人对物质文明的向往。传教士原来的目的是传布耶稣基督的福音,结果却无意中为洋货开拓了市场。

我不是说传教士应对中国现代商业的成长负主要责任,但是他们至少在这方面担任了一个角色,而且是重要的一角,因为他们深入到中国内地的每一角落。主角自然还是西方列强的商船和兵舰。基督教传教士加上兵舰,终于逼使文弱的、以农为本的古老中国步上现代工商业的道路。

我曾经目睹买办阶级的成长以及士大夫阶级的没落。我自己也几乎参加了士大夫的行列,但是最后总算偷偷地溜掉了。所谓买办阶级,就是本国商人和外国商人之间的中国人。外国商人把货运到上海、天津等通商港埠,这些货品再通过买办,从大商埠转销到各城镇村庄。买办们在转手之间就可以大笔地

enterprising and fortunate entered the new business of dealing directly or indirectly in foreign goods. Some became very rich and many others well to do. The less fortunate were left behind, to go on tilling their land or to remain in their old trades. As the land was less remunerative and the old trades fast deteriorating in the face of foreign competition, the old economic structure began rapidly to break down. Naturally a number of people were thrown out of economic gear. These unfortunates, jealous of the newly rich and either dissatisfied with their old occupations or deprived of them, became desperate. The flood was surging against the water gate—the autumn flood, symbolic of the turmoil that was to banish peace from my village.

One autumn afternoon as I was running in the fields I heard the frantic sounding of a gong. As the crier approached our village, I heard his cry that the dike had broken through and the flood was coming. I ran back home as fast as I could and told everyone I met on the way.

Everyone got busy at once. We got ready boats, wooden bathtubs, or anything that would float, waiting for the calamity to arrive. Some even chose tall trees for their future abode. None of us slept well that night. The next morning the flood entered our gate and the spearhead of water glided like a giant serpent into our courtyard. By noon, children had begun to row in bathtubs in the hall.

The dike was repaired with sandbags and the Tsao-ao River ceased to overflow. The flood stayed in our village and surrounding districts for about a week, then gradually emptied into the lower lands and disappeared through the rivers into the sea, and all the crops with it.

After a week or so, late in the afternoon a large boat was seen plying toward our village with many people aboard. It docked near our house and they began to disembark. As a precaution we closed our gates. They stormed the main gate with heavy granite slabs and finally it crashed down like an avalanche. The crowd forced their way in. The leader, muscular and heavy built, with his queue round the top of his head, came into the courtyard with his followers after him. He shouted, "We are hungry and want to borrow rice." The crowd joined in chorus. They searched the barn but did not touch it; they wanted to "borrow." Finally, through the mediation of a neighboring farmer, several bushels of rice were "loaned" to them and they embarked with it and sailed away. This was the first intimation of troubles to come.

赚钱，因此吃这一行饭的人也就愈来愈多。事业心比较强、际遇比较好的人，纷纷加入直接间接买卖外国货的新行业。有的人发大财，有的人则丰衣足食。际遇比较差的可就落了伍，有的依旧种田耕地，有的则守在旧行业里谋生。田地的出息有限，旧行业在外国竞争之下又一落千丈，于是旧有的经济制度很快地就开始崩溃了。结果是一大群人无可避免地失了谋生糊口的机会。这些不幸的人，一方面嫉妒新兴的暴发户，一方面又不满于旧日的行业，或者根本丧失了旧有的职业，结果就铤而走险。曹娥江大潮正在冲激着水闸，象征着即将破坏蒋村安宁的动乱正在奔腾澎湃。

一个秋天的下午，我正在田野里追逐嬉戏，忽然听到一阵紧急狂骤的锣声。敲锣的人一面狂奔着，一面高喊堤塘已经冲塌了，洪水正向村中漫过来。我拼命跑回家里，并把这消息告诉路上所碰到的一切人。

大家马上忙作一团。我们赶快准备好船只、木浴盆，以及所有可以浮得起来的东西，以便应付即将来临的灾难。有的人则决定爬到大树上去暂避。第二天早晨，洪水已经冲进我家的大门，水头像巨蟒一样奔进院子。到了中午时，小孩已经坐上浴盆，在大厅里划来划去了。

堤塘缺口终于用沙包堵住，曹娥江也不再泛滥了。洪水在我们村里以及邻近村庄停留约一星期，然后慢慢退到低地，最后随江河入海，同时卷走了所有的稻作。

大约一星期以后，一只大船在傍晚时分载着许多人向我们村庄划过来。这只船在我家附近停下，船上的人也纷纷离船上岸。我们为防意外，赶紧闭起大门。他们用大石头来捣大门，最后终于排闼而入。领头的人身材魁伟，显然孔武有力，辫子盘在头顶上。他带着一伙人走到天井里，高喊："我们肚子饿，我们要借粮。"其余人也就跟着呐喊助威。他们搜索了谷仓，但是没有马上动手搬；他们要"借"。最后经过隔壁一位农人的调停，他们"借"走了几担谷子以后，就回船启航了。这是随后发生的一连串变乱的首次警号。

One incident after another of the same kind but of more serious nature happened in neighboring villages. It started with "borrowing" but ended in robbing. It spread like fire and the scant government forces in the country could not stop it. Moreover, robbery of foodstuffs was not liable to capital punishment and only capital punishment could have checked it, at least temporarily.

The thing dragged on till winter and then the first robbery of a felonious nature took place in the village of the Suns. The victim was a Mr. Sun who owned a prosperous lumber business in Shanghai. His father had amassed a fortune in that port by doing construction work for foreign "hongs" or companies.

It was a cold winter night and everybody had gone to bed early to keep warm. Someone noticed through the window against the background of darkness a column of torchlights moving along the highway toward the village of the Suns. As the lights came near the village a volley of shots was heard. It was bandits. They forced open the gates of Mr. Sun's house and seized all the treasure they could carry—valuable fur coats, silver pieces, jewels, etc. They took Mr. Sun, tied him to the end of a long bamboo pole, and thrust him into the canal. People found him the next morning by pulling up the pole.

Waves of robbery spread through the villages. Overnight the peace and tranquility that the villagers had been enjoying for centuries vanished. Night after night we could not sleep in peace. My father bought revolvers and outmoded guns from Shanghai. All of us, including children, began to practise shooting. Even the birds had no peace, for we took them as our living targets. We went to bed by turns, some keeping a night watch. When we heard dogs barking we fired a few shots in the air as a warning to bandits, real or imaginary; to save ammunition we often mixed firecrackers with gunshots.

This sort of thing could not go on indefinitely. Reluctantly my father gathered together the members of his family and moved to Shanghai.

Meanwhile, during the two years previous to our move I had continued my education at a neighboring provincial city. When I was still studying at the family school, my father asked me one day whether I would like to enter business as a career or prepare for government service. My two elder brothers had both decided for the latter. Father said he would like me to think it over carefully before coming to a decision.

性质相近然而比较严重的事件，接二连三地在邻村发生。开始时是"借"，随后就变质为抢劫。抢劫事件像野火一样到处蔓延，乡间微薄的官兵武力根本无法加以阻遏。而且抢粮食不能处以极刑，但是在那种情势下，恐怕只有极刑才能加以遏止，至少暂时不至如此猖獗。

"借粮"的事件一直延续至那年冬天。不久之后，杀人掳掠的暴行终于在孙庄首次发生。被害的孙君在上海有一爿生意兴隆的木行。孙君的父亲曾在上海承包"洋行"的营造工程而发了大财。

那是一个凛冽的冬夜，孙庄的人很早就躲到被窝去了。有人从窗子里发现黑暗中有一队火把正从大路上向孙庄移动。火把临近孙庄时，大家听到一阵枪声。强盗来了！强盗冲开孙家的大门，抢走了孙家所有的金银财帛——名贵的羊裘皮袄、金银器皿、珍珠宝石，无一幸免。他们并且掳走了孙君，把他绑在一根长竹竿的顶端，然后又把他压到河底。第二天孙家的人拖起竹竿才发现他的尸体。

抢劫的风潮迅速蔓延到各村庄。几百年来乡村人们所享受的和平与安宁，一夜之间丧失殆尽。我们没有一夜能够安稳地睡。我父亲从上海买来了手枪以及旧式的长枪。大家开始练习放枪，小孩子也不例外。我们拿鸟雀当活靶，因此连鸟雀都遭了殃。我们轮班睡觉，值班的人就负责守夜。一听到犬吠，我们就向空放枪警告盗匪，自然有时是虚惊，有时却的确把强盗吓跑了。为了节省弹药，我们常常在枪声中夹带些爆仗。

永远这样紧张下去究竟不是事。父亲最后无可奈何地带了一家大小搬到上海住下来。

我们搬家之前的两年内，我曾在绍兴继续我的学业。我还在家塾里念书的时候，父亲曾经问我将来愿意做生意还是预备做官。我的两位哥哥都已经决定步入仕途。父亲要我决定之前，仔细考虑一番。

The honor of service to the state had attracted young people for generations. It was only natural that I should be strongly inclined to it. On the other hand, the life of the newly rich, who could enjoy the luxury of the many new and ingenious imported manufactures, was also a temptation. The choice between honor and wealth was more or less contingent upon the ideas and ideals already instilled into one's mind.

I had been told that the people of China fell into four classes. The highest and governing class was the scholars. Next in order came the farmers, who supplied the people with food. The artisans—the third class—manufactured goods for the use of the people. The last were the traders, who transported goods from where there was plenty to where there was a scarcity. Each class had its function to perform in society, but the scholars were the governors of all. So, theoretically speaking, if philosophers were not to be kings, they were at least to be ministers of the state. As there was no hereditary aristocracy in China, the scholars were aristocrats not by birth but by personal endeavor. It was proverbial that a *Hsiu-tsai*, or person possessing the First Degree by having passed the Imperial civil examinations for that initial degree, was an embryo prime minister to the Imperial Court. Then why should I go into business, which later in life would exclude me from the class of the learned aristocracy?

Thus my mind was set to learning. Of course I understood only vaguely what it meant; to me it was only a steppingstone to something higher up. There were many farmers in our village. There were also a number of businessmen who traded in Shanghai and brought back many interesting things: penknives, whistles, rubber balls, dolls, popguns, watches, and the like. As regarded the artisans, an elder of our clan was a carpenter, as also were his sons. A distant uncle was a silversmith who made rings, bracelets, and trinkets to adorn the ladies of the villages. Of the scholars, another uncle—my mother's brother—was one. He had passed the First Degree but stopped short of the other two. There were carved panels with golden inscriptions hanging high in our Ancestral Hall and tall flagpoles standing before it in honor of clansmen who had been successful in the examinations. I remember that one day the magistrate of our hsien came to a neighboring village to probe a murder case. Did I not see the golden button at the top of his red-tasseled hat, and the string of beads round his neck? Did I not see how his sedan chair was lined with green felt and borne by four persons—each wearing a tall black cone-shaped hat, like a gigantic ice-cream cone, with a feather tilting from the pointed top; and how, as he proceeded in his chair, a pair of gongs kept

做官可以光宗耀祖，几百年来，年轻人无不心向往之。自然我也很希望将来能做官。在另一方面，新近发财的人可以享受新颖奇巧的外国货，这般人的生活也是一种强烈的引诱。名利之间的选择，多少与一个人思想中所已灌输进去的观念和理想有点关联。

我听人家说，我们中国人分为士、农、工、商四个阶级。虽然每一阶级在整个社会里都有特定的任务，士大夫都是统治阶级，因此也是最尊荣的一级，依照亚里士多德的主张，哲学家当为国王，所以我们可以说，哲人、学士如果做不到帝王，至少也应该是公卿、宰相。中国的贵族阶级除极少数例外，都不是世袭的，而是由于本身努力达到的。俗语说：秀才是宰相的根苗。如果我去经商，那么将来不就与功名无缘了吗？

因此我决心续求学问。自然，我当时对学问的意义并不十分了解；我只觉得那是向上层社会爬的阶梯。在我们村子里，农、工、商三类人都不稀罕。种田的不必说了，商人也不少。好多人在上海做生意，从上海带回来很多好玩的东西：小洋刀、哨子、皮球、洋娃娃、汽枪、手表等等，多不胜举。至于工匠，我们的一位族长就是木匠，他的儿子们也是的。一位远房叔叔是银匠，专门打造乡村妇女装饰的指环、手镯、钗簪之类。至于读书的人，那可不同了。凡是族人之中有功名的，家庙中都有一面金碧辉煌的匾额，举人以上的家庙前面还有高高的旗杆，悬挂他们的旗帜。我还记得有一天县太爷到邻村查办命案，他乘坐一顶四人扛抬的绿呢暖轿，红缨帽上缀着一颗金顶，胸前挂着一串朝珠。四名轿夫每人戴着一顶尖锥形的黑帽，帽顶插着一根鹅毛。暖轿前面有一对铜锣开道，县太爷

sounding to announce the presence of His Excellency and that the people must show respect? He was the governor of our district and had, as it were, power over our lives and fortunes. What stuff was he made of? A scholar.

Yes, I knew what a scholar was and the advantage of being one. He might climb up, rung by rung, to the top of the ladder and some day become a very high official, sipping Imperial tea in the majestic palace at Peking. Can the reader blame a village boy like me, whose steps had never carried him more than a few miles from his own village, for aspiring to be a scholar? My childish mind pondered the Imperial honors which were the scholar's due. I imagined myself growing larger and larger in importance year by year, passing one examination after another from the lowest to the highest, till one day I should be made a high official—much higher than the magistrate—attired in an embroidered gown with a red button on my hat, a long string of beads, and all the other Imperial honors imaginable, coming back home before the eyes of the awe-inspired folk of the village. How wonderful! All these pictures unrolled enticingly. What a bright future lay before me—but only if I applied myself to the study of the classics.

Again, my early schooling, although distasteful to me, had instilled into my mind somewhat vaguely the importance of learning above everything else. Officials of the state were selected through civil examinations and only people who possessed learning could expect to pass them. Officials were honored because learning itself was honored in China.

My own decision was finally to acquire more learning in preparation for the civil examination, to which my father readily agreed. As our family school was inadequate for my further education, I was sent to an advanced school in Shaoshing, the prefectural capital, about forty miles from the village. My two elder brothers had gone there the year before. We went in a small, slender boat, propelled by a long oar pushed by foot power on one side and a short one held by hand as a helm on the other. Along the way I saw on the river banks many pailous standing in rows—pillared arches erected in memory of virtuous widows. River towns appeared at almost regular intervals with their busy traffic on both land and water. We started early in the morning and arrived at the prefectural capital next day in the afternoon after stopping for the night at a large town.

The Sino-Occidental School, as its name implied, offered not only Chinese studies but also courses in Occidental subjects. This was a new departure in Chinese education. Here my mind began to come into contact with Western knowledge, however poorly explained and

所经之处，老百姓就得肃静回避。他是本县的父母官，我们老百姓的生命财产都得听他发落。他的权势怎么来的？读书呀！

于是我知道了读书人的地位，也知道做一名读书人的好处。他可以一级一级地往上爬，甚至有一天当了大官，还可以在北京皇宫里饮御赐香茗呢！像我这样的一位乡下孩子，足步向未逾越邻近的村镇，他希望读书做官应是很自然的事。我幼稚的心灵里，幻想着自己一天比一天神气，功名步步高升，中了秀才再中了举人，中了举人再中进士，终于有一天当了很大很大的官，比那位县知事要大得好多好多，身穿蟒袍，腰悬玉带，红缨帽上缀着大红顶子，胸前挂着长长的朝珠，显显赫赫地回到故乡，使村子里的人看得目瞪口呆。这些美丽的憧憬，在我眼前一幕幕展开，我的前程多么光明呀！只要我能用心熟读经书就行了。

我的童年教育虽然枯燥乏味，却也在我的思想里模模糊糊地留下学问重于一切的印象。政府官吏都是经过科举选拔的，但是只有有学问的人才有希望金榜题名。官吏受人敬重，是因为学问本身在中国普遍受人敬重的关系。

因此我最后决定努力向学，准备参加科举考试。父亲自然欣然同意，家塾的教育是不够的，因此父亲把我送到离村约四十里的绍兴府去进中西学堂，我的两位哥哥则已先我一年入学。我们是乘条又小又窄的河船去的。小船的一边是一柄长桨，是利用脚力来划的，另一边则是一柄用手操纵的短桨，作用等于船舵。沿岸我们看到许多纪念烈女节妇的牌坊。沿岸相隔相当的距离就有一个比较热闹的市镇。我们一大早动身，中途在一个大镇过了一夜，第二天下午就到了府城。

顾名思义，中西学堂教的不但是我国旧学，而且有西洋学科。这在中国教育史上还是一种新尝试。虽然先生解释得很粗浅，我总算

superficial. My acquaintance with the West had been limited to imported manufactured articles. A mind filled with gods, goddesses, ghosts, fairies, and timeworn traditions was now setting forth to meet some mental imports from the West.

The first and most surprising thing I learned in this school was that the earth is round like a ball. To me it was decidedly flat. I was dumfounded on being further told that lightning is created by electricity and is not the reflection from the mirror of a goddess; that thunder is a by-product of the same electricity and not the beating of a drum by the god of thunder. In elementary physics I learned how rain is formed. It made me give up the idea that a gigantic dragon showers it from his mouth like a fountain high above in the clouds. To understand the meaning of combustion was to banish the idea of fire gods from my mind. One after another, the gods worshiped by my people melted away in my mind like snowmen under the sun. It was the beginning of what little science I know and the end of animism in me. The habit I had formed in my simple nature study in the village, of observing and reasoning without knowing the significance of it, was carried over into the school. As before, I was quite good in reasoning but deficient in memory, and therefore always ready to give up what I had in memory for new ideas that seemed reasonable.

The major part of the curriculum, however, still consisted of literary studies: Chinese literature, classics, and history. There was a considerable amount of memory work to do. As I was not good at it, my name always appeared in the lower middle of the school examination list. I was mediocre in the school, falling far short of brilliance; this was the opinion of my teachers and so it was my own opinion of myself.

Foreign languages were divided into three sections: English, French, and Japanese. I took English and later also Japanese. My Japanese teacher was a Mr. Nakagawa, from whom I learned a correct pronunciation, English was taught us by a Chinese teacher, and his pronunciation of the language was so incorrect that in later years I had to spend much painful time unlearning it. He started us off wrong at the very beginning, even mispronouncing the alphabet. An extreme example is the letter Z, which he called "ütsai."

In the school, in 1898, I heard that Kang Yu-wei and Liang Chi-chao, two liberals from south China who had become unofficial advisers to Emperor Kwang-hsü, had succeeded in persuading the Emperor to abolish the civil examinations and establish instead schools along Western lines throughout China. The old scholars were shocked by the

开始接触西方知识了。在这以前，我对西洋的认识只是限于进口的洋货。现在我那充满了神仙狐鬼的脑子，却开始与思想上的舶来品接触了。

我在中西学堂里首先学到的一件不可思议的事是地圆学说。我一向认为地球是平的。后来先生又告诉我，闪电是阴电和阳电撞击的结果，并不是电神的镜子里发出来的闪光；雷的成因也相同，并非雷神击鼓所生。这简直使我目瞪口呆。从基本物理学我又学到雨是怎样形成的。巨龙在云端张口喷水成雨的观念只好放弃了。了解燃烧的原理以后，我更放弃了火神的观念。过去为我们所崇拜的神佛，像是烈日照射下的雪人，一个接着一个溶化。这是我了解一点科学的开端，也是我思想中怪力乱神信仰的结束。我在乡村里曾经养成研究自然的习惯，我喜欢观察，喜欢说理，虽然有时自己根本就不知道其中的深意。这种习惯在中西学堂里得到继续发展的机会。我还是像过去一样强于理解而不善记忆，凡是合理的新观念我都乐于接受，对记忆中的旧观念则弃如敝屣。

中西学堂的课程大部分还是属于文科方面的：中国文学、经书和历史。记忆的工作相当多，记忆既非我之所长，我的考试成绩也就经常在中等以下。我在学校中显得庸庸碌碌，较之当时头角峥嵘的若干学生，显有逊色。教师们对我的评价如此，我自己也做如是观。

校中外国语分为英文、日文、法文三组。我先选修英文，后来又加选日文。我的日文教师是中川先生，我从他那里学到了正确的日文发音。英文是一位中国老师教的，他的英语发音错得一塌糊涂，后来我千辛万苦才算改正过来。他一开始就把我们导入歧途，连字母发音都咬不准。最可笑的是他竟把字母 z 念成"乌才"。

一八九八年，我在学校里听到一个消息，说是光绪皇帝听了康有为和梁启超的话，已经决定废科举，办学校。这使老一辈的学人

news. But the reform was short lived. The Empress Dowager came back into power; Kang Yu-wei and Liang Chi-chao fled to Japan. China was to go on along the old line. When I came home for the vacation I saw the Imperial Edict, printed in bold letters in both the Chinese and Manchu languages on a large yellow paper, posted on the walls in a busy street, ordering the arrest of the two scholar-statesmen. It looked as if the reform were buried forever.

Shaoshing is a city full of historical interest. It was the capital of the ancient kingdom of Yueh (2068-334 B.C.)[2]. In 494 B.C., during the reign of King Kou-chien, Yueh was defeated by the kingdom of Wu with its capital at Soochow. The king of Yueh adopted a "twenty-year plan" by which, within ten years, he made his country prosperous and populous and in another ten succeeded in training his people in the arts of war. Meantime he discarded all the comforts that belong to a king, taking very coarse food and sleeping on a rough bed while the king of Wu reveled in luxuries. At the end of twenty years, in 473 B.C., King Kou-chien delivered a deathblow at Wu.

This historical episode has been proverbial ever since, serving as an example for all who hope to rise again after a defeat, whether in private enterprise or national affairs. It illustrates patience, courage, endurance, self-denial, and careful planning. I absorbed this lesson in history right on the spot, and no one could help being impressed by it.

Here also the South Sung emperors (1127-1276 A.D.)[3] made their sojourn when the Tartars had overrun north China and the capital had to be moved to Hangchow. Their Imperial mausoleums could be seen not far from the prefectural capital.

This district, with Shaoshing as its center, supplied lawyers for the whole country. In every yamen or government office throughout the country, large or small, no business could be carried on without a Shaoshing lawyer. And Shaoshing wines were the best in China. Famous scholars, philosophers, poets, and calligraphers who made history in their respective fields were born and lived in the prefecture of Shaoshing. It contained six districts, of which my own, Yuyao, was one.[4]

Shaoshing was also famous for its beautiful scenery. Winding creeks, bridge-spanned canals, rivers, mirrored lakes, and gentle hills together formed a landscape which scholars and philosophers found congenial.

大惊失色。但是康、梁的维新运动有如昙花一现，不久慈禧太后再度垂帘听政，康有为和梁启超亡命日本。中国又回到老路子，我放假回到乡村时，看到大街的墙上张贴着黄纸缮写的圣旨，一面是汉文，一面是满文，写的是通缉康、梁的命令。看起来，维新运动就此寿终正寝了。这个维新运动，以后叫做戊戌政变[5]，是中国近代思想史的一个转折点。虽不为革命党人所乐道，而历史的事实却不能因政见不同而抹杀的。我记得梁氏逝世的消息传到南京以后，蔡子民先生和我两人曾在中央政治会议提请国民政府明令表扬其功业。适值胡展堂先生为主席，一见提案，面孔涨得通红，便开口大骂。于是我们自动把提案取消了事。

绍兴的名胜古迹很多，它原是古代越国的都城。越王勾践在纪元前四九四年被以苏州为京城的吴王夫差所击败。勾践定下"二十年计划"，卧薪尝胆，生聚教训，终于在纪元前四七三年击败骄奢淫逸的吴王夫差，复兴越国。

勾践卧薪尝胆、雪耻复国的故事，差不多已经成为家喻户晓的格言。这则历史教训使一切在公私事业上遭受挫折的人重新燃起希望，它说明了忍耐、勇气、刻苦和详密计划的重要性。我在勾践卧薪尝胆的故址领受这个历史教训，自然印象特别深刻。

南宋（纪元一一二七——一二七六）的高宗也曾在绍兴驻节。当时金兵南侵，宋康王渡江南迁，京城也从开封迁到杭州，离绍兴府城不远，还有南宋皇帝的陵寝。

绍兴师爷是全国皆知的。全国大小衙门，几乎到处有绍兴师爷插足，绍兴老酒更是名震遐迩。绍兴府更出过许多历史上有名的学者、哲学家、诗人和书法家。绍兴府包括八个县，我的故乡余姚便是其中一县。

绍兴的风景也很有名，这里有迂回曲折的小溪、桥梁密布的小河、奔腾湍急的大江、平滑如镜的湖泊，以及蜿蜒起伏的丘陵，山光水色使学人哲士留连忘返。

I studied in Shaoshing for two years. My mental horizon rapidly widened. I was made to understand the significance of the Sino-Japanese War of 1894: Japan's victory over China was due to the former's adoption of Western learning. Emperor Kwang-hsü's reforms were inspired by Japan's success in the war. China was to make her erstwhile enemy her teacher. This was why the school offered a course in the Japanese language.

At the end of two years, when bandits made life in the village untenable, my father took me to Shanghai with the rest of the family. My eldest brother had died a year earlier. Here I was put temporarily in a Catholic school to continue my English study. The instruction was given by a French Brother. The pupils were told to call him "Bladda." As he was a foreigner his pronunciation of the language, I imagined, must be good; it was obviously different from that of the Chinese teacher. For instance, he taught us to say "dat" instead of "zat" and "bladda" instead of "bloder." The reader can imagine what curious English we acquired. But I did not stay long in the school. As there was no suitable school in Shanghai for me to go to, Father sent my brother to learn English from an American lady and made me study under him. He thus acted as a comprador of English teaching. I was much dissatisfied with the arrangement, but my father thought it a very clever scheme because it would save money.

Shanghai by 1899 was a small city with a few thousand arrogant foreigners. But the city was well governed, with clean, wide streets and electric or gas lights. I thought the foreigners were wonderful. They knew the secret of electricity. They had invented the steam engine and built steamboats. They took the place of my old gods, who had melted away in the face of my instruction in science, and occupied my mind as new ones. At the same time they served as new devils, too, for their arrogance coupled with the clubs of the policemen, frightened me. In the list of regulations displayed at the entrance of a park on the banks of the Huang-pu River, Chinese as well as dogs were forbidden admission.

This said much. The foreigner appeared to my mind half divine and half devilish, double-faced and many-handed like Vishnu, holding an electric light, a steamboat, and a pretty doll in one set of hands, and a policeman's club, revolver, and handful of opium in the other. When one looked at his bright side he was an angel; on the dark side he was a demon.

我在绍兴读了两年书，知识大增。我开始了解一八九四年中日战争的意义：日本战胜我国是吸收了西洋学术的结果。光绪皇帝的维新运动是受了这次失败的刺激。中国预备学敌人的榜样，学校里有日文课程就是这个道理。

在绍兴的两年学校生活结束以后，乡村里盗警频仍，使我们无法再安居下去。于是父亲带了我们一家迁到上海。我的大哥已在搬家的前一年亡故。到了上海以后，我暂时进了一家天主教学校继续念英文，教我们英文的是一个法国神父。我心里想，这位英文先生既然是外国人，发音一定很准确。他的发音与我过去那位中国先生确乎迥然不同，过去那位先生把"兄弟"念成"布朗德"，现在的法国先生却教我们念"布拉达"。后来我才发现那不是英国音或美国音，而是法国音。不过我在这个天主教学校里的时间不久。因为一时找不到合适的学校，父亲就让我二哥到一位美国太太那里学英文，二哥又把学到的英文转授给我，因此二哥就成为学英文的"掮客"了。我对这办法很不满意，但是父亲认为这是很聪明的安排，因为这样可以省钱。

上海在一八八九年前后还是个小城，居留的外国人也不过三四千，但是这些洋人却都趾高气扬，自视甚高。市政倒办得不错，街道宽大清洁，有电灯，也有煤气灯。我觉得洋人真了不起，他们居然懂得电的秘密。他们发明了蒸汽机，又能建造轮船。他们在我的心目中已经成为新的神，原先心目中的神佛在我接受科学知识之后已经烟消云散了。但是有时候他们又像是魔鬼，因为他们不可一世的神气以及巡捕手中的木棒使我害怕，外滩公园门口挂一个牌子写着："犬与华人不得入内"。犬居华人之上，这就很够人受的了。在我的心目中，外国人是半神半鬼的怪物，很像三头六臂的千手观音，三只手分别拿着电灯、轮船、洋娃娃，另外三只手分别拿着巡棍、手枪、鸦片。从某一边看，他是天使；从另一边看，他却是魔鬼。

Western civilization, as viewed by the Chinese in China's recent history, has been either one way or the other at different periods or among different groups of individuals. Li Hung-chang saw the importance of the dark and devilish side and built a navy to beat the devil by his own weapons. Emperor Kwang-hsü saw the importance of the bright and godly side and tried to establish a new school system. The Empress Dowager and the Boxers saw the curse of the devilish side and tried to oust the devils with China's own obsolete arms. The trouble was that the god was strong for the very reason that at times he could be devilish; the devil was powerful because at times he could be godly. He was one and indivisible—you had either to take him as a whole or not at all. Was not Japan the example? Make your erstwhile enemy your teacher!

We lived in Shanghai for about two years, and this home, too, we left hurriedly one night when we were informed that the Empress Dowager had sent instructions to viceroys throughout the country to put all foreigners to death. It was 1900 and the beginning of the Boxer War in North China. The "Boxers" were a fanatical cult claiming magical powers; gymnastics formed a part of their program—hence the name by which they became known. They meant to destroy all foreign manufactured goods and kill every person found in possession of them. They wanted to kill all the foreigners who brought in these terrible things and destroyed their trade. Churches, schools, missionaries, and Christians were all guilty of introducing these poisonous manufactures into China. Get rid of these people by killing them, with swords, knives, magic! Destroy foreign properties by setting them on fire.

The Imperial Court for its own part wanted to destroy all the crazy ideas of foreign origin introduced by Kang Yu-wei and Liang Chi-chao, so that nothing like the reforms of 1898 could happen again. Thus the Boxers wanted to get rid of the manufactured goods and the Empress Dowager and her court wanted to get rid of foreign mental goods; both came from one source—the foreigners. Kill them all! In the beginning of the industrial revolution in England people smashed the machines which destroyed their livelihood. The Boxers went a bit too far. They destroyed the human "machinery" too.

In the south people looked at the foreigner in a different light. They welcomed foreign manufactures but did not understand that it was this very thing that caused the banditry. They put the blame on the obnoxious taxes of the Imperial government and the corruption and incompetence of its officials. So they wanted a revolution.

中国人对西方文明的看法总不出这两个极端，印象因人而异，也因时而异。李鸿章看到西方文明丑恶狰狞的一面，因此决定建立海军，以魔鬼之矛攻魔鬼之盾。光绪帝看到西方文明光明和善的一面，因此想建立新式的学校制度。慈禧太后和义和团看到可憎的一面，想用中国的陈旧武器驱逐魔鬼。麻烦的是这位怪物的黑暗面和光明面是不可分的。它有时像是佛法无边的神，有时又像狰狞凶残的魔鬼，但是它凭藉的力量是相同的。我们要就不接受西方文明，要接受就得好坏一齐收下。日本就是一个很好的榜样。没奈何，我们只好向我们过去的敌人学习了。

我们在上海住了将近两年。有一天晚上，我们听说慈禧太后已经命令各省总督把所有的外国人一齐杀光。于是我们连夜举家迁离上海，那是一九〇〇年的事，也就是义和团战争的开始。义和团的人自称能用符咒对付刀枪子弹，拳术也是训练节目之一。因此，义和团有拳匪之称。他们预备破坏一切外国制造的东西，同时杀死所有使用外国货的人。他们要把运进这些可恶的外国货而阻绝他们生路的洋人统统杀光。把这些害人的外国货介绍到中国来的教会、学校、传教士、基督徒都罪无可逭。用刀剑、法术把这些人杀光吧！放把火把外国人的财产统统烧光！

朝廷本身也想把康有为、梁启超介绍进来的外国思想一扫而光，免得有人再搞什么维新运动。义和团要消灭物质的外国货，而慈禧太后则想消灭精神上的外国货。不论是物质上的或者精神上的，反正都是外国货，都是外国人造的孽。杀呀！杀光外国人！工业革命开始时，英国人曾经捣毁了威胁他们生活的机器。义和团做得更彻底，他们要同时破坏血肉构成的"机器"。

南方的人对外国人的看法稍有不同，他们欢迎外国货，他们不觉得外国货是盗匪的起因，他们认为毛病在于清室的苛捐杂税以及官吏的腐败无能。他们要革命。

The people and the Imperial Court in the north were right in holding the foreigners responsible for destroying their trades, but found a wrong solution in smashing the "human machinery." The people of the south had a wrong reason in holding the Imperial government responsible for their plight, but did the right thing in starting a revolution. History seems to consist of a series of accidents, illogical reasoning, and unexpected results, in which the great men appearing on the scene are but the instruments of Fate.

Foreigners cursed banditry in China, but did not know that their own manufactures had caused it in the beginning. In my childhood days we all feared tigers, ghosts, and bandits, but all were imaginary; we only saw them in picture books. Then suddenly the bandit appeared in real life—as if a tiger should dash into your house or a ghost chase you. Finally we dreaded the bandits and forgot about tigers and ghosts.

北方的老百姓和朝廷，认为外国人杜绝了他们的生路，那是对的。但是他们想藉破坏血肉构成的"机器"来解决问题却错了。南方的人认为朝廷本身的腐败是苦难唯一的原因，想不到更大的原因是洋货进口。推理是错了，但是展开革命的行动却是对的。历史似乎包括一连串的意外事件、不合逻辑的推理和意想不到的结果。历史上的风云人物似乎不过是命运之神摆布的工具而已。

外国人咒骂中国的盗匪，殊不知盗匪正是他们自己的货品所引起的。在我的童年时代里，大家都害怕老虎、鬼怪和强盗，但是实际上并没有真的老虎、鬼怪或强盗。我们只在图画书中看到这些东西。忽然之间，强盗在实际生活中出现了，好像是老虎冲进你的居室，也像是鬼怪在你背后紧追不舍。最后我们所惧怕的是强盗，老虎和鬼怪却都被遗忘了。

CHAPTER 6   FURTHER EDUCATION

Thus at the age of fifteen I was brought back home by my father. We were afraid that the Boxer War might extend to Shanghai and so returned to the village; but after a short stay, as the bandits became worse, we moved to Yuyao, the district capital, to live. There I was sent to a local school to study English and arithmetic, and studied Chinese under a private tutor.

After a year or so I went to Hangchow, capital of the province of Chekiang. This was the center of the silk industry in China and also one center of the tea trade. Hangchow silk and tea were famous all over the country.

Hangchow is well known for its scenic beauty. To one side of the city the Chien-tang tides rush up from Hangchow Bay. On the other is the West Lake, mirrored against a blue sky with reflections of temples and villas perched on the surrounding hills. The city was known as a paradise on earth. This was the city that Marco Polo adored in his travels, and it was the ancient capital of King Chien-liao, who kept his domain in peace through long years of incessant invasions and wars in China. Here the South Sungs made their capital for a hundred and fifty years, and here famous poets and men of letters lived. It is a city rich in historical records and monuments. The Imperial Library was filled with valuable books. It was the right place for young scholars to nurse themselves to grow.

In this city of learning I stumbled accidentally into a backward school, a local Christian academy run by an American missionary. Here I hoped that at least I might learn English well. The atmosphere was far from congenial. The principal was a carpenter by trade; this pious American had been carried to China by his religious zeal. He had done some missionary work in my prefecture before being given charge of the academy. As he taught nothing except the Bible, I did not know how much he knew, and since learning was honored in China the carpenter-teacher evoked secret contempt in the hearts of his pupils. My English teacher was a man of vulgar manners, a new convert whose soul may have been saved but whose tongue remained distinctly heathen. I had tramped from this school to that trying to find a really good English teacher, but to my great disappointment I was still simply chasing after shadows.

陆 继续就学

在我十五岁的时候，父亲又带我回到故乡。我们怕义和团之乱会蔓延到上海，因此就回到乡下去住。在蒋村住了不久，乡下土匪愈闹愈凶，又迁到余姚城里，我在余姚县里的一所学校里念英文和算术，另外还请了一位家庭教师教中文。

大概一年之后，我到了杭州。杭州是浙江的省会，也是我国蚕丝工业的中心和五大茶市之一。杭州的绸缎和龙井茶是全国闻名的。

"上有天堂，下有苏杭"，杭州的风景更是尽人皆知。城东南有杭州湾的钱塘大潮；城西有平滑如镜的西湖，湖边山麓到处是古寺别墅。马哥·孛罗游记中就曾盛道杭州的风景。杭州是吴越和南宋的故都，南宋曾在这里定都一百五十年之久，因此名胜古迹很多。墨人骚客更代有所出。湖滨的文澜阁收藏有四库全书及其他要籍，正是莘莘学子潜心研究的好去处。

我在这个文化城中瞎打瞎撞，进了一所非常落伍的学校。校长是位木匠出身的美国传教士。我以为在这所教会学校里，至少可以学好英文，事实上却大谬不然。这位传教士抱着一股宗教热忱来到中国，在主持这所教会学校之前，曾经在我的故乡绍兴府传过教。因为他只教《圣经》，我也摸不清他肚子里究竟有多少学问。在我们学生的心目中，士、农、工、商，士为首，对木匠出身的人多少有点轻视。我的英文教师更是俗不可耐的人物。他入教不久，灵魂也许已经得救，但是那张嘴却很能够使他进拔舌地狱。我为了找位英文好教师，曾经一再转学，结果总使我大失所望。

It was compulsory in the academy to attend exercises in the chapel every morning. We sang hymns in Chinese. Sometimes the clever pupils saw fit to render them in paraphrases which gained more popularity among us than the hymns. In spite of Sunday schools and morning exercises my mind was closed tight as a clam against any spiritual foreign elements. Having got rid of its spirits, ghosts, and gods, it was reluctant to admit any new elements of similar nature. And indeed, ever since that time I have remained an agnostic, trying to find immortality rather in this world than in the next. This conforms with the basic teachings of Confucius.

The only respectable buildings on the campus of the academy were the chapel and the residence of the principal. The students lived in cell-like mud sheds, and classes were held there or in the shabby dining hall.

Out of curiosity some pupils liked to loiter around the principal's house. These unwelcome guests were often told to keep away. Usually they obeyed and walked off, but on one occasion a student rebelled and got into a quarrel with a teacher who happened by.

A crowd began to gather. The student accused the teacher of slapping his face and wept to draw the ready sympathy of the mob. The commotion spread like fire and within a few minutes the majority of the student body had joined in demanding the immediate dismissal of the teacher. The demand being refused by the principal, the crowd became enraged and emotions soared to the highest pitch. The principal told them bluntly that if they did not like the school they could leave. In about two hours the whole school walked out.

This marked the end of my education in a missionary school and I had no regret. The sooner I left the better.

One may ask why such a thing should happen, all of a sudden. It was not a mere outburst of ugliness on the part of unruly students. The slap was only a trigger pulled on a loaded gun; the explosive charge is not to be identified with a little missionary academy. This was part of a country-wide student rebellion against school authority. Even a backward missionary school in Hangchow was not exempt.

The rebellion had started in Nanyang College in Shanghai during the previous year. A student had left an inkstand on his professor's chair and the professor had sat on it. His clothes being stained, he got very angry;

在这所教会学校里，学生们每天早晨必须参加礼拜。我们唱的是中文赞美诗，有些顽皮的学生就把赞美诗改编为打油诗，结果在学校里传诵一时。虽然我也参加主日学校和每天早晨的礼拜，我心灵却似紧闭双扉的河蚌，严拒一切精神上的舶来品。我既然已经摆脱了神仙鬼怪这一套，自然不愿再接受类似的东西。而且从那时起，我在宗教方面一直是个"不可知"论者，我认为与其求死后灵魂的永恒，不如在今世奠立不朽根基。这与儒家的基本观念刚好符合。

校园之内唯一像样的建筑是礼拜堂和校长官舍。学生则住在鸽笼一样的土房里，上课有时在这些宿舍里，有时在那间破破烂烂的饭厅里。

大概是出于好奇吧，学生们常常喜欢到校长官舍附近去散步。校长不高兴学生走进他的住宅，不速之客常常被撵出来。有一次，一位强悍的学生说什么也不肯走开，结果与一位路过的教员发生冲突。

围观的人渐聚渐多。那位学生说先生掴他的耳光，同时放声大哭，希望引起群众的同情。这场纷扰遂即像野火一样波及全校。学生会多数决议，要求校长立即开革那位打人的教员。校长断然拒绝学生的要求，群众的情绪愈涨愈高。校长冷然告诉学生说：如果他们不喜欢这个学校，就请他们卷铺盖。不到两个小时，全体学生都跑光了。

我所受的教会学校教育就此结束。但我毫不后悔，我巴不得早一天离开这个学校。

或许有人要问：为什么这样的事会突然发生呢？其实这只是学生桀骜难驯的表现而已，那耳光不过是导火线。这类事件也绝不局限于这所小小的教会学校，学生反抗学校当局已经成为全国的普遍风气。

一年以前，上海南洋公学首先发生学潮。一位学生放了一瓶墨水在教授的坐椅上，教授不注意一屁股坐了上去，弄得全身墨迹。

it was reported to the president and a few suspects were dismissed. There followed a clash between the college authorities and the student body, the latter supported by a number of faculty members. Eventually all the students walked out.

The younger generation was changing, and it was a change from submission to rebellion. Dismayed at the encroachment of foreign powers upon China, people blamed the Imperial Court for it. The students, inflamed and aroused by Dr. Sun Yat-sen's revolutionary propaganda, were ready to strike whenever there might be opportunity and at anything they could get hold of. They delivered their first blows at the school authorities who were handiest to them.

The Provincial College of Chekiang followed suit. A minor fracas between a student and a sedan chair bearer of the Imperial governor who was visiting the college set off the incident. All the students went on strike in consequence and left the college in a body. Many incidents of like nature occurred in other schools, with eventual disruption of a number of institutions of new learning. It spread throughout the country.

The new elements in the country sympathized with the strikes and blamed the authorities for their despotism; the old elements condemned the students in no uncertain terms and sympathized with the school authorities. Whatever one's opinion, few realized that this was the eve of a revolution. From the time of these early student rebellions to the Revolution of 1911 which marked the birth of the Republic of China was only eight short years.

It was the rebellion of the coming intelligentsia against the class of old literati who controlled China, intellectually and socially as well as politically. With the introduction of the theory of evolution—with special reference to the struggle for existence and the survival of the fittest— and other scientific ideas, the mental attitude of the young generation was undergoing a radical change in social and political philosophy. Eighteenth-century concepts of individual freedom encountered the nineteenth-century industrial revolution: freedom in the form of rebellion against established authority, and industrial revolution in the form of imported products which doomed the old trades to decay. China's old structure was crumbling and the new one was yet to be built.

There was a general unrest throughout the country. Poverty, bandits, famine, plague, official corruption, ignorance of world affairs, and the pinch of foreign aggressions—all were contributing factors. The students,

教授盛怒之下报告了校长，接着几个嫌疑较大的学生被开除。这引起了学生会和学校当局之间的冲突，学生会方面还有许多教授的支持。结果全体学生离开学校。

年轻的一代正在转变，从驯服转变为反抗。一般老百姓看到中国受列强的侵略，就怪清廷颟顸无能；受到国父革命理论熏陶和鼓励的学生们则热血沸腾，随时随地准备发作。首当其冲的就是学校当局。

浙江省立高等学堂接着起了风潮。起因是一位学生与来校视察巡抚的一名轿夫发生龃龉，结果全校罢课，学生集体离开学校。类似的事件相继在其他学校发生，卒使许多学府弦歌中辍。学潮并且迅速蔓延到全国。

思想较新的人同情罢课的学生，斥责学校当局过于专制；思想守旧的人则同情学校当局，严词谴责学生。不论是同情学生或者是同情学校当局的，似乎没有人体会到这就是革命的前夕，从学生初闹学潮开始，到一九一一年辛亥革命成功、中华民国诞生为止，其间不过短短八年而已。

这种反抗运动可说是新兴的知识分子对一向控制中国的旧士大夫阶级的反抗，不但是知识上的反抗，而且是社会的和政治的反抗。自从强调物竞天择、适者生存的进化论以及其他科学观念输入中国以后，年轻一代的思想已经起了急剧的变化。十八世纪的个人观念与十九世纪的工业革命同时并临：个人自由表现于对旧制度的反抗；工业革命则表现于使中国旧行业日趋式微的舶来品。中国的旧有制度正在崩溃，新的制度尚待建设。

全国普遍显现扰攘不安。贫穷、饥馑、瘟疫、贪污、国际知识的贫乏以及外国侵略的压力都是因素，青年学生不过是这场战乱中的

the young blood, merely took the lead. It was not an insignificant inkstand, nor the slapped face of a pupil in a missionary school, nor any altercation between a student and a chair bearer that set educational institutions ablaze throughout China.

After leaving the academy our youthful student body organized a school for themselves—the "School of Reforms and Progress." The name was suggested by Chang Pin-ling, one of the famous revolutionary scholars of our time. Our ambition was to make the school as great one day as Oxford or Cambridge. Pretty soon, as was natural, we found ourselves disillusioned. The student body dwindled in the course of half a year to a few elected officers. When these few found no one to re-elect them, they also departed to seek educations elsewhere.

For my part, I registered at Chekiang College, under a new name lest the college authorities find me *persona non grata*. I took the entrance examination, passed it, and was admitted. The college had just been reorganized after the strike and was the highest institution of learning in the Province of Scholars, as our province was known. Its forerunner had been Chiou Shih Shu-yuan, or the "School for Seeking What Is Right." It is the proper frame of mind for a scholar to seek what is right, and this was the attitude of Chinese scholars of former generations. This had been a school similar to the Sino-Occidental School of Shaoshing, an old-style Chinese school whose curriculum included some foreign languages and science teaching. As the new subjects grew in importance and were allotted more time it developed into a new type of school and was renamed Chekiang College.

Situated in the provincial capital and maintained by the government, the college served as a center of cultural movements in the province. The curriculum was very similar to that of the Sino-Occidental School, but the courses were more advanced, more various, and better taught, with less sheer memory work. It was a modern school in the making.

I had been trotting along in the dark since entering the school in Shaoshing. My mind always rushed for the place where I caught a glimpse of bewitching light and groped in some other direction when it elusively disappeared. By this time, however, I saw things in much clearer perspective. I had begun to study world history in English. At first

急先锋而已，使全国学府遍燃烽火的，不是一只无足轻重的墨水瓶，不是一个在教会学校里被刮了耳光的学生，也不是一次学生与轿夫之间的龃龉而已。

我们离开那所教会学校以后，我们的学生会自行筹办了一个学校，取名"改进学社"。这个名称是当时著名的学者章炳麟给我们起的。这位一代大儒，穿了和服木屐，履声郭橐，溢于堂外。他说，改进的意思是改良、进步。这当然是我们愿意听的。我们的妄想是，希望把这个学校办得和牛津大学或者剑桥大学一样，真是稚气十足。但是不久我们就尝到幻灭的滋味。不到半年，学生就渐渐散了，结果只剩下几个被选担任职务的学生。当这几位职员发现再没有选举他们的群众时，他们也就另觅求学之所去了。

我自己进了浙江高等学堂。我原来的名字"梦熊"已经入了闹事学生的黑名单，因此就改用"梦麟"注册。我参加入学考试，幸被录取。当时的高等学堂，正当罢课学潮之后重新改组，是一向有"学人之省"之称的浙江省的最高学府。它的前身是求是书院。"求是"是前辈学者做学问的一贯态度。求是书院和绍兴的中西学堂有很多相似的地方，课程中包括一些外国语和科学科目。后来新学科愈来愈见重要，所占时间也愈来愈多，求是书院终于发展为一种新式的学校，同时改名为浙江高等学堂。

这个学堂既然办在省城，同时又由政府负担经费，它自然而然地成为全省文化运动的中心。它的课程和中西学堂很相似，不过功课比较深，科目比较多，先生教得比较好，全凭记忆的工作比较少。它已粗具现代学校的规模。

我自从进了绍兴的中西学堂以后，一直在黑暗中摸索。看到东边有一点闪霎的亮光，我就摸到东边；东边亮光一闪而逝以后，我又连忙转身扑向西边。现在进了浙江高等学堂，眼前豁然开朗，对一切都可以看得比较真切了。我开始读英文原版的世界史。开始时

it seemed as difficult to understand the doings of other peoples as when one tries to understand the behavior of the masses, but gradually I began to see, albeit dimly, the development of Western civilization. This was of course only in a very general and vague way. But my interest in Western history was aroused and a foundation laid for further study.

Here I was in the midst of intellectual activities. Through reading, lectures, and conversation, my information about China and the world was accumulating. I grew familiar with some forty centuries of China's history, with a fair understanding of the causes, as given by the great historians, of the rise and fall of many dynasties. This served as the basis for a comparative study of Western history later on.

In the field of contemporary history there was plenty of material. The Sino-Japanese War of 1894, of which I had learned from the misleading colored pictures in my childhood; the short-lived reforms of Kang Yu-wei and Liang Chi-chao in 1898, which had taken place during my stay in the Sino-Occidental School, the Boxer War of 1900, news of which I learned at such close range in Shanghai; and the Russo-Japanese War of 1904 which was even then raging (with China's overwhelming sympathy for Japan)—each and all furnished rich materials for thought and study.

One might study history backward, too: there was the Sino-French War in 1885 in which China lost Indo-China; the Taiping Rebellion (1851-1864) and the ever-victorious army of Generals Gordon and Ward; the Opium War of 1840, as a result of which China lost Hongkong; and if one went farther back there was the coming of the Jesuits during the later Ming and early Ching periods, and the travels of Marco Polo during the Yuan or Mongol Dynasty; still farther back China had relations with the Roman Empire.

Liang Chi-chao's *Young China*, an encyclopedic monthly published in Tokyo, furnished a great variety of materials ranging from short stories to metaphysics and including elementary science, history, politics, biographies, literature, etc. His lucid pen was capable of making people understand almost any subject new or difficult to the reader. This was very important at a time when there was a need to introduce Western ideas into China. His style was clear, persuasive, and easy to follow and therefore very profitable reading for students. I was one among thousands who came under his influence. I think this great scholar did more than anyone else in his time to popularize modern knowledge among the rising generation. His was the fountain of wisdom from which every young man drew to quench his thirst for the new learning.

似乎很难了解外国人民的所作所为，正如一个人试图了解群众行动时一样困难。后来我才慢慢地了解西方文化的发展。自然那只是一种粗枝大叶而且模模糊糊的了解，但是这一点了解已经鼓起我对西洋史的兴趣，同时奠定了进一步研究的基础。

在浙江高等学堂里所接触的知识非常广泛。从课本里，从课外阅读，以及师友的谈话中，我对中国以及整个世界的知识日渐增长。我渐渐熟悉将近四千年的中国历史，同时对于历代兴衰的原因也有了相当的了解。这是我后来对西洋史从事比较研究的一个基础。

近代史上值得研究的问题就更多：首先是一八九四年使台湾割让于日本的中日战争，童年时代所看到的彩色图画曾使我对它产生错误的印象；其次是一八九八年康有为和梁启超的维新运动，那是我在中西学堂读书时所发生的；再其次是一九〇〇年的义和团战争，我在上海时曾经听到许多关于义和团的消息；然后是一九〇四年的日俄战争，我在杭州念书时正在进行。每一件事都有丰富的资料足供研究而且使人深省。

我们也可以用倒卷珠帘的方式来研究历史：一八八五年的中法战争使中国丧失了越南；[1]太平天国始于一八五一年而终于一八六四年，其间还出现过戈登将军和华德将军的常胜军；一八四〇年鸦片战争的结果使中国失去了香港；如果再往上追溯，明末清初有耶稣会教士来华传教，元朝有马哥·孛罗来华游历；再往上可以追溯到中国与罗马帝国的关系。

梁启超在东京出版的《新民丛报》是份综合性的刊物，内容从短篇小说到形而上学，无所不包。其中有基本科学常识，有历史，有政治论著，有自传，有文学作品。梁氏简洁的文笔深入浅出，能使人了解任何新颖或困难的问题。当时正需要介绍西方观念到中国，梁氏深入浅出的才能尤其显得重要。梁启超的文笔简明、有力、流畅，学生们读来裨益非浅，我就是千千万万受其影响的学生之一。我认为这位伟大的学者，在介绍现代知识给年轻一代的工作上，其贡献较同时代的任何人为大。他的《新民丛报》是当时每一位渴求新知识的青年的智慧源泉。

Politically he stood for constitutional reforms under the reigning dynasty. Meanwhile the revolutionaries were publishing a number of periodicals to sponsor Dr. Sun Yat-sen's radical idea that for China a republican form of government was better than a monarchy and that China must be governed by the Chinese[2] and not by the corrupt and degenerate Manchus. That published by the Chekiang students in Tokyo was a monthly: *Tides of Chien-tang.* This magazine attacked the reigning dynasty so fiercely that it was barred from the mails, among other like periodicals, by the postal authorities. But the movement had the sympathy of the Tokyo government and the tabooed periodicals therefore flowed continuously from Japan, where they were published, into the International Settlement of Shanghai where Chinese jurisdiction reached only partially. So Shanghai became a clearinghouse for revolutionary ideas, and from there the literature was smuggled into other cities by sympathizers as well as profit makers.

Chekiang College itself was deluged with pamphlets, magazines, and books of revolutionary propaganda; some depicting the atrocities committed by the Manchus during their invasion of China[3], others describing their misrule and the unequal treatment of Manchus and Chinese under the existing regime. The students devoured them voluptuously. No power on earth could stop them.

Moreover, concrete examples of Manchu misrule and incompetence could be found just outside the college gate. Within the city walls of Hangchow was a walled city for the Manchus who were stationed there as a garrison to watch over the Chinese. I was warned not to enter it; anyone did so at his own risk. More than two hundred years earlier this city within a city had been set aside exclusively as barracks for the Manchu soldiers in Hangchow. After them their children's children had lived there, nominally as soldiers, for generations until they were killed by the Taipings during the siege of the capital. Intermarriage between Chinese and Manchus was in general forbidden, but Manchus were allowed to marry Chinese women if they preferred, although such marriages were rare. When the civil war was over, a part of the garrison stationed at Chingchow in Hupeh Province was moved to Hangchow to fill the vacancy. Some of these were still living and spoke Hupeh dialect; most of them had died, but their children lived there and still clung to the dialect of their fathers. Thus they were easily detected by the natives of Hangchow. But the third generation had begun to speak the local Hangchow tongue.

　　在政治上，他主张在清廷主持之下进行立宪维新。这时候，革命党人也出版了许多刊物，宣传孙中山先生的激烈思想。中山先生认为共和政体胜于君主立宪，同时他认为中国应由中国人自己来统治，而不应由腐败无能的满洲人来统治。浙籍学生在东京也出版了一个定名《浙江潮》的月刊。这个杂志因为攻击清廷过于激烈，以致与若干类似的杂志同时被邮政当局禁止寄递。但是日本政府却同情中国留学生的革命运动，因此这些被禁的杂志仍旧不断地从日本流入上海租界。因此上海就成为革命思想的交易所，同情革命的人以及营求厚利者再从上海把革命书刊走私到其他城市。

　　浙江高等学堂本身就到处有宣传革命的小册子、杂志和书籍，有的描写清兵入关时的暴行，有的则描写清廷的腐败，有的则描写清廷对满人和汉人的不平等待遇。学生们如饥似渴地读着这些书刊，几乎没有任何力量足以阻止他们。

　　事实上，清廷腐败无能的实例，在校门之外就俯拾即是。杭州城墙之内就有一个满洲人住的小城，里面驻扎着监视汉人的"旗兵"。两百多年前，政府特地划出这个城中之城作为驻扎杭州的"旗兵"的营房。这些旗兵的子子孙孙一直就住在这里，名义上仍旧是军人。满汉通婚原则上是禁止的，但是满人如果愿意娶汉人为妻是准许的，实际上这类婚姻很少就是了。太平军围城时，杭州的旗人全部被杀。内战结束以后，原来驻扎湖北荆州的一部分旗兵移驻杭州，来填补空缺。这些从荆州来的旗人当时还有健在的，而且说的是湖北话。虽然他们多数已经去世，但是他们的子女仍旧住在那里，而且说他们父辈所说的方言。道地杭州人很容易察觉这些旗人的湖北口音。但是从第三代开始，他们就说杭州的本地方言了。

They sent ten of their boys to study at the college. These youths behaved wisely toward the revolutionary movement in the college by pretending not to know of it. One of them, of Mongol origin, actually told me he was in favor of a revolution against the Manchu Dynasty as he was a non-Manchu in spite of being a Manchu "soldier."

These so-called Manchu soldiers were no soldiers at all; they were just the same as civilians. They had families and reared children in the so-called barracks and knew nothing of the arts of war. The only difference was that they lived on government rations and had no occupation. Theirs was a sort of parasitic life, and they degenerated physically, mentally, and morally. They haunted the teahouses on the West Lake, some of them in the fashionable manner carrying a bird in its cage, and people generally kept away from them. They would slap anyone who offended them. These living examples of degeneration, corruption, and arrogance woke hatred and contempt in the hearts of the young students. It was just as effective as revolutionary propaganda, if not more so.

While we got our mental food from Liang Chi-chao, we drew our emotional nourishment from Dr. Sun Yat-sen and his sympathizers. Generally speaking, it is emotion that leads to action when a decisive hour comes; when that hour came in China Dr. Sun, both dreamer and man of action, won a decisive victory over the new literati who stood for constitutionalism.

Such was the general atmosphere of Chekiang College. Similar conditions also prevailed in other institutions. I was interested in all these activities. I liked to get hold of information and to think with the materials thus secured, and also to feel and to act. But nothing carried me away entirely. To play safe I still planned to take the Imperial civil examination, still the only road to a government position except by way of revolution, which seemed long and difficult to me. I was at times timid and shy, at others bold and reckless, and therefore did not trust my own temperament. So I often acted cautiously, feeling my way before making a definite move. Especially at any crossroads, I would consider again and again before coming to a decision. In case of doubt I was apt instead to sit by the roadside and indulge in daydreams. But once a decision was made I would stick to the end. I made mistakes in life, but never so fatally as to be swept away by the advancing tides.

　　当时的浙江高等学堂里有十名旗人子弟。这几位青年人对学校中的革命运动装聋作哑，应付得很得当。其中一人原是蒙古人的后裔，他甚至告诉我，他也赞成革清朝的命，因为他虽然是旗"兵"，却不是满人。

　　这些所谓旗兵，实际上绝对不是兵；他们和老百姓毫无区别。他们在所谓"兵营"里娶妻养子，对冲锋陷阵的武事毫无所知。唯一的区别是他们有政府的俸饷而无所事事，他们过的是一种寄生生活，因之身体、智力和道德都日渐衰退。他们经常出入西湖湖滨的茶馆，有的则按当时的习尚提着鸟笼到处游荡，一般老百姓都敬而远之。如果有人得罪他们，就随时有挨揍的危险。这些堕落、腐化、骄傲的活榜样，在青年学生群中普遍引起憎恨的鄙夷。他们所引起的反感，比起革命宣传的效果只有过之而无不及。

　　我们从梁启超获得精神食粮，孙中山先生以及其他革命志士，则使我们的革命情绪不断增涨。到了重要关头，引发革命行动的就是这种情绪。后来时机成熟，理想和行动兼顾的孙中山先生终于决定性地战胜主张君主立宪的新士大夫阶级。

　　这就是浙江高等学堂的一般气氛。其他学校的情形也大都如此。我对这一切活动都感兴趣。我喜欢搜求消息，喜欢就所获得的资料加以思考分析，同时也喜欢使自己感情奔放，参加行动。但是我常常适可而止。为求万全，我仍旧准备参加科举考试。除了革命，科举似乎仍旧是参加政府工作的不二途径，并且我觉得革命似乎遥遥无期，而且困难重重。我有时候非常胆小而怕羞，有时候却又非常大胆而莽撞，因此我对自己的性格始终没有自信。所以我的行动常常很谨慎，在采取确切的行动之前，喜欢先探索一下道路。尤其碰到岔路时，我总是考虑再三才能作决定。如果犹豫不决，我很可能呆坐道旁，想入非非。但是一旦作了决定，我必定坚持到底。我一生犯过许多错误，但没有犯不可挽回的错误，所以没有让时代潮流把我卷走。

CHAPTER 7   IMPERIAL CIVIL EXAMINATION

Early one morning, as the time for the civil examination drew near, I started for Shaoshing where the examination was to be held for our district. The luggage man slung his bamboo pole over his shoulder with my suitcase and bamboo basket roped to one end and bedding outfits balancing the other. I followed on his heels. As my luggage swung out of the college gate a teacher who happened to see me smiled and wished me good luck.

After passing through many granite-paved streets and zigzag narrow Hangchow alleys, we came to the banks of the Chien-tang River. I measured my steps along a gangway of narrow, frail planks a quarter of a mile long, with the tides flowing underneath, leading to the waiting ferryboat. The boat was plied by several heavy oars, with the occasional help of sails. It glided along in leisurely fashion. As it could only be controlled by heading against the tide, the slow speed was further reduced and it took us two hours to cross. None of us imagined then that within some thirty years a long steel bridge would span the river, with trains and cars passing over it.

I then took a sedan chair through miles of mulberry groves to a busy trading city, where I embarked for Shaoshing, arriving next morning after a night on the boat, which was packed with passengers like sardines. One had to lie flat and straight; if you tried to move your legs you found your allotted space gone; if you tried to turn on your side there was no space left to lie flat again.

In Shaoshing I got a room with board in a fan maker's family. The place was small and dark and filled with strange odors from certain vegetable oils used to make fans. In the evening I studied by a vegetable-oil lamp which did not give enough light to read small letters without straining one's eyes. We refrained from using kerosene because of the inflammable materials that filled the place. In the dark we could not walk without stumbling over some sort of stuff for making fans.

The examination began with roll call at the entrance of the Examination Hall at about four o'clock in the morning. The early autumn morning was chilly. A large crowd of literati, several thousand strong and each wearing a red-tasseled hat—without a button—and carrying a lantern gathered around the spacious courtyard. At the entrance to the hall the Prefect sat in stately dignity at a long desk. He wore a

柒 参加郡试

郡试快到了。一天清早，我从杭州动身往绍兴去，因为我们那一区的郡试是在绍兴举行。行李夫用一根扁担挑起行李走出校门，我紧紧地跟在他的后面。扁担的一端系着一只皮箱和一只网篮，另一端是铺盖卷。走到校门口，碰到一位教师，他向我微微一笑，并祝我吉星高照。

穿过许多平坦的石板路，又穿过许多迂回狭窄的小巷，我们终于到了钱塘江边。渡船码头离岸约有一里路，我小心翼翼地踏上吱吱作响的木板通过一条便桥到达码头。渡船上有好几把笨重的木桨，风向对时也偶然张起帆篷。船行很慢，同时是逆水行驶，所以整整化了两个小时才渡过钱塘江。当时谁也想不到三十年之后竟有一条钢铁大桥横跨宽阔的江面，桥上还可以同时行驶火车和汽车。

上岸以后雇了一乘小轿。穿过绵亘数里的桑林，到达一个人烟稠密的市区，然后转船续向绍兴进发，船上乘客挤得像沙丁鱼。我们只能直挺挺地平躺着睡，如果你缩一缩腿，原来放腿的地方马上就会被人占据；如果你想侧转身睡一下，你就别想再躺平。

在船上过了一夜，第二天早晨到达绍兴。寄宿在一个制扇工匠的家里，房间又小又暗，而且充满了制扇用的某种植物油气味。晚上就在菜油灯下读书，但是灯光太暗，看小字很吃力。我们不敢用煤油灯，因为屋子里到处是易燃的制扇材料，黑暗中摸索时还常要跌跤。

考试开始时，清晨四点左右大家就齐集在试院门前，听候点名。那是一个初秋的早晨，天气相当冷。几千位考生挤在院子里，每人头上戴着一顶没有顶子的红缨帽，手里提着一个灯笼、一只考篮。大厅门口摆着一张长桌。监考官就是绍兴知府，昂然坐在长桌后面。

red-tasseled hat with a blue crystal button at the top, a black jacket over a deep blue gown, and a chain of beads around his neck. This was his full official attire. With a vermilion pen in his hand he began to call the roll. As he went down the list a man standing by him called out in long-drawn tones the name of each candidate, who promptly sang out at the top of his voice, "Here! So-and-so, the guarantor." Immediately the guarantor sang his own name in acknowledgment of the sponsorship. The Prefect then glanced about quickly to see if anything was wrong and made a red dot above the name with his vermilion pen.

The candidate was then let in. His hat and clothes were searched to see that he carried no notes with him. Anything found written on paper would be confiscated.

The candidates moved on in files to their respective seats, which were numbered, each finding his place accordingly. The names on the examination papers were written on detachable slips to be torn off before the papers were handed in. Each paper was also numbered in a sealed corner, which was not opened until the papers were marked and the successful candidates selected, so as to prevent any possible favoritism. Toward the end of the Manchu Dynasty, when corruption ran rampant in many branches of government office, the Imperial examination system remained independent and free alike of external interference and internal corruption. This was one reason why the degrees conferred were so much honored in China.

Questions were limited to the Confucian classics and this was why a candidate must commit to memory all the texts in the classics. This I had done through years of laborious conning in my country school and the Sino-Occidental School in Shaoshing. Questions were shown to the candidates by means of cubic lanterns, on the screens of which the questions were written; they were lighted with candles so that the black letters on the white screens could be seen distinctly at a distance. Bearers raised the lanterns high above their heads and carried them up and down the aisles several times, so that none could miss them.

About noon officials went around to check on how far the candidates had gone with their essays and set on each paper a seal at the spot to which the lines had run. At about four in the afternoon cannon began to roar, marking the first call for the collection of papers. The gates were flung open and the band began to play. Candidates who were able to answer the first call handed in their papers and made their way out slowly through the gates with music playing and an anxious crowd waiting.

他戴着蓝色晶顶的红缨帽，穿着深蓝色的长袍，外罩黑马褂，胸前垂着一串朝珠。那是他的全套官服。他提起朱笔顺着名单，开始点名。他每点一个名，站在他旁边的人就拖着长腔唱出考生的名字。考生听到自己的名字以后，就高声答应："有！某某人保。"保的人也随即唱名证明。监考官望一眼以后，如果认为并无舛错，就用朱笔在考生名字上加上红点。

考生点名后就可以进考棚了。他的帽子和衣服都得经过搜索，以防夹带，任何写了字的纸头都要没收。

考生鱼贯进入考棚，找出自己的位置分别就座。座位都是事先编好号码的。考卷上有写好考生姓名的浮签，缴卷时就撕去浮签。考卷的一角另有弥封的号码，录取名单决定以后才开拆弥封，以免徇私舞弊。清末时，政府各部门无不百弊丛生。唯有科举制度颇能保持独立，不为外力所染。科举功名之所以受人器重，大概就是这个缘故。

考试的题目不出四书五经的范围，所以每个考生必须把四书五经背得烂熟。我在家塾里以及后来在绍兴中西学堂里，已经在这方面下过苦功。题目写在方形的灯笼罩子上，白单子上写着黑字，灯笼里面点着蜡烛，因此从远远的地方就可以看得很清楚。提灯笼的人把灯笼擎得高高的，在考生座位之间的甬道上来回走好几次，所以大家都不会看漏题目。

将近中午时，办事人员开始核对考生的进度，每一份考卷的最末一行都盖上印子。下午四点钟左右，炮声响了，那是收卷的第一次讯号。大门打开，吹鼓手也呜呜啦啦开始吹奏起来。考生缴了卷，在乐声中慢慢走出大门，大门外亲戚朋友正在焦急地等待着。

After everyone had made his exit the gates were closed again. The second call was made about an hour later with the same ceremony. The third or final call was made about six, with both cannon and band remaining silent.

We had about a week or ten days to wait for the results of the examination. In the interim there was plenty of time for amusement. Bookstores, large and small, were found everywhere near the Examination Hall. There were chess stands, temporary restaurants with famous Shaoshing wines and delicious dishes at moderate prices, and traveling theatres where we could go and enjoy ourselves.

On the day when the results were to be made public a large crowd waited anxiously in front of a high, spacious wall opposite the entrance of the Examination Hall. Cannon and band announced the moment when the list of names, or rather numbers, of the successful candidates was issued. The numbers were set down in a circular formation instead of in a column, so as to avoid having a top and bottom to the list.

I was pleasantly surprised to find my own number in big black letters among the others in the circle on the enormous oblong paper posted on the wall. To make sure I rubbed my eyes and looked at it several times. When I was sure they had not deceived me, I elbowed through the packed crowd and hastened back to my lodging house. As I made my way out I noticed a man with an open umbrella which caught on a railing. When he jerked it off the umbrella went upward, looking like a giant artichoke, but in his excitement he kept on running and paid no attention to it.

The second session of the examination came within a few days. Everyone who had passed the first had reason to worry, since some would be eliminated. I was lucky in the second trial. In the list of names which was posted on the wall I found mine somewhere in the middle rows.

The third and final session was merely perfunctory. In addition to an essay we were supposed to write down from memory a section of the "Imperial Instructions in Morals"; in reality each of us had with us a copy of the text, which we were allowed to carry into the Examination Hall and which we copied outright. The Imperial Examiner appeared in person to supervise the final examination. His official title I learned

缴了卷的人完全出来以后，大门又重新关上。第二次缴卷的讯号大约在一小时以后发出，同样鸣炮奏乐。第三次下令收卷则在六点钟左右，这一次可不再鸣炮奏乐。

考试以后，我们要等上十天、八天，才能知道考试结果。因此放榜以前我们可以大大地玩一阵。试院附近到处是书铺，我常碰到全省闻名的举人徐锡麟，在书铺里抽出书来看。我认识他，因为他曾在绍兴中西学堂教算学。想不到不出数年，他的心脏被挖出来，在安徽巡抚恩铭灵前致祭，因他为革命刺杀了恩铭。街头巷尾还有象棋摊子，棋盘两边都写着"观棋不语真君子，落子无悔大丈夫"两句俗语。街上有临时的酒楼饭馆，出售著名的绍兴酒和价廉物美的菜肴。一毛钱买一壶酒。醉蚶、糟鸡、家乡肉，每盘也只要一毛。如肯费三四毛钱，保管你买得满面春风，齿颊留香。城里有流动的戏班子，高兴的时候，我们还可以看看戏。

放榜的那一天，一大群人挤在试院大门前一座高墙前面守候。放榜时鸣炮奏乐，仪式非常隆重。榜上写的是录取考生的号码，而非姓名。号码排成一圆圈，以免有先后次序的分别。

我发现自己的号码也排入圆圈，列在墙上那张其大无比的长方形榜上，真是喜出望外。号码是黑墨大字写的，但是我还是不肯相信自己的眼睛，连揉了几次眼，发现自己的号码的的确确排在榜上的大圈圈内，这才放了心。连忙挤出人群，回到寄宿的地方。在我往外挤的时候，看到另一位考生也正在往外跑。他打着一把伞，这把伞忽然被一根栅栏钩住，他一拖，伞就向上翻成荷叶形。可是这位兴奋过度的考生，似乎根本没有注意他的伞翻向天了，还是匆匆忙忙往前跑。

几天之后，举行复试。复试要淘汰一部分人，所以初试录取的还得捏一把汗。复试时运气还算不错。放榜时，发现自己的名字列在居中的某一行上。

第三次考试只是虚应故事而已。除了写一篇文章以外，名义上我们还得默写一段《圣谕广训》（皇帝训谕士子的上谕）；但是我们每人都可以带一册进考场，而且老实不客气地照抄一遍。这次考试由学政（俗称学台）亲自莅场监考。试院大门口的两旁树着两根

from the inscription on two identical pennants about fifteen feet long which streamed in the air from flagpoles standing symmetrically at either side of the entrance. It read: "The Imperial Vice-Minister of Rites and Concurrently Imperial Examiner of Public Instruction for the Province of Chekiang, etc."

Early in the morning, some days later, I was awakened from slumber by the rapid beating of a tom-tom outside my window. It was an official reporter coming to announce the award of the First Degree—*Wu-shen*, popularly known as *Hsiu-tsai*. The official announcement, which was printed in bold block prints on a piece of red paper about six feet by four, read as follows:

> His Majesty's Imperial Vice-Minister of Rites and Concurrently Imperial Examiner of Public Instruction for the Province of Chekiang, etc., wishes to announce that your honorable person, Chiang Monlin, is awarded the Degree of Wu-shen and entitled to enjoy the privilege of entering the District Government School as a government scholar.

The "district school" was an empty Confucian temple with one official in charge who acted as the "government teacher" but in fact never taught anyone or anything. One found, actually, neither school nor teacher; what was called a school was only symbolic. Yet I had to pay the traditional entrance fee of $100—which I paid only partially, through bargaining.

After the examination the pendulum of life swung back once again to my new education. In a few days I went back to Chekiang College. In leaving, I learned from my landlord that one of my fellow lodgers had complained to him in a rage that the Imperial Examiner was so blind as to pass a man almost illiterate, like me, and neglect him, who possessed great literary merits. Such are the hazards of examinations!

Back at the college I plunged at once into studies again and found myself in the midst of algebra, physics, zoölogy, history, and so on. By way of extracurricular activity I indulged in reading revolutionary literature and discussed contemporary politics with my fellow students.

Imperial examination days and Chekiang College were worlds apart! It seemed a transformation overnight from misty, immutable medievalism to the whirlpool of a new revolutionary world. I felt as if what had happened had been a dream.

旗竿，旗竿上飘着长达十五尺的长幡，幡上写的就是这位学台的官衔。记得他的官衔是："礼部侍郎提督浙江全省学政……"

再过几天之后，我一大早就被窗外一阵当当小锣惊醒。原来是试差来报喜。我已经考取了附生，也就是平常所说的秀才。试差带来一份捷报，那是一张大约六尺长，四尺宽的红纸，上面用宋楷大字写着：

"贵府相公某蒙
礼部侍郎提督浙江全省学政某考试录取余姚县学附生"

所谓"县学"只有一所空无所有的孔庙，由一位"教谕"主持，事实上这位"教谕"并不设帐讲学，所谓"县学"是有名无实的。按我们家庭经济状况，我须呈缴一百元的贽敬，拜见老师，不过经过讨价还价，只缴了一半，也并没有和老师见过面。

当讨价还价正在进行的时候，父亲恼怒了说，孔庙里应该拜财神才是。旁边一位老先生说，那是说不得的。从前有一位才子金圣叹，因为讥笑老师，说了一句"把孔子牌位取消，把财神抬进学宫"的话，奉旨杀了头。临刑前这位玩世不恭的才子叹道："杀头至痛也，圣叹于无意中得之，岂不快哉。"

郡试以后，又再度回到浙江高等学堂，接受新式教育。我离开绍兴时，房东告诉我，一位同住在他店里的考生愤愤不平地对他说，学台简直瞎了眼，居然取了像我这样目不识丁的人，其意若曰像他那样满腹经纶的人反而落第，真是岂有此理。我笑笑没说什么，考试中本来不免有幸与不幸的！

回到学校以后，马上又埋头读书，整天为代数、物理、动物学和历史等功课而忙碌，课余之暇，又如饥似渴地阅读革命书刊，并与同学讨论当时的政治问题。郡试的那段日子和浙江高等学堂的生活恍若隔世。静定的、雾样迷濛的中世纪生活，似乎在一夜之间就转变为汹涌的革命时代的漩涡。我像是做了一场大梦。

After two months it was time for the winter vacation. I was called back home by my father to receive congratulations from relatives and friends upon my success. I was now nineteen. My close relatives saw a bright future for me; if the *feng-shui* of my ancestral tombs were favorable I would go right along, passing the two remaining examinations to receive the highest degree, to the glory of family, relatives, and above all, our ancestors whose spirits were in heaven. My second brother had passed his civil examination a few years before me; he was now a student at the Imperial University of Peking, of which I was to be Chancellor after some fifteen years—unpredictable chance.

An announcement printed on a big piece of red paper like the one I had received in Shaoshing was presented by official reporters, to the beating of a tom-tom, to my relatives and family friends. On the day of celebration I dressed in a blue satin gown and wore a red-tasseled hat with a silver button on top. Several hundred relatives and friends, including women and children, came to feast for two days. The spacious guesthall was decorated with artistic red lanterns and an orchestra played Chinese tunes. The happiest man there was my father, who cherished the hope that some day his son might become a grand minister at His Majesty's Imperial Court. For my part, I was puzzled. I was torn between two opposing forces, one pulling toward the old and the other toward the new. "What shall I do? What shall I do?" a voice cried out within me.

After three weeks the college reopened for the new session. Once more I swung back again to my studies in the new learning. I stayed for about half a year, leaving before the summer vacation. All the conflicting ideas, as between new and old, constitutional reforms and revolution, buzzing around in this topsy-turvy world of mine, were more than an immature mind could endure. I became restless and often had a fantasy in which, by a sort of somersault, I rocketed high into the air and then whirled down rapidly to the ground, where I burst to bits and was gone forever.

Being born in a family which had a few cases of insanity among my close relatives, I wondered sometimes whether I, too, had inherited a faint streak of instability which might occasionally tip the scale a little in my otherwise well-balanced temperament. I had been told, moreover, by my father and my granduncle that my ideas and actions during childhood had been quite different from those of the rest of the children. I still remember how my granduncle scolded me one day, remarking that

两个月以后，寒假到了。奉父亲之命回到乡间，接受亲戚朋友的道贺。那时我是十九岁，至亲们都希望我有远大的前程，如果祖坟的风水好，很可能一步一步由秀才而举人，由举人而进士，光大门楣，荣及乡里，甚至使祖先在天之灵也感到欣慰。二哥已早我几年考取了秀才，那时正在北京大学（京师大学堂）读书。当时的学生们听说京师大学四个字，没有不肃然起敬的。想不到十五年之后我竟为时会所迫承乏了北京大学的校长职务。回想起来，真令人觉得命运不可捉摸。

在绍兴时曾经收到一份捷报，不久，试差又用一份同样以红纸写的捷报，敲着铜锣分向我家乡的亲戚家属报喜。开筵庆祝的那一天，穿起蓝绸衫，戴了一顶银雀顶的红缨帽。好几百亲戚朋友，包括妇孺老少，齐来道贺，一连吃了两天喜酒。大厅中张灯结彩，并有吹班奏乐助兴。最高兴的自然是父亲，他希望他的儿子有一天能在朝中做到宰相，因为俗语说："秀才为宰相之根苗"。至于我自己，简直有点迷惘。两个互相矛盾的势力正在拉着，一个把我往旧世界拖，一个把我往新世界拖。我不知道怎么办。

在乡间住了三个星期，学校重新开学，我又再度全神贯注地开始研究新学问。在浙江高等学堂再逗留了半年光景，到暑假快开始时，又离开了。满脑子矛盾的思想，简直使尚未成熟的心灵无法忍受，新与旧的冲突，立宪与革命的冲突，常常闹得头脑天旋地转，有时觉得坐立不安，有时又默坐出神，出神时，会觉得自己忽然上冲霄汉，然后又骤然落地，结果在地上跌得粉碎，立刻被旋风吹散无踪了。

我的近亲当中曾经发现有人患精神病，我有时不禁怀疑自己是否也有点神经质的遗传。父亲和叔祖都说过，我小时候的思想行动本来就与常儿不同。我还记得有一天伯祖骂我，说我将来如不成君子

when I grew up I would become either a wise man or a rascal; to which, not knowing the meaning quite clearly, I secretly replied to myself that I wanted to be a wise man.

Was I crazy in this crazy world? At least one problem always remained clear in my mind: how to save China from dismemberment by the foreign Powers. Revolutionary ideas were now fast gaining ground in the minds of students throughout the country. As more and more of them joined the movement, the influence of Dr. Sun Yat-sen grew wider and wider. The days of the reigning dynasty were numbered.

On my part, I longed for a better and more westernized school. For by this time I could see that the wind blew in the direction of westernization, irrespective of whether China had constitutional reforms or revolution. One morning as I passed unintentionally by a passageway where students were forbidden, I met the proctor, who asked me what I was doing there. On the spur of the moment I improvised the story that my mother was ill and had written me to come home.

"That's too bad," he said. "You had better go right away."

I went back to my dormitory, packed up everything, and left the college that same morning. I took a small steamboat, chugging along the Grand Canal, down to Shanghai. There I took the entrance examination for Nanyang College and passed it. This was the year 1904, when the Russo-Japanese War was raging in all intensity for the control of Manchuria[1].

必成流氓。虽然不大明白这话的意思，但是我心里想，一定要做君子。

这个世界的确是个疯狂的世界，难道我也真的发了疯吗？至少有一个问题在脑子里还是很清楚的：那就是如何拯救祖国，免受列强的瓜分。革命正迅速地在全国青年学生群中生根发展。投身革命运动的青年学生愈多，孙中山先生的影响也愈来愈广。清室覆亡已经近在旦夕了。

我渴望找个更理想、更西化的学校。因为这时候已经看得清楚：不论立宪维新或者革命，西化的潮流已经无法抗拒。有一天早晨，无意中闯进禁止学生入内的走廊，碰到了学监。他问有什么事，我只好临时扯了个谎，说母亲生病，写信来要我回家。

"哦！那太不幸了。你还是赶快回家吧！"学监很同情地说。

回到宿舍，收拾起行李，当天上午就离开学校，趁小火轮沿运河到了上海。参加上海南洋公学的入学考试，结果幸被录取。那是一九〇四年的事。为争取满洲控制权的日俄战争正在激烈进行。

CHAPTER 8   WESTERNIZATION

China was now definitely on the track of westernization, whatever her struggles between old and new, between constitutionalism and revolution. The victory of Japan over Tsarist Russia gave further impetus to her reforms along new or Western lines. By this time about fifty thousand Chinese students had gathered about Tokyo, a center of the new knowledge. In the meantime the government had begun a series of reforms; new educational, military, and police systems were adopted, all copied after the Japanese models. Many believed that the Western systems and institutions which had been assimilated by the Japanese and adapted to Japanese life were more suitable to Chinese conditions than purely foreign forms. That is to say, China was to receive Western civilization via Japan. There were others, however, who held that if she must introduce Western civilization for her rejuvenation, why should she not go direct to the West for it?

I was one of those who believed in the direct route. In spite of the persuasions of friends studying in Japan, I stuck stubbornly to my belief. I entered Nanyang College with a view to preparing myself for American universities. As all the textbooks on Western subjects were in English, it suited me splendidly.

The college had been organized with the advice of Dr. John C. Ferguson, a former American missionary who only recently died in New York, and its preparatory department was run along the lines of an American high school. So it was most convenient as the final step to an American college. There were several American teachers who taught us modern subjects. After two years there I could read English fairly well, although I was still quite deficient in speaking. The language was not taught by phonetic methods and I found my tongue too stiff to follow.

The curriculum was divided into two groups, one of Chinese and the other of Western subjects. I always stood high in both, once winning honors in the two examinations simultaneously. The principal summoned me and paid me high compliments, to my great satisfaction.

The college was laid out and built according to Western plan; the main building had in its center a clock tower which could be seen several miles away. In front of a row of buildings was a vast football field, green and well kept. Football and baseball were encouraged by the college

捌 西化运动

虽然新旧之争仍在方兴未艾，立宪与革命孰长孰短亦无定论，中国这时已经无可置疑地踏上西化之路了。日本对帝俄的胜利，更使中国的西化运动获得新的鼓励，这时聚集东京的中国留学生已近五万人，东京已经成为新知识的中心。国内方面，政府也已经开始一连串的革新运动，教育、军事、警政都已根据日本的蓝图采取新制度。许多人相信：经过日本同化修正的西方制度和组织，要比纯粹的西洋制度更能适合中国的国情，因此他们主张通过日本接受西洋文化。但是也有一班人认为：既然我们必须接受西洋文明，何不直接向西洋学习？

我是主张直接向西方学习的，虽然许多留学日本的朋友来信辩难，我却始终坚持自己的看法。进了南洋公学，就是想给自己打点基础，以便到美国留学。这里一切西洋学科的课本都是英文的，刚好合了我的心意。

南洋公学开办时，采纳了美国传教士福开森博士的许多意见。南洋公学是交通大学的前身，交通大学附近的福开森路，就是为纪念这位美国传教士而命名的。南洋公学的预科，一切按照美国的中学学制办理，因此南洋公学可说是升入美国大学的最好阶梯。学校里有好几位讲授现代学科的美国人。在校两年，在英文阅读方面已经没有多大困难，不过讲却始终讲不好。学校教的英文并不根据语音学原理，我的舌头又太硬，始终跟不上。

课程方面分为两类，一类是中国旧学，一类是西洋学科。我在两方面的成绩都还过得去，有一次还同时侥幸获得两类考试的荣誉奖。因此蒙校长召见，谬承奖勉。

校舍是根据西洋设计而建筑的，主要建筑的中心有一座钟楼，数里之外就可以望见。有一排房子的前面是一个足球场，常年绿草如茵，

authorities and games and sports, generally indulged in by the students. Intercollegiate track and field games were held twice a year, with thousands of spectators.

Born physically frail, I began to realize that a healthy body was necessary for a healthy mind. Besides daily exercise and some sports of the lighter kind, I adopted a course of physical culture for myself. Every morning at about six I practised with dumbbells for half an hour, and again for fifteen minutes in the evening before going to bed. I kept this up for three years without interruption and after that time found myself in good health and always in a cheerful mood.

Spender's principles of education—consisting of three elements: the intellectual, moral, and physical—had by now been introduced into China. So to make up my moral education I reviewed some of the Confucian classics and studied the Sung and Ming philosophers and biographies of great men in history, both Chinese and Western, with a view to imitating their conduct. I entered selected parts of their savings and doings in my diary as I came across those that struck me. Then I did some careful thinking about them, tried to act on them, and watched the results, which were also entered into the diary for further examination.

It was exciting whenever I discovered that Chinese and Western ideas regarding certain matters were similar or almost identical. When they were I knew that in acting in accordance with them I would be guided by a universal truth. When discrepancies occurred I studied them and tried to find out the reasons for them. In this way I unconsciously made a comparative study of morals, or rules of conduct, of East and West. The most important result was that I learned to differentiate essentials from nonessentials and the fundamental from the superficial in moral ideas.

Henceforth I began to be more positive, more definite, more self-confident in steering my life on troubled waters. For moral ideas are the charts by means of which a life of action is directed.

I began to see the oneness of East and West and appreciate the dictum of Lu Hsiang-shan, a Sung philosopher, that "the sages born of the Eastern sea will have the same mind and therefore the same reason as the sages of the Western sea." I also began to see unity in chaos, for I came to realize that essentials are but few, while to know the similarities, differences, or contrasts among them is to clarify each and all of them. It was the buzzing of trifling things that made you dizzy. So I followed the teachings of Mencius and Lu Hsiang-shan that in learning we must

而且打扫得很整齐。学校当局鼓励学生玩足球和棒球，学生们对一般的运动也都很感兴趣。

我生来体弱，进了南洋公学以后，开始体会到要有高深的学问，必须先有强健的体魄。除了每日的体操和轻度的运动之外，还给自己定了一套锻炼身体的办法。每天六点钟光景，练习半小时的哑铃，晚间就寝前再练一刻钟。继续不断地练了三年，此后身体一直很好，而且心情也总是很愉快。

包括德、智、体三要素的斯宾塞尔教育原则这时已经介绍到中国。为了发展德育，就温习了四书，同时开始研究宋明的哲学家以及历代中外伟人的传记，希望借此学习他们的榜样，碰到认为足资借鉴的言行时，就把它们摘录在日记本上。然后仔细加以思考，试着照样去做，同时注意其成绩。这些成绩也记载在日记上，以备进一步的考核。

每当发现对某些问题的中西见解非常相似、甚至完全相同时，我总有难以形容的喜悦。如果中西贤哲都持同一见解，那末照着做自然就不会错了。当发现歧见时，就加以研究，设法找出其中的原因。这样就不知不觉地做了一项东西道德行为标准的比较研究。这种研究工作最重要的结果是学到了如何在道德观念中区别重要的与不重要的，以及基本的与浮面的东西。

从此以后，对于如何立身处世开始有了比较肯定、比较确切、也比较自信的见解，因为道德观念是指导行为的准绳。

我开始了解东西方的整体性，同时也更深切地体会到宋儒陆象山所说的"东海有圣人出焉，此心同，此理同。西海有圣人出焉，此心同，此理同"的名言。同时开始体会到紊乱中的统一，因为我发现基本道理原极有限，了解这些基本道理之间的异同矛盾正可以互相发明，互相印证。使我感到头晕眼花的只是细微末节的纷扰而已。孟子和

grasp the essentials and neglect the trifles and make our own reasoning power the sole arbiter. Thus I began to establish myself on the solid rock of reasoning instead of traditional beliefs. I felt as if I had stripped off clothes that were altogether too tight and stepped forth naked and free.

However, reason does not exist in a vacuum. I indulged in too much thinking, which led to nothing but disappointment. But the way to right thinking had to start from thinking itself, and learning to think by experience. You cannot teach a person how to think if he does not think at all. My belief here was reinforced in later years in America by reading John Dewey's *How We Think*, to which I owed much.

It is the teaching of the Confucian school that mental culture is the starting point of personal culture, which in turn will serve as the foundation for statecraft. Therefore, in order to save China, save yourself first. So I devoted myself to study and thinking, to physical exercise and to proper conduct. This was, as I understood it, the way to personal culture which would some day serve as the foundation for rendering service to the state.

While I was still at Nanyang College the Imperial Court took a definite step in educational reform by abolishing—in 1905—the agelong system of civil examinations; by this act the door to the past was closed to the younger generation once and for all. The decree was prompted by the victory of Japan over Russia. To replace the old, a new educational system was inaugurated, modeled after the Japanese, which in turn had been introduced to Japan from the West. China was now surely on the road to westernization.

For some time past Shanghai had been the center of a fugitive cultural movement in China. Harbored in the International Settlement and the French Concession, where Chinese jurisdiction reached to only a very limited extent or so far as international or French authorities might agree, Chinese intellectual and revolutionary leaders made their homes and enjoyed freedom of speech and publication. Here political fugitives and men of radical thought, or those so considered at the time, gathered to discuss, elucidate, and publish their ideas. Life here was comparable to that in one of the old Greek city-states—thinking was free and active.

For my own part, in addition to my training at Nanyang I joined in various activities as a junior member, more by way of learning than active participation. On Saturdays and Sundays I frequented especially Chi-fang,

陆象山告诉我们，做学问要抓住要点而舍弃细节，要完全凭我们的理智辨别是非。于是我开始发展以理解为基础的判断能力，不再依赖传统的信仰。这是思想上的一次大解放，像是脱下一身紧绷绷的衫裤那样舒服而自由。

但是，理解力也不能凭空生存。想得太多，结果除失望外一无成就，这样是犯了孔子所说的"思而不学"的毛病。当然，导向正确思想的途径还是从思想本身开始，然后从经验中学习如何思想。你不可能教导一个根本不用脑筋的人如何去思想。后来我留美时读到杜威的《我们如何思想》，使我的信念更为加强。

儒家说，正心诚意是修身的出发点，修身则是治国、平天下的根基。因此，我想，救国必先救己。于是决心努力读书、思考，努力锻炼身体，努力敦品励行。我想，这就是修身的正确途径了，有了良好的身心修养，将来才能为国服务。

在南洋公学读书的时候，清廷终于在一九○五年采取了教育改革的重要步骤，毅然宣布废止科举。年轻一代迷恋过去的大门从此关闭。废科举的诏书是日本战胜帝俄所促成的。代替科举的是抄袭自日本的一套新教育制度。日本的教育制度是模仿西方的。追本溯源，中国的新教育制度仍旧来自西方。中国现在总算不折不扣地踏上西化的途程了。

在这以前，上海曾经是我国革命分子文化运动的中心。中国的知识分子和革命领袖，躲在上海公共租界和法租界，可以享受言论自由和出版自由。政治犯和激烈分子在租界里讨论，发表他们的见解，思想自由而且蓬勃一时，情形足与希腊的城邦媲美。

我自己除了在南洋公学接受课本知识之外，也参加了各式各样的活动，但是学习的性质居多，谈不到积极工作。到礼拜六和礼拜天时，

a teashop on Foochow Road where all the students of Shanghai sipped their tea and indulged in lively discussions. No student of those days can forget the unique figure of the king of rogues, or "King Hsu," who was an inseparable part of the teahouse, selling revolutionary literature to the students. He was dressed in shabby Western clothes with a grey greasy cap on his head, his queue being cut. Among his revolutionary wares he included a pamphlet, *A New Treatise on Sex Problems*, which he explained was to catch the attention of the reading public. Nobody ever knew his name or where he lived. Any book on revolution nominally tabooed by the municipal authorities by request of the Chinese government could be secured through him.

In the same year that civil examinations were abolished the Tung Men Huei—the "Revolutionary Union," predecessor of the Kuomintang—was organized by Dr. Sun Yat-sen in Tokyo with several hundred students joining, and Dr. Sun was elected president. This was the year of the Portsmouth Treaty, signed by Japan and Russia to end the Russo-Japanese War. After this victory over one of the Western Powers Japan was now ready to launch aggression on China. This was a bare ten years before she delivered her famous Twenty-One Demands, and only sixteen years before the Mukden Incident which led to full-fledged war in 1937.

In Shanghai a boycott movement against American goods was proceeding in all intensity as a protest against the passing of the Chinese Exclusion Act by the American Congress. Students and merchants joined in calling from door to door on Chinese shopkeepers, urging them not to sell American merchandise. The shopkeepers tried to get rid of their boycotted goods as fast as possible at very moderate prices and a number of people were happy to buy them at the back door. Mass meetings were held in which fierce speeches against the exclusion act were made. At one of them the speaker stamped on the platform so hard that the sole of his shoe fell off and was flung into the audience while waves of laughter rang through the hall.

Another important incident, in the following year, was the agitation by the gentry of Chekiang and Kiangsu Provinces and the students and merchants of Shanghai against construction of the Soochow-Hangchow-Ningpo Railway by British capital. There were public demonstrations in the form of mass meetings, circular telegrams, and soapbox orations, and subscriptions were opened for shares in the railway with a view to building it with Chinese capital. The line was changed to run via

常常到福州路的奇芳茶馆去坐坐。那时候，上海所有的学生都喜欢到"奇芳"去吃茶，同时参加热烈的讨论。茶馆里有一位叫"野鸡大王"的，每日在那里兜售新书，他那副样子，去过"奇芳"的人没有一个会忘记的。他穿着一身破烂的西装，头上戴着一顶灰色的满是油垢的鸭舌头帽。他专门贩卖革命书刊给学生，他的货色当中还包括一本叫《性学新论》的小册子，据他解释，那只是用来吸引读者的。谁也不知道他的名字。吴稚晖先生说，他知道他是谁，并告诉了我他的名字，我却忘记了。我们也不晓得他住在什么地方。任何革命书刊都可以从他那里买得到。这些书，因租界当局应中国政府之请，在名义上是禁止贩卖的。

科举废止的同一年，孙中山先生在东京组织同盟会，参加的学生有好几百人，中山先生被选为主席。这一年也就是日本和俄国签订《朴茨茅斯条约》，结束日俄战争的一年。日本在击败西方列强之一的俄国以后，正蠢蠢欲动，预备侵略中国。十年之后，日本向中国提出著名的二十一条要求，十六年以后，发动九·一八沈阳事变，最后终于在民国二十六年与中国发生全面战争。

当时，上海正在热烈展开抵制美货运动，抗议美国国会通过排华法案。学生和商人联合挨户劝告中国商店店主不要售卖美国货。店主亟于卖掉被抵制的货品，只好削价脱售，有许多顾客倒也乐于从后门把货色买走。群众大会中，大家争着发表激烈演说，反对排华法案。有一次会中，一位慷慨激昂的演说者捶胸顿足，结果把鞋跟顿掉了。鞋跟飞到听众头上，引得哄堂大笑。

翌年也发生一件重要的事情。江浙两省的绅士同上海的学生和商人联合起来反对英国人投资建筑苏杭甬铁路。示威的方式包括群众大会、发通电、街头演说等等，同时开始招股准备用本国

Shanghai, Hangchow, and Ningpo; Shanghai being substituted for Soochow by the curious reasoning that the latter, an inland city, would thus be spared foreign influence, which was bound to increase with a railway. The British gave in as to the route, though the agitation was unsuccessful in obtaining Chinese capital ownership, and the railway was begun the next year.

Students all over China remained quiet in the schools during those years, partly because of their wider interests in activities outside school and partly because they themselves had wearied of the meaningless troubles they gave the school authorities. Nevertheless, they now turned their attention to the school cooks who prepared food for them. Each student paid six dollars a month for his food in Shanghai; in the interior, three dollars. One could not, therefore, expect very much from the cook, but the students were dissatisfied with what they got. They complained of the coarse rice and the poor quality of meat and vegetables, often demanding additional dishes—generally fried eggs, which were easy to prepare. Eggs were cheap in China then, about fifty or sixty for a dollar. Sometimes the students smashed the plates or bowls or beat up the cooks. No school was free from "strikes in the dining hall" as they were called.

In 1907 a short-lived revolution broke out in Anking, provincial capital of Anhwei. The leader was Hsu Shih-ling, police taotai (chief of police) of that province. He had been a teacher in the Sino-Occidental School in Shaoshing, where I received my early education in Western learning—where I first learned that the earth is round. He was a Chu-jen, the Second Degree awarded through the Imperial civil examinations; had taught in the school for a few years and then gone to Japan to study. Returning to China, he bought the office of taotai with fifty thousand dollars borrowed from friends and was appointed for the province of Anking. With the police under his control, he shot the governor with his own hand and started a coup d'état in the provincial capital. With two personal followers and the police force he occupied the arsenal, training its several cannon on the entrance. Not being adepts in military art, they were unable to make the guns work and soldiers rushed in and arrested him. One of his followers, Chen, was killed in action while the other, Ma, was arrested later.

Ma had been a schoolmate of mine at Chekiang College in Hangchow, and on their way from Japan to Anking he and Chen had stopped in Shanghai, where they came to see me almost every day. They talked

资金建筑这条铁路，路线要改为由上海经杭州到宁波。以上海代替苏州的理由很奇怪，说苏州是个内陆城市，铁路不经过苏州，可以使苏州免受外国的影响。英国人对路线让步了，铁路也在第二年动工兴建。

那几年里，全国各校的学生倒是都能与学校当局相安无事，一方面是因为他们对校外活动的兴趣提高，另一方面是因为他们对于给学校当局找些无谓的麻烦已经感到厌倦。不过，他们却把注意力转移到为他们做饭的厨子身上去了。当时上海学生的伙食费是每月六块钱；在内地，只要三块钱。因此饭菜不会好到哪里去。但是学生对伙食很不满意，不是埋怨米太粗糙，就是埋怨菜蔬质地太差，因此常常要求加菜——通常是加炒蛋，因为炒蛋最方便。当时鸡蛋也很便宜，一块钱可以买五六十个。有时候，学生们就砸碎碗碟出气，甚至把厨子揍一顿。几乎没有一个学校没有"饭厅风潮"。

一九O七年，安徽省城安庆发生了一次昙花一现的革命。革命领袖是徐锡麟，我们在前面曾提起他过。他是安徽省警务督办，曾在绍兴中西学堂教过书，我们在前面也曾经提及。（中西学堂就是我最初接触西方学问的地方，我在那里学到地球是圆的。）他中过举人，在中西学堂教过几年书以后，又到日本留学。他回国后向朋友借了五万块钱，捐了道台的缺，后来被派到安庆。他控制了警察以后，亲手枪杀安徽巡抚，并在安庆发动革命。他同两名亲信带了警校学生及警察部队占领军械库，在库门口架起大炮据守。但是他们因缺乏军事训练，无法使用大炮，结果被官兵冲入，徐锡麟当场被捕。他的两位亲信，一名叫陈伯平的阵亡了，一位叫马子夷的事后被捕。

马子夷是我在浙江高等学堂的同学，他和陈伯平从日本赴安庆时，曾在上海逗留一个时期。两个人几乎每天都来看我，大谈革命

at length about the revolutionary movement, which they believed was the only course for China's salvation, and asked me to go to Anking with them; but a cousin of mine, the manager of a native bank, advised me rather to take a trip to Japan. During summer vacation I took the opportunity of going with a friend to Tokyo, where an exposition was being held. Ma and Chen and I dined in farewell at the I-tse-hsiang Restaurant the evening before my departure, and they also left the next day for Anking, aboard a Yangtze steamer which took them up the river to their fatal destination.

My first experience on an ocean-going steamer was rather thrilling. Everything was novel to me. The flush toilet was a wonder. The Japanese *boysans* (cabin boys) were courteous. We reached Nagasaki the next morning and were impressed with the beautiful scenery in that port. In the afternoon we passed Shimonoseki, well known in China for Li Hung-chang's visit to it and for the peace treaty concluded in 1895 and known by that name. We landed at Kobe and from there took a train to Tokyo, getting off at Shimbashi Station. A friend of mine who was studying in Tokyo took me to a small hotel, the Kimigayokan in the Koishikawa district. The street was unpaved and muddy on that rainy day.

I visited the exposition in Ueno Park dozens of times and was impressed with the industrial development of Japan. In a war museum where prizes of war were shown I was very much ashamed to see the Chinese flags, uniforms, and weapons seized in the Sino-Japanese War and I tried vainly to dodge the eyes that stared at me. In the evening the park was illuminated with thousands of electric lights and the happy populace of Tokyo paraded on the grounds with myriad lanterns in their hands, shouting *Banzai*! They were intoxicated with the victory over Russia two years earlier and still went wild about it. On my part, I stood alone at the top of an imitation hill and watched the parade passing. I was so much moved that tears rolled down my cheeks.

Early one morning, within a week or so of my arrival, the *neisan* or chambermaid brought me a Japanese paper from which I learned of Hsu Shih-ling's revolution in Anking and its failure. I would have been killed if I had gone there with my two friends.

The general impression I had of Japan was very favorable. The whole country was a garden. The people were well dressed, their cities clean. They were perhaps inwardly conceited, but courteous to strangers.

运动。他们认为革命是救中国的唯一途径，还约我同他们一道去安庆。但是一位当钱庄经理的堂兄劝我先到日本去一趟。那年暑假，就和一位朋友去东京，顺便参观一个展览会。我们离沪赴日的前夕，马子夷、陈伯平和我三个人在一枝香酒楼聚餐话别。第二天我去日本，他们也搭长江轮船赴安庆。想不到一枝香酒楼一别竟成永诀。

初次乘大洋轮船，样样觉得新奇。抽水马桶其妙无比。日本茶房礼貌周到。第二天早晨，我们到达长崎，优美的风景给我很深的印象。下午经过马关，就是李鸿章在一八九五年与日本签订《马关条约》的地方。我们在神户上岸，从神户乘火车到东京，在新桥车站落车。一位在东京读书的朋友领我们到小石川二十三番君代馆住下。东京的街道当时还没有铺石子，更没有柏油，那天又下雨，结果满地泥泞。

我到上野公园的展览会参观了好几十趟，对日本的工业发展印象很深。在一个展览战利品的战迹博物馆里，看到中日战争中俘获的中国军旗、军服和武器，简直使我惭愧得无地自容。夜间整个公园被几万盏电灯照耀得如同白昼，兴高采烈的日本人提着灯笼在公园中游行，高呼万岁。两年前，他们陶醉于对俄的胜利，至今犹狂喜不已。我孤零零地站在一个假山顶上望着游行的队伍，触景生情，不禁泫然涕下。

到日本后约一星期，君代馆的下女在清晨拿了一份日文报纸来，我从报上获悉徐锡麟在安庆起义失败的消息。如果我不来日本而跟那两位朋友去安庆，恐怕我不会今日在此讲"西潮"的故事了。

我对日本的一般印象非常好。整个国家像个大花园，人民衣饰整饬，城市清洁。他们内心或许很骄傲，对生客却很有礼貌。

Compulsory education made the general level of the people much higher than in China, and this was perhaps the secret of Japan's becoming a world Power. These were the impressions I carried home after a month's stay.

Pretty soon I began to work hard again at the college. The following year, during the summer vacation, I went to Hangchow to take the Chekiang provincial examination for scholarships to study in America. Having failed, I got a few thousand dollars from my father and prepared to go to California for further study.

强迫教育使国民的一般水准远较中国为高，这或许就是使日本成为世界强国的秘密所在。这是我在日本停留一月后带回来的印象。后来赴美国学教育学，也受这些感想的指示。但是国家兴衰事情并不如此简单，让我等机会再谈罢。

不久以后，又开始为学校功课而忙碌。第二年暑假，跑到杭州参加浙江省官费留美考试，结果未被录取。于是向父亲拿到几千块钱，预备到加利福尼亚州深造。

PART TWO

第二部　留美时期

AMERICAN YEARS

CHAPTER 9   FURTHER "WEST"

With part of the money my father gave me I bought hats, shoes, clothes, and other necessary things, and a first-class ticket to San Francisco. The rest I converted into American gold dollars at the rate of two Mexican to one. My queue I got rid of at a barbershop. When the barber applied a pair of long scissors to my hair I felt as if I were on the guillotine—a chill stole all over me. With two quick, heavy cuts my queue fell off and I felt as if my head had gone with it. It was given back to me wrapped in paper and I threw it into the ocean on my way to America.

I acquired a doctor's certificate and a passport, based on Section 6 of the immigration law admitting students, and went to the American Consulate General in Shanghai for a visa. This done, I secured my ticket and boarded an American Mail liner for San Francisco. It was late August, 1908. There were about a dozen Chinese students on the same boat. Leaving the shores of my country seemed to cut away the last link that connected me with my earlier life. I was lucky in being a good sailor and was never sick during the twenty-four long days aboard ship. Perhaps this was due to the practice I had had in swinging for several weeks before embarking. I was good at it, for swinging is a Chinese garden pastime.

The liner was much larger and more luxurious than the Japanese steamer I had taken to Kobe the previous year. The most striking thing to me on board was the dancing. Brought up in a society where men and women did not mix freely, I could not at once reconcile myself to it. But after watching it several times I began to appreciate the beauty of it.

On the day of our arrival at San Francisco a port doctor came on board and carefully examined the eyes of Chinese students to see whether any of us had any trace of trachoma.

The first thing I had felt on landing was the power of the state through the instrumentality of the immigration officials and police. I began to wonder why the people of a republic enjoyed less individual freedom than did the people of China, which was an absolute monarchy. In China we scarcely felt the influence of the state. "Heaven is high above and the Emperor is far away."

We stopped over in San Francisco for a few hours to visit Chinatown. Then two of us who were bound for the University of California were taken to Berkeley by the president of the Chinese Students' Alliance there. In the evening we dined at a restaurant in Berkeley, the Sky Light,

玖 负笈西行

我拿出一部分钱，买了衣帽杂物和一张往旧金山的头等船票，其余的钱就以两块墨西哥鹰洋对一元美金的比例兑取美钞。上船前，找了一家理发店剪去辫子。理发匠举起利剪，抓住我的辫子时，我简直有上断头台的感觉，全身汗毛直竖。咔嚓两声，辫子剪断了，我的脑袋也像是随着剪声落了地。理发匠用纸把辫子包好还给我。上船后，我把这包辫子丢入大海，让它随波逐浪而去。

我拿到医生证明书和护照之后，到上海的美国总领事馆请求签证，按照移民条例第六节规定，申请以学生身份赴美。签证后买好船票，搭乘美国邮船公司的轮船往旧金山。那时是一九〇八年八月底。同船有十来位中国同学。邮船启碇，慢慢驶离祖国海岸，我的早年生活也就此告一段落。在上船前，我曾经练了好几个星期的秋千，所以在二十四天的航程中，一直没有晕船。

这只邮船比我前一年赴神户时所搭的那艘日本轮船远为宽大豪华。船上最使我惊奇的事是跳舞。我生长在男女授受不亲的社会里，初次看到男女相偎相依、婆娑起舞的情形，觉得非常不顺眼。旁观了几次之后，我才慢慢开始欣赏跳舞的优美。

船到旧金山，一位港口医生上船来检查健康，对中国学生的眼睛检查得特别仔细，惟恐有人患砂眼。

我上岸时第一个印象是移民局官员和警察所反映的国家权力。美国这个共和政体的国家，她的人民似乎比君主专制的中国人民更少个人自由，这简直弄得我莫名其妙。我们在中国时，天高皇帝远，一向很少感受国家权力的拘束。

我们在旧金山逗留了几个钟头，还到唐人街转了一趟。我和另一位也预备进加州大学的同学，由加大中国同学会主席领路到了卜技利。晚饭在夏德克路的天光餐馆吃，每人付两角五分钱，

on Shattuck Avenue, each paying twenty-five cents for a dinner which consisted of soup, beef stew, and a piece of pie, with bread and butter and a cup of coffee. I took a room at Mrs. Coole's house on Bancroft Way. She was a talkative, elderly lady, very kind to the Chinese students. She told me that I must turn off the light before going out and shut off the water after washing; that I must not throw peanuts into the flush toilet or leave my money on the table; that in leaving the room I needn't lock the door, but if I preferred I might leave the key under the mat. "If you want anything," she said, "you just tell me. I know how a stranger must feel in a foreign country. Make yourself at home." Then she bade me good night and left the room.

As I had arrived in San Francisco too late to enter the fall session of the university, I had to wait for the next term. Meantime I got a coed of the university to coach me in English at fifty cents an hour. I spent all my time studying English; I read the *San Francisco Chronicle* regularly every morning and subscribed to a weekly magazine, *The Outlook*, for more serious study. By the aid of Webster's *Collegiate Dictionary*, which was always at hand and to which every doubtful word was referred, my vocabulary increased day by day and at the end of four months I could read papers and magazines quite freely.

In the beginning I found myself partially blind, deaf, and dumb so far as the English language was concerned. These difficulties had to be surmounted before I could hope to get along well in the university. By concentration and perseverance the first obstacle was largely overcome in the first four months and it was only a matter of time to reduce it completely. The second had to be removed gradually by listening to conversations and lectures. It was easier to understand lectures because they were in the form of organized thought and were slower and more distinct in delivery. Conversations were generally wider in range and carried on in a rapid succession of varied or disconnected groups of ideas in which one had difficulty in following the thread of thought. To listen to a play at the theatre was midway between the two.

It was most difficult, however, to overcome the dumbness. First of all, I had been started off wrong from the very beginning in China. The wrong habits were deeply rooted and it took time to dislodge them. In the second place, as I was ignorant of phonetic methods the mere effort to imitate a word did not necessarily lead to a correct pronunciation.

吃的有汤、红烧牛肉、一块苹果饼和一杯咖啡。我租了班克洛夫路的柯尔太太的一间房子。柯尔太太已有相当年纪，但是很健谈，对中国学生很关切。她吩咐我出门以前必定要关灯；洗东西以后必定要关好自来水龙头；花生壳决不能丢到抽水马桶里；银钱决不能随便丢在桌子上；出门时不必锁门；如果我愿意锁门，就把钥匙留下藏在地毯下面。她说："如果你需要什么，你只管告诉我就是了。我很了解客居异国的心情。你就拿我的家当自己的家好了，不必客气。"随后她向我道了晚安才走。

到卜技利时，加大秋季班已经开学，因此我只好等到春季再说。我请了加大的一位女同学给我补习英文，学费每小时五毛钱。这段时间内，我把全部精力花在英文上。每天早晨必读《旧金山纪事报》，另外还订了一份《展望》周刊，作为精读的资料。《韦氏大学字典》一直不离手，碰到稍有疑问的字就打开字典来查，四个月下来，居然字汇大增，读报纸、杂志也不觉得吃力了。

初到美国时，就英文而论，我简直是半盲、半聋、半哑。如果我希望能在学校里跟得上功课，这些障碍必须先行克服。头一重障碍，经过四个月的不断努力，总算大致克服了，完全克服它也不过是时间问题而已。第二重障碍要靠多听人家谈话和教授讲课才能慢慢克服。教授讲课还算比较容易懂，因为教授们的演讲，思想有系统，语调比较慢，发音也清晰。普通谈话的范围比较广泛，而且包括一连串互不衔接而且五花八门的观念，要抓住谈话的线索颇不容易。到剧院去听话剧对白，其难易则介于演讲与谈话之间。

最困难的是克服开不得口的难关。主要的原因是我在中国时一开始就走错了路。错误的习惯已经根深蒂固，必须花很长的时间才能矫正过来。其次是我根本不懂语音学的方法，单凭模仿，

For there are wide gaps between the tone uttered and the ear that hears it, and between ear and tongue—the ear does not necessarily catch the right tone, nor does the tongue always follow the ear in reproducing it. Moreover, California was not so hospitable a land socially for the Chinese as to make one feel congenial or at ease; I was always overconscious of this, slow to mingle with others and shy when others tried to approach me. Thus many available social connections were cut off, and as language improves only with intercourse, the improvement in the spoken language was indeed very, very slow. This hampered my participation in discussions, both in the classroom and out of it, when I later entered the university. As a rule I remained mute in class and when a question was put to me responded only by a blush. My professors were very considerate and on no occasion tried to exact an answer. Perhaps they realized my social plight, or excused me simply because I was a foreigner. At any rate, from my examination papers—in most cases above "B" grade—they knew I did my classwork conscientiously in spite of muteness.

Time flew—it was soon Christmas. On Christmas Eve I dined alone at a restaurant with better food than on the first occasion, and a larger bill. After dinner I strolled about the streets watching the happy family gatherings through the windows where curtains were not drawn. Christmas trees, some lighted with tiny electric lights and some with candles, were everywhere.

With a few Chinese friends on New Year's Eve I went across the bay to San Francisco. From the ferry we could see at a distance, on the other side of the bay, the Clock Tower bejeweled with hundreds of lights. Moving through the crowd to the exit on landing, one heard the player pianos going full tilt for their nickel's worth. As I followed the packed crowd streaming slowly along the main street, flooded with lights, my ears were deafened by toy bugles and rattles. People took particular pleasure in blowing and rattling at the ears of pretty ladies, who returned the compliment good-naturedly with smiles at the merrymakers. Paper streamers floated in the air and were strung around people's necks. Confetti showered on the crowd like many-colored snow. I branched off to Chinatown, where I found throngs admiring the window decorations with their Oriental touch. Firecrackers made you feel that you were celebrating New Year's Eve in China.

不一定能得到准确的发音。因为口中发出的声音与耳朵听到的声音之间，以及耳朵与口舌之间，究竟还有很大的差别。耳朵不一定能够抓住正确的音调，口舌也不一定能够遵照耳朵的指示发出正确的声音。此外，加利福尼亚这个地方对中国人并不太亲热，难得使人不生身处异地、万事小心的感觉。我更特别敏感，不敢贸然与美国人厮混，别人想接近我时，我也很怕羞。许多可贵的社会关系都因此断绝了。语言只有多与人接触才能进步，我既然这样固步自封，这方面的进步自然慢之又慢。后来我进了加大，这种口语上的缺陷，严重地影响了我在课内课外参加讨论的机会。有人问我问题时，我常常是脸一红，头一低，不知如何回答。教授们总算特别客气，从来不勉强我回答任何问题。也许他们了解我处境的窘困，也许是他们知道我是外国人，所以特别加以原谅。无论如何，他们知道，我虽然噤若寒蝉，对功课仍旧很用心，因为我的考试成绩多半列在乙等以上。

日月如梭，不久圣诞节就到了。圣诞前夕，我独自在一家餐馆里吃晚餐。菜比初到旧金山那一天好得多，花的钱，不必说，也非那次可比。饭后上街闲游，碰到没有拉起窗帘的人家，我就从窗户眺望他们欢欣团聚的情形。每户人家差不多都有满饰小电灯或蜡烛的圣诞树。

大除夕，我和几位中国同学从卜技利渡海到旧金山。从渡轮上可以远远地看到对岸的钟楼装饰着几千盏电灯。上岸后，发现旧金山到处人山人海。码头上候船室里的自动钢琴震耳欲聋。这些钢琴只要投下一枚镍币就能自动弹奏。我随着人潮慢慢地在大街上闲逛，耳朵里满是小喇叭和小鼗鼓的嘈音，玩喇叭和鼗鼓的人特别喜欢凑着漂亮的太太小姐们的耳朵开玩笑，这些太太小姐们虽然耳朵吃了苦头，但仍然觉得这些玩笑是一种恭维，因此总是和颜悦色地报以一笑。空中到处飘扬着五彩纸条，有的甚至缠到人们的颈上。碎花纸像彩色的雪花飞落在人们的头上。我转到唐人街，发现成群结队的人在欣赏东方色彩的橱窗装饰。噼噼啪啪的鞭炮声，使人觉得像在中国过新年。

When the clock struck midnight people began to shout "Happy New Year!" at the tops of their voices, and to blow horns and shake rattles. More confetti and more streamers. This was my first New Year in America and I was impressed with the good-naturedness of the American crowd and the spontaneous play spirit of the grownups. They were a young race in their merrymaking.

I got back home quite late and pleasantly tired, went to bed, and slept soundly until late in the morning. After breakfast I took a walk in the residential section of Berkeley. The houses on the gentle slopes of the Berkeley hills were surrounded with flower beds and green lawns. Roses were in full bloom in the mild California winter, for Berkeley, like Kunming in China, is blessed with perennial spring.

After the New Year I looked forward to the beginning of the second term of the university in February. With new hopes and vigor I worked hard at my language study. When the term drew near I applied for admission on credits from Nanyang College in Shanghai and was entered in the College of Agriculture, with Chinese as a substitute for Latin.

Here I must explain why I turned to agriculture when my preparation was along literary lines. This was not a happy-go-lucky move as it might have been with many a young student; it had been carefully considered and decided upon in all seriousness. Since China was mainly agricultural, the improvement of agriculture, as I saw it, would bring happiness and prosperity to the largest number of people in China; moreover, I had always taken delight in plants and animals since my early years in the village, where farming was the main current of life. For national as well as personal reasons, therefore, agriculture seemed the most appropriate study to pursue. Another minor consideration was that as I was born a delicate child my health could be improved by having plenty of fresh air in the country.

I took botany, zoölogy, hygiene, English, German, and physical culture for the term—a period of three hours a week for each course except the last, which took six hours. We were told to buy textbooks at a bookstore on College Avenue, so I went to the store and asked, among other things, for so-and-so's *Bo'tany*, with the accent on the second syllable.

"What is it you want?" the sales clerk demanded. I repeated the word with the same accent. He shook his head. "Sorry, haven't got it."

　　午夜钟声一响，大家一面提高嗓门大喊"新年快乐！"一面乱揿汽车喇叭或者大摇响铃。五光十色的纸条片更是漫天飞舞。这是我在美国所过的第一个新年。美国人的和善和天真好玩使我留下深刻的印象。在他们的欢笑嬉游中可以看出美国的确是个年轻的民族。

　　那晚回家时已经很迟，身体虽然疲倦，精神却很轻松，上床后一直睡到第二天日上三竿起身。早饭后，我在卜技利的住宅区打了个转。住宅多半沿着徐缓的山坡建筑，四周则围绕着花畦和草地。玫瑰花在加州温和的冬天里到处盛开着，卜技利四季如春，通常长空蔚蓝不见朵云，很像云南的昆明、台湾的台南，而温度较低。

　　新年之后，我兴奋地等待着加大第二个学期在二月间开学。心中满怀希望，我对语言的学习也加倍努力。快开学时，我以上海南洋公学的学分申请入学，结果获准进入农学院，以中文学分抵补了拉丁文的学分。

　　我过去的准备工作偏重文科方面，结果转到农科，我的动机应该在这里解释一下。我转农科并非像有些青年学生听天由命那样的随便，而是经过深思熟虑才慎重决定的。我想，中国既然以农立国，那末只有改进农业，才能使最大多数的中国人得到幸福和温饱。同时我幼时在以耕作为主的乡村里生长，对花草树木和鸟兽虫鱼本来就有浓厚的兴趣。为国家，为私人，农业都似乎是最合适的学科。此外我还有一个次要的考虑，我在孩提时代身体一向羸弱，我想如果能在田野里多接触新鲜空气，对我身体一定大有裨益。

　　第一学期选的功课是植物学、动物学、生理卫生、英文、德文和体育。除了体育是每周六小时以外，其余每科都是三小时。我按照指示到大学路一家书店买教科书。我想买植物学教科书时，

I pointed to the book on the shelf. He smiled and said, "Oh, excuse me, you mean 'botany.'"

I was glad to have the book and also to learn the right pronunciation of the word. Again, we were told to observe certain plants in the botanical garden. Failing to locate the place, I asked a janitor where the 'botanical garden was—with the accent on the first syllable.

"What?" he said. I repeated.

"Oh, oh—you mean the bo'tanical garden," he responded after a moment, enlightened.

I would have liked to swear in good American slang if I had learned any. Years after, when I related the incident to an American friend in Peking, he told me the story of a Frenchman who was asked what difficulties he found in speaking English. The Frenchman replied with characteristic gesture, "Oh, English is easy—but the *abominable accent!*" pronouncing the last words in French. Indeed, the *abominable accent* has discouraged many a student who has tried to learn English and found himself caught in an intricate maze. Of course there are rules by which one can somewhat steer his way. But there are too many exceptions; often the exceptions are the rule, so that one has to consider each case and acquire them all gradually and with great pains.

I studied botany and zoölogy with great interest. I still remember the jocular remarks of the professor of botany as we were being taught to use the microscope, "Don't think you're going to see through the microscope a fly as big as an elephant. No—you can't see even a section of the fly's leg."

My interest in the observation of nature had its roots in the naïve nature study which, during my school days in China, I carried on outside of school as a sort of diversion after the day's tiresome classical study. My improvised observations years before and my interest in botany and zoölogy now all proceeded from a common source—curiosity. The one great difference lay in the tool used. The microscope is an extension of the eye and enables you to see minute particles which the naked eye can never hope to reach. Use of this tool has led to the discovery of microbes, whose limitless numbers are comparable to the stars—which in turn are studied by another extension of the eye, the telescope. I longed to make

说了半天店员还是听不懂，后来我只好用手指指书架上那本书，他才恍然大悟。原来植物学这个名词的英文字（botany）重音应放在第一音节，我却把重音念在第二音节上去了。经过店员重复一遍这个字的读音以后，我才发现自己的错误。买了书以后心里很高兴，既买到书，同时又学会一个英文字的正确发音，真是一举两得。后来教授要我们到植物园去研究某种草木，我因为不知道植物园在哪里，只好向管清洁的校工打听。念到植物园的植物这个英文字时，我自作聪明把重音念在第一音节上，我心里想，"植物学"这个英文字的重音既然在第一音节上，举一反三，"植物园"中"植物"一字的重音自然也应该在第一音节上了。结果弄得那位工友瞠目不知所答。我只好重复了一遍，工友揣摩了一会之后才恍然大悟。原来是我举一反三的办法出了毛病，"植物（的）"这个字的重音却应该在第二音节上。

可惜当时我还没有学会任何美国的俚语村言，否则恐怕"他×的"一类粗话早已脱口而出了。英文重音的捉摸不定曾经使许多学英文的人伤透脑筋。固然重音也有规则可循，但是每条规则总有许多例外，以致例外的反而成了规则。因此每个字都得个别处理，要花很大工夫才能慢慢学会每个字的正确发音。

植物学和动物学引起我很大的兴趣。植物学教授在讲解显微镜用法时曾说过笑话："你们不要以为从显微镜里可以看到大如巨象的苍蝇。事实上，你们恐怕连半只苍蝇腿都看不到呢！"

我在中国读书时，课余之暇常常喜欢研究鸟兽虫鱼的生活情形，尤其在私塾时代，一天到晚死背枯燥乏味的古书，这种肤浅的自然研究正可调节一下单调的生活，因而也就慢慢培养了观察自然的兴趣。早年的即兴观察和目前对动植物学的兴趣，有一个共通的出发点——好奇，最大的差别在于使用的工具。显微镜是眼睛的引伸，可以使人看到肉眼无法辨别的细微物体。使用显微镜的结果，使人发现多如繁星的细菌。望远镜是眼睛的另一种引伸，利用望远镜可以观察无穷无数的繁星。我渴望到黎克天文台

a pilgrimage to Lick Observatory to see the world's largest telescope, but for some reason or other did not go. Instead I paid twenty-five cents to look into a telescope on the streets to see the planets and was thrilled to behold silvery Saturn in its shining ring, sailing in the blue sky as I had seen it on a celestial map in school.

I stayed in the College of Agriculture for half a year. One of my friends had meanwhile been urging me to take up some branch of social science instead of a practical science like agriculture. He argued that though agriculture was very important, there were other studies more vital for China; unless we could solve our political and social problems in the light of modern developments in the West we could not very well solve the agricultural ones. Moreover, my world outlook would be limited, in agriculture, to a practical science and would not embrace anything beyond the narrow scope of that special field.

As I had studied Chinese history as well as the general outlines of Western history, and was familiar with the general development of national strength in various countries at various times, I could very well appreciate my friend's advice. It set me thinking, for I was again at the crossroads and must sooner or later make a final decision. As I have mentioned, I was always careful in making any decision as to a new field which would determine my future course of life.

Early one morning, on my way to a barn to watch the milking, I met a number of fresh-looking youngsters—pretty girls and lively boys—on their way to school. Suddenly an idea struck me: I am here to study how to raise animals and plants; why not study how to raise men? Instead of going to the barn I went up into the Berkeley hills and sat under an old oak tree overlooking beautiful sunlit San Francisco Bay and the Golden Gate. As I gazed into the bay, thoughts on the rise and decline of the successive dynasties in China presented themselves one after another. All of a sudden I saw as if in a vision children emerging like water nymphs from the waters of the bay and asking me to give them schools. I decided to take education as my major, in the College of Social Science.

It was already late in the morning when I rushed down from the hills, went directly to the Recorder's Office to see Mr. Sutton, and asked to be transferred from the College of Agriculture to that of Social Science. After some argument the transfer was granted. In the fall of 1909 I began to take courses in logic, ethics, psychology, and English history, and was thus launched on what became my real college career.

去见识见识世界上最大的一具望远镜，但是始终因故不克遂愿。后来花了二毛五分钱，从街头的一架望远镜去眺望行星，发现银色的土星带着耀目的星环，在蔚蓝的天空中冉冉移动，与学校里天体挂图上所看到的一模一样。当时的经验真是又惊又喜。

在农学院读了半年，一位朋友劝我放弃农科之类的实用科学，另选一门社会科学。他认为农科固然重要，但是还有别的学科对中国更重要。他说，除非我们能参酌西方国家的近代发展来解决政治问题和社会问题，那末农业问题也就无法解决。其次，如果不改修社会科学，我的眼光可能就局限于实用科学的小圈子，无法了解农业以外的重大问题。

我曾经研究过中国史，也研究过西洋史的概略，对各时代各国国力消长的情形有相当的了解，因此对于这位朋友的忠告颇能领略。他的话使我一再考虑，因为我已再度面临三岔路口，迟早总得有个决定。我曾经提到，碰到足以影响一生的重要关头，我从不轻率作任何决定。

一天清早，我正预备到农场看挤牛奶的情形，路上碰到一群蹦蹦跳跳的小孩子去上学。我忽然想起：我在这里研究如何培育动物和植物，为什么不研究研究如何培育人才呢？农场不去了，一直跑上卜技利的山头，坐在一棵古橡树下，凝望着旭日照耀下的旧金山和金门港口的美景。脑子里思潮起伏，细数着中国历代兴衰的前因后果。忽然之间，眼前恍惚有一群天真烂漫的小孩，像凌波仙子一样从海湾的波涛中涌出，要求我给他们读书的学校，于是我毅然决定转到社会科学学院，选教育为主科。

从山头跑回学校时已近晌午，我直跑到注册组去找苏顿先生，请求从农学院转到社会科学学院。经过一番诘难和辩解，转院总算成功了。从一九〇九年秋天起，我开始选修逻辑学、伦理学、心理学和英国史，我的大学生涯也从此步入正途。

My student life moved along in an atmosphere of intellectual activity. Days and months rolled on smoothly and pleasantly. As the sands of time gathered, so grew my knowledge.

In logic I learned that thinking has its method—that is to say, we must think logically. There is a difference between inductive and deductive thinking. Observation is very important in inductive thinking, so I wanted to practice it. I began to observe the many things I came across on campus or near the university. Why were cows belled? Why do the leaves of the eucalyptus hang vertical? Why are all California poppies yellow?

One morning as I was walking along the slopes of the Berkeley hills I noticed a pipe from which water was flowing. Where did the water come from? I followed up the pipe line, which led me to the source, and rejoiced over the discovery. Quite high on the hills I began to wonder what was on the other side of them. I climbed over one hill after another and found that there were endless hills, higher and higher as I went farther and farther. Finally I gave up and took a path which led down to a number of farmhouses, finding by the way creeks and woods which I enjoyed immensely.

Of course the endless chain of observation running merely from one thing to another could lead only to disappointment. Finally I learned that observation must have a definite object and a definite purpose, not ramble aimlessly. The astronomer observes the stars, the botanist the growth of plants. Later I came to know that there is another kind of observation, a sort of controlled observation called experiment, by means of which scientific discoveries are made.

In the field of ethics I learned that there is a difference between ethical principles and rules of conduct. The principles tell you why certain accepted rules are desirable at certain stages of civilization, while the rules themselves merely exact observance without inquiry into the underlying principles and their relation to modern society.

As life in China was governed by accepted rules of conduct, the inquiry into their underlying principles created storms in my mind. The old moral foundations which we had taken as final truths began to rock as in an earthquake. Moreover my professor, Harry Overstreet, was not the kind of traditional teacher who simply believed in accepted truths

岁月平静而愉快地过去，时间之沙积聚的结果，我的知识也在大学的学术气氛下逐渐增长。

从逻辑学里我学到思维是有一定的方法的。换一句话说，我们必须根据逻辑方法来思考。观察对于归纳推理非常重要，因此我希望训练自己的观察能力。我开始观察校园之内，以及大学附近所接触到的许许多多事物。母牛为什么要装铃？尤加利树的叶子为什么垂直地挂着？加州的罂粟花为什么都是黄的？

有一天早晨，我沿着卜技利的山坡散步时，发现一条水管正在汩汩流水。水从哪里来的呢？沿着水管找，终于找到了水源，我的心中也充满了童稚的喜悦。这时我已到了相当高的山头，我很想知道山岭那一边究竟有些什么。翻过一山又一山，发现这些小山简直多不胜数。越爬越高，而且离住处也越来越远。最后只好放弃初衷，沿着一条小路回家。归途上发现许多农家，还有许多清澈的小溪和幽静的树林。

这种漫无选择的观察，结果自然只有失望。最后我终于发现，观察必须有固定的对象和确切的目的，不能听凭兴之所至乱观乱察。天文学家观察星球，植物学家则观察草木的生长。后来我又发现另外一种称为实验的受控制的观察，科学发现就是由实验而来的。

念伦理学时，我学到道德原则与行为规律的区别。道德原则可以告诉我们，为什么若干公认的规律切合某阶段文化的需要；行为规律只要求大家遵守，不必追究规律背后的原则问题，也不必追究这些规律与现代社会的关系。

在中国，人们的生活是受公认的行为规律所规范的。追究这些行为规律背后的道德原则时，我的脑海里马上起了汹涌的波澜。一向被认为最终真理的旧有道德基础，像遭遇地震一样开始摇摇欲坠。同时，赫利·奥佛斯屈里特教授也给了我很大的启示。传统的教授通常只知道信仰公认的真理，同时希望他的学生们如此做。

and expected his students to do likewise; his searching mind led me to peer into every crevice in the foundation stones of moral principle. In class there were lively discussions, which I refrained from joining partly because of my deficiency in the spoken language and partly owing to shyness, which grew in me out of a sense of inferiority. For around the year 1909 China was in the darkest period of her recent history and we had very little self-confidence about her future. But I pricked up my ears and listened like an intelligent dog to its master, understanding the meaning but unable to talk.

We were required to read Plato, Aristotle, the Gospel of St. John, and Marcus Aurelius, among other sources. I was impressed with the all-searching mind of the Greeks as revealed through the two Greek philosophers; I felt that while the Confucian classics were richly tinged with moral sense, the Greek philosophers were permeated by all-piercing intellect. This led me later on to a study of Greek history and a comparative study of ancient Greek and Chinese thought. It also led me to understand what an important part Greek thought has played in modern European civilization, and why Greek has been regarded as an indispensable part of a liberal education.

With St. John I began to appreciate the meaning of love as preached by Jesus, stripped of creed and church. It is indeed the highest ideal to "love your enemy." If one could really love one's enemy there would be no enemy.

"Can you love your enemy?" the professor asked the class. There was no answer.

"I can't," the attentive dog yelped.

"You can't?" he smiled.

I quoted Confucius, "Love those who love you, but be fair to your enemy." Upon this he commented, "It's quite sensible, isn't it?" The class made no response. As we dispersed a young American boy came up to me and patted me on the shoulder. "Love your enemy! Tommyrot, eh?"

Marcus Aurelius talked like a Sung philosopher. He meditated and discovered reason as the measure of all conduct. Translated and put among the Sung philosophers, he could easily have passed for one of them.

奥佛斯屈里特教授的思想却特别敏锐，因此促使我探测道德原则的基石上的每一裂缝。我们上伦理学课，总有一场热烈的讨论。我平常不敢参加这些讨论，一方面由于我英语会话能力不够，另一方面是由于自卑感而来的怕羞心理。因为一九〇九年前后是中国现代史上最黑暗的时期，而且我们对中国的前途也很少自信。虽然不参加讨论，听得却很用心，很像一只聪明伶俐的小狗竖起耳朵听它主人说话，意思是懂了，嘴巴却不能讲。

我们必须读的参考书包括柏拉图、亚里士多德、约翰福音和奥里留士等。念了柏拉图和亚里士多德之后，使我对希腊人穷根究底的头脑留有深刻的印象。我觉得四书富于道德的色彩，希腊哲学家却洋溢着敏锐的智慧。这印象使我后来研究希腊史，并且做了一次古代希腊思想和中国古代思想的比较研究。研究希腊哲学家的结果，同时使我了解希腊思想在现代欧洲文明中所占的重要地位，以及希腊文被认为自由教育不可缺少的一部分的原因。

读了约翰福音之后，我开始了解耶稣所宣扬的爱的意义。如果撇开基督教的教条和教会不谈，这种"爱敌如己"的哲学，实在是最高的理想。如果一个人真能爱敌如己，那末世界上也就不会再有敌人了。

"你们能够做到爱你们的敌人吗？"教授向全班发问，没有人回答。

"我不能够，"那只一直尖起耳朵谛听的狗吠了。

"不能够？"教授微笑着反问。

我引述了孔子所说的"以直报怨，以德报德"作答。教授听了以后插嘴说："这也很有道理啊，是不是？"同学们没有人回答。下课后一位年轻的美国男同学过来拍拍我的肩膀说："爱敌如己！吹牛，是不是？"

奥里留士的言论很像宋朝哲学家。他沉思默想的结果，发现理智是一切行为的准则。如果把他的著述译为中文，并把他与宋儒相提并论，很可能使人真伪莫辨。

Things European or American I always measured with a Chinese yardstick. This is the way that leads from the known to the unknown. To gain new experience based upon and constructed out of past experiences is the way to new knowledge. For example, a child who has not seen an airplane can be made to understand it by reference to the flying bird and a "boat with wings." A child who has not seen a bird or a boat cannot easily be made to understand an airplane. A Chinese student learns to understand Western civilization only in the light of what he knows of his own. The more he knows of his own culture, the better able he will be to understand that of the West. Thus arguing in my mind, I felt that my midnight lucubrations on the Chinese classics, history, and philosophy in school in China were not labor lost. Only because of those studies was I now in a position to absorb and digest Western ideas. My work hereafter, I thought, is to find out what China lacks and take what she needs from the West. And in the course of time we will catch up with the West. With these views I grew more self-confident, less self-conscious, and more hopeful for the future.

My interests among the fields of knowledge were indeed rather broad. I took ancient history, English history, the history of philosophy, political science, and even Russian literature in English translation. Tolstoy absorbed me, especially his *Anna Karenina* and *War and Peace*. I attended many public lectures given by prominent scholars and statesmen and thus heard Santayana, Tagore, David Starr Jordan, Woodrow Wilson—then president of Princeton—and many other scholars. Science, literature, the arts, politics, and philosophy all interested me equally. I heard Taft and Roosevelt. "I took the Panama Canal and let Congress debate about it," said the latter in one of his lectures in the Greek theatre. His emphasis and characteristic gestures still stand out clearly in my memory.

Traditional education in China seemed narrow, but within its walls one found a diversity of subjects almost encyclopedic. This apparently narrow education, it is not paradoxical to say, furnished the basis for a broad view of knowledge. My diversity of interests probably derived from my past training in that traditional body of thought. The ancient classics contain many branches of knowledge: history, philosophy, literature, political economy, government, war, diplomacy, and the like. They have

对于欧美的东西，我总喜欢用中国的尺度来衡量。这就是从已知到未知的办法。根据过去的经验，利用过去的经验获得新经验也就是获得新知识的正途。譬如说，如果一个小孩从来没有见过飞机，我们可以解释给他听，飞机像一只飞鸟，也像一只长着翅膀的船，他就会了解飞机是怎么回事。如果一个小孩根本没有见过鸟或船，使他了解飞机可就不容易了。一个中国学生如果要了解西方文明，也只能根据他对本国文化的了解。他对本国文化的了解愈深，对西方文化的了解愈易，根据这种推理，我觉得自己在国内求学时，常常为读经史子集而深夜不眠，这种苦功总算没有白费，我现在之所以能够吸收、消化西洋思想，完全是这些苦功的结果。我想，我今后的工作就是找出中国究竟缺少些什么，然后向西方吸收所需要的东西。心里有了这些观念以后，我渐渐增加了自信，减少了羞怯，同时前途也显得更为光明。

我对学问的兴趣很广泛，选读的功课包括上古史、英国史、哲学史、政治学，甚至译为英文的俄国文学。托尔斯泰的作品更是爱不释手，尤其是《安娜·卡列尼娜》和《战争与和平》。我参加过许多著名学者和政治家的公开演讲会，听过桑太耶那、泰戈尔、大卫、斯坦、约登、威尔逊（当时是普林斯顿校长）以及其他学者的演讲。对科学、文学、艺术、政治和哲学我全有兴趣。也听过塔虎脱和罗斯福的演说。罗斯福在加大希腊剧场演说时，曾经说过："我攫取了巴拿马运河，国会要辩论，让它辩论就是了。"他演说时的强调语气和典型姿势，至今犹历历可忆。

中国的传统教育似乎很褊狭，但是在这种教育的范围之内也包罗万象。有如百科全书，这种表面褊狭的教育，事实上恰是广泛知识的基础。我对知识的兴趣很广泛，可能就是传统思想训练的结果。中国古书包括各方面的知识，例如历史、哲学、文学、政治经济、政府制度、军事、外交等等。事实上绝不褊狭。古书之外，

never been narrow. After the classics, scholars were initiated into even such practical arts as agriculture, irrigation, astronomy, and mathematics. Thus the traditional Chinese scholar was no narrow specialist but had a broad foundation for learning. Moreover, an open-minded search for truth was the aim of Confucian scholars. Their deficiencies seemed to lie in the fact that their knowledge was rather limited to books. Book knowledge can be narrow in another sense.

In school I remember I was given a rhymed book which contained a great variety of subjects, starting with astronomy and geography and going on down to vegetables and insects, including between them such topics as cities, commerce, farming, travel, inventions, philosophy, government, and so on. Rhymes are easier to learn by heart and even at the moment of writing I am still able to recite a great part of that rhymed encyclopedia.

The Berkeley hills with their moss-green oaks and scent-laden eucalyptus, their fields of golden poppies and gardens of crimson roses bathed in smiling California sunshine, served as an ideal nursery for the native sons of the Golden West. I felt ever-grateful to share in the care and protection of my Western Alma Mater, in whose lap her foster son from the ancient Eastern empire was nursed to grow.

In this climate in which there was no very cold winter nor any very hot summer, it was indeed pleasant to live in a sort of perpetual spring for four long, enjoyable years. There was no rain to interrupt outdoor life except for winter showers which turned the grass on the hills green again and washed the roses in the gardens clear as with morning dew. Otherwise no inclement weather interrupted the performances in the Greek theatre, surrounded by its forest of eucalyptus. Shakespearean plays, Greek dramas, Sunday concerts, and public lectures were given in the open air. Not far away were the athletic fields in which intercollegiate games and track meets took place. Young Apollos strove hard for the fame of their alma mater. Beauty, health, and intellect were cultivated at the same time. *Mens sana in corpore sano*—was this ancient Greece re-enacted?

Almost in the center of the campus stood the campanile towering high above the other buildings. At the main entrance leading to College Avenue was Sather Gate with nude carvings standing out in vivid relief

学生们还接受农业、灌溉、天文、数学等实用科学的知识。可见中国的传统学者绝非褊狭的专家，相反地，他具备学问的广泛基础。除此之外，虚心追求真理是儒家学者的一贯目标，不过，他们的知识只限于书本上的学问，这也许是他们欠缺的地方。在某一意义上说，书本知识可能是褊狭的。

幼时曾经读过一本押韵的书，书名《幼学琼林》，里面包括的问题非常广泛，从天文地理到草木虫鱼无所不包，中间还夹杂着城市、商业、耕作、游记、发明、哲学、政治等等题材。押韵的书容易背诵，到现在为止，我仍旧能够背出那本书的大部分。

卜技利的小山上有长满青苔的橡树和芳香扑鼻的尤加利树；田野里到处是黄色的罂粟花；私人花园里红玫瑰在温煦的加州太阳下盛放着。这里正是美国西部黄金世界，本地子弟的理想园地。我万幸得享母校的爱护和培育，使我这个来自东方古国的游子得以发育成长，衷心铭感，无以言宣。

加州气候冬暖夏凉，四季如春，我在这里的四年生活确是轻松愉快。加州少雨，因此户外活动很少受影响。冬天虽然有阵雨，也只是使山上的青草变得更绿，或者使花园中的玫瑰花洗涤得更娇艳。除了冬天阵雨之外，几乎没有任何恶劣的气候影响希腊剧场的演出，剧场四周围绕着密茂的尤加利树。莎翁名剧、希腊悲剧、星期演奏会和公开演讲会都在露天举行。离剧场不远是运动场，校际比赛和田径赛就在那里举行。青年运动员都竭其全力为他们的母校争取荣誉。美育、体育和智育齐头并进。这就是古希腊格言所称"健全的心寓于健全的身"——这就是古希腊格言的实践。

在校园的中心矗立着一座钟楼，睥睨着周围的建筑。通到大学路的大门口有一重大门，叫"赛色门"，门上有许多栩栩如生的浮雕

which invoked protests from parents who had daughters at the university. "Let girls see more of these nude figures of boys and they will be cured of their false decency," remarked my professor of ethics. We had Venus and other goddesses of the ancient Greeks in our reading rooms in the old library (later torn down when the new Doe Library was built), but there was no criticism from the parents of boys. When I saw these Greek figures for the first time I wondered why the authorities should put such "indecent" things at the fountain of wisdom. But later I assumed that they were meant to teach the idea of *mens sana*—sometimes translated as "a beautiful mind in a beautiful body." For with the Greeks beauty, health, and wisdom are one and indivisible.

The performance of *A Midsummer Night's Dream* among the oak groves on campus was really a masterpiece of beauty. Youth, love, beauty, and joy of life are all vividly portrayed in the pleasant masquerade.

Greek-letter fraternity and sorority houses were numerous on the campus. I was told what a wonderful life the members enjoyed together, but I had not visited any until on one occasion I was invited on a bargain—I was to vote for members of that fraternity for class president and other officers. They canvassed the whole class from a list; when they came to a classmate who was likely to vote for their opponents they would say "No good!" and mark the name "NG."

I was received with such cordiality as one would remember a lifetime. The vote was cast next day and I kept faithfully to my promise, for a "Chinaman's" word is as good as gold. I was glad to have made friends with quite a few fellow students during the campaign.

A few days after the election, for some occasion which I don't remember now, a bonfire was made. The glow of the flames lit up the happy faces of the young people. Boys and girls sang, ending each song with college yells. The crackling of the burning logs, the giggles of the girls and the shouts of the boys still echo in my ears. There in the light I came across a fellow student for whom I had cast my vote. To my great surprise his cordiality toward me had already turned to indifference. This is how things go in the world! His kindness to me had been paid for by my vote; the bills being paid, the account was squared—neither owed anything to the other. Thereafter I exchanged no more votes for cordialities and never again voted in college elections.

裸像。这些裸像引起许多女学生的家长抗议。我的伦理学教授说："让女学生们多看一些男人的裸体像，可以纠正她们忸怩作态的习惯。"老图书馆（后来拆除改建为陀氏图书馆）的阅览室里就有维纳斯以及其他希腊女神裸体的塑像。但是男学生的家长从未有过批评。我初次看到这些希腊裸体人像时，心里也有点疑惑，为什么学校当局竟把这些"猥亵"的东西摆在智慧的源泉。后来，我猜想他们大概是要灌输"完美的思想寓于完美的身体"的观念。在希腊人看起来，美丽、健康和智慧是三位一体而不可分割的。

橡树丛中那次《仲夏夜之梦》的演出，真是美的极致。青春、爱情、美丽、欢愉全在这次可喜的演出中活生生地表现出来了。

学校附近有许多以希腊字母做代表的兄弟会和姊妹会。听说兄弟会和姊妹会的会员们欢聚一堂，生活非常愉快。我一直没有机会去作客。后来有人约我到某兄弟会去作客，但是附带一个条件——我必须投票选举这个兄弟会的会员出任班主席和其他职员。事先，他们曾经把全班同学列一名单，碰到可能选举他们的对头人，他们就说这个"要不得！"同时在名字上打上叉。

我到那个兄弟会时，备受殷勤招待，令人没齿难忘。第二天举行投票，为了确保中国人一诺千金的名誉，我自然照单圈选不误，同时我也很高兴能在这次竞选中结交了好几位朋友。

选举之后不久，学校里有一次营火会。究竟庆祝什么却记不清楚了。融融的火光照耀着这班青年的快乐面庞。男男女女齐声高歌。每一支歌结束时，必定有一阵呐喊。木柴的爆裂声，女孩子吃吃的笑声和男孩子的呼喊声，至今犹在耳际萦绕。我忽然在火光烛照下邂逅一位曾经受我一票之赐的同学。使我大出意外的是这位同学竟对我视若路人，过去的那份亲热劲儿不知哪里去了！人情冷暖，大概就是如此吧！他对我的热情，我已经以"神圣的一票"来报答，有债还债，现在这笔账已经结清，谁也不欠谁的。从此以后，我再也不拿选举交换招待，同时在学校选举中从此没有再投票。

In the basement of North Hall was a student "co-op," at the entrance of which was a sign which read, "In God we trust, all others pay cash." The most prosperous business in the co-op was the sale of hot dogs at five cents apiece (cash). They tasted fine.

One memorable character on the campus—probably forgotten by my contemporaries but not by me—was the aged janitor of the philosophy building. He was tall and spare, with a very straight carriage. His eyes were deep-sunk in their sockets and his grey eyebrows grew very long, almost covering his eyes, like a Pekingese toy dog. From under his brows one could see him twinkling with friendliness and warmth of heart. We took a mutual liking to each other. After classes and sometimes on Sundays I was a frequent visitor to the basement where he had lived from the time when the university was a small college.

He had been a soldier and fought many battles under the Union flag in the Civil War. He lived in memories of the past and related to me many stories of the war and of his childhood. From him I learned that conditions in America in older days—it is almost a century now—were not very much better than in China then; in some respects worse. He told me that there had existed in his youth many kinds of money: English pounds, French francs, and Dutch guldens. I heard Lyman Abbott speak of this several years later in New York. Modern sanitation seemed to him nonsense. Once he showed me a roll of toilet paper and said, "Nowadays people die young with these sanitary things. We didn't have any sanitation or what you call modern medicine. Look at me, how healthy I am at my age!" He stood erect like a soldier at attention for me to look at him.

West Point was also a joke to him. "You think they can fight? No! They're puffed up by uniforms and sure know how to dress in a parade. But fighting—no. I can teach 'em. In one battle I killed a whole lot of rebels singlehanded. If they want to learn to fight, let 'em come to me!"

He still harbored a grudge in his heart against the Confederates after these long years. He said he once found a rebel lying wounded after a battle was over and tried to help him. "You know what that crittur did?

在"北楼"的地下室里，有一间同学经营的"合作社"，合作社的门口挂着一块牌子，上面写着："我们相信上帝，其余人等，一律现钱交易。"合作社里最兴隆的生意是五分钱一个的热狗，味道不错。

学校里最难忘的人是哲学馆的一位老工友，我的先生同学们也许已经忘记他，至少我始终忘不了。他个子高而瘦削，行动循规蹈矩。灰色的长眉毛几乎盖到眼睛，很像一只北京叭儿狗，眼睛深陷在眼眶里。从眉毛下面，人们可以发现他的眼睛闪烁着友善而热情的光辉。我和这位老工友一见如故，下课以后，或者星期天有空，我常常到地下室去拜访他，他从加州大学还是一个小规模的学校时开始，就一直住在那地下室里。

他当过兵，曾在内战期间在联邦军队麾下参加许多战役。他生活在回忆中，喜欢讲童年和内战的故事。我从他那里获悉早年美国的情形。这些情形离现在将近百年，许多情形与当时中国差不多，某些方面甚至还更糟。他告诉我，他幼年时美国流通好几种货币：英镑、法郎，还有荷兰盾。现代卫生设备在他看起来一文不值。有一次他指着一卷草纸对我说："现代的人虽然有这些卫生东西，还不是年纪轻轻就死了。我们当时可没有什么卫生设备，也没有你们所谓的现代医药。你看我，我年纪这么大，身体多健康！"他直起腰板，挺起胸脯，像一位立正的士兵，让我欣赏他的精神体魄。

西点军校在他看起来也是笑话，"你以为他们能打仗呀？那才笑话！他们全靠几套制服撑场面，游行时他们穿得倒真整齐。但是说到打仗——差远了！我可以教教他们。有一次作战时，我单枪匹马就把一队叛军杀得精光，如果他们想学习如何打仗，还是让他们来找我吧！"

虽然内战已经结束那末多年，他对参加南部同盟的人却始终恨之入骨。他说，有一次战役结束之后，他发现一位敌人受伤躺在地上，他正预备去救助。"你晓得这家伙怎么着？他一枪就向我

He fired right at me." He leveled his angry eyes at me steadily as if I had been the culprit. "What did you do?" I ventured. "I shot the beast dead right on the spot," was the reply.

To me this old soldier-janitor was an inseparable part of the university. He thought himself so, too, for he had seen the place grow.

射过来！"他瞪着两只眼睛狠狠地望着我，好像我就是那个不知好歹的家伙似的。我说："那你怎么办？""我一枪就把这畜生当场解决了。"他回答说。

这位军人出身的老工友，对我而论，是加州大学不可分的一部分，他自己也如此看法，因为他曾经亲见加大的发育成长。

CHAPTER 10   CHINA IN AMERICA

Before the end of October of my first year in America an important change had taken place in China. This was the death, in rapid succession, of the Emperor Kwang-hsü and the Empress Dowager. There were two versions to the story; one was that she died first, whereupon he was murdered by her followers in the fear that he would come back into power. The other was that, near death, she sent a eunuch to Yun Tai—the island palace in the Imperial Chung Hai Park where this strong-willed woman had kept her Imperial consort imprisoned ever since the short-lived reforms of 1898—who informed the Emperor, always in poor health, that Her Majesty the Illustrious Buddha, as she was called, wished him as a favor to take the medicine she sent. According to this version the poor imprisoned Emperor understood the message and obeyed, succumbing to the poison in a short time. The fact was made known to her before she died and she ordered the issue of an Imperial Edict by which the death of the Emperor was announced and his nephew, little Pu-yi, made successor to the throne.

Whatever the truth of it, the unanimous opinion of the Chinese students in Berkeley was that with the death of the "old woman," as the Empress Dowager was disrespectfully called, there would be plenty of trouble in China. It proved to be so. For with a baby Emperor on the throne and his inexperienced father, Tsai Hsun[1], as Prince Regent, the authority of the Manchu Dynasty fell into meteoric decline until its last vestige was swept away three years later by the Revolution of 1911.

In 1909 I had joined as an editorial writer the *Chinese Free Press*, Dr. Sun Yat-sen's revolutionary organ in San Francisco. One evening in the fall of that year, with my co-editor Liu Chun-yu, I called for the first time on Dr. Sun Yat-sen at a hotel on Stockton Street on the outskirts of Chinatown. My heart throbbed with excitement as we entered. Dr. Sun received us cordially in his room. It was a small room with a couch, several chairs, and a small desk. There was a wash basin by the window. The curtains were drawn.

Mr. Liu introduced me to the esteemed leader of China's revolutionary movement. His magnetic personality was such as to win the confidence of any who had a chance to meet him. Dr. Sun's ample and majestic forehead and strong dark brows gave signs of a forceful intellect

拾 美国华埠

我到美国第一年的十月底以前，中国发生了重大的变故，光绪皇帝和慈禧太后相继去世。关于这件事，在美国的中国学生队里有两种不同的传说：一说慈禧太后先去世，她的亲信怕光绪皇帝重掌政权，于是谋杀光绪皇帝以绝后患。另一说法是慈禧太后临死前派了一名太监到囚禁光绪的瀛台，告诉病弱的光绪帝说："老佛爷"希望他服用她送去的药，光绪帝自然了解太后的用意，就把药吞服了，不久毒发身亡。慈禧太后驾崩以前，已经接到光绪帝服毒死亡的报告，于是发下圣旨，宣布光绪之死，并由光绪的小侄子溥仪继承皇位。

不论这些说法的真确性如何，在卜技利的中国学生一致认为"老太婆"（这是大家私底下给慈禧太后的诨号）一死，中国必定有一场大乱。后来事实证明确是如此。溥仪登基以后，他的父亲载沣出任摄政王。皇帝是个小孩子，摄政王对政务也毫无经验，因此清廷的威信一落千丈，三年以后，辛亥革命成功，清室终于被推翻。

我早在一九〇九年参加《大同日报》担任主笔。这报是孙中山先生在旧金山的革命机关报。那一年的一个秋天晚上，我与《大同日报》的另一个编辑，以后在国内大名鼎鼎的刘麻哥成禹，初次晋谒孙先生。他住在唐人街附近的史多克顿街的一家旅馆里。我进门的时候，因为心情紧张，一颗心怦怦直跳。孙先生在他的房间里很客气地接见我们。房间很小，一张床，几张椅子，还有一张小书桌。靠窗的地方有个小小的洗脸盆，窗帘是拉上的。

刘麻哥把我介绍给这位中国革命运动的领袖。孙先生似乎有一种不可抗拒的引力，任何人如果有机会和他谈话，马上会完全信赖他。他的天庭饱满，眉毛浓黑，一望而知是位智慧极高、意念坚强的

and indomitable will. His clear, inviting eyes revealed his candor of thought and warmth of heart, while his compressed lips and set jaw made people readily understand that he was a man of courage and decision. His general build was muscular and sturdy, giving the impression of strong nerves and steady emotions. In conversation his line of argument was clear and convincing, whether you agreed with him or not; unless you wished to discontinue he would keep on untiringly expounding his theories to you. He spoke slowly but distinctly and one felt behind his words a deep sincerity. He also listened easily yet was not slow to catch essential points.

Later I found him to be an ardent reader of a variety of books, both Chinese and English. He saved all the money he could to buy books. He was a slow reader but had an extraordinary retentive power. Dr. Sun's wide reading gave him a clear understanding of the development of both Chinese and Western civilizations.

He enjoyed jokes—though he seldom jested—laughing heartily when a good one was recounted to him.

He liked fish and vegetables for his meals, but seldom touched meat and preferred Chinese to Western cooking. "Chinese food is the best in the world," he would say.

Dr. Sun was a real democrat. He lectured in the streets of Chinatown in San Francisco. With banners of the Nationalist party streaming in the air, he would stand on the sidewalk and talk to the crowd gathering around him. He understood the psychology of the man in the street and could reduce his own language to the simplest terms. "What is revolution?" he would ask rhetorically. "Down with the rule of the Manchus!" The crowd understood and joined in in chorus. Then he would go on explaining in very simple language why the Manchus must be done away with and what he would do when a republican form of government was established in China—how many benefits the people would reap from a new regime.

He would often size up an audience to which he was about to speak, choose an appropriate subject, and improvise a suitable discourse, expressing himself with great eloquence. He usually carried the audience with him to the very end. He was always ready to speak for he possessed a remarkable ability to carry it with him.

人物。他的澄澈而和善的眼睛显示了他的坦率和热情。他的紧闭的嘴唇和坚定的下巴，则显示出他是个勇敢果断的人。他的肌肉坚实，身体强壮，予人镇定沉着的印象。谈话时他的论据清楚而有力，即使你不同意他的看法，也会觉得他的观点无可批驳。除非你有意打断话头，他总是娓娓不倦地向你发挥他的理论。他说话很慢，但是句句清楚，使人觉得他的话无不出于至诚。他也能很安详地听别人讲话，但是很快就抓住人家的谈话要点。

后来我发现他对各种书都有浓厚的兴趣，不论是中文书，或者英文书。他把可能节省下来的钱全部用来买书。他读书不快，但是记忆力却非常惊人。孙先生博览群书，所以对中西文化的发展有清晰的了解。

他喜欢听笑话，虽然他自己很少说，每次听到有趣的笑话时总是大笑不止。

他喜欢鱼类和蔬菜，很少吃肉类食物。喜欢中菜，不大喜欢西菜。他常说："中国菜是全世界最好的菜。"

孙先生是位真正的民主主义者，他曾在旧金山唐人街的街头演说。头顶飘扬着国民党的党旗，他就站在人行道上向围集他四周的人演说。孙先生非常了解一般人的心理，总是尽量选用通俗平易的词句来表达他的思想。他会故意地问："什么叫革命？""革命就是打倒满洲佬。"听众很容易明白他的意思，因此就跟着喊打倒满洲佬。接着他就用极浅近的话解释，为什么必须打倒满洲佬，推翻满清建立共和以后他的计划怎么样，老百姓在新政府下可以享受什么好处等等。

在开始讲话以前，他总先估量一下他的听众，然后选择适当的题目，临时决定适当的讲话的方式，然后再滔滔不绝地发表他的意见。他能自始至终把握听众的注意力。他也随时愿意发表演说，因为他有惊人的演说天才。

Dr. Sun's deep understanding of human nature, his intense love of his country and people, and his insight into what China needed in building up her new nationhood gave him unquestioned leadership in the development of young China. Between travels in the southern and eastern states and in Europe he came back every so often to San Francisco, where Liu Chun-yu and I had the pleasure of seeing him whenever he came.

On October 8, 1911, at about eight o'clock in the evening, Dr. Sun came into the editorial room of the *Chinese Free Press* wearing a dark overcoat and a derby hat. He appeared happy, though not in the least excited, as he said calmly that from news he had received through certain sources things seemed to be turning out well—the group of people who had laid plans for revolution in Hankow and Wuchang were ready for action. Two days later news reached San Francisco that revolution had broken out in Wuchang. This was the revolution of October 10, 1911, which eventually overthrew the Manchu Dynasty. On that day the Republic of China was born.

Urgent cablegrams advised Dr. Sun to come back to lead the revolution. He left San Francisco and returned to China by way of Europe. On January 1, 1912, he was inaugurated at Nanking as Provisional President of the Republic, and China entered on a new life.

Under Dr. Sun's guidance, for three consecutive years Liu Chun-yu and I wrote editorials for the *Chinese Free Press*, each of us at first writing one every other day. We supplied these articles to the paper while studying at the university, often burning midnight oil to finish a piece for the next morning's issue. The university work was by no means light and we felt—especially myself—the burden of this extra labor. After the successful revolution Liu went back to China and I had to bear the brunt of the daily editorial war. Though I felt deeply for the future of my country, the constant practice of writing against my will ultimately killed in me all interest in writing. In the unremitting pressure and rush under which I labored, the quality of production deteriorated and I formed the habit of loose and hurried thinking and careless choice of words. Sometimes my thought flowed reluctantly as water through a clogged pipe, but the words still rushed from my pen like a swarm of aimless wanderers. I was rather exasperated at these unwelcome guests. I would, however, let them go since they filled up the columns.

孙中山先生对人性有深切的了解，对于祖国和人民有热烈的爱，对于建立新中国所需要的东西有深邃的见解。这一切的一切，使他在新中国的发展过程中成为无可置辩的领袖。他常常到南部各州、东部各州去旅行，有时又到欧洲，但是经常要回到旧金山来，每次回到旧金山，我和刘麻哥就去看他。

一九一一年十月八日，大概晚上八点钟左右，孙先生穿着一件深色的大衣和一顶常礼帽，到了《大同日报》的编辑部。他似乎很快乐，但是很镇静。他平静地告诉我们，据他从某一方面得到的消息，一切似乎很顺利，计划在武汉起义的一群人已经完成布署，随时可以采取行动。两天以后，消息传至旧金山，武昌已经爆发革命了。这就是辛亥年十月十日的武汉革命，接着满清政府被推翻，这一天也成为中华民国的国庆日。

在孙先生的指导之下，我和刘麻哥为《大同日报》连续写了三年的社论。开始时我们两人轮流隔日撰写。我们一方面在加大读书，一方面为报纸写社论，常常开夜车到深夜，赶写第二天早上见报的文章。大学的功课绝不轻松，我们，尤其是我，深感这种额外工作负担之重。成功以后，刘麻哥回国了，我只好独立承当每日社论的重任。我虽然深深关切祖国的前途，但是这种身不由己的经常写作，终于扼杀了我一切写作的兴趣。我一直在无休无止的压力下工作，而且仓促成文，作品的素质日见低落，而且养成散漫而匆促的思想习惯，用字也无暇推敲。有时思想阻滞，如同阻塞的水管里的水滴，但是笔头的字还是像一群漫无目的的流浪者涌到纸上。我对于这些不速之客实在生气，但是我还是由他们去了，因为他们至少可以填满空白。

When I first took the job I found a real pleasure in writing, fitting words to thoughts like coins into a slot machine. Only when I tried to jam all the coins into the slots at once, the machine got clogged and refused to take in the superfluous ones, which spilled all around the floor, so to speak. This is how meaningless words fill space when you are forced to write in a rush.

After my graduation in 1912 I gave up the job and felt a great release. Thereafter I feared writing as a schoolboy would Latin composition. When labor is drudgery and done in a hurry as well, no good work will come of it. The bad habits thus formed were difficult to eradicate for years after.

On the Pacific coast during my college days about fifty thousand Chinese immigrants clustered around the centers in the various cities—Sacramento, San Francisco, Oakland, San José, Los Angeles, and others—with isolated small groups or individuals dotting the smaller towns and villages. These centers were called Chinatowns. Chinatown in San Francisco was the largest of all, with a Chinese population of more than twenty thousand. The main street was originally Dupont Street, but its name was afterward changed to Grant Avenue, for what reason I do not know. Grant Avenue was a very prosperous street. Oriental bazaars, Chinese restaurants known as "chop suey houses," fortunetelling stands, gambling houses in the guise of social or literary clubs, and temples for worship of Chinese gods—called "joss houses"—attracted the attention of tourists, sight-seers, and pleasure-seekers. Once a pretty young American told me that she had seen a wonderful thing in an Oriental bazaar—a Buddha sitting in an artichoke; and had eaten bird's nest soup, sharks' fins, and chop suey in a Chinese restaurant. She was much excited over it. Her younger sisters listened with wondering eyes and gaping mouths. "I declare!" said the grandmother, looking over her spectacles while her hands were busy with her knitting.

"How do you eat soup with chopsticks?" a younger sister asked curiously.

"As you do with your soda straws, my young lady," said I. All joined in the laughter.

　　最初担任这份工作时，对于写作的确非常有兴趣，字斟句酌，务求至当。这情形很像选择适当的钱币，使它能投进自动售货机的放钱口。如果你匆匆忙忙希望把一大把钱币同时挤进放钱口，机器自然就阻塞了，多余的钱怎么也放不进去，结果就散落一地。一个人不得不在匆忙中写文章，情形就是这样，结果是毫无意义的一大堆文字浪费了篇幅。

　　一九一二年毕业后，我终于放弃了这份工作，心里感到很轻松。从此以后我一直怕写文章，很像美国小学生怕用拉丁文作文一样。工作如果成为苦差，并且必须在匆忙中完成，这种工作绝无好成绩。这样养成的坏习惯后来很难矫正。

　　在我四年的大学时期里，约有五万华侨集中在西海岸的各城市，包括萨克拉孟多、旧金山、屋岺、圣多谢、洛杉矶等，另外还有零星的小群华侨和个人散布在较小的城镇和乡村。华侨集中的区域就叫唐人街或中国城，也称华埠。旧金山的华埠是美洲各城中最大的一个，共有华侨两万余人。主要的街道原来叫杜邦街，后来改称葛兰德路，究竟为什么改，我不知道。葛兰德路很繁华。东方古董铺、普通称为"杂碎馆"的中国饭馆、算命测字的摊子、假借俱乐部名义的赌场、供奉中国神佛的庙宇等等，吸引了无数的游客和寻欢作乐的人。有一个年轻美丽的美国人告诉我，她曾在一家东方古董铺中看到一件非常稀奇的东西——一尊坐在一朵莲花座上的大佛；她还在一家中国饭馆吃过鸟巢（燕窝）、鱼翅和杂碎。她对这一切感到新奇万分，说得手舞足蹈。她的妹妹们都睁着眼睛、张着嘴巴听她。"真的啊！"她的老祖母从眼镜上面望着她，两只手则仍旧不停地织着毛线。

　　"你用筷子怎么喝汤呢？"一位小妹妹满腹狐疑地问。

　　"正像你用麦管吸汽水一样吸汤呀！小妹妹。"我代为回答，引得大家大笑。

In small towns my countrymen kept laundry establishments. Day in and day out they washed and washed from dawn till dusk and often late into the night. The reason many American families liked to send their laundry to the Chinese was because hand wash did not wear out the materials as easily as machines. These hard-working sons of the Celestial Empire saved every bit of their earnings by living a frugal life; they slung silver or gold pieces into the savings bags hidden under their beds and made liberal contributions to the cause of Dr. Sun's revolutionary movement or sent money home to support their families and relatives in Canton, thus helping to enrich the villages of their province.

Kwangtung was the richest province of China, not only because the people did prosperous business in Hongkong and elsewhere but because it was the reservoir into which gold trickled from all parts of the world where there were Chinese colonies—Malaya, the Dutch East Indies[2], the Philippine Islands, North and South America, etc. It was from this province that most of the émigrés from China originally came.

The Chinese working and living in foreign lands, numbering in the millions, were not there to exploit. Rather, their labor has been exploited. They had no capital other than the flesh and blood they were given in their mothers' wombs. With hard work, frugality, and endurance, they labored like bees carrying their tiny specks of Sweetness from distant flowers to build up honeycombs in China. There was no political power to back them up, and they carried no guns. They helped to build railroads, open mines, raise rubber; in return for their labor they received a few dollars or shillings or rupees or guldens for a day's hard work. Some, to be sure, especially in Singapore and the Dutch East Indies, became rich and owned palatial mansions and villas, living like maharajahs. A number rose to the level of the middle class and owned property. But the rich and well to do were in the minority; the rank and file had to work hard, and only by hard work managed to make a living and put by some savings.

Among the Chinese in America there were neither very rich nor very poor. Most of them were honest, hard-working people. Almost all had some savings to contribute to that great reservoir, the province of Kwangtung. Their mode of life was mainly Chinese. Taking a boat along the Sacramento River, one would see Chinese towns or villages perched on the banks with bold Chinese signboards in front of the shops. One felt as if he were sailing on the Yangtze River or the Grand Canal in China.

也有许多华侨开洗衣店。他们一天到晚忙着浆洗衣服，常常忙到深夜。许多美国家庭喜欢把衣服送到中国洗衣店洗，因为手洗不像机器那样容易损坏衣服。这些来自"天朝"的子孙，节衣缩食省下有限的一点钱，把省下的钱装在袋里藏在床下。但是他们却慷慨地捐钱给孙中山先生的革命运动，或者把钱寄回广东，扶养他们的家人或亲戚，同时使他们的故乡变为富足。

广东是中国最富的省份，一方面是广东人在香港以及其他地方经商发财的关系，另一方面也是因为各地华侨把积蓄汇回广东的缘故。华侨遍布于马来西亚、印度尼西亚、菲律宾及南美、北美各地。各地的华侨多半是从广东或福建来的。

上千万的华侨生活在外国，他们在外国辛勤工作从不剥削别人，相反地，他们的劳力却常常受到剥削。他们除父母所赐的血肉之躯外，别无资本。他们像一群蜜蜂，辛勤工作，节衣缩食，忍气吞声，把花蜜从遥远的花朵运送到中国的蜂房。他们得不到任何政治力量的支持，他们也没有携带枪炮到外国来。他们帮着居留地的人民筑路、开矿、种植树木，以一天辛劳的工作换回几个美金或先令。不错，有些人，尤其是在新加坡和印度尼西亚，的确发了财，住着皇宫样的大厦和别墅，生活得像印度的土大王，另一些人也跻入中产阶级，买田置产，但是富有的和小康的究竟还是少数。大多数的华侨必须辛勤工作，而且只有辛勤工作才能糊口或稍有积蓄。

在美国的华侨，没有很富的，也没有很穷的。多数都是老实可靠、辛勤工作的人。几乎所有的人都寄一点钱回广东。他们的生活方式主要是中国式的。你如果乘一只船沿萨克拉孟多江航行，你可以看到两岸散布着一些华侨城镇和村落，店铺门前挂着大字书写的中文招牌如"长途粮食"、"道地药材"等类。你可能以为自己是在沿着长江或运河航行呢。

I landed once at one of these Sacramento River Chinatowns and stayed with the owner of an asparagus plantation, Tin San, a friend of Dr. Sun Yat-sen. He treated me to tender asparagus, fat and juicy. Thereafter, whenever I had asparagus for dinner I thought of him. He had a cannery for this delicious vegetable, under American brand names. So I often think that some of the American canned asparagus may have been raised and canned by the Chinese. His way of making money was really good and ingenious. He kept places of amusement for his men, arguing that they must have some diversion after the day's work and if he had not established these houses they would go to other places run by his neighbors. He wanted the water to flow into his own gardens, so to speak, to feed his own plants. His plants—or rather dollars—did indeed grow from the voluntary contributions of his men to these amusement places.

The Chinese immigrants in America as well as elsewhere were truly loyal sons and daughters of that Flowery Kingdom. The men wore queues and some of the women even practised foot-binding. In the streets of Chinatown in San Francisco one could find fortunetellers. One such man who was telling a white man's fortune said to him, "Good luck. By and by, plenty of money." A Negro standing by wanted to have his fortune told and was very much pleased to hear the same words repeated to him. Everything would have been all right if the prophet had stopped there. But he went on to say, "By and by, no more black. Like him—" pointing with his index finger at the white man. The Negro instead of being pleased got mad and kicked over the fortuneteller's stand. This was a case where compliments, overdone, become insults.

There were grocery stores selling salt fish, eels, edible snakes, bean sauce, sharks' fins, birds' nests, dried abalones, and other Cantonese stuff brought to America from Canton or Hongkong. Once I went to one of the groceries and tried to buy something. Failing to make the man understand my poor Cantonese dialect, I wrote on paper what I wanted. An old woman standing by saw my writing and being ignorant of the fact that China has only one written language for the whole country, despite her many dialects was surprised and asked, if this Chinese cannot speak Chinese (meaning Cantonese), how can he write it? A group of curious people gathered around me. One who could speak enough mandarin to make me understand asked, "Have you ever been in the provincial capital of Canton?" "No," I replied. "Then where did you do your shopping?"

有一天，我曾经在萨克拉孟多江沿岸的一处中国城上岸，访一位芦笋园的主人。这位主人叫丁山，是孙中山先生的朋友，他拿鲜嫩的芦笋招待我，非常肥美多汁，后来一吃到芦笋，我总要想起他。他还有一间制造芦笋的罐头厂，所制的罐头借用美国商标出售。因此我常常想，美国的某些芦笋罐头，可能就是华侨种植和装罐的。他赚钱的办法的确好，而且很巧妙。他为工人开设了许多娱乐场所，他说，工人们辛苦了一天，必须有散散心的地方；如果他不开办娱乐场所，工人们就会找到他的邻居所开的娱乐场所去。他的用意是"肥水不流外人田"。结果到他娱乐场所来玩的人，都贡献了一点"肥水"，他的财产也就愈来愈多了。

在美国以及世界各地的华侨，真不愧为炎黄裔胄。男子留着辫子，女人甚至还缠足。在旧金山的华侨街头，可以发现卖卦算命的摊子。有一位算命先生告诉一位来算命的白人说："好运道，快快的，大发财。"旁边一位黑人也想算算命，算命先生把同样的话重复一遍，黑人大为得意。如果这位算命先生说到此地为止，自然太平无事，但是他偏偏要画蛇添足，对黑人说："快快地，不再黑，像他——"同时用手指着那位白人。黑人气得一脚踢翻算命摊子，阿谀过分成为侮辱，此即一例。

华侨还有许多杂货店，出售咸鱼、鳗鲞、蛇肉、酱油、鱼翅、燕窝、干鲍以及其他从广州或香港运到美国的货色。有一次，我到一家杂货铺想买一些东西。但是我的广东话太蹩脚，没法使店员明白我要买的东西。只好拿一张纸把它写下来，旁边站着一位老太婆只晓得中国有许多不同的方言，却不晓得中国只有一种共同的文字，看了我写的文字大为惊奇，她问店里的人：这位唐人既然不能讲唐话（她指广东话），为什么他能写唐字呢？许多好奇的人围住我看，有一位稍稍懂点普通话的人问道："你到广州省城去过没有？"我回答说："没有。""那末你过去在那里买东西呢？"

"Shanghai," I laughed, and went away with a bottle of bean sauce and a package under my arm.

Schools in Chinatown still stuck to the old curriculum. Pupils were taught to read aloud the old books just as I had been taught in China. The American schools not far away had no influence on them.

These were the times before the revolution. After that date Chinatown began to change, for China herself was changing—changing rapidly. In the course of a few years the fortunetellers disappeared. The number of queues fast decreased until they were gone. The young girls stopped their foot-binding. The schools were reformed and adopted a modern curriculum; more children were sent to near-by American schools. Chinatown resisted the influence of its American neighbors but followed in the footsteps of the mother country in reforms and mode of living. These loyal sons and daughters of China!

"上海。"我笑着夹起一瓶酱油和一包货物走了。

唐人街的学校仍旧保持旧式的课程。学生们要高声朗诵古书；和我小时候的情形一模一样。离唐人街不远的美国学校对它们毫无影响。

这是辛亥革命以前的情形。革命以后，唐人街开始起了变化，因为中国本身也在变化，而且是急剧的变化，短短几年之内，算命卖卦的不见了。辫子的数目也迅速减少，终至完全绝迹。青年女子停止缠足，学校制度改革了，采用了新式的课程；送到附近美国学校上学的孩子逐渐增加。唐人街虽然想抗拒美国邻居的影响，但是祖国有了改革，而且在生活方式上有了改变以后，这些忠贞的炎黄裔胄也终于亦步亦趋了。

CHAPTER 11   NEW YORK

As the years went on my mental horizon extended and I became more and more self-confident. In 1912 I was graduated with honors in education and went to Columbia University in New York City for my postgraduate work.

Here I learned the method and acquired the spirit of scientific research as applied to social phenomena. Among the professors who taught me untiringly, from whom I drew my inspiration and to whom I am greatly indebted, there is one I wish to mention particularly because of his connection with Peking University. He is Professor John Dewey, who taught Dr. Hu Shih and myself at Columbia, and later through his writings, lectures, and personal contacts with contemporary thinkers in China, during his two-year sojourn as visiting professor at the National University of Peking, influenced Chinese educational theories and practice to a great extent. His pragmatism finds its counterpart in the practical Chinese mentality. But he warned us that "if a thing is too practical it becomes impractical."

Of the years at Columbia I shall not speak in detail. They were most enriching. I was now acclimated to America and to the language and could absorb what came within my orbit with less overwhelming effort of adaptation.

In New York I was impressed by the skyscrapers, the rapid circulation of subways and elevated trains, the dazzling lights of moving advertisements on the tops of tall buildings; the theatres, night clubs, hotels, and restaurants; fashionable Fifth Avenue, Greenwich Village, the East Side slums, and so on.

On the social side one found Yankees, Irish, Poles, Italians, Greeks, Jews, all living side by side in a neighborly way, and a few thousand of my own countrymen clustered around Chinatown. In my time there were in the great metropolis five hundred Chinese restaurants catering to the public. The agglomerated cosmopolitan mass of the city population, with its politicians, gangsters, scholars, artists, financiers, industrialists, multimillionaires, slum-dwellers, and many others, was fundamentally an American product. There is nothing further from the truth than to say, "When you get into New York, you get out of America." America alone

拾壹 纽约生活

时间一年一年地过去，我的知识学问随之增长，同时自信心也加强了。民国元年，即一九一二年，我以教育为主科，历史与哲学为两附科，毕业于加大教育学系，并承学校赠给名誉奖，旋赴纽约入哥伦比亚大学研究院续学。

我在哥大学到如何以科学方法应用于社会现象，而且体会到科学研究的精神。我在哥大遇到许多诲人不倦的教授，我从他们得到许多启示，他们的教导更使我终生铭感。我想在这里特别提一笔其中一位后来与北京大学发生密切关系的教授。他就是约翰·杜威博士。他是胡适博士和我在哥伦比亚大学时的业师，后来又曾在北京大学担任过两年的客座教授。他的著作、演讲以及在华期间与我国思想界的交往，曾经对我国的教育理论与实践发生重大的影响。他的实验哲学与中国人讲求实际的心理不谋而合。但是他警告我们说："一件事若过于注重实用，就反为不切实用。"

我不预备详谈在哥大的那几年生活，总之，在那几年里获益很大。我对美国生活和美国语言已感习惯，而且可以随时随地从所接触的事物汲取知识而无事倍功半之苦。

纽约给我印象较深的事物是它的摩天大楼、川流不息的地道车和高架电车、高楼屋顶上的炫目的霓虹灯广告；剧场、影院、夜总会、旅馆、饭店；出售高贵商品的第五街、生活浪漫不拘的格林威治村、东区的贫民窟等等。

在社会生活方面，新英格兰人、爱尔兰人、波兰人、意大利人、希腊人、犹太人等各族杂处，和睦如邻，此外还有几千名华侨聚居在唐人街附近。当时在这个大都会里的中国菜馆就有五百家之多。纽约市密集的人口中龙蛇混杂，包括政客、流氓、学者、艺术家、工业家、金融巨子、百万富翁、贫民窟的贫民以及各色人等，但是基本上这些人都是美国的产物。有人说："你一走进纽约，就等于

is capable of producing such a great, highly industrialized city and vast melting pot. There was little racial friction. For in New York anyone can do anything he likes if he knows how to stay inside the law. Everyone is permitted to go his own way if he observes a certain degree of public decency. Anyone can expound his theories of society and government if he can find an audience.

Liberty within the orbit of the law and freedom of thought and speech within the domain of reason had free play. Great industries, international banking and big business, and the utilization of invention, engineering, and material resources to the fullest extent, all showed the spirit and application of Americanism. In New York one found it in concentrated form. In the midst of this concentration the eye of the observer is easily dazzled by the glaring lights, thus losing sight of Americanism in its normal state as one would see it elsewhere in America.

During the summer vacations I would go to the Adirondacks. One summer, with a few Chinese friends, I went to Rainbow Lake and camped on one of its hilly islets. In the daytime we went boating and fishing on near-by lakes. Our catches were quite rich—pike weighing over ten pounds were among our prizes for a day's work and pleasure. Big fat frogs were found a-plenty around the island on which we camped. I had learned to catch frogs in my village childhood in China and carried the art over to America. A rod, a string, and a hook rounded out of a good-sized needle with a piece of red cloth attached to it were sufficient for frog fishing; the improvised outfit worked wonders. Usually we could catch two dozen of them in an hour. This was more than enough for two delicious meals a day. The people living around the lake had never eaten frogs—they admired our art of frog fishing but at the bottom of their hearts must have thought, "The heathen Chinee is peculiar."

In the evenings we often joined their barn dances to the tune of the fiddle played by the host. One of the songs they all sang, a part of which still lurks in my recollection, runs something like this:

All the hinges are rusty

And the doors are falling down,

The roof lets in sunshine and rain—

离开了美国。"事实上大谬不然。只有美国这样的国家才能产生这样高度工业化的大都市，也只有美国才能出现这种兼容并蓄的大熔炉。种族摩擦的事可说绝无仅有。一个人只要不太逾越法律的范围，就可以在纽约为所欲为。只要他不太违背习俗，谁也不会干涉他的私人行动。只要能够找到听众，谁都可以评论古今，臧否时政。

法律范围之内的自由，理智领域之内的思想自由和言论自由在纽约发挥得淋漓尽致，大规模的工商业，国际性的银行业务，发明、机械和资源的极度利用，处处显示美国主义的精神和实例。在纽约，我们可以发现整个美国主义的缩影。我们很可能为这个缩影的眩目的外表所迷惑而忽视美国主义的正常状态，这种正常状态在美国其余各地都显而易见。

暑假里我常常到纽约州东北部的阿地隆台克山区去避暑。有一年暑假，我和几位中国朋友到彩虹湖去，在湖中丛山中的一个小岛上露营。白天时我们就到附近的小湖去划船垂钓。钓鱼的成绩很不错，常常满载而归，而且包括十斤以上的梭鱼。我们露营的小岛上，到处是又肥又大的青蛙，我幼时在我们乡下就曾学会捉蛙，想不到到了美国之后居然有机会大显身手。一根钓竿，一根细绳，一枚用大小适度的针屈曲而成的钓钩，再加一块红布就是钓蛙的全副道具了。这些临时装备成绩惊人，我们常常在一小时之内就捉到二十多只青蛙，足够我们大嚼两餐。彩虹湖附近的居民从未吃过田鸡，他们很佩服我们的捉蛙技术，但是他们的心里一定在想："这些野蛮的中国人真古怪！"

晚上我们常常参加附近居民的仓中舞会，随着主人弹奏的提琴曲子婆娑起舞。我还依稀记得他们所唱的一支歌，大意是：

所有的户枢都长了锈，

门窗也都歪斜倾倒，

屋顶遮不住日晒雨漏，

And the only friend I have

Is the little yellow dog

On the trail behind the bush.

This reflects the loneliness of a solitary hermitage in the mountain region, but to the city-dwellers it depicted a charming, quiet life.

Sometimes we penetrated into virgin forests where the luxuriant leaves veiled the sky like thick clouds. The junipers growing along the trail gave out their aromatic scent, and we picked fragrant evergreen branches to make pillows which would bring nature to our beds and send out floating odors to sweeten our gentle sleep.

Sometimes we lost our way back in the dense woods. We would listen then for the whistle of a train to lead us to the railroad tracks. Experience taught me later to take a compass when going into the woods.

To go back to city life after staying in the country for some time is really a pleasure. The city looks refreshed when you come back to it; the country seems doubly enchanting if you go there from the city. It is all because of the change, the contrast. When foreigners go to China they are often charmed with the complacent Chinese life and with the scenery. A Chinese in a foreign land is often delighted with its city life. So you frequently find a Westerner more enthusiastic about things Chinese than the Chinese themselves, and vice versa. It is a change, a contrast, which breaks monotony and refreshes the mind. But the intrinsic values of things are not altered by these changes of mental approach.

During my student days in New York Sino-Japanese relations took a turn which left the two countries at loggerheads later on. After some fifty years of reforms, Japan showed her strength in 1894 by delivering a blow at China. Instead of resentment and enmity, China returned good for evil. The unfriendly act, contrary to expectations, invoked rather the admiration and gratitude of the Chinese people—admiration for Japan's great reforms, accomplished in the short span of fifty years, and gratitude for thus awakening China to her future possibilities. It rekindled the dying flame of hope in China's heart. For some time thereafter she lived under inspiration drawn from Japanese example.

> 我的唯一的朋友，
> 是灌木丛后面的，
> 一只黄色的小狗。

这支歌反映山区孤村生活的孤独和寂寞，但是对城市居民而言，它却刻画了一种宁静迷人的生活。

我们有时也深入到枝叶蔽天的原始森林里。山径两旁的杜松发散着芬芳的气息。我们采撷了这些芳香的常绿枝叶来装枕头，把大自然带回锦衾之中，阵阵发散的芳香更使我们的梦乡充满了温馨。

有时我们也会在浓密的树林中迷途。那时我们就只好循着火车汽笛的声音，找到铁路轨道以后才能回来。经过几次教训以后，我们进森林时就带指南针了。

在乡下住了一段时间之后，重新回到城市，的确另有一番愉悦之感。从乡村回到城市，城市会显得特别清新可喜；从城市到了乡村，乡村却又显得特别迷人。原因就是环境的改变和鲜明的对照。外国人到中国时，常常迷恋于悠闲的中国生活和它的湖光山色；而中国人到了异国时却又常常留恋外国的都市生活。因此我们常常发现许多欧美人士对中国的东西比中国人自己更喜爱。在另一方面，也有许多中国人对欧美的东西比西洋人自己更喜爱。这就是环境改换和先后对照的关系，改换和对照可以破除单调而使心神清新。但是事物的本身价值并不因心理状态的改变而有所不同。

我在纽约求学的一段时期里，中日关系突起变化，以致两国以后势成水火。日本经过约五十年的维新之后，于一八九四年一击而败中国，声威渐震。中国人以德报怨，并未因战败而怀恨在心。这次战衅反而意外地引起中国人对日本的钦仰和感激——钦仰日本在短短五十年内所完成的重大革新，感激日本唤醒中国对自己前途的乐观。甲午之战可说燃起了中国人心中的希望。战后一段时期中国曾力求追随日本而发奋图强。

Students went to Japan by thousands every year to study. China's new military, police, and school systems were developed and headed by students returned from Japan. Through Japan, China began to see the significance of Western civilization. The Russo-Japanese War gave further impetus to China's reforms—Japan was held in the hearts of the Chinese as an idol.[1]

China absorbed Western civilization gradually through her neighbor, but soon realized that the currents flowing in Japan, from which she drank the waters of modern wisdom, had their source in Europe or America. It was a happy coincidence that America returned the Boxer indemnity; China used it to send more students to the United States than she had done before. Students had previously been sent to Europe and America on government scholarships or by private means, but the number was small. Those who returned direct from the West now grew in numbers and began to occupy some of the key positions in government, industry, commercial enterprise, and educational fields. Missionaries, especially American, helped to educate the youth of the country through mission schools.

Thus, culturally speaking, China began to drift away from Japan. The Japanese idol dwindled in Chinese hearts. And the Japanese were not aware of it.

Taking advantage of the first World War, in 1915 Japan suddenly delivered to Yuan Shih-kai's government the famous Twenty-One Demands, enforcement of which would have reduced China to a Japanese protectorate. This rash act grew out of the upset of the balance of power in the Far East, owing to the preoccupation of the Western Powers with the war and the rapid decline of the military might of Tsarist Russia. It turned China's face once and for all toward the West, and the consequent parting of the ways of the two countries was to change the course of international politics in the years to come. Had Japan been farsighted enough to lend a helping hand to her neighbor in her period of distress,

China would have remained a friend. What would have been the effect of this union upon World War II?

While I was in New York the substance of the Twenty-One Demands was allowed to leak out by the Chinese Legation at Washington. It created consternation in all the capitals of the Western Powers. A boycott of Japanese goods spread like wildfire throughout China as a feeble protest,

　　每年到日本留学的学生数以千计。中国在军事、警务、教育各方面都采取了新制度，而由留日返国的学生主其事。中国开始从日本发现西方文明的重要。日俄战争更使中国的革新运动获得新动力——日本已成为中国人心中的偶像了。

　　中国通过她的东邻逐渐吸收了西方文明，但是中国不久发现，日本值得效法的东西还是从欧美学习而来的。更巧的是美国退还了八国联军之后的庚子赔款，中国利用庚款选派了更多的留美学生。在过去，中国学生也有以官费或自费到欧美留学的，但是人数很少，现在从西洋回国的留学生人数逐渐增加，而且开始掌握政府、工商业以及教育界的若干重要位置。传教士，尤其是美国的传教士，通过教会学校帮助中国教育了年轻的一代。

　　因此，中国与日本的文化关系开始逐渐疏远，中国人心目中的日本偶像也渐行萎缩，但是日本人却并未意识到这种转变。

　　日本利用第一次世界大战的机会，在民国四年即一九一五年突然向袁世凯政府提出著名二十一条要求，如果中国接受这些要求，势将成为日本的保护国。日本之所以突然提出二十一条，是因为西方列强在战事进行中自顾不暇，同时帝俄军事力量急剧衰退，以致远东均势破坏。中国既受东邻日本的逼迫，乃不得不求助于西方国家，中日两国从此分道扬镳，此后数十年间的国际政治也因而改观。如果日本具有远大的眼光，能在中国的苦难时期协助中国，那末中日两国也许一直和睦相处，而第二次世界大战的情形也就完全不同了。

　　驻华盛顿的中国大使馆经政府授意把二十一条要求的内容泄漏了，那时我正在纽约读书。这消息使西方各国首都大为震惊。抵制日货运动像野火一样在中国各地迅速蔓延以示抗议，

but the Japanese navy was concentrated at important Chinese ports and her armed forces mobilized in south Manchuria and Shantung. On May 7, 1915, four months after the presentation of the demands, Japan sent an ultimatum to Yuan Shih-kai and two days later it was accepted.

By force of circumstances the demands in the course of time dwindled to virtually nothing. But the admiration and gratitude of China were thus turned into fear and suspicion which were to grow in the hearts of her millions. Thereafter, whatever Japan had to say China received with suspicion; whatever she did China watched with fear. The more she professed sincerity, the more China suspected a sinister design behind it.

"Why don't you love us as we love you?" our neighbor would ask. "How can we love you when you make love with the bayonet?" we would reply.

"Why should China play off the Western Powers against Japan?" a Japanese general asked me one day, a few years before the Mukden Incident.

"To maintain the balance of power and thus save China from being swallowed up by you," I replied frankly.

"Japan swallow up China! How could we? It's silly."

"It is not silly, General. Didn't Japan deliver us her Twenty-One Demands during the last war, when the Powers were preoccupied? If those demands had been carried into effect, Japan would be in a position to gobble up all China."

"So, so—?" said the general, as if in surprise.

"Yes, yes," I replied briefly.

但是日本军舰已经结集在中国的重要口岸，同时日本在南满和山东的军队也已经动员。民国四年即一九一五年五月七日，也就是日本提出二十一条要求之后四个月，日本向袁世凯提出最后通牒，袁世凯终于在两天之后接受二十一条要求。

后来情势演变，这些要求终于化为乌有，但是中国对日本的钦慕和感激却由此转变为恐惧和猜疑。从此以后，不论日本说什么，中国总是满腹怀疑，不敢置信；不论日本做什么，中国总是怀着恐惧的心情加以警戒。日本越表示亲善，中国越觉得她居心叵测。

我们的东邻质问我们："你们为什么不像我们爱你们一样地爱我们？"我们回答说："你们正在用刺刀谈恋爱，我们又怎么能爱你们？"

九·一八事变前几年，一位日本将官有一天问我："中国为什么要挑拨西方列强与日本作对？"

"为保持均势，以免中国被你们并吞。"我很坦白地回答。

"日本并吞中国！我们怎么会呢？这简直是笑话。"

"一点也不笑话，将军。上次大战时列强自顾不暇，日本不是曾经乘机向中国提出二十一条要求吗？如果这些要求条条实现，日本不是就可以鲸吞中国吗？"

"哦，哦——？"这位将军像是吃惊不小的样子。

"一点不错。"我直截了当地回答。

PART THREE

第三部　民国初年

THE NEW CHINA

CHAPTER 12   RAPID CHANGES

In the midst of American mobilization for a European war for the first time in her history, in June, 1917, I left for home with mixed feelings. The last night I spent in Hartley Hall at Columbia my mind was too much occupied to sleep and I lay the whole night in meditation. The hours ebbed away until the early, summer dawn came in at the window through the creeping vines. The morning air was mild and the petals of the roses were dew-laden. Near by, on the granite steps of the library, the Alma Mater was smiling her grave smile as if wishing her foster son Godspeed. As I stood at the window looking out on the familiar scene that had meant so much to me those five years, tears began to well up in my eyes. Was I to be torn away once and for all from the fountain of wisdom, leaving my friends behind? But it was my duty to go home, just as it had been my privilege to come.

In the afternoon I boarded a train at Grand Central for a city in Ohio. As the train crawled out of the station I kept looking back at the waving hands of my American friends, boys and girls, until they were lost to sight.

One friend accompanied me to Ohio to visit with friends of his there, and we were welcomed to the family by its charming hostess. The host had some sort of business in that city. There was no son in the family; the girl was the sunshine in the house. She was an attractive brunette with an oval face, and the warmth that poured from her young heart would endear her to anyone who met her.

We stayed for about two weeks. It was in the midst of registration and draft; the first groups gathered, marched on the streets, and were sent off for training. The sidewalks were thronged with people. Mothers, sweethearts, and friends bade good-by to their soldiers with kisses, tears, and throbbing hearts.

We formed rowing parties on moonlit ponds dotted with islets of gold and silvery lilies. Fireflies twinkled like moving stars. Fish splashed. The girls sang together—I still remember one of the songs they loved to sing:

The June air is warm and tender.

Why do you hold your petals to display?

Are you afraid someone will

Come and steal your heart away?

拾贰 急剧变化

　　我在民国六年即一九一七年六月间离美返国，美国正为有史以来第一次参加欧战而忙着动员。离美前夕，心情相当复杂，那晚睡在哥伦比亚大学的赫特莱楼，思潮起伏，一夜不曾阖眼。时间慢慢消逝，终于东方发白。初夏的曙光从窗外爬藤的夹缝漏进房里。清晨的空气显得特别温柔，蔷薇花瓣上满积着晶莹的露珠。附近图书馆前石阶上的圣母铜像，似乎怀着沉重的心情在向我微笑道别，祝她抚育的义子一帆风顺。我站在窗前伫望着五年来朝夕相伴的景物，不禁热泪盈眶。难道我就这样丢下我的朋友，永远离开这智慧的源泉吗？但是学成回国是我的责任，因为我已享受了留美的特权。那天下午我在中央车站搭火车离开纽约前往俄亥俄州的一个城市。火车慢慢移动离开车站时，我不住地回头望着挥手送别的美国朋友，直到无法再看到这些青年男女朋友的影子时才坐下。

　　一位朋友陪我到俄亥俄州去看他的朋友。男主人有事进城去了，由漂亮的女主人招待我们。主人家里没有男孩，只有一位掌上明珠。这位黑发女郎明媚动人，长着一张鹅蛋脸，而且热情洋溢，真是人见人爱。

　　我们在那里住了两星期，正是大家忙着登记应召入伍的时候，第一批新兵正在集合出发，队伍浩浩荡荡经过大街，开往营地受训。街道两旁人山人海，母亲们、爱人们、朋友们纷纷向出征的勇士道别，有的拥吻不舍，有的泪流满面，就是旁观的人也为之鼻酸。

　　作客期间，我们曾经数度在月明之夜划船游湖。湖上遍布着满长金色和银色水仙花的小屿。萤火虫像流星样在夜空中闪烁。鱼儿在月色下跳跃戏水。女孩子们则齐声欢唱。我还记得一支她们喜欢唱的歌：

　　　　六月的空气温暖而清新。

　　　　你为什么不肯打开你的瓣儿？

　　　　难道你怕会有人

　　　　悄悄地偷走你的心？

The frogs echoed with their ungainly chorus. The girls sang and sang until the breezes of late evening brought a chilly warning. Then we would all go ashore and walk home over the dew-laden grass under the slanting moon.

Time flew and soon the two enjoyable weeks came to an end. I said good-by to my friends and took a train for San Francisco. When the ocean liner steamed gently out of the Golden Gate I stood on the deck facing east thinking of my friends in New York. Good-by, my friends! Good-by, America!

It was still summer in Shanghai. The city had changed much during my absence of nine years. Many streets were wider and better paved. New roads had been built beyond the limits of the Foreign Settlement. Department stores, fashionable hotels, roof gardens, amusement parks, and cabarets had multiplied. Shanghai had caught up with the spirit of New York.

The number of schools had increased manyfold in the city during the years of my absence; all but a few, however, were supported by private or Chinese government sources—these few had been established years before by the international municipal government. I suppose the revenues of the Settlement must have increased a hundred times since these few outmoded schools had been founded decades earlier. But let the Chinese remain ignorant—they would be easier to control and exploit.

The young girls had bobbed their hair and wore short skirts up to their knees in the fashion of the day. No—excuse me—I mean they wore gowns down to their knees, For the dress of the modern Chinese girl was very sensible. It consisted of a straight piece of silk hanging from the shoulders, longer or shorter according to fashion. This had been originally the Manchu gown, and Chinese girls had adopted it after the downfall of the dynasty some six years earlier.

Here, there, and everywhere on the streets high-heeled shoes adorned the dainty feet of young women. When one heard quick heels tapping the sidewalks one felt at once that the rising generation were radically different from their mother. The old modesty had disappeared. They were also better-developed physically, however, thanks to the modern shoes. In the old days women had practiced foot-binding. The movement to free women's feet, as a part of China's reform program, began around

青蛙们也嘶着粗野的歌喉随声和唱，女孩子唱了一支又接着一支，直到晚风带来寒意，大家才意识到夜色已深。于是我们弃舟登岸，在斜泻而下的月色中踏着遍沾露珠的草地回家。

时间在不知不觉间飞逝，两个礼拜的愉快生活旋告结束。我向朋友们道别，搭了一辆火车去旧金山。邮船慢慢离开金门海口时，我站在甲板上望着东方，心里念念不忘在纽约的朋友们。再会吧，朋友们！再会吧，美国！

回到上海时还是夏天。离开九年，上海已经变了。许多街道比以前宽阔，也比以前平坦。租界范围之外也已经铺筑了许多新路。百货公司、高等旅馆、屋顶花园、游乐场、跳舞场都比以前多了好几倍。上海已经追上纽约的风气了。

离开祖国的几年之内，上海的学校也增加了好几倍；但是除了少数例外，所有学校的经费都是由私人或中国政府负担的。少数例外的学校是多年以前公共租界当局兴办的。自从这些落伍的学校在几十年前创立以来，租界当局的收入我想至少已经增加百倍。但还是让中国人永远无知无识罢——这样，控制和剥削都比较方便。

年轻女孩子已剪短头发，而且穿起高齐膝盖的短裙，哦！对不起，我说错了，我的意思是指她们穿了仅到膝盖的旗袍，当时流行的式样就是如此。当时中国摩登女子的这种衣服是相当有道理的，从肩到膝，平直无华，料子多半是绸缎，长短随时尚而定。这原是满洲旗人的长袍，于清朝进关时男子被迫而穿着的，满清覆亡以后也被汉家女子采用，因此称为"旗"袍。

到处可以看到穿着高跟鞋的青年妇女。当你听到人行道高跟皮鞋的急骤的笃笃声时，你就知道年轻的一代与她们的母亲已经大不相同了。过去的羞怯之态已不复存在。也许是穿着新式鞋子的结果，她们的身体发育也比以前健美了。从前女人是缠足的。天足运动是中国改革运动的

the time of the Russo-Japanese War and went on rather slowly until after the Revolution of 1911. I think the high heels helped to accelerate it, for women were surely more ready to give up the practice of squeezing their little daughters' feet into tiny slippers when they saw others wearing dainty high heels.

Men had dropped their queues but still clung to the long gown. It was funny to see a long gown without a queue. But before long I found myself one of the multitude, for Chinese clothing is more convenient and comfortable. No one can resist the temptation of being comfortable and convenient at the same time—it is a matter of practical common sense.

There were still a few individuals who wore queues, especially among the old men. They did not see any sense in getting rid of it; the queue had grown on Chinese heads for more than two centuries and it would do no harm to have it for a few centuries more. There are always die-hards in any movement.

In America I had measured things American by the Chinese yardstick. Now I reversed the process, measuring things Chinese with the American yardstick, or most likely with a sort of hybrid stick, neither Chinese nor American but something of both, or vacillating between the two.

I pitied the rickshaw coolies who ran for a few coppers, out of breath, their sweating tanned backs turned toward you in the hot summer sun. It was something inhuman, my American yardstick would say. Once in a while I came across some of the beastly foreigners who kicked them like dogs—but no, in America I never saw a man kick a dog. Blood rushed to my head and I often wanted to kick back at the human beasts, but refrained from venting my noble sentiments when I saw extraterritoriality looming large behind them. Then I reverted to my ancestral patience. "Coward!" the American yardstick would say. "Patience," returned the Chinese stick of my forefathers. Stop using these rickshaws and have more buses and tramways. But what were the poor coolies to do to eke out their meager subsistence? Return to the farms? No, they were surplus farmers. Three ways were open to them: to turn bandit with the strong, petty thieves with the weak, or beggars with the still weaker. Well then, let them pull the rickshaws. Here you are in a vicious circle.

一部分，开始于日俄战争前后，但是在辛亥革命成功以前进展始终很慢。我想高跟鞋可能是促使天足运动迅速成功的原因，因为女人们看到别人穿起高跟鞋婀娜多姿，自然就不愿意再把她们女儿的足硬挤到绣花鞋里了。

男子已经剪掉辫子，但是仍旧没有舍弃长衫，因为大家已经忘记了长衫本来就是旗袍。穿着长衫而没有辫子，看起来似乎很滑稽。但是不久之后，我也像大家一样穿起长衫来了，因为无论革命与不革命，旗袍究竟比较方便而且舒服。谁也不能抵抗既方便又舒服的诱惑，这是人情之常。

也有一些人仍旧留着辫子，尤其是老年人。他们看不出剪辫子有什么好处。辫子已经在中国人头上养了两百多年，就让它再留几百年也无所谓。任何运动中总不免有死硬派的。

在美国时，我喜欢用中国的尺度来衡量美国的东西。现在回国以后，我把办法刚刚颠倒过来，喜欢用美国的尺度来衡量中国的东西，有时更可能用一种混合的尺度，一种不中不西、亦中亦西的尺度，或者游移于两者之间。

我可怜黄包车夫，他们为了几个铜板，跑得气喘吁吁，汗流浃背，尤其在夏天，烈日灸灼着他们的背脊，更是惨不忍睹。我的美国尺度告诉我，这太不人道。有时我碰到一些野兽似的外国人简直拿黄包车夫当狗一样踢骂——其实我说"当狗一样踢骂"是不对的，我在美国就从来没有看见一个人踢骂过狗。看到这种情形，我真是热血沸腾，很想打抱不平，把这些衣冠禽兽踢回一顿。但是一想到支持他们的治外法权时，我只好压抑了满腔气愤。我想起了"小不忍则乱大谋"的古训。"懦夫！"我的美国尺度在讥笑我。"忍耐！"祖先的中国尺度又在劝慰我。大家还是少坐黄包车，多乘公共汽车和电车罢！但是这些可怜的黄包车夫又将何以为生？回到乡下种田吗？不可能，他们本来就是农村的剩余劳力。摆在他们面前的只有三条路：身强力壮的去当强盗，身体弱的去当小偷，身体更弱的去当乞丐。那末怎么办？还是让他们拖黄包车罢！兜了半天圈子，结果还是老地方。

Build up industry, it will give them employment. But industry is impossible without a stable government. A stable government is hardly possible when there are so many surplus farmers in the country, always ready to join mercenary armies and fight for the warlords who pay them or who let them loose to plunder the people. Here is another vicious circle, difficult to break.

There was an improvement in the notice boards of the Settlement public parks. The list of regulations forbidding the entrance of Chinese as well as dogs now displayed the modified clause: "Respectable Chinese only are admitted." At last even the arrogant foreigners had begun to be aware that there was something to be respected rising in China.

So much for Shanghai.

The great eastern seaport and trading center was now connected by rail with Soochow to the west and Hangchow to the south cities both regarded as paradises on earth. The line ran from Soochow farther west to Nanking, connected by a ferry across the Yangtze River; and north through Tientsin to Peking, then capital of the Republic. The southern branch stopped at Hangchow and remained as yet to be connected with Ningpo.

My home was not very far from Ningpo, native city of Generalissimo Chiang Kai-shek. It is one of the five treaty ports but has never come into any considerable importance as a port, for the rapid growth of Shanghai as one of the great ports of the world overshadowed it. Three lines had ships running between Shanghai and Ningpo nightly, both incoming and outgoing; two of these were British companies and the third the China Merchants Navigation Company. These ships were the models for the steamless paddle-wheel "steamboat" my father had built so many years earlier and failed to make go. My brother and I took a second-class cabin on one of these boats.

There was not much change in the life of the passengers in twenty years. The gangways and decks were packed with human sardines and one could hardly set foot on the floor without stepping on somebody. We went on board about five in the afternoon to occupy our berths. Hawkers came by in great numbers, selling every kind of goods that a household might need, mostly imported manufactures. Fruit sellers brought bananas, apples, and pears on board. My brother and I had an argument. He wanted to buy the partly rotten fruit because it was much cheaper. "No," I argued, "you will pay much more for the doctor's bill."

那末就发展工业，让他们去做工吧。但是没有一个稳定的政府，工业又无法发展。农村里农夫过剩，只要军阀们肯出钱，或者肯让他们到处掳掠，这些过剩的农夫随时可以应募当兵，在这种情形下，欲求政府稳定势不可得。因此发展工业的路还是走不通。

租界公园门口的告示牌已经有了改进，"犬与华人不得入内"的禁条已经修改为"只准高等华人入内"。甚至一向趾高气扬的洋人，也开始发现有些值得尊重的东西，正在中国抬头。

关于上海的事，暂时谈到此地为止。

上海这个华东大海港和商业中心，现在已经与向有人间天堂之称的苏州和杭州由铁道互相衔接。由上海到苏州的铁路再往西通到南京，在下关渡长江与津浦铁路衔接，往北直通天津和当时的首都北京。上海往南的铁路止于杭州，尚未通到宁波。

我的家乡离宁波不远。宁波虽是五口通商的五口之一，但是始终未发展为重要的商埠，因为上海迅速发展为世界大商埠之一，使宁波黯然无光。宁波与上海之间有三家轮船公司的船只每夜对开一次；两家是英国公司，第三家就是招商局。许多年前我父亲曾经拿这些轮船作蓝本，打造没有锅炉而使用手转木轮的"轮船"，结果无法行驶。我从上海经宁波还乡，与我哥哥搭的就是这种轮船的二等舱。

事隔二十年，乘客的生活无多大改变。过道和甲板上乘客挤得像沙丁鱼，一伸脚就可能踩到别人。我们为了占住舱位，下午五点钟左右就上了船。小贩成群结队上船叫卖，家常杂物，应有尽有，多半还是舶来品。水果贩提了香蕉、苹果和梨子上船售卖。我和哥哥还因此辩论了一场。哥哥要买部分腐败的水果，因为比较便宜。"不行，"我说，"买水果的钱固然省了，看医生的钱却多了。"

"Ha, ha! I have been eating rotten pears and apples for years," he said. "They taste better. I have no trouble from them." He picked up a big, partly decayed red apple, bit off the bad parts and ate the rest. I shuddered. He laughed.

Before dawn we passed the fortresses of Ningpo Harbor, which fired a cannon ball that hit and killed a French admiral in the Sino-French War of 1885.

Day dawned. Clamorous voices from the dock rose to my ears. Streams of porters rushed up, fighting for luggage. The slightest negligence would find your possessions removed without permission. My brother and I elbowed down through the packed crowd, closely following our porters lest they walk off with our belongings.

Ningpo was practically the same as it had been nine years earlier. The air was laden with the smell of salt fish. I felt at home with this smell, for salt fish had been a staple food since childhood. Ningpo is a fishing town and large quantities of salt are produced not far away. We followed our porters to the station and found a train waiting to depart for Yuyao, our home city. Along the railroad I saw miles of well-cultivated fields cushioned with rippling rice that flowered in the autumn morning sun, unfolding like a never-ending scroll of landscape painting before the windows of the moving train. The morning air was stimulating and laden with the scent of flowering rice. Oh—this is my homeland!

As the train pulled into the Yuyao station my heart throbbed with excitement. We crossed the river by a long stone bridge built centuries ago. The ebb tide was racing down the river; through the arches of the bridge anglers could be seen casting their lines in the flowing water. The bridge was called Wu-shen, meaning "brave and victorious," because at the bridgeheads some four centuries ago people fought from time to time to defend the city against the invasions of pirates of uncertain origin from the Japan Sea. The Chinese believed they were Japanese, but Japanese historians deny it.

It was late in the morning when we hurried into the courtyard steeped in brilliant autumn sun. My father stood on the granite steps leading to the spacious hall. He was somewhat aged, his hair turning grey; otherwise in good health and splendid spirits. His kind eyes and smiling lips glowed with the tender emotions that flow from the heart of a loving parent. Before him my brother and I bowed three times in respect; the old way of kowtowing on one's knees had, among certain sections of the people, passed into history with the vanished dynasty.

"哈，哈——我吃烂梨子、烂苹果已经好几年，"他说，"烂的味道反而好。我从来没有吃出过毛病。"他随手捡起一个又大又红，然而烂了一部分的苹果，咬掉烂的一部分，其余的全部落肚，我耸耸肩膀，他仰天大笑。

天亮前我们经过宁波港口的镇海炮台。一八八五年中法战争时镇海炮台曾经发炮轰死一位法军的海军上将。

天亮了，码头上的喧嚷声震耳欲聋。脚夫们一拥上船拼命抢夺行李。一个不留神，你的东西就会不翼而飞。我和哥哥好容易在人丛中挤下跳板，紧紧地钉在行李夫的背后，唯恐他们提了我们的东西溜之大吉。

宁波几乎与九年前一模一样。空气中充塞着咸鱼的气味。我对这种气味颇能安之若素，因我从小就经常吃咸鱼。宁波是个鱼市，而且离宁波不远的地方就盛产食盐。我们跟着行李夫到了车站，发现一列火车正准备升火开往我的家乡余姚。沿铁道我看到绵亘数里的稻田，稻波荡漾，稻花在秋晨的阳光下发光，整齐的稻田在车窗前移动，像是一幅广袤无边的巨画。清晨的空气中洋溢着稻香，呵，这就是我的家乡！

火车进余姚车站时，我的一颗心兴奋得怦怦直跳。我们越过一座几百年前建造的大石桥，桥下退落的潮水正顺着江流急泻而下。从桥洞里还可以看到钓翁们在江边垂钓。这桥名曰武胜桥，意指英武常胜。因为四百年前当地居民为保卫余姚县城，曾与自日本海入侵的倭寇屡次在桥头堡作战。这些倭寇大家都认为就是日本人。

我们跑进院子时，秋阳高照，已是晌午时分。父亲站在大厅前的石阶上，两鬓斑白，微露老态，但是身体显然很好，精神也很旺健。他的慈祥眼睛和含笑的双唇洋溢着慈父的深情。我兄弟两人恭恭敬敬地向他老人家行了三鞠躬礼。旧式的叩头礼在某些人之间已经随着清朝的覆亡而成为历史陈迹了。

Father had given up his queue but still wore Chinese slippers. He did not say much: silence conveyed much more than words on such an occasion. Then we all entered the hall. Stiff-backed chairs arranged symmetrically along the walls showed little sign of change in his way of living. The couplet panels inlaid with mother-of-pearl shone on the back walls. On the right side one read: "Fishes have greater freedom in the vastness of the sea," and on the left: "Birds take broader liberty in the wide span of the sky." Between the two panels was a painting of bamboo shadows which seemed to bend in an autumn breeze, all the leaves pointing with the wind. These things all speak of a contented, quiet, and unchanging life.

Behind the hall was a narrow strip of back yard. Miniature mountain scenes set in large rectangular pots brought landscape within the high walls. Tiny temples and pagodas perched on the miniature mountains, and dwarf trees that looked centuries old grew around them. Little monkeys with still smaller babies sitting innocently by their side sat here and there in the quiet recesses of the mountains. They all looked so cute that I wished some of them could grow life sized and jump into my lap. There was a tiny bamboo grove flourishing around a toy pavilion. Goldfish snapping at the air and shrimps stretching out their claws for food all enjoyed undisturbed life in the imitation ponds. All of this led one's mind to nature.

On hearing of my return old Mr. Liu came to call in the afternoon. He had told me stories in my childhood. How we children loved him! That day he recounted many amusing things. He described how the people acted on learning of the successful revolution. All the queues in the city vanished overnight. Young people bought foreign clothes and looked like monkeys in them. And how the short skirts and bobbed hair invaded the city later on! But for him the cutting of the queue that had grown on his head for more than seventy years was sufficient support of the revolution and the Republic. At first he wondered how the world could go on without an emperor sitting upon the dragon throne in Peking, but after some time he was sure that a republic with a president had the same power of maintaining peace and order in the country. At any rate, he said, "Heaven is high above and the Emperor is far away." It was up to the local authorities to do their job of maintaining peace, and they did it well.

父亲已经剪掉辫子，但是仍然穿着旧式布鞋。他说话不多；在这种场合，沉默胜似千言万语。我们随即进入大厅。直背的椅子靠墙很对称地排列着，显见他的生活方式仍然很少改变。正墙上悬着镶嵌贝壳的对联，右联是"海阔凭鱼跃"，左联是"天空任鸟飞"。对联的中间是一幅墨竹，竹叶似乎受秋风吹拂，都倾向一边。这一切很可以显示一种满足的，安静的，而且安定的生活。

大厅后面有一个小院子，长方形的大盘子里堆砌着山景，因此使高墙的院子里平添山水之胜。小寺小塔高踞假山之上，四周则围绕着似乎已历数百年的小树。山坳里散坐着小小的猴子，母猴的身旁则偎依着更小的小猴，这些微小的假猴显得如此玲珑可爱，我真希望它们能够变成活猴一样大小而跳进我的怀里。小寺小塔之外还有一个小凉亭，亭边长着一丛篁竹。假池子里则有喋喋的金鱼和探鳌觅食的小虾。这一切的一切，都使人有置身自然之感。

刘老丈听说我回家了，当天下午就来看我。在我童年时代，刘老丈曾经讲许多故事给我们听，小孩子们都很喜欢他。那天下午，他讲了许多有趣的故事。他告诉我，老百姓们听到革命成功的消息时欢喜得什么似的。城里的人一夜之间就把辫子剪光了。年轻人买了西装，穿起来很像一群猴子。他又告诉我，短裙与短发如何在后来侵入县城。革命以后，他那留了七十多年的辫子居然也剪掉了，可见他对革命和民国仍然是很赞成的，起先他有点想不通，没有皇帝坐龙庭，这个世界还成什么样子？但是过了一段时期以后，他才相信民国的总统，照样可以保持天下太平。他说，反正天高皇帝远，地方治安本来就靠地方官府来维持。民国以来，地方官府居然做得还不错。

When the Taipings had invaded the city some half century before, he said, heads went off shoulders with the queues. Now we lost only our queues and retained our heads. Talking thus, he touched his grey head with his bony fingers in such a comical way that it made everybody laugh. At dusk, after an early supper, in taking his leave he happened to slip on the steps leading to the courtyard. Someone rescued him, holding him up by the arms. He shook his head and joked, "Three thousand years ago Grandfather Chiang at the age of eighty met King Wen and helped him to build a new kingdom. Now Grandfather Liu at the same age may meet King Nian of the other world and help him to govern his invisible realm." He laughed heartily and went away in good spirits.

Several days later word came that "Grandfather" Liu had passed into the invisible realm. For me, I lost my childhood friend and old companion, and there were no more stories from his endless fountain of wit.

A school which my sister and I had established some fifteen years earlier had been turned into a district government school for girls. A hundred girls or so were studying there. They ran and laughed in the playgrounds and rode high in the air on the swing. A new generation of womanhood was in the making. They played Western tunes on a portable organ; "Swanee River" and "Tipperary" and popular Chinese tunes were wafted through the doors and over the walls.

I stayed at home about a week and then went to the country to pay a visit to the village of the Chiangs. There the children of my childhood had grown to maturity. The grownups of older days had come to old age, their hair turning grey. The old people of days gone by had retired to their graves, except for a few who were still alert, witnessing the turns of fortune in the village.

The village did not look as bad as I anticipated. The banditry of early days had subsided, for people had now adjusted themselves to new trades and many had gone to Shanghai, which was able to accommodate larger numbers as commerce and industry expanded. Change, like birth, gives pain, but after the delivery the mother comes back to her normal state and feels happy with the newly born. Change that China had once hated had come to stay, ever deepening and widening, until she was constantly on the onward march—whither and for what purpose her teeming millions knew not.

他说，五十年前太平军侵入县城时，许多脑袋连辫子一起落了地，现在我们虽然丢掉辫子，脑袋总还存在。他一边说，一边用他皮包骨的手指摸着脑袋，样子非常滑稽，因此引得大家都笑了。那天晚饭吃得比较早，饭后他告辞回家，暮色苍茫中不留神在庭前石阶上滑了一跤，幸亏旁边有人赶紧抓住他的肩膀，搀住他没有跌伤。他摇摇头自己开自己的玩笑说："三千年前姜太公八十遇文王，我刘太公八十要见阎王了。"说罢哈哈大笑，兴高采烈地回家去了。

几天之后消息传来，刘太公真地见阎王去了。对我而言，我失去了一位童年时代的老朋友，而且再也听不到这位风趣的老人给我讲故事了。

十五年前左右，姊姊和我创办的一所学校现在已经改为县立女子学校。大概有一百名左右的女孩子正在读书。她们在操场上追逐嬉笑，荡秋千荡得半天高。新生一代的女性正在成长。她们用风琴弹奏《史华尼河》和《迪伯拉莱》等西洋歌曲，流行的中国歌更是声闻户外。

我在家里住了一星期左右，随后就到乡下去看看蒋村的老朋友。童年时代的小孩子现在都已成人长大，当时的成年人现在已经是鬓发斑白的老人。至于当年的老人，现在多已经入土长眠，只有极少数历经村中沧桑的老人还健在。

村庄的情形倒不像我想像中的那样糟。早年的盗匪之灾已经敛迹，因为老百姓现在已经能够适应新兴的行业，而且许多人已经到上海谋生去了。上海自工商业发展以后，已经可以容纳不少人。任何变革正像分娩一样，总是有痛苦的。但是在分娩以后，产妇随即恢复正常，而且因为添了小宝宝而沾沾自喜。中国一度厌恶的变革现在已经根深蒂固，无法动摇，而且愈变愈厉，中国也就身不由己地不断往前迈进——至于究竟往那里跑，或者为什么往前跑，亿万百姓却了无所知。

My aunt whom I called the Great Mother had been bedridden for months. She was very happy on seeing me, made me sit by her side and stretched out her feeble hands to touch mine. She told me all about the births, marriages, and deaths which had occurred in the village in the last sixteen years. The world was not the same as before, she said. So many changes and so many new things had come in. Women did not weave and spin any more because foreign cloth was much cheaper, and better too. They had not much to do now; some spent their time in quarrels with their neighbors and others devoted themselves to Buddha. The younger ones went to school. Girls made hair nets and crocheted napkins to be exported to America. There was good money in it, she said. The boys were sent as apprentices to factories and machine shops in Shanghai. They took to new trades and made more money. There was now a dearth of farm hands in the village, but there were no more bandits. Tranquility and peace had come to stay. When dogs barked at night people did not have to be anxious for their safety as they had ten years before.

But something very bad she noticed in the girls and boys who had been in schools. They called the worship of gods a superstition. They said that the burning of paper money before our ancestors was silly. To them there were no kitchen gods. All the images of gods in the temples were only blocks of wood and lumps of clay. They thought these images ought to be flung into the river, so as to banish superstition along with them. They said girls had the same rights as boys. The girls said they had the right to marry by their own choice, and to remarry after a divorce or the death of their husbands. The foot-binding of old days was a cruel and inhuman practice, they said. Foreign pills were much better than Chinese herbs. They said there was no such thing as ghosts or transmigration of the soul. Nothing would be left after death but a heap of chemical compounds. They said the only immortality was to render services to the people and the country.

She shook her head and sighed. "Do they teach these things in

America?" she asked. I smiled. Apparently she did not like my smile. Perhaps she suspected that the crazy Americans were responsible for teaching Chinese boys and girls these silly notions, for she told me that an American missionary lady had come some time earlier to tell her not to worship idols.

A fat black cat leapt up on her bed and began purring around her pillows. "Are there cats in America?" she asked feebly. I said yes, and saw that she was already asleep. I left her with the purring cat whose soft paws rested upon her pillows and touched her cheek.

　　我的大伯母已经卧病好几个月，看到我回家非常高兴，吩咐我坐到她的床边，还伸出颤巍巍的手来抚摸我的手，她告诉我过去十六年中谁生了儿子，谁结了婚，谁故世。她说世界变了，简直变得面目全非。女人已经不再纺纱织布，因为洋布又好又便宜。她们已经没有多少事可以做，因此有些就与邻居吵架消磨光阴，有些则去念经拜菩萨。年轻的一代都上学堂了。有些女孩则编织发网和网线餐巾销售到美国去，出息不错。很多男孩子跑到上海工厂或机械公司当学徒，他们就了新行业，赚钱比以前多。现在村子里种田的人很缺乏，但是强盗却也绝迹了。天下大概从此太平无事，夜里听到犬吠，大家也不再像十年前那样提心吊胆。

　　但是她发现进过学校的青年男女有些事实在要不得。他们说拜菩萨是迷信，又说向祖先烧纸钱是愚蠢的事。他们认为根本没有灶神。庙宇里的菩萨塑像在他们看来不过是泥塑木雕。他们认为应该把这些佛像一齐丢到河里，以便破除迷信。他们说男女应该平等。女孩子说她们有权自行选择丈夫、离婚或者丈夫死了以后有权再嫁，又说旧日缠足是残酷而不人道的办法，说外国药丸比中国药草好得多。他们说根本没有鬼，也没有灵魂轮回这回事。人死了之后除了留下一堆化学元素的化合物之外什么也没有了。他们说唯一不朽的东西就是为人民、为国家服务。

　　一只肥肥的黑猫跳上床，在她枕旁咪咪直叫。她有气无力地问我："美国也有猫吗？"我说是的。再一看，她已经睡熟了。我轻轻地走出房间，黑猫则仍在她枕旁呼噜作响，并且伸出软绵绵的爪子去碰碰老太太的脸颊。

My niece, who had been listening all the time, ran out after me. She put her tongue between her teeth for a moment and said mischievously, "Grandma is too old for the change." After a month or so the old lady left this crazy, changing world.

I went to visit with another aunt of mine, whom I called Third Mother. She was a strong elderly lady. Her husband, my "Third Father," owned large farms. There were chickens, ducks, geese, and pigs in abundance. My aunt told me the tragedy of a childhood friend of mine who had speculated in gold in Shanghai and incurred heavy losses. He had lost his job and retired to his home village. The year before, he had committed suicide by taking a big dose of opium. His widow and children were destitute and one of the children had drowned in the canal while fishing for shrimp under the big soap tree.

My aunt snatched a big fat capon which struggled and screamed in her hands and dressed it herself. Later a delicious chicken dinner was served, with fish and shrimp in addition.

My uncle told me that people had used chemical fertilizers for cabbages the year before, and these grew to such enormous size that they thought the abnormal growth must contain poison. So they pulled them up and threw them away. But he kept his, bought them cheap from others, and salted them. They were tender and delicious. A wise old man he was.

An old woman who had held me in her arms when I was a baby came to the village to see me. She must have been over ninety and was partially deaf, yet had walked from her own village some four miles away. She examined me from top to toe and was satisfied to find nothing strange about me. This big boy was once a small, skinny child, she said, and very naughty. He bit his own brother on the knee and left purple marks on it. Then he cried and blamed his brother's knee for having hurt his teeth.

"Do you remember the two brothers who divided their father's property into equal parts when he died?" she asked. They had each got a wing of their father's house and had set a bamboo partition in the middle of the hall, which was thus evenly divided so that each could get an exactly equal portion. One kept a cow in his part and the other retaliated by making his a piggery. They even sawed the boat in two equal halves. The wicked brothers—may the gods curse them! Then there came a fire and turned their house into ashes. Heaven must have eyes.

　　我和大伯母谈话时，我的侄女一直在旁边听着。我走出房间以后，她也赶紧追了出来。她向我伸伸舌头，很淘气地对我说："婆婆太老了，看不惯这种变化。"一个月之后，这位老太太终于离开这个疯狂的不断在变的世界。

　　接着我去拜望三叔母，她的年岁也不小了，身体却很健旺。我的三叔父有很多田地，而且养了许多鸡、鸭、鹅和猪。三叔母告诉我一个悲惨的故事。我的一位童年时代的朋友在上海，做黄金投机生意，蚀了很多钱，结果失了业，回到村里赋闲。一年前他吞鸦片自杀，他的寡妇和子女弄得一贫如洗，其中一位孩子就在皂荚树下小河中捉虾时淹死了。

　　三叔母捉住一只又肥又大的阉鸡，而且亲自下厨。鸡烧得很鲜美，鸡之外还有鱼有虾。

　　三叔父告诉我，上一年大家开始用肥田粉种白菜，结果白菜大得非常，许多人认为这种大得出奇的白菜一定有毒，纷纷把白菜拔起来丢掉。但三叔父却不肯丢，而且廉价从别人那里买来腌起来。腌好的咸菜香脆可口，这位老人真够精明。

　　小时候曾经抱过我的一位老太婆也从村子里来看我。她已经九十多岁，耳朵已经半聋，却从她的村子走了四里多路来看我。她仔仔细细地把我从头到脚端详一番，看我并无异样才安了心。她说，这位大孩子从前又瘦又小，而且很顽皮。他曾经在他哥哥的膝头咬了一口，留下紫色的齿印，结果自己号啕大哭，怪哥哥的膝盖碰痛了他的牙齿。

　　"你记不记得那两位兄弟在父死之后分家的事？"她问我。两兄弟每人分到他们父亲的房子的一个边厢，又在大厅的正中树了一片竹墙，把大厅平分为二。一位兄弟在他的那一半厅子里养了一头牛，另一位兄弟气不过，就把他的半边厅子改为猪栏来报复。他们父亲留下一条船，结果也被锯为两半。这两位缺德兄弟真该天诛地灭！后来祝融光顾，他们的房子烧得精光。老天爷是有眼的！

They sold the lot and a big house of foreign style was later built on it. It belonged to a rich merchant who was in business in Shanghai. When the house was completed she paid a visit to it and got into such a labyrinth of passageways and stairs and doors that she was confused and could not find her way out. She tried the soft chairs and spring beds and was frightened when she sank deep into them. The most curious thing to her was the machine which the owner of the house had brought from Shanghai. When the wheels turned swiftly it lit up bulbs all over the house. The night was as brilliant as day.

The boy who took charge of the machine was the son of her neighbors. He had learned to operate it in Shanghai. She would never have thought that stupid boy could manipulate such an intricate piece of machinery. She stood far away from the swiftly turning wheels lest she be caught and turned into sausage or tough meat balls.

Another curious thing she noticed was that there was no Kitchen God in the kitchen. And the family worshiped no ancestors. The kitchen gods she did not mind so much, but how could a family have no ancestors? The master of the house believed a sort of religion which precluded the worship of other gods. She would not like to belong to that religion, because she wanted to go to any temple she chose and worship any gods she wanted to. She wondered how a god could be so jealous as to forbid people to worship other gods. She was willing to worship that god, for the man in his temple gave her quinine pills which cured her malaria last summer; but she wanted to bend her stiff knees to other gods also to ask for blessings.

She said she had scarcely enough to eat and often went hungry. My father gave her a monthly allowance in rice as a charity, but since her orphaned granddaughter had come to live with her the small girl ate a portion of it. I pulled out a twenty dollar bill and squeezed it into her hands. She scurried away happily, muttering, "From his childhood I know he is a kind-hearted boy, a kind-hearted boy."

Late one afternoon I made a visit to my mother's tomb. A pair of candles and a bunch of incense sticks were displayed before it. The air was still and streaks of smoke from the incense went straight up in the air. Instinctively I bent my knees to the ground and kowtowed. My childhood memories revived. Everything seemed to have happened only yesterday. I felt as if I were still a child paying respects to my mother. I wished her

他们把那块地基卖掉了。一位在上海做生意的富商后来在这块地上建了一座大洋房。洋房完工时，她曾经进去参观，转弯抹角的走廊、楼梯和玻璃门，弄得她头昏眼花，进去以后简直出不来。她试过沙发和弹簧床，一坐就深陷不起，真是吓了一大跳。最使她惊奇的是屋主人从上海买来的一架机器。轮子一转，全屋子的灯泡都亮了，黑夜竟同白昼一样亮。

管机器的是她邻居的儿子。他是在上海学会开机器的。她做梦也想不到这位笨头笨脑的孩子居然能够拨弄那样复杂的一件机器。她离得远远地看着飞转的轮子，唯恐被卷进去碾成肉浆。

她还注意到另一件怪事：厨房里没有灶神。这一家人而且不拜祖先。厨房里没有灶神，她倒不大在乎，但是一个家庭怎么可以没有祖宗牌位？据说屋主人相信一种不拜其他神佛的教。她可不愿意信这个教，因为她喜欢到所有的庙宇去跑跑，高兴拜哪位菩萨就拜哪位。她倒也愿意拜拜屋主人相信的那位"菩萨"。因为上一年夏天她发疟疾时，那个"庙"里的先生曾经给她金鸡纳霜丸，结果把她的病治好了。但是她希望也能向别的菩萨跪下来叩头，求它们消灾赐福。

她说她穷得常常无以为炊，饿肚子是常事。我父亲已经每月给她一点米救济她，但是她的小孙女死了父母，现在靠她过活，因此吃了她一部分粮食。我拿出一张二十元的钞票塞在她手里。她高高兴兴地走了，嘴里咕噜着："从小时候起，我就知道这孩子心肠好，心肠好。"

有一天傍晚，我去祭扫母亲的坟墓，坟前点起一对蜡烛和一束香。没有风，香烟袅袅地升起。我不知不觉地跪倒地上叩了几个头，童年的记忆复活了，一切恍如隔昨。我似乎觉得自己仍然是个小孩子，像儿时一样地向母亲致敬，我希望母亲的魂魄能够

spirit could welcome me with open arms and caress me. I wished I could curl up on her lap and listen to her soothing lullabies. All my thoughts and feelings reverted to childhood days. My mother had died when I was only seven, so I had not much experience in mother love. Perhaps an imaginary mother was even tenderer and sweeter than a real one. A dead mother could not spank you and would not get cross with you when you were naughty.

From the village I walked some three miles through the rice fields to the railway station, on the banks of a placid lake, the reservoir that irrigated thousands of acres of land. It is surrounded on three sides by mountains famous for berries and bamboo shoots. Here I took a train to the bank of the Tsao-ao River. The railway bridge was uncompleted, for the materials ordered from Germany had been held up by the war. Construction of the railroad to Hangchow had also been suspended. A steamship line supplied the missing link. Most travelers took steamships and left the small boats struggling for existence.

I arrived at the Chien-tang River late in the afternoon and crossed it in twenty minutes by a steam ferry. The rowed ferryboats of my high-school days had disappeared.

By sunset I found myself in Hangchow, comfortably settled in a hotel overlooking the West Lake. The sun was sinking behind the thunder peaks, casting red, golden, and purple beams up into the sky. On one side the needle-sharp Pao Su Pagoda stood clear on the mountaintop in the evening light, while directly opposite, in the valley across the lake, the squat Thunder Peak Pagoda was silhouetted against the distant shady blue mountains. Tiny pleasure boats dotted the rippling lake. Fish splashed in the water. Birds flew homeward. Villas and temples perched on the mountainside were gradually enveloped by a thin veil of evening mist, leaving only the streams of smoke from their chimneys standing motionless in the still air. An utter peacefulness stole over me. Despite all modernism, the West Lake retained its enchantment as of old.

But things had changed. My reverie was soon broken by the tapping of the high heels which adorned the short-skirted, bobbed-haired young women of fashion parading the lake boulevard. This new section of the city had been during my school days the seat of the Tartar or Manchu garrison. The Revolution of 1911 had razed it to the ground and upon its ruins a new town had been built, with wide streets and ugly-looking

张着双臂欢迎我，抚慰我。我希望能够爬到她怀里，听她甜美的催眠曲。我的一切思想和情感都回复到童年时代。母亲去世时我才七岁，因此我对母爱的经验并不多，也许想像中的母亲比真实的母亲更温柔、更亲密。至少，死去的母亲不会打你，你顽皮，她也不会发脾气。

从村子里到火车站，大约有三里路，中间是一片稻田。车站建在一个平静的湖泊岸旁，这个湖叫牟山湖，土名西湖，是一个灌溉好几万亩田的蓄水库。湖的三面环山，山上盛产杨梅和竹笋。我步行至车站以后就搭了一列火车到曹娥江边。铁路桥梁还没有完成，因为从德国订的材料因第一次世界大战影响迟迟未能到达，所以靠渡船渡江。通往杭州的铁路工程也因缺乏材料停顿了。从此到杭州的一大段空隙由轮船来衔接。多数旅客都愿意乘轮船，因为橹船太慢，大家不愿乘坐，所以旧式小船的生意非常清淡。

傍晚时到达钱塘江边，再由小火轮渡过钱塘江，只花二十分钟。我中学时代的橹摇的渡船已经不见了。

日落前我到了杭州，住进一家俯瞰西湖的旅馆。太阳正落到雷峰塔背后，天上斜映着一片彩霞。一边是尖削的保俶塔在夕阳余晖中矗立山顶，它的正对面，短矮的雷峰塔衬着葱翠的山色蹲踞在西湖另一边的山坳里。玲珑的游船点缀着粼粼起绉的湖面。鱼儿戏水，倦鸟归巢，暮霭像一层轻纱，慢慢地笼罩了湖滨山麓的丛林别墅。只有缕缕炊烟飘散在夜空。我感到无比的宁静。时代虽然进步了，西湖却妩媚依旧。

但是许多事情已经有了变化。我的冥想不久就被高跟鞋的笃笃声给粉碎了，一群穿着短裙，剪短了头发的摩登少女正踏着细碎的步子在湖滨散步。湖滨路在我中学时代原是旗下营的所在。辛亥革命铲平了旗下营，后来一个新市区终于在这废墟上建立起来，街道宽阔，

buildings in semi-foreign style. In place of medieval barracks, restaurants, theatres, wine-shops, and tea pavilions had sprung up, and an amusement park, all catering to weekend tourists who came by railway from Shanghai. Hangchow had become a tourist center.

Chekiang College, which I had attended years before, was closed and the buildings had been turned into offices for the new governor. The once-palatial yamen of the Imperial governor had burned during the revolution, leaving a vast rectangular space in the heart of the city overgrown with wild plants and grass.

Revolution had come to Hangchow without shedding a drop of blood. The commanders of the new army met and sent a few pieces of light artillery into the streets in the dark of night. Without firing a shot they forced the Imperial governor of the province to surrender. The army then set his yamen on fire as a symbol of the revolution and the city was lit up with its flames. The Manchu garrison entrenched itself in its own walled city but surrendered after negotiations in which it was promised that no one would be molested. Mr. Kwei Han-hsiang, a Manchu leader, accepted the terms on behalf of the garrison. He was, however, seized by his personal enemies and shot, on the false charge that he was plotting a revolt. It was a case of sheer murder. The newly elected governor, Tang Shuo-chien, a famous old litterateur, was indignant over this cowardly act and threatened to resign, but the matter was patched up until he was called to Nanking to take up the portfolio of Minister of Communications under the presidency of Dr. Sun Yat-sen.

Northeast of the modern town which had replaced the Manchu city, rows of shacks, totaling five hundred rooms, had been erected to house the families of the former garrison. Some had already melted away into the vast ocean of China's multitudes and left their houses vacant. In the course of a few years all the remnants of the once-conquering race had vanished into the common stream of life of the once-conquered. The Manchus were gone forever. Pictures of their lives still linger in my memory, but the stories about them have sunk into folklore. It is left to history alone to tell the rise, decline, and fall of the Manchu Dynasty.

The quaint old teahouses at which I used to sip my tea quietly with the lake view filling the windows had disappeared in the face of the diabolic modernization; only one or two lingered to recall the memories of the good old days. This was the kind of time-mellowed teahouse I still loved to frequent. I would go there and read Tang poems over a cup of Hangchow tea. It took one back to the dear old days.

但是两旁的半西式的建筑却并不美观。饭馆、戏院、酒店、茶楼已经取代古老的旗下营而纷纷出现，同时还建了湖滨公园，以便招徕周末从上海趁火车来的游客。杭州已经成为观光的中心了。

我在十多年前读过书的浙江高等学堂已经停办，原址现已改为省长公署的办公厅。从前宫殿式的抚台衙门已在革命期间被焚，在市中心留下一片长满野草闲花的长方形大空地。

革命波及杭州时不曾流半滴血。新军的将领会商之后黑夜中在杭州街头布下几尊轻型火炮，结果未发一枪一弹就逼得抚台投降。新军放了把火焚毁抚台衙门，算是革命的象征，火光照得全城通红。旗下营则据守他们的小城作势抵抗，后来经过谈判，革命军承诺不伤害旗下营的任何人，清兵终于投降。旗人领袖桂翰香代表旗下营接受条件。但桂本人却被他的私人仇敌藉口他阴谋叛乱抓去枪毙了。新当选的都督汤寿潜是位有名的文人，对于这件卑鄙的事非常气愤，闹着要辞职。但是这件事总算没有闹僵，后来汤寿潜被召至南京，在临时大总统孙中山先生之下担任交通部长。

旗下新市区的东北已经建了五百间平房，安置旧日旗兵的家属。有些旗人已经与汉人熔于一炉而离开了他们的安置区。几年之后，全体旗人都失去踪迹，一度养尊处优的统治者已经与过去的被统治者汇为一流了。旗人从此成为历史上的名词，他们的生活情景虽然始终回旋在我的记忆里，但是有关他们的故事已经渐渐成为民间传说。至于清朝的崛起与没落，且让史家去记述罢！

从前的文人雅士喜欢到古色古香的茶馆去，一面静静地品茗，一面凭窗欣赏湖光山色，现在这些茶馆已经为不可抵御的现代文明所取代，只有一两家残留的老茶馆使人发怀古之幽情，这种古趣盎然的茶馆当然还有人去，泡上一杯龙井，披阅唐宋诗词。这样可以使人重新回到快乐的旧日子。

I have said that the city was the center of the silk industry. Some factories had introduced textile machines, but many of the smaller establishments still retained the hand looms. A college of engineering had been established in which practical courses in textiles were given. Graduates who had taken courses in mechanical engineering set up small machine shops in the city, with machines run by electricity. The city now had electric light and a telephone system. Hangchow seemed on the eve of industrialization.

I stayed for about a week, visiting many historical sites to refresh my boyhood memories. As I wandered away from the center of commercial activity I found the old life less affected by modernization. The charm of old days still remained intact in the mountain regions and out-of-the-way villages. The monasteries surrounded by tall trees and bamboo groves stood as calmly as they had centuries ago. The life of the monks had undergone little change; they chanted their Buddhist hymns as before. The villagers raised their tea and mulberry leaves as their forefathers had done. A few imported articles were to be seen here and there, but the quantity was negligible. However, the spearhead of future modernization had already reached them—in the schools, where modern textbooks were in use. The mental attitude of the coming generation was changing, under the influence of modern education, in spite of unchanged ways of living. Seeds of new ideas sown in the minds of the young were bound to sprout in the course of time.

我曾经提到杭州是蚕丝工业的中心。若干工厂已经采用纺织机器，但是许多小规模的工厂仍旧使用手织机。一所工业专科学校已经成立，里面就有纺织的课程。受过化学工程教育的毕业生在城市开办了几家小工厂，装了电动的机器。杭州已经有电灯、电话，它似乎已经到了工业化的前夕了。

　　我大约逗留了一个星期，重游了许多少年时代常去的名胜古迹。离商业中心较远的地方，我发现旧式生活受现代文明的影响也较少。在山区或穷乡僻壤，旧日淳朴的生活依然令人迷恋。参天古木和幽篁修竹所环绕的寺庙仍然像几百年以前一样的清幽安静。和尚们的生活很少变化，仍旧和过去一样诵佛念经。乡下人还是和他们的祖先一样种茶植桑，外国货固然也偶然发现，但是数量微不足道。不过，现代文明的前锋已经到达，学校里已经采用现代课本。在现代教育的影响下，虽然生活方式未曾改变，新生一代的心理却正在转变。播在年轻人心中的新思想的种籽，迟早是会发芽茁长的。

CHAPTER 13   WARLORDS

In my youthful days I noticed that civil ranks came invariably above the military. Imperial officers wore buttons of different colors at the tops of their red-tasseled hats. The red button was highest in rank; next came the pink, then dark blue, brilliant blue, white, and finally golden, the lowest. Often my wondering eyes watched a military pink-button, though higher in rank, bowing before a blue-button civil official. It was explained to me that the Imperial system had chosen to put the military under control of the civil in order to eliminate the evils of military dictatorship in the country. Through centuries of history we had learned that when the country came under the control of warlords it was divided into spheres of influence; the authority of the Imperial Court became a mere shadow and peace and order vanished like a bubble. We learned this lesson from the later Tangs. Thus there was a popular saying that "good iron is not to be beaten into nails, and good men are not to be made into soldiers." We were taught to look down upon soldiers. I remember that a man of questionable character in one of our neighboring villages joined the army, and when he came home on leave we used to avoid him like a plague. It was borne in upon us that soldiers were a bad lot, something to be despised, feared, and detested.

On the other hand, when a country sank into military impotence it lost all power of resistance before the onslaught of powerful invaders; thus it was that the Sungs fell into the hands of the Mongols and the Mings into the hands of the Tartars. So we were between the devil and the deep sea. What should be our choice?

China must be saved—saved from powerful invaders by land on the north and by sea from the east and south. What, then, was to be done? Build up a modern army in which modern weapons of war would be employed and soldiers well trained and imbued with patriotism. How could we look down upon soldiers? They were the defenders of the land, the saviors of China from partition by the Western Powers. Despise them? By no means—we must elevate and honor them, even worship them. Or who would join the army?

Our people began to argue in their minds. As necessity is the mother of invention, we organized a modern army with imported weapons, modern uniforms, and military bands. Once I saw such an army on the march, bugles blowing, drums beating. It was inspiring. I imagined myself grown up and joining them in the march—marching to victory!

拾叁 军阀割据

年轻时我注意到文官总比武官高些。朝廷命官红缨帽的顶子分几种不同的颜色。阶级最高的是红顶子，其次是粉红的，再其次是深蓝的、翠蓝的和白色的，最后是金黄的也就是最低的一级。我常常看到戴粉红顶子的武官向阶级比较低的蓝顶子文官叩头，心里觉得很奇怪。据说历朝皇帝深恐武官擅权跋扈，所以特意让文官控制武官。历史告诉我们，国家一旦受军阀控制，必定要形成割据的局面。晚唐的历史就是最好的教训，俗语说："好铁不打钉，好男不当兵。"因此大家都瞧不起军人。记得邻村有一位品行不端的人去当兵，在他告假返乡时，大家把他看做瘟神似的，都远远地避开他。我们有个牢不可破的观念，认为当兵的都是坏人，可鄙可怕而且可憎。

在另一方面，国家的武力如果一蹶不振，碰到外来侵略就毫无能力抵抗了。宋朝亡于蒙古人，明朝亡于满洲鞑靼，情形就是如此。前临深渊，后是魔鬼，我们究将何去何从？

最要紧的是救中国——北方由陆路来的和东南由海道来的强敌都得应付。那末，怎么办？赶快建立一支装备现代武器的现代化军队吧！士兵必须训练有素，而且精忠报国。我们怎么可以瞧不起军人呢？他们是保卫国土的英雄，是中国的救星，有了他们，中国才可以免受西方列强的分割。鄙视他们，千万不可以——我们必须提高军人的地位，尊敬他们，甚至崇拜他们。不然谁又肯当兵？

大家的心理开始转变了。穷则变，变则通：我们建立了一支现代化的军队，装备外国武器，穿着新式制服，而且还有军乐队。我见过这样的一队现代军队的行军阵容，洋鼓洋号前导，精神饱满，步伐整齐，令人肃然起敬。我看得出神，恍惚自己已经成人长大，

Meanwhile I found my real self standing among the silent crowd and watching, overwhelmed with joy. It was my first glimpse of a modern army. Yes—we must honor the soldiers and the commanding officers. Hereafter only good men should be made into soldiers. We must depend upon them to regain the past glories of China. In the old armies of yesterday the soldiers wore jackets and carried bows and arrows, or in some cases obsolete guns discarded and sold to China by European countries. How different from the modern army of today!

While I was studying at Chekiang College in Hangchow I saw a former student who had just come back from a military academy in Tokyo on a visit to the college. He was in military uniform, spick and span, carrying a sword in its shining sheath. A future great general of the Chinese army—how our hearts rushed out to him!

There were a number of embryo generals of that kind who came back from Japan and were entrusted with the duty of organizing new armies. In the course of a few years army units had been organized and stationed at various strategic centers in the country. China was armed, armed to defend herself.

Then came the Revolution of 1911. The revolutionary armies were perhaps not so well trained as the government armies, but commanders and men were full of patriotism and ready to sacrifice their lives for their country. The new armies of the government went over, one after another, to Dr. Sun Yat-sen. Within a few months the agelong Imperial regime had vanished like a ghost at the least rustle of leaves into the dark night. Waves of enthusiasm spread far and wide over the country. China was reborn with little regret for the past and great hopes for the future. Let the Manchus lament their mistake in forming a new army, and let the people be overjoyed by the splendid actions of these modern-trained generals.

But the hour of triumph passed. The candle flickered out in dark streaks of smoke. The generals of the new army had little pity for the

Manchus and less love for the revolution; they had tasted power and resolved to keep it. As appetite grows with eating, they longed for larger and higher power, and so fought among themselves for it.

Dr. Sun Yat-sen had returned to China in 1912. After negotiations between the revolutionaries and the Peking government the dynasty agreed to abdicate and the Republic was established. Little Pu-yi was

正在行列中迈步前进——向胜利进军，我站在静静围观的群众中，心里喜不自胜。这是我首次看到现代的军队。是的，我们必须尊敬士兵和军官。从此以后，只有好男才配当兵。我们必须依赖他们恢复中国过去的光荣。从前的旧式军队中，士兵穿着马甲，佩着弓箭，或者背着欧洲国家废弃不用卖给中国的旧枪。与今天的现代军队比起来真是差得太远了！

我在杭州浙江高等学堂读书时，一位高等学堂的老学生刚从日本士官学校回来探望师友。他穿着崭新的军服，腰旁佩着长剑，剑鞘闪闪发光。这就是中国军队的未来将领，我们无不怀着钦敬的心情热烈地欢迎他。

许多这样的未来将领正从日本回国，受命组织新军。几年之内新军部队渐次建立，驻在国内各军略要地。中国已经武装起来保卫她自己了。

不久辛亥革命爆发，革命军的训练也许不及政府军那样精良，但是革命的将领和士兵却充满着爱国热情，随时准备为国牺牲。革命号角一响，政府新军相继向孙中山先生投诚。短短几个月之内，统治了中国几百年的满清帝室就像秋风扫落叶般消逝了。全国人民欢欣鼓舞，中国已经获得新生，前途光明灿烂。满清政府训练新军，结果自速灭亡，让他们去自怨自艾吧！让我们为这些受过现代训练的将领的优越表现欢呼！

但是胜利的狂欢不久就成为过去。庆祝的烛光终于化为黑烟而熄灭。新军将领们对满清反目无情，对革命更无所爱。他们已经尝到权势的滋味，绝不肯轻易放弃；而且食髓知味，渴望攫取更大更高的权势，结果你抢我夺，自相残杀起来。

孙中山先生已经在民国元年即一九一二年回国。革命军和满清政府谈判结果。宣统皇帝决定退位，民国接着成立。革命军同意

allowed by agreement to retain residence in the Forbidden City, ancient palace of the emperors of China. A constitution was to be drafted, providing for a President and a National Assembly; meanwhile the Provisional Assembly elected Dr. Sun Yat-sen Provisional President of the Republic.

After a short time he resigned in favor of Yuan Shih-kai, who was later elected President by the National Assembly, more or less through coercion and intrigue. Political power again slipped into the hands of the reactionaries. Yuan was a mandarin of the monarchical regime who had begun the training of a modern army. He had fallen into disfavor with the Imperial Court but had been recalled to Peking when the revolution broke out.

Dr. Sun believed that the most important service he could render China was to build railroads; he was content to be at the head of China's national railways and let Yuan Shih-kai hold the reins of government. But he was soon to be disillusioned. When Yuan came into power he knew very well that his strength lay in the army under his control. The National Assembly he regarded as a mere necessary evil; so long as he controlled the army it could prove at worst no more than a nuisance to him. With strong armies behind him the new head of the state usurped all sorts of powers that did not properly belong to the President. He employed methods of intimidation and resorted to the dastardly means of assassination. Politically, he knew the trick of "divide and rule" and fostered dissension in Dr. Sun's Nationalist, or Kuomintang, camp. He went further and encouraged political parties to multiply, so that the influence of the Nationalist party would be further reduced.

Then he took steps to remove its military power. He first assassinated its political leader, Mr. Sung Chiao-ren, on his way to Peking from Shanghai. Then he removed all the Nationalist military governors of the southern provinces by a stroke of the pen, thus provoking those provinces in order to crush them. Dr. Sun Yat-sen attempted a second revolution, but failed. Yuan Shih-kai had by this time almost the whole country under his military control and took steps to disqualify the Kuomintang members of the National Assembly on account of the "rebellion." With the south crushed his appetite grew; he longed for more power and glory. In 1915, as he was about to proclaim himself Emperor of a new Chinese Empire, the provinces revolted, whereupon he abandoned his monarchical scheme and soon died, broken-hearted.

让小溥仪仍旧住在紫禁城里。革命人士准备草拟宪法，成立参议会，选举总统，不久临时参议会选举孙中山先生为中华民国临时大总统。

中山先生不久辞职，让位给袁世凯。后来新选的国会选举袁世凯为总统，不过，那多少是威胁利诱的结果。于是政权又再度落到反动分子的手里去了。袁世凯原来是清朝的官吏，负责训练新军，他一度失宠于清廷，革命爆发后被召回北京。

孙先生认为他对国家所能提供的贡献，最重要的还是建筑铁路，因此他甘愿主持国有铁道而让袁世凯统治国家。但是孙先生不久就觉醒了。袁世凯上台时，他很清楚他的实力在于他所控制的军队。他把国会看做一个惹人讨厌却又无可避免的东西，不过他想，只要他能够控制军队，国会除了给他一点小麻烦外，绝对奈何他不得。这位国家的新元首在强大的军队支持之下，竟然篡窃了许多并不属于总统的权力。他随时威胁恐吓异己，甚至不惜采取卑鄙的暗杀手段。在政治上，他很懂得"分而治之"的那一套，竭力在中山先生的国民党内部制造摩擦。他更进一步鼓励成立许多小政党，企图削弱国民党的势力。

他接着采取步骤来削除国民党的武力。他首先暗杀国民党的政治领袖宋教仁，接着下令解除南方各省所有国民党将领督军职务，企图激起各省的反抗，然后加以武力扫荡。孙中山先生想发动二次革命而没有成功。这时候袁世凯差不多已经以武力控制全国，于是借口这次"叛变"，预备取消国会中国民党籍议员的资格。南方被他镇压住以后，他的野心愈来愈大，亟欲攫取更大的权力和尊荣。民国四年他正预备自立为皇帝时，各省纷纷通电反对，因此被逼放弃皇帝梦，旋即忧伤而死。

In 1917 Dr. Sun Yat-sen finally entrenched himself in Canton, hoping to form a nucleus of an army in preparation for a new revolution to dethrone the warlords, only to find himself overthrown in 1929 by the warlord of Canton, Chen Chun-ming. In the next year, however, he succeeded in organizing a new Kuomintang government there, in a reinvigorated Nationalist movement to which the Russians gave some assistance after an agreement between himself and an unofficial Russian adviser. But this was only a beginning. After the death of the ambitious and unscrupulous Yuan Shih-kai the country as a whole remained divided among the warring provinces and political turmoil continued for twelve long years until Generalissimo Chiang Kai-shek unified it in 1928, after the triumph of the Nationalist movement.

For sixteen years after the founding of the Republic China was in the grip of warlords. One civil war after another, often supported by foreign interests, devastated the country, bringing innumerable hardships to the people and paving the way for Japanese aggression. The cause of revolution seemed to be doomed. Victorious generals, elated, reached for more and more power. Wounded lions and tigers fell in ignominy and with their tails between their legs limped into the foreign concessions or settlements of Tientsin or Shanghai to lick their wounds and wait for opportunities to come back. When opportunity came they sneaked out, entered the arena again, and caused more suffering to the people.

The soldier, who had been once despised and then honored, was now again despised.

民国六年（一九一七年），孙中山先生在广州建立根据地，希望在那里成立一支军队的核心，发动新革命而推翻军阀，不料在民国十一年（一九二二年）反被广州军阀陈炯明所推翻。不过翌年孙先生终于在广州成立新政府，国民革命运动声势得以重振。但这仅是一个开端。自从野心勃勃而不择手段的袁世凯死了以后，中国一直四分五裂，各省之间内战频仍，政局扰攘达十二年之久，直到民国十七年（一九二八年）蒋总司令北伐成功，国家才重归统一。

　　中华民国成立以后，十六年来中国一直掌握在军阀手里。内战一次接着一次发生。这些内战多半还是外国势力怂恿和支持的。内战的结果，国力损耗，民生凋敝，并且为日本侵略铺了路。革命前途似乎黑暗一片。内战中获胜的军阀趾高气扬，野心愈来愈大，不断争取更大的权力。被击败的军阀则夹起尾巴躲在天津和上海的租界里待机再起，机会一来就重启战衅，使人民又增加一场灾祸。

　　一度被鄙视、后来受尊重的军人，现在又再度被人鄙视了。

CHAPTER 14   INTELLECTUAL AWAKENING

From Hangchow I went to Shanghai, where I entered the Commercial Press—the largest publishing company in China—as one of its editors. Board and lodging were accorded me at the headquarters of the Kiangsu Provincial Education Association, in return for which I served as a member of the executive committee. But I was not yet old enough to be pinned down to a desk and resigned at the end of a year. My financial arrangements with the publishing company were cleared within another year.

Together with friends I began to issue a monthly, *The New Education*, published under the auspices of the National University of Peking and the Kiangsu Education Association. I was editor-in-chief. Six months after its inception the magazine had reached a circulation of ten thousand. Its chief aim was to "develop individuality and attain social progress." Encouragement of liberal ideas as against purely traditional thought was what the monthly stood for.

These were the times immediately after the European war when liberalism and democracy were in vogue all over the world and Wilsonian ideals had caught the imagination of the thinking minds of China. Chinese youth was imbued with the new ideas that came in torrents from postwar Europe and America. Newspapers and magazines devoted large sections to international news and developments. China was beginning to think with the world.

La Jeunesse, a radical magazine launched by Chen Tu-hsiu some years before and then taken up by a group of professors in the University of Peking, was advocating democracy and modern science for the rejuvenation of China. In introducing new elements of thought it was quite natural that they should fiercely attack the old beliefs and traditions. Some contributors even went so far as to cry "Down with the Confucian shops!" While all this evoked strong antagonism from the reading public, the youth of the country caught the spirit of the intellectual revolt.

In 1918 Dr. Sun Yat-sen came to reside in Shanghai. As we have seen, the government of the young Republic was having its ups and downs and had come partially under the sway of independent warlords. The Kuomintang, or Nationalist, party of Dr. Sun was strongest in the south and here, in 1917, a government was set up, separate from the Peking regime, to maintain the principles for which the revolutionaries had labored and re-established them throughout the country. Now, however, the veteran leader left his southern government in Canton under the

拾肆 知识分子的觉醒

我从杭州到上海以后就进当时最大的书局商务印书馆当编辑，同时兼了江苏省教育会的一名理事，膳宿就由教育会供给。但是年轻人干不惯磨桌子的生活，一年之后我就辞职了。与商务印书馆之间的银钱往来也在翌年清结。

我与几位朋友在国立北京大学和江苏省教育会赞助下开始发行《新教育》月刊，由我任主编。杂志创办后六个月就销到一万份。它的主要目标是"养成健全之个人，创造进化的社会"。

那时正是欧战后不久，自由与民主正风靡全世界，威尔逊主义已引起中国有识之士的注意。中国青年正浸淫于战后由欧美涌至的新思想。报纸与杂志均以巨大篇幅报导国际新闻和近代发展。中国已经开始追上世界的新思潮了。

《新青年》正在鼓吹德先生与赛先生（即民主与科学），以求中国新生。这本思想激进的杂志原为几年前陈独秀所创办，后来由北京大学的一群教授共同编辑。《新青年》在介绍新思想时，自然而然对旧信仰和旧传统展开激烈的攻击。有些投稿人甚至高喊"打倒孔家店"！这些激烈的言论固然招致一般读者的强烈反感，但是全国青年却已普遍沾染知识革命的情绪。

孙中山先生于民国七年移居上海。我们前面已经谈过新诞生的民国的坎坷命运，而且一部分正受着割据各省的军阀统治。中山先生的国民党，最强大的据点是南方和上海。民国六年（一九一七年），国民党成立新政府对抗北京政席，以求维护革命人士所致力的原则，并进而推广于全国。当时广州的南方政府是由总裁控制的。

control of a Directorate. The political views of its members did not go beyond their noses, a brevity of outlook to which Dr. Sun could not subscribe. So he settled down in Shanghai to work on his plan for the industrial development of China.

His vision carried him far beyond the political squabbles of the time and his plan, if successfully carried into effect, was one which would relieve the poverty of the people, bring prosperity to the country, and put China on the level of modern industrialized nations of the world. According to Dr. Sun, China's industrial reconstruction fell into four categories: clothing, food, shelter, and transportation, All are necessary for the livelihood of the people and with these elements in view he planned the industrial development of the country.

He worked out a system of railroads and highways to cover all important commercial and military routes in the vast territory of China. He planned ports and harbors through which China's future commerce could flow abundantly. He outlined a project for river conservation, irrigation, and reclamation which would feed millions more in the country. He worked out a scheme for the development of natural resources and for the building up of both heavy and light industries. Seeing China far on the road of deforestation, he made plans to reforest great areas of central and north China.

He laid down two principles or categories under which industry was to be developed: (1) that which could be maintained as private enterprise was to be under private ownership, while (2) that which was beyond the capacities of individual citizens to undertake, or tended to create monopoly, was to be under state ownership. The government was to encourage private enterprise and to protect it by law. Obnoxious taxes must be abolished, the currency system must be improved and unified. Official interference and obstacles must be removed and communications developed to insure an easy flow of trade.

Railroads and highways, river conservation, irrigation, and reclamation, ports and harbors and the like, were to come under state control. The government was also to develop coal and iron resources in Shansi, and establish iron and steel works on a large scale. Foreign capital was to be welcomed and foreign experts employed.

Dr. Sun Yat-sen was the first Chinese statesman to have modern scientific training. His knowledge of scientific data and his mathematical accuracy were amazing. In planning China's industrial development he himself drew up maps and charts and collected his data and checked them carefully. He was familiar with such details as the depths and

若干参加分子的政治见解非常肤浅，孙先生无法同意，乃离粤北上定居沪渎，从事中国实业计划的研究。

他的目光远超乎当时的政治纷争之外，他的实业计划如果顺利实现，可以解除人民贫困，促使国家富强，并使中国跻于现代工业化国家之林。根据中山先生的计划，中国的工业建设分为食衣住行四大类。这些都是人民生活所必需的，孙先生就根据这些因素计划中国的工业建设。

他设计了贯串中国广大领土内所有重要商业路线和军运路线的铁路网和公路网；他定下发展中国商埠和海港计划；他也定下疏浚河流、水利建设、荒地开垦等的计划大纲。他又设计了发展天然资源和建设轻重工业的蓝图。他鉴于中国森林砍伐过度，又定下在华中华北造林的计划。

他对工业发展规定了两个原则：（一）凡是可以由私人经营的就归私人经营；（二）私人能力所不及或可能造成垄断的则归国家经营。政府有责鼓励私人企业，并以法律保护之。苛捐杂税必须废除，币制必须改善并予统一。官方干涉和障碍必须清除，交通必须发展以利商品的流通。

铁道、公路、疏浚河流、水利、垦荒、商埠、海港等都规定由国家主持。政府并须在山西省建立大规模的煤铁工厂。欢迎外国资本，并将雇用外国专家。

孙中山先生是中国第一位有过现代科学训练的政治家。他的科学知识和精确的计算实在惊人。为了计划中国的工业发展，他亲自绘制地图和表格，并收集资料，详加核对。实业计划中所包括的

gradations of the riverbeds and harbors which came under his plan. Once I gave him a map of the Huai-ho Conservancy; he at once spread it on the floor and began to study it seriously. Later it was seen hanging on the walls of his study.

After a careful investigation of the various phases of industrial reconstruction and how they might be dealt with, he wrote it all out in English. Madame Sun Yat-sen did all his typing, while David Yui and I were entrusted to go over the manuscripts carefully. Data were checked over and suggestions gladly considered. Any project that Dr. Sun worked on, political, philosophical, scientific, or whatever, was carried out with great enthusiasm. His broad-mindedness echoed every suggestion or criticism that was offered him.

Because in his views and plans he was ahead of his time he was often exasperated at the shortsightedness of his contemporaries, who frequently dismissed his projects with the proverbial saying, "It is easy to know but difficult to do." From the beginning of his revolutionary movement some forty years earlier he had met with the same stubborn obstacle. So he wrote an essay on "Psychological Reconstruction for China" in which he advanced the theory that it is difficult to know but easy to do. Here he brought out a significant difference between Chinese and Western thought. The practical-mindedness of his own people often unduly emphasized the difficulties—imaginary or real—that lay in the way of practice, at the cost of neglecting the principles underlying the practice. A mind used to handling abstractions and generalizations and familiar with the process of seeking out the basic principles involved in any problem would find it easy to understand what Dr. Sun Yat-sen had in view. For minds, on the other hand, habitually intent on short-range practical results and impatient of deeper effort it was difficult to appreciate what he stood for. In China, during the declining days of the Imperial regime, men of strong will and determination to carry out reforms were not lacking, but those who perceived underlying causes and could lay plans which would strike at the root of things were rare. Dr. Sun, who possessed a clear understanding of the development of Western civilization as well as vision for the future development of China, could not but appreciate the importance of the kind of knowledge which implies foresight, or seeing beyond immediate needs, and a clear understanding of problems.

河床和港湾的深度和层次等细节他无不了如指掌。有一次我给他一张导淮委员会的淮河水利图，他马上把它在地板上展开，非常认真地加以研究。后来我发现这幅水利图在他书房的壁上挂着。

在他仔细研究工业建设的有关问题和解决办法以后，他就用英文写下来。打字工作全部归孙夫人负责，校阅原稿的工作则由余日章和我负责。一切资料数字都详予核对，如果有什么建议，孙先生无不乐予考虑。凡是孙先生所计划的工作，无论是政治的、哲学的、科学的或其他，他都以极大的热忱去进行。他虚怀若谷，对于任何建议和批评都乐于接受。

因为他的眼光和计划超越了他的时代，许多与他同时代的人常常觉得他的计划不切实际，常常引用"知之非艰，行之唯艰"的传统观念来答复他。他对这些人的短视常常感到困扰。当他在四十年前倡导革命运动时，他就曾遭遇到同样的障碍。后来他写了一篇叫《心理建设》的文章，提倡知难行易的学说。中西思想重点不同的地方其中之一就是中国人重应用，而西洋人重理知。中国人重实际，所以常常过分强调实践过程中的困难，有时是实在的困难，有时只是想像的，以致忽视实际问题背后的原理原则。凡是经常接触抽象原则和理论的人，或者熟悉如何由问题中找出基本原则的人，都不难了解中山先生的立论。在另一方面，凡是惯常注重近功实利而不耐深思熟虑的人，可就不容易了解中山先生的主张了。在清室式微的日子里，中国并不缺乏锐意改革的人，但是真能洞烛病根，且能策定治本计划的人却很少。孙先生深知西方文化的发展过程，同时对中国的发展前途具有远大的眼光，因此他深感超越近功近利的原理原则的重要，他知道只有高瞻远瞩的知识才能彻底了解问题的本质。

Once knowledge of this fundamental sort is secured there is no inherent difficulty in carrying it into effect. The real difficulties lie in discovering it. Indeed, even lacking essential knowledge, if one is willing to follow the direction of those who know, as masons and carpenters follow the architect, he may have no difficulty in executing a complex plan. Thus it is very plain in the field of medicine that to diagnose a case is often more difficult than to apply the cure. A medical student knows well that he must have a grasp of biological sciences such as physiology and anatomy before he is in a position to study medical science, and he has had to learn even more general science, such as physics and chemistry, before studying biological sciences. And each science is the result of centuries of research by men who have loved knowledge. Therefore it is very clear that the process of learning medical science is more laborious than the practice of medicine.

Dr. Sun's practical-minded contemporaries wanted to get things done without taking much interest in studying the underlying causes of conditions in China in the light of knowledge gained from history, sociology, psychology, science, or the like; or making plans for the country accordingly. They branded his plans as visionary and impractical. Unaware of the problems which lay beyond their "practical" mental horizon, they did not realize that their own difficulties usually arose from lack of knowledge, or an insufficient or superficial knowledge of problems—certainly, in any case, not alone from lack of practical ability. What they thought they knew was often limited to immediate personal experience or empirical reasoning. Such knowledge is not only easy to obtain but dangerous as a basis for practice.

To the Western mind these are mere philosophical squabbles of theory and practice, or knowledge and conduct—and what have they to do with revolution and reconstruction in China? Yet Dr. Sun Yat-sen was very serious about it, considering psychological reconstruction the first step to successful reconstruction in other realms, whether political, industrial, or social. "Overpractical becomes impracticable," Professor Dewey said to him. "No one in the West would think that 'to know' is an easy matter."

Amid the revolutionary atmosphere of the intellectual world and my own inspiring contact with Dr. Sun, *The New Education* stood

只要我们把握这种基本的知识，实践起来就不会有不可解除的困难了。真正的困难在于发见基本的道理。事实上，不但真知灼见的事情，必能便利地推行，而在许多地方，即使所知不深，亦能推行无阻。例如水泥匠和木匠，只要他们照着建筑师的吩咐去做，即使他们不懂得建筑学，也照样能执行复杂的建筑蓝图。医药方面的情况更明显，诊断常常比用药困难，医科学生知道得很清楚，在研究医学之前，他必须对生理学和解剖学先有相当的了解，而在研究生理学和解剖学之前则又得先研究物理与化学等普通科学。每一种科学都是许多为学问而学问的人们经过几百年继续不断研究所积聚的结果。由此可见医学的基础知识之获得比行医远为艰难。

与孙先生同时代的人只求近功，不肯研究中国实际问题的症结所在，希望不必根据历史、社会学、心理学、科学等所得的知识，就把事情办好，更不愿根据科学知识来订定国家的建设计划。因此他们诬蔑孙先生的计划是不切实际的空中楼阁。他们的"现实的"眼光根本看不到远大的问题，更不知道他们自己的缺点就是无知和浅见，缺乏实际能力倒在其次。以实在而论，他们自己认为知道的东西，实只限于浅薄的个人经验或不过根据一种常识的推断。这样的知识虽然容易获得，但以此为实践基础反常常会遭受最后的失败。

在西洋人看起来，这些或许只是理论与实践，或者知识与行为的哲学论争，似乎与中国的革命和建设不发生关系。但是中山先生却把它看得很严重，认为心理建设是其他建设的基础，不论是政治建设、实业建设或社会建设。有一天我和罗志希同杜威先生谒见孙先生谈到知难行易问题，杜威教授对中山先生说："过重实用，则反不切实用。没有人在西方相信'知'是一件容易的事。"

《新教育》月刊，一方面受到思想界革命风气的影响，一方面

pedagogically for initiative, the needs of children, and much that John Dewey stands for in his *Democracy and Education*. As regarded Chinese principles of education, it stood for Mencius' ideas on human nature: that it is good. Hence education means a proper development of what there is in the child. As a matter of fact, in its main current Chinese education had followed since Confucius the principle that human nature is all-good. The trouble was that as the centuries accumulated, what is good in human nature came to mean certain moral precepts shrouded in age-worn tradition. Thus while in theory it was very modern, in practice it might lead miles away from original principles. "Development of nature" may in fact come to mean mere conformity to traditional morals, and this is what happened in China.

With the introduction into Chinese thought of Rousseau, Pestalozzi, Froebel, and later Dewey, the Mencian principles came into better perspective and shed a more living light. Children of China were to be set free of hard and fast rules of conduct and traditional moral ideas incongruous to modern society. Thus children must be led to think for themselves and helped to solve their own problems in accordance with their needs and not those of grownups, They should be led to an interest in nature and in their environment. In accordance with the principles of child psychology, a child must be treated as such; he is not a little man and must not be stuffed with knowledge only, much less with books. Education should help a child to grow—mentally, physically, and socially.

Such were the lines of thought that guided the policies of *The New Education*. As the reader will easily see, it fell in line with the current revolutionary thought of the country. The intellectual ties between *The New Education*, and the professors and students of Peking University, the whirlpool of intellectual revolt, drew me the next year to that much-troubled institution as professor of education and Acting Chancellor.

因为我个人受到中山先生的启示，所以在教学法上主张自发自动，强调儿童的需要，拥护杜威教授在他的《民主与教育》中所提出的主张。在中国的教育原理方面，《新教育》拥护孟子的性善主张，因此认为教育就是使儿童的本性得到正常的发展。事实上孔子以后，中国教育的主流一直都遵循着性善的原则。不过年代一久，所谓人性中的"善"就慢慢地变为受古代传统所规范的某些道德教条了。因此我们的主张在理论上似很新鲜，实践起来却可能离本来的原则很远很远。所谓"发展本性"在事实上可能变为只是遵守传统教条，中国发生的实际情形正是如此。

自从卢梭、裴斯塔洛齐、福禄培，以及后来的杜威等人的学说被介绍至中国思想界以后，大家对孟子学说开始有了比较清晰的认识，中国儿童应该从不合现代需要的刻板的行为规律中解放出来。我们应该诱导儿童自行思想，协助他们根据他们本身的需要，而不是根据大人的需要，来解决他们自己的问题。我们应该启发儿童对自然环境的兴趣。根据儿童心理学的原则，儿童只能看做儿童；他不是一个小大人，不能单拿知识来填，更不应拿书本来填，教育应该帮助儿童在心智、身体和团体活动各方面成长。

这些就是指导《新教育》的思想原则。读者不难觉察，这与当时国内的革命思想是恰好符合的。《新教育》月刊与北京大学师生间知识上的密切关系，终于使我在第二年跑进这个知识革命的大漩涡，担任了教育学教授，并于校长蔡先生请假时代理校长。

CHAPTER 15   PEKING UNIVERSITY AND THE STUDENT REVOLT

If you throw a stone into a body of still water, rings of waves begin to rise and travel farther and farther, ever widening and extending away from the center. In Peking, capital of China during five dynasties and more than ten centuries—the seat of conservatism where the Empress Dowager ruled the country from her dragon throne—stood the oldest modern institution of learning in the country, known as the National University of Peking. It was the only landmark left by Emperor Kwang-hsü's short-lived reforms of 1898. The brief tide of reform had ebbed and vanished into history; only a few scattered shells remained, witness to the vicissitudes of fortune in that placid ancient capital. But the university, in which were clustered the living shells that contained pearls, was destined to make valuable contributions to culture and thought within the short span of one generation.

The man who threw the stone of intellectual revolt into that placid water was Dr. Tsai Yuan-pei, who in 1916 became Chancellor of the university. Dr. Tsai was an eminent scholar of China's ancient culture, but imbued with the spirit of Western scholarship and especially the spirit of free inquiry which prevailed in the Hellenic world. His belief in "knowledge for knowledge' sake," in contrast to the "learning for its practical use" of Chinese thought, had its foundation in a thorough knowledge of ancient Greek culture. His views on knowledge were essentially the same as those of Dr. Sun, but the latter had acquired his outlook from the natural sciences, Dr. Tsai his from a study of Greek philosophy.

This renowned scholar preferred the appreciation of beauty to belief in religion. Here we find an interesting blending of Greek and Chinese culture. The traditional love of nature of the Chinese scholar and the Greek sense of beauty working together in Dr. Tsai's mind resulted in a love for Western sculpture and Chinese carvings; Chinese landscape painting and Western portraits; both Chinese and Western architecture, and Chinese and Western music. His views on religion were essentially

Chinese: religion is but part of morality. He wanted to elevate the moral sense of youth to a higher level by love of beauty. It was an ancient Chinese belief that there is no greater moral force than that of music. Good morals had their foundation in well-balanced emotions, which could only be brought about by the fine arts and music or poetry, which is closely allied to music.

拾伍 北京大学和学生运动

如果你丢一块石子在一池止水的中央，一圈又一圈的微波就会从中荡漾开来，而且愈漾愈远，愈漾愈大。北京曾为五朝京城，历时一千余年，因此成为保守势力的中心，慈禧太后就在这里的龙座上统治着全中国。光绪皇帝在一八九八年变法维新，结果有如昙花一现，所留下的唯一痕迹只是国立北京大学，当时称为京师大学堂或直呼为大学堂，维新运动短暂的潮水已经消退而成为历史陈迹，只留下一些贝壳，星散在这恬静的古都里，供人凭吊。但是在北京大学里，却结集着好些蕴蓄珍珠的活贝；由于命运之神的摆布，北京大学终于在短短三十年历史之内对中国文化与思想提供了重大的贡献。

在静水中投下知识革命之石的是蔡子民先生（元培）。蔡先生在一九一六年（民国五年）出任北京大学校长，他是中国文化所孕育出来的著名学者，但是充满了西洋学人的精神，尤其是古希腊文化的自由研究精神。他的"为学问而学问"的信仰，植根于对古希腊文化的透彻了解，这种信仰与中国"学以致用"的思想适成强烈的对照。蔡先生对学问的看法，基本上是与中山先生的看法一致的，不过孙先生的见解来自自然科学，蔡先生的见解则导源于希腊哲学。

这位著名的学者认为美的欣赏比宗教信仰更重要。这是希腊文化交融的一个耐人寻味的实例。蔡先生的思想中融合着中国学者对自然的传统爱好和希腊人对美的敏感，结果产生对西洋雕塑和中国雕刻的爱好；他喜爱中国的山水画，也喜爱西洋油画；对中西建筑和中西音乐都一样喜欢。他对宗教的看法基本上是中国人的传统见解；认为宗教不过是道德的一部分。他希望以爱美的习惯来提高青年的道德观念。这也就是古语所谓"移风易俗莫大于乐"的传统信念。高尚的道德基于七情调和，要做到七情调和则必须透过艺术和与音乐有密切关系的诗歌。

Dr. Tsai had great faith in natural science. He not only trusted it to yield inventions, engineering, and other benefits, but believed it would foster the mental habits of methodical thinking and research which led to the discovery of general truths, the foundation of all true knowledge.

In his younger days his brilliance was less veiled in modesty. When he was principal of the Sino-Occidental School at Shaoshing which I attended in my boyhood, one evening at a banquet, after a few cups of Shaoshing wine, he stood up and announced at the top of his voice that the reforms of Kang Yu-wei and Liang Chi-chao were too superficial, since they retained the Manchu court to lead them. "I, Tsai Yuan-pei, will not do that. Unless you overthrow the Manchus no reforms will be possible!" He shouted it out, raising his right arm over his head.

Dr. Tsai in his early years wrote essays full of brilliant and stimulating ideas contrary to the common practice of writing in the days of civil examinations. My uncle King told me of a strange essay of his which began, "In sex, food, and drinking human desires lie." He handed in his paper to the Imperial examiners after the time limit. The night was getting on to the small hours and the eyes of the examiners were heavy with sleep. His paper was accepted and he passed the examination for the Second Degree—Chu-jen, or the Promoted Scholar. In the following years he achieved the Third or highest degree—Chin-shih, or Advanced Scholar—when still under thirty. He subsequently entered Hanlin Academy, composed of the highest ranking scholars, which has since ceased to exist.

In his later years he was the personification of what is best in a Chinese scholar, with a broad mind open to Western ideas. His eyes, looking over his spectacles, were alert but calm; his speech easy, clear, fluent, and sincere, though often drowned in a monotone. He never let harsh words cross his thin lips, but when he was indignant his utterance was quick, weighty, and concise—as clearly to the point as a judge rendering judgment or a dagger popping out from under soft velvet cotton.

He was of a light build but his movements were steady. His artistic fingers would run deftly through the pages as he read, as if he read by paragraphs, even by pages, his quick sight grasping essential points and his retentive memory keeping knowledge in store. His love of nature and the arts made his emotions tranquil, thoughts lofty, tastes refined, manners sincere and modest, and ways of living simple and retired. His broad-mindedness was as responsive to every shade of opinion, criticism, or suggestion "as a hollow in the mountains that echoes with every vibration of sound."

蔡先生崇信自然科学。他不但相信科学可以产生发明、机器，以及其他实益，他并且相信科学可以培养有系统的思想和研究的心理习惯，有了系统的思想和研究，才有定理定则的发现，定理定则则是一切真知灼见的基础。

蔡先生年轻时锋芒很露。他在绍兴中西学堂当校长时，有一天晚上参加一个宴会，酒过三巡之后，他推杯而起，高声批评康有为、梁启超维新运动的不彻底，因为他们主张保存满清皇室来领导维新。说到激烈时，他高举右臂大喊道："我蔡元培可不这样。除非你推翻满清，否则任何改革都不可能！"

蔡先生在早年写过许多才华横溢、见解精辟的文章，与当时四平八稳、言之无物的科举八股适成强烈的对照。有一位浙江省老举人曾经告诉我，蔡元培写过一篇怪文，一开头就引用《礼记》里的"饮食男女，人之大欲存焉"一句。缴卷时间到时，他就把这篇文章缴给考官。蔡先生就在这场乡试里中了举人。后来他又考取进士，当时他不过三十岁左右，以后就成为翰林。

蔡先生晚年表现了中国文人的一切优点，同时虚怀若谷，乐于接受西洋观念。他那从眼镜上面望出来的两只眼睛，机警而沉着；他的语调虽然平板，但是从容、清晰、流利而恳挚。他从来不疾言厉色对人，但是在气愤时，他的话也会变得非常快捷、严厉、扼要——像法官宣判一样的简单明了，也像绒布下面冒出来的匕首那样的尖锐。

他的身材矮小，但是行动沉稳。他读书时，伸出纤细的手指迅速地翻着书页，似乎是一目十行地读，而且有过目不忘之称。他对自然和艺术的爱好使他的心境平静，思想崇高，趣味雅洁，态度恳切而平和，生活朴素而谦抑。他虚怀若谷，对于任何意见、批评或建议都欣然接纳。

In such a scholar the government of Li Yuan-hung, then President of the Republic, found a chancellor for the university. Under his administration the institution underwent a radical change. Science was put on an equal footing with literature, which had reigned in the realm of knowledge in China from time immemorial. History, philosophy, and the classics were studied in the light of modern scientific method. The spirit of knowledge for its own sake was encouraged. Scholars of old conservative schools, new schools, and radical schools were all given an equal chance. Old literati with queues hanging down their backs who still retained faith in a monarchical regime sat shoulder to shoulder with men of radical thought, discussing problems, joking and laughing at the same dinner table. Free inquiry into problems, of knowledge, culture, family, social relations, and political systems was found in the classrooms, seminars, and social gatherings.

It was the intellectual life of ancient China of the pre-Ching period or ancient Greece of the times of Socrates and Aristotle re-enacted. Dr. Tsai was the old, wise Socrates of China, and would have suffered the same fate had he not had sympathizers on a nationwide scale, especially among the Kuomintang members who had a strong hold in Canton. Yet by conservative Chinese and foreigners alike the university was accused of advocating "A-three-ism"—no religion, no government, and no family— just as Socrates was accused by the ancient Greeks of corrupting the souls of young men. No argument could dispel these unfounded suspicions. History alone would disprove them, as it has absolved Socrates.

I have said that Dr. Tsai advocated esthetics as a substitute for religion, and free inquiry as a means of approach to truths. Mr. Chen Tu-hsiu, Dean of the College of Literature, advocated science and democracy as the twin weapons to modernize China. Free inquiry led to freedom of thought. Science sapped the old beliefs. Democracy meant the assertion of popular rights. Meanwhile Dr. Hu Shih, professor of philosophy, worked for a literary revolution by which the language in common use by the people was to replace the classical language as a medium of thought and expression. The colloquial, or common written language, is nearer to the Chinese spoken language and therefore easier to learn, to write, and to understand. It is a better and easier medium for the expression of thought. Its use was to popularize knowledge, hitherto a monopoly of classical scholars. The movement developed a host of young writers

　　当时的总统黎元洪选派了这位杰出的学者出任北大校长。北大在蔡校长主持之下，开始一连串的重大改革。自古以来，中国的知识领域一直是由文学独霸的，现在，北京大学却使科学与文学分庭抗礼了。历史、哲学和四书五经也要根据现代的科学方法来研究。为学问而学问的精神蓬勃一时。保守派、维新派和激进派都同样有机会争一日之短长。背后拖着长辫、心里眷恋帝制的老先生与思想激进的新人物并坐讨论，同席笑谑。教室里，座谈会上，社交场合里，到处讨论着知识、文化、家庭、社会关系和政治制度等等问题。

　　这情形很像中国先秦时代，或者古希腊苏格拉底和亚里士多德时代的重演。蔡先生就是中国的老哲人苏格拉底，同时，如果不是全国到处有同情他的人，蔡先生也很可能遭遇苏格拉底同样的命运。在南方建有坚强根据地的国民党党员中，同情蔡先生的人尤其多。但是中国的和外国的保守人士却一直指责北京大学鼓吹"三无主义"——无宗教、无政府、无家庭——与苏格拉底被古希腊人指责戕害青年心灵的情形如出一辙。争辩不足以消除这些毫无根据的猜疑，只有历史才能证明它们的虚妄。历史不是已经证明了苏格拉底的清白无罪吗？

　　我已经提到蔡先生提倡美学以替代宗教，提倡自由研究以追求真理。北大文学院院长陈仲甫（独秀）则提倡赛先生和德先生，认为那是使中国现代化的两种武器。自由研究导致思想自由；科学破坏了旧信仰，民主则确立了民权的主张。同时，哲学教授胡适之（适）那时正在进行文学革命，主张以白话文代替文言作表情达意的工具。白话比较接近中国的口语，因此比较易学，易懂。它是表达思想的比较良好也比较容易的工具。在过去知识原是士大夫阶级的专利品，推行白话的目的就是普及知识。白话运动

throughout the country. After a few years the Ministry of Education made compulsory the use of the vulgate as a medium of instruction in all elementary schools.

The university was an oasis in the intellectual desert of Peking. But the seeds of intellectual revolt grew in that small green spot with remarkable rapidity. Within three years the whole institution was filled with it.

In that vigorous atmosphere of intellectual activity a mental and moral unrest developed among the students. I have related earlier how, under the influence of French eighteenth-century political idealism with its catchwords of Liberty, Equality, and Fraternity, and as a revolt against established authority which the youth of the nation believed responsible for retarding China's progress and thus inviting the encroachment of foreign Powers, students had gone on strike against their school authorities upon the slightest pretext. This first happened in Shanghai in 1902. The first student revolt had spent itself in the course of a few years and degenerated into strikes against the school cooks. In the end the authorities outwitted the students by handing the management of the kitchens over to the student body. Isolated cases of strikes still persisted for some years. In one instance this ended in tragedy when a dozen students in the provincial high school at Hangchow died of arsenic poisoning which the cooks put in their rice as a revenge. I went to the school after the outrage and found a large number of youths moaning in their beds, while a dozen caskets stood in the open-air gymnasium waiting for relatives to take them for burial.

While the spirit of revolt in the form of school strikes was gradually spending itself, its force turned inward into revolutionary ideas which gained much wider ground outside the schools in the form of a political revolution, resulting ultimately in the downfall of the Manchus in 1911.

The second student revolt burst out suddenly in Peking on May 4, 1919, the eighth year of the Republic. What happened was this. From the peace conference in Paris news reached China that Tsingtao in the Shantung Peninsula, a German-leased port taken from German hands during the war by the Japanese, had been awarded to Japan by the victorious Powers. As China had declared war against Germany, the leased territory should in all justice have been returned to China.

　　推行结果，全国各地产生了无数的青年作家。几年之后，教育部并下令全国小学校一律采用白话为教学工具。

　　北大是北京知识沙漠上的绿洲。知识革命的种籽在这块小小的绿洲上很快地就发育滋长。三年之中，知识革命的风气已经遍布整个北京大学。

　　这里让我们追述一些往事。一个运动的发生，绝不是偶然的，必有其前因与后果。在知识活动的蓬勃气氛下，一种思想上和道德上的不安迅即在学生之中发展开来。我曾经谈过学生如何因细故而闹学潮的情形，那主要是受了十八世纪以自由、平等、博爱为口号的法国政治思想的影响，同时青年们认为中国的迟迟没有进步，并且因而招致外国侵略应由清廷负其咎，因此掀起学潮表示反抗。

　　第一次学潮于一九〇二年发生于上海南洋公学，即所谓罢学风潮。我在前篇已经讲过。几年之后，这种学生反抗运动终至变质而流为对付学校厨子的"饭厅风潮"。最后学校当局想出"请君入瓮"的办法，把伙食交由学生自己办理。不过零星的风潮仍旧持续了十五六年之久。有一次"饭厅风潮"甚至导致惨剧。杭州的一所中学，学生与厨子发生纠纷，厨子愤而在饭里下了毒药，结果十多位学生中毒而死。我在惨案发生后去过这所中学，发现许多学生正在卧床呻吟，另有十多具棺木停放在操场上，等待死者家属前来认领葬殓。

　　表现于学潮的反抗情绪固然渐成过去，反抗力量却转移到革命思想上的发展，而且在学校之外获得广大的支持，终至发为政治革命而于一九一一年推翻满清。

　　第二度的学生反抗运动突然在一九一九年（民国八年）五月四日在北京爆发。此即所谓五四运动。事情经过是这样的：消息从巴黎和会传到中国，说欧战中的战胜国已经决定把山东半岛上的青岛送给日本。青岛原是由中国租借给德国的海港，欧战期间，日本从德国手中夺取青岛。中国已经对德宣战，战后这块租地自然

The whole nation was indignant over the news. Students in Peking, under the leadership of the National University group, demonstrated against the signing of the Versailles Treaty. Three thousand students held mass meetings and paraded in the streets demonstrating against acceptance of the terms, shouting "Return Tsingtao to China!" "Boycott Japanese goods!" "Down with the traitors!" Banners streamed in the air bearing the same slogans.

The Peking government, despite the efforts of Dr. Sun Yat-sen's Kuomintang or Nationalist party in Canton and its adherents elsewhere, was still under the thumb of military men and ruled China with a mere semblance of the democracy and parliamentary procedure which the revolution had labored so earnestly to establish. Among its influential high officials were three members of a notoriously pro-Japanese group. Their sympathies were well known. These men—Tsao Ru-lin, Minister of Communication; Chang Chung-hsiang, Chinese Minister of Tokyo; and Lu Chung-yu, another minister—now became the targets of student wrath. The crowd streamed to the residence of Tsao, where secret meetings were supposed to have been going on; they broke in, and combed the house for the three "traitors." Tsao and Lu escaped by the back door; Chang was caught by the mob and badly beaten. Leaving him for dead, the students dispersed, in their retreat smashing everything in sight and setting the place on fire.

Meanwhile, the armed police and gendarmery had thrown a cordon around the house. They arrested some sixty students and sent them to headquarters. The rest—about a thousand strong—followed after, each claiming individually to have been responsible for the outbreak and asking to be arrested. Finally all were put under heavy military guard in the compounds of the Law College of the university.

News concerning the demonstration was strictly censored. Some students outwitted the government, however, by sending a cable through a foreign agency in one of the foreign concessions of Tientsin, and this cable was the sole source of the news that appeared in Shanghai papers on the morning of the fifth.

I was at breakfast on May 5 when the newspapers reached me. On their front pages appeared in bold letters a news item something as follows:

毫无疑问地应该归还中国。消息传来，举国骚然。北京学生在一群北大学生领导下举行示威，反对签订凡尔赛和约。三千学生举行群众大会，并在街头游行示威，反对接受丧权辱国的条件，高喊"还我青岛！"、"抵制日货！"、"打倒卖国贼！"写着同样的标语的旗帜满街飘扬。

当时的北京政府仍旧在军人的掌握之下，仅有民主政体和议会政治的外表，在广州的中山先生的国民党以及其余各地的拥护者，虽然努力设法维护辛亥革命所艰辛缔造的民主政制，却未著实效。北京政府的要员中有三位敢犯众怒的亲日分子。他们的政治立场是尽人皆知的。这三位亲日分子——交通总长曹汝霖，驻日公使陆宗舆，和另一位要员章宗祥[1]——结果就成为学生愤恨的对象，群众蜂拥到曹宅，因为传说那里正在举行秘密会议。学生破门而入，满屋子搜索这三位"卖国贼"。曹汝霖和陆宗舆从后门溜走了；章宗祥则被群众抓到打伤。学生们以为已经把他打死了，于是一哄而散，离去前把所有的东西砸得稀烂，并且在屋子里放了一把火。

这时武装警察和宪兵已经赶到，把屋子围得水泄不通。他们逮捕了近六十位学生带往司令部，其余的一千多名学生跟在后面不肯散，各人自承应对这次事件负责，要求入狱。结果全体被关到北京大学第三院（法学院），外面由宪警严密驻守。

有关这次游行示威的消息，遭到严密的检查与封锁。但是有几个学生终于蒙过政府的耳目，透过天津租界的一个外国机构发出一通电报。这电报就是五号上海各报新闻的唯一来源。

五号早晨报纸到达我手里时，我正在吃早餐。各报的首页都用大字标题刊登这条新闻，内容大致如下：

> Students in Peking demonstrated against the signing of the Versailles Treaty. Three pro-Japanese high officials—Tsao, Lu, and Chang—were beaten by the students. The residence of Tsao Ru-lin was burned. Several thousand have been detained under heavy armed guard in the Law College of the National University of Peking. Ringleaders were arrested and their state is unknown.

There were no further details.

The whole city was excited by the news. In the afternoon public organizations such as educational associations, chambers of commerce, and provincial and local guilds sent telegrams to the Peking government demanding the dismissal of the three high officials and the release of the students arrested or detained. Through the following day all Shanghai waited anxiously for a reply from the government but there was none. Then the students of the city went on strike, making the same demands as the public organizations, and went forth lecturing on the streets.

Next morning schoolboys and girls went by hundreds from door to door on Nanking Road, the main street of Shanghai, begging the shopkeepers to go on strike. Some in sympathy and others out of fear closed their doors. Many followed suit in imitation of their neighbors. In about an hour's time all the Nanking Road shops were closed as tight as clams. Police interfered but to no avail.

The shop strike spread like fire. By noon all Shanghai was shut. Thousands of people wandered about the streets and traffic was almost blocked. Settlement police became powerless. Boy and girl scouts went out as police to keep order and direct traffic. To see order maintained in the crowded streets by bobbed-haired girl scouts was something novel in the International Settlement of Shanghai. Both Chinese and foreigners wondered why the crowd willingly obeyed the orders of young boys and girls while showing such an ugly temper toward the police.

Within a few days the student strike had grown into a nationwide movement. Shops and commercial houses closed in all the cities near

Shanghai. As Shanghai was the center of commerce in the lower Yangtze Valley, these cities were paralyzed when the heart of the great metropolis ceased to beat, and suspended their affairs, not necessarily out of sympathy for the students.

Settlement authorities were alarmed when employees of the water works and the electric company wanted to join the strike. Through the mediation of the chamber of commerce and student representatives they

北京学生游行示威反对签订凡尔赛和约。三亲日要员曹汝霖、陆宗奥、章宗祥遭学生围殴。曹汝霖住宅被焚，数千人于大队宪警监视下拘留于北京大学第三院。群众领袖被捕，下落不明。

除此简短新闻外，别无其他报导。

这消息震动了整个上海市。当天下午，公共团体如教育会、商会、职业工会等纷纷致电北京政府，要求把那三位大员撤职，同时释放被捕或被扣的学生。第二天一整天，全上海都焦急地等待着政府的答复，但是杳无消息。于是全市学生开始罢课，提出与各团体相同的要求，同时开始进行街头演说。

第二天早晨，各校男女学生成群结队沿着南京路挨户访问，劝告店家罢市。各商店有的出于同情、有的出于惧怕，就把店门关起来了。许多人则仿照左邻右舍的榜样，也纷纷关门歇市。不到一个钟头，南京路上的所有店户都关上了大门了，警察干涉无效。

罢市风声迅即蔓延开来，到了中午时，全上海的店都关了。成千成万的人在街头聚谈观望，交通几乎阻塞。租界巡捕束手无策。男女童子军代替巡捕在街头维持秩序，指挥交通。由剪了短发的女童子军来维持人潮汹涌的大街的秩序，在上海公共租界倒真是一件新鲜的事。中国人和外国人同样觉得奇怪，为什么群众这么乐意接受这些小孩子的指挥，而对巡捕们却大发脾气。

几天之内，罢课成为全国性的风潮，上海附近各城市的商店和商业机构全都关了门。上海是长江流域下游的商业中心，这个大都市的心脏停止跳动以后，附近各城市也就随着瘫痪，停止活动，倒不一定对学生表同情。

租界当局听说自来水厂和电灯厂的雇员要参加罢工，大起惊慌。后来经过商会和学生代表的调停，这些人才算被劝住没有罢工。各方

were persuaded to stick to their jobs. The pressure continued for more than a week and the Peking government finally gave in. The three pro-Japanese officials resigned and all the students were set free.

With country-wide sympathy behind them, students everywhere were intoxicated by their success. Thereafter there was no peace for institutions of learning, or for the government. The students of Peking, having won their victory, continued to agitate against corruption in the government and the old traditions which, they thought, enslaved the minds of young people. They had won over the government because they had national sentiment behind them. Everybody in China would have liked to join the demonstrations and parades against the signing of the Versailles Treaty. The students, who were better organized, more articulate, more impulsive and less hesitant, took the lead and thus plucked at the heartstrings of the nation.

When the pro-Japanese officials had resigned and the students had been released by the government—when the general strike had been called off in Shanghai and elsewhere—the incident was considered closed, for the time being at least. But the university itself became a problem. Chancellor Tsai Yuan-pei, apparently shocked by the violence, had resigned and quietly left Peking. He went first to Tientsin, then to Shanghai, and finally slipped into Hangchow, where he lived in a friend's house on the historic West Lake, surrounded by gentle hills, enjoying nature as a traditional scholar of the old days. Despite repeated persuasions he declined to go back to the university. He said that he had never intended to incite the students to revolt, but that in demonstrating against acceptance of the Shantung clause of the Versailles Treaty they had acted on patriotic impulses which could hardly be condemned. As regarded the university, he thought that thenceforth it would be difficult to maintain discipline, as the students were likely to be intoxicated with the cup of success. Once they tasted power there would be no end to their appetite. This was the stand he took in regard to the student movement. The belief that he was always ready to encourage a student revolt was far from the truth.

Finally he approved my going to Peking to take charge of the university for him. I consented rather reluctantly. With the heavy responsibilities thus thrust upon me, I went to Peking in July with one of

压力继续了一个多星期，北京政府终于屈服，亲日三官员辞职，全体学生释放。

各地学生既然得到全国人士的同情与支持，不免因这次胜利而骄矜自喜。各学府与政府也从此无有宁日。北京学生获得这次胜利以后，继续煽动群众，攻击政府的腐败以及他们认为束缚青年思想的旧传统。学生们因为得到全国舆情的支持，已经战胜了政府。参加游行示威，反对签订凡尔赛和约，是每一个中国人都愿意做的事。学生们因为有较好的组织，比较敢言，比较冲动，顾虑比较少，所以打了头阵，并且因此拨动了全国人民的心弦。

亲日官员辞职，被捕学生释放，上海和其他各地的全面罢课罢市风潮歇止以后，大家以为"五四"事件就此结束，至少暂时如此。但是北京大学本身却成了问题。蔡校长显然因为事情闹大而感到意外，这时已经辞职而悄然离开北京，临行在报上登了一个广告引《白虎通》里的几句话说："杀君马者道旁儿，民亦劳止，汔可小休。"他先到天津，然后到上海，最后悄然到了杭州，住在一个朋友的家里。住处就在著名的西湖旁边，临湖依山，环境非常优美，他希望能像传统的文人雅士，就此息隐山林。虽然大家一再敦劝，他仍旧不肯回到北大。他说，他从来无意鼓励学生闹学潮，但是学生们示威游行，反对接受凡尔赛和约有关山东问题的条款，那是出乎爱国热情，实在无可厚非。至于北京大学，他认为今后将不易维持纪律，因为学生们很可能为胜利而陶醉。他们既然尝到权力的滋味，以后他们的欲望恐怕难以满足了。这就是他对学生运动的态度。有人说他随时准备鼓励学生闹风潮，那是太歪曲事实了。

他最后同意由我前往北京大学代理他的职务。我因情势所迫，只好勉强同意担负起这副重担，我于是在七月间偕学生会代表张国焘乘了火车，前赴北京。到了北京大学，初次遇见了当时北大学生，以后任台大校长的傅孟真（斯年），现在台湾任"国史馆长"的罗志希（家伦）。两位是北大"五四"的健将，不但善于谋略，而且各自舞着犀利的一支笔，好比公孙大娘舞剑似的，

the student delegates. The student body convened in a mass meeting of welcome, and this was the gist of my first speech to them:

> Your patriotic motives in the recent demonstrations are to be highly commended. But if you keep on doing this your valuable time will be wasted and the existence of the institution where you drink at the fountain of wisdom will be endangered. A new nation is not made in one day, and certainly not by demonstrations alone. The demonstrations are trifles in comparison with the work you have to do in classrooms, in the library, in laboratories, and in seminars...

After the storm the clouds began to disperse and a clear day emerged. Dr. Tsai returned to his office in September.

The university was again reorganized, on a sounder basis. The office of dean of administration was created to take charge of the business side of the university. Existing offices were modified and systematized into an organic whole. The dean of faculties was responsible for academic affairs. The Academic Council, members of which were elected by the professors with the deans as ex officio members, was the highest legislative body, empowered to pass on university regulations, grant degrees, and enforce discipline among the students. Various executive committees were set up to perform administrative functions. The university was put on a basis of faculty control. Academic freedom, faculty control, and a fearless spirit of searching for truth were the guiding principles in administration. Student self-government was encouraged as a step to democracy.

For seven long years, in spite of intermittent strikes and demonstrations, the university sailed along under full canvas on the rough sea of political turmoil, with men of courage and foresight at the helm. The number of volumes in the library was vastly increased, laboratory equipment much improved. Scholars of international fame such as John Dewey and Bertrand Russell were invited to join the university as visiting professors.

The two Western philosophers contributed their part to the great intellectual movement in China. Dewey directed the young minds of

China to the study of educational and social problems in accordance with the needs of the individual and society. It is true that the very act of thinking of problems in this way led naturally to the creation of other problems which caused trouble in such a static society as that of China

光芒四照。他们约好了好多同学，组织了一个新潮社，出版了一种杂志，叫做《新潮》，向旧思想进攻。我现在写《西潮》，实在自从"五四"以后，中国本土，已卷起了汹涌澎湃的新潮，而影响了中国将来的命运。然而"五四"之起因，实为第一次世界大战后，欧洲帝国主义之崩溃，以及日本帝国主义的猖狂。所以毕竟还是与西潮有关。

我到校以后，学生团体开了一个欢迎大会。当时的演说中，有如下一段：

"……故诸君当以学问为莫大的任务。西洋文化先进国家到今日之地位，系累世文化积聚而成，非旦夕可几。千百年来，经多少学问家累世不断的劳苦工作而始成今日之文化。故救国之要道，在从事增进文化之基础工作，而以自己的学问功夫为立脚点，此岂摇旗呐喊之运动所可几？当法国之围困德国时，有德国学者费希德在围城中之大学讲演，而作致国民书曰：'增进德国之文化，以救德国。'国人行之，遂树普鲁士败法之基础。故救国当谋文化之增进，而负此增进文化之责者，惟有青年学生。……"

暴风雨过去以后，乌云渐散，霁日重现，蔡先生也于九月间重回北大复职视事。

北大再度改组，基础益臻健全。新设总务处，由总务长处理校中庶务。原有处室也有所调整，使成为一个系统化的有机体，教务长负责教务。校中最高立法机构是评议会，会员由教授互选；教务长、总务长，以及各院院长为当然会员。评议会有权制订各项规程，授予学位，并维持学生风纪。各行政委员会则负责行政工作。北大于是走上教授治校的道路。学术自由、教授治校，以及无畏地追求真理，成为治校的准则。学生自治会受到鼓励，以实现民主精神。

此后七年中，虽然政治上狂风暴雨迭起，北大却在有勇气、有远见的人士主持下，引满帆篷，安稳前进。图书馆的藏书大量增加，实验设备也大见改善。国际知名学者如杜威和罗素，相继应邀来校担任客座教授。

这两位西方的哲学家，对中国的文化运动各有贡献。杜威引导中国青年，根据个人和社会的需要，来研究教育和社会问题。无庸讳言的，以这样的方式来考虑问题，自然要引起许多其他的问题。在当时变化比较迟钝的

in those days. Hu Han-min, a Kuomintang leader, once told me that it was Dewey's teaching that caused unrest in the schools. But he ignored the fact that there were many student strikes under the Imperial regime during prerevolutionary days; as well as the fact that Dewey's teaching, which interested the students in social problems, thus helped the movement against the warlords later on.

It was due to Russell that young minds began to get interested in principles of social reconstruction, which roused them against both religion and imperialism. To the missionaries and members of the British Legation he was an unwelcome guest. He lived in a Chinese hotel and refused to see officials of his own legation. I heard one of them express the view that his coming to China was a matter for regret. In Peking Mr. Russell contracted a serious case of pneumonia and at one time the doctors gave up hope. On his recovery I heard a missionary lady say, "That's too bad." I repeated it to Mr. Russell, who laughed heartily.

During those days of freedom of thought in China just after the first World War, thinking about either social problems or social principles created storms in the thinking mind and waves of emotion in the feeling heart. This prepared the way for the further introduction of Western ideas from postwar Europe. All the "isms" had full play in China. While the intellectuals on the whole moved along the line of Western democracy, a section of them, inspired by the success of the Russian revolution of 1917, were attracted to the ideology of Marxism. Chen Tu-hsiu, editor of *La Jeunesse*, resigning from his deanship at the University of Peking, became the leader of a Chinese Communist movement. The anti-imperialist movement against Japan also prepared the ground for general sympathy among intellectuals for the Russian Revolution. In 1923 the Third International sent Mr. Joffe to Peking to make contact with Chinese intellectuals, and one evening at a dinner given in his honor at the Chih-ying Restaurant in Peking, Dr. Tsai made a speech of welcome in which he said, "The Russian Revolution has given great inspiration to the revolutionary movement in China."

Russia had repeatedly announced that she was ready to give back to China the Chinese Eastern Railway[2] in north Manchuria, and wished China success in getting rid of both the warlords and the imperialistic Powers that had a grip on the country. This good will of Soviet Russia toward China was welcomed by all the intellectuals as well as by the people as a whole. Among other things, it paved the way for the growth of Communism in China.

中国实际社会中自然会产生许多纠纷。国民党的一位领袖胡汉民先生有一次对我说，各校风潮迭起，就是受了杜威学说的影响。此可以代表一部分人士对于杜威影响的估计。他的学说使学生对社会问题发生兴趣也是事实。这种情绪对后来的反军阀运动却有很大的贡献。

罗素则使青年人开始对社会进化的原理发生兴趣。研究这些进化的原理的结果，使青年人同时反对宗教和帝国主义。传教士和英国使馆都不欢迎罗素。他住在一个中国旅馆里，拒绝接见他本国使馆的官员。我曾经听到一位英国使馆的官员表示，他们很后悔让罗素先生来华访问。罗素教授曾在北京染患严重的肺炎，医生们一度认为已经无可救药。他病愈后，我听到一位女传教士说："他好了么？那是很可惜的。"我转告罗素先生，他听了哈哈大笑。

第一次世界大战后，中国的思想界，自由风气非常浓厚，无论是研究社会问题或社会原理，总使惯于思索的人们难于安枕，使感情奔放的人们趋向行动。战后欧洲的西洋思想就是在这种气氛下介绍进来的。各式各样的"主义"都在中国活跃一时。大体而论，知识分子大都循着西方民主途径前进，但是其中也有一部分人受到一九一七年俄国革命的鼓励而向往马克思主义。《新青年》的主编陈独秀辞去北大文学院院长的职务，成为中国共产运动的领袖。反对日本帝国主义的运动也促使知识分子普遍同情俄国革命。第三国际于一九二三年派越飞到北京与中国知识分子接触。某晚，北京撷英饭店有一次欢迎越飞的宴会。蔡校长于席中致欢迎词说："俄国革命已经予中国的革命运动极大的鼓励。"

俄国曾经一再宣布，准备把北满的中东铁路归还中国，并且希望中国能够顺利扫除军阀，驱除侵略中国的帝国主义。苏俄对中国的这番好意，受到所有知识分子以及一般老百姓的欢迎。这种表面上友好表示的后果之一，就是为苏俄式的共产主义在中国铺了一条路。

Meanwhile, eminent scientists from European and American universities came to guide students in scientific research. A number of periodicals were issued by the faculties as well as by the students. Music and art clubs, athletic associations, library and science associations sprang up in abundance. A society for the study of Marxian theories was established under the leadership of Professor Li Ta-chao. The student army corps, organized some time earlier to give military training to the students, was growing in size. The university gates were flung open to girls—Peking University was the first institution of higher learning in the history of education in China to accept women on an equal footing with men. Faculty and students, immersed in an atmosphere of academic freedom and free inquiry, worked in unison, happy and contented.

The influence of the university was far-reaching. From every intellectual pebble thrown into the waters of ancient Peking waves traveled to every corner of the land. Even the middle schools of the country—the equivalent of American high schools—copied its organization, introducing freedom of thought and opening their doors to girls. Progressive newspapers, magazines, and political parties echoed every movement of the university. In this atmosphere the influence of the Kuomintang revolution extended far and wide, while at the same time the Communist party began to take shape.

The conflicts of the warlords meanwhile roared intermittently around the ancient capital. In one of these internecine wars the gates of Peking were all closed for almost a week. Fighting was going on some ten miles outside the city. It usually began at nightfall and lasted until dawn. Once we went to watch the artillery fire from the top of Peking Hotel. It was like watching a fire on the other side of a river; you got the entertainment of a bonfire at the expense of others without incurring the risk of being licked by the flames. A crossfire of tracers spanned the earth in the dark night like multitudes of rainbows crossing each other. The roar of cannon set the roof trembling as if in a mild earthquake. From dusk till dawn there was no pause in the fighting. When I went home to bed I could not turn my ears to the pillow, for the thundering of the cannon seemed much louder that way. So I lay flat in bed with my eyes toward the ceiling and noticed that the beautifully painted shades of the electric lights were swinging slightly. Glasses rattled. Wolfy, my German police dog, kept moaning, unable to enjoy her usual peaceful slumber on the floor.

在这同时，许多留学欧美大学的杰出科学家也纷纷回国领导学生，从事科学研究。教员与学生都出了许多刊物。音乐协会、艺术协会、体育协会、图书馆协会纷纷成立，多如雨后春笋。教授李守常（大钊）并领导组织了一个马克思主义研究会。当时北京报纸附栏，称这研究会为"马神庙某大学之牛克斯研究会"，不过作为嘲笑之对象而已。马神庙者北京大学所在地也。此时北大已经敞开大门招收女生。北大是中国教育史上第一所给男女学生同等待遇的高等学府。教员和学生在学术自由和自由研究的空气里，工作得非常和谐而愉快。

北大所发生的影响非常深远。北京古都静水中所投下的每一颗知识之石，余波都会到达全国的每一角落。甚至各地的中学也沿袭了北大的组织制度，提倡思想自由，开始招收女生。北大发起任何运动，进步的报纸、杂志和政党无不纷起响应。国民革命的势力，就在这种氛围中日渐扩展，同时中国共产党也在这环境中渐具雏型。

军阀之间的冲突正在这古都的附近间歇进行着。在这些时断时续的战事中，北京各城门有一次关闭几达一星期之久。枪炮声通常在薄暮时开始，一直持续到第二天早晨。有一次，我们曾经跑到北京饭店的屋顶去眺望炮火，那真叫做隔岸观火，你可以欣赏夜空中交织的火网，但是绝无被火花灼伤的危险。炮弹拖着长长的火光，在空中飞驰，像是千万条彩虹互相交织。隆隆的炮声震得屋顶摇摇晃晃，像是遭到轻微的地震。从黄昏到清晨，炮火一直不停。我回家上床时，根本不能把耳朵贴着枕头睡，因为这样炮声显得特别响亮。因此我只能仰天躺着睡，让耳朵朝着天花板，同时注意到电灯罩子在微微摇晃。玻璃窗也嘎嘎作响。我有一只德国种的狼犬，名叫狼儿，它被炮声吵得无法再在地板上安睡，一直哼个不停。它的耳朵一贴到地板，

As soon as she laid her ear to the floor, she would start, get up, groan, dart for the door, and scratch it violently, thinking that these abominable sounds came from beneath the floor of my bedroom. The next morning I scolded her for being naughty the previous night. She stared at me with guilty eyes. From the breakfast table I called to her but she did not respond. I never saw her again. Presumably she wandered away in search of a land of peace where no mocking devils would pound the ground at night and she could sleep well. But I am afraid she was sorely disappointed.

On one of those days in the besieged city I took a walk with a friend along Shun-ching-men Street. People went about their business as usual, without a trace of excitement. As usual, people were pulling or being pulled in rickshaws. We turned at Hsi-tan Pailou into Hsi-ching-an-chieh and then into Central Park. The yellow enamel tiles of the imposing towers on the Wu Gate of the palace glittered in the slanting autumn sun against the cloudless blue. We chose a spot under the spreading branches of one of the ancient spruces planted there in rows and squares by early Manchu emperors centuries ago. The air was laden with their fragrance and light winds brushed our faces with the soothing odor. We sat at a table listening to the gossip at neighboring tables. People all talked about the war and wondered which side was going to win and who was going to have Peking as a spoil of war; all seemed to be utterly unconcerned. What is the use of worrying? Peking had seen many wars and vicissitudes of fortune but remained the same, as the towers of the Wu Gate bore silent witness.

"Let's order a fish for dinner and see whether we get it, with the city gates all closed," said my friend.

A waiter came with a fish wriggling in his hand. "How would you like to have it?"

"Two ways. Split it in half—one half fried with sweet-and-sour gravy spread on top; the other half cooked with bean sauce." The fish came. One of the two halves tasted stale.

"Why, one half of the fish was from a dead one," said my friend to the waiter, who bowed and smiled.

"Oh, I see. The fish sailed in over the city wall. The side that hit the ground was dead, while the other was still alive," I said. When the waiter came back again my friend snatched one of the empty wine jars on the table and showed it to him. "What! You have given us an empty jar."

它就惊跳起来，哼唧几声之后，它冲到房门旁，拼命在门上抓，它一定以为怪声是我卧房的地板下面发出来的。第二天早上，我骂了它一顿，说它前一晚不该那么捣乱。它似乎自知理屈，只用两只眼睛怯生生地望着我。早餐时我到处找不到狼儿，从此再不见它的踪影。大概它跑出去想找块安静地，夜里不会有恶作剧的魔鬼在地下大敲大擂，好让它安安稳稳地睡觉。不过，我想它大概是很失望的。

有一天，我和一位朋友在围城中沿着顺城门大街散步。老百姓还是照常操作，毫无紧张的样子。拉黄包车和坐黄包车的也与平常毫无异样。我们从西单牌楼转到西长安街，然后又转到中央公园。皇宫前午门谯楼上的黄色琉璃瓦，在夕阳下映着澄碧的秋空闪闪发亮。我们在一颗古柏的浓荫下选了一个地方坐下。这些古老的柏树是几百年前清朝的开国皇帝种植的。有的排成长列，有的围成方形。空气中充塞着柏树的芳香，微风带着这些醉人的香味吹拂着我们的面庞。我们围坐在桌子旁，静听着邻座酒客的议论。大家都在议论战事，猜测着谁会胜利，谁将入据北京。谁胜谁败，大家好像都不在乎。操心又怎么样？北京已经见过不少的战事，饱经沧桑之后，北京还不是依然故我？沉默的午门谯楼就是见证。

"城门都关了，不知道我们能不能叫个鱼吃吃。"我的朋友说。

堂倌拿了一条活生生的鱼来问我们："先生们喜欢怎么个烧法？"

"一鱼两吃。一半醋溜，一半红烧。"

鱼烧好端上来了，有一碟似乎不大新鲜。

"这是怎么回事？这一半是死鱼呀！"我的朋友质问堂倌，堂倌鞠了一躬，只是嘻嘻地笑。

"哦，我知道了！这条鱼一定是从城墙跳进来的。碰到地的一边碰死了，另一边却仍然活着。"我代为解释。堂倌再度跑过来时，我的朋友从桌上抓起一把空酒壶，翻过来给他看。"怎么！你给我们一把空酒壶呀！"

"Sorry." The waiter was smiling. "The liquor has evaporated." He immediately brought us a new one. Of course both were charged to our account.

We went back home at dusk. That night the fighting ceased. I thought of Wolfy. She must have slept in peace somewhere in the city. The next morning we found the government had changed hands. The palace remained the same. The people went about as usual. The city was undisturbed. The gates were flung open, and thousands of people from the country streamed in with vegetables, meat, eggs, and fish. Donkeys, mules, and camels followed in the wake of the pedestrians. Children gathered empty cannon shells and shrapnel from the battleground and sold them in the streets for a few dollars. Out of these shells we made flower vases.

Many people outside the city lost their property, a number of them lost their lives. I lost my Wolfy.

On the whole the losses to property and life in the various war areas during those long, distressing years were negligible. It was the unsettled state of mind, the disruption of communications, the ruined finances, the disturbances of order and upset of administrative machinery of the government—above all, the obstruction of the tranquil flow of blood in the veins of national life—that reduced China to such a paralyzed state that she became an easy prey to the aggressor neighbor. The division of the country made any nationwide constructive plan for the country well-nigh impossible. Unification was what China needed.

I acted for the second time for Chancellor Tsai when he went for a visit to Europe. At this time a letter from Dr. Sun Yat-sen lauded the movements in the university and ended in the following words: "Lead the three thousand disciples to help the cause of revolution."

Dr. Sun did not live to see his hopes come true, but only a few years later his successor, General Chiang Kai-shek, led the Nationalist army sweeping down from Canton to the Yangtze Valley, then to the Yellow

River Valley, and finally to Peking, treading the path psychologically prepared for the new Nationalist victory by the revolutionary movements which had started in Peking and permeated the minds of all classes of people in the country.

"对不起，"堂倌笑嘻嘻地说，"酒烫跑了！"他马上给我们重新拿了一壶。当然，两壶酒都记在我们账上。

我们在黄昏时回家。那天晚上，战斗停止了，我又想起狼儿。这一晚，它大概可以在城里找个地方，安静地睡一觉了。第二天早上，我们发现政府已经易手。皇宫依然无恙。老百姓照常过活。各城门大开，成千成万的人从乡下挑着蔬菜、肉类、鸡蛋、鱼虾涌进北京城。小孩子们在战场上捡起废弹壳，以几块钱的代价在街头出售。许多人拿这些炮弹壳制花瓶。

城外有些人家破人亡，我亦失掉了我的狼儿。

一般而论，在这些漫长痛苦的日子里，因战事而丧失的生命财产并不严重。使中国陷于瘫痪而成为邻邦侵略之目标的，实为人心之动荡，交通之破坏，经济之崩溃，以及国民安定生活之遭破坏。国家陷于四分五裂，全国性的建设计划几乎成为不可能。中国当务之急就是统一。

蔡校长赴欧旅行时，我又再度代理北大校长。这时我接到中山先生一封信，对北大的各种运动大加奖誉，最后并勉励我"率领三千子弟，参加革命"。

孙先生可惜未能在有生之年看到他的希望实现，不过短短数年之后，他的继承人蒋总司令，率领革命军从广州北伐，所向披靡，先至长江流域，继至黄河流域，终至底定北京。开始于北京，随后遍及全国各阶层的革命运动，已先为这次国民革命军的新胜利奠定了心理的基础。

CHAPTER 16   YEARS OF TROUBLES

The students after their May 4 victory were indeed intoxicated with the cup of success as Chancellor Tsai, Dr. Hu Shih, and others had predicted. It was beyond their power or any other power in the country to stop, for the root of discontent lay deep in the political, social, and intellectual soil of China. In the schools the students usurped the right of the authorities to engage or dismiss a teacher. Failing to meet their demands, the administration invariably faced a strike. The students struck against teachers who required a severe examination or stood for sterner discipline. They demanded subsidies from the schools for their traveling expenses during spring vacation, or money for student activities. They demanded free copies of the lecture notes (a kind of course syllabus). It was a matter of trying to get as much as possible out of the school in every conceivable way, never thinking of their duties toward it. They were intoxicated with power; their selfishness ran wild. The mere word "discipline" found them with rolling eyes, lips curled, and teeth bared, ready to fall upon you in packs.

Once the senate of the University of Peking passed a regulation that all students must pay for the copies of lecture notes provided by the university. This touched their private pocket. A crowd of several hundred demonstrated against the rule. Chancellor Tsai arrived on the scene and told them that they must obey the university regulations. His words fell upon deaf ears. The mob streamed into the classrooms and offices to find those responsible for the "obnoxious" rule. The Chancellor told them that he alone was responsible.

"You cowards!" he shouted indignantly, rolling his sleeves up to his elbows and shaking his fists in the air. "I'll fight a duel with any one of you who dares. If anyone dares to touch his teachers, I'll knock him down."

The crowd stood in a semicircle in front of him. As the Chancellor moved toward them they stepped back, always keeping at a safe distance. This quiet scholar, tame as a lamb in daily life, was suddenly transformed into a moral lion.

The crowd dwindled; he walked to his office. About fifty students still waited outside the door demanding the abrogation of the rule. The corridor was packed with spectators curiously looking on. The thing came to a deadlock. The Dean of Faculties, Ku Men-yu, brought about a settlement by promising to see that the assessment of lecture note fees was postponed—indefinitely, of course.

拾陆 扰攘不安的岁月

蔡校长和胡适之他们料得不错，学生们在"五四"胜利之后，果然为成功之酒陶醉了。这不是蔡校长等的力量，或者国内的任何力量所能阻止的，因为不满的情绪已经在中国的政治、社会和知识的土壤上长得根深蒂固。学校里的学生竟然取代了学校当局聘请或解聘教员的权力。如果所求不遂，他们就罢课闹事。教员如果考试严格或者赞成严格一点的纪律，学生就马上罢课反对他们。他们要求学校津贴春假中的旅行费用，要求津贴学生活动的经费，要求免费发给讲义。总之，他们向学校予取予求，但是从来不考虑对学校的义务。他们沉醉于权力，自私到极点。有人一提到"校规"他们就会瞪起眼睛，噘起嘴巴，咬牙切齿，随时预备揍人。

有一次，北大的评议会通过一项办法，规定学生必须缴讲义费。这可威胁到他们的荷包了。数百学生马上集合示威，反对此项规定。蔡校长赶到现场，告诉他们，必须服从学校规则。学生们却把他的话当耳边风。群众涌进教室和办公室，要找主张这条"可恶的"规定的人算账。蔡校长告诉他们，讲义费的规定应由他单独负责。

"你们这班懦夫！"他很气愤地喊道，袖子高高地卷到肘子以上，两只拳头不断在空中摇晃。"有胆的就请站出来与我决斗。如果你们那一个敢碰一碰教员，我就揍他。"

群众在他面前围了个半圆形。蔡校长向他们逼进几步，他们就往后退几步，始终保持着相当的距离。这位平常驯如绵羊、静如处子的学者，忽然之间变为正义之狮了。

群众渐渐散去，他也回到了办公室。门外仍旧聚着五十名左右的学生，要求取消讲义费的规定。走廊上挤满了好奇的围观者。事情成了僵局。后来教务长顾孟余先生答应考虑延期收费，才算把事情解决。所谓延期，自然是无限延搁。这就是当时全国所知的北大讲义风潮。

Among the worst agitators, who usually took cover behind the crowd to shout their shrill accusations, I noticed a tall young man, too tall to be hidden by the crowd. I did not know him—he was not among those whose names were later struck from the university register. But a number of years afterward, when I saw him as a puffed-up official, I recognized him at once. His countenance was unmistakable; his shouts still rang in my ears. He had developed into a skillful politician and unscrupulous grafter, and died a rich man a few years after the war.

In another demonstration several years later against myself for refusal to listen to their demands, a number of students closed the gates of the compound and thus shut me in my office. Dr. Hu Shih telephoned to ask whether I would like police to break the siege, but I replied in the negative. The gates were closed for two hours. Those who wanted to leave after their classes clamored from inside, while others who wanted to come in to attend courses echoed without. At length the ringleaders, no longer able to withstand the protests of their fellow students, opened the gates. As I came out of my office a score or two of them followed, vociferously denouncing me. Turning my head, I saw a few at close range. The university senate decided to dismiss those whose names I could remember or afterward ascertained.

Several years later as I was walking on the campus of the Central Aviation School, transferred from Hangchow to Kunming during the war, a fine-looking young officer stepped forward and after a military salute told me that he was a student dismissed from the National University of Peking. At once I recognized his honest-looking face and fine, strong physique. The ugliness I had seen in his face as he dogged my steps that day of demonstration was all transformed into shining happy eyes and smiling lips. We were happy to see each other. The president of the school told me later that he was one of the best flyers and instructors they had.

These instances are indicative of the fact that the student demonstrations contained all elements. Those who honestly believed in their cause, rightly or wrongly, and were willing to be responsible for what they had done, often turned out to be good citizens, while the sneaky fellows often proved undesirable elements in society.

The students usually took as their target some international problem which the government was not in a position to solve, or had failed to solve to the satisfaction of the people. Thus they always carried with

闹得最凶的人往往躲在人们背后高声叫骂，我注意到这些捣乱分子之中有一位高个子青年，因为他个子太高，所以无法逃出别人的视线。我不认识他，后来被学校开除的一批人之中，也没有他的名字。若干年之后，我发现他已经成为神气十足的官儿，我一眼就认出他来。他的相貌决不会让人认错，他的叫骂声仍旧萦回在我的耳畔。他已经成为手腕圆滑的政客，而且是位手辣心黑的贪员，抗战胜利后不久故世，留下一大堆造孽钱。

几年之后，发生了一次反对我自己的风潮，因为我拒绝考虑他们的要求。一群学生关起学校大门，把我关在办公室。胡适之先生打电话给我，问我愿不愿意找警察来解围，但是我谢绝了。大门关闭了近两小时。那些下课后要回家的人在里面吵着要出去，在门外准备来上课的人则吵着要进来。群众领袖无法应付他们自己同学的抗议，最后只好打开大门。我走出办公室时，后面跟着一二十人，随跟随骂着。我回过头来时，发现有几个学生紧钉在我背后。北大评议会决定开除我所能记得的以及后来查出的闹事学生。

好几年以后，我偶然经过昆明中央航空学校的校园。航空学校原来在杭州，战时迁到昆明。忽然一位漂亮的青年军官走到我面前，他向我行过军礼告诉我，他就是被北京大学开除的一位学生。我马上认出他那诚实的面孔和健美的体格。闹学潮时紧迫在我背后所表现的那副丑恶的样子已经完全转变了，他的眼睛闪耀着快乐的光辉，唇边荡漾着笑意。这次邂逅使我们彼此都很高兴。航空学校的校长后来告诉我，这位青年军官是他们最优秀的飞行员和教官之一。

这些例子足以说明学生运动中包含各式各样的分子。那些能对奋斗的目标深信不疑，不论这些目标事实上是否正确，而且愿意对他们的行为负责的人，结果总证明是好公民，而那些鬼头鬼脑的家伙，却多半成为社会的不良分子。

学生们所选择的攻击目标，常常是政府无法解决或者未能圆满解决的国际问题。因此，他们常能获得国人的同情；他们的力量

them the sympathy of the country; herein lay their power. As "incidents" grew in number between China and Japan, their demonstrations were naturally interpreted by the Japanese as an anti-Japanese movement. The root of the trouble lay in the Twenty-One Demands and in the Shantung question created by the Versailles Treaty. After the balance of power in the Far East was upset, Japan enjoyed almost exclusive privileges in strangling China. The policy of partitioning China had given way to the Open Door policy, which was fundamentally dependent upon a balance of power; once this balance was kicked over, China had only two alternatives—to submit to the domination of Japan or fight it out alone every step of the way.

So the students fought, first with demonstrations, strikes, and boycotts against Japanese goods, then turning their attack on the government at Peking, which they believed responsible for all evils. When they found nothing internationally or nationally important to fight, they fought the school authorities. The cause lay in the psychological unrest of youth. Once they were aroused to act, it tended to express itself; to repress emotions that ran so high would have been difficult.

A number of student groups, among them the young Communists, turned their attention to the labor movement and the labor unrest which was then brewing in the treaty ports. Railway and factory workers began to show activity and agitation, which spread like patches of oil. Soon they joined the students in mass meetings and parades. The labor movement was no negligible weapon. With it the Kuomintang government in Canton once devastated Hongkong with a general strike, reducing the British island colony to a commercial and industrial desert, as it were, for eighteen months.

Nationwide anti-British feeling had been provoked in Shanghai on May 30, 1925, when International Settlement authorities gave orders to shoot into a crowd of sympathizers with the labor movement there, gathered on Nanking Road. A few were killed and many wounded. Under the leadership of both the Kuomintang and the Communists a general strike of laborers, merchants, and students followed. Once more Shanghai was a dead city. On June 23 students, workmen, merchants, and soldiers in Canton demonstrated in sympathy against the British. As the crowd passed through the outskirts of the Foreign Settlement the

也就在此。中日之间的"事件"日渐增多以后，学生的示威游行常常被日本人解释为反日运动。纠纷的根源在于二十一条要求和凡尔赛和约所引起的山东问题。自从远东均势破坏以后，日本几乎享有控制中国的特权。门户开放政策已经取代瓜分中国的政策。但是门户开放政策必须以均势为基础，均势一旦破坏，中国只有两条路可走——一条路是任由日本宰割，另一条路就是自我振作，随时随地与日本打个分明。

学生们决定奋起作战，起先是游行、示威、罢课和抵制日货，接着就转而攻击北京政府，因为他们认为一切毛病都出在北京政府身上。他们发现没有重要的国际问题或国内问题足资攻击时，他们就与学校当局作对。原因在于青年心理上的不稳。一旦他们受到刺激而采取行动时，这种不稳的情绪就爆发了。想压制这种澎湃的情绪是很困难的。

若干学生团体，包括青年共产党员，开始把他们的注意力转移到劳工运动以及工人的不稳情绪上。沿海商埠的工人正蠢蠢欲动。铁路工人和工厂工人已开始骚动，而且蔓延各地。他们不久就与学生携手，参加群众大会和游行。劳工运动是不可轻侮的武器。在广州的国民党政府，曾以总罢工瘫痪香港，使这个英国殖民地在工商业上成为荒漠，历时十八月之久。

全国性的反英情绪是民国十四年的上海"五卅惨案"激起的。五月三十日那一天，一群同情劳工运动的人在上海大马路（南京路）游行示威，公共租界当局竟然下令向群众开枪，好几个人中弹身死，伤者更不计其数。工人、商人和学生在国民党及共产党领导之下，随即发动全面罢工、罢市、罢课，上海再度变为死城。六月二十三日，广州的学生、工人、商人和军人继起响应，发动反英示威游行。群众行近沙面租界时，驻防英军

British garrison fired on them. As a result of the firing Hongkong went on a general strike which rendered the British colony a dead city. At the instigation of the students Chinese employees of the British Legation at Peking also went on a sympathetic strike, which left these diplomatic officials without cooks or boys for some time.

After the workers had joined the student movement, the number of demonstrators was increased by thousands. Often one would see a vast motley crowd in the mass meetings or parading on the streets of Peking, shouting slogans and waving banners. In one of these meetings a White Russian, shuddering, remarked that he had seen many such mass meetings in Russia—the sure signs of an impending revolution—and he wondered whether it was safe for him to stay in China.

The workers, like the students, when there was no more important demonstration to make, turned their hostility against their employers. There was little peace for the factories. However, it was much easier for the central or local government to deal with striking workmen than with students. In many instances they stopped the strikes by force of arms, in some cases simply firing on the strikers with machine guns.

Supposing that this would be an effective way to stop all strikes, the government under Tuan Chi-jui gave orders to train machine guns on a crowd of students gathering around the executive mansion. I had previously been informed that the government had given the order to fire if the students besieged the building, and I warned them of the danger and tried to prevent them from participating; but they formed in lines on the campus, ready to march, and refused to listen to me. No sooner had they approached the entrance of the mansion than bullets rained upon them.

About four o'clock in the afternoon news reached me of the tragedy. At once I rushed to the scene. The open space in front of the official residence of Tuan Chi-jui was literally covered with bodies of young boys and girls. It was difficult to distinguish the dead from the dying.

Ambulances came and picked up all who showed any sign of life. About two dozen remained lifeless on the ground. A number died on the way to hospitals and still more lost their young lives on the operating table. We checked with the various hospitals and found that the casualties ran up over a hundred. This did not include those who left after receiving first aid.

又向群众开枪。于是香港各界亦开始罢工、罢市、罢课，使香港也变为死城。北京英国使馆的华籍雇员，在学生煽动之下，也进行同情罢工，致使这批英国外交官员很久都没有厨子和听差侍候。

自从工人运动与学生运动彼此呼应以后，游行示威者人数动以万计，北京不时有各色人等参加的群众大会出现，街头游行行列常常长达数里，群众手摇旗帜，高呼口号，无不慷慨激昂。一位白俄看到这种情形时，不觉怵然心惊。他曾经在俄国看到不少这样的集会，他说这是革命即将来临的征兆，因此他担心是否能继续在中国平安住下去。

学生们找不到游行示威的机会时，曾经拿学校当局作为斗争的对象，工人的情形亦复如此。他们找不到示威的对象时，就把一股怨气发泄在雇主的身上。不过，中央政府或地方政府对付罢工工人，可比对付学生简单多了。他们有时用武力来弹压罢工工人，有时就干脆拿机关枪来扫射。

段祺瑞执政的政府显然认为机关枪是对付一切群众行动的不二法门，因此，在一群学生包围执政府时，段执政就老实不客气下令用机关枪扫射。我在事前曾经得到消息，说政府已经下令，学生如果包围执政府，军队就开枪。因此我警告学生不可冒险，并设法阻止他们参加；但是他们已经在校内列队集合，准备出发，结果不肯听我的劝告。他们一到了执政府，子弹就像雨点一样落到他们头上了。

我在下午四点钟左右得到发生惨剧的消息后马上赶到出事地点。段执政官邸门前的广场上，男女学生伤亡枕藉，连伤者与死者都难辨别。救护车来了以后，把所有留着一口气的全部运走，最后留下二十多具死尸，仍旧躺在地上。许多重伤的在送往医院的途中死去，更有许多人则在手术台上断了气。我们向各医院调查之后，发现死伤人数当在一百以上。这个数目还不包括经包扎后即行回家的人在内。

This dastardly action of the Tuan Chi-jui government drew a wave of protest from the whole country, and its resultant unpopularity was among the reasons for its later downfall.

Besides the factors I have mentioned, the most important element in making the students so powerful and uncontrollable at this period was the fact that most of them were the sons and daughters of the ruling classes of China. A revolt of students meant, so to speak, a revolt of sons and daughters against their fathers. The most knotty problem a parent had to face was that of a rebellious son or daughter, especially when his children's actions enjoyed the popular support of his neighbors. Workmen were a different proposition; neither their parents nor relatives held any power in the government or in society. So it was their lot to submit to the whips of policemen or the bayonets of armed forces. Only when they were under the guidance of, or in co-operation with, the students was their power strongly felt.

The student movement was further fortified by the sympathy of teachers within the schools and Kuomintang members and Communists outside of them. Other political forces were also involved. So the movement grew in complexity and magnitude. There were always teachers behind it, from its beginning in 1919. Even during the first student revolt under the Imperial regime there had been teachers behind the movement.

A strike of teachers, to support their demands for payment of arrears of salary owed them by the government at Peking, caused further complications. The poor teachers in the university and in seven other government colleges were very irregularly paid. Often they received only half a month's salary in two or three months. When they demonstrated they could usually squeeze out from a half to one month's salary from the Ministry of Education.

Once several hundred teachers, supported by a still larger number of students, occupied the premises of the Ministry demanding payment

of their arrears. The presidents of the eight government institutions
went to act as intermediaries. Teachers and students coerced the vice-
minister and all the presidents into marching to the presidential mansion
to demand their pay. At the exit of the Ministry the vice-minister refused
to go any farther on the pretext that it was raining. A student walking
beside him opened his umbrella and handed it over, saying brusquely,
"Here is an umbrella," and the vice-minister took it from him and

段祺瑞政府的这种行动，引起全国普遍的抗议，段政府后来终于
垮台，此为原因之一。

学生势力这样强大而且这样嚣张跋扈，除了我前面所谈到的原因
之外，另一原因是这些学生多半是当时统治阶级的子女。学生的反抗
运动，也可以说等于子女对父母的反抗。做父母的最感棘手的问题就
是对付桀骜不驯的子女，尤其是这些子女的行为偏偏又受到邻居们的
支持。工人们的情形可就不同了；他们的父母或亲戚，既不是政府大
员，也不是社会闻人，因此他们命中注定要挨警察的皮鞭或军队的刺
刀。只有在学生领导之下，或者与学生合作时，工人才能表现较大的
力量。

学生运动在校内享有教师的同情，在校外又有国民党员和共产党
员的支持，因此势力更见强大。此外还牵涉到其他的政治势力。故而
情形愈来愈复杂，声势也愈来愈浩大。学生运动自从民国八年开始以
来，背后一直有教员在支持。就是满清时代的首次学潮，也是教员支
持的。

后来教员也发生罢教事件，要求北京政府发放欠薪，情势更趋复
杂。北大以及其他七个国立大专学校的教员，一直不能按时领到薪
水。他们常常两三个月才能领到半个月的薪俸。他们一罢课，通常可
以从教育部挤出半个月至一个月的薪水。

有一次，好几百位教员在大群学生簇拥之下，占据了整个教育部
的办公厅，要求发放欠薪。八个国立学校的校长也到了教育部，担任
居间调停的工作。教员与学生联合起来，强迫马邻翼教育次长和八位
校长一齐前往总统府，要求发薪水。这位次长走到教育部门口时，藉
口天在下雨，不肯继续往外走。一位走在他旁边的学生汪翰，马上把
自己的雨伞打开递给他，并且很直率地说："喏，这把雨伞你拿去！"

marched on reluctantly. The presidents followed grudgingly after. As the crowd approached the entrance of the mansion the gendarmery and police closed the gates. Teachers and students clamored for admittance. Suddenly the gates were flung open and swarms of armed police and gendarmes streamed out with bayonets and rifle butts, stabbing and beating at random. Aged teachers and young girls alike fell into the ditches with hands muddy and faces bleeding, screaming and crying. The president of the College of Law lay on the ground as if dead. A professor of political science argued with the soldiers as to why they should be so unsympathetic as to insult the hungry teachers. A professor of Chinese literature with a big lump on his forehead, his nose bleeding, shouted at them, "You fight your own people. Why don't you fight the Japanese?"

This professor was taken to the French Hospital, where a former provincial governor was sent by the government to offer its apology. The professor's aged mother was sitting by.

"This boy is my only son. The government almost killed him. I demand the reason why?"

To this the former governor replied, "Never mind, Aunty, I am a good fortuneteller. By looking at my cousin's countenance I can see he has a great future before him. Don't worry, dear Aunt, the government is sorry for the misbehavior of the ignorant soldiers. Aunt, I apologize to you."

The old lady was humored into calmness, while everyone in the room repressed his laughter. The faces of the teachers in their hospital beds all lighted up at this humor in the midst of tragedy.

Thus it went. On another occasion the teachers streamed into the Ministry of Finance, demanding their arrears of salary. All the members of the Ministry sneaked out the back doors, leaving the buildings empty behind them. Once the students, in disapproval of government policy toward a certain foreign Power, forced themselves into the Ministry of Foreign Affairs and smashed the big looking glass and quite a few nice chairs. Students, teachers, and workers all joined in strikes against the government in Peking and the aggressor Powers that encroached upon the rights of China. In bad years not a month passed without strikes of some sort.

To be president of a university in those days was really more than a headache. Funds came from the government only occasionally—usually a year or two in arrears. While students demanded more freedom of action,

于是这位次长只好无可奈何地继续前进，后面跟着八位心里同样不怎么乐意的校长。群众走近总统府时，宪兵、警察赶紧关起大门。教员与学生在门外吵着要进去。忽然大门打开了，大群武装宪警蜂拥而出，刺刀乱刺，枪把乱劈。上了年纪的教员和年轻的女学生纷纷跌到沟里，有的满身泥泞，有的一脸血迹，叫的叫，哭的哭，乱成一片。法政大学校长王家驹像死人一样躺在地上。北大政治学教授李大钊挺身与士兵理论，责备他们毫无同情心，不该欺侮饿肚皮的穷教员。北大国文系教授马叙伦额头被打肿一大块，鼻孔流血，对着宪兵大喊："你们只会打自己中国人，你们为什么不去打日本人？"

这位马教授后来被送到法国医院诊治，政府派了一位曾任省长的要员前往慰问并致歉意。坐在病榻旁的马教授的老母说：

"这孩子是我的独子，政府几乎要他的命，请问这是什么道理？"

曾任省长的那位要员回答道："老伯母请放心，小侄略知相法，我看这位老弟的相貌，红光焕发，前途必有一步大运。老伯母福寿无疆，只管放心就是。至于这些无知士兵无法无天，政府至感抱歉。老伯母，小侄向您道歉。"

老太太居然被哄得安静下来，病房里其余的人却几乎笑出声来了。躺在医院病床上的其他教员，也都因为这位要员的风趣而面露笑容。

这件事情总算这样过去了。另有一次，教员们拥到财政部要求发放欠薪，部里的人一个个从后门溜走，结果留下一所空房子。有一次学生们因为不满政府应付某一强国的外交政策，冲进外交部打烂一面大镜和好些精致的座椅。学生、教员和工人联合起来罢工罢课，反对北京政府和侵略中国权益的列强。多事的那几年里，差不多没有一个月不发生一两次风潮，不是罢课就是罢工。

在那时候当大学校长真是伤透脑筋。政府只有偶然发点经费，往往一欠就是一两年。学生要求更多的行动自由，政府则要求维持秩序，

the government desired order and discipline. For whatever happened, in or out of the school, the president was responsible. In demonstrations, parades, and riots, he was called upon either to stop one party or to help another. Every time the telephone rang his heart beat against his ribs, and he was rewarded for untiring work only by the grey hair that grew rapidly on his head.

The writer does not speak idly. After setting down the events in these pages he again spent a night of nightmare, seeing at one moment young boys and girls lying dead on the streets of Peking, at another the gendarmery besieging the university and demanding the surrender of ringleaders. Nor, when he started and woke, and lay sleepless with his head upon the pillows, could he shut out by closing his eyes the unfolding pictures of that tragic record.

Sipping tea under a scent-laden spruce in Peking's Central Park, an old scholar made a remark to me which was, I think, typical of those bad days of the strikes.

"Strikes here, there, and everywhere—strikes yesterday, today, tomorrow and every day. Mr. Chancellor, what are you going to do about them? When is the thing going to end? Someone has said that the new spirit is born, but I say the old tranquil spirit is dead!"

严守纪律。出了事时，不论在校内校外，校长都得负责。发生游行、示威或暴动时，大家马上找到校长，不是要他阻止这一边，就是要他帮助那一边。每次电话铃声一响，他就吓一跳。他日夜奔忙的唯一报酬，就是两鬓迅速增加的白发。

我讲这些话，决不是开玩笑。我记下这些往事以后，又做了场恶梦，有时看到青年男女横尸北京街头，有时又看到宪兵包围北京大学要求交出群众领袖。梦中惊醒之后，辗转反侧无法安枕，一闭上眼睛，一幕幕的悲剧就重新出现。

有一天，我和一位老教授在北京中央公园的柏树下喝茶。这位老教授曾经说过一段话，颇足代表当时扰攘不安的情形。

"这里闹风潮，那里闹风潮，到处闹风潮——昨天罢课，今天罢工，明天罢市，天天罢、罢、罢。校长先生，你预备怎么办？这情形究竟到哪一天才结束。有人说，新的精神已经诞生，但是我说，旧日安宁的精神倒真是死了！"

PART FOUR

第四部　国家统一

UNIFICATION

CHAPTER 17   AN EXPERIMENT IN CONSTITUTIONALISM

During the warlord regime one evening the Soviet Ambassador at Peking gave a banquet at the Embassy to leading men of the city. About sixty people were present. When the roast suckling pigs were passed round the table some of the guests looked at the steaming roast and burst into subdued giggles, while out of the corners of their eyes they glanced at the President and Vice-President of the National Assembly, who were among the guests. The contagious giggles spread until the whole table caught them except the two officials, who pulled long faces but remained calm. Finally I saw somebody whisper in the ear of the Soviet Ambassador and he, too, succumbed to the contagion.

The story was this. In the old days when the Dutch Indies needed labor, owners of rubber plantations and mines resorted to getting laborers from China by fraudulent means. By painting a rosy picture of the prospects and offering a sum of money, labor agencies in China enticed workers to cross the sea to the islands and there sold them to the development companies with or without the knowledge of the human goods. These unfortunate people were called "pigs" because they had been sold for money like the meanest livestock.

During the early years of the Republic the irregular practices of certain members of the National Assembly became so notorious and contemptible that people reminiscently called them "pigs," since they were willing to sell themselves to the highest bidder. The great majority of members were upright men, but they were unorganized and therefore powerless to check their fellow members. They, too, were so unfortunate as to be tagged with the epithet. When bad men combine the good must associate; if they do not, it is their own fault and they have only themselves to blame.

The idea of a written constitution for China had been introduced from America. The Constitution of the United States was an embodiment of ideas and beliefs of the American people and grew out of the life of the people. The Constitution of China was a copy of imported ideas, adopted according to the fancy of those who drafted the document and alien to the habits and ideas of the Chinese.

During the Imperial regime, in the last few years before the revolution, the provincial assemblies representing the gentry class achieved creditable results because their main interests were more or less

拾柒 宪政的试验

　　军阀时代的一天晚上，俄国驻北京大使加拉罕举行宴会，招待当地首要。出席宴会的约有六十人。上菜上到烤乳猪时，席上一些客人，一面斜眼看看在座的国会议长、副议长，一面望着热气蒸腾的烤乳猪，不觉掩嘴而笑。这种吃吃的笑声，迅即传染到全体宾客，只有那位议长和那位副议长，板起面孔装聋作哑。最后我看到有人向苏俄大使咬耳朵，弄得这位大使也忍俊不止。

　　这里头有个典故。从前印尼的橡园主人和矿场老板，常常以不法手段向中国招募工人。中国的劳工招募所，就把南洋说得天堂似的，花点钱把工人诱骗到南洋群岛，转卖给当地的开发公司。这些被当做货色出卖的可怜虫就叫"猪仔"。他们有的是自甘卖身，有的根本糊里糊涂就被当猪一样卖掉了。

　　民国初年，国会的议员受贿舞弊，弄得声名狼藉，普受鄙视，许多人就骂他们是"猪仔议员"，因为他们只看谁出价高，就把自己卖给谁。当然，绝大多数的议员是正直无私的，但是这些人毫无组织，因此也就无法制止其中的败类。于是"猪仔"之名就普遍加在国会议员的头上了，坏人营私结党时，好人也必须团结一致，要不然，好人蒙冤不白，那是自作自受。有一次他们在万牲园里的豳风堂宴会，有人把豳字解作"猪积如山"，一时全城传诵，此后议员们就不敢再在那里请客了。

　　中国成文宪法的观念是从美国介绍来的。美国的宪法是美国人民思想信仰的具体表现，而且是根据人民的生活发展而来的。中国的宪法只是抄袭外国的观念，起草宪法的人随意取舍，根本没有考虑到中国人的生活习惯或思想观念。

　　革命前的帝政时代末年，由绅士阶级组成的省咨议局倒是成绩斐然，因为他们的目标大致相同，而且绅士阶级里也不乏领袖

the same and there was leadership in that class. The Imperial governor of the province had enough prestige to serve as a check to the assembly. Little or no political squabbling went on in the assembly to obscure the larger issues. The bills passed were generally for the welfare of the people of the province. Little or no corruption was known.

In 1912, when Dr. Sun Yat-sen was Provisional President of the Republic at Nanking, the National Assembly showed healthy signs of becoming a modern parliament, for its members represented revolutionary interests and there were revolutionary leaders to guide it. Dr. Sun's prestige as Chief Executive was high. But when the Assembly came under Yuan Shih-kai, trouble began to brew. This autocratic and reactionary President was hated by the revolutionary leaders and the President hated them in turn. With a strong army in his hands he resorted to intimidation, thus setting a very bad precedent for future development of the legislative body. To illustrate the ludicrously bad effect of this technique on the morale of the members, I may relate here an incident which occurred during Yuan's election to the presidency. Photographers covered the event. In those days indoor picture-taking involved the use of flashlight powder, which exploded noisily with a dazzling light. On this occasion, taking it for a bomb explosion, people ran wildly for safety. One member ducked under a table, shouting, "I voted for Yuan Shih-kai!" Quite a few lost their slippers (Chinese masculine footgear is comfortably loose) and were obliged to look for them after the scare was over. The episode ended with the impeachment of the secretary-general for allowing photographers to frighten the Assembly by a "bomb."

Under Yuan's presidency the activity of the half dozen political parties degenerated into mere political squabbling. Party and personal feelings ran high. The Assembly, discredited in the eyes of the people, was finally washed away in the tides of Yuan's maneuvers for a monarchy and the restoration movement of Chang Hsun. These movements failed, however, and the National Assembly was restored. Political power was now divided among the military governors of the provinces, the shadowy central government in Peking having neither prestige nor power to control the Assembly. Through corruption Tsao Kun, a northern warlord, got himself elected President, and the prestige of the national legislative body sank rapidly as subsequent developments led ever downward to new lows of political integrity.

Quite a number of representatives were elected through corruption. Ku Hung-min, a well-known cynical scholar of international fame, told me that during an election he got eight hundred dollars from a man who

人才。同时各省巡抚威望甚高，足以约束省咨议局。碰到重大问题时，咨议局里很少发生政治纠纷。通过的议案大致都是为省民谋福利的，贪污舞弊绝无仅有。

民国元年，中山先生在南京任临时大总统时，参政会颇有成为现代国会的迹象，因为参政员代表革命利益，而且有革命领袖在领导工作，孙先生担任总统，众望所归，威望一时无两。后来袁世凯继任总统，国会里就有了纠纷了。革命领袖憎恶专制反动的袁世凯，袁也憎恶革命领袖。但因他掌握军队，不惜以武力恐吓国会议员，为此后国会发展史上开了恶例。我不妨在这里举一个例子，藉以说明恐吓手段对议会风气所产生的恶劣影响。事情发生在选举袁世凯为总统的时候，选举时有摄影师在场拍照。当时室内照须用镁光粉，点燃镁光粉时会发出炫目的闪光和震耳的响声。镁光粉爆炸时，许多人以为是炸弹，纷纷夺路逃命。有一位议员躲到桌子底下，高喊："我选举的是袁世凯！"另外有些人则落掉鞋子，事情过去以后到处找鞋。这场戏终以弹劾国会秘书张公权为结束，说他不该让摄影师以"炸弹"惊扰国会。

在袁世凯担任总统期间，经常活动的五六个政党之间纠纷迭起，派系之争和意气之争非常激烈。这个被老百姓瞧不起的国会后来终于被袁世凯称帝运动以及张勋复辟运动的潮流所卷走。不过两次运动相继失败，国会亦告恢复。政治权力一部分操在各省督军手里，一部分操在有名无实的北京中央政府手里。这时的北京政府，已经威信扫地，无力控制国会。北方军阀曹锟贿选获任总统之后，国会威信一落千丈，此后情势演变，国会声望更是每况愈下。

国会议员之中，许多是贿选而来。享誉国际、愤世嫉俗的学者辜鸿铭告诉我，有一次选举时，曾有一位哥伦比亚大学毕业的陈博士，

bought his vote. He took the money but did not go to the polls. Instead he went to Tientsin and spent all the money there. Later, at an international party in the Grand Hôtel de Pékin, Ku got hold of the man and pointing to him said to the gathering, "This man wanted to buy me for eight hundred dollars. Gentlemen, do you think Ku Hung-min is so cheap?"

When undesirable elements came into the Assembly in this manner, even though the number was not large they naturally made it look like an auction house, representation being sold to the highest bidder.

The students of Peking now directed their attack upon the "House of Corruptions." One afternoon several thousand boys and girls surrounded the Assembly and demanded that a certain bill concerning educational measures be deleted from the agenda. There was a clash between the police on duty there and the student body. Some of the students became so incensed that a few days later they smuggled in three bombs from Tientsin intended for the Assembly. They were persuaded not to carry out this violence and the bombs were taken outside the city and thrown into a river. A few weeks later a fisherman caught one of them and shook it in his hands to find out what was inside. Bang! The bomb went off and carried with it the hands and head of the inquisitive fisherman. Police assumed that it had been dropped there in the days of the revolution and no investigation was made.

Conflicts between the Assembly, and the students continued. The Assembly members tried at first to assert their right as representatives of the people. The students retorted, calling them by their now familiar contemptible name. The Assembly tried to impeach the Chancellor of the National University of Peking; the students retaliated by staging mass demonstrations in which flags bearing the likeness of a pig streamed in the air amid threats to smash the Assembly. Finally the Assembly, conscious of its weakness, declared a truce by letting the universities and students alone. Ku Hung-min, whose cynical views made him contemptuous of students and representatives alike, said to me one day, "You believe in democracy. But to me it is demo-crazy."

If an institution is hated by the public it may still have some grounds to exist; but when it is sniffed and mocked at, even though for the acts of a mere minority, the whole suffers from the inadequacy of the part and goes down together like a sinking boat. So it was with the Assembly in the early phases of constitutional government in China. At length some of the warlords snatched the opportunity to brush it aside as a scrap of paper.

出八百大洋收买他的选票，他把钱收下了，跑到天津逛了一趟胡同，根本没有去投票。后来在北京饭店的一次国际性聚会上，辜鸿铭碰到这位贿选的人，他指着这人对大家操英语说："这家伙要拿八百块钱买我，各位先生，你们看我辜鸿铭真的这么贱吗？"

若干不良分子就是这样混进国会的，虽然这种人数目不多，但是已足以使国会显得有点像拍卖场，谁出钱最高，就把议席卖给谁。

北京学生现在开始把他们的攻击目标移到这个"腐败之家"头上了。有一天下午，好几千男女学生包围了国会，要求取消议程上若干有关教育的议案。结果学生与守卫警察发生冲突。若干学生气愤之余，竟在几天之后从天津偷运来三颗炸弹准备去炸议会。这事被我们劝阻了，总算没有见诸行动，炸弹也运出城外丢到河里。几个礼拜之后，一位渔夫捡到其中的一颗炸弹，他把炸弹提在手里摇来摇去，希望弄清楚里面究竟是什么东西。轰隆一声，炸弹爆炸，炸得这位好奇的渔人血肉横飞。警方认为这颗炸弹是革命时期投进河去的，因此根本未进行任何调查。

国会与学生之间的冲突仍然不断发生。国会议员最先想确立人民代表的权威，学生们却反唇以"猪仔"相讥。国会预备弹劾北大校长，学生就发动示威游行，高举画着猪猡的旗帜，并且扬言要捣毁国会。国会自知本身有弱点，最后只好高悬免战牌，不敢再将学校与学生的虎须。愤世嫉俗的辜鸿铭既看不起学生，也看不起议员，他有一天对我说："你相信民主，这实在是民狂。"

如果一个机关只是被公众憎恨，它也许仍旧有存在的余地，如果这个机关成为公众冷讽热嘲的对象，即使那是为了其中少数人的行为，多数人也会因此遭殃，而整个机关也就像沉船一样难逃劫数了。中国宪政初期的国会，情形就是如此。后来有些军阀抓住机会，干脆把它一脚踢开。

The story of constitutionalism in the days of the warlords had, of course, two sides to it. On the one hand, the warlords wrecked it by intimidation through force and by corruption with money. They had no prestige, no principle, and no policy by which to guide a democratic body. After Yuan Shih-kai, the power of the central government was a political shadow, the real power being divided among the provinces by the warring rulers who set themselves above the law. What they knew was the military strength of their feudal armies. The central government was not a position to have any principle or policy; fundamentally it was worthy neither of support nor of opposition.

On the other side, most members of the Assembly were little concerned with national interests. Their preoccupations were either provincial or local, or still worse, personal. National interests they conceived only vaguely, and they themselves were therefore not in a position to have any coherent guiding principles or policy on national issues. Consequently no leadership was possible except in matters of local or personal interest. The Chinese people love freedom but were inexperienced in organized democracy—in other words, in constitutionalism. They did not see the importance of it. For China to follow the constitutional pattern of the West without its background was to hitch China's wagon to the Western star. It was small wonder that the experiment failed miserably.

With this failure before his eyes Dr. Sun Yat-sen devised a system of tutelary government as a steppingstone to constitutional government in his plan for an organized democracy for China. According to this scheme the period of national unification was to be followed by what might be called government in a state of tutelage—i.e., government by the Kuomintang—as a transition to the full-fledged constitutional form. And when the Kuomintang came to power in 1927 the tutelary government at Nanking was indeed meant to offset the bad effects of the corrupt National Assembly, which had become a headache to the entire country. During the next ten years the Nationalist party, under the leadership of

Generalissimo Chiang Kai-shek, dislodged many a local warlord from the provinces and achieved to a large extent the unification of the country. The danger to national existence brought upon China by the Japanese militarists further intensified the unification.

Unification of the country was a necessary condition to constitutionalism. With respect for the law on the part of governing and governed alike—with the principles laid down by Dr. Sun Yat-sen, and with efficient leadership both in the government and in the National Assembly—China will be on the road to successful constitutionalism and organized democracy.

　　我们可以从两个不同的角度来看军阀时代的宪政。一方面是军阀以威胁利诱来破坏宪政，他们没有领导民主团体的威信、原则或政策。袁世凯垮台以后，中央政府的权力已经名存实亡，实际权力操纵在互相残杀的各省督军手里。他们根本不理什么叫法律，他们只晓得自己持有封建军队的武力。中央政府既不能维持宪政原则，也不能确立治国政策，事实上这个政府已经无足轻重，不值得拥护也不值得反对。

　　在另一方面，国会里的议员，很少有人关心国家利益。他们念念不忘的只是他们本省的或本地的利益，甚至只是本身的利益。他们对国家利益的观念，本来就很模糊，因此对国家大事也就不可能有整套的指导原则或政策。除了地方事件或私人利益之外，既无组织，亦无领导。中国人爱好自由，但是对有组织的民主政治，也就是对宪政，却无经验，也不懂组织对民主的重要。中西国情不同，想使中国遵循西洋的宪政规模，无异赶东方之车，朝向西方的一颗星走着。宪政试验的失败，实在毫不足奇。

　　中山先生有鉴于此，所以在他的民主宪政计划中，设计了训政制度，作为过渡到宪政政府的跳板。依照他的计划，先有军政时期以达国家统一，接着是一个以党领政的训政时期，最后才过渡到正式的宪政时期。民国十六年，北伐成功，国民党在南京建立训政政府，锐意革除国会的腐败风气。此后十年间，国民党在蒋委员长领导下，铲除军阀，统一全国。日本军阀所导致的国难，使统一的局面更为加强。

　　国家统一是实行宪政的先决条件。孙中山先生已经制定建国的原则，只要政府与国会能有坚强的领导，人民与政府一致尊重法律，中国无疑地将在民主宪政的道路上大步迈进。

CHAPTER 18   THE DEATH OF DR. SUN YAT-SEN

Death calls before Victory descends upon my country.

Patriots that come after me will forever think of the tragedy in tears.

The above lines are from a poem by a famous general who was sent to defend China against an invasion of the Tartars in the twelfth century. They apply only too truly to the death of Dr. Sun Yat-sen. The great leader had struggled in the cause of revolution for forty long and strenuous years, and death snatched him away when the nation needed him for its regeneration.

In the spring of 1925 he had been for some months in poor health as a result of his untiring work for the country. Having admitted the Communists to the Kuomintang he went one step further. Seeing China still a divided house and knowing that strength lay in union, in response to an invitation of the northern generals he came from Canton to Peking to discuss a plan to unify the country. On his way north he made a trip to Japan in an effort to convince the Japanese people that a strong and unified China would be beneficial to that country. When he arrived at Tientsin he fell sick. He was carried from that port to the capital, accompanied by Madam Sun Yat-sen. But he was too ill to discuss plans and could only lie in bed. The doctors of the Peking Union Medical College were at their wits' end. Dr. Hu Shih recommended a Chinese herb doctor. Dr. Sun declined to take the Chinese medicine. He said that as a physician himself he knew that an herb doctor might sometimes cure a disease where scientific medicine failed. "A ship without a compass may reach its destination," he said, "while that which has one may not come to port. But I prefer to sail with that scientific instrument." However, he was persistently advised to take the Chinese medicine, and to meet the wishes of his friends he at length consented. But the ship without a compass did not reach port.

Dr. Sun was presently transferred from the Medical College to the home of Dr. Wellington Koo. This magnificent house, built in the seventeenth century, had once belonged to a famous beauty, Chen Yuan-yuan, wife of General Wu San-kwei of the Ming Dynasty, who surrendered to the Manchus and conducted them inside the Great Wall, so the story goes, in order to rescue the lady from the hands of the bandit leader Li Shih-chung.

拾捌 中山先生之逝世

出师未捷身先死，
长使英雄泪满襟。

此为杜甫咏诸葛武侯之句，宋宗泽元帅假以自挽者也。如果拿这两句诗来描写中山先生之死，真是再恰当没有了。这位伟大的领袖，致力国民革命达四十年之久，不幸在国家建设正需要他的时候，死神就把他攫走了。

民国十四年（一九二五年）春天，孙先生因为宵旰勤劳的结果，几个月来身体一直不怎么好。他在容许共产党参加国民党以后，更采取了进一步的行动。他鉴于中国仍旧陷于分裂，同时鉴于只有团结才能产生力量，乃毅然应北洋军阀之邀，离粤北上，到北京讨论统一国家的计划。北上途中，他曾绕道访问日本，希望说服日本朝野，使他们相信强大统一的中国是对日本有利的。到达天津时，他竟病倒了。我到天津谒见孙先生及夫人并报告北京政情后，不日返京。过了几天，大家把他从天津护送到北京，我赴车站往迎。……先生到北京后病势仍是很重，无法讨论统一计划，且一直卧床不能起身。执政段祺瑞托称足疾亦未往谒。北京协和医院的医师对先生的病均告束手，胡适之先生推荐了一位中医陆仲安。但是孙先生不愿服中药。他说，他本身是医生，他知道现代医药束手时，中医的确有时也能治好疑难的病症。他说："一只没有装罗盘的船也可能到达目的地，而一只装了罗盘的船有时反而不能到达。但是我宁愿利用科学仪器来航行。"朋友仍旧一再劝他吃点中药，他不忍过于拂逆朋友的好意，最后终于同意了。但是这只没装罗盘的船却始终没有到达彼岸。

孙先生自协和医院移住顾少川（维钧）寓。顾寓宽敞宏丽，建于十七世纪，原为著名美人陈圆圆的故居。陈为明将吴三桂之妻，据说吴三桂为了从闯王李自成手中抢救陈圆圆，不惜叛明降清，并引清兵入关。

On the morning of March 12, 1925, a telephone call from Ma Soo informed me that Dr. Sun was nearing his end. I hastened to his temporary residence. When I entered the chamber Dr. Sun Yat-sen was beyond speech. A moment earlier he had muttered, "Peace, struggle, save China..." These were his last words. We retired to the reception hall and looked at each other in silence. "Is there any chance for the Doctor to recover?" whispered an aged Kuomintang member. All shook their heads, stifling the word upon their lips.

Silence gathered and deepened until one could hear it. Minute melted insensibly into minute. Some leaned against the wall, staring blankly at the painted ceiling. Others sank into the comfortable sofas and closed their eyes. A few tiptoed to the chamber and back without a word.

Suddenly everybody in the hall was alert, listening to sobs barely audible from the bedroom. The faint sounds gave way to a chorus of loud cries—the great leader had passed into history. As we entered the death chamber I saw that Dr. Sun's countenance was serene, as if he were asleep. His son, Sun Fo, was sitting on a bench at the bedside staring into space like a man of stone. Madam Sun bent over the edge of the bed with her face buried in the soft mattress, shaking with sobs that would break one's heart. Wang Chung-huei, standing at the end of the bed, was rocking convulsively, wailing and wiping away his tears with a handkerchief. The elder statesman Wu Chi-huei stood with his hands clasped behind him and tears welling up in his eyes.

As Dr. Sun's body was carried out of the hall covered with a big national flag, Mr. Borodin, the Soviet adviser, said to me sadly that if he could have lived a few years or even a few months longer things would have been very different.

An autopsy made at the Medical College proved that cancer of the liver had caused his death.

Dr. Sun's body lay in state in one of the former palace halls in Central Park. Every day for a week at least twenty to thirty thousand people came to pay their last respects to their leader. The funeral procession, four or five miles long, was joined by all the students from elementary schools up to colleges, and by teachers, government officials, tradesmen, workers, and farmers, a hundred thousand strong.

The casket was placed temporarily in a stone pagoda in Pi-yun Ssu, the Purple Cloud Temple in the Western Hills, about fifteen miles from

民国十四年三月十二日早晨，行辕顾问马素打电话来通知我，孙先生已入弥留状态。我连忙赶到他的临时寓所。我进他卧室时，孙先生已经不能说话。在我到达前不久，他曾经说过："和平、奋斗、救中国。……"这就是他的最后遗嘱了。大家退到客厅里，面面相觑。"先生还有复原的希望吗？"一个国民党元老轻轻地问。大家都摇摇头，欲言又止。

沉默愈来愈使人感到窒息，几乎彼此的呼吸都清晰可闻。时间一分一秒无声地过去，有些人倚在墙上，茫然望着天花板。有些人躺在沙发上，闭起眼睛沉思。也有几个人蹑手蹑脚跑进孙先生卧室，然后又一声不响地回到客厅。

忽然客厅里的人都尖起耳朵，谛听卧室内隐约传来的一阵啜泣声，隐约的哭声接着转为号啕痛哭——这位伟大的领袖已经撒手逝世了。我们进入卧室时，我发现孙先生的容颜澄澈宁静，像是在安睡。他的公子哲生先生坐在床旁的一张小凳上，呆呆地瞪着两只眼，像是一个石头人。孙夫人伏身床上，埋头在盖被里饮泣，哭声凄楚，使人心碎。汪精卫站在床头号啕痛哭，同时拿着一条手帕擦眼泪。吴稚晖老先生背着双手站在一边，含泪而立。

覆盖着国旗的中山先生的遗体舁出大厅时，鲍罗廷很感慨地对我说：如果孙先生能够多活几年，甚至几个月，中国的局势也许会完全改观的。

协和医院检验结果，发现中山先生系死于肝癌。

孙先生的灵柩停放在中央公园的社稷坛，任人瞻仰遗容。一星期里，每天至少有两三万人前来向他们的领袖致最后的敬意。出殡行列长达四五里，执绋在十万人以上，包括从小学到大学的全部学生、教员、政府官员、商人、工人和农人。

灵柩暂停厝在离北京城约十五里的西山碧云寺石塔里。石塔

Peking. This picturesque pagoda was built centuries ago under Tibetan influence, of white marble with a pointed top of gilded bronze. It perches majestically on the south side of Purple Cloud Mountain, surrounded by tall pine trees, and overlooking a sea of whispering pines which sound like waves in the spring breeze and scent the air with their fragrance. The sky was serene. Streams wound their way among the moss-grown rocks. The bells in the eaves of the temple chimed melodiously in the wind.

Dr. Sun, who had lived a life of science and struggle, now rested in peace amid the beauty of art and nature.

......

建于数百年前，略带西藏风味，由白色大理石建成，塔尖是镀金的青铜打造的。石塔高踞碧云寺南方，四周古松围绕，春风中松涛低吟，芬芳扑鼻。碧空澄澈，绿茵遍地，潺潺的溪水和碧云寺的檐角的铃声相应和，交织成清轻的音乐。

毕生致力于科学和奋斗的孙先生，现在终于在艺术与自然交织的优美环境中安息了。

…… ……

按：罗家伦先生主编《国父年谱》七三八页对中山先生民国十四年于北平治疗情形，曾有刊载，志录如下：

十八日自协和医院移居铁狮子胡同行辕。是日，先生离协和医院，乘医院特备汽车，缓驶至铁狮子胡同行辕。家属及友好同志，多以为医院既经宣告绝望，仍当不惜采取任何方法，以延长先生寿命。于是有推荐中医陆仲安者，因陆曾医治胡适博士，若由胡进言，先生或不峻拒。乃推李煜瀛（石曾）赴天津访胡（时胡适有事赴津），告以来意，约其同归。胡初以推荐医生责任太重，有难色。后抵京见汪兆铭等，力言侍疾者均惶急万状，莫不以挽救先生生命为第一，且因先生平时对胡甚客气，换一生人往说，或可采纳。胡乃偕陆同往。胡先入卧室进言。先生语胡曰："适之！你知道我是学西医的人。"胡谓："不妨一试，服药与否再由先生决定。"语至此，孙夫人在床边急乘间言曰："陆先生已在此，何妨看看。"语讫即握先生腕，先生点首，神情凄惋，盖不欲重拂其意，乃伸手而以面移向内望。孙夫人即转身往床之内方坐下，目光与先生对视。

CHAPTER 19   THE ANTI-WARLORD CAMPAIGN

Years of student demonstrations and strikes coupled with internecine wars had sapped the strength of the government in Peking. In the provinces the warlords ruled like maharajahs. The power of the overlord in Peking at any one time depended upon the good will and support of the provinces which had easy access to the city. As its roots in the provinces weakened, the tree of power in Peking grew shaky. No sooner had one warlord entered the capital to take over the reins of government—either himself or through a puppet of his creation—than another would conspire to overthrow him and come to power in turn; when public sentiment as revealed in student demonstrations ran high against the regime in power, some other provincial general was always ready to take advantage of it. Through intrigue, civil war, coups d'état, or reshuffled combinations of power, the government changed hands constantly. During my first nine years in Peking I witnessed so many changes that the rapid shift of scene left in my memory only a jumble of disconnected, though vivid, pictures of the tragicomedy. I could imagine myself a pyramid sitting in the Egyptian desert, watching utterly unconcerned the constant coming and going of caravans and listening to the camel bells chiming their sad tunes.

Financial stringency was acute for the Peking government. National revenues were detained by the warlords in the provinces and spent in maintaining their private armies or to enrich their own coffers. A portion of the money that came to the central government, usually through loans from banks at exorbitant interest, had to go to military expenditure to placate the insatiable warlords who supported the government. Salaries, not only of teachers, as we have seen, but also of government employees and of diplomatic officials stationed in foreign lands, were left unpaid for months at a time or even years.

"What is the future of the Peking government?" asked an American diplomat one day.

"It will dry up like a clam and only the shell will remain," I replied.

The situation grew worse year after year until the last vestige of the public respect due to a government was gone. The students helped to destroy its prestige and the warlords buried it in the Peking dust.

拾玖 反军阀运动

　　学生游行罢课闹了好几年，加上军阀互相残杀，北京政府的力量终于一蹶不振，军阀则像印度土大王一样统治各省。在北京的中央政府首脑，无时不需要邻近各省的支持，如果军阀一翻脸，随时可以长驱直入北京城。北京政府在各省的根基愈来愈脆弱，政权本身亦随之摇摇欲坠。某一军阀进入北京接收政权，另一军阀马上阴谋取而代之。当政的人如果遭遇民意的强烈反对，例如学生游行示威，其他军阀便利用机会从中取利。权谋、内战、政变，各种政治力量纵横捭阖的结果，北京政府随时在更换主人。我在北京的最初九年之中，所看到的变迁实在太多了，留在记忆中的是一大堆乱糟糟的悲喜剧场面。我像是埃及沙漠中一座金字塔，淡淡遥望着行行列列来来往往的驼影，反映在斜阳笼罩着的浩浩平沙之上，驼铃奏出哀怨的曲调，悠扬于晚红之中。

　　北京政府的经济状况非常窘困，国库应有的收入，都被各省军阀扣留，用以维持他们的私人军队或径入私人腰包。中央政府通常只能以极高的利息向银行借一点钱，这一点钱之中的一部分，还得用于笼络支持政府然而需索无餍的军阀。我们前面已经提到教员薪水拖欠的情形。不但教员如此，就是政府官员和驻外使节的薪水，也往往一欠就是好几个月，甚至好几年。

　　"北京政府的前途究竟怎么样呢？"有一天，一位美国外交官这样问我。

　　"它会像河滩失水的蚌，日趋干涸，最后只剩下一个蚌壳。"我回答说。

　　情势一年不如一年，终至老百姓对政府的最后一点敬意也消失了。学生帮同破坏了它的威信，军阀们则把它整个埋葬在北京的尘土里。

　　数年后在美国遇见那位美国朋友，他问我是否忘了蚌壳的故事，我说没有。

In the meantime the Kuomintang movement in Canton grew in strength by leaps and bounds. It had enjoyed public faith for some time, especially among intellectuals and students, and even won the sympathy of certain enlightened generals of the north—for among the warring northern generals enlightened ones were not lacking. In the basket of rotten oranges it was possible to find a few good ones.

Even after the death of Dr. Sun Yat-sen the spirit of the Nationalist party of China remained undaunted. Dr. Sun's nucleus of an army kept on growing at Huang-pu Military Academy near Canton, of which General Chiang Kai-shek was the president. In the course of a few years General Chiang's newly trained Nationalist troops were ready to deliver a deathblow to the warlords of the north. In 1927 this army of the Nationalist government of the Kuomintang swept northward at lightning speed through the heart of the country to Hankow, and another wing moved along the coast to Hangchow. In a pincer movement the two converged on Nanking, which was made capital of the Nationalist government when the victorious armies entered the city.

That same year, at about the time the Nationalist army started its northern expedition, a notorious warlord, Chang Chung-chang, entered Peking. This renowned leader had the physique of an elephant, the brain of a pig, and the temperament of a tiger. His powerful paws were always ready to snatch at any person he disliked or at any good-looking woman he coveted. I saw him several times in a peace-preserving committee of which I was a member, and felt that he was dangerous even to look at. When I was informed by Sun Pao-chi, ex-premier of the Peking government, that I was on the blacklist, and news reached me in the evening of the execution of Shao Piao-ping, editor of the newspaper *Ching Pao*, I began to see the shadows of those powerful claws. Without hesitating I got into the car of Dr. Wang Chung-huei, who happened to call on me, and went directly to the Legation Quarter, where I got a room in the Hôtel des Wagons Lits. Here I stayed for three months and passed my time in studying calligraphy.

There were several others in similar plight; Dr. Chu Chia-hua, professor of geology and now director of the Academia Sinica, was one. Quite a few friends ran in from time to time to visit us. But spending

在那时候，广州的国民革命运动则以一日千里之势在发展，国民党的革命运动一直享有大众的支持，尤其是知识分子和学生，甚至连北洋军阀中的一些开明分子也同情国民党。一篮烂橘子里，有时也能找出几个好的来的。

中山先生虽然逝世了，国民党的精神却始终未沮丧。孙先生所建立的革命武力核心，继续在蒋介石将军为校长的黄埔军校发展茁壮，短短几年之内，蒋将军的国民革命军已经完成训练，随时可予北洋军队以致命的打击。民国十六即一九二七年，革命军以雷霆万钧之势长驱北伐，左翼直入华中而下汉口，右翼循闽浙沿海北上而达杭州，继以钳形攻势会师南京。革命军攻克南京后，遂以南京为国民政府首都。

国民革命军开始北伐的那一年，北洋军阀张宗昌亦于同时入据北京，这位声名狼藉的军阀，体健如牛，脑笨如猪，性暴如虎。他的利爪随时会伸向他不喜欢的任何人，或者他垂涎的任何漂亮女人。我曾在一个治安委员会席上见过他几面，当时我是这个委员会的委员之一。他那副尊容，真叫人望而生畏。京报编辑邵飘萍被枪毙的那天晚上，北京政府的前总理孙宝琦告诉我，我的名字已经上了黑名单，我感觉到魔爪的影子已经向我伸过来了。刚好王亮畴（宠惠）来访，我不假思索，连忙跳上他的军警不会盘查的红牌汽车，直驶东交民巷使馆界，在六国饭店僻室住下。第二天跑到美国使馆向一位美国朋友开玩笑说："我天天叫打倒帝国主义，现在却投入帝国主义怀抱求保护了。"还有校长室秘书政治学教授李守常（大钊）、女生张挹兰等六七人先后逃入使馆界旧东清铁路办事处躲避。他们后来被张作霖派兵捕去，处绞刑而死。我在六国饭店住了三个月，经常以写字消遣。

同住在六国饭店的亦有几个人，地质学教授，以后任中央研究院院长朱骝先（家骅）就是其中之一。好些朋友不时探望我们，

three months in even a de luxe prison was no fun at all. We plotted escape and at length, when the situation was somewhat eased, sneaked out one after another. A very able young lady, the wife of a friend of mine, planned my escape. Acting as my wife she escorted me to the East Station without our being noticed by the police. Every casual look from a stranger startled me, though I remained outwardly calm. Following a stream of passengers I boarded a train to Tientsin and from there went by British merchant liner to Shanghai.

On the boat I met Dr. Chu Chia-hua, who from Shanghai was to proceed to Canton, where he later became president of the Sun Yat-sen University. For my part, I went to Hangchow. As the railway from Shanghai had been cut I reached the city by a roundabout way. At this time, before the Nationalist army commanded by General Ho Yin-chin reached the province, the governor appointed by Peking was attempting to revolt against the northern government and go over to the southern side. I called on him, and he revealed to me his plan for joining the southern camp. He told me that he had sent about a thousand men along the railway to the Kiangsu border, where the line was already cut.

I thought privately that he must be intoxicated with the cup of other people's success, or he would not attempt to fight an enemy at least ten times stronger than himself. I left Hangchow again the next morning by the roundabout route back to Shanghai. Within a few weeks his army was utterly routed by northern forces. When they entered Hangchow he was captured and executed.

Then the tables were turned on the northern warlords and Nationalist forces entered the city. Again I went there. Hangchow welcomed the Nationalist army with open arms. Thousands of spectators lined up along the streets with smiling faces to see the victorious modern-equipped troops march through the city. I stood watching in the crowd with my heart thumping against my ribs in ecstasy. After some sixteen years the good name of a modern army in China was once more established.

In about a year's time, in 1928, General Chiang Kai-shek was ready to launch his northern expedition. The army under his command crossed the Yangtze River and moved along the Tientsin-Pukow Railway with Peking as its objective. When it reached the outskirts of Tsinanfu, capital of Shantung Province, the Japanese—fearing a unified China—moved

但是在那里关了三个月，即使那是一个豪华"监狱"，也有点吃不消。我们一直在设法逃出北京，后来局势比较松弛一点时，就相继溜出来了。我的一位朋友有一位年轻能干的太太，我之能够逃出北京，就是她一手策划的。她冒充我的太太，同乘一轮古老的马车陪送我到东车站，一路上居然逃过警察的耳目。陌生人望我一眼，都会使我心惊肉跳，虽然我在外表上仍旧竭力装作若无其事的样子。我挤在人潮中搭上一辆去天津的火车，然后从天津搭英国商船到上海。

在船上碰到朱骝先，他正预备转道上海赴广州，后来他出任广州中山大学校长。我本人则由上海转赴杭州。当时沪杭铁路已告中断，因此我只好绕道赴杭。这时何敬之将军（应钦）所率领的国民革命军尚未到达浙江，北京政府委派的浙江省长正准备起义反抗北洋政府向国民革命军输诚。我去拜访他时，他向我透露了参加南方集团的计划。他告诉我，他已经派了一千人沿铁路进驻江苏边境，江浙之间的铁路已告中断。

我心里想，他准是被别人的胜利陶醉了，否则他怎么会企图与实力强他十倍的敌人作战呢？第二天早晨，我就离开杭州，绕道重回上海。几星期以后，他的军队被北军打得落花流水。北军进杭州时，他被捕处决。

不久北洋军阀命运逆转，国民革命军进占杭州。我也再度回到西子湖畔。杭州人热烈欢迎国民革命军。这些现代装备的军队胜利进军杭州时，成千成万的市民满面笑容地列队欢迎。我站在人丛中观望，一颗心高兴得怦怦乱跳。经过十六年之后，一支现代化的中国军队的信誉又重新建立起来了。

大约一年之后，蒋总司令在民国十七年即一九二八年完成部署，准备继续北伐。他指挥的军队渡过长江，沿津浦路向北京推进。北伐军抵达山东济南府边缘时，日本人惟恐中国统一，

troops from Tsingtao down along the Tsingtao-Tsinan Railway to that capital under the pretext of protecting their vested interests and the lives and properties of the Mikado's subjects. This was intended to frustrate the unification plan by provoking an "incident," i.e., an open clash between China and Japan. The Japanese army murdered the Commissioner of Foreign Affairs and his staff in Tsinanfu, hoping that China would retaliate.

With foresight and forbearance and a sound strategy, the General saved his army and his hopes of unification by turning the spearhead of his forces away from Shantung, quickly crossing the Yellow River, and marching right on to Peking. The Japanese were thus outwitted and left to fight shadows.

Peking fell when the Nationalist army arrived. The giant of hollow papier-mâché toppled over before the merest breath of wind from the south.

When the Nationalist army entered Hangchow the year before, I had been appointed a member of the provincial government and Commissioner of Education. Thus in Hangchow, capital of Chekiang Province and city of my boyhood days, my experience in government administration began. The provincial government was formed with a council in charge. Before the national government in Nanking was organized, all the members of the council, with its chairman, were appointed by the supreme commander of the Nationalist army, General Chiang Kai-shek.

Five members of the council acted concurrently as Commissioners of Civil Affairs, Finance, Military Affairs, Reconstruction, and Education. Above the provincial council was a branch council of the central political council of the Kuomintang, of which I was appointed secretary-general. This council was in charge of general policy for the province and gave orders to the provincial government to execute. It was later abolished as conditions in the province gradually settled down.

The provincial government was imbued with the same spirit of reform and reconstruction as the national government of Nanking, whose broader program we shall take up in the next chapter. The provincial reconstruction plan was rather ambitious, but after a revolution it was necessarily handicapped by lack of funds. So it concentrated on building more roads. Within a few years many roads were built—in the capital

藉口保护在山东的权益和日本皇民的生命财产，竟由青岛派兵沿胶济路向济南推进。他们的目的是制造"事件"，以破坏中国的统一计划。所谓"事件"，自然就是中日之间公开冲突。日军在济南府残杀山东交涉员及其僚属，希望藉此激起中国的报复行动。

蒋总司令洞烛日人阴谋，深恐小不忍而乱大谋，决定暂避其锋，把国民革命军的前头部队调离山东，并以迅雷不及掩耳的手段渡过黄河，直逼北京。因而国民革命军未遭阻挠，统一目标亦赖以实现。日本军队在山东终于扑了空。

国民革命军到达后，北京随即陷落，北京政府的纸老虎被南风一吹就倒了。

民国十六年国民革命军进杭州时，我被任为省政府委员兼教育厅长。我在政府中担任工作的经验也就在杭州开始了。杭州是浙江的省会，也是我青年时代读书的地方。省政府由省政府委员会组成。国民政府在南京成立以前，所有省府委员以及主席都是由国民革命军总司令蒋介石将军委派的。

省府委员之中有五位分别兼任民政厅长、财政厅长、军事厅长、建设厅长和教育厅长。省府委员会之上则有国民党中央政治会议浙江分会，负责全省一般政策，政策决定后即下令省政府执行。会议主席由省主席张静江先生担任，由我任秘书长。这是我第一次担任国民党要职。后来省境情势渐趋稳定，政分会遂告撤销。

省政府和南京的国民政府一样充满着改革和建设的精神，中央政府的重大施政，我将在下一章加以叙述。省政府的建设计划相当庞大，但是革命之后，此项计划难免受经费支绌的限制。因此只能将工作集中在铺筑公路上面，几年之内的确铺了不少公路。省城本身

itself the provincial council ran a pencil through the map of the city and ordered roads to be built accordingly. After two years Hangchow was blessed with many wide streets within the city and roads running along the shores and on the dikes across the West Lake, leading to scenic spots in the Western Hills. A highway linked the city with Shanghai, and this brought many week-end motorists. In the short span of three years everyone noticed how the city had changed. New buildings shot up like mushrooms in the city, around the lake, and in the mountains. The population increased and business prospered.

Many electric plants were set up in local areas. In some rural districts gas pumps were installed to irrigate the rice fields. As Chekiang was the center of silk production, scientific sericulture was started by the government: silkworm eggs were raised scientifically and distributed to the silk producers at cost. The first year strong objections were raised to the new eggs, for the silk producers became suspicious of them under the influence of egg producers who followed traditional methods. But results speak louder than false propaganda; the second year there was more demand for new eggs than the government could supply.

In order to reform the land tax system a general survey was made of agricultural land in the province, and this continued for many years following. In contrast to the drastic methods adopted by the Communists in their dealing with agrarian problems, these were tackled in Chekiang by the mild means of a general 25 per cent reduction of the land rent paid by the tillers to the owners. As a rule the tenant farmers paid about 25 per cent of their main crop as rent; the reduction lowered this figure to 18.75 per cent.[1] As the rates of land rent had existed through centuries and the method and basis of calculation varied in different localities, the tenant farmers of some localities were much benefited, while elsewhere the rule for reduction caused great friction between owners and tenants. Lawsuits streamed in to the Land Rent Reduction Commission. There was so much confusion throughout the province that after some years the scheme was finally abandoned. Shen, the moving spirit in rent reduction, was assassinated for causes still undetermined.

Later, a campaign against illiteracy was launched. After some six or seven years the number of short-term schools to teach the reading and writing of the more commonly used characters had increased by thousands alongside the regular elementary schools.

也有许多道路经省政府指定拓宽或添建。两年之后，杭州城内已经添筑了许多宽阔的马路。西湖沿岸和苏堤也辟了马路，直达西山各名胜，另有一条公路与上海衔接，招来了不少度周末的游客。短短三年之内，杭州已经焕然一新了。市区之内，西湖之滨，以及湖边山麓，新建洋房别墅像雨后春笋一样出现，人口激增，商业也盛极一时。

各县市也新建了许多电灯厂。若干乡村里还装设了蒸汽帮浦灌溉稻田。因为浙江是丝织业中心，政府开始提倡科学养蚕法，以科学方法培育蚕种，然后转售给养蚕的人。头一年里，科学蚕种曾经引起强烈的反对，因养蚕的人受了以传统方法培育蚕种的人的影响，对于科学蚕种发生怀疑。但是事实胜于雄辩，第二年中，政府出产的新式蚕种已经供不应求。

为了改善田租制度，政府举办全省耕地调查，工作继续了好几年。浙江省所采用的办法，与共产党对农地所采的激烈手段适成对照。浙江省采取一种比较温和的"二五减租"办法，也就是佃农付给地主的田租普遍减低百分之二十五。佃农通常以主要作物收获的百分之五十付给地主田租，"二五减租"以后，佃农就只要付收成的百分之三七点五了。田租的租率已经维持了几百年，计算方法各地互有差别，实行"二五减租"以后，有些地方的佃农得到很大的利益，在另一些地方，这个减租办法却在地主与佃农之间引起严重的纠纷。减租委员会所收受的讼案多如山积，全省各地普遍发生纠纷，减租办法终于几年之后放弃。推行减租最力的沈玄庐（定一）被暗杀，死因迄今未明。

不久之后，扫除文盲运动开始。经过六七年时间，除了普通的小学之外，短期的民众识字班增加了几千个。

A new experiment was made in the educational system of the province. The National University of Chekiang was organized with the writer as president. The university was not only to take charge of higher education but also to control the public school system in the province. The office of commissioner of education was abolished and the president of the university was made a member of the provincial government. Two other provinces followed suit with their respective university and school systems. After two years of trial, internal troubles and political complications grew in the other provinces, and the whole system was accordingly abolished in 1929 during my term of office as national Minister of Education. Thus the person by whose hands it was sent to the grave was the one who had nursed it to grow with much work and thought.

I stayed a full year in Hangchow and the next year went back forth between Hangchow and Nanking, where I was appointed Minister of Education of the national government while concurrently holding the presidency of the University of Chekiang. In 1929 I gave up the latter post and stayed in Nanking for another year, when I was forced to resign from the Ministry of Education as a result of disagreement with some of the elder statesmen regarding a question of educational policy.

省内的教育制度进行一次新试验。国立浙江大学成立，由我担任校长。浙大不但主持高等教育，并且主管全省公立学校。教育厅取消，浙大校长则成为省府委员。另外两省也继起仿效，各自成立大学。经过两年的试验，另外几省发生内部纠纷和政治争执，整个制度终于在民国十八年即一九二九年废止，那时我任国民政府教育部长，所以培植这个制度和埋葬这个制度的都是我自己。

我在杭州整整住了一年，翌年膺任教育部长，同时兼任浙江大学校长，因此经常往返京杭之间。民国十八年，我辞去浙大校长兼职，在南京再住了一年，后以中央大学易长及劳动大学停办两事与元老们意见相左，被迫辞职。

我当时年壮气盛，有决策，必贯彻到底，不肯通融，在我自以为励精图治，在人则等于一意孤行。我本世居越中，耳濡目染，颇知绍兴师爷化大为小、化小为无的诀窍。今背道而驰，自然碰壁。武力革命难，政治革命更难，思想革命尤难，这是我所受的教训。

在我辞职的前夜，吴稚晖先生突然来教育部，双目炯炯有光，在南京当时电灯朦胧的深夜，看来似乎更觉明显。他老先生问我中央、劳动两校所犯何罪，并为两校讼冤。据吴老先生的看法，部长是当朝大臣，应该多管国家大事，少管学校小事。最后用指向我一点，厉声说道："你真是无大臣之风。"

我恭恭敬敬地站起来回答说：

"先生坐，何至于是，我知罪矣。"

第二天我就辞了职，不日离京，回北京大学去了。刘半农教授闻之，赠我图章一方，文曰："无大臣之风。"

CHAPTER 20   THE RISE OF THE KUOMINTANG TO POWER

After the fall of Peking the country was once more a political whole. The capital of all China was moved to Nanking and remained there. Peking, meaning "North Capital," was changed to Peiping, "Peace in the North," an old name of the city before it was known to the world.

Peking had been the capital of five dynasties—the Liao, King, Yuan (Mongol), Ming, and Ching (Manchu)—over a period of more than a thousand years, and now ceased to be the capital. But it still remained the center of culture and art. The official dialect or language spoken by many of the educated classes in China in addition to their local dialects, used in broadcasting stations and taught in schools, had its home in Peking.

There were two main reasons why Nationalist China shifted the capital from the Yellow River Valley in the north to the Yangtze Valley in the south. The first was that the revolutionary spirit had permeated the latter area, which was therefore fertile soil where it was easier for the new spirit to take firm root, while the Yellow River Valley was the home of the reactionary warlords. Secondly, the Yangtze Valley was the seat of China's financial power, which could provide the government with necessary funds.

Nanking had been the capital for the Taipings, from 1851 to 1864. When they were dislodged from their last stronghold the city was devastated, and has never recovered its past glories. There were more ruins, wheat fields, vegetable gardens, and orchards than streets with buildings in that walled enclosure. The streets were narrow, rough, and filthy, the electric light no better than vegetable-oil lamps. A foot messenger was often speedier than a telephone call.

In the earlier periods of history this city on the bank of the Yangtze was a center of culture and refinement, especially in the time of the southern dynasties. Its life of wine, women, and song dwelt in the memories of generations of literary men, poets, and artists. The Ching-huai Canal, connecting lakes of luxuriant lilies, traversed the city crowded with singing houseboats lit up by painted lanterns and lavishly decorated with articles of art. On either bank of the canal, as a boat sailed leisurely by, there unrolled before one's eyes endless rows of restaurants, and rooms elaborately furnished with painted columns and bamboo screens for literary, artistic, or musical entertainments. The air was laden with enchanting tunes and soothing scents that flowed out from behind the bamboo screens.

贰拾 国民党之出掌政权

国民革命军攻克北京以后，中国重归统一，首都亦由北京迁至南京，北京则改为北平。

北京曾为辽、金、元、明、清五代的首都，历时一千余年。现在国都固然改定为南京，北平却仍旧是文化和艺术的中心。中国知识阶级除了本地方言之外所说的，以及广播电台所采用和学校所教授的"官话"或"国语"就是以北京方言做基础的。

国民政府从北方黄河流域迁都南方的长江流域，主要原因有二。第一个理由是革命精神已经弥漫长江流域，因此也是革命精神比较容易生根的肥沃土壤，黄河流域则是反动军阀的根据地。第二个理由：长江流域是中国金融力量的中心，足以供应政府必需的经费。

在一八五一年至一八六四年之间，南京曾是太平天国的首都。太平军溃败以后，南京破坏殆尽，而且始终不曾恢复旧观。城内的废墟、麦田、菜圃、果园比盖了房子的街道还多。街道狭窄，路面高低不平，而且肮脏不堪，电灯昏暗如菜油灯。差个专人送信往往比打电话还快。

这座雄踞扬子江边的古城，在古时是文物教化的中心，尤其是在南朝时代，所谓南朝金粉是也。女人、醇酒、清歌、妙舞一直萦回在历代骚人墨客的记忆里。秦淮河横越城内，连接了盛长百合的湖泊。河上满是金碧辉煌高悬彩灯的画舫。秦淮河两岸酒楼歌榭栉比，雕梁画栋，门口挂着竹帘子，妙曼的曲调和醉人的幽香从竹帘后一阵阵飘送出来，此所谓：

> "此曲只应天上有，
> 人间哪得几回闻。"

Such was the city in days of old. But Nanking was of strategic military importance. In every major war in the country this city was destined to suffer devastation. After every conflict its glories passed into memory, and from memory it was rebuilt upon its ruins when peace came. And from the memory of the past, as it was recorded, I have depicted a part of the old life of Nanking.

Since the Taipings, however, it has never recovered its ancient beauty. It is as if the successive restorations were only copies, done by some vulgar artist, of the original picture; after repeated copying the color of the original was lost and only vulgarity remained. From time to time, in periods after the Southern Sungs (1127-1276), scholars of puritanic bent or stoic leanings objected to the type of effeminate refinement which grew up along the Ching-huai, now but an empty name with pleasant associations. But we must aver that the wrong lay not in enjoying the refinements of life but in the neglect of work and duty which should go with enjoyment. If there were only work and no play, Jack would be a dull boy. The stoic ways of living which came into vogue with the philosophers of the Sung Dynasty bequeathed to China generations of dull Jacks who knew neither play nor the right sort of work. They killed art, and with art, life. They attacked bad morals, but countenanced that abominable and most immoral institution, the foot-binding of women. Compare with this life in the Tang Dynasty (618-905), when work and play went hand in hand and a healthy civilization shone like the brilliant sun upon all its neighbor nations! Think of the Tang dances (mind you, there was no foot-binding then), music, sports, poetry, painting, and calligraphy; and then of its great generals and their glorious armies. During the Tang period Chinese civilization reached its zenith. After the Tangs came declining days. In the time of the Northern Sungs art persisted but the martial spirit waned, until finally the philosophers of the South Sungs with their asceticism and moral speculation killed the arts both of peace and of war.

The Ching-huai Canal still ran through the city of Nanking. The houseboats and the apartments were there, too. But the forms, the quality, and the content were all changed. The refinement of life had disappeared with the flowing waters of the Yangtze, into the Yellow Sea.

When the Nationalist army entered Nanking a new spirit was born—a spirit of reform and reconstruction. Modern science was to revitalize the arts of days past. Upon the debris of the partly ruined city a modern town was built with asphalt roads traversing all sections. Trees were planted and parks designed and developed. Automatic telephones, light, and water were installed. An aerial map was made from the seaplanes of the American gunboats stationed at Nanking. On the basis of this map a new city was planned. The Commission of City Planning, of which the writer was a member in his capacity as Minister of Education, worked for more than a year with an American architect of wide experience in Chinese

这就是旧日京华。但是南京是战略要地，国内每有重大战事，南京必定要遭一场浩劫，每经一次战祸，它的精华也就失去其大半。战事结束，和平重临，南京又会在废墟上重建，恢复旧日的光辉。我所描写的往昔金陵生活，就是根据历史记载而来的。

不过，自从太平天国灭亡，劫后南京一直未曾恢复昔日的美丽。历次重建似乎只是庸俗艺匠对于古本的临摹，经过一再临摹之后，原作的光彩渐渐消失，留下的只是俗不可耐的赝品。

秦淮河仍旧在南京城内流过，画舫歌榭也依然存在。但是形式、素质和内容都远非昔比了。风雅的生活已经随滚滚江流冲走了。

国民革命军进入南京以后，一种新精神随之诞生——一种改革和建设的精神。大家要拿现代科学来复兴往昔的艺术。在这疮痍满目的废墟上，一座柏油马路四通八达的现代城市建立起来了。街道旁栽种了葱翠的树木，供市民游息的公园也先后开始设计和建立。自动电话、电灯和自来水也装设了，停泊南京附近的美国兵舰的水上飞机则从空中测绘了一幅南京地图，南京的新都市计划就是根据这幅地图设计的。国民政府成立了首都建设设计委员会，我以教育部长的身分成为该委员会的委员之一。这个设计委员会在一位美国建筑师的协助下，辛勤工作了一年多。这位美国建筑师对北京的

architectural design in the enchanted city of Peking. The commission planned to retain as far as possible the grandeur and beauty of Chinese architecture together with the convenience and hygienic installations of a modern city.

Old, dilapidated buildings were torn down to make way for new roads and houses. Commerce began to prosper. Modern theatres multiplied to accommodate the growing population. The canal and the lakes were dredged and old temples and other public buildings repaired.

The Central Museum was built to house a part of the treasures from the Palace Museum of Peking, and an underground safety vault constructed for them, of reinforced concrete, in a hill which would be immune to air bombing. For the directors foresaw the impending Japanese aggressions against the new capital. As the situation in the north grew worse and war clouds hung thick over this side of the Great Wall, the more valuable treasures of Peking were moved by hundreds of trainloads to Nanking, and before the fall of the new capital to the Japanese all had been transported for safekeeping to eaves in the mountains of the interior.

The gigantic steel gate of the museum vault, with its intricate combination locks, was a piece of American ingenuity which humbled the Japanese. As reported from the occupied city, they worked on the locks for several days and finally gave up.

The buildings of the Ministries of Communications and of Railways were of reinforced concrete with modern lighting system ventilation, and conveniences. But their architectural design was altogether Chinese, with enamel tiles, painted columns, artistic windows, and other exterior decoration. These two imposing buildings stood opposite each other on Chung-shan Road, the main artery of traffic in the new metropolis, as monuments to China's old glory adapted to modern needs. Other buildings were planned and designed, but on account of the war they all had to be postponed.

The Sun Yat-sen Mausoleum, with blue enamel tiles and white marble columns, stood on the Purple Mountains outside the city overlooking the hilly valley and the winding Yangtze. Flights of granite steps led up to the tomb of the father of the Chinese Republic. The mountains were reforested with trees from various parts of China. Flowering plants and fruit trees decorated the gentle slopes. An athletic field and stadium with a swimming pool were built at the foot of the mountain.

A new model village was built in the rolling valley. A general plan was first laid out by the government, with roads, drainage, telephone and

中国宫殿式建筑很有研究，委员会的目标是尽量保持中国建筑的宏伟和华丽，同时兼有现代都市的便利和卫生设备。

陈旧倾圮的建筑被拆除了，以便铺筑道路或重建新屋。商业日渐发达，现代戏院倍增，人口急速增加。秦淮河和湖泊——加以疏浚，古刹和其他公共建筑也都开始修葺。

政府建造了中央博物院，来陈列北平故宫博物院的一部分珍品，而且在南京城内朝天宫一座小山里，造了一个不虞空袭的钢骨水泥的地下室，来保藏贵重文物。因为中央博物院的董事们早已预料到日本不久即将发动对华侵略，南京当然是他们的攻击目标。华北局势恶化，长城战云密布之时，故宫博物院的贵重宝藏即以数百辆火车运至南京，并且在南京失陷之前，全部转运内地，保留于山洞石室之中。

交通部大楼和铁道部大楼都是钢骨水泥的建筑，里面有现代的照明、通风等设备。但是它们的建筑图样却是完全中式的，釉瓦、雕梁、画栋、花窗，以及其他古色古香的装潢。这两幢雄伟的建筑峙立在新都交通要道中山路的两旁，成为配合现代需要的中国古代艺术的纪程碑。其他的建筑也已设计好蓝图，后以战事影响而告搁置。

中山陵位于城外紫金山之麓，上覆琉璃瓦，柱子全部是白色大理石。陵前有层层叠叠步步高升花岗岩的石阶。山上栽种着从全国各地移来的不同林木。山坡上点缀着各种各样的花木和果树，山脚建造了一个运动场和游泳池。

政府在南京附近规划了一个示范新村，由市府设计包括道路、下水道、电话、电灯、学校等的建设蓝图。几年之内，私人新建

lighting systems, and school buildings. In the short space of a few years new houses sprang up like mushrooms, with ample space around them for Oriental gardens. Trees grew and plants flowered; the birds sang and streams flowed. Old ways of living gave place to a new life in which science and art, work and pleasure, nature and human endeavor, went hand in hand.

Such was the nucleus which, it was hoped, would grow and some day transform every corner of the land. It was a modest beginning but had already borne fruit. For the new village movement had within a few years reached a number of cities and their surrounding areas. It was only a matter of time and further economic development for the new villages to change the mode of living of young China.

We could not very well expect that all trouble from the warlords would end with the downfall of Peking. Their seat of government was gone, but their real power was entrenched in the provinces. The country was vast and communications poor. These conditions and the unsettled state of mind in the country afforded them good opportunities to nurse their ambitions. At any favorable moment they were always ready to snatch more power; they lurked in the provinces like germs in the blood, ready to attack when the body weakened. In ten years, from the time his victorious army entered Peking to the eve of the Sino-Japanese War, Generalissimo Chiang Kai-shek had not a day's rest in his effort to unify the country.

Like the Roman generals who bound their ancient empire together by roads, he was not unmindful of the need to build more roads and railways and air lines. With Nanking as a center, highways, railways and airways were made to radiate from the capital to the provinces. A part of the communication system had existed before the Nationalist government came to power; with this as a basis it built new roads to make connections and extensions. Air lines were established to distant cities. From the new capital one could fly to Peking, Kaifeng, Sian, and Lanchow in the north;

to Fuchow, Canton, and Kunming in the south; in the west to Hankow, Chungking, and Chengtu.

New railways were built to connect Hankow with Canton and Kowloon, just opposite Hongkong. If the Japanese had not at this time started trouble in Manchuria, a continuous journey would have been possible in 1931 from either Hongkong or Shanghai to Paris by rail. A through train ran from Shanghai via Nanking, Tsinan, and Tientsin outside the Great Wall, and via Mukden to Tsitsihar in north

房屋已到处矗立，房屋周围都有广大的空地，辟为东方式的花园。树木葱翠，花枝招展，小鸟啁啾，溪水低吟，古老的生活方式已为新生活所取代，科学与艺术，工作与娱乐，天工与人力，齐头并进，相得益彰。

这就是实验中的胚芽，大家希望它发展滋长，将来有一天可以推广到全国的每一角落。这只是个平凡的开端，但是已经有了相当的成果，因为这个新村运动已经在数年之内推广到许多大城市及其附近地区。如果持之以恒，而且经济有进一步的发展，这些新村势将使新中国的生活方式全面改观。

我们无法奢望北京政府垮台之后，军阀们随之销声匿迹。他们的实力仍旧根深蒂固地盘据在各省。中国幅员辽阔，交通不便，兼以人心未定，凡此种种，无不使军阀们蠢蠢欲动。时机一到，他们就企图扩张势力：他们像血液中的细菌一样潜伏在各省，身体衰弱，就会乘机偷袭。蒋总司令从挥军攻克北京到对日抗战的前夕，十年间为统一国家，真是宵旰辛劳，席不暇暖。

罗马帝国的将军们曾以纵横辐辏的道路巩固其帝国，蒋总司令也深知开辟公路、铁路和航空线的重要。他以南京为中心，建筑了向各省辐射的公路、铁路和航空线。国民政府成立以前，交通网的一部分业已存在。国民党执政以后，就以原有的交通网为基础，新建了许多支线和衔接线。边远城市则辟航空线以资联系。从新首都北飞可达北平、开封、西安和兰州，南飞可达福州、广州和昆明，西航则达汉口、重庆及成都。

连接汉口与广州及香港对岸九龙的新铁路也筑成了。如果日本不在此时侵略东北，我们很可能在民国二十年（一九三一年）就可以从香港或上海乘火车直达巴黎。如果从上海出发，可搭直达车经南京、济南到天津，从天津搭北宁路出长城到沈阳，从沈阳搭中国自建而与日人

Manchuria, by Chinese railroads built parallel to the Japanese-owned South Manchurian Railway[1]. A branch line from Tsitsihar connected with the Trans-Siberian Railway. The progress of unification in China and the building of these parallel lines prompted the Japanese to try to take Manchuria, or the "Three Eastern Provinces," at a stroke—which became known to the world as the "Mukden Incident" of September 18, 1931.

Along the coast the gap between the Chien-tang and Tsao-ao rivers on the Shanghai-Hangchow-Ningpo line was filled, but the laying of track was suspended when war broke out. The new line between Soochow and Hangchow, however, was completed before hostilities began. Another new line from Hangchow running west to Kiangsi was finished just before the war and during the war was prolonged farther west to Hunan, where it connected with the Canton-Hankow Railway. The line was also further extended to Kweilin, capital of the southwest province of Kwangsi.

Highways were extended more rapidly. The Nanking-Hangchow highway was built during my sojourn in Nanking and I had the pleasure of going through it before it was opened to traffic. It traversed the richest sections of Chekiang and Kiangsu Provinces. As the car wound its way along Tai Lake one felt like stopping for a few days to sit under the pine trees and watch the sails rise or vanish over the horizon in the sunset. The fishermen cast their nets and drew up shining carp from the water. Tai is one of the five largest lakes in China, irrigating millions of acres of fertile land in the two most populous and cultured provinces of the country.

This highway also passed through a bandit-infested region, but the bandits disappeared when the road was opened because troops could be rushed to the spot.

Local troubles sometimes brewed as fast as construction progressed. At times the railway and highway lines had to run a race with disturbance in areas without modern roads. The rebellion in Fukien Province a year before the war was frustrated by central troops rushed down through the then newly built Hangchow-Kiangsan Railway and along the roads also newly built, from Hangchow to that province.[2] More roads meant less rebellion and less banditry, aside from the easy flow of products from one locality to another.

Communication is the key to modernization and reforms and to the discovery of possibilities of future development of the country. Thus the Nationalist government began its reconstruction program with the building of roads and railways. This was also the way to secure the unification of the country; any local rebellion could be put down easily if

所有的南满铁路平行的长春铁路到齐齐哈尔；从齐齐哈尔有铁路支线与西伯利亚铁路连接。中国统一努力的进展以及在东北自建铁路，促使日人企图一举而占满洲（即东三省），乃在民国二十年（一九三一年）九月十八日挑起"沈阳事件"，亦即"九·一八事变"。

沪杭甬铁路钱塘江至曹娥江之间的一段缺口也填补起来了，但是铺轨工作却因战事发生而停止。不过苏州与杭州之间的苏杭铁道刚在战事开始以前就铺筑完成了。另一条从杭州到江西的浙赣铁路刚好在抗战前完成，抗战期间更西延至湖南境内，在株洲与粤汉路衔接。后来湘桂铁路完成，再往西可以直达广西的桂林。

公路的发展更为迅速。京杭国道是在我居留南京期间建成的，在这条公路正式开放以前，我曾经很荣幸地参加通车典礼。京杭国道穿越江浙两省最富庶的地区。当车子沿太湖奔驰时，我们真想留下来小住几天，坐在松树之下，眺望着远帆在夕阳余晖中出没。渔人们在湖边撒网捕鱼，渔网中跳跃着金鳞闪灿的鲤鱼。太湖是我国五大湖之一，湖水灌溉了我国人口最密、文化最高的江浙两省千万亩肥沃的农田。

京杭国道同时经过一个盗匪如毛的区域，但是公路通车以后，盗匪随之销声匿迹，因为现在如遇匪警，军队可以随时赶到出事地点了。

建设进展之时，各地也不断发生事故。有时缺乏现代道路的地区发生变乱，铁路和公路常常需要以赛跑的姿态赶筑到出事地点。抗战前一年，福建省发生叛变，中央军迅速沿新筑成的浙赣铁路及公路从杭州赶赴福建，变乱旋即敉平。铁路公路愈多，叛乱与盗匪也愈会减少，各地间货运赖以畅流更不必说了。

交通是现代化和改革的关键，也是发现国家未来发展机会的钥匙。因此国民政府的建设计划就从建筑铁道公路着手。交通建设也是确保国家统一之一法，如果有完善的道路可资利用，地方性变乱很容易

good roads were available. Again, better and more communication means more travel and quicker exchange of ideas. Beautiful scenery hitherto hidden in inaccessible parts of the country suddenly opened to the appreciative eyes of scholars, painters, poets, and lovers of nature.

Under the influence of the Nationalistic government the provinces themselves began to build more roads. Existing roads were fast extended after the Kuomintang came to power. During the war, troops were freely shifted on these roads from one province to another. A year or two before the war a motor trip was made from Nanking to Kunming—that is, from the east coast to the southwest frontier city, the starting point of the Burma Road.

In the field of administration an attempt was made to increase the efficiency of official business. New filing systems for official documents were devised and put into trial use. The form of language in official documents was simplified.

A civil examination system was again inaugurated, but to the disappointment of those who had seen the old Imperial days, without the pomp and honors that had greeted the successful candidates.

A new code of civil law was drafted. The status of women was raised to the same level as that of men. Daughters were to inherit property of their parents as hitherto only sons had done. Freedom of marriage was granted to the parties concerned when they came to legal age. A mutual agreement of the parties concerned is sufficient for legal divorce.

The school curriculum was standardized and the proportion of science teaching increased. Physical training was emphasized. New laws were promulgated governing the universities, and the Central Research Institute, Academia Sinica, etc., were established to carry on research in science, history, economics, and engineering.

The obnoxious internal customs system of *likin*, which we shall see more of in the next chapter, was abolished. Government finance was put on a sounder basis. National currency was standardized, government banks reorganized. The circulation of silver was later suspended and only government bank notes allowed to circulate; during the war we began to realize the importance of this move, for if we had had to rely upon bulky silver as the medium of exchange it would have been well-nigh impossible to carry on the long years of war, while if the shift had been made in wartime it would have caused great confusion.

就可以敉平。除此之外，交通愈便利愈发达，人民交往也愈频繁，观念交流也愈容易。偏僻地区的名胜风景，旦夕之间就成为学者、画家、诗人和爱好自然者的徜徉之所了。

各省在国民政府影响之下也开始修筑更多的道路。原有道路在国民党执政以后很快就开始修补拓展。因之抗战期间军队得以在各省之间畅通无阻。抗战前一两年，旅客可以从南京坐汽车直达昆明，换一句话说，可以从华东沿海直达西南边城，也就是滇缅公路的起点。

在行政方面，政府正设法增加行政效率。政府设计了一种新式的档案处理办法并在各机关试行。公文程式也经过简化。

文官考试制度重新恢复，但是见过清朝科举制度的人也许会失望，因为考试录取的人已经不再有从前那种煊赫的排场和荣耀。

新的法典也开始拟订。妇女的地位提高到与男人一样。过去只有儿子可以继承父亲的产业，现在女儿也享有同等的继承权了。男女到达结婚年龄就可以享受婚姻自由。只要当事两边协议，就可构成合法的离婚。

学校课程统一，科学钟点增加，体育普遍受重视。管理大学的法律也公布了。中央研究院等机构先后成立，以进行科学、历史、经济学和工程等的高深研究。

厘金制度宣告废止。对于这种苛扰的国内关卡制度，我们将在下章再加论列。政府财政基础渐见巩固，全国币制统一，政府所属的各银行也加以改组。不久之后，银元禁止流通，一律改用法币，抗战期间我们开始了解此一措施的重要，如果我们一直依赖笨重的银子作交易的媒介，势将无法进行长期抗战，如果在抗战期间才能进行币制改革，也必定要引起严重的紊乱。

From 1927, when the capital was established at Nanking, to 1937, when the Japanese army fired its first shots at the Marco Polo Bridge, only ten short years were allowed to the Nationalist government to do its job. During these ten years intermittent rebellions and other obstacles retarded the progress of reforms and reconstruction, yet in this brief time 7,300 kilometers of railway were constructed, in contrast to 8,300 kilometers during the last fifty years. More than 100,000 kilometers of highway were built, and 33,000 kilometers of new telegraph lines were added to those already in existence.[3] Yet naturally there could be only a moderate beginning in each phase of construction in so short an interval, and so it must be considered.

......

从民国十六年（一九二七年）定都南京开始，到民国二十六年（一九三七年）芦沟桥事变止，其间只有短短十年工夫让国民政府从事建设。十年之间还有断续的变乱和其他障碍阻滞改革和建设的进展，但在这短期间内，居然建筑了四千五百多公里的铁路，而在过去五十年内所建的铁路也不过一万六千公里而已。十年之内建筑的公路超过十万公里，新添电报线路则在一万多公里以上。在这样短的时间之内，自然各方面的建设成就都很有限，评断成绩时，不能不考虑到时间因素。

....

PART FIVE

第五部　中国生活面面观

SOME ASPECTS OF
CHINESE LIFE

CHAPTER 21   THE "LEAKAGE" SYSTEM

Foreigners coming to China for the first time used often to meet with the annoying practice of petty "squeeze" among their servants and cooks and naturally felt that something must be wrong with China. But they would presently be informed by old China hands, familiar with the China of Imperial days and the later regimes of the warlords, that the practice of "squeeze" was not only to be found in servant circles but also among those higher up. "Squeeze is a national system," they would say and cite concrete examples to illustrate their point.

This reference to happenings of bygone days that lingered in their memories would focus the eyes of the newcomers on remnants of the dark side of Chinese life which are fast passing, and the effect has been to throw a veil over unprejudiced minds in their effort to see the living, new China of today. This is very unfortunate for foreign observers who have tried to understand China, and unfair to both this and the last generation of Chinese leaders, who endured hardships and sacrificed their lives for reforms in China's national life.

I propose now to paint a dark, vivid, and real picture of Chinese economic life in the past, without exaggerating or minimizing—which I hope I can do even better than the old China hands.

Anyone who witnessed the downfall of the Imperial regime must be aware that one of the main factors which caused the Manchu government to lose control of the country was its decrepit system of public finance. Large numbers of public servants were paid only nominal salaries and left to finance themselves by *Lou-kwei*, or the "leakage" system. This practice deprived them of any sense of public morality and caused them to countenance corruption as a matter of course. The Imperial government connived at the irregular gains of its officials, and the officials in turn connived at those of their subordinates. The poisonous sap circulated in the whole tree of state, reaching to every twig of every branch and every leaf on each twig. It flowed through all the roots of the tree and every rootlet.

From the government offices through which public revenues passed, the government required only certain fixed amounts to be forwarded to the national treasury. The officials in charge of the revenues could, by various means and all sorts of excuses and plausible reasons, attach a variety of fees to the regular taxes. In this way, for every tael of silver that flowed into the government treasury at least the same amount or even more would be diverted to "leakage" funds. In the later years of the Imperial regime more wine leaked into private cups than remained in the public barrel. The government, finding itself parched as a fish in a dry pond, pressed hard for more money—whence still more "leakage" for public servants and heavier burdens for the people.

贰壹 陋规制度

　　凡是亲见清室覆亡的人都知道：满清政府失败的主要原因之一就是财政制度的腐败。公务人员的薪水只是点缀品，实际上全靠陋规来维持。陋规是不公开的公家收支，为政府及社会所默认的。以现在用语来说，好像我们大家所称的黑市。这种办法削弱了公务人员的公德心，也使他们把不规则的收入看成理所当然的事。清廷对官吏的这种收入视若当然，常说"规矩如此"，竟把陋规变成规矩了。这些官吏对下属营私舞弊也就开只眼闭只眼。如果拿一棵树来比喻政府的话，这种陋规的毒汁可以说已经流遍树上的每一枝叶，每一根芽。

　　政府只要求税收机关向国库缴纳定额的税款。主持税收的官吏可以利用各式各样的藉口和理由，在正规赋税之外加征各种规费。这样一来，如果有一两银子到了国库，至少也另有一两银子成了陋规金。在满清末年，"漏"入私人腰包的钱远较缴入国库的钱为多。清廷需用浩繁，只好一味向官吏需索。官吏向民间搜刮，结果官场陋规愈来愈多，人民负担也愈来愈重。乾隆皇帝几次下江南，开支浩大，都靠官吏孝敬、民间搜刮而来，清代在乾隆朝为极盛时代，而衰运亦在此时开始。

Failing to realize funds by taxation or other means, such as offering public offices for sale, the Imperial government resorted to borrowing from foreign sources by awarding them concessions for building railroads or opening mines. This was to quench thirst by drinking poison. It may be remembered that the nationalization of railways in Szechuan Province, as a preliminary step to awarding the building rights to foreign concerns, pulled the trigger for the Revolution of 1911.

But as to the "leakage" system and how it worked. China was then divided into some twenty-two provinces, comprising about two thousand hsien. The chief executive of the hsien was the magistrate, who took charge of all financial matters and concurrently filled the role of administrator of justice in his district. His salary—not more than a few taels a month—was nominal. All expenses incurred by the holder of the office had to be paid out of "leakage" funds. When higher officials of the Imperial government passed through his district he had to entertain them and secure for them all the "necessities" required for their travel. To the entourage of any higher official he had to offer "presents," usually in the form of money.

On the banks of the Yaokiang River just outside the city wall of my native Yuyao stood a welcome pavilion at which the magistrate welcomed passing officials of higher rank. One sunny afternoon some forty years ago I noticed crowds gathering at a distance, near the pavilion. I joined them and watched the landing of the Imperial Examiner and his entourage, on their way to Ningpo to hold civil examinations in that prefecture. On the previous day the magistrate had "caught," or requisitioned, many houseboats from the people and the one set aside for the Imperial Examiner was loaded with sealed cases, their contents known only to those who had prepared them.

I watched the party change boats. The Imperial Examiner stepped into the most prominent; the sails were set and the little flotilla with the officials and "leakage" gifts on board floated downriver with the ebbing tide to the seaport city of Ningpo. Under that inspiration I said to myself that from now on I must study hard, so that some day I myself might be an Imperial Examiner blessed with such mysterious gifts as lay hidden in those cases.

Regular "gifts" had to be presented to the secretaries of the civil governor (*fantai*) of the province. Failing that, a magistrate could not expect them to speak kind words for him to the governor and would

清代后期，征税与捐官等方法均未能使清廷达到筹款的目的，因此不得不乞灵于借贷外债，而以让渡铁路建筑权或矿产开采权为交换条件。这自然是饮鸩止渴的办法。现在或许还有人记得清廷将四川省内铁路收归国有，以为转让筑路权予外国公司之张本，结果触发了辛亥革命的导火线。时遭光绪帝国丧，地方士绅披麻带孝，头顶"德宗景皇帝神位"，长跪于总督衙门之前，哭呼先帝，保佑四川，不使铁路收归国有，弄得政府啼笑皆非。

所谓陋规制度究竟是怎么一种办法呢？中国当时分为二十二行省，大约包括两千个县。县的行政首长是知县，他不但掌管一县的财政，同时还是一县的司法官。他的薪水每月不过数两银子，简直微不足道。因此他的一切费用都只能在陋规金上开支。如果上级官员经过他那一县，他除了负责招待之外，还得供应旅途一切需要财物。对于上级官员的随员也得送"礼"，所谓"礼"通常都是送的钱。

我的故乡余姚城外的姚江岸上有一座接官亭，这是各县都有的。如果有上级官员过境，知县就在亭里迎候。大约六十年前的一个下午，我发现亭子附近聚了一大堆人。我赶过去一看，原来是大家在观望学台和他的随行人员纷纷下船；有些上岸。这位学台正预备去宁波主持郡试。前一日，知县已经从老百姓手中"抓"去好几条大船，那条专为这位学台预备的船上装了好几只加封条的箱子，至于箱子里面装些什么，自然只有经手的人才知道了。

我遥望着学台等一行换了船，学台踏上最华丽的一只，随后这只载着官吏和陋规礼金的小型舰队就扬帆顺着退潮驶往宁波去了。那种气派使我顿生"大丈夫当如是也"的感触。我心里说从今以后一定要用功读书，以便将来有一天也当起学台享受封藏在箱子里面的神秘礼物。

知县还得经常给藩台的幕僚送礼，否则他就别想他们给他在藩台面前说好话；如果搞得不好，这些师爷们还可能在公事上吹毛求疵呢。

find them faultfinding in his official relations with the governor's office. Added together, the amount required for plain sailing in his career was by no means small. Human nature also made him not unmindful of the necessity to provide for a rainy day. And he had his family and followers to support.

Candidates for magistracy who had pull were covetous of the districts with large revenues. I remember that in the hsien in which we lived during my school days no magistrate had ever held office for more than a year. The regular term of office was three years, in which a magistrate could realize approximately a hundred thousand dollars. In those times this sum was considered very great. So the governor appointed acting magistrates, whose term was usually one year. In this way there would be more chances for expectant magistrates to share the profit.

When a magistrate retired from office after the expiration of his term and paid an official call on the governor, he was usually asked by his superior whether his district had been a good one, meaning how much he had got out of the "leakage" funds. His friends and relatives also asked him the same question by way of starting a conversation.

The higher the rank of the official through whose hands the government revenues passed, the more "leakage" flowed into his private coffer. The taotai of Shanghai was known to reap a profit of some 100,000 taels a year. Governors and viceroys of rich provinces and the powerful princes and grand ministers in Peking usually enjoyed large yearly incomes.

The system was upheld even by the great statesman and scholar, General Tseng Kuo-fan, who put down the Taiping Rebellion for the Manchu Dynasty. In one of his letters he argued that "leakage" was indispensable to the smooth running of the government; the expenses incurred by an official were great and he had a family and relatives to provide for. The system was countenanced by scholars as well. In his diary a famous scholar-official who lived in Peking during the Hsien-feng and Tung-chi period complains that Viceroy Chang Chi-tung presented him with only a small "gift." A later entry reads something like this: "Went to Tao Ren Pavilion in the afternoon to sip tea. Chang Chi-tung entered. I pretended not to see him and left the place." This may be safely interpreted to mean that the famous viceroy had offended the prominent scholar by presenting him with too small a gift from his "leakage" funds.

各种礼金加起来，一个知县为保宦海一帆风顺所化的钱就很可观了。同时人情世故也告诉他必须未雨绸缪，何况他还得养活一家大小以及跟随他的一班人呢！

有靠山的候补知县无不垂涎收入比较大的县份。以我的故乡余姚县而论，就我所能记忆的，没有一个知县在我们的县里任职一年以上。正常的任期是三年，一位知县如果当上三年，大概可以搜刮到十万元叮当作响的银洋。这在当时是很大的数目。因此藩台只派些代理知县，任期通常一年。这样一来，候补知县们的分肥机会也就比较多了。

知县任满离职时，通常都得正式拜望藩台一次，藩台总要问一声他的缺好不好。当时对于所补的职位叫做缺，也就是等于问他得到了多少陋规金，他的亲朋戚友与他谈话，也常常以同样的问题做开场白，说"老兄你的缺想必很好罢"。

经手政府收支的官吏，官阶愈高，"漏"入他私人腰包的数目也愈大。据说上海道台每年可以获利十万两银子。所以上海道的缺，是全国缺中最肥的。富庶省份的藩台、督抚以及北京有势力的王公大臣，每年的收入也都很可观。

连平定太平天国之乱的学者政治家曾国藩也赞成陋规制度。他曾在一封信里为陋规制度辩护，认为要顺利推行政务，就不得不如此；他说一个官吏的必要开支太大，而且还得赡养一家和亲戚。咸丰同治年间住在北京的名士李莼客曾在日记里抱怨总督张之洞送他的"礼"太轻。过了几天日记里又有一段记载，为："午后至陶然亭，张之洞来，我避之。"可见张之洞从陋规金中提出来赠与李莼客的礼太轻，结果就得罪了这位名士了。

During the Imperial regime promising candidates could keep servants with very little pay or none at all. The servants would stick to their masters through thick and thin for years, hoping that some day when luck fell into the laps of their masters they too could share the "leakage" with their lords. When luck did come master and servant alike would strive to make it still leakier, so that each and all could have cupfuls of this wine to their hearts' content. If luck failed to appear they would keep on waiting until the last ray of hope was gone. Under pressure of starvation some unfortunate masters found relief in the rope, with which they ended their lives. In Hangchow during my school days the news circulated by word of mouth that an expectant magistrate, idle for years, had hanged himself on a New Year's Eve when his creditors pressed him hard for the money he owed them.

The poisonous sap penetrated even to the households of the well to do. The cook would poke "holes" in his vegetable and meat baskets in order to make them "leak." Servants got something from the purchases they made for the household—especially in Peking the shops always added a certain percentage to the price for the servants who made the purchase.

The practice of "leakage" even went abroad and found its way into the household of Napoleon. Napoleon had a Chinese cook who served his master very faithfully. On his deathbed this great French general remembered his faithful servant, saying, "Treat him well because his country will be one of the greatest in time to come. But the Chinese love money. Give him five hundred francs." On the other hand, the Dean Lung Professorship of Chinese Literature in Columbia University was established in memory of a Chinese laundryman with the money earned by a lifetime of washing. Before his death Dean Lung handed over a bag of gold to his master and asked him to do something good for China. The master, adding a sum to it, established the chair in memory of the patriotic laundryman.

The practice of "leakage" permeated the entire system of *likin*. And *likin*, like a gigantic octopus with tentacles reaching to every communication line in the country, sucked the blood out of the trade and commerce of the nation. It had been installed during the Taiping Rebellion to raise war funds for the support of the Imperial army. The Taipings were gone, but the obnoxious system was there to stay.

在满清时代，有前程的候补官员只要化很少的钱，甚至不必出钱，就会有仆从跟随他们。这些仆从们也会含辛茹苦地追随不舍，希望有朝一日他们的主人时来运转，他们也就可以分享陋规了。如果真的吉星高照，主子和奴才就沆瀣一气，大刮一笔。如果流年不利，官爵迟迟不能到手，仆从们也还株守不去，直至最后一线希望消灭时为止。一些倒霉的主人，受不住饥寒煎熬，只好投缳自尽，以求解脱。我在杭州读书时，曾经听说有一位赋闲多年的候补知县，因为受不住债主催逼，结果在大除夕自缢了。

变相的陋规恶习甚至流布于小康之家，厨子买菜时要揩油，仆人购买家用杂物时也要捞一笔。尤其在北平，仆人们来买东西时，商店照规矩会自动把价格提高一成，作为仆人们的佣金，这在北平通俗叫做"底子钱"。

这种变相的陋规之风甚至吹到外国而进入拿破仑的家里。拿破仑有个中国厨子，服务周到而热心。这位伟大的法国将军临死时记起他的忠仆，就吩咐他的左右说："你们要好好地待他，因为他的国家将来是要成为世界最伟大的国家之一的。不过这位中国朋友很爱钱的，你们给他五百法郎罢！"自然，中国人并非个个如此。哥伦比亚大学的丁良（译音）中国文学讲座基金，就是为纪念一位中国洗衣工人而设的，基金的来源是他一生辛勤浆洗衣服的积蓄。丁良临死时把一袋金子交给他的东家，托付他做一点有益于中国的事。这位东家就拿这笔钱，再加上他自己的一笔捐款，在哥大设置了中国文学讲座，来纪念这位爱国的洗衣工人。

陋规之风更弥漫了整个厘金制度，厘金制度像一个硕大无朋的章鱼把它的触须伸展到全国的每一条交通线上，吮吸着国内工商业的血液。厘金是在太平天国时期设置的，旨在筹措战费以供应清廷士卒。太平军虽然被平定，厘金却始终未取消。

It worked this way. Anyone who knew how to "squeeze" the people would bid—say two hundred thousand dollars a year—to government agents for the right to run the *likin* at a certain station or a number of stations established at points on the highway where merchandise passed from one city to another. The person who won the bid would become *likin* commissioner at that station or group of stations and had the right to assess duties on the goods passing through. If he could realize a sum of three hundred thousand dollars within the year, he would turn over two hundred thousand to the government and keep the remainder for himself and his partners. So he would make most goods dutiable in order to swell his private fortune.

Once I saw a boat loaded with watermelons passing under the bridge at a station. It was stopped by a long bamboo hook from shore and several inspectors jumped down and began to thrust iron rods into the melons. The owner begged them to desist and promised to pay any amount they demanded. The "duties" were paid; the poor farmer sailed on.

I remember how small traders and farmers hated *likin*. Everybody would have liked to smash the stations to pieces. Once a group of young scholars going by boat to take an Imperial examination passed by a *likin* station, ignoring the order to stop. The inspectors detained the boat and began to search their belongings. The scholars leaped ashore, entered the station, and smashed everything they could lay their hands on. Only the flag, emblem of the authority of the Imperial government, was left drooping in the air with its inscription: "To Collect *Likin* by His Majesty's Orders." Triumphantly the scholars departed under the gaze of the admiring crowd.

After the Revolution of 1911 the "leakage" system was gradually suppressed, and the system of *likin* was abolished later on. Higher salaries were paid to officials. But cases of corruption were still frequent. The practice persists among servants in the form of petty "squeeze." A lady once scolded her cook for being too greedy in getting his "squeeze," and got into a quarrel with him. Someone remarked that he was as greedy as a hungry wolf, to which he replied, "If one were not greedy, he would not become a cook."

In one of the embassies in Peking the ambassador's cook charged ten cents for an egg, while his secretary's cook charged his master five cents. "Why should I have to pay more for an egg than the wife of our secretary?" asked the ambassador's wife. "Madam, the ambassador receives a higher salary than

厘金方面的陋规大致是这样的：凡是懂得如何敲诈老百姓的人都可以向政府经纪人出价投标，只要他出价高，譬如说一年二十万块钱，他就可以获得在某一关卡或若干关卡征收厘金的权利。这些关卡通常设在官道上的货物必经之地，得标的人就成为此一关卡的厘卡委员，受权向过往的货物征税。如果他能在一年之内收到三十万块钱，他把二十万缴交政府，其余的钱就归他本人及其合伙者所有。因此他规定大多数的货物都得抽税，以便充实他们的私囊。

有一次我看到一条装西瓜的木船从关卡附近的一座桥下经过。这条船马上被岸上伸下来的一根竹柄挠钩拦住了，同时岸上跳下好几位稽查，用铁棒往西瓜堆里乱戳乱擤。西瓜主人慌了手脚，哀求他们手下留情，同时答应他们，要缴多少税收就缴多少税。"税"缴过以后，这位可怜的农夫才得继续鼓棹前进。

小商人和农夫对厘金无不深恶痛绝，如果有机会，每一个人都愿意把关卡砸个稀烂。有一次，一群青年士子乘船去参加科举，途经一处厘金关卡，卡上着令停船，他们根本不予理睬。稽查们扣住船只，并且开始搜检行李。这群士子蜂拥上岸，冲进关卡，见物就砸，结果把关卡打得落花流水。只留下那面象征朝廷权威，上面写着"奉旨征收厘金"的旗子低垂在空中，围观的群众以不胜钦慕的目光伫望着这些士子扬长而去。

辛亥革命以后，陋规制度逐渐被戢止，厘金制度亦于稍后废止。官吏的薪俸也提高了。但是贪污案件还是屡见不鲜，仆役间的揩油风气迄今未衰。有一位太太骂她的厨子揩油揩得太贪心，结果与厨子大吵其架。有人批评这厨子贪心得像条饿狼，他的答覆是："如果一个人不贪心，他也就不会当厨子了。"

北京某大使馆的厨子每买一个鸡蛋，就向主人索价一毛，大使秘书的厨子为主人买蛋，却只索价五分钱一只。大使夫人问："为什么我买鸡蛋要比秘书太太多化钱呢？"她的厨子答道："太太，大使的薪水

the secretary," was the reply. Owners of cars often found their gas tanks "leaky," because the drivers helped themselves to cupfuls of gasoline. Unwarranted repairs made bills for maintenance mount up.

Since the Nationalist government came to power in 1927 China has been endeavoring to check the occasional corruption in the government. Severe punishment has been meted out to offenders. However, the legacy from centuries of the "leakage" system, which existed even before the Manchus, is difficult to discard totally within a few years or even a generation. Under the leadership of Generalissimo Chiang Kai-shek official corruption has been reduced to a few isolated cases. With the introduction of a modern financial system and the gradual enlightenment of public conscience, China has done much in checking these malpractices. As the technique of government improves with time, she will attain the level of a modern, well-organized country in which more efficient methods of taxation and effective control of public finance will be devised.

The Chinese have always trusted in the intrinsic good of human nature, believing that evils arise only from perversion of that good through negligence or lack of proper education. It was the decrepit system of public finance that caused China's trouble in this respect, not lack of a sense of moral responsibility. But the system had such a demoralizing influence on public practice that we still suffer from its effects.

Concrete examples have shown us that the remedy lies in building up a good system to supersede the bad ones. It is not sufficient merely to abolish the bad. The customs administration organized by the British for China was free of the bad influence of "leakage." Employees were properly trained and adequately paid. Ample pensions were given them after retirement. Patronage was little known. The control of this important branch of national revenue by foreign governments as a guarantee for the payment of indemnities and foreign debts has been humiliating and extremely dangerous to national integrity, but the adequate system of revenue built up as a by-product is an unintended blessing to China.

The postal administration was organized under the Western system. It has been running efficiently since its inception—even long years of civil war did not disrupt its work. Ever since the Japanese aggression started it has been marvelous to see letters circulating in the occupied areas as freely as in Free China. Mail carriers have constantly crossed the firing lines to deliver the mails entrusted to them.

要比秘书先生的高呀！"汽车主人也常常发现汽油箱"漏"油，原因就是司机"揩"油。不必要的修理，更使保养费大得惊人。

自从民国十六年（一九二七年）国民党执政以来，中国一直在设法阻遏政府中的贪污风气，并且规定了几种对贪污舞弊的严厉罚则。但是陋规制度在清朝以前就已存在。数百年的积习，不是几年之内，甚至二三十年之内所能完全革除的。自从现代财政制度建立，公家道德逐渐提高以后，中国已经革除了很多积弊。行政技术正与时俱进，相信她在不久的将来一定可以达到组织健全的现代国家的水准，征收赋税和控制财政的有效办法也会渐次建立。不幸当时内乱外患并乘，致使功败垂成。

我们中国人一向相信人之初性本善，认为邪恶的产生只是缺乏正当的教育而使善良的本性湮没，中国社会风气的败坏导源于腐朽的财政制度，而非缺乏责任感。但是这种制度对社会风气产生极大的不良影响，因此我们迄今仍蒙受其遗毒。

实际的例子已经指出，补救之道在于建立良好的制度，来接替腐败的制度。单单废止坏制度，还是不够的。英国人为中国建立的关税制度，一开始就摆脱了陋规的恶劣影响。海关雇员都经过良好的训练，薪俸也相当优厚，退休之后还有充裕的养老金。徇情偏私的情形很少发生。中国为了保证偿付外债而把国家重要收入的控制权交付给外国政府，这原是国家的奇耻大辱，而且严重威胁到主权的完整，但是因此而建立关税制度却是中国的意外收获。

邮政也是根据西方制度建立的。创办迄今，行政效率始终很高。就是在漫长的内战时期，邮递工作也从未中断。抗战期间，日军占领区与中国大后方之间，邮递一直畅通无阻，邮差们常常穿越火线把邮件送达收件人手里。

The salt administration is another example. Even during the long years of Japanese aggression the people have been adequately supplied with this daily necessity.

The Huang-ho Commission was well known formerly for its "leakage" system; indeed, the famous Shantung and Honan cuisines were the product of the rich appetites and well-lined coffers of the gluttonous commissioners of the Huang-ho works. In the same way, Yangchow cooking became renowned through the epicurean salt merchants of Yangchow.

With the formation of a Huang-ho Conservancy Board with modern trained engineers in charge of the conservation work, the "leakage" system itself was cast into the river and flowed down into the Yellow Sea. The gluttons disappeared with their system; only the art of cooking remains. Yangchow delicacies, too, are still admired by men of good taste, while the innovators who introduced them are gone and forgotten since the introduction of the salt gabelle, a modern, well-organized system of salt administration.

With well-organized administration, a well-trained and well-paid personnel, tenure of office ensured and adequate pensions provided after retirement, the good that is in human nature has full play.

It may be said that these successes have depended on foreign assistance. But let me ask: Are they due alone to the good morals of the foreigners—or rather to the good system they have introduced into China? Without personal integrity no such system would work, yet could we depend on foreign morals alone to obtain the desired results? Could a handful of foreign experts on top be powerful enough to check the irregular practices of hundreds and thousands of Chinese personnel? It is through the co-operation of the rank and file of Chinese employees under a good system that the customs, salt, and postal administrations have been successful. This is what Mencius, disciple of Confucius, has said: "Good morals alone will not make a good administration; systems alone will not carry the work to the desired ends."

The modern banking system and railway administration in China are also commendable examples. The banks and railways on the whole run efficiently and are free of gross maladministration of funds.

Modern universities in China are further examples of honest administration of funds, aside from their stand for intellectual honesty. Teachers have worked hard, through privations on account of the abnormally high cost of living during the war, to maintain their standards

盐务机构是另一实例。八年抗战期间，人民的这种日用必需品始终供应无缺。

治黄河的河督衙门从前一向以陋规制度闻名于世；事实上著名的山东菜和河南菜就是这些食厌珍馐、腰缠万贯的治黄老爷们光顾的结果。同样地，扬州菜之所以出名，就是因为贪图口福的扬州盐商而来。

黄河水利委员会成立以后，改由受过现代训练的工程师主持疏浚工作，陋规制度也就随滚滚河水冲入黄海去了。老饕已随陋规制度消失，只有烹饪艺术依旧存在。美食家至今对扬州菜赞不绝口，但是自从组织完善的现代盐务制度建立以后，倡导扬州菜的盐商已无法立足了。

这些成就可以说是依赖外国协助而来的。但是我要请问：这些成就究竟由于外国人的良好道德，还是由于他们介绍到中国来的良好制度呢？没有健全的品德，这些制度固然无法实行，但是单凭外国人的道德难道就能收到预期的效果吗？单凭少数高居要津的外国专家就能够制止千千万万中国职员的不法行为吗？海关、盐务、邮政之所以成功，还是靠良好制度下的基层中国职员的通力合作。这就是孟子所谓："徒善不足以为政，徒法不足以自行。"

中国的现代银行制度和铁道管理也是值得称道的实例。一般而论，银行与铁路的行政效率都很高，而且没有银钱上的重大舞弊案件。

中国的现代大学除了实事求是的学术立场之外，也是经费从无私弊的又一实例。抗战期间，因为物价高昂，教授生活非常清苦，但是他们始终辛苦工作，力求维持学术水准。绝大多数的学生，

of scholarship. The majority of students coming under the good influence of the teachers and the university organization cannot but form healthy ideas and correct habits as regards honest and efficient administration of public funds, along with the modern training they have received. And we must remember that in their hands the future of China lies.

Above all, the attitude toward the administration of public funds has basically changed. In the old days the "leakage" system was connived at or even admired. At present it is disliked and reviled by all intelligent people. This change of public sentiment will have an important bearing, given modern methods, upon the future handling of funds in all spheres of public administration.

It is more difficult to eradicate the practice of "squeeze" among servants, cooks, and chauffeurs. Perhaps it will take a generation or two to alleviate the economic status of these people; until that is done, we cannot very well expect that they will drop their bits of "sweets." Perhaps by then it will be difficult in any case to find people to work as household servants. Yet in my six years of sojourn in Kunming during the war I have met with one cook, one man servant, one maid, and one chauffeur in our employ who never "squeezed." Our present cook and man servant have a spotless record as regards money matters.

Let the reader turn the leaves of a textbook of European history to the period just before the French Revolution; let him glance through the constitutional development of England or the history of India in the times of Warren Hastings; he will readily agree with the writer that the "leakage" system of China was but a mild form of corruption. Yet, along with other forces, it did gradually sap the vitality of a reigning dynasty, once very powerful, and render it in the end financially anemic and politically impotent. Finally the Manchu Empire crumbled like a house of cards before the moral force of Dr. Sun Yat-sen.

除了接受现代训练之外，在教授和大学当局的良好影响之下，对于如何诚实而有效地运用公款，也自然养成正确的观念和良好的习惯。

最重要的是对公款处理的态度已经起了根本的转变，过去大家都默认甚至赞扬陋规制度，到了抗战以前的几年，有识之士不但讨厌它而且随时加以讥讽，这种风气的转变，再加采用现代方法，当时我们相信对于将来公共行政各方面的经费处理，必将发生重大良好的影响。

要消灭仆役、厨子和司机的揩油行为可难得多了。或许要经过五六十年之后才能提高这些人的经济地位，在他们的经济地位确切提高以前，我们无法奢望他们临财不苟。如果真的到了那一天，也许我们已经不容易找到愿意当家庭仆役的人了。抗战时我在昆明居留的八年期间，我倒在我的佣人中碰到过一位男仆、一位女佣和一位司机从来没有揩过油。

CHAPTER 22 · SOCIAL STRUCTURE AND SOCIAL PROGRESS

It has been a common belief that China's four hundred million people were as loosely connected as the sands of the sea. It would be nearer the truth to say that her great population is—or was—segmented into many small self-governing units. Chinese democracy has consisted of tens of thousands of such units, loosely knit together by a common language, a common culture, and common ideals of life achieved through centuries of cumulative effort. These units, large or small, developed on a basis of family, trade, and tradition. Individuals were bound by these common ties to each self-governing group and so were more intimate with the members of their own group than with a broader society. They understood local problems better than national ones. This was the fundamental reason the constitutional National Assembly failed to work, and this was why the people allowed themselves to be governed by warlords. It was the frame of mind that gave birth to the nationwide idea in Imperial days, often quoted here, that "Heaven is high above and the Emperor is far away."

Individuals, unless they broke with society in some way, were always part of the unit, but the units were not well cemented by any effective national organization. This was a strong point as well as a weakness in China's national life—a strength because it made China democratic and enduring through ages of war and invasion, and a weakness because it made her central authority impotent and rendered her vulnerable to the attack of invaders.

The existence of these units in Chinese life has its historical background. They came into being by the slow work of centuries. As the Chinese gradually moved into the less populated or unpopulated areas, they went in groups to form separate colonies which grew into self-governing villages or communities. The vast Chinese Empire was built up by centuries of peaceful colonization[1] of outlying territory by just such social clusters. In recent years, by a study of the dialects of China, we have been able to trace the path of this development. The Cantonese dialect is found to be closely related to the spoken language of the Tang Dynasty. We may reasonably infer that the predominant part of the population of Canton are descendants of the Tangs. Later arrivals, forming their own distinct groups, spoke a quite different dialect known as *Hak-ka*, which shows the language characteristics of recent centuries. Even along the Yangtze Valley the slight difference in dialect in various localities affords a subtle record of the stages of colonization.

贰贰 社会组织和社会进步

一般人都说中国的四万万人像一盘散沙，如果说中国的人是由许多自治的小单位构成的，倒更切近事实。中国的民主体制包括千千万万的这种单位，由几千年来累积下来的共同的语言、共同的文化和共同的生活理想疏松地联系在一起。这些或大或小的单位是以家庭、行业和传统为基础而形成的。个人由这些共同的关系与各自治团体发生联系，因此团体内各分子的关系比对广大的社会更为亲切。他们对地方问题比对国家大事了解较深。这就是立宪国会失败的症结，也是老百姓听凭军阀统治的原因。我们在前面曾经一再提到"天高皇帝远"的观念，帝制时代的这种观念就是上述心理状态产生的。

个人如非因特殊事故与所属社会破裂，永远是小单位的一部分，但是各单位之间并无全国性的组织使其密切团结。这是中国国民生活中的优点，同时也是弱点。好处在于使中国生活民主，虽经数百年之战乱以及异族[2] 之入侵而仍能屹立无恙，坏处在于中央政权软弱无能，因而易遭异族侵凌。

中国人民生活中这些单位的存在是有它历史的背景的。它们是几千年历史演变的结果。我们的祖先逐渐向人口比较稀少的地区迁移时，他们总是成群结队而行，在各地构成许多独立的部落，这些部落后来便发展为自治的村庄或乡镇。广大的中华帝国就是千百年来由这些聚族而居者向边疆和平原拓殖而形成的。近年来由于研究中国各地方言的结果，我们已经追溯出这种发展的途径。我们发现广东话与唐朝的口语有密切的关系，因此我们可以推断多数的广东人是唐朝的后裔。迁到广东较晚的移民又另行形成不同的部落，所说的方言也迥然不同，那就是我们所谓的客家话。客家话所显示的语言特征是属于近世纪的。甚至长江流域各地方言之间的些微差别，也可以隐约显示拓殖过程中的先后。

The migration of the Chinese population to the south was hastened in the tenth century by the downfall of the Tangs when north China was devastated by invaders from outside the Great Wall. The southern provinces, especially Kwangtung, Hunan, and Chekiang, which were not vulnerable to the successive invasions and were less affected by intermittent wars, became reservoirs of Chinese culture destined to irrigate the vast territory of New China in the last fifty years.

If a reform was to be truly effective in the direction of national unity and coherence, it had to touch the age-old local units by effecting some sort of change in the family, the trades, and tradition. And inversely, since these units were knit together by a common language and culture and common ideals of life, any modification of culture and ideals through the common language would be bound to affect the life of these social clusters and consequently of the country.

China was first set on the road to change when foreign manufactures began to affect the trades. Thus one of the three strands that bound her society was loosened. That was the early stage of change when she first came under modern influence, and the process was unconscious. Then the introduction of modern ideas through books and newspapers and the school system further weakened the already slipping knot by loosening the strand of tradition. The last remaining element, that of family ties, had finally to give way with the other two.

The loosening of these three ties which bound people to their local units caused years of disturbance. Individuals groping for new effective bonds created trouble of many sorts. The students were the first to be affected by the new ideas and it was they who started the trouble; workers in the new industries lost their old trade bonds and they, too, joined the students in troublemaking, as we have seen. The internecine wars of the warlords, the failure of constitutionalism, and the existence of the demoralizing "leakage" system neither prevented the disintegration of the old social organizations nor retarded social progress to any great extent. The troubles caused by the warlords were but ripples on China's vast social sea. The undercurrent went on swirling under the surface, with or without them, or the debased National Assembly, or the "leakage" system. These were evils in the superstructure merely; the self-governing units themselves remained temperamentally peaceful and morally clean.

第十世纪，唐朝灭亡，中国北方普遍遭塞外入侵的异族蹂躏，因而也加速了中国人口的南迁。南方各省，尤其是广东、湖北和浙江一带，不易遭受外族的侵略，所受战祸较轻，因此就成了中国文化的蓄水库，并在过去六七十年内灌溉了新中国大块的土地。

如果要使某一改革对国家统一与团结切实有效，这种改革必须直接使这些古老的区域单位在家庭制度上、行业上和传统上发生某种程度的变化，反过来说，这些单位系共同的语言、文化和生活理想所维系，那么任何经由共同语言所产生的文化和理想的变化，也势必影响这些社会集团的生活，并且进而影响国家的生活。

外国商品开始影响中国行业时，中国就开始变化了，维系中国社会的三条绳索之一因而松散。这是受现代影响的最初改变，这种改变人们是不大知道的。以后现代思想经由书籍、报纸和学校制度等输入中国，又松散了传统这一条绳索。最后留下来的一条绳索——家庭的联系，也终于不得不随其他两条绳索一起松散。

人们因探索新的有效的团结而引起各式各样的纷乱。首先受到新思潮影响的是学生，首先闹事的也是他们；新兴工业的工人丧失了旧日行业的维系力量，因此也就跟着学生一起滋生事端。军阀之间的内战，宪政的失败，以及败坏风气的陋规制度，既未阻止旧有社会组织的瓦解，亦未阻滞社会的进步。军阀所引起的祸患只是中国广大的"社会之海"面上的泡沫。不论有没有互相残杀的军阀，或者声誉扫地的国会，或者败坏风气的陋规，海面底下的潜流仍在滚滚而进。军阀、国会、陋规只是浮面上的祸患，那些自治单位本身仍然宁静如恒，在道德方面也洁净无瑕。

In the long course of history, especially since the latter days of the Tang Dynasty, China has been weak in national defense because her invaders have all been organized on a war footing while she was organized on a basis of peace. Defense forces have had to be drawn from peaceful communities and maintained by a central authority which was a mere superstructure above a peace-loving society.

The Chinese under the leadership of the Mings overthrew the Yuans or Mongols not so much through their own military might as because of the failing strength of the Mongols. Through long years of wars on two continents the military force of the descendants of Genghis Khan had spent itself. Under Chung Chu, second emperor of the Ming Dynasty, China succeeded in organizing a strong army which conquered a great part of Manchuria during his reign; but this military power gradually weakened after his death. When the warlike Manchus rose outside the Great Wall the Mings were helpless in the face of Tartar invasion, and the Ming Dynasty gave way to the Ching or Manchu Dynasty without much effective fighting. After more than a century in China the Manchus in turn were contaminated by the peaceful spirit of the Chinese, and when the Western Powers attacked China with gunboats she was again helpless.

Studying the past, Japan assumed that history would repeat itself and on this assumption began her continental campaign against China in 1894. Up to that year she was right. But Chinese history then began to shift its course as China learned the "tricks" of Western civilization. Japan was either unaware of this change or tried to nip it in the bud. In either case she did not hesitate to launch a new continental campaign some thirty years later, and was surprised to find that a stumbling block had risen in her way.

This was China's social progress. Japan had seen at the top the weak and corrupt Imperial Peking government whose financial strength had been sapped by the "leakage" system; later she saw on the surface the warring warlords; but she was blind to the undercurrents which had slowly but persistently moved in China's immense ocean during the last fifty years.

In the old days organized national ties had existed in secret societies. The members lived outside the village units, gathering around large cities and along commercial routes. Their main purpose was mutual protection against oppression, but this sometimes degenerated into illicit trade.

在悠久的历史过程中，尤其在唐朝末年以后中国的国防一直很脆弱，因为侵略她的异族全部组织严密，随时准备作战，而中国的社会组织却是升平世界的产物。国防部队是由太平无事的社会中征募来的，维持这些军队的中央政府也只是一个和平社会上层的空架子。

明室领导下的汉族之所以能推翻蒙古人所建立的元朝，并非由于汉人本身的军事力量，而是由于蒙古人本身力量的衰竭。成吉思汗的子孙在欧亚两大陆连年征战之后，武力已消耗殆尽。中国在明成祖御宇期间，曾经组织成一支强大的军队，并且征服了满洲的大部分；但是成祖驾崩以后，这支军队的实力也就日趋式微。骁勇善战的满洲人在关外崛起以后，明室对鞑靼入侵简直束手无策，结果没有经过激烈战斗，明朝就亡在满洲人手里了。满清入主中国一百余年以后，结果也染上了汉人的和平习气，等到西方列强的兵舰来攻击中国时，清室也是同样束手无策。

日本研究历史的结果，认为历史是会重演的，因此就在一八九四年发动对中国大陆的攻击。到那一年为止，日本的设想并没有错。但是自从中国学到西方的"诀窍"以后，中国的历史演变途径就开始转向了。日本不是对这种转变懵然无知，就是有意防患于未然。无论动机如何，日本终于在三十年之后又向中国大陆发动了另一次战争。结果发现她的途程上障碍重重，使她大感意外。

日本遭遇的障碍就是中国的社会进步，日本已经看到高踞中国社会之上的腐败无能的北京帝制政府，这个政府的财政力量已经被陋规制度腐蚀殆尽；稍后日本又在水面上看到互相征战的军阀；但是她对过去五十年间在中国的浩瀚海洋之中缓慢地、然而不断地流动的潜流，却茫然无知。

在过去，秘密帮会是全国组织的维系力量。帮会弟兄生活于乡村单位之外而聚集于大城市附近或通商孔道。他们的主要目的是互相保护，抵制压迫，但是这种动机有时候会堕落为不法买卖。他们在内乱时

They were powerful in time of internal rebellion but not of much use against foreign aggression. They lacked new ideas and the notion of social progress was alien to them.

But now, on the fringes of the many thousands of self-governing units in the country there had gathered people imbued with national ideas as against local prejudices and newly learned patriotism as against family loyalty. These individuals hummed like honeybees round a hive and gradually gathered in clusters along the edges. More and more individuals sneaked out to join those outside. As the clusters grew in size, they began to make intrusions into the hive and affected the life of the whole colony. At the same time they began to organize themselves into a national union, so to speak, and took China as their common hive.

Such was the growth of China's modern national institutions. The process was hastened by the rapid extension of communication: steam navigation, highways, railroads, and airways. Educational associations, chambers of commerce, labor unions—scientific, engineering, and political science societies and other bodies—all were organized on a national basis. Political parties, whether the Kuomintang or those whose views were opposed to it, all led the people to think along national lines. The universities took members of the family and molded them into leaders of the nation. Schools instilled national consciousness and patriotism into the formative minds of the new generation.

In spite of continuous civil wars, even before the unification of the country the number of public schools had multiplied in all the provinces. Private citizens established private schools as a way of expressing their patriotism. These millions of elementary school graduates, entering thousands of local self-governing communities, spread ideas of patriotism even to the humble hamlets of the interior.

Once, traveling in the interior during the fight along the Great Wall, I saw a solitary small boy playing soldier. He took a tree for his imaginary enemy and stabbed it with his dagger. Then he imagined that his enemy struck back. He made gestures of defending himself, then fell to the ground with his eyes closed and whispered to himself, "I die for my country." Evidently he was defending the country against the Japanese invasion. During the later war, after a few of the Chungking people had deserted to the Japanese, way back in the hinterland I saw a little boy digging a small grave with a spade. When the work was done he put a sign on the grave: "The Traitor." In one mountainous region, where the

可以表现相当大的力量，但是以之应付外国侵略却无多大用处。他们缺乏现代思想，也不懂什么叫社会进步。

现在的情形可不同了，全国千千万万自治单位的边缘，已经围集了充满国家观念和爱国热情的人，他们反对地域偏见和家族观念。这些人像蜜蜂一样绕着蜂巢喧嚷不休，最后就在蜂巢边缘聚集起来。从蜂巢里面溜出来参加巢外集团的个人愈来愈多。外面围集的群众数量增加以后，他们开始闯进蜂巢，终至影响了整个社会的生活。同时他们开始把自己组织为全国性的社会，拿中国作为他们的共同蜂巢。

中国现代的全国性社团就是这样形成的。轮船、公路、铁路、航空等交通网的迅速扩展，更加速了社团发展的过程。教育会、商会、工会、科学团体、工程学会、政治学会等社团都纷纷成立全国性组织。所有政党，包括国民党以及意见与其相左的政党，都鼓励人民考虑全国性的问题。大专学校吸收了家庭的分子，而把他们塑造成国家的领袖。学校都在努力把国家民族观念和爱国心灌输到新生一代正在发育的心灵里。

虽然内战频仍，各省的公立学校甚至在国家统一之前就已经增加了好几倍。私人常常以创办学校来表达他们的爱国忠忱。千千万万的小学毕业生，跑进本乡本土的自治社会，把爱国观念散布到全国的每一角落。

中日正沿长城作战时，我在内地旅行，途中看到一个孤单的小孩在扮军人作游戏。他把一棵树当作假想敌，拿他的匕首猛刺这棵树。然后他又想像敌人向他还击，他装出自卫的姿势，接着躺倒在地上，闭起眼睛自言自语说："我为国牺牲了！"显然地他在想像自己为保卫国家而抵抗日本侵略。抗战后期，我在后方边荒地区看到一个小孩拿铲子挖了一个小坟。坟挖成以后，他在坟上立了一个木牌，上书"汉奸"。那时少数重庆政要已经出亡投靠日本去了。

nearest school was miles away, a mining engineer saw small boys writing on the walls of their village: "Long live the Three People's Principles of Dr. Sun Yat-sen." These instances show the growth of the national bonds that were taking the place of local ones.

Under the influence of the new education, organized into a national school system, children all over the country now made paper airplanes and sailed them in the air. They made toy water pumps and built toy automobiles. They began to be mechanically minded—a good groundwork for future industrialization of the country.

The growth of light industries in recent years has drawn more and more individuals from the local units and they have begun to associate into a national body instead of local guilds. Radio has brought new ideas to the people through the air. Customs, superstitions, dialects, folksongs, religions, domestic industries, and the economic condition of the tottering local trades and of the suffering farmers have been investigated and studied scientifically from data gathered by institutions of higher learning and learned societies. China has begun to know herself through scientific research.

The turmoils of half a century had set the people thinking. Their attitudes toward life began to change. They tried to create a new stability out of chaos by forming effective national bonds to hold China together in the face of invasion and by working for the progress of the country. This new social and national consciousness was not yet strong enough to face modern warfare with full force. But it was formidable enough to offer stubborn resistance, with indomitable will.

有一次，一位矿冶工程师经过某山区，那里离最近的学校也有好几里路，他却看到几位小孩在他们村庄墙上书写"三民主义万岁！"这些例子可以显示全国性的团结力量已经代地方性的维系力量兴起了。

小孩子们在新的教育制度影响之下，大家都能拿纸折飞机抛在空中滑翔。他们制造小小的抽水机，也能做玩具汽车。他们开始养成研究机械的习惯，这对国家的未来工业化运动也是个良好的基础。

近年来轻工业的发展，从地方单位吸收了许多人，他们开始彼此联系，组成全国性的团体。广播从空中给人民带来许多新观念。风俗习惯、迷信、方言、民歌、宗教、家庭工业、垂危的本地行业及苦难农民的经济情况，都经过仔细调查，并且根据高等学府和学术团体所收集的资料很科学地加以研究。中国已开始从科学研究中了解她自己了。

五十年的动荡已经促使人们思索，他们的人生观开始转变了。他们希望在侵略威胁下从事有效的组织，以团结全国的力量，同时为国家的进步辛勤工作，期望能在混乱中创造安定。这种新生的社会意识和国家意识或许还不够坚强，因为它还不能充分应付战争。但是这种意识可以产生坚忍不拔的意志来进行坚强的抵抗。从这一方面来看，社会意识和国家意识的力量是惊人的。

CHAPTER 23   ENCHANTED CITY OF PEKING

As Paris has inherited the spirit of the ancient Roman Empire, Peking has inherited that of the Chinese Empire of the old glorious days. Paris is the city of cities in the West, Peking in the East. Of Paris you feel that it is not only a city of Frenchmen but also your own; so Peking is not the city of the Chinese alone but universal. In both Paris and Peking one says, "This is my city, where I would like to live."

I lived in Peking for fifteen years until the Evil One dislodged me in 1937. As I look back to the old days there even the annoying dust of Peking is rich in pleasant associations. I miss it and long for it. In the early morning when the rising sun cast its beams upon the paper windows, with shadows of creeping vines dancing upon them, you would see a thin layer of dust sprayed evenly upon your mahogany desk from the night before. It was a pleasure to dust it off carefully with a feather duster. Then you would dust the brush-holder carved with landscapes, and the carved ink stone once owned by famous scholars of past centuries who dusted and washed it centuries before you. And you would do the same for the porcelains of Chien-lung, the bronzes of the Chow Dynasty, the oracle bones of the Shang period—used for divination four thousand years ago—and other timeworn treasures. Even the books, printed long before the West knew anything of the art and lying peacefully on your shelves, did not escape your attention. Let your fingers touch the covers; you would find that the dust did not grudge its favor.

Then you felt that you had done well your morning's preliminary work. The sunlit windows with their dancing shadows now smiled before you. The spotless desk with its ageless pieces of art displayed before your eyes beckoned you on. With a tranquil mind and contented heart you set to your day's work.

In such an atmosphere of antiquity you might read of the period when Confucius taught his disciples; or when the Nestorians came to the glorious empire of the Tangs; or the Jesuits made their astronomical instruments at the Ming court; or Buddha preached his doctrine of eternity; or Napoleon carried his campaign into Russia and drank oil from the street lights; or Genghis Khan sent his invincible armies to the Danube basin, founded an empire on two continents, and made Peking the capital of one of his sons. In Peking one could read history in its

贰叁 迷人的北京

　　正像巴黎继承了古罗马帝国的精神，北京也继承了中华帝国黄金时代的精神。巴黎是西方都市之都，北京则是东方的都市之都。如果你到过巴黎，你会觉得它不但是法国人的首都，而且是你自己的城市；同样地，北京不仅是中国人的都市，也是全世界人士的都市。住在巴黎和北平的人都会说："这是我的城市，我愿意永远住在这里。"

　　我在北京住了十五年，直到民国廿六年（一九三七年）抗战开始，才离开北京。回想过去的日子，甚至连北京飞扬的尘土都富于愉快的联想。我怀念北京的尘土，希望有一天能再看看这些尘土。清晨旭日初升，阳光照射在纸窗上，窗外爬藤的阴影则在纸窗上随风摆动。红木书桌上，已在一夜之间铺上一层薄薄的轻沙。拿起鸡毛帚，轻轻地拂去桌上的尘土，你会感到一种难以形容的乐趣。然后你再拂去笔筒和砚台上的灰尘；笔筒刻着山水风景，你可以顺便欣赏一番，砚台或许是几百年来许多文人学士用过的，他们也像你一样曾经小心翼翼地拂拭过它。乾隆间出窑的瓷器，周朝的铜器，四千年前用于卜筮的商朝甲骨，也有待你仔细揩擦。还有静静地躺在书架上的线装书，这些书是西方还不懂得印刷术以前印的。用你的手指碰一碰这些书的封面，你会发现飞扬的尘土已经一视同仁地光顾到这些古籍。

　　拂去案头杂物上的灰尘，你会觉得已经圆满地完成这一早晨的初步工作。阳光映耀，藤影摇曳的纸窗在向你微笑，纤尘不染的书桌以及案头摆设的古董在向你点头；于是你心满意足地开始处理你这一天的工作。

　　这种古色古香的气氛可以使你回想到孔夫子设帐授徒的春秋时代；或者景教徒初至中国的唐朝时代；或者耶稣会教士在明朝制造天文仪器的时代；或是拿破仑长驱直入俄罗斯，迫得饮街灯灯油的时代；或者回想到成吉思汗派遣他的常胜军直入多瑙河盆地，建立横跨欧亚两大洲的蒙古帝国，并且把北京定为他的一位儿子的京城[1]。我们可以

true perspective. For this city was as grand as nature itself and as old as history. As a capital it has witnessed the rise and fall of five dynasties— dynasties came and were gone, but Peking remained.

The palace buildings were all rectangular and symmetrically arranged like an armchair, with a vast rectangular courtyard in the middle in which stood proudly the giant incense burners of gilded bronze whose smoke, when incense was burning, streamed to the sky. Bronze deer stood in rows and pairs of crouching lions of stone or bronze guarded the entrances. Over a hundred of these courtyards with imposing buildings on three sides were fitted together like the squares of a chessboard in the Forbidden City, which was shut in by rectangular yellow walls with yellow-roofed towers standing out against the sky at the four corners. The Mongols began it, the Mings rebuilt it, and the Manchus improved it to its present form.

The yellow enamel tiles of the roofs shone under the brilliant sun in a speckless blue sky. At dusk or before dawn the triumphal towers of Wu Men—the main entrance of the Forbidden City—silhouetted against the pale sky, looked like castles in the air. On a cloudless moonlit night they made one feel that he was near some fairy palace of the moon which he might admire but not reach.

Before the little Emperor Pu-yi, who reigned over this city within the city of Peking, was ousted from the Forbidden City by General Fung Yu-hsiang in 1926, semimonthly audiences were granted to the remnants of Manchu officialdom. Attired in the quaint old Manchu costumes the officials clustered around the back doors of his toy empire seeking admittance.

A few days after the coup d'état I went into the palace to witness a government committee sealing, house by house, the doors of the halls. A few of the eunuchs were still retained, from whom I got quite a bit of information about life in the palace and stories of the doings of emperors and empresses, princes and princesses, of bygone days.

One story was about the large looking glass which ran from the ceiling to the bottom of the wall. The Empress Dowager loved to sit opposite it so that she could see for herself how stately she was. One day the governor of Shensi was granted an audience by Her Majesty. As he entered the door he saw her in the mirror and bent his knees before the image, kowtowing.

从北京正确地了解历史，因为北京不仅像大自然一样伟大，而且像历史一样悠久。它曾是五个朝代的京城，一代继替一代兴起，一代又接着一代灭亡，但是北京却始终屹立无恙。

皇宫建筑都是长方形的，而且很对称地排得像一张安乐椅，中间有一个宽阔的长方形天井，天井中央摆着一只青铜镀金的大香炉，点了香，香烟就袅袅地升入天空。宫门前站着一排排的铜鹿，宫门口则有雄踞着的一对石狮或铜狮把守。这种三面围着雄伟建筑的天井，数在一百以上，星罗棋布在紫禁城内，紫禁城的周围是一座长方形的黄色城墙，城墙四角矗立着黄瓦的碉楼。北京皇城由元朝开始建造，明朝时曾予改建，清朝再予改良而成目前的形式。

碰到晴空澄碧、艳阳高照的日子，宫殿屋顶的黄色釉瓦就闪耀生辉。在暮霭四合或曙色初露之时，紫禁城的大门——午门——上的谯楼映着苍茫的天色，很像半空中的碉堡。在万里无云的月夜，这些谯楼更像是月亮中的神仙官阙，可望而不可即。

民国成立以后，满清的末朝皇帝溥仪暂时仍统治着北京的这个城中之城，少数残留的清廷官吏还每隔半月觐见一次。这些官吏穿着旧日满清官服聚集在紫禁城的后门听候召见，仍执君臣之礼。民国十三年（一九二四年）冯玉祥入京，终于把溥仪逐出紫禁城。

政变后不久，我受命入故宫监督政府的一个委员会逐屋封闭各门。当时宫内还留有几个太监，我从他们口中得到好些有关宫廷生活的知识，以及过去许多皇帝、皇后、王子、公主等等的趣闻轶事。

其中一则故事涉及一面从天花板一直垂到墙脚的大镜子，据说慈禧太后喜欢坐在镜子前面，看看她自己究竟多威严。有一天陕西抚台奉命入宫觐见，他进门后首先看到镜子里的太后，于是马上跪倒对镜中人大叩其头。

"What did the Empress Dowager do? I suppose she was angry," I said.

"No, no. She smiled and said to him kindly, 'You are seeing me in the mirror.'"

I met some of the eunuchs who attended the princes at the palace school for princes and found them to be all illiterate. Imperial household regulations forbade them to have an education, so that they would remain ignorant of what was taught in the school.

Perched on frames hanging in the veranda, red, yellow, and blue parrots talked the language of the princesses who had spent much time in teaching them. "Please come in. Guests coming. Bring tea..." said the blue one to me, and the red and yellow ones echoed, "Bring tea! Bring tea!" This was the first time I ever saw a blue parrot. Goldfish—black, white, red, and gold varieties—many of them almost a foot long, darted in the palace ponds, their periscope eyes looking skyward while their multiple fan-shaped silken tails waved gracefully in the water.

The living quarters of Pu-yi looked vulgar. A cheap-looking long foreign table stood in the middle of the hall with a few ugly chairs at either side. A pair of pink glass vases decorated the table. It was more like a second-rate country inn in America than the residence of an emperor of China. All the fine furniture and art treasures had been pushed aside and bundled up in the background. The vulgar Western civilization of the treaty ports had invaded the palace; nothing could be more out of place. Cheap magazines were scattered about. Half an apple, freshly cut, and a newly opened box of biscuits lay on the table. Apparently the Emperor had been taken by surprise and left the place as it was at the moment.

When the sealed doors were subsequently opened for a methodical checking over of the art treasures, the variety of beautiful objects was amazing. There were watermelons carved out of jade which looked like real ones, porcelains the color of "blue skies after a shower," bronzes that had witnessed thirty centuries of peace and war, and Imperial seals of jade which had set their mark on many an important document.

Among the famous paintings of the Tang, Sung, Yuan, Ming, and Ching periods were landscapes depicting the beauty and harmony of nature which invited you to step in and enjoy a tranquil life; horses that looked ready to trot out from the picture; fish that seemed to be swimming in water; geese hissing and honking as if painted in sound;

"那末太后怎么样呢？我想她一定很生气吧！"我说。

"哦，不，不！她笑了，而且很和蔼地对他说："你弄错了，那是镜子呀。""

我遇到几个曾经侍候过王子读书的太监，但是这几个太监竟然全都目不识丁。宫廷规矩禁止他们受教育，因此他们对于王子念些什么始终毫无所知。

走廊上挂着许多鸟架，上面站着红色、黄色以及蓝色的鹦鹉，嘴里说着公主们花了不少时间教它们的话，"请进！客来了。倒茶……"一只蓝色的鹦鹉这样对我说，那只红色的和那只黄色的跟着喊："倒茶！倒茶！"这是我第一次看到蓝色的鹦鹉。金鱼在宫中的水池中追逐嬉戏，有白色的、黑色的、红色的和金色的。其中有许多几乎长达一尺，它们的潜望镜一样的眼睛朝天望着，它们的丝绸样的尾巴好像几柄相连的扇子在水中摇曳生姿。

溥仪住的宫殿看起来很俗气，大厅中央摆着一张似乎很粗俗的长长的外国桌子，桌子四周放着几张丑陋的椅子。桌子上摆着一对红色的玻璃花瓶。这房间看起来倒很像美国乡下的次等客栈，真想不到就是中国皇帝的居室。所有的精美家具和艺术珍品已经被弃置而收拾到后宫去了。通商口岸的粗俗的西方文明已经侵入到皇宫；对照之下，使人觉得没有再比这更不调和的了。低级杂志四散各处，新切开的半只苹果和一盒新打开的饼干还放在桌子上。溥仪显然因事起仓卒，匆匆出走，无暇收拾房间。

后来各宫启封清点艺术珍藏时，奇珍拱璧之多实在惊人。其中有足以乱真的玉琢西瓜，有"雨过天青"色的瓷器，有经历三千年沧桑的铜器，还有皇帝御用的玉玺。

唐宋元明清的历代名画，更是美不胜收。有些山水画，描写大自然的美丽和谐，使人神游其中，乐而忘返；有些名家画的鸟维妙维肖，跃然纸上；鱼儿遨游水中，栩栩如生；鹅嘶鸡啼，如闻其声；

bamboo shadows that appeared to bend in the autumn breeze; lotus leaves fresh with morning dew; orchids that seemed to pour forth their mild scent into the air. Great painting in China meant to render not the likeness alone but the motion, sound, color, characteristics—all that would stir the imagination and evoke feeling. In other words, it tried to paint the spirit of the subject.

For two years the committee, with a staff of over a hundred persons, ransacked every recess of the vast palace for treasures of art and checked many hundreds of thousands of articles accumulated through generations of emperors. Some of the storerooms were sealed with spider webs and others had dust ankle deep, a sure sign that they had been a no-man's-land for a century or more. Some treasures had lain there unnoticed for many, many years, no one knew how long.

At long last the palace was thrown open to view and the Palace Museum established to exhibit its treasures. The public, especially the younger generation, opened their eyes at the riches and wonderful achievements of Chinese art through the centuries. Peking was already a center of art; connoisseurs were many and artists not lacking, and with the opening of the Palace Museum the city was much enriched. Things heretofore secluded in the depths of the palace were now revealed for anyone to see—things previously accessible only to the royal family were now open to the common people.

As science is the expression of the mind in knowing and searching for the laws of nature, art is the expression of the heart in feeling their reality. Art is an expression of the life of the people who create it, and makes life richer and more enjoyable. Science is the product of the activity of the mind in satisfying its intellectual interest, and creates material prosperity. In modern civilization the two must join hands to make life complete.

There was a chain of three lakes—the South, Middle, and North "Seas"—to the left of the Forbidden City, with camel-back bridges spanning the creeks between them, trees centuries old along the shores, lilies growing luxuriantly in the water, and pavilions perched on the surrounding heights with golden enamel tiles, vermilion columns, and artistically painted beams. A fish caught some time ago in the lake, so the story has it, bore a gold plate with the sign of "Yung-lo" of the Ming Dynasty (1368-1643).

竹影扶疏，迎风摇曳；荷塘新叶，晨露欲滴；兰蕙飘香，清芬可挹。中国的名画，不仅力求外貌的近似，而且要表现动态、声音、色泽和特征，希望启发想像，甚至激发情感。换一句话说，就是要描摹事物的神韵。

这个委员会包括一百多职员，两年中翻箱倒箧，搜遍了皇宫的每一角落，把历代帝王积聚下来的千万件奇珍异宝一一登记点验。有些仓库密密层层满是蜘蛛网，有些仓库的灰尘几乎可以淹没足踝，显见已经百年以上无人问津。有些古物已经好久没有人碰过，究竟多少，谁也不知道。

最后故宫终于开放，同时故宫博物院成立，主持古物展览事宜。一般民众，尤其是年轻的一代，总算大开眼界，有机会欣赏几百年来中国艺术丰富而伟大的成就。北京本来就是艺术中心，鉴赏家很多，艺术家也不少，故宫博物院开放以后，更使北京生色不少。过去深藏在皇宫后院的东西，现在大都可以欣赏了，过去只有皇室才能接触的东西，现在已经公诸大众。抗战初期，政府就把故宫古物南运，由北平而南京而西南内地。战后运回南京。复因战乱而运至台湾。现在台中所陈列之古物，就是从北平故宫运来的。

科学是心智探究自然法则的表现，艺术则是心灵对自然实体所感所触的表现。艺术是人生的一种表现，它使人生更丰富，更美满；科学是心智活动的产物，旨在满足知识上的欲望，结果就创造物质文明。在现代文明里，艺术与科学必须携手合作，才能使人生圆满无缺。

紫禁城之西，有三个互相衔接的湖，叫南海、中海和北海，湖与湖之间的小溪上有似驼背形的石桥，沿湖遍植百年古木，湖里盛开着荷花，环湖的山峰上矗立着金黄色琉璃瓦、朱红柱子和雕梁画栋的亭子。据说有一次在湖中捕到一条鱼，鱼身上还挂着一块写着明朝（一三六八———一六四三）永乐年间放生的金牌。

In the Middle Sea was Yun Tai, an islet surrounded by lotus where the Emperor Kwang-hsü was imprisoned by the Empress Dowager after the unsuccessful reforms of 1898 and where he died broken-hearted in 1909[2]. On the island was a group of palace buildings with spacious courtyards. Moss-grown trees stood high above the yellow tiles of an intricate system of halls, pavilions linked together with winding corridors of vermilion beams and columns. Miniature hills with rocks and caves brought mountain scenes into the Imperial gardens. How much the unfortunate Emperor enjoyed life in his beautiful prison only Kwang-hsü and those who were with him could tell. During the long days of his lonely existence he was perpetually tortured by ailments of mind and body until death relieved him.

Water was formerly conducted into the lakes through stone conduits connected with springs in the Western Hills. Parts of these pipes still lay along the highways. The drainage system in Peking was a great engineering feat of the old days. Underground aqueducts resembling modern subway tunnels were constructed to drain the sewage from the city. During the latter part of the Manchu Dynasty they were all choked, but the system of yearly inspection of the drainage was still retained to the last days of the regime. In the early days inspectors were ordered to walk through the tunnels to see whether any section needed repair. Later, when passage was obstructed by deposits of dirt, they deceived the eyes of their superiors by a cunning method of cheating: two inspectors in uniform climbed down at one end of the aqueduct and stayed there, while another pair in identical uniforms, hidden at the other end, appeared as the inspector general rode by on his horse. The example illustrates how the spirit of the system had evaporated through years of stagnation while the system still remained as a symbol. This happened in many departments of the Imperial government in the later years. It was small wonder that the government of Imperial China had become a mere symbol.

Peking was a city of trees. In the spacious courtyards and gardens of private residences were moss-grown trees which shot heavenward with a wide spread of branches and luxuriant leaves. If you stood on Coal Hill or some other height, the city seemed to be built in a forest. Wide streets running parallel and crosswise like the lines in a checkerboard traversed the "Bois de Boulogne" of Peking. By an old Imperial rule trees might be planted but never cut down in the capital. With the years people forgot about the rule but had acquired the good habit of loving trees—

中海之中有个瀛台，那是一个周围遍植荷花的小岛，一八九八年维新运动失败后，光绪皇帝就被慈禧太后囚禁在瀛台，后来在一九〇九年死在那里。小岛上建着许多庭院宽敞的宫殿。长着绿苔的古树高高地俯盖着设计复杂的宫殿上的黄瓦，各亭台之间有迂回曲折的朱红色的走廊互相连接。御花园中建有假山，洞穴怪石毕具，使人恍如置身深山之中。至于不幸的光绪皇帝是否在这美丽的监狱里乐而忘忧，那恐怕只有光绪皇帝自己和跟随他的人才知道了。在他被幽禁的寂寞的日子里，他一直受着身心病痛的困扰，最后还是死神解脱了他的痛苦。

湖水原先是用石渠从西山转引来的泉水。公路旁边至今仍可发现部分残留的渠道。北京的下水道系统更是旧日的一项伟大的工程成就。用以排泄市内污水的地下沟渠很像现代地道车的隧道。到了清朝末期，所有这些下水道都淤塞了，但是每年检查下水道一次的制度却维持到清朝末年。早年时，检查人员必须身入下水道，从这一头查到那一头，看看有没有需要修补的地方。后来下水道垃圾淤塞，这些检查人员就用一种非常巧妙的手段欺蒙他们的上司：两个穿制服的检查员在下水道的一端爬下去躲起来，另外两个穿着同样制服的检查员则预先躲在另一端，检查官骑马到了出口处时，事先躲在那里的检查员也就爬出来了。这个例子也说明了这个下水道系统表面上虽然仍旧存在，但是它的精神却因多年来阳奉阴违的结果而烟消云散了。满清末年，这类事情在政府各部门都有发生，所以清廷终于只剩下一个空架子，实在毫不足奇。

北京满城都是树木。私人住宅的宽敞的庭院和花园里到处是枝叶扶疏、满长青苔的参天古木。如果你站在煤山或其他高地眺望北京，整个城市简直像是建在森林里面。平行交叉的街道像是棋盘上纵横的线条交织着北京的"林园"。根据由来已久的皇家规矩，北京城里只许种树，不准砍树。年代一久，大家已经忘记了这规矩，

an instance in which the spirit got into the veins of the people while the system was forgotten. Here lies a secret of China's regeneration.

Few of those who have lived in Peking will fail to retain the pleasant memory of its palaces and other public buildings with their gleaming tiles under the cloudless blue. Imperial parks and gardens were blessed with junipers planted in rows and squares centuries ago and filling the air with soothing scent. Restaurants with exquisite cuisine were always ready to satisfy the wants of the epicure. Curio shops displayed antiques and jades, catering to connoisseurs. Public and private libraries preserved centuries of wisdom on their shelves and in archives. Most remote of all were the oracle bones which threw light on that misty era of Chinese history, the Shang Dynasty (1766-1122 B.C.)[3]. And there was the awe-inspiring Altar of Heaven, which made one feel the grandeur of nature and the sublimity of the spirit of man.

Only yesterday, comparatively speaking—in 1898—the modern National University of Peking was founded as a direct successor to the centuries-old Imperial Academy, *Kuo-tse-chien*, in an atmosphere of centuries of accumulated culture. This institution served both as a center of the old culture and a fountain of new wisdom. Scholars, artists, musicians, writers, and scientists came to Peking to develop their minds and enrich their hearts in the congenial atmosphere of the ancient city. There the inspiration of the past, the influence of contemporary thought, and hope for the future flowed into one inseparable stream of wisdom, and the youth of the country came and drank at its fountain.

却在无形中养成爱护树木的良好习惯——这个例子说明了制度本身虽然已经被遗忘，但是制度的精神却已深植人心。中国新生的秘密就在这里。

在北京住过的人，很少人会忘记蔚蓝天空下闪闪发光的宫殿和其他公共建筑。颐和园和公园里有几百年前栽种的古松。有的成行成列，有的则围成方形，空气中充塞着松香。烹调精美的酒楼饭馆随时可以满足老饕们的胃口。古董铺陈列着五光十色的古玩玉器，使鉴赏家目不暇接。公共图书馆和私人图书馆的书架上保存着几千年来的智慧结晶。年代最久的是商朝（公元前一七六六——前一一二二）的甲骨，这些甲骨使我们对中国历史上雾样迷濛的时代开始有了概念。此外还有令人肃然起敬的天坛。它使我们体会到自然的伟大和人类精神的崇高。

现代的国立北京大学于一八九八年成立，直接继承了国子监的传统，在几百年积累下来的文化氛围中，北京大学的成立几乎可以说只是昨天的事。北大不仅是原有文化的中心，而且是现代化智慧的源泉。学者、艺术家、音乐家、作家和科学家从各方汇集到北京，在这古城的和谐的氛围中发展他们的心智，培育他们的心灵。古代的文物，现代思想的影响，以及对将来的希望，在这里汇为一股智慧的巨流，全国青年就纷纷来此古城，畅饮这智慧的甘泉。

CHAPTER 24   LIFE IN THE FOUR CITIES

Hangchow was the city of natural beauty; Shanghai that of foreign manufactures; Nanking, of revolutionary spirit; Peking, of the golden age—of art and leisure. In my childhood I was reared in a small village in Chekiang, lived among the farmers and craftsmen and played with their children. During my boyhood I was educated in the city of Hangchow and later in Shanghai. When I returned from America my work required that I live, first in Shanghai, then in Peking, then in Nanking and Hangchow, and finally again in Peking until the beginning of the war.

As to their geography, Peking stands in the northern plain not far from the seaport of Tientsin, in the Huang-ho (Yellow River) Valley. It is a northern city, while the other three are southern cities of the Yangtze basin. Hangchow is situated on the banks of the river Chien-tang, where Hangchow Bay begins to spread its broad waters out to the ocean. In the old days Hangchow and Peking were connected by the Grand Canal, 2,074 kilometers long, which crosses both the Yangtze and the Yellow River. The Canal is still partly navigable to the present day.

Northeast of Hangchow, Shanghai perches on the banks of the Whangpoo River, which empties near the mouth of the Yangtze into the Yellow Sea—a body of water which is an integral part of the Pacific, different only in name. Nanking lies a little inland, farther north and west of the other two, along the southern bank of the Yangtze. Not far down the river from it the Grand Canal crosses the Yangtze at Yangchow, where Marco Polo resided as magistrate under the Mongol Dynasty. The four cities are all connected now by railways. Generally speaking, they all border on the Pacific.

The southern cities of the lower Yangtze Valley have approximately the same climate. Spring and autumn days are very pleasant. Sprouting willows are signs of the coming of spring—joyous spring seekers pluck the budding branches and bring them home to decorate their doors as symbols of welcome. When the leaves turn red they tell the coming of fall, and the crimson leaves in the setting autumn sun lend inspiration to poets. The damp season falls in spring, when there is plenty of rain; during the other seasons sunshine and rain are about evenly distributed. Summer and winter are not severe.

貳肆 杭州、南京、上海、北京

杭州富山水之胜，上海是洋货的集散地，南京充满了革命精神，北京则是历代的帝都，也是艺术和悠闲之都。我出生在浙江省的一个小村里，童年时生活在农夫工匠之间，与他们的孩子共同嬉戏。少年时代在杭州读书，后来又在上海继续求学。留美回国以后，因为工作的关系先住在上海，继至北京、南京、杭州，最后又回到北京，一直到抗战开始。

就地理来说，北京位于黄河流域的华北平原，离天津不远。其余三地则是长江流域的南方城市。杭州位于杭州湾口钱塘江之岸，与北京之间从前有运河可通。运河全长二〇七四公里，横越长江黄河两大河，至今仍有一部分可通舟楫。一千三百多年前，隋炀帝动员全国人力，筑此运河，河成而隋亡。唐皮日休有诗云：

"人道隋亡是此河，至今千里赖通波。
若无水殿龙舟事，共论禹功不较多。"

上海在杭州的东北，踞黄浦江之岸。黄浦江位于长江口而入黄海，所谓黄海实际上是与太平洋不可分的一部分，仅仅名称不同而已。南京离海较远，位于沪杭两地的西北，雄踞长江南岸。自南京沿长江东下可达扬州，运河即在此越江入江南，马哥·孛罗曾在元朝扬州当过太守。北京、南京、上海、杭州四城之间现在均有铁路互通，也可以说是太平洋沿岸的城市。

长江下游的江南都市，气候大致差不多，春秋两季的天气尤其温煦宜人。杨柳发芽就表示春天到了，游春的人喜欢采摘新枝回家装饰门户，表示迎春。树叶转红则表示秋天到了，夕阳红叶曾给诗人带来不少灵感。春天有一段雨季，雨水较多，其余三季晴雨参半，夏天不太热，冬天也不太冷。

The soil is fertile. Rice is the chief product. Sericulture is a family industry. Fish, shrimps, crabs, eels, pork, mutton, beef, vegetables, and fruits abound. Out of these materials the famous Yangchow cuisine was created.

Shanghai was the financial center of the Yangtze Valley. It owed its growth to the commercial and industrial activities of the foreigner. Foreign capital was the foundation of its economic structure and foreign merchants and capitalists its aristocrats, before whom all the Chinese living in the city bowed their heads. These foreigners lived a life by themselves. Even if they had been there for several decades, China remained to many of them a *terra incognita*. They lived in beautiful mansions with spacious gardens and were served like lords by obedient Chinese servants. The masters got rich by exploitation and the servants got their modest share of profit by petty "squeeze." Their clubs excluded the Chinese worth knowing; their libraries excluded the books that were worth reading. Their minds were full of arrogance, ignorance, bigotry, and racial prejudice, but were closed like clams to such science and art as the great masters of their own people had created and were creating, and to the new ideas and new movements that were growing in China or in their own countries. Their life had no higher ideal than the amassing of money.

Second in rank to these foreigners, the Chinese compradors shared their masters' ignorance and their money. Compradors of foreign banks and concerns were held in high esteem by the Chinese merchants. When they looked up to their masters and opened their mouths for a bone, their compatriots wagged their tails sympathetically, their mouths watering. The compradors, like alchemists, spent their time turning coppers into silver, while their foreign masters transformed silver into gold. They spent a part of their silver in getting concubines; their masters were much smarter and spent only gold on their "friends."

The third class of people in Shanghai were the merchants and shopkeepers. They waited on the doorsteps of the compradors to buy foreign manufactured goods. When they made money they sent it back home to buy land. Occasional visits to their families, who as a rule lived in their native villages, towns, or cities, brought "inspiration" to the provincial folk, and thus more relatives came back to Shanghai to share their business.

I can speak of these things that existed in Shanghai with intimacy and without exaggeration, for many of my relatives were merchants and

土壤非常肥沃，主要农作物是稻，养蚕是普遍的家庭工业。鱼、虾、蟹、蚌、鳗、牛、羊、猪、蔬菜、水果遍地皆是，著名的扬州菜就是拿这些东西来做材料的。

上海是长江流域的金融中心。上海的繁荣应该归功于外国人的工商活动，外国资本是上海经济结构的基础，外国商人和资本家因而成为上海的贵族阶级，住在上海的人都得向这些洋人低头。这些洋人有他们自己的生活圈子，许多外国人虽然在上海住了几十年，中国对他们却仍然是个"谜样的地方"。他们住在富丽幽邃的花园洋房里，有恭顺的中国仆人们侍候着，生活得有如王公贵族。主人们靠剥削致富，仆人们则靠揩油分肥。他们的俱乐部拒绝华人参加，似乎没有一个华人值得结识；他们的图书馆也没有一本值得一读的书。他们自大、无知、顽固，而且充满种族歧视，就是对于他们自己国内的科学发明和艺术创造也不闻不问，对于正在中国或他们本国发展的新思想和潮流更无所知。他们唯一的目标就是赚钱。

地位仅仅次于这些洋人的是中国买办，他们像洋主子一样无知，也像洋主子一样富足。中国商人非常尊敬外国银行里和洋行里的买办。买办们张大嘴巴向洋主子讨骨头时，他们的同胞也就流着口水，不胜羡慕地大摇其尾巴。买办阶级很像炼金术士，可以点铜成银，他们的洋主子则点银成金。买办们花了一部分银子去讨小老婆，他们的洋主子却高明多了，只要在"女朋友"身上花点银子。

上海的第三等人物是商人。他们从买办手中购买洋货，赚了钱以后就汇钱回家买田置产。他们偶然回乡探亲时，自然而然触动了乡下人的"灵机"，因此到上海做生意的人也愈来愈多。

我所谈的上海种种情形，多半是身经目睹的，绝无夸张之词，因为我的许多亲戚就是在上海做生意的，其中有些还是买办。我对

some were compradors in that city. I know well their mode of life and their ways of thinking; I also knew quite a few foreigners there and have heard many stories about them. Enlightened foreigners, especially the Americans whom I knew well, shook their heads with knit brows when we talked about Shanghai.

The fourth class were the factory workers. They were surplus farmers or those who had given up farming to come to the great city to make more money. They were slum-dwellers.

The fifth and last were the rickshaw coolies, who came from the poor districts north of the Yangtze. These human animals pulled and ran like horses on their two hind legs, with small carriages rolling after them. This cheaper and handier means of communication kept Shanghai constantly in motion—the coolies kept the blood circulating in the city's business veins.

These five classes of people together formed what came to be called the "Settlement mind"—the mentality which grew in the Foreign Settlement of Shanghai. It is a mind which worships power and admires superficialities. Power, whether financial, military, extraterritorial, or in any other form, superficiality bordering on vulgarity in painting, calligraphy, singing, music, and every phase of life. These reigned supreme in Shanghai. *Hai-pai*, or the "Shanghai School," was the epithet invented for this kind of mentality; the opposite is *Ching-pai*, or the "Peking School," which admires the arts in their deeper meaning and strives for perfection. Shanghai was a financial sea but an intellectual desert.

People were all busy as ants at their hoarding. The more they piled up, the more they were admired. In Shanghai both Western and Chinese civilizations were at their worst. The Chinese misinterpreted the West and foreigners misunderstood the Chinese; the Chinese hated the foreigners, who in turn despised the Chinese, both with reason. But they had one thing in common—their equally deculturated state; and one mutual understanding—hoarding. These two elements welded Chinese and foreigners together in a common brotherhood of money. "You exploit me, I squeeze you."

There were oases in the desert, and in them lay the redeeming feature of Shanghai. In the first decade of the century extraterritoriality here afforded a refuge and clearinghouse for revolutionary ideas and literature. The seeds of the theory of evolution and the ideas of democracy were first sown in these oases and blown far and wide to

他们的生活思想知道得很清楚；同时，我认得不少住在上海的外国人，也听过不少关于他们的故事。开明的外国人，尤其是我所熟悉的美国人，每当我们谈起上海，总是紧蹙双眉，摇头叹息。

第四等人是工厂工人。他们是农村的过剩人口，因为在农村无法过活，结果放弃耕作而到上海来赚钱。他们是贫民窟的居民。

第五等人，也就是最低贱的一等人，是拉人力车的苦力。他们多半是来自江北的贫苦县份。这些名为万物之灵的动物，拖着人力车，像牛马一样满街奔跑。这种又便宜又方便的交通工具使上海的活动川流不息，使上海商业动脉中的血液保持循环的，就是人力车苦力。

这五等人合在一起，就构成了一般人所说的"租界心理"，一种崇拜权势、讲究表面的心理。权势包括财力、武力、治外法权等等，表面功夫则表现于绘画、书法、歌唱、音乐，以及生活各方面的肤浅庸俗。我们通称这种"租界心理"为"海派"，相对的作风则叫"京派"，也就是北京派。"京派"崇尚意义深刻的艺术，力求完美。上海是金融海洋，但是在知识上却是一片沙漠。

上海人一天到晚都像蚂蚁觅食一样忙忙碌碌。他们聚敛愈多，也就愈受人敬重。在上海，无论中国文化或西洋文明都是糟糕透顶。中国人误解西方文明，西洋人也误解中国文化；中国人仇恨外国人，外国人也瞧中国人不起，谁都不能说谁没有理由。但是他们有一个共通之点——同样地没有文化；也有一个共同的谅解——敛财。这两种因素终使上海人和外国人成为金钱上的难兄难弟。"你刮我的钱，我揩你的油。"

沙漠之中还是有绿洲的，上海的可取之处也就在此。在本世纪的最初十年里，治外法权曾使上海成为革命思想和革命书籍的避难所和交换处。进化论和民主思想的种籽最初就散播在这些绿洲上，

the intellectual centers of China. While in other parts of China they grew into giant trees, in international Shanghai they remained dwarfs. In the 'twenties a rapid growth of Chinese industry took place in and around the Settlement, protected from the exploitation of warlords by the same extraterritoriality. When returned students came into financial and industrial power, the Chinese began to put into use foreign tricks of management and production, learned, however, more often directly from Europe and America than from the foreigners of Shanghai.

The life of Peking must be painted in other colors, as we have already seen. Aside from beautiful palaces and Imperial gardens, one's first impression was that there seemed to be only two classes of people in the city: those who pulled rickshaws and those who were pulled in them. But when you lived there longer you discovered that there were various classes among those who rode. It would be difficult to find any "top" classes; there were simply people of various professions coexisting side by side in a good, neighborly way. In the old days the Manchus were born aristocrats, but these had now vanished into the multitude. All men were born equal and their differences were of their own making. The only aristocracy was that of learning—the painters, the calligraphers, the poets, the philosophers, the historians, the literary men, and in recent times also the scientists and engineers.

The connoisseurs of art who could put their finger on the genuine amid the counterfeit; the craftsmen who made a thousand and one articles of art; the booksellers who were living bibliographies and the seal carvers who could make you feel your name worth preserving in artistic seals; the rug designers who beautified your floors and brightened up your living quarters—all lived side by side in the enjoyment of knowing or making things for the enjoyment of others. Knowledge and crafts were the keynote of life in Peking.

All could find some leisure in the day to enjoy beautiful things in many different ways. You might drop into an old, dingy-looking bookstore, converse with the man in charge and glance over the books on the shelf; you would feel that your mind was being led into the treasure of knowledge of the past and of the present. You might spend two or three hours there if you liked—when you left you would be invited courteously to come again. You need not buy unless you wanted to.

之后又随风飘散到中国各文化中心。科学和民主的种籽在其他各地发育滋长为合抱大树，在上海却始终高不盈尺。在民国十年到二十年间，上海因受治外法权的庇护，军阀无法染指，上海及其附近地区的工业曾有急速的发展。留学生回国掌握金融和工业大权以后，中国更开始利用管理和生产上的外国诀窍，不过这些诀窍多半是直接从欧美学来的，与上海的外国人关系较小。

北京的生活可就不同了。除了美丽的宫殿和宫内园苑之外，我们第一个印象是北京城内似乎只有两个阶级：拉人力车和被人力车拉的。但是你在北京住久了以后，你会发现被人力车拉的也分好几个阶级。不过要找出一个"上层"阶级倒也不容易，大家和睦相处，所不同的只是职业而已。在过去，旗人出生以后就是贵族；但这些贵族现在已经与平民大众融为一体。大家都生而平等，要出人头地，就得靠自己努力。唯一的贵族阶级是有学问的人——画家、书法家、诗人、哲学家、历史家、文学家以及近代的科学家和工程师。

一眼就能辨别真伪的艺术鉴赏家，制作各式各样艺术品的工匠，脑中装着活目录的书商，替你篆刻图章，使你俨然有名重百世之感的金石家，美化你的客厅卧室的地毯设计师，大家融融泄泄地生活在一起，有的陶醉于自己的鉴赏力，有的则以能为别人制造艺术品而自豪。鉴赏、技艺也是北京生活的特征。

差不多每一个人都可以抽空以不同的方式来欣赏美丽的东西。你可以逛逛古老的书铺，与店主人聊上一阵，欣赏一番书架上的古籍和新书，神游于古今知识的宝库之中，只要你有兴致，你不妨在这里消磨两三个钟头，临走时店伙会很客气地请你再度光临。除非你自己高兴，你不一定要买。

You might go into a curio shop if you felt like it, to look over all the beautiful things, both genuine and clever imitations, and enjoy them to your heart's content. You would be always welcome whether you bought or not at the time. But once you became interested you would very likely spend the last dollar you had counted on for supper.

You might go to a theatre and hear the singing of some of the great actors. It was perfect in every detail, touching the strings of your heart, which vibrated with every note. Or you could go to the Palace Museum and admire the treasures of art created by geniuses of the past. In this atmosphere of arts that always strive after perfection and the deeper meaning of life there grew up the mentality I have just mentioned which came to be called Ching-pai.

If you preferred you might go to the Imperial Gardens and sit under the moss-grown trees sipping tea, or upon the ancient rocks on one of the artful little miniature hills, watching the geese swimming in the pond. On holidays one could go by donkey, rickshaw, or automobile to the Western Hills to see historic spots and breathe air laden with the fragrance of hoary pines.

In seeking wholesome pleasures scholars, artists, craftsmen, scientists, and engineers all united in their enjoyment of old Peking. At work, they carried on their activities in widely diverse fields. The scientists worked in their laboratories to make contributions to the stock of human knowledge, the engineers went back to their slide rules and drawing tools, the scholars buried themselves in books to reconstruct from the past ideas and ideals for the future. The craftsmen produced more beautiful goods; the artists, having drawn inspiration from nature and from the past, cast their mental images on paper or in other materials with their deft fingers.

Years of trouble and war had left Peking undisturbed. Governments had come and gone but the fine old city remained the same. As we have seen, the name was changed to Peiping when the capital of China was removed to Nanking. Peiping, however, still remained Peking and has a good chance to be the capital again in the future. With the shift of the capital a portion of Peking went to the new seat of government—some of the scholars and artists, the architectural design and treasures of art—but the atmosphere and flavor of Peking remained unchanged. Railways and airplanes kept the blood of the two cities interflowing to mutual advantage.

如果你有兴致，你可以跑进古董铺，欣赏书画珠宝，包括贵重的真品和巧妙的赝品。无论你买不买，都会受到欢迎，但是等到你真的对这些东西发生兴趣时，就是要你拿出留着吃晚饭的最后一块钱，你也在所不惜了。

你也可以跑到戏园里去，欣赏名伶唱戏。他们多半唱得无懈可击，声声动人心弦。要不然你就跑到故宫博物院，去欣赏历代天才所创造的艺术珍品，我在前面所提到的"京派"作风就是在这种永远追求完美、追求更深远的人生意义的氛围下产生的。

如果你高兴，你也可以跑到皇宫内苑所改的"中央公园"，坐在长满青苔的古树下品茗，或是坐在假山的古石上闲眺池中的白鹅戏水。在星期天，你可以骑驴，或者坐人力车，或者乘汽车到西山去凭吊名胜古迹，呼吸充塞着古松芳香的空气。

寻求正当娱乐时，学者、艺术家、工匠、科学家和工程师一致欣赏古老的北京。工作时，他们各自在不同的行业上埋头努力。科学家们在实验室里从事研究，希望对人类的知识宝库提供贡献；工程师拿起计算尺和绘图仪器，设计未来建设的蓝图；学者们埋头在书堆里，希望从历史教训里找寻未来的理想；工匠们在努力创造美丽的器皿；艺术家们从自然和历史文物里获得灵感，用灵巧的手指把心目中的形象表达于画纸或其他材料。

连年战乱并没有使北京受到多大的影响，政府虽然一再易手，这个可爱的古城仍然还是老样子。我在前面曾经提到，国都迁移南京以后，北京已经改名为北平。但是在精神上，北平仍旧是北京，随着国都的迁移，北京的一部分也转到政府的新址，例如一部分学者和艺术家、建筑式样和艺术珍藏，但是北平的气氛和情趣却始终未变。铁路和飞机使这两个城市的血液彼此交流，结果两蒙其利。

Nanking is different. It is a city that had to be built upon ruins. In the new capital there reigned a spirit of building up the new structure and tearing down old remains. In Peking, people were nurtured on old glories while they cast their minds into the future. But Nanking had no past to rely upon except memories; everything had to be built anew. Therefore in the collective mind all was thinking, planning, and work, and life kept pace with these activities. Everybody was busy attending meetings and carrying out orders. The atmosphere was always tense. The leisurely spirit of Peking could not have flowered in Nanking.

On the streets pedestrians hustled, rickshaw coolies dashed by; even the inert donkeys fell in with the rapid flow of traffic with hurried steps. Every month new streets shot through old blocks and new houses sprang up like mushrooms. Everywhere was growth—rapid growth.

Even pleasure had to be secured through hard work. Restaurants served delicious food in congested corners, waiting for new quarters under construction. People planned gardens and waited impatiently for the trees to grow. Things you wanted had to be improvised. Without constant constructive activity you fell out of line and were left behind; you had to keep up with the spirit of the time. After some six or seven years of hard work Nanking became a new and prosperous city. Old ruins were fast disappearing while the spirit of thinking, planning, and work was constantly growing, and it radiated to other cities in the provinces and into the future of the country.

Your mind ran ahead into the future to catch up with the spirit of progress in the world. But your steps were necessarily slower—too slow to keep pace with your mind. You can plant trees but you cannot make them shoot skyward overnight; railways and highways must be laid yard by yard; policies of reform have to be carried out day by day. Then, you would think, what is all this hustle and bustle for?

What people sometimes felt about their effort may be summed up in words current and typical in those times: "Discussions ended with no decisions, decisions ended with no actions, and actions ended with no results." It was not really as bad as that. But one thing was certain: people felt their work did not measure up to the efforts made. And that was the spirit of progress.

南京和北平不同，它是个必须从废墟上重建的城市。新都里充满着拆除旧屋、建筑新厦的精神。北京的人固然也憧憬着未来，他们却始终浸淫于旧日的光辉里，但是南京除了历史记忆之外，并无足资依赖的过去，一切都得从头做起。因此大家都在思考、计划和工作，生活也跟着这些活动而显得紧张。每个人都忙着开会和执行命令。空气永远是那么紧张，北京的悠闲精神无法在南京发荣滋长。

街上行人熙来攘往，人力车夫争先恐后，就是懒洋洋的驴子也受了急急忙忙的行人车辆的感染而加紧了脚步。每月都有新道路和新建筑出现，到处在发展，而且是急速地发展。

甚至连娱乐都得花很大气力去争取。饭馆只能在拥挤的角落里供应饭菜，新店面尚未建筑完工。人们在花园里栽花种木，焦急地等待着花木长大。你需要东西全得临时设法。除非你不断地积极工作，你就会落伍；你必须努力不懈，才能追上时代精神。经过六七年的辛勤工作之后，南京终于成为崭新而繁荣的都市了。旧日废墟正在迅速地消失，思考、计划和工作的精神不断在发展，而且扩散到各省的其他城市，国家的前途也因而大放光明。

你为了追赶上世界的进步潮流，计划或许很远大，甚至已经跑在时代的前头，但是实际行动势必无法赶上你的思想。你可以栽花种木，但是你不能使它们在一夜之间长大成荫；铁路公路必须一尺一码地铺筑，改革计划也不能在旦夕之间实现。于是，你可能要问：我们又何必这样惶惶不可终日呢？

当时有几句流行的话，颇足代表一般人的感慨，这几句话是："议而不决，决而不办，办而不通。"当然，实际的情形并不至于如此之糟，但是有一件事情是无可置疑的：大家都觉得他们的工作成绩不如理想。其实，这就是进步的精神。

Hangchow had something of all three of the other cities, yet it was different from them all. It was like Peking in its old culture, for it is the capital of a province of scholars; yet it lacked the grandeur of the former capital of China. Like Shanghai it was tinged with commercialism, yet more lightly, while the absence of foreign overlords left the city freedom for self-expression. It was something like Nanking in its spirit of reforms and reconstruction. But it was provincial-minded, as Peking and Nanking were national-minded. Hangchow is the city of a province in China, while the others are cities of China.

The great asset of the city is the West Lake, which not only supplied the richness of nature but retained the pleasant associations of generations of poets and scholars who once lived there. Hangchow's shortcomings also lie in its historic scene. For its people so treasured the lake that they could not look beyond its horizons; they fooled themselves into thinking it greater than the Pacific Ocean and as alluring as the veriest Paradise on earth. They were, in fact, hypnotized into believing the proverbial saying: "In the heavens you have Paradise and on earth you have Soochow and Hangchow." Just forget Soochow, they would think; Hangchow is here and Paradise is with us.

So Hangchow is West-Lake-minded. If you stayed there too long you were in danger of being engulfed, like the lovers of the South Seas; you would grow and wither there, and become complacent in life.

But the spirit of reforms and reconstruction emanating from Nanking awakened Hangchow from its slumber. Rubbing its eyes, it began to see the possibilities of future development of the province and the part it was to play in the rebuilding of China.

Peking, too, had its broad and tranquil water view. Outside the walled city, from the tops of the Western Hills, one had a bird's-eye panorama of the valley with the river Yunting winding its gentle way through vast tracts of cultivated land. The pagodas in the city were visible to the east.

To the west the Marco Polo Bridge spanned the river where it lay like a sleeping dragon undisturbed through peace and war. Under this long, historical bridge the muddy, loess-laden water flowed steadily, day and night, month after month and year by year.

　　杭州与前面所谈的三个城市都有一点相像，但是与它们又都不同。在古文化上，杭州有点像北京，因为它是"学人之省"的首府，但是缺少北京的雄伟。杭州像上海一样带点商业色彩，但是色调比较清淡，同时因为没有洋主子存在，故有表现个性的自由。在改革和建设的精神上，它有点像南京，但是气魄较小。杭州究竟只是中国一省里的城市，北京和南京却是全国性的都市。

　　杭州最大的资产是西湖。西湖不但饶山水之胜，而且使人联想到历代文人雅士的风流韵事，但是杭州的缺点也就在此。因为杭州人把西湖视如拱璧，眼光也就局限于此；他们甚至自欺欺人地以为西湖比太平洋还伟大，并且足与天堂媲美。他们已经被"上有天堂，下有苏杭"的俗谚所催眠而信以为真。他们想：且别管苏州怎么样，杭州就在这里，所以这里也就是天堂。

　　自我来台湾以后，从经验中证实，苏杭确是天堂，因为既无地震，又无台风。

　　杭州人的心目中只有西湖，你如果在这里住得太久，你不免有沉醉于西湖的危险。此种情况，自古已然。昔人有诗为证云：

　　　　"山外青山楼外楼，西湖歌舞几时休。
　　　　暖风吹得游人醉，却把杭州作汴州。"

　　但是，从南京传播过来的改革和建设的精神终于把杭州从沉醉中唤醒了。揉揉眼睛以后，它渐渐看出浙江省未来发展的远景以及它在重建中国的过程中所应担负的任务。

　　北京也有它辽阔宁静的一面。从城外西山之顶可以鸟瞰北京内外：永定河蜿蜒于广漠的田野之间；向东可以看到城内的塔尖；向西可以看到横跨永定河之上的芦沟桥，它像一条沉睡的巨龙，不理会战争，也不理会和平，在这条年代久远的长桥之下，挟着黄沙的河水日以继夜地、经年累月地奔流着。

The name "Yunting" means "perpetual stability" or "everlasting peace." Was peace everlasting? The Chinese cherished that hope, and so we gave the river its name and then did little to make the peace secure. Finally it slipped from our hands and vanished into the flowing water under that very bridge. For at that bridge, on July 7, 1937, the first shots were fired by the Japanese army in the undeclared war which ultimately set all China aflame. Japan had become intoxicated with the cup of seeming success. And in the Japanese magic box the flames of China were transformed into a streak of lightning that blasted Pearl Harbor on December 7, 1941.

"永定"是"永远安定"或者"永久和平"的意思。和平真能永维不坠吗？国人存着这个希望，因此也就给这条河取了这么个名字。但是我们并未努力保持和平，结果和平从我们手上溜走，随着芦沟桥下的河水奔腾而去。民国二十六年（一九三七年）七月七日，日本军队未经宣战而发动了对芦沟桥的攻击，终使烽火燃遍了整个中国。为步步胜利所陶醉的日本，把在中国的战火日积月累的贮蓄在魔盒里滋长，终至民国三十年（一九四一年）十二月七日变为一道金光向珍珠港闪击。

PART SIX

第六部　抗战时期

WAR

CHAPTER 25   MANCHURIA AND KOREA

In the summer of 1918, some nineteen years before the outbreak of actual war between Japan and China, I made a trip with a friend, Huang Yen-pei, to Manchuria. As this is the area where Japanese aggression in China began, it will not be inappropriate to describe how it appeared in those early years.

We took a train from Shanghai to Nanking, and thence, from across the Yangtze at Pukow, went by the Tientsin-Pukow Railway to Peking. From Pukow north, for two days and a night, the train traversed a vast plain. The dry dust, the arid yellow soil, and the cornfields in this enormous plain of the northern section of the country, which I was visiting for the first time, contrasted greatly with the humid black earth, winding creeks, rice fields, and hilly valleys of the south in which I was born and reared.

I wondered whether the difference in geographical surroundings between north and south had much to do with the difference in physical and mental make-up of their respective peoples. The eastern coastal provinces of Chekiang and Kiangsu, where my ancestors had lived for generations and indeed for many centuries, were the regions in China which, down the long avenue of history, had produced great numbers of scholars, artists, and statesmen. But northern Kiangsu, together with that part of northern Anhuei through which we now traveled, struck me as the poorest part of the country, where deforestation was extreme and the frequent floods of the Huai River played havoc among the population.

Then we came to the Yellow River Valley—to Shantung, the northern coastal province where people were tall, muscular, and hard working, but much crowded through overpopulation—and finally to Peking. From the capital, of whose parks and palaces, museums and gardens, I then had my first glimpse, we continued to Mukden by the Peking-Mukden Railway, passing through Shanhaikwan Pass, the coastal terminal of the world-famous Great Wall of China which, like a gigantic dragon, runs hundreds of miles from Kansu to the coast, separating China proper[1] from Manchuria and Mongolia. Before the train went through the pass we heard cicadas singing in chorus on the leaves of summer trees, just as noisily as in every other part of China. But as soon as we crossed the pass, all the trees were silent, without those singing homopterous insects. They lived and sang only inside the Great Wall!

贰伍 东北与朝鲜

民国七年（一九一八年）夏天，也就是中日战争爆发前十九年，我曾经和一位朋友到东北去过一趟。日本侵略中国是从东北开始的，我们且来看看民国初年时那里的情形。

我们从上海搭火车到南京，在下关渡长江到浦口，再搭津浦铁路火车到北京，自浦口北上，火车穿越广漠的平原，一共走了两天两夜。这还是我第一次经过这一区域。飞扬的沙尘，干旱的黄土，以及遍野的玉蜀黍，与江南潮湿的黑土，蜿蜒的溪涧，连绵的稻田和起伏的丘陵，适成强烈的对比。

我心里想，北方与南方地理环境的不同，可能与两地人民体魄和心理的差异有很大的关系。我的祖先几百年来所居住的华东江浙两省，曾在历史上出过无数的学者、艺术家和政治家；但是我现在经过的苏北和皖北却似乎是全国最贫穷的地区，境内树木砍伐殆尽，淮河更不时泛滥成灾。

车离苏北进入黄河流域的山东省境。山东是华北的沿海省份之一，人民个子高大，肌肉结实，生活勤劳，但是人烟过于稠密，省民不得不向外谋发展。最后我们到了北京，使我有机会初次瞻仰故都的公园、宫殿、博物院和花园。我们从北京循京奉铁路续向沈阳进展，途经长城的终点山海关。全球闻名的万里长城，西起甘肃的嘉峪关，像一条巨龙蜿蜒而东，以迄于渤海岸的山海关，把中国本部与满洲及蒙古隔为两半。在火车穿越山海关以前，我们随处可以听到知了（蝉）在枝头此唱彼和，喧闹的情形与中国其他各地完全一样。但一出山海关就不闻蝉声了。原来知了只在长城以内生长、歌唱。

We came at night into Mukden station, in the Japanese settlement of the city. The streets were dotted with Japanese shops and looked like a small city in Japan. Penetration of the Japanese in Manchuria was already a fact—nothing short of victorious war could stop it. Historically Manchuria, together with that vast territory to the west called Mongolia, had been the center of China's[2] troubles. From time to time the peoples of these great areas—the Huns, the Mongols, and the Tartars—made inroads inside the Great Wall and wrought havoc there. The Japanese were to be modern Tartars after entrenching themselves in Manchuria.

We saw a number of officials working under General Chang Tso-lin, the local warlord in power, and learned much about Manchuria from them. We wanted to interview the general but were advised by friends not to do so. Mukden, former capital of the Manchus before they conquered China some three hundred years ago, was the capital of Fengtien Province, over which Chang Tso-lin ruled. We visited the Imperial Manchu mausoleums near the city, where Manchu emperors were buried before they came inside the Great Wall.

From Mukden we traveled by the South Manchurian Railway, owned and operated by the Japanese, to Kuan-cheng-tse, which was later—after the Mukden Incident of 1931—renamed Shinching, or Seijo, and made capital of the Japanese-made puppet empire of Manchukuo. Here the penetration was very evident. Japanese shops were everywhere to be seen.

On both sides of the railroad endless miles of luxuriant wheat nourished in the virgin soil of Manchuria bore witness that this tremendous area of north China beyond the Great Wall was the richest portion of China and could well support the tens of thousands of immigrants that flowed yearly from Shantung and Hopei Provinces into this northernmost part of the Chinese Republic. To cut off Manchuria from China was to deprive her of lebensraum and suffocate the provinces in the Yellow River Valley.

Kuan-cheng-tse was the terminal of the Japanese-owned South Manchurian Railway and the starting point of the Chinese Eastern

Railway, formerly owned and operated by Tsarist Russia. This company had inherited a legacy of corruption from the tsarist regime and the line was operated by a gang of corrupt White Russian employees. People who bought tickets had to fight for a seat on the train, while free riders occupied comfortable compartments. Theft was rampant. One passenger who slept with his shoes on in an upper berth next morning found one of them gone. He stared at his shoeless foot and wondered how the shoe

　　我们在夜色苍茫中到达沈阳，车站建在城内的日本租界里。街头到处是日本商店，很像日本的一座小城。日本势力侵入满洲已经是铁的事实，除非中国与日本一决雌雄，否则这种情势绝无法遏止。在历史上，满洲和蒙古一直是中国祸患之源。这两个广大区域里的民族如匈奴、蒙古和鞑靼，不时越过长城入侵，致令中原板荡，民不聊生。日本人一旦盘据满洲，势将成为现代的鞑靼。

　　我们拜访了好几位在当地军阀张作霖手下做事的官员，从他们那里听到许多关于满洲的情形。我们原来打算去看张作霖，但是被朋友劝住了。沈阳是奉天省的省会，也是三百年前满洲人征服中国以前的京城。我们参观了沈阳附近的皇陵，清兵入关前的清室诸王就葬在那里。

　　我们从沈阳搭日本人经营的南满铁路到宽城子。宽城子就是我们现在所知道的长春市，民国二十年（一九三一年）九·一八事变后一度改名新京而成为伪满洲国的首都。日本势力侵入宽城子的迹象非常显著，日本商店随处可见。

　　铁道两旁是一望无际的麦田，繁茂的麦穗说明了长城之外这块辽阔的处女地正是中国最富庶的地方，供应每年从山东、河北来的千万移民，绰有余裕。从中国抢走东北等于剥夺了她的生存空间，并使黄河流域的省份窒息而死。

　　宽城子是日人经营的南满铁路的终点，也是原由帝俄经营的中东铁路的起点。中东铁路公司承袭了沙皇政府的腐败作风，由一群贪污无能的白俄雇员在管理。买了票的乘客上车时还得争夺座位，不买票坐霸王车的人反而大模大样占据着舒适的车厢。扒窃之风非常猖獗。有一位乘客，穿着皮鞋睡在卧车的上铺，早上醒来，发现一只皮鞋已经不翼而飞。他眼睁睁地望着那只失掉鞋子的脚，想不通

could have been stripped off without his knowing it; and I wondered what was the earthly use of stealing one shoe without the other. All passengers kept a watch on their belongings after this strange incident. As a precaution my companion hid his supply of rubles in the pockets of his underwear and slept with his Chinese gown on. The next morning the rubles were gone. On our return trip, at Harbin station as I was talking to a Chinese customs official—an American—through a window of the train, I felt somebody meddling with my hip pocket. Before I could turn around my own rubles were gone.

The dilapidated city of Harbin, international metropolis of the extreme north, was a meeting place of East and West. Poor Chinese and Russian children in rags played together in the streets and intermarriages were frequent. Children spoke a sort of hybrid language, part Chinese and part Russian. The free mixing of the poorer classes of inhabitants of Harbin was something novel to me. The bigoted foreigners of Shanghai looked down upon the poorer classes of Chinese as something that would contaminate them. Perhaps this was because few poverty-stricken Europeans ever came to stay in Shanghai.

The streets of Harbin, once well paved, had gone unrepaired for years. The carriages in which we rode bounced up and down on the rough ground so badly that comfort was a negligible factor—we had constantly to grasp at something to avoid being thrown out. The sewers were choked up. After a shower the streets turned into rivers in which the water often came up to one's knees. We met a number of people from south China who were in trade there. All the merchants did prosperous business in that frontier city by speculating in wheat, soy beans, and minerals. So long as their business was good they had no time to worry about the dilapidated state of the Russian-developed city.

We went to Kirin, capital of Kirin Province—one of the three provinces of Manchuria—and were impressed with its beautiful scenery. The city is situated on the banks of the Sungari River. Climbing to the temple on the hill in the city and looking down over the widest part of the river, one saw that it was like a lake, and I was reminded of West Lake at Hangchow. The river was rich in fish. The best fish I ever tasted was whitefish from the Sungari. In old Imperial days this delicious fish found its way only to the tables of the Imperial Court and the princesses and

鞋子被人脱走时他为什么毫无知觉。我也想不通，偷鞋子的贼光偷一只鞋子究竟有什么用途。这件怪事发生以后，全体乘客都小心翼翼地守着自己的行李不敢离开。我的那位朋友为了保险起见，赶紧把携带的卢布塞到内衣口袋里，晚上并且穿着长衫睡觉。第二天早上他的卢布仍然不翼而飞。回程经过哈尔滨车站时，我从车窗探身与中国海关的一位美国官员谈话，我发觉有人摸我臀部的裤袋。我还来不及转身，自己的卢布也不见了。

破败的哈尔滨市是我国最北的国际都市，也是东方与西方的交会地，衣衫褴褛的中俄两国的穷孩子在街头一道玩耍，中俄通婚的事也屡见不鲜。小孩子们说着一种混杂的语言，一半中文，一半俄文。哈尔滨贫苦居民不分畛域地交往相处，对我倒是一件新鲜的事。在上海，顽固的洋人总是瞧不起比他们穷的中国人，把中国人看成瘟疫似的。这或许是因为很少赤贫的欧洲人到上海来住的缘故。但是最重要的原因，还是俄国多混血儿。鞑靼与斯拉夫血统合流已经有相当的年代了。

从前平坦整洁的哈尔滨街道，已经多年未曾修整。我们所坐的马车，在崎岖的路面经过时，忽上忽下地颠簸震荡，我们必须经常紧紧抓住一点东西，才不致于跌出车外，舒服不舒服自然谈不到了。下水道大部淤塞。一阵暴雨之后，街道便成泽国，积水深可没胫。我们曾经碰到不少从南方来的人在这里做生意。这城里的商人们靠小麦、大豆和矿砂的投机居奇，全都利市百倍。他们只知道赚钱，可没有时间理会这个俄国人发展起来的城市究竟残破到什么程度。

我们随后又到吉林省城吉林，当地优美的风景给我们很深的印象。吉林城建筑在松花江北岸，爬上城内山头的寺庙眺望江景，宽阔处有如湖泊，使我想起了杭州的西湖。江中盛产鱼鲜，松花江的白鱼是大家公认最为鲜美的一种鱼。帝制时代，只有皇帝、后妃以及王公大臣才有吃到白鱼的口福。北京郊外青龙桥在夏季有白鱼市，

grand ministers. Ginseng, the life-sustaining drug that China treasured, was also indigenous to the province; large quantities found their way every year inside the Great Wall to all the provinces.

We paid a short visit to Tsitsihar, capital of the province of Heilungkiang. There we experienced an abrupt turn of summer to winter. Overnight we noticed that the green leaves began to wither and drop from their branches. This was the northernmost city within Chinese boundaries; we could go no farther unless we went on to Siberia by the branch line which connected with the Trans-Siberian Railway.

Returning to Harbin, we chartered a steamboat and sailed down the gentle Sungari to Fuchin Hsien. For two days and a night we enjoyed the mountain scenery on both sides, while mountain islands wreathed in virgin forest appeared here and there in the winding river. The evening was blessed with a brilliant moon in a clear sky, the air crisp in the northern summer night. The moon was reflected from the water, which broke into ripples of silver as our boat plowed calmly through. Often the Sungari itself appeared to have ended in a lake, with dark forested mountains rising ahead of us against the moonlit sky. But as we drew near the river suddenly opened to left or right, and as our boat changed its course and curved gradually around the mountains, the river seemed to straighten out and roll down ahead beyond the horizon.

Fukchin, or Fuchin Hsien, was a city of granaries. The wheat and soy beans produced in the surrounding hundreds of square miles all were brought to this frontier city. In the winter it was defended against possible attacks of bandits—the "Red Beards"—by walls built round it with bricks of ice which melted away in summer when the defense was less necessary. Everyone carried a gun and knew how to use it. The new stock of Chinese in the frontier provinces was primitive, full of fighting spirit, and not burdened with the overrefinements of old culture. What a contrast with the overcivilized stock inside the Great Wall! Before the war we drew our best fighters in the Chinese Air Forces from this strong stock from the virgin soil of Manchuria.

Our final destination was Lu-pu Hsien and the plantation of a friend of ours. This district was situated at the sharp end of that spearhead of land where the Sungari and Amur rivers meet and flow concurrently into the Huen-tung—the lower part of the Amur. We went by small boat down the

因为慈禧太后常在颐和园驻跸避暑。直到北伐以前，我们在青龙桥还可买到白鱼。大家相信能够延年益寿的人参也是吉林的特产，每年有大量的人参运入关内，销售各省。

我们又到黑龙江的省会齐齐哈尔逗留了一个短时期，我们在那里经历了一次气候由夏转冬的急遽变化。我们发现绿叶在一夜之间枯萎，纷纷从枝头飞坠。齐齐哈尔已经是中国境内最北的都市，除非搭乘连接西伯利亚铁路的支线火车前往西伯利亚，我们已无法再往北前进。

回到哈尔滨以后，我们包了一只汽船，沿平静的松花江顺流驶往富锦县。舟行两日一夜，沿途饱览山光水色，曲折迂回的江上不时出现原始森林遮掩着的岛屿，夜间月明如洗，北国夏夜的空气更是清新凉爽。月亮倒映在河水里，我们的船缓缓经过时，水面激起银鳞似的微波。松花江本身也常常有山穷水尽疑无路的情境，江水似乎汇为湖泊，森林覆盖得黑森森的山峰，常常在月色辉映中横阻去路。但是当我们驶近山麓时，江流会或左或右忽然回转，我们的船也绕山而过，河道再度向前平伸，江水继续向天边外滚滚奔流而去。

富锦县是个农仓林立的城市。周围几百里内所出产的小麦和大豆都运集在这个边城里。冬天里四周用冰砖筑起城墙，以防止土匪"红胡子"的袭击。入夏冰砖融化，因为夏天盗匪较少，防务也可以稍稍松弛。这里每个人都带着枪，也都知道如何放枪。这些边陲省份的人民仍然保持着原始作风，充满了战斗精神，未曾因古老文化的熏染而变得文弱，与长城以内的老大民族适成强烈的对比。抗战前，中国空军就曾从东北处女地的这群强壮的人民中吸收了大批最优秀的斗士。

我们的最终目的是罗甸县和我们一位朋友的农场。罗甸县在黑龙江与松花江汇合处三角地带的尖端，黑龙江下游与松花江合流后叫混同江。我们从富锦改乘小船顺流而下，于傍晚到达罗甸，当晚

river, arriving at dusk, and were put up for the night in a small lonely hut with thatched roof. A section of the broad brick bed was already occupied by an old woman and a cat, the remainder being set aside to accommodate us. Two pigs lay comfortably on the mud floor, snoring occasionally. Mosquitoes and bedbugs annoyed us the whole night.

Long before dawn we set out for the plantation. A party of four, we trotted on horseback in single file through miles of woods and wheat fields. Before we reached our destination the sun had begun to come up over the horizon. Mountains were barely visible in shady outlines on the Russian side of the Amur Valley. Horseflies began to gather and the animals bled profusely; I was riding a white horse, whose coat showed streaks of blood running down. We did our best to chase away the flies with a horsetail duster. At about six in the morning we came to a plantation run by a Dane. We were told that a band of Red Beards had visited the place a week before. The walls were riddled with bullets.

We arrived at our destination at about eight. The plantation yielded fairly good profits for the first few years of cultivation in that virgin soil, but bandits were the real problem. A few months earlier the "Little White Dragon" and his band had paid them a visit and carried away a large portion of the cattle and poultry. The bandits were on friendly terms with the people on the plantation, apparently, and exchanged their bad guns for good ones. "After all," said the manager, "the bandits are really not so bad, but if the Japanese should get control of this part of the country it would be the end of us all."

This was the final point of our northern journey. At the southern tip of the Manchurian mainland we also visited Dairen[3] and Port Arthur[4], both Japanese-leased territories. Dairen was a commercial port through which soy beans were exported in immense quantities. Port Arthur was a naval base, the key to Manchuria, over which the Japanese fought the Russians in 1904. The defeat of Tsarist Russia had resulted in a transfer of the lease to Japanese hands. With railways starting from Port Arthur and Korea and running through south Manchuria, the Japanese had already got control of the heart and veins of the Chinese Three Eastern Provinces.

We wandered about the naval base for a day and climbed many hills trying to get a bird's-eye view. Finally, on top of one of them, in the slanting sun we came across a stone monument inscribed with the famous lines of the Tartar general who conquered the Sungs in 1276: "March an

寄宿在一个孤零零的小茅屋里，宽阔的砖炕的一部分已经睡着一位老太婆和一只小猫，剩下的一角就用以安顿我们。泥地上睡着两只肥猪，它们似乎睡得很安稳，时而发出重浊的鼾声。蚊子和臭虫扰得我们整夜不能入睡。

天亮以前我们就起个大早望农场进发。一行四人骑着马，鱼贯穿越连绵数里的树林和麦田。在我们到达目的地以前，太阳已经爬上树梢。黑龙江彼岸俄罗斯境内的山岭依稀可辨。马蝇渐聚渐多，咬得我们坐骑血流如注。我骑的是一匹白马，马身上血流如汗，下垂如柳条。我们只有用马尾鬃制的蝇拂尽力驱逐这些马蝇。早上六点钟光景，我们到达一个丹麦人经营的农场，据说一星期前曾有一伙红胡子光顾这里。各处墙壁弹痕累累。

我们在八点钟左右到达目的地。在最初几年里，这块处女地上所经营的农场，每年种植的收益相当不错，真正的问题在乎盗匪。几个月以前，"小白龙"曾经带着一伙人到农场来光顾一次，掳走大批的鸡鸭牛羊。土匪们似乎对农场上的人相当友善，还用他们的破枪枝换走一批新枪。农场经理说："无论如何，土匪并不如想像中的那么坏。如果日本人控制东三省，那我们就真的完蛋了。"

罗甸县是我们这次北行的终站，在满洲大陆的南端，我们曾访问过日本的租借地大连与旅顺。大连是个商港，东北的大豆就是由这里大量出口的。旅顺港是个海军基地，也是东北的门户，一九〇四年日俄战争就为此而发。帝俄失败以后，租借权也就转入日人之手。从旅顺和朝鲜开始而贯穿南满的铁路已使日本人控制了东三省的心脏和动脉。

我们在这海军基地漫游了一天，爬上许多山头，希望能够鸟瞰全港。夕阳衔山时我们终于在一处山头上看到一个石碑，碑上刻着日本东乡大将引金人的两句诗云：

army of a million men to the West Lake and mount, on horseback, the first peak of the Wu Mountains."[5] At Hangchow, overlooking the lake, the Sungs had established their capital in 1127. To follow in the Tartar's steps was the dream of Admiral Togo and his people after the Russo-Japanese War. And after some thirty years the dream came true, when a Japanese army entered Hangchow after the fall of Shanghai.

Korea was the springboard by means of which Japanese imperialism leapt to the mainland of Asia. It was over Korea that China and Japan clashed in 1894. The Sino-Japanese War for control of that ancient kingdom was the starting point of Japan's aggression on the continent. It opened a new chapter of China's history—the chapter which was to see China's reforms, revolutions, wars, sufferings, humiliation, and eventual westernization and modernization.

After our trip to Manchuria we turned off to Korea. Crossing the Yalu River which forms the boundary line between China and her erstwhile protectorate, we arrived by train at Chemulpo. From there we proceeded to Seoul, capital of the country.

The Japanese governor general of Korea resided in the capital. His imposing, Western-style office building was located right in front of the royal palace, as if put there purposely to insult the Korean kings. The kings were gone, but the palace remained to endure the humiliation of being put back into the background.

The royal palace looked exactly like the Chinese Imperial Palace in Peking, but on a very much smaller scale, rather like a toy palace. In the old times, when the Chinese Imperial ambassador condescended to call, the king had to descend from the granite steps to meet the honored guest in the courtyard. If the ambassador had an Imperial Edict to deliver, His Majesty had to bend his knees in receiving the Imperial favor.

At the back of the palace was a Chinese pavilion in which the princesses performed the ancient Chinese dances of the Tang Dynasty.

In Korea as well as Japan, ancient Chinese customs still prevailed. Their pronunciation of Chinese words, their customs, dances, music, and ways of living could all be traced back to influences of the Tang era. As I stood in the pavilion gazing up at the mist-mantled hills of Seoul, my mind reverted to the glorious times of that dynasty (618-905) when Chinese civilization shone as brilliant as the sun in a clear sky, casting its beams far beyond the horizon upon such lands as Japan, Korea, and Indo-China.

"拥兵百万西湖上，
立马吴山第一峰。"

南宋曾在一一二七年建都杭州，吴山第一峰就在西湖之滨，金人则于一二七六年征服南宋。**⁶**日俄战争以后，东乡大将和他同胞的梦想就是步武金人的后尘。大约三十年之后，这个梦想居然实现。继攻陷上海之后，日军终于进占杭州，骑马登上吴山第一峰。

朝鲜是日本帝国主义到达亚洲大陆的跳板。一八九四年的中日战争就是因为朝鲜而引起的。为控制这个古老王国而起的中日战争是日本侵略亚洲大陆的开端，也为中国历史揭开了新的一页，接着而来的是中国的维新运动、革命、内战、灾祸、国耻以及西化运动和现代化运动。

我们在游历满洲以后就转往朝鲜。我们坐火车渡过鸭绿江到达仁川，由仁川续行到达朝鲜京城汉城⁷。

日本的朝鲜总督就住在汉城。雄伟的西式总督府建在王宫的正前面，像是故意要侮辱朝鲜国王似的。国王已经不再存在，王宫却仍留在那里忍受被挤在总督府背后的侮辱。

王宫与北京的中国宫殿一模一样，不过规模却小得多，所以只能算是小型宫殿。据熟悉李朝掌故的韩人某君对我说：中国钦差来访时，李王必须降阶亲迎；如奉上谕，李王尚须跪接圣旨。

王宫的后面有个中国式的亭，嫔妃们就在这亭子里表演唐朝时的中国古代歌舞。在朝鲜和日本，古代的中国风俗习惯至今仍风行不衰。他们对中国字的发音，他们的风俗习惯、舞蹈、音乐和生活方式都可追溯到唐代的影响。当我站在那个亭子里眺望着笼罩在烟雾里的汉城小山时，我不禁神驰于唐朝（六一八——九〇五）的辉煌时代，当时的中国文化有如丽日中天，光芒四射，远及日本、朝鲜

The offshoots of Chinese civilization grew, were preserved and later rejuvenated in Japan, whereas in Korea and Indo-China they grew and withered. The mother country of this glorious civilization had changed its manners, customs, and ways of life as the waves of invasion swept over it. Japan, which succeeded in building up a new civilization in the last century by the introduction of Western civilization upon a foundation of Chinese Tang culture, had gobbled up Korea, and as appetite grew with eating, was on the way to swallow up China, her teacher and benefactor. But Japan taught China a lesson in her turn: how to build a strong new nation upon a foundation of old civilization. Hence China's reforms, revolutions, westernization, and modernization.

While I mused thus over the past and the future, sunshine was peeping through the clouds and the mist was fast fading from the Seoul hills. The Korean who had taken me there, an old Chinese scholar, was standing by in silence but now called my attention to a dinner engagement. We left the pavilion and passed the spot where the Princess Ming was assassinated, presumably by the Japanese for her sympathy toward China. "I know what you have been thinking," said the old scholar. "It is too late for my country now. Our kings preferred dances to the affairs of state. But China, which is your country and may be regarded as mine, has a bright future. I am old now. Brother, you are young. Do your best for China."

The dinner was ready at the Chinese Consulate General, formerly the residence of China's special ambassador. What had happened behind the doors of this historic mansion during the quadrangular love affairs of China, Tsarist Russia, and Japan in courtship of the Korean lady, only those who participated knew. History gives bare outlines only; personal records, if any, remain yet unpublished. Matters have had to be left to the imagination of posterity.

Life in Seoul was being fast engulfed in Japanization. Japanese bazaars, banks, shops, and restaurants occupied prominent sections of the streets. Managers of big business, government officials, and teachers of the more important schools were all Japanese. The life of the vanquished people was fast receding into the background, like their palace. Here and there you would see Koreans squatting complacently on the sidewalks with long stick-like pipes in their mouths, puffing to their heart's content, and women walking leisurely by with heavy loads on their heads. Some of the old type of school, in which Confucian classics were

和越南等地，成了一个远东文化圈。这个灿烂的文化的祖国已因历经外族入侵而改变了她的风俗习惯和生活方式。十九世纪时，日本在中国唐朝的文化基础上吸收了西洋文明而创立了一种新的文化，终于并吞了朝鲜，而且食髓知味，正预备鲸吞她的恩师中国。但是日本倒也给了中国一个教训：如何在古文化的基础上建立一个富强的新中国。中国的一连串改革、革命、西化运动和现代化运动也就是这样开始的。

在我思前想后的当儿，太阳已经从云层后面探出头来，汉城山头的烟雾也很快消散了。引我到王宫去的是位精通汉学的韩国老学者，他一直默然站在我旁边，这时才提醒我晚上的一个宴会。我们离开亭子后经过闵妃被刺的地方，据说闵妃因同情中国而遭日人暗杀。"我知道你心里在想什么，"这位老学者对我说，"我国现在要振作也太晚了。我们的国王已经因沉湎声色歌舞而贻误国事。但是中国是有光明的前途的，中国是你的国家，也可以看作我的祖国。我已经老了，老弟，你还年轻，你好好地为中国努力吧！"

我们到达中国总领事馆时，晚餐已经准备好了。总领事馆在从前是中国特使的官邸。中国、帝俄和日本竞争这位朝鲜小姐的四角恋爱期间，这座历史性的大厦里面究竟有过什么活动，恐怕只有参与其事的人才知道。历史记载只给我们一个模糊的轮廓；私人记录即使有，也迄今未发表。一切情形只能凭后人想像了。

汉城的生活正在迅速地日本化。日本的商场、银行、店铺和饭馆，占据着大街闹市。大企业的经理、政府官员、重要学府的教员全都是日本人，被征服者的生活习惯，正像他们的皇宫一样，正在步步往后退缩。街头不时可以碰到朝鲜人蹲踞在人行道上，嘴里衔着长烟筒，吞云吐雾，悠然自得；妇女们头上顶着沉重的篮子，悠闲地在街上走过。几处讲授四书五经的老式学校已有无法维持

taught, had been left to struggle for existence. I went into such a school, which had one old scholar of the classics as teacher and a dozen pupils squatting around him on the matting. The Koreans and Japanese still kept the ancient Chinese way of squatting on their heels on the floor. It was slightly heated from beneath even in summer and was kept as clean as a bed. The pupils had to learn the Chinese classics by heart as I had done in childhood. Although they used the same textbooks they pronounced the words quite differently. Like the Japanese and the Indo-Chinese, they had been influenced by the Tang pronunciation.

All the people wore padded cotton stockings even in summer. I asked the reason and was informed that the earth was cold in the northern country. Yet they all wore white linen gowns which were quite cool.

The Koreans as well as the Japanese and Indo-Chinese loved Chinese landscape painting, calligraphy, and poetry. But each of the three peoples retained their own individual characteristics. As it was with their arts, so it was with their lives. Korea and Indo-China had come more under the Ming influence in later centuries while Japan, beyond the sea, escaped it. Moreover, the seafaring people of Japan were highly adventurous and therefore kept the martial spirit of ancient China, while the Koreans and Indo-Chinese were touched more deeply with that complacency that tinged Chinese life in later centuries. The system of civil examinations which conferred so much honor upon scholars in China found its way to Korea and Indo-China, but stopped at the gates of Japan.

In its relation to China the younger generation in Korea was undergoing a change under the pressure of Japanese-controlled modern schools, in which the sacred person of the Mikado was worshiped, the virtues of the Japanese exalted to the skies, and the vices of the Chinese amplified to monstrous proportions. If the attitude of young Koreans toward Japan was hatred, toward China it was contempt. While the older generation lamented the passing of the good old ways of Chinese culture, the young people were made to think that they were now the blessed subjects of the Mikado's glorious empire.

之势。我曾经去过这样的一所学校，那里有一位教经书的老先生，十多位学生则围着他蹲踞在垫席上。朝鲜人和日本人仍旧保持着中国的古代方式，蹲踞在地板上。地板下面即使在夏天也用温火烘着，垫席打扫得和床铺一样清洁。学生们必须背诵中国经书，和我童年时的情形完全一样。虽然他们采用同样的课本，字句发音却迥然不同。他们像中国的广东和日本、越南一样，中国字的发音和唐朝人的读法相似或竟相同。

所有人都穿着棉絮布袜，夏季也不例外。我问他们这是什么道理，他们说是因为北方的土地太寒。但是他们身上却都穿着非常凉爽的白色麻布长衫。

朝鲜人、日本人和越南人，都爱好中国的山水画、书法和诗词。但是这三个民族都保持着他们自己的特色。艺术方面如此，生活方面亦然。朝鲜和越南后来受明朝的影响较大；日本则为海洋所隔离，且明代与德川幕府，彼此均以锁国为政策，故所受影响不多。此外，以海为家的日本人富于冒险精神，因此保持着古代中国的尚武精神；朝鲜人和越南人则深受明以后几百年来中国崇尚文事的影响。授予中国文人莫大尊荣的科举制度曾经传入朝鲜和越南，却止于日本大门之外。

朝鲜的年轻一代因受日本人控制下的现代学校的影响，对中国的态度已有急剧的转变；在这些学校里，日本天皇被奉为神明，日本人的优点被捧上天，中国人的缺点则被过分描写。如果说朝鲜青年对日本的态度是仇恨，那么对中国的态度就是鄙夷。年老的一代惋叹充满中国文化的黄金时代已成为过去，年轻的一代虽有少数人认为自己是大日本帝国的天皇子民，而大多数的青年却仍仇视日本。

CHAPTER 26   WAR CLOUDS DEEPENING

In October, 1930, after my resignation from the office of Minister of Education in the national government, I had gone back to Peking—now called Peiping. Again I was entrusted by Generalissimo Chiang Kai-shek, then President of the Executive Yuan (the title of the executive branch of government), with charge of the National University of Peking.

The number of student demonstrations was very much reduced. When the capital was moved to the south the focus of political activities went with it. There was not much left for students to demonstrate against except for occasional outbursts provoked by Japanese aggression, which had started in Manchuria and was now fast extending inside the Great Wall.

On the morning of September 19, 1931, as I was sitting at my desk in the Chancellor's office of the university, a telephone call brought me the fatal news of the previous day. Japan had delivered a blow at Mukden and the Chinese troops had evacuated the city to avoid a clash.

......

A few months later I made the trip back to the south. The afternoon of January 28, 1932, I went to Shanghai station to take the train back to Peiping. As I entered a sense of utter strangeness stole over me—the station looked as quiet as a deserted village. A station guard told me that there was no outgoing train. "It looks as if the Japanese are ready for a blow," he said. "You had better leave here right away. Something may happen any minute."

That night I was suddenly wakened by the roar of cannon, followed by the rat-tat-tat of machine guns. I jumped from my bed and followed the stream of guests to the roof of the hotel. The sky was red with the glow of fires that leapt out here and there from the vicinity of the station. Japanese aggression seemed to have followed on my very heels from north to south. The next morning I went up again to the roof and my heart ached with the sight of the *Commercial Press* Library on fire. Several Japanese bombers kept on bombing the building of the *Commercial Press*. The dark smoke rose heavenward, carrying with it scraps of scorched paper which floated in the sky and sailed idly over the roofs. The print still visible on some of the fragments read dearly "*The Commercial Press*."

贰陆 战云密布

　　我辞卸国民政府的教育部长以后，于民国十九年（一九三〇年）十月回到北京——这时已改称北平。但北京大学校名以历史关系名未改。旋奉当时任行政院长的蒋委员长之命，再度承乏北京大学校务。

　　学生游行示威的次数已大见减少。国都迁往南方以后，政治活动的重心已跟着转移，学生们示威反对的对象已经不多，只有日本的侵略偶然激发学生的示威行动。日本在东北发动侵略以后，此时已经向关内迅速扩展。

　　民国二十年（一九三一年）九月十九日早晨，我正坐在北大校长室里办公，忽然电话传来前一天发生的惊人消息：日本人已经在沈阳发动突击，国军为避免冲突，已撤出沈阳。

　　…… ……

　　几个月以后，我因事回到南方。民国二十一年（一九三二年）一月二十八日下午，我前往上海车站，准备搭火车回北平。进车站后，发现情势迥异平常，整个车站像荒凉的村落。一位车站警卫是认识我的，他告诉我，已经没有往外开的车子。"看样子，日本人马上要发动攻击了。"他说，"你最好马上离开这里。恐怕这里随时要出事呢！"

　　那天夜里，我突然被一阵炮声惊醒，接着是一阵轧轧的机枪声。我从床上跳起来，随着旅馆里的人跑到屋顶观望。天空被车站附近射出来的炮火映得通红。日本侵略似乎已经追在我脚跟后面，从北方到了南方，我所住的十层高楼的旅馆在租界以内，日本炮火不会打过来的。我同一班旅客都作隔岸观火。隆隆的大炮声、拍拍的机枪声终宵不断。第二天早晨，我再度爬上屋顶，发现商务印书馆正在起火燃烧，心里有说不出的难过。好几架日本轰炸机在轮番轰炸商务印书馆的房子。黑烟冲天，纸片漫天飞舞，有些碎纸片上还可以看到"商务印书馆"的字样。

The Japanese had opened an attack on Shanghai. It resulted in the bitterest fighting before 1937, but China was finally forced to accept terms under which Japanese troops were permitted to remain in the city.

For seven years, from 1930 to 1937, I was at the helm of the university, endeavoring to steer that ship of learning through the rough seas of Sino-Japanese conflict. With the aid of many friends—particularly Dr. Hu Shih, Mr. V. K. Ting, and Mr. Fu Shih-nian—the university sailed smoothly with only an occasional trimming of her canvas.

The standard of science teaching and research was raised. A serious study was made of Chinese history and literature. The faculty had ample time for research and the students were led to direct their attention to study; the whirlpool of revolutionary activity and student demonstration was gradually transformed into a center of learning. During all these years there was only one demonstration worth recording, As the Japanese forces drove rapidly inside the Great Wall the students in Nanking and Shanghai clamored for war. Demonstrations on a large scale were frequent in the capital and the students in Peiping wanted to join the movement. One day a crowd of students tried to take a south-bound train at the East Station. Being refused entrance to the train itself, the boys and girls lay on the track day and night to prevent it from leaving the station. At length a few hundred were allowed to go and join their comrades in Nanking.

Seeing that war clouds hung thick over our heads, during the next years we tried to gain time by sailing along the shallows of caution, not venturing on those high seas where we would be bound to clash full-force with the Japanese tidal wave. But our caution was not timidity. When Japanese scholars, fifth columnists in disguise, came to pay "respects" to the "center of culture" (which really meant to them the center of the anti-Japanese movement), we talked frankly with them. One, I remember, spoke at length about cultural relations with our professors and was told that we did not see any cultural relations between the two countries but only the military ambition of Japan. "Give up your military ambition and

China and Japan will co-operate well."

These men—geologists, economists, biologists, and other scholars—came to us from time to time seeking the "friendship" of the university. They all complained about our anti-Japanese movement. We told them

日本已经展开对上海的攻击。结果引起一场民国二十六年（一九三七年）以前最激烈的战事，但是中国终于被迫接受条件，准许日本在上海驻兵。

从民国十九年到二十六年的七年内，我一直把握着北大之舵，竭智尽能，希望把这学问之舟平稳渡过中日冲突中的惊涛骇浪。在许多朋友协助之下，尤其是胡适之、丁在君（文江）和傅孟真（斯年），北大幸能平稳前进，仅仅偶尔调整帆篷而已。

科学教学和学术研究的水准提高了。对中国历史和文学的研究也在认真进行。教授们有充裕的时间从事研究，同时诱导学生集中精力追求学问，一度曾是革命活动和学生运动漩涡的北大，已经逐渐转变为学术中心了。七年之中只有一次值得记录的示威运动。当日军迅速向长城推进时，京沪一带的学生大声疾呼，要求政府立即对日作战。大规模的示威游行不时在南京发生，北平的学生也亟欲参加此一救国运动。有一天，一大群学生聚集东火车站，准备搭乘南下的火车。军警当局不准他们上车，这班男女青年就日夜躺卧在铁轨上，不让火车出站。最后当局只好让几百名学生南下，与他们在南京的同志会师。

我们头上的乌云愈来愈密，此后几年中我们为了争取时间，只好小心翼翼地在浅水里缓缓前进，不敢闯进急流，以免正面撞上日本侵华的浪潮。但是我们的谨慎是与懦怯不同的。每当日本的第五纵队伪装的学者来这"文化中心"（实际上他们却把北大看成反日运动的中心）"拜访"时，我们总是毫无保留地表示我们的态度。记得有一位日本学者曾经对北大教授们滔滔不绝地大谈中日文化关系，结果我们告诉他，除了日本的军事野心之外，我们可看不出中日之间有什么文化关系存在。"只要你们肯放弃武力侵略的野心，中日两国自然就能携手合作的。"

这些学者，包括地质学家、经济学家、生物学家等等，不时来拜访我们，希望争取北大的"友谊"。他们一致埋怨我们的反日运动。

that anti-Japanese we were not, but anti-Japanese-militarism we were. Their minds, however, were set on the strangulation of China; nothing short of a complete surrender could change their course.

Meanwhile the Japanese Kwantung army stationed in Manchuria made rapid inroads inside the Great Wall. The Chinese army fought against the intruders along the Wall, then in the northern part of Hopei Province, and finally withdrew to Peiping and its vicinity. Wounded soldiers streamed in and all the hospitals were filled. A hospital was established supported by faculty members. Wives and young co-eds acted as nurses. Here I came into close contact with the fighting forces and learned their psychology. In conversations at their bedsides the soldiers showed no sign of weakness toward the Japanese. They attributed their defeat to the lack of modern weapons, especially guns, which permitted the enemy to break through the Chinese wall of human flesh.

I wish to remind the reader that this undaunted spirit of the Chinese army built a wall of flesh and blood for the defense of their country against the steel and fire of the enemy. It enabled China to fight on and on for eight long, suffering years, with millions of dead and wounded, without a murmur. China lost many battles but was still winning the war.

When the fighting was going on along the Great Wall, General Ho Yin-chin, Minister of War, came to Peiping to direct the operations. He and I wanted to effect a truce in order to gain time. I went to call on Sir Miles Lampson, the British Ambassador, to sound out his feelings as to acting as mediator. He said that Mr. Suma of the Japanese Embassy had intimated to him that the Japanese, too, desired a truce. Cables were sent to London and the reply permitted Sir Miles to act as mediator. Washington was informed through the good offices of Mr. Nelson Johnson, the American Ambassador. But the plan fell through when the Foreign Minister, Lo Wen-kan, told the British Embassy in Nanking that no one was authorized to deal with a foreign country but himself.

Then the Japanese forces broke through the defense lines along the Great Wall and swept down toward Peiping. The city was about to be evacuated.

As I was laid up in the Peking Union Medical College after an appendix operation, I was not informed. But early in the morning I heard Japanese planes droning over our heads and smelt something wrong. I got permission from the doctor in charge to leave the hospital and limped

我们告诉他们，我们不一定是反日，不过我们反对日本军国主义却是真的。但是他们一心一意要灭亡中国，除了中国完全投降，他们绝不会改变方针。

这时，驻屯东三省的日本关东军正迅速向长城之内推进。国军先沿长城浴血奋战，继在河北省北部步步抵抗，最后终于撤退到北平及其近郊。伤兵络绎于途。各医院到处人满。北大教职员也发动设立了一所伤兵医院，由内子陶曾毂主持院务，教职员太太和女学生充任职员和看护。因为这医院的关系，我与作战部队有了较密切的接触，同时，获悉他们的心理状态。他们认为作战失利完全是由于缺乏现代武器，尤其是枪支，因而以血肉之躯筑成的长城，终被敌人冲破了。

国军以血肉筑成长城抗御敌人的弹雨火海，主要的凭藉就是这种不屈不挠的精神。这种精神使中国在漫长痛苦的八年之中愈战愈勇，虽然千千万万的人受伤死亡，中国却始终连哼都不哼一声。我们虽然节节失利，却终于赢得战争。

战事正在沿长城进行时，当时的军政部长何敬之（应钦）将军曾亲至北平指挥作战。他和我都希望能达成停战以换取时间。我访晤英国大使蓝浦生，探询他有无出任调人之意。他说日本大使馆的须磨先生曾经对他暗示，日本也希望停战。蓝浦生大使当即拍电报向伦敦请示，伦敦覆电同意由他出任调人。我们经由美国驻华大使詹森先生把这件事通知华盛顿。但是这个计划终于胎死腹中，因为当时的外交部长罗钧任（文干）告诉在南京的英国大使馆说，除了他本人之外，谁也无权与外国办交涉。

不久日军突破国军沿长城布置的防线，步步向北平逼近，北平军民已开始准备撤退。

我当时因为割盲肠之后正躺在北京协和医院，对外面的情形很隔膜。有一天清早，我听到日本飞机在头上盘旋，直觉地感到情势不妙。我得到主治医生的许可，忍痛步行到何敬之将军的寓所。

to the residence of General Ho Yin-chin, who was surprised to see me still in the city and informed me that the Japanese were about to attack. I made plans to leave the next day.

Next morning at dawn my telephone rang. It was the general. "A truce has been arranged—you don't have to leave the city." At once I telephoned Dr. Hu Shih.

"Why, the Japanese planes are droning over our heads," he said.

"I have just received a message from General Ho Yin-chin to that effect," was all I could say. But the Tangku Agreement had been signed for China at midnight by Huang Fu, by the terms of which the Japanese forces were to halt after occupying the northern part of Hopei.

The Japanese, having occupied this area and established a puppet "autonomous government" there, urged the Chinese commander of the remaining Hopei forces to co-operate by establishing an autonomous government in Peiping. Rumors circulated widely in the city that the commander, General Sung Chieh-yuan, would give in to the Japanese. In this momentary crisis the university professors issued a statement that they were unconditionally opposed to the so-called autonomous movement in north China. The general, in point of fact, did not comply.

One afternoon a month or two later a Japanese gendarme called on me in the university. "The Japanese garrison in the Legation Quarter invites you to go there and talk over some matters which they wish to understand and which need explanation," he announced. I promised to go in an hour, and he left.

Before dark I went alone to the Japanese barracks in the Legation Quarter, after informing my family and some of my friends. As I entered the offices of General Kawabe I heard the click of the key which meant that the door was locked behind me. A Japanese colonel stood up and said, "Please be seated." I took the seat and out of the tail of my eye saw a soldier standing by the door with a drawn revolver.

"Our commanding general invites you to come here and wishes

to know why you carry on an extensive propaganda against Japan." He offered me a cigarette as he spoke.

"What do you mean? I carry on anti-Japanese propaganda—? Nothing of the sort," I replied, accepting the cigarette.

"Then did you sign that statement opposing the autonomous movement?"

他见我还留在北平城内，很感意外。他告诉我日军马上会发动攻击，劝我快离开北平，于是我准备第二天就离开。第二天早晨，我的电话响了，是何将军打来的："我们已经谈妥停战，你不必走了。"我马上打电话把这消息转告胡适之。

"真的吗？日本飞机还在我们头上盘旋呢！"他说。

"何敬之将军刚刚打电话来这样说的。"我所能回答的也仅此而已。后来才知道黄膺白（郛）已代表中国在午夜签订塘沽协定，根据此项协定，日军在占领河北省北部以后，将暂时停止前进。

日军占领上述地区后，就在当地成立"自治政府"，并催促留在河北的国军司令官与他们合作，在北平也成立一个"自治政府"。北平城内谣言满天飞，说河北省境内的司令宋哲元将军即将对日本人屈服。北大教授就在这紧急关头发表宣言，声明誓死反对华北的所谓"自治运动"。事实上，宋哲元将军也并没有答应日本人的要求。

一两个月以后的一个下午，一个日本宪兵到北大来找我。"日本在东交民巷的驻防军请你去一趟，谈谈他们希望了解并且需要你加以解释的事情。"他这样告诉我。我答应在一小时之内就去，这位日本兵也就告辞回去了。

我把这件事通知家里的几位朋友之后，在天黑以前单独往东交民巷日本兵营。我走进河边将军的办公室以后，听到门锁咔嚓一声，显然门已下了锁。一位日本大佐站起来对我说："请坐。"我坐下时，用眼睛扫了旁边一眼，发现一位士官拔出手枪站在门口。

"我们司令请你到这里来，希望知道你为什么要进行大规模的反日宣传。"他一边说，一边递过一支香烟来。

"你说什么？我进行反日宣传？绝无其事！"我回答说，同时接过他的烟。

"那末，你有没有在那个反对自治运动的宣言上签字？"

"Yes, I did. It is our internal problem. It has nothing to do with an anti-Japanese movement."

"You wrote a book in which you attacked Japan."

"Show me the book."

"Then you are a friend of Japan?"

"Not exactly. I am a friend of the Japanese people, but an enemy to Japanese militarism, just as I am an enemy to Chinese militarism."

"Well, you know, there is some misunderstanding about it in the Kwantung army. Would you go there and have a talk with General Itagaki at Dairen?" The telephone rang and the colonel answered, then turned to me. "A special coach has been prepared for you. Would you go to Dairen tonight?"

"No, I will not."

"Don't be afraid. The Japanese gendarmes will go with you for your protection."

"I am not afraid. If I had been I would not have come here alone. If you want to use force, go ahead—I am in your hands. But I advise you not to. You will become a laughingstock when the world, including Tokyo, is informed that the Japanese army has abducted the Chancellor of Peking University."

His face changed color and he looked as if I were now a problem to him. "Please don't be afraid," he said casually.

"Afraid? No, no. Confucius has told me as well as you to remain calm in the face of danger. You believe in Bushido. Bushido would not harm a defenseless person." I puffed the cigarette calmly.

The telephone rang again, and again he turned to me. "Well, Chancellor Chiang, the general wanted me to thank you for your visit. You may wish to go to Dairen some other time—whenever you like. Thank you. Good-by." The key clicked again. The colonel helped me with my overcoat, accompanied me to my car, and opened the car door. Darkness had already fallen.

The following afternoon General Sung Chieh-yuan sent a major general to advise me to leave Peking lest he should be unable to protect me. I thanked his representative and said that I would remain on my own responsibility.

"是的，我签了名的。那是我们的内政问题，与反日运动毫无关系。"

"你写过一本攻击日本的书。"

"拿这本书出来给我看看！"

"那末你是日本的朋友吗？"

"这话不一定对。我是日本人民的朋友，但是也是日本军国主义的敌人，正像我是中国军国主义的敌人一样。"

"呃，你知道，关东军对这件事有点小误会。你愿不愿意到大连去与坂垣将军谈谈？"这时电话铃响了，大佐接了电话以后转身对我说："已经给你准备好专车。你愿意今晚去大连吗？"

"我不去。"

"不要怕，日本宪兵要陪你去的，他们可以保护你。"

"我不是怕，如果我真的怕，我也不会单独到这里来了。如果你们要强迫我去，那就请便吧——我已经在你们掌握之中了。不过我劝你们不要强迫我。如果全世界人士，包括东京在内，知道日本军队绑架了北京大学的校长，那你们可就要成为笑柄了。"

他的脸色变了，好像我忽然成了一个棘手的问题。"你不要怕呀！"他心不在焉地说。

"怕吗？不，不。中国圣人说过，要我们临难毋苟免，我相信你也一定知道这句话。你是相信武士道的，武士道绝不会损害一个毫无能力的人。"我抽着烟，很平静地对他说。

电话又响了，他再度转身对我说："好了，蒋校长，司令要我谢谢你这次的光临。你或许愿意改天再去大连——你愿意什么时候去都行。谢谢你。再见！"门锁又是咔嚓一响。大佐帮我穿好大衣，陪我到汽车旁边，还替我打开汽车门。这时夜色已经四合了。我独自到日本兵营，也有朋友说我不应该去的，听日本人来捕好了。他们敢么？

第二天下午，宋哲元将军派了一位少将来劝我离开北平，因为他怕自己无力保护我。我向他的代表致谢，不过告诉他，我将继续留在北平负起我的责任。

I stayed on, but nothing happened to me. Occasionally some Koreans came to the university and acted very queer—these incidents were reported to me but I did not pay much attention to them. Then the tactics of the Japanese changed. General Matsumoro was sent to Peiping as special agent of the Japanese army. He made friends with me and came to my house often. He denounced the Japanese general for grilling me at the Legation barracks, and for about half a year we were very friendly. At the end of his term of office he came in full military uniform to say good-by. He told me that he was being sent to Hailar, on the border between Manchuria and Siberia, to command a cavalry division, and said that he was afraid the war clouds were deepening and that a clash between China and Japan would be very unfortunate. "If the war should come," he said, "the Japanese army would go as far as Hankow."

"Yes, General, I agree with you. If our two countries should be so unfortunate as to come to an open clash, international complications might arise and all the Japanese navy be sent to the bottom of the sea, and the Island Empire might be reduced to a few tiny dots on the map of the Pacific Ocean."

He sighed and said, "That may be. But Japan would still be an independent nation, while China will be destroyed by the Western Powers."

"It may be so. Next time we meet I hope we shall not embrace each other, weeping for what we have done so foolishly. No matter what happens in the future, General, let us remain friends." We parted with heavy hearts.

General Imai succeeded him. He called on me and I returned his call. We talked quite frankly along the same lines as I had talked with his predecessor. Once two members of the Japanese House of Peers called. One had formerly been governor of Formosa. After looking around to see whether anyone was within hearing he inquired in a whisper who had been the person responsible for detaining me in the Japanese barracks. I told him it was Takahashi. He shook his head and said, "Ridiculous."

The Japanese had found out by now that the University had no immediate desire to start an anti-Japanese movement and they hoped to win it to the Japanese side by making friends with leading members of

不久以后，蒋委员长因陈辞修将军北上之便，亦来代表慰问。

我继续在北平住下来，而且居然平安无事。偶然也有些朝鲜浪人到北大来寻衅找岔，这些事曾经一一报告给我知道，但是我并未予以重视。不久日本人的策略开始转变了。松室孝良将军受命来北平担任日军的特别代表。他与我交了朋友，常常到我家里来。他大骂那位日本将军不该在东交民巷兵营折磨我。大概半年光景，我们私人之间一直保持非常友好的关系。他任期届满时，穿了全副武装来向我辞行。他告诉我，他已奉命调往东北与西伯利亚交界的海拉尔去指挥一个骑兵师。他说战云愈来愈低，如果中国与日本真的发生冲突，那是很不幸的。"战事一旦发生，"他说，"日军势将深入汉口。"

"是的，将军，我同意你的看法。两国之间不幸而发生公开冲突，很可能会引起国际纠纷，那时整个日本舰队都可能葬身海底，日本帝国会缩小为太平洋地图上的几粒小黑点。"

他叹了一口气："那当然也可能。但是日本仍旧是独立的国家，中国却不免要被西方列强消灭了。"

"也可能如此。下次碰面时，希望我们不必为愚蠢的作为而抱头痛哭。不管将来发生什么事情，将军，希望我们永远是朋友。"我们就这样怀着沉重的心情分别了。战事结束若干年后，我经过东京偕内子陶曾毂往访，相对话旧，不禁感慨系之。

接替他的是今井将军。他来拜访我，我也曾去回拜。我们谈得很坦白，和我跟松室孝良谈话的情形大致相似。有一次，日本贵族院的两位议员来访，其中一位曾任台湾总督。四顾无人之后，他低声问我，在东交民巷日本兵营拘留我的是谁。我告诉他是高桥。他摇头说：

"岂有此理！"

这时候日本人已经明白，北大并无意于马上发起反日运动，他们希望能与北大里的主要教授建立友谊，而把北大拉到日本这一边。

the faculty. Both sides were cautious in dealing with each other and the tension between the university and the Japanese army was somewhat eased.

General Tashiro came to Tientsin as commander of the army there. The Japanese had treaty rights, with other Powers, to station troops in that city. The general came to Peiping and gave a banquet, to leading Chinese and Japanese officials, military as well as civil. In a speech at the banquet he advocated economic co-operation between China and Japan. Some of the Chinese officials responded but spoke rather equivocally. On the score of economic co-operation I remained as silent as a sphinx except for occasional jokes at the table. To my great surprise a telegram came to me in code from Nanking a few days later, informing me that the Japanese Embassy had intimated to the Ministry of Foreign Affairs that the Chancellor of Peking University supported Sino-Japanese co-operation.

This was how the Japanese worked on China. The procedure seemed to be: first sweet words, then political intrigue, then intimidation, again sweet words, and finally blitzkrieg. The order might vary somewhat, but they never deviated from their fundamental course—the subjugation of China. This was also the way the Japanese went about dealing with America before Pearl Harbor.

双方来往都很审慎，北大与日军之间的紧张情势至此已渐渐缓和了。

后来田代将军来到天津担任当地驻军司令。日本以及其他列强，因条约规定有权在天津驻军，田代特地跑到北平来，设宴招待中日双方文武要员。田代在席间发表演说，鼓吹中日经济合作，中国官员也曾有人继起发言，但是措词都相当含糊。我除了吃饭时偶尔说笑外，对于经济合作问题始终不发一言。几天之后，忽然南京来了密电，告诉我，日本大使馆已经暗示外交部，说北大校长支持中日合作。

这就是日本人对付中国的手段。程序大概是：先来一套甜言蜜语，继之挑拨阴谋，然后威胁恫吓，接着又是甜言蜜语，最后施行闪电攻击。先后次序可能有所改变，但是从来不离征服中国的基本方针。日本人在珍珠港事变以前对付美国的，也是这一套。

CHAPTER 27   WAR

When Peiping was Peking, the city was a center of intellectual activities and the student movement. When it became Peiping it turned into the center of Sino-Japanese conflict. During the early months of 1937 one incident after another happened in the vicinity. The arrow was drawn and must in time fly. With lightning speed it went off at the Marco Polo Bridge. On the night of July 7 the Japanese army under cover of darkness suddenly shelled the outskirts of the city from their side of the bridge, and the Chinese army stationed in the city returned fire.

I was at Kuling, a summer resort on the middle Yangtze, when the war god descended upon Peiping. Generalissimo Chiang Kai-shek had summoned a group of intellectuals for discussion of national problems in the cool Kuling mountains during those hot summer days. The sky was clear and patches of shade from the trees made lacelike patterns on the green lawns. One day after lunch, as I was resting in a one-room cottage, one of a group of houses the Generalissimo had set aside for his guests, and was looking through the window into a tall shady tree and listening to the singing of the cicadas, Chen Tsang-po, editor of the *Central Daily News*, broke the quiet of the noon hour by knocking at the door with the news that the Japanese had struck at Marco Polo Bridge the previous night. I leapt from the bed and inquired for further details. There were none.

We discussed the possibilities. As I was fresh from Peiping he asked my opinion from what I knew of conditions in the city. I told him that from my impression of the Japanese commanding generals there and their conservative views, the thing looked like another local incident. The Japanese plan seemed to be to bite off the Chinese cheese piece by piece, and I was not inclined to think they were ready to swallow the whole chunk. But by this policy of slow motion—gnawing off a bit from time to time and slowly accumulating, day after day—in a few years they would have entrenched themselves firmly in north China and it would be difficult to dislodge them. The Yangtze Valley would be at their mercy.

Japan had swallowed up Manchuria by a slow process and had then come to north China. What Manchuria was to north China, so north China was to the south. The same method and the same process. That seemed to be the policy of the Japanese vis-â-vis China.

There was desultory fighting for some days. Twelve days later, as skirmishing went on outside the city, Generalissimo Chiang Kai-shek, in an address to several thousand officers from various armies in the country

贰柒 抗战初期

未改名北平以前的北京是文化活动和学生运动的中心，易名以后则变为中日冲突的中心。民国二十六年（一九三七年）之初，北平附近事端迭起，战事已如箭在弦上，不得不发。七月七日的晚上，终于发生芦沟桥事变。日军在夜色掩护下发动攻击，从芦沟桥的彼端向北平近郊进袭，城内驻军当即予以还击。

战神降临北平时，我正在庐山。当时蒋委员长在这华中避暑胜地召集了一群知识分子商讨军国大事，有一天午后，天空万里无云，树影疏疏落落地点缀着绿油油的草地。蒋委员长曾经为他的客人准备了许多简单雅洁的房子，我吃过午饭正在一幢单开间独立的宿舍里休息，一面眺望着窗外一棵枝叶扶疏的大树，一面谛听着枝头知了的唱和。忽然《中央日报》程社长沧波来敲门，告诉我日军在前一晚对芦沟桥发动攻击的消息，我从床上跳起来追问详情，但是他所知也很有限。

我们曾经讨论可能的发展。因为我刚从北平来，他问我，根据我所知道的北平情况，对时局有何看法。我告诉他，以我对当地日军司令官的印象以及他们的保守见解来判断，这次事变似乎仍旧是地方性事件。日本的计划似乎还是蚕食中国，一时恐怕尚无鲸吞的准备。但是蚕食的结果，日本很可能在数年之内即根深蒂固地盘据华北而无法撼其分毫，到那时候，长江流域也就危在旦夕了。日本已经以渐进的方式吞噬东北而进窥华北，将来华北对华中、华南的局势亦复如是。同样的方法，同样的过程。这似乎就是日本对付中国的政策。

战事断断续续相持了好几天。十二天以后，北平城外的零星战事仍在进行，蒋委员长在牯岭对几千名在庐山训练团受训的将领演说，

who were under training in the Kuling Training Center, expressed the view that the Japanese were about to launch a general war against China and we must get ready to defend the country at any cost. "But if such a general war should start," he said, "we must be ready to sacrifice... It will be a long war and the longer it drags on, the more we shall suffer."

It was the first time I had heard him speak in such unequivocal terms of the Japanese question. General Chen Chun, General Hu Chung-nan, and other commanding generals of the Chinese armies who later distinguished themselves at the various fronts were among the listeners. A few days after this speech Generalissimo Chiang Kai-shek returned to Nanking by air and the commanding generals rejoined their respective armies. With some of my friends I flew to the capital and tried to get back to Peiping, but northbound trains were all suspended.

In about two weeks the war was spreading like a flood in the vicinity of Peiping. General Sung Chieh-yuan fought gallantly as casualties mounted. The commander of the Japanese army, Tashiro, with whose conservative views regarding China problems I was well acquainted, fell ill and the radical younger officers got control of the Japanese forces. After a few days General Tashiro died. Was it illness, suicide, or assassination? Rumors were rampant but nobody could find out the truth. General Sung Chieh-yuan still clung to the idea of localizing the incident and urged the central government troops, which were being rushed northward, to stop at Paoting. And at Paoting, accordingly, they made a halt.

But the Japanese army, now under the direction of young officers, did not stop; Sung's forces were attacked by the enemy right and left and on all sides. One of the commanding generals died in action. Finally General Sung withdrew from Peiping and the Japanese entered the city without firing a shot.

Now the Japanese had control of Peiping. Would north China suffer the same fate as Manchuria after they occupied Mukden some six years earlier? Would Japan stop at north China for the moment, wait a few years more, and use that base for a further attack on south China? Or was she tired of waiting—would she strike at south China with a single blow and get the thing done, once and for all? Either way seemed possible. The plan of slow motion seemed on the whole more dangerous to China. All the ranking officers in Nanking and the military leaders in the provinces favored a country-wide resistance to the aggression. All China—officials, generals, and the people—stood up as one man to face the greatest calamity in history to fall upon the country.

认为日本即将对中国发动全面攻击，呼吁大家准备不计代价保卫国家。他说："全面战争一旦开始，我们必须随时准备牺牲。……这次战争必将旷日持久，时间拖得愈长，我们的牺牲也就愈大。"

在这次演说里，我初次听见蒋委员长称呼侵华的日军为倭寇，并表示对日问题的坚决主张。倭寇这个名词，在一般听众或不甚注意，但在明代长期遭倭寇蹂躏的宁波和绍兴人，听到这种称呼，就会觉得事态严重。当时的听众之中有陈诚将军、胡宗南将军，以及其他后来在各区建立殊勋的许多将领。这次演说后不久，蒋委员长飞返南京，各将领亦分别返防。我和几位朋友飞到南京，希望赶返北平，但是北上火车已全部停顿。

在此后的两个星期内，战事像洪水一样泛滥北平附近。宋哲元将军英勇奋战，部下伤亡惨重。日军司令田代对中国问题的看法一向很保守，我知道得很清楚，不幸田代忽然病倒，思想激进的少壮军官遂得控制日本部队。数日后田代去世。究竟是病故、自杀或被杀，虽然谣言满天飞，谁也弄不清楚底细。宋哲元将军仍旧希望把事件局部化，要求兼程北上的中央政府军队暂时停留在保定。结果中央部队就在保定留下来了。

但是现由少壮军人指挥的日本军却并未停止前进；宋哲元将军的部队四面八方受到攻击。一位高级将领并在作战时阵亡。宋将军不得已撤出北平，日军未经抵抗即进入故都。

日军已经控制北平了，华北是否会像沈阳陷落后的东北，遭逢同样的命运呢？日本会不会在华北暂时停下来，在华北等上几年，然后再以之为攻击南方的基地呢？日本是不是已等得不耐烦，准备一举攻下南方而图一劳永逸呢？二者似乎均有可能。日本的渐进政策似乎对中国更危险。南京的高级官员以及各省的军事领袖全都赞成全面抵抗侵略。结果全国上下，包括政府官员、军事将领和平民百姓，万众一心，一致奋起应付空前的国难。

Meanwhile Japan began to dispatch troops to Shanghai from across the sea. China at the same time rushed her own troops down the Yangtze to the same port. In that small area, face to face, were massed tens of thousands of men. A tiny spark would set off a terrific explosion in the powder magazine. It was immaterial which side should strike it first— whether by the accidental discharge of a gun by a careless soldier without orders, or by the policy of men high up in power.

The Japanese army knew very well that the men responsible for the Mukden Incident, such as Generals Honjo and Doihara, had received the highest rewards and honors for their meritorious acts. Those responsible for the Marco Polo Bridge Incident were to receive like honors, there was no doubt. Who could blame the commanding generals from across the sea for aspiring to similar rewards?

All of us in Nanking knew that the thick war clouds hanging over the whole country were bound to break into a storm. I left for Hangchow by motorcar to stay with a friend in a villa on the historic West Lake. In the serene quiet of the place I had a chance to muse over the past and think of the future. Every day, and every succeeding night, we expected a clash between the two opposing forces in that tightly congested area of Shanghai. Every now and then my friend, Wang Wen-po, telephoned to Shanghai to inquire about the situation. On August 12 the voice at the other end replied abruptly, "No news. Tomorrow at ten, at ten. That's all." The receiver was hung up.

Next morning the fatal hour struck. Smoke rose sky-high. Bombers from both sides blasted the lines of the opposing forces. A full-scale war had begun. There would be no more local incidents, no more piecemeal ways. Japan must either gobble up all China or give it up. But gobble she could not—quite, and give up she would not. It was bound to be a long-drawn-out war.

Two days later, on a cloudy afternoon, I was sitting under a willow tree watching the fish shuttling back and forth in the shallows of the lake. Peals of thunder were audible over the other side of the city. The telephone rang for me. "Hello—do you hear that?" More thunder. "Yes, it's thundering."

"No—the enemy is bombing our airfield."

Seven bombers had flown over from Formosa without escort. They were met by Chinese fighters stationed at Hangchow and five were shot down on the spot. The remaining two flew for their lives and were forced to land at some distance. The pilots were captured, and we learned that

这时候，日本已开始派遣军队循海道开抵上海。中国也在同时派军队沿长江东下赶到沪渎。在这小小的区域里，已有好几万军队结集对峙着，战事一触即发。究竟那一方面先发第一枪都无关宏旨，不论是一位粗心大意的士兵无意中走火，或者是掌握大权者的决策。

日军官兵大家都知道，制造沈阳事变的负责将领如本庄繁和土肥原等均曾因功而获得最高级的勋奖。一手制造芦沟桥事变的人，无疑地也会获得同样的勋奖。谁又能怪渡海而来上海的日军将领也想一显身手呢？

我们在南京的人都知道，密布在全国上空的乌云势将迸发为狂风暴雨。我离开南京循公路到杭州，在湖滨一位朋友的别墅里住了几天，我们没有一天不担心，在淞沪对垒的中日军队会发生冲突。我的朋友王文伯不时打长途电话到上海探问情况。八月十二日，上海方面的回答很短促："没有消息。明天十点钟，十点钟，再见！"接着电话就挂断了。

第二天早上十点钟，历史性的时刻终于来临。浓烟上冲霄汉，双方的轰炸机交互炸射敌方阵地，全面战争已经开始了。从此不再有地方性的事件，也不再有蚕食的机会。日本要就一口吞下中国，要就完全放弃。但是吞下去倒也不容易，放弃吗？她又舍不得。这局面注定是一场长期战争。

两天以后，一个乌云密布的下午，我正坐在柳荫下欣赏湖边浅水中鱼儿穿梭往返，城的这一边隐隐传来阵阵雷声。有人打电话给我："喂！你听到没有？"接着又是一阵雷声。"是呀，在打雷。"

"不是——敌人在轰炸我们的机场！"

七架没有战斗机掩护的木更津队轰炸机已经从台湾松山机场飞到杭州。驻扎笕桥的中国战斗机当即升空拦击，并当场击落其五架，其余两架夺路逃命，但是也在离杭州不远处被迫降落，飞行员被俘。

they had been told by their commanding officers that there were no fighter planes in China.

Next day the Japanese bombed Nanking. In the beginning of the war the enemy dropped only one bomb at any one place, so that all their bombs were scattered. This caused much less damage than concentrated bombing, which they learned a year later from the Russians at Changkaofen, a border town between Manchuria and Siberia where they had a clash with Soviet forces.

My friend Wang Wen-po was a member of the Chekiang provincial government and Commissioner of Reconstruction. He had to get busy. Hundreds of trucks were taken over from the bus lines and munitions shipped to the front in them. Once a fleet of some twenty such trucks was sent to the front. It ran into the rear of the enemy and was fired upon. One truck driver got out of his car and hid in the fields; under cover of darkness he crawled on his stomach through the enemy lines and came back to Hangchow. A few days later he found another truck and dashed off again for the front.

Refugees from Shanghai poured into Hangchow. The temples were filled with women and children. Humble huts in the mountains were turned into temporary homes for fashionable young ladies. They talked and laughed as if nothing had happened to them. The Chinese were always in good humor even in time of danger.

A friend of mine, formerly a cotton magnate, came to Hangchow with his daughters and young children and lived in a temple up in the mountains. He told me that he would like to build a house for his family.

"What for?" I asked.

"I should like to stay in Hangchow during the war in Shanghai," he said.

I was surprised at his idea of the war. I told him that he had better move into the interior as the war would surely spread to Hangchow and all coastal cities and perhaps up the Yangtze as far as Hankow. He was stunned and could not believe my words. Five years later I met him in Chungking, where he told me that he and his family had left Hangchow before war descended upon the West Lake.

In Nanking a plan was afoot for the evacuation of three of the northern universities: Peking and Tsinghua Universities in Peiping and Nankai University in Tientsin. These three institutions were to combine into

我到绍兴专员公署去看一位俘虏，据他说，他们在台湾的指挥官曾经告诉他们，中国根本没有战斗机。

第二天，日军开始轰炸南京。战事刚开始时，日本人在一个地方只丢一个炸弹，所以他们所有的炸弹都是分散的。这种轰炸方式所造成的损害远较集中轰炸为小。一年之后，日军与俄军在伪满与西伯利亚交界处的张高峰[1]发生冲突，日本人才从俄国学到集中轰炸的战术。

我的朋友王文伯是浙江省政府委员兼建设厅厅长。战事开始以后，他的工作自然跟着紧张起来了。他调集了好几百辆公路车，把军火运给前方。有一次，大约二十辆车子结队驶往前方，结果这队车辆误入敌人后方而遭围攻。其中的一位司机跳下车子躲在田野里，后来借夜色掩护爬出敌人阵地回到杭州。几天之后，他找了另外一辆卡车，又再度上前线担任运输工作去了。

难民从上海像潮水一样涌到杭州。庙宇里住满了妇孺老幼。山区的小茅屋也成了衣装入时摩登小姐的临时香闺。她们还是像以前一样谈笑，似乎根本没有发生过任何变故。我们中国人就有这点本领，即使身临危难，也常能处之泰然。

我有一位朋友，本来是上海的棉纱大王，"八·一三"战事发生后，带着他的子女逃到杭州，暂时住在山中的一所庙宇里。他告诉我，他预备给他的家人盖一幢房子。

"为什么？"我问他。

"上海作战期间，我想在杭州住下来。"他说。

我真想不到他对这次战争有这样的看法。我劝他最好还是迁到内地去，因为战事必定要蔓延到杭州以及所有的沿海城市，甚至可能远及华中的汉口。他听到这些话，好像没法相信似的。五年之后，我在重庆碰到他，他告诉我，他们一家人在战火扩及杭州以前就离开西湖了。

与北方三个大学有关的人士正在南京商议学校内迁的计划。大家有意把北平的北京大学、清华大学和天津的南开大学从北方撤退

a union university at Changsha; an inland city on the upper Yangtze. Hu Shih telephoned from the capital and asked me to go back to Nanking to put the scheme into effect. I did not welcome the idea but was finally forced to accept the plan. There are things in the world which you do not want to do but must do in the end, willy-nilly. Like war itself: when war comes, you find yourself fighting whether you like it or not. This was my attitude toward the associated university.

Knowing that I would be unable to see my father's home again before the end of the war and that the hazards of war are difficult to foresee, I borrowed a Buick from a friend and drove home. My father, now very old, was all smiles. When I left again for Nanking I told him that China would be reborn through fire and blood.

"What do you mean?" he asked, giving me a steady look from his twinkling eyes.

"The thing is this. The war will be a long war. Hundreds and thousands of houses will be burned and thousands and millions of lives will be lost. This is what I mean by fire and blood. And in the end China will emerge victorious."

When I left him I had the feeling that most probably I would not see my beloved father again, to whom I owed so much and had returned so little. When bombs visited the native city of my boyhood days, he moved into the mountains and there enjoyed his trees, flowers, and birds. After two years of war he got up early one morning as usual and felt dizzy. He went back to bed and there his spirit fled, at the age of nearly eighty. He was but one of many indirect casualties of war. War is rather hard on old people.

I stayed at Nanking for several days and then boarded a steamer sailing upriver for Hankow. Near the docks wooden boxes containing government archives, books of the Central University library, and art treasures from the Palace Museum were piled high along the banks of the Yangtze, ready for shipment. And on the way to Hankow we met boat after boat packed with troops steaming down the river to reinforce Shanghai.

From Hankow I took the Canton-Hankow Railway to Changsha. On the way we met trainloads of troops crowded in open cars, coming up to Hankow from Canton and Kwangsi. The war was now really on a national footing, not a mere local war as heretofore. The spirit of the fighting men was high. I asked where they were going.

"Fight the Japs!" they replied with zest.

而在长沙成立联合大学。胡适之从南京打电话给我，要我回到南京商量实施这个计划的办法。我经过考虑，勉强同意了这个计划。

我晓得在战事结束以前恐怕没有机会再见到父亲和我的老家。而且战局前途很难逆料，因此我就向朋友借了一辆别克轿车驶回家乡。这时父亲年纪已经很大，看到我回家自然笑逐颜开。我离家重返南京时告诉父亲说，中国将在火光血海中获得新生。

"你这是什么意思？"他目不转睛地望着我，双目炯炯有光。

"事情是这样的：这次战争将是一次长期战争，千千万万的房屋将化为灰烬，千千万万的百姓将死于非命。这就是我所说的火光血海，最后中国将获得胜利。"

当我向父亲告别时，我心里有一个感觉，怕自己从此没有机会再见我所敬爱的父亲了。父亲所施于我的实在太多了，但是我所报答他的却又如此之少。后来我的家乡遭到轰炸时，他迁到山中，以栽花养鸟自娱。战事发生两年以后的一个早上，他像平常一样起得很早，他忽然感到有点头晕，回到卧室，即告去世。享年八十。他不过是战争的间接受害者之一。战争对老年人实在是很大的磨难。

我回南京逗留几天之后就搭轮溯江而至汉口，码头附近沿江堆积着大批木箱，里面装着政府的档案、中央大学图书馆的书籍和故宫博物院的古物（即现在台中之古物）。从南京至汉口途中，我们曾碰到满载军队的船只，顺流东下增援上海。

我从汉口搭粤汉铁路赴长沙，沿途碰到好几批军队挤在敞篷车里，由广东、广西向北开往汉口。这次战争现在的的确确是全国性的，不再像过去一样是地方性的战事了。士兵们的斗志非常激昂，我问他们往哪里去。

"打日本鬼！"他们异口同声地说。

CHAPTER 28   LIFE IN CHANGSHA

Changsha is an inland city. For the first time in my life I lived far away from the sea. Even in America I had stayed first in California for four years and then in New York for another five, always on the seacoast. Living in an inland city I felt a kind of dryness in spite of the damp climate and Tung-ting Lake not far away. My ideal of a place to live was in the mountains near a vast plain or on the plain near the mountains, in either case not far from the sea. Away from the sea, the sense of space in my mind seemed to fill up with solid earth. I began to feel somewhat uncomfortable.

When I arrived at Changsha Mei Yi-chi, President of Tsinghua University, was already there. To run a university in troubled times is something of a headache. To do it during a war, in conjunction with two other institutions not lacking in the diverse personalities and idiosyncrasies common to university professors, was worse. With the worries of war and anxiety as to my family and friends in the war zones or occupied areas, it was more than nay health could endure. "Headache" is a figurative term, but real stomach trouble saps one's spirit and physical vigor. In spite of frequent stomachaches I had to exert myself to help my colleagues steer our precarious craft with its mixed crew over a rough sea.

Teachers and students of the three component institutions flocked to Changsha. Some came by sea from Tientsin, taking a British steamer to Hongkong and then a plane or the Canton-Hankow Railway; others took the Peiping-Hankow Railway to Hankow and then the Canton-Hankow line to Changsha. Within a few weeks some two hundred professors and over a thousand students had gathered around the Changsha Bible School, which the Union University rented as its temporary home. Books and laboratory apparatus were bought and shipped in from Hongkong. In less than two months the university was in full swing.

Owing to lack of space in the city the College of Literature moved to the sacred mountains of Nan-yu. I made two trips there, and these are among my pleasantest recollections of this part of the country. On one of them I wandered with friends deep into the mountains on a three-day jaunt, crossing on our way the road by which a fugitive Ming emperor passed to the southwest almost three centuries ago to avoid capture by

貳捌 战时的长沙

　　长沙是个内陆城市。住在长沙的一段时期是我有生以来第一次远离海洋。甚至在留美期间，我也一直住在沿海地区，先在加利福尼亚住了四年，后来又在纽约住了五年。住在内陆城市使我有干燥之感，虽然长沙的气候很潮湿，而且离洞庭湖也不远。我心目中最理想的居所是大平原附近的山区，或者山区附近的平原，但是都不能离海太远。离海过远，我心目中的空间似乎就会被坚实的土地所充塞，觉得身心都不舒畅。

　　我到达长沙时，清华大学的梅贻琦校长已经先到那里。在动乱时期主持一个大学本来就是头痛的事，在战时主持大学校务自然更难，尤其是要三个个性不同、历史各异的大学共同生活，而且三校各有思想不同的教授们，各人有各人的意见。我一面为战局担忧，一面又为战区里或沦陷区里的亲戚朋友担心，我的身体就有点支持不住了。"头痛"不过是一种比喻的说法，但是真正的胃病可使我的精神和体力大受影响。虽然胃病时发，我仍勉强打起精神和梅校长共同负起责任来，幸靠同仁的和衷共济，我们才把这条由混杂水手操纵的危舟渡过惊涛骇浪。

　　联合大学在长沙成立以后，北大、清华、南开三校的学生都陆续来了。有的是从天津搭英国轮船先到香港，然后再搭飞机或粤汉铁路火车来的，有的则由北平搭平汉铁路火车先到汉口，然后转粤汉铁路到长沙。几星期之内，大概就有两百名教授和一千多名学生齐集在长沙圣经学校了。联合大学租了圣经学校为临时校舍。书籍和实验仪器则是在香港购置运来的，不到两个月，联大就粗具规模了。

　　因为在长沙城内找不到地方，我们就把文学院搬到佛教圣地南岳衡山。我曾经到南岳去过两次，留下许多不可磨灭的回忆。其中一次我和几位朋友曾深入丛山之中畅游三日，途中还曾经过一条山路，明朝末年一位流亡皇帝（永历帝）在三百年前为逃避清兵追赶

the Manchus. A stone tablet in his memory stands there to this day, with the names of all the officials who followed him inscribed upon it. Oddly, at one of the temples we visited, a tree planted by the fleeing emperor had grown into a crooked shape looking like an old, old man taking a rest after a very long journey. We were now treading the same path, standing in the same temple. For what reason? Foreign invasion from the north, which had troubled China through ten centuries.

The first night we stopped at the Fang-kwang Temple. Here a famous Ming scholar passed the remainder of his life after the fall of the Ming Dynasty. It was a clear night—the full moon sailed low over the mountains in the empty sky. I had never seen the moon look so low and so near, as if one could poke one's fingers in its smiling face.

The second night we stopped at a monastery near the highest peak of the sacred mountains. A spring gushes from the very top of the peak, and a temple is perched there. This is the house of the Fire God and a symbol of the ancient practical wisdom that water should always be ready near fire, which may thus be controlled.

Near this temple we saw the sun come up next morning, a wonderful sight. It rose out of a sea of clouds, first sending up violet, golden, pink, and blue tints through the cloud bank and then emerging to lie like a golden ostrich egg on a white velvet cushion. All of a sudden it split into four brilliant oranges, then in the flash of a few seconds merged again into one great ball. For some moments it seemed to change color with every fraction of a second, as if with the turning of a moving-picture color camera. Then it stopped, glowed mellow gold for a few instants, and finally became a great ball of fire from which we had to turn our eyes. The icebergs of cloud disappeared and the still waves vanished. Only a thin layer of mist veiled the valleys down below. Through it one could see chimneys sending up their smoke in the mild morning sun.

Pilgrims came by thousands to the sacred mountains. Many walked from several hundred miles away. Old and young, rich and poor, all joined in common worship of the Buddha.

Changsha is the capital of Hunan Province, a center of rich rice production feeding many millions of people outside its boundaries. Fish, shrimp, eels, and turtles from the river Hsiang were abundant, oranges

曾经走过这条山路。现在路旁还树着一个纪念碑，碑上刻着所有追随他的臣子的名字。在我们经过的一所寺庙里，看见一棵松树，据一位老僧说是永历帝所手植的。说来奇怪，这棵松树竟长得像一位佝偻的老翁，似乎是长途跋涉之后正在那里休息。我们先后在同一的路上走过，而且暂驻在同一寺庙里，为什么？同是为了由北方来的异族入侵。一千多年来，中国始终为外来侵略所苦。

第一夜我们住宿在方广寺。明朝灭亡以后，一位著名的遗老即曾在方广寺度其余年。那天晚上夜空澄澈，团圞明月在山头冉冉移动，我从来没有看到过这样低、这样近的月亮，好像一伸手就可以触到它这张笑脸。

第二夜我们住在接近南岳极峰的一个寺院里。山峰的顶端有清泉汩汩流出，泉旁有个火神庙。这个庙颇足代表中国通俗的想法，我们一向认为火旁边随时预备着水，因为水可以克火。

第二天早晨，我们在这火神庙附近看到了日出奇观，太阳从云海里冉冉升起，最先透过云层发出紫色的光辉，接着发出金黄色、粉红和蓝色的光彩，最后浮出云端，像一个金色的鸵鸟蛋躺卧在雪白的天鹅绒垫子上。忽然之间它分裂为四个金光灿烂的橘子，转瞬之间却又复合为一个大火球。接着的一段短暂时刻中，它似乎每秒钟都在变换色彩，很像电影的彩色镜头在转动。一会儿它又暂时停住不动了，四散发射着柔和的金光，最后又变为一个耀目大火球，使我们不得不转移视线。云海中的冰山不见了，平静的云浪也跟着消逝，只剩下一层轻雾笼罩着脚下的山谷。透过轻雾，我们看到缕缕炊烟正在煦和的旭日照耀下袅袅升起。

来南岳朝山进香的人络绎于途，有的香客还是从几百里之外步行来的。男女老幼，贫贱富贵，都来向菩萨顶礼膜拜。

长沙是湖南的省会，湖南是著名的鱼米之乡，所产稻米养活了全省人口以外，还可以供应省外几百万人的食用。湘江里最多的是鱼、虾、鳝、鳗和甲鱼，省内所产橘子和柿子鲜红艳丽。贫富咸宜的

and persimmons bountiful. Pork was tender and full of flavor. The bean curd, China's national food for rich and poor alike, was as pure and smooth as thickened milk. The only drawback was the high humidity—there were far more rainy or cloudy days in a year than sunny ones.

Every time I went up by airplane from the city, as I sometimes had to do, I thought of the crystal palace deep in the sea where the king of dragons lives, as we all learned in Chinese fairy tales. There would still be clouds above my head, while down below mist enveloped the city like the white around the yolk of an egg. Farther up, there would be another ceiling of cloud without a streak of sun.

The people were healthy, independent, and hard working. They loved to fight. The slightest provocation would find them ready for combat, whether vocal or by fists. At highway stations one often saw signs: DO NOT QUARREL and DO NOT FIGHT. Rickshaw coolies sauntered along the streets and refused to run. If you told a coolie to run faster he would invariably say, "You pull the rickshaw—I'd like to see you run." While the temper of the people was quick, their movements were slow. Here was a case where temper and tempo did not go together.

They were frank and sincere, not easily influenced by other people's opinions. They would be either your friends or your enemies, with no halfway between. They are good soldiers. "No Hunanese, no army." It was by his Hunan army that Tseng Kuo-fang defeated the Taipings in 1864. Even now no Chinese army is found without some soldiers from Hunan. It is the Sparta of China.

The Japanese invaded Changsha three times in the course of the war, and three times suffered defeat there. The people co-operated with the national army wholeheartedly, through blood and fire.

In Changsha we had news of the war in Shanghai. For three long months Chinese troops of flesh and blood held at bay the Japanese army of fire and steel. Finally the Chinese army withdrew to save further futile sacrifice. Now the enemy converged on Nanking. An exodus of the population from the capital began—thousands of people streamed along the highway to Changsha. Trains of trucks and cars miles long poured into the city. Suddenly it was congested with refugees. Some ministries of the government moved to Changsha, others to Hankow.

豆腐洁白匀净如浓缩的牛奶。唯一的缺点是湿气太重，一年之中雨天和阴天远较晴天为多。

我每次坐飞机由长沙起飞时，总会想到海龙王的水晶宫。我的头上有悠悠白云，脚下则是轻纱样的薄雾笼罩着全城，正像一层蛋白围绕着蛋黄。再向上升更有一层云挡住了阳光。在长沙天空飞行终逃不了层层遮盖的云。

湖南人的身体健壮，个性刚强，而且刻苦耐劳，他们尚武好斗，一言不合就彼此骂起来，甚至动拳头。公路车站上我们常常看到"不要开口骂人，不要动手打人"的标语。人力车夫在街上慢吞吞像散步，绝不肯拔步飞奔。如果你要他跑得快一点，他准会告诉你"你老下来拉吧——我倒要看看你老怎么个跑法"。湖南人的性子固然急，但行动却不和脾气相同，一个人脾气的缓急和行动的快慢可见并不一致的，湖南人拉黄包车就是一个例子。

他们很爽直，也很真挚，但是脾气固执，不容易受别人意见的影响。他们要就是你的朋友，要就是你的敌人，没有折衷的余地。他们是很出色的军人，所以有"无湘不成军"的说法。曾国藩在清同治三年（一八六四年）击败太平军，就是靠他的湘军。现在的军队里，差不多各单位都有湖南人，湖南是中国的斯巴达。

抗战期间，日本人曾三度进犯长沙而连遭三次大败。老百姓在枪林弹雨中协助国军抗敌，伤亡惨重。

在长沙我们不断有上海战事的消息。国军以血肉之躯抵御日军的火海和弹雨，使敌人无法越过国军防线达三月之久。后来国军为避免继续作无谓的牺牲，终于撤出上海。敌军接着包围南京，首都人民开始全面撤退，千千万万的人沿公路涌至长沙。卡车、轿车成群结队到达，长沙忽然之间挤满了难民。从南京撤出的政府部会，有的迁至长沙，有的则迁到汉口。

Before long the Japanese army entered Nanking, where animal instincts ran wild in the Japanese soldier. Women were raped to death and fleeing people were machine-gunned at random. Military trucks ran through streams of people on the streets. The atrocities committed by the Japanese will remain forever a black spot in human history.

At the turn of the new year the Japanese army headed upriver toward Nanchang. It seemed to be approaching Changsha, while the Chinese army was concentrated around Hankow. The capital of Hunan Province was now vulnerable to enemy attack. I flew to Hankow to sound out the Generalissimo as to the removal of the Union University still farther inland. I interviewed first the Minister of Education, Chen Li-fu, who advised me to see the Commander in Chief. So I went to call on him. He agreed that the university ought to move farther west, and I suggested that we move to Kunming, which had access to the sea through the Yunnan-Indo-China Railway. He readily agreed and suggested that someone go there first to select a site for the university.

The month of January, 1938, passed in preparation for the removal. Books and scientific apparatus were packed and trucks and gasoline bought. In February, as the preparations were almost complete, I flew to Hongkong, where I took a French liner to Haiphong in French Indo-China. Thence I went by train to Hanoi, capital of the French colonial government, and from there to Kunming by the Yunnan-Indo-China Railway through one of the most mountainous regions of China.

日军不久进入南京，士兵兽性大发。许多妇女被轮奸杀死，无辜百姓在逃难时遭到日军机枪任意扫射。日军在南京的暴行，将在人类历史上永远留下不可磨灭的污点。

新年里，日军溯江进逼南昌。中国军队结集在汉口附近，日军则似有进窥长沙模样。湖南省会已随时有受到敌人攻击的危险。我飞到汉口，想探探政府对联大续迁内地的意见。我先去看教育部陈立夫部长，他建议最好还是去看总司令本人。因此我就去谒见委员长了。他赞成把联大再往西迁，我建议迁往昆明，因为那里可以经滇越铁路与海运衔接。他马上表示同意，并且提议应先派人到昆明勘寻校址。

民国二十七年（一九三八年）正月，就在准备搬迁中过去了。书籍和科学仪器都装了箱，卡车和汽油也买了。二月间，准备工作已经大致完成，我从长沙飞到香港，然后搭法国邮船到越南的海防。我从海防搭火车到法属越南首府河内，再由河内乘滇越铁路火车，经过丛山峻岭而达昆明。

CHAPTER 29   INDO-CHINA AND BURMA

Just as, some twenty years earlier, I had found the ancient Chinese ways of life still persisting in Korea, so now, taking the opportunity of going to Kunming by way of Indo-China, I found there the same ancient Chinese ways. Like the Koreans, they wore a dress similar to that of the Ming Dynasty. Their pronunciation of Chinese words stemmed from that of the Tang Dynasty; villages, cities, and administrative districts bear Chinese names pronounced somewhat after the Tang fashion.

The French preferred for general use a romanization of the Annamese language, which is itself a modified form of Chinese. I must admit that it is much easier for the common people to learn. But this romanized Annamese will further widen the gap between China and Indo-China.

The capital of Annam[1], where the titular emperor, Pao-dai, lived, was very much like the palace of the former Korean kings and, again, like the Imperial Palace in Peking on a much smaller scale. Indeed, the court of Annam looked like a living branch of the Imperial Ming Court. The French had preserved it as a sort of living museum, while the Japanese preferred to transport the Korean king to Tokyo and make a Japanese out of him.

I was told that the first ancestor of the emperor of Annam was buried on a hill in Kunming. For he was Chinese. One afternoon, later, I tried to locate the grave but failed to find it.

While Hanoi, capital of the French colonial government, had become a French city with wide streets and imposing public buildings, the peasants lived in miserable villages which seemed to be sinking down into the earth. Liberty, Equality, and Fraternity! Colonial governments are an anachronism and bad as a system, for the governors are there for exploitation and not interested in the welfare of the governed, which is contrary to modern theory of government.

Here I wish to make one exception: the colonial government of the Philippine Islands. The Americans had an ideal—to raise the people to a higher level of civilization. The American colonial government in the Philippines established a system of public schools not inferior to American schools. I went to the Philippines in 1931. Everywhere I saw schools in which history, literature, science, and democratic ideals were taught. The United States endeavored to make the Philippine Islands a republic in the image of her own.

贰玖 日军入侵前夕之越南与缅甸

我由长沙绕道越南赴昆明途中，发现越南也保留着许多古代中国的风俗习惯，正如二十多年前我在朝鲜所发现的。越南人与朝鲜人一样，穿着一种近似明朝服饰的衣服。他们念中国字时，发音与唐代语言相像；乡村、城市和行政区也采用中国地名，这些地名的读音多少与唐代的读音相似。亦可以说与广东音相似。

越文是中文的一种变体，在一般用途上，法国人却宁取一种拉丁化的越文。这种拉丁化文字在一般人学起来自然容易得多，但以此为表达高深思想之工具是不够的。

越南国王保大在顺化的宫殿很像过去朝鲜李王的宫室，但是与北京的紫禁城比起来，规模同样地小得多了。事实上，越南皇宫很像明朝皇宫残留的一枝，法国人一直保留着越南皇宫，拿它作活的博物馆看待，日本人却宁愿把朝鲜国王送到日本，想把他改造为日本人。

有人告诉我，越南王的始祖葬在昆明某山头，因为他本来是中国人。后来有一天下午，我曾经去找越南王陵寝的故址，结果没有找到。

法国殖民地政府的所在地河内已经发展为现代化的法国城市，街道宽阔，公共建筑巍然矗立。但是一般农民所住的乡村却肮脏破落，与河内相较，真有天渊之别。自由、平等、博爱，原来如此！殖民地政府是一种时代的倒置，也就是非常倒退的制度，总督们到殖民地来只是为了剥削榨取，对人民的福利漠不关心，这与现代的政治原理恰恰背道而驰。

不过，我想在这里声明一句：菲律宾的殖民地政府应该例外。美国人有一个理想——提高菲人的文化水准，美国在菲律宾的殖民政府，在当地建立了一种足与美国学校媲美的学校制度。我曾在民国二十年（一九三一年）去过菲律宾，所到之处，学校都在传授历史、文学、科学和民主思想。美国正按照自己的模型，致力建设菲律宾为一民主共和国。菲律宾在欧美人殖民地制度下，获得两大贡献。一是西班牙人留下来的天主教。二是美国人留下来的民主制度和言论自由。

Britain had to depend on her colonies for her national existence; France had to be fed with riches from her colonies. Each was interested in the welfare of the governed peoples only in the sense that the geese should be kept alive to lay more golden eggs. In Korea and Formosa Japan was pressing the geese flat in order to squeeze the eggs out of them. Before the war Japan had amassed a great fortune from trade with China. But she was not satisfied; she wanted to make China a vast colony so as to be completely free to squeeze that giant goose.

The British way of keeping the geese alive was rather ingenious. They controlled the key industries and let the natives live on what was left. Let the geese feed on the corn and fish they can catch in the pond. So the geese were happy with their corn and small fish and the owners were happy with their golden eggs. The British never interfered with the customs, manners, superstitions, or beliefs of the governed peoples, and the natives could enjoy their life undisturbed except in matters affecting public health. For public health concerns alike both governors and the governed; you cannot segregate contagious disease or pestilence. Roads, too, were built and maintained, for peace and order and commerce depend upon good roads. Defense was built up only to the extent required to put down rebellions within the colony; to defend it against attacks from some other Power was left to the prestige of the British Empire, and when that prestige weakened the colony was at the mercy of a powerful neighbor. This was how Hongkong and Burma were temporarily lost, and this was why Britain was so jealous for her prestige, especially in the Far East.

Burma borders on the southwest corner of Yunnan. I went there as leader of a goodwill mission just about a year before Pearl Harbor. The British way of governing colonies was clearly evident. I saw the oil refineries, lumber mills, and rice mills—these were key industries and were under British control. Other things were left to the Burmese. Sacred cows roamed the streets in Rangoon without interference from the police. Here, there, and everywhere were temples with their gilt pagodas and monks respected by both the governors and the governed. The Burmese enjoyed an undisturbed life under British rule; the geese, swimming in their pond, were satisfied with their fish and corn, and as far as I could see showed no sign of unrest. And the owners got their golden eggs.

But the light that shone brilliantly in the homeland of the governors could not be altogether smothered in the colonies. In India Gandhi went unmolested except for imprisonment in times of crisis. Such instances

英国的生存寄托在殖民地上，法国也得靠殖民地的资源维持生存。如果说英法对殖民地人民的福利还没有完全漠视的话，那也只是为了养活母鸡，好让它多生一些蛋而已。

英国人养鸡生蛋的方法更是妙不可言，他们控制了主要的工业，而让当地人民在余留的行业上自觅生路。让鸡到田野里自行寻觅谷粒小虫充饥。鸡能找到谷粒小虫就心满意足了，养鸡的人则捡起晶莹的鸡蛋笑逐颜开。英国人从来不干涉殖民地人民的风俗或迷信思想，除了影响公共卫生的事情以外，当地人民可以自由自在地过活而不受干扰。因为公共卫生不但与被统治者有关，与统治者也有同样的关系，传染病或瘟疫是不认肤色人种的。道路修得宽敞平坦，而且保养得很好，因为治安和商业是要靠良好的道路来维持的。防御力量只建立到足以镇压当地叛乱的程度，抵御其他强国的攻击则有赖大英帝国的威望。这种威望衰退时，殖民地就不免要受强邻的觊觎了。香港和缅甸一度失陷就是这个道理，英国这样珍惜她的威望，尤其是在远东的威望，也是这个道理。

缅甸与云南省的西南角接壤，珍珠港事变前约一年，我曾经奉命组织一个友好访问团到缅甸，我参观过炼油厂、锯木厂和碾米厂，这些都是缅甸的主要工业，统由英国控制，其余的行业则留归缅甸人经营。被视为神圣的牛只闲荡仰光街头，警察从来不加干涉。到处是寺院，院内矗立着镀金的宝塔，生活着普受统治者及被统治者尊崇的僧侣。缅甸人在英国统治之下自由过活，像一群吃饱了小虫谷粒的母鸡悠然自得，至少，我看不出一点不满的情绪，养的人则心满意足地捡取他们的鸡蛋。

但是总督们在祖国照耀出来的光明在殖民地里却不能完全隔绝。在印度，甘地的行动一直不受干扰，只有在紧急危难时才

would be dealt with underhandedly in the colonies of certain other European nations. But Great Britain, that land of liberty, could not help shedding some of her light through the clouds of a colonial sky. There are signs that Britain is on the road to a more enlightened policy toward her colonies. I hope that these streaks of light will be broadened to strong beams of liberty, illuminating the peoples she is entrusted to lead. British friends, give them more of that light which you have so plentifully in the British Isles. Chuck overboard the anachronisms!

As far as types of civilization are concerned, the former kingdom of Annam, now a part of Indo-China, is Chinese, while Burma is Indian. The palace of the former king of Burma at Mandalay is Indian in architectural design. The names of the cities and towns bear no trace of Chinese origin. The Annamites, like the Chinese, eat with chopsticks; the Burmese, like the Indians, with their fingers. Yet both Annam and Burma, as we have seen earlier, were formerly tributaries of China, and their loss was part of her awakening.

When Burma fell to British hands the royal family escaped into Yunnan and is supported by the provincial government down to this day, although its title is only nominal now. Its children and grandchildren entered Chinese schools and became Chinese. But they are known to the people of Tengtsung in Yunnan as descendants of the Burmese royal family, whose ancestors once reigned over the kingdom of golden pagodas and yellow-robed monks from their peacock throne in the royal palace at Mandalay.

遭受监禁。像甘地的这种行动，在某些欧洲国家的殖民地里或许早已受到阴毒的处置了。但是大不列颠究竟是自由之邦，自由的光辉不免要透过殖民地上空的云层而惠及当地人民。各种迹象显示，英国对殖民地正在采取一种比较开明的政策。我希望这些照射到海外殖民地的微光能扩大为强烈的自由火炬，引导殖民地人民向光明的前途迈进。

就文化形态而言，越南王国是属于中国型的，缅甸则是印度型的。从前缅甸国王在曼达来的宫殿就是印度式的建筑。城镇的地名也看不出与中国有丝毫的渊源。越南人和中国人一样，吃饭时用的是筷子；缅甸却和印度人一样用手指。但是越南和缅甸在过去曾一度尊重中国的宗主权，中国在两国宗主权的丧失是中国觉醒的原因之一。

缅甸落入英人手中以后，缅甸的王室就逃到云南，生活费用一直由云南省政府供给，不过缅甸王的头衔已经有名无实了。缅王的子孙后来进了中国学校，结果归化为中国人。但是云南腾冲一带的人仍旧知道，这些缅甸王室后裔的祖先，曾经在曼达来皇宫的雀屏宝座上，统治过有镀金宝塔和黄袍僧人的王国。

CHAPTER 30   THE MIGRATION OF UNIVERSITIES

The migration of universities from the coastal provinces where Chinese institutions of higher learning were originally centered to the hinterland of China was a direct sequel to the outbreak of war. Besides the three I have mentioned, other institutions located nearest to the scene of war and likely to be first affected moved gradually toward the interior. As a result there were toward the end of the war some twenty universities and colleges, with a total enrollment of about sixteen thousand students, boys and girls, newly established in Free China.

These institutions were scattered all over the interior provinces. They were housed either in temples or in the buildings of local schools. Some were able to rent private mansions when no public buildings were available. Still others had to put up temporary shacks. All brought with them such scientific apparatus and books as conditions permitted. The amount was of course negligible, yet even this scanty equipment was not infrequently ruined by the deliberate and merciless bombing of the enemy.

A large number of the students were from the occupied areas. Their support from their parents was naturally cut off; some even lost track of their families in the war zones. It may be noted, also, that some parents in the occupied areas deemed it wise, when questioned, to report as dead sons who were actually studying in Free China. The national government in Chungking consequently allotted large sums of money to care for these helpless students.

As the Japanese invasion began in north China the universities first affected were naturally those located in the areas of Tientsin and Peiping. When the two cities were occupied many students and faculty members, realizing the futility of expecting to have any spiritual freedom at the point of the invader's bayonet, went south or elsewhere to join their universities. Two combined universities were established by order of the national government then at Nanking: one at Changsha as I have related, and the other at Sian in the northwest. The Northwestern Union University consisted of two former national universities and two colleges.

It was later moved from Sian to Hanchung and has since been broken up into more or less its original components.

As the war spread to other parts of China, universities which had hitherto been able to remain where they were had now to follow our example. Thus the National Central University was moved from the former capital to the war capital of Chungking; Chekiang University was moved from Hangchow to the interior province of Kweichow; Chungshan University was moved from Canton in south China to Yunnan in the southwest.

叁拾 大学逃难

中日战争爆发以后，原来集中在沿海省份的大学纷纷迁往内地，除了我前面提到过的北大、清华、南开三所大学之外，接近战区以及可能受战争影响的高等学府都逐渐向内地迁移，到抗战快结束时，在内地重建的大学和独立学院，数目当在二十左右，学生总数约一万六千人。

这些学府四散在内地各省。有的借用庙宇祠堂，有的则借用当地学校的一部分校舍上课。公共建筑找不到时，有的学校就租用私人宅院，也有些学校临时搭了茅篷土屋。所有学校都已尽可能带出来一部分图书仪器，数量当然很有限，然而就是这一点点简陋的设备也经常受到敌机故意而无情的轰炸。

许多学生是从沦陷区来的，父母对他们的接济自然断绝了；有些学生甚至与战区里的家庭完全音信不通。有些在沦陷区的家长，虽然明知子弟在内地读书，遇到敌伪人员查问时，宁愿把儿子报成死亡，以免招致无谓的麻烦。后来由政府拨了大笔经费来照顾这些无依无靠的学生。

因为日本侵略是从华北开始的，所以最先受到影响的大学自然是在平津区的学校。平津区陷敌以后，许多教员和学生知道在侵略者的刺刀下绝无精神自由的希望，结果纷纷追随他们的学校向南或其他地方转进。当时政府尚在南京，看到这种情形，便下令在后方成立两个联合大学，一个在长沙，另一个在西北的西安。西北联大包含过去的两个国立大学和两个独立学院。它后来从西安迁到汉中，因为校舍分散，结果多少又回复了原来各单位的传统。

战事蔓延其他各地以后，原来还能留在原地上课的大学也步我们的后尘内迁了。结果国立中央大学从南京搬到战时首都重庆，浙江大学从杭州搬到贵州，中山大学从广州搬到云南。

I shall describe in some detail the former Union University in Changsha: how it was organized—or associated, to use a better term—and later transplanted from Changsha to Kunming. The story may serve as an example of the handling of other migrating universities.

As I have already related, the Union University at Changsha was formed by the association of three former Peiping and Tientsin universities by order of the Ministry of Education, then at Nanking. They were the National University of Peking, the oldest and the first government-sponsored modern university in China; the National Tsinghua University; and Nankai University at Tientsin. The presidents of these three institutions were made members of the presidium. All their faculty members and students were turned over to the Union University. Classes were resumed at Changsha by November 1, 1937, with an enrollment of approximately 1,250 students from the three universities, and an additional 220 students from other institutions which had also been moved. The latter were admitted as visiting students. The university was in fairly good shape, though equipment and facilities were meager. The spirit among the professors and students was excellent; the reading rooms were, for the most part, packed with students despite the handful of books available. But early in 1938—that is, after the fall of Nanking—things changed. Japanese planes made Changsha one of their bombing objectives. A prolonged stay in the city was perilous, so with the approval of the government, after the completion of a semester's work the Union University moved, at the end of February, 1938, southwest to Kunming.

The migration from Changsha to Kunming was made in two groups: some three hundred male students with a few professors constituted themselves a walking party, hiking from Changsha in Hunan through the mountainous province of Kweichow all the way to the remote city of Kunming in Yunnan—a trek of 3,500 *li*, or approximately 1,160 miles, accomplished over a period of two months and ten days. The others, numbering about eight hundred, rode from Changsha to Canton on the much-bombed Canton-Hankow Railway, thence by boat to the British colony of Hongkong, and again by boat to Haiphong. From here they traveled by the French Indo-China Railway to Kunming, their final destination. The rail-boat and boat-rail trip required from ten to fourteen days, depending upon connections. Over three hundred and fifty students remained in Changsha to join the various war organizations.

　　我想详细地叙述一下长沙临时大学的情形，它是怎么联合起来的，后来又如何从长沙迁移到昆明。这故事也许可以说明一般大学播迁的情形。

　　我在前面已谈到，长沙临时大学是原在北平和天津的三所大学奉教育部之命联合而成的。这三所大学就是国立北京大学、国立清华大学和私立南开大学。三所大学的校长成立校务委员会，教职员全部转到临时大学。民国二十六年（一九三七年）十一月一日在长沙复课，注册学生有从原来三个大学来的约一千二百五十人，以及从其他大学转来的二百二十名借读生。虽然设备简陋，学校大致还差强人意，师生精神极佳，图书馆图书虽然有限，阅览室却经常座无虚席。但是民国二十七年初，也就是南京失陷以后，情形可不同了。日本飞机把长沙作为轰炸目标之一。在长沙久留是很危险的，结果临时大学在第一学期结束后，经政府核准于二十七年二月底向西南迁往昆明。

　　从长沙西迁昆明是分为两批进行的，一批包括三百名左右男生和少数教授，他们组织了一个徒步旅行团，从湖南长沙穿越多山的贵州省一直步行到云南的昆明，全程三千五百公里，约合一千一百六十哩，耗时两月零十天。另外一批约有八百人，从长沙搭被炸得疮痍满目的粤汉路火车到广州，由广州坐船到香港，再由香港转到海防，然后又从海防搭滇越铁路到达昆明。他们由火车转轮船，再由轮船转火车，全程约耗十至十四天，视候车候船的时日长短而有不同。另有三百五十名以上的学生则留在长沙，参加了各种战时机构。

After its removal to Kunming the title "Union University" was changed to the present name: National Southwest Associated University. As Kunming had no immediately available and suitable buildings to put at the disposal of the newcomers, the university—called "Lienta" from the abbreviation of its Chinese name—decided to locate its College of Arts and College of Law and Commerce at Mengtsz, probably the second largest city in the province, and keep the College of Science and Engineering in Kunming. When classes began in early May, 1938, there were around thirteen hundred students in the total enrollment for these four colleges of Lienta. In September of the same year the two colleges at Mengtsz moved back to Kunming, where the housing problem had become less acute as all the local middle schools had by then been moved to the country and their school buildings could be rented. The "happy-double-union" was celebrated by the founding of a teachers' college by order of the national government at Chungking. Enrollment in the five colleges, comprising twenty-six departments, increased to two thousand.

In September, 1939, Lienta again grew in size. There were by now over three thousand students. The university was fortunate, as its hundred shacks, built in the past ten months, could then be used to accommodate the growing student body. At the close of the war we had about five hundred professors, assistants, and administrative officers and three thousand students. Most of the latter came from the occupied areas and had to cross more than one firing line to reach the free zone; they went through much hardship and suffering, and others lost their lives before they could reach Free China.

My son, a student in Chiao-tung University in Shanghai, on his way to join me at Kunming met with several incidents. Once, on a dark night, with a number of friends he tried to go by small boat under a bridge guarded by the enemy and was shot at. On another occasion the party traveling ahead of his lost one of its members, who was arrested by the enemy and his head was later found by his friends dangling from a tree.

The son of a friend of mine came from Peiping to Kunming, traversing many firing lines in the north, and was shot at by the enemy several times. Often he had nothing to eat during the day and had to walk miles under cover of night. He had left Peiping with his brother, who was arrested by the Japanese guard at the station and sent to a detention camp because something was found in his pocket which identified him as a student. They had disguised themselves as apprentices of a shop. When the identity of such a person was established it was a serious offense.

搬到昆明以后，"长沙临时大学"即改名"国立西南联合大学"，简称"联大"。因为在昆明不能立即找到合适的房子容纳这许多新客，联大当局决定把文学院和法商学院设在云南第二大城蒙自。民国二十七年五月初联大开课时，四个学院的学生总数约在一千三百人左右。同年九月间，文学院和法商学院由蒙自迁回昆明，因为当地各中学均已迁往乡间，原有校舍可以出租，房间问题已不如过去那么严重。这时适值联大奉教育部之令成立师范学院，真是"双喜临门"。五院二十六系的学生人数也增至二千人。

二十八年九月间，联大规模再度扩充，学生人数已达三千人。联大过去十个月来新建造的百幢茅屋刚好容纳新增的学生。抗战结束时，我们共有五百左右的教授、助教和职员以及三千学生。多数学生是从沦陷区来的。他们往往不止穿越一道火线才能到达自由区，途中受尽艰难险阻，有的甚至在到达大后方以前就丧失了性命。

我的儿子原在上海交通大学读书，战事发生后他也赶到昆明来跟我一起住。他在途中就曾遭遇到好几次意外，有一次，他和一群朋友坐一条小船，企图在黑夜中偷渡一座由敌人把守的桥梁，结果被敌人发现而遭射击。另一次，一群走在他们前头的学生被敌人发现，其中一人被捕，日人还砍了他的头悬挂树上示众。

我有一位朋友的儿子从北平逃到昆明，在华北曾数度穿越敌人火线，好几次都受到敌人射击。他常常一整天吃不到一点东西，晚上还得在夜色掩护下赶好几里路。他和他的兄弟一道离开北平，但是他的兄弟却被车站上的日本卫兵抓走送到集中营去了，因为他身上被搜出了学生身分的证件。他们是化装商店学徒出走的，但是真正的身分被查出以后，就会遭遇严重的处罚。

It was reported that the basement of the College of Literature in the University of Peking had been turned into a dungeon in which terror reigned. I had no way to verify actual conditions there, but later met a former student of mine who had been arrested and imprisoned for two years before he managed to leave Peiping for Free China. He said that he was sent there for a "treat." The place was a living hell. Water was forced into his nose until he lost consciousness. When he came to, a Japanese gendarme by the name of Uyemura told him that he deserved the treatment because his alma mater was responsible for this terrible war in which Japan had suffered so much. "No pity!" said Uyemura in a rage. "Let the punishment fit the crime!" Three times he was thus "treated," fainting each time. In that dungeon he saw other tortures which do not befit my pen to describe. The shrieks of the girls and the groans of the boys turned that seat of learning into an inferno where Satan had his day.

While the students left in Peiping moaned under torture, the university in Kunming was blasted by enemy bombs. The bombing was done deliberately, since the seat of the university was outside the city wall with no military objective near by. Many buildings were destroyed, including the stacks of the main university library and some of the science laboratories. About one third of the university buildings were rendered useless and had to be rebuilt as fast as possible. Despite all this, the spirit of the students was wonderful. As a rule they studied hard in these trying circumstances, with meager food and poor living conditions.

This migration of institutions of learning from the seacoast to the interior has an important bearing on the future development of China's hinterland. The presence of a large number of intellectuals in various localities in the interior will exercise a strong influence upon the mental outlook of people in those localities. Moreover, students as well as teachers who have lived for a long time along the coast with only a local knowledge of the country have now had an opportunity to learn actual conditions in the interior, which has given them a better perspective on conditions in the vast country as a whole.

The migration of universities, combined with the removal of industries, both government and private, and of skilled laborers, engineers, experts, and managers, was indeed epoch-making. In the postwar period ahead of us the development of China in regions far from the coast, hitherto inaccessible to Western influence, will have a better chance than ever before.

据说北大文学院的地下室已经变为恐怖的地牢。我无法证实这些传说，不过后来我碰到一位老学生，在他设法逃出北平到达大后方以前，曾经被捕坐了两年牢。据他说，他曾被送到北大文学院地下室去受"招待"。那简直是活地狱。敌人把冷水灌到他鼻子里，终至使他晕过去。他醒过来时，日本宪兵上村告诉他，北大应该对这场使日本蒙受重大损害的战争负责，所以他理应吃到这种苦头。上村怒不可遏地说："没有什么客气的，犯什么罪就该受什么惩罚！"他曾经连续三次受到这种"招待"，每次都被灌得死去活来，他在那个地牢里还看到过其他的酷刑，残酷的程度简直不忍形诸笔墨。女孩子的尖叫和男孩子的呻吟，已使中国历史最久的学府变为撒旦统治的地狱了。

留在北平的学生在敌人的酷刑下呻吟呼号，在昆明上课的联大则受到敌机的无情轰炸。轰炸行为显然是故意的，因为联大的校址在城外，而且附近根本没有军事目标。校内许多建筑都被炸毁了，其中包括总图书馆的书库和若干科学实验室。联大的校舍约有三分之一被炸毁，必须尽速再建。但是敌机的轰炸并没有影响学生的求学精神，他们都能在艰苦的环境下刻苦用功，虽然食物粗劣，生活环境也简陋不堪。

学术机构从沿海迁到内地，对中国内地的未来发展有很大的影响，大群知识分子来到内地各城市以后，对内地人民的观念思想自然发生潜移默化的作用。在另一方面，一向生活在沿海的教员和学生，对国家的了解原来只限于居住的地域，现在也有机会亲自接触内地的实际情况，使他们对幅员辽阔的整个国家的情形有较真切的了解。

大学迁移内地，加上公私营工业和熟练工人、工程师、专家和经理人员的内移，的确具有划时代的意义。在战后的一段时期里，西方影响一向无法到达的内地省份，经过这一次民族的大迁徙，未来开发的机会已远较以前为佳。

CHAPTER 31   AT THE TERMINAL CITY OF THE BURMA ROAD

With the migration of the universities, I came to stay for the duration of the war at Kunming, terminal city on the Burma Road. Before Pearl Harbor I made one visit to Burma and many to Indo-China and Hongkong; all were connected with Kunming by air. After the capitulation of France, Indo-China was given over to Japan virtually without a fight. So we built the Burma Road to connect the city with Rangoon. After Pearl Harbor Burma, too, was lost to the enemy. Land communications with Haiphong in Indo-China and Rangoon in Burma were cut. Kunming was now bottled up. Lend-Lease ammunition ceased to flow into the city except by air over the "hump" of the Himalayas which separates China from the land of Buddha.

In the last few years I have visited Chungking by air many times and once also Chengtu, capital of Szechuan Province. The hilly wartime national capital of China is situated on the banks of the Yangtze River within the Yangtze gorges. The city is built on hills. Its narrow strip of land is girdled by the Yangtze on the south and the Kialing River on the north, the two rivers merging into the greater Yangtze at the easternmost point of the narrow strip. Thus Chungking looks like a tiny peninsula. Most of the houses are built upon terraces, and dugouts were made at their back doors or under the buildings through the granite hills. For several years Japanese planes rained explosives on the defenseless city day after day, night after night, month after month. But the capital remained undaunted. Buildings were hit and destroyed and rebuilt by tens of thousands, yet comparatively few lives were lost. The enemy tried to bomb the wartime government out of its capital, but the city still stands like the pyramids, which have endured their many centuries of hardship and will stand many centuries more. Chungking embodies to perfection the spirit of stubborn resistance against the Japanese invaders.[1]

To the west of the hilly capital, about half an hour distant by air, is the flat city of Chengtu. This walled city is as spacious as Peking. The streets are wide. The atmosphere is also somewhat like that of the former capital. The irrigation system at Kwan Hsien, established some twenty centuries ago, waters over a million acres of fertile land in the Chengtu Valley. Serious flood or drought are almost unknown. This immense, rich valley kept the people in Chungking and the army stationed in the province and adjacent districts amply fed.

叁壹 战时之昆明

　　北大等校内迁以后，我也随着迁居滇缅路的终点昆明。珍珠港事变爆发以前，我曾一度去过缅甸，并曾数度赴法属印度支那及香港。当时以上数地与昆明之间均有飞机可通。法国对德投降以后，日本不战而下法属印度支那，因此我们就筑了滇缅路与仰光衔接。珍珠港事变以后，缅甸亦陷敌手，我国与法属印度支那的海防以及缅甸的仰光，陆上交通均告断绝，昆明亦陷于孤立状态。租借法案下运华的军火，只好由空运飞越隔绝中印两国的喜马拉雅山的"驼峰"，才免于中断。

　　抗战期间，我曾数度坐飞机去重庆，也曾一度去过四川省会成都。重庆是战时的首都，位于嘉陵江与长江汇合之处。嘉陵江在北，长江在南，重庆就建在两江合抱的狭长山地上，看起来很像一个半岛。房子多半是依山势高下而建的，同时利用屋后或屋基下的花岗岩山地挖出防空洞，躲避空袭。日本飞机经年累月，日以继夜地滥炸这个毫无抵抗力的山城，但是重庆却始终屹立无恙。成千累万的房屋被烧毁又重建起来，但是生命损失却不算太大。敌人企图以轰炸压迫战时政府迁出重庆，但是陪都却像金字塔样始终雄踞扬子江头，它曾经受过千百年的磨练考验，自然也能再经千百年的考验。重庆可以充分代表中国抵抗日本侵略的坚忍卓绝的精神。

　　重庆之西约半小时航程处是平坦的成都市。成都和北平差不多一样广大，街道宽阔，整个气氛也和故都北平相似。成都西北的灌县有两千年前建设的水利系统，至今灌溉着成都平原百万亩以上的肥沃土地。严重的水灾或旱灾几乎从来没有发生过。这块广大丰饶的平原使四川成为"天府之国"，使重庆人民以及驻防省境和附近地区的军队，粮食得以供应无缺。

When we moved our university to Kunming we had in mind the possibility of importing books and scientific instruments from Europe and America through Indo-China. But after the fall of Canton the main line for the supply of munitions was cut and shipments were diverted to the Indo-China-Yunnan route. The congestion on the railway precluded the shipment of nonmilitary cargoes. Only a small fraction of our shipments was allowed to trickle in.

Meanwhile all the cities along the Yangtze River fell one after another into the hands of the enemy, up to I-chang, not far from the Yangtze gorges. Finally that too failed to stem the tide of advancing enemy might and went under the heel of the invader.

Kunming felt the pinch of every adversity of war. What most affected the daily life of the people was the rising cost of living. When we came there, in the second year of war, rice per Chinese bushel (eighty kilograms) cost $6 in Chinese currency. When it had increased by degrees to $40 a bushel one of our professors of economics predicted that after a few months it would rise to $70. People laughed at him. But it did go to $70. The capitulation of Indo-China and the loss of Burma both severely affected the price of commodities.

The first noticeable rise in prices came after the first bombing of the city by enemy planes. The country people were afraid to come in, and fewer vegetables and meats were brought to market. The shopkeepers worried over the safety of their goods and raised prices to cover their possible loss. The embargo on certain imported goods also affected the prices of similar or allied home products. Thus the embargo on kerosene raised the prices of vegetable oils. The rise in price of vegetable oils carried with it an increasing price for lard. When lard went up, pork followed suit. One thing thus led to another. The upward run of prices naturally gave rise to a host of hoarders. Hoarding in turn aggravated the price situation. When the swing of the pendulum went higher on one side, momentum brought it high again on the other.

The thing to have done, of course, was to control prices by controlling commodities from the very beginning of the war; not try to regulate prices after it was too late. I was told by a British friend that British farmers made a good deal of profit out of the First World War, but that farm products were controlled at the beginning of this war. Since this was the first modern war on a large scale in China, she had no past experience of such problems.

学校初迁昆明之时，我们原以为可经法属印度支那从欧美输入书籍和科学仪器，但是广州失陷以后，军火供应的干线被切断，军火都改经滇越线运入。滇越铁路军运频繁，非军用品根本无法挤上火车。我们运到越南的图书仪器，只有极少一部分获准载运入滇。

这时候，长江沿岸城市已相继陷入敌手，日军溯江直达宜昌，离长江三峡只是咫尺之遥。最后三峡天险也无法阻遏敌人的侵略狂潮而遭到铁骑的蹂躏。

每当战局逆转，昆明也必同时受到灾殃。影响人民日常生活最大的莫过于物价的不断上涨。抗战第二年我们初到昆明时，米才卖法币六块钱一担（约八十公斤）。后来一担米慢慢涨到四十元，当时我们的一位经济学教授预言几个月之内必定会涨到七十元，大家都笑他胡说八道，但是后来一担米却真的涨到七十元。法属安南投降和缅甸失陷都严重地影响了物价。

物价初次显著上涨，发生在敌机首次轰炸昆明以后，乡下人不敢进城，菜场中的蔬菜和鱼肉随之减少。店家担心存货的安全，于是提高价格以图弥补可能的损失。若干洋货的禁止进口也影响了同类货物以及有连带关系的土货的价格。煤油禁止进口以后，菜油的价格也随之提高。菜油涨价，猪油也跟着上涨。猪油一涨，猪肉就急起直追。一样东西涨了，别的东西也跟着涨。物价不断上涨，自然而然就出现了许多囤积居奇的商人。囤积的结果，物价问题也变得愈加严重。钟摆的一边荡得愈高，运动量使另一边也摆得更高。

控制物价本来应该从战事刚开始时做起，等到物价已成脱缰野马之后，再来管制就太晚了。一位英国朋友告诉我，英国农人在第一次世界大战时曾经大发其财，但是第二次大战一开始，农产品就马上受到管制了。这次战争在中国还是第一次大规模的现代战争，所以她对这类问题尚无经验足资借鉴。

The climate of Kunming is really ideal. Situated in the semitropical zone at an altitude of six thousand feet, the city is something like a great summer resort. But because of its size the inhabitants do not think of it as such. It is perpetual spring. The rainy season falls in summer, when, frequent showers cool off the summer days. During the other seasons most of the days are filled with smiling sunshine cast upon the luxuriant growth in the fields from a cloudless blue sky.

Flowers abound in that climate and fruits are plentiful. Melons, eggplant, and citrons grow to enormous sizes. People do not have to work hard to make a living; they enjoy a complacent life and take things in leisurely fashion. Newcomers from the coastal provinces were at first exasperated by the slowness of the inhabitants, but they themselves gradually melted into that sea of tranquility.

The people of Kunming were quite concerned about the flow of thousands of refugees into the city from the coast. Many brought large sums of money and spent it freely. The local people blamed them for the increasing cost of living. The city was crowded with fashionable young ladies and well-dressed folk from the coast. In the evenings they rubbed shoulders with native citizens on the sidewalks of the main streets of Kunming. House rents rose fast. Hotels were all filled to capacity; on arrival people often found no place to stay. New houses shot up like mushrooms. Old houses destroyed by bombs were rapidly restored. Yet the population grew faster than houses could be built to accommodate it.

Within the few years of the war Kunming was transformed. The old tranquil scene was filled with truck drivers, war profiteers, contractors, engineers, and manufacturers. Munitions trucks shuttled through the outskirts of the city.

The natural and historic surroundings, however, remained unchanged. Kunming Lake, which flows into the Yangtze and over two thousand miles into the Yellow Sea,[2] remained as placid as before. Fish and duck enjoyed their watery life as in days of old. Historic temples with quaint trees around them perched on the hills overlooking the wide span of the rippling lake. The Buddhist monks chanted their prayers as others had done centuries ago. Looking over the lake to the horizon I often wondered: If a sealed bottle with letters in it were thrown into the water, might it not be carried by the outgoing current down the Yangtze, passing through Chungking, I-chang, Hankow, Kiu-kiang, Anking, and Nanking

　　昆明的气候非常理想，它位于半热带，海拔约六千呎，整个城有点像避暑胜地。但是因为它的面积大，居民并不认为它是避暑胜地。昆明四季如春，夏季多雨，阵雨刚好冲散夏日的炎暑。其他季节多半有温煦的阳光照耀着农作密茂的田野。

　　在这样的气候之下，自然是花卉遍地，瓜果满园。甜瓜、茄子和香橼都大得出奇。老百姓不必怎么辛勤工作，就可以谋生糊口；因此他们的生活非常悠闲自得。初从沿海省份来的人，常常会为当地居民慢吞吞的样子而生气，但是这些生客不久之后也就被悠闲的风气同化了。

　　昆明人对于从沿海省份涌到的千万难民感到相当头痛。许多人带了大笔钱来，而且挥霍无度，本地人都说物价就是这批人抬高的，昆明城内到处是从沿海来的摩登小姐和衣饰入时的仕女。入夜以后他们在昆明街头与本地人一齐熙来攘往，相互摩肩接踵而过。房租迅速上涨，旅馆到处客满，新建筑像雨后春笋一样出现。被飞机炸毁的旧房子，迅速修复，但是新建的房子究竟还是赶不上人口增加的速度。

　　八年抗战，昆明已变得面目全非。昔日宁静的昆明城，现已满街是卡车司机，发国难财的商人，以及营造商、工程师和制造厂商。军火卡车在城郊穿梭往返。

　　自然环境和名胜古迹却依然如昔。昆明湖的湖水仍像过去一样平滑如镜，依旧静静地流入长江，随着江水奔腾两千哩而入黄海。鱼儿和鹅鸭仍像往昔一样遨游在湖中。古木围绕的古寺雄踞山头，俯瞰着微波荡漾的辽阔湖面。和尚还是像几百年前的僧人一样念经诵佛。遥望天边水际，我常常会想入非非：如果把一封信封在瓶子里投入湖中，它会不会随湖水流入长江，顺流经过重庆、宜昌、汉口、

to the sea near Shanghai? And perhaps some fisherman might pick it up and forward it to my native land of Chekiang. It was, of course, only the dream of an exile thinking of home.

A network of aqueducts, built between two parallel embankments protected by age-old spruces, conducts water to irrigate tens of thousands of acres of fertile land. The embankments are wide enough to run a horse on; one could trot leisurely along this endless trail for miles in the forest of scent-laden spruce, traversing the luxuriant fields.

In the city a stone tablet marking the spot where the last refugee emperor of the Mings was strangled to death looks tragically down the slope at the passers-by. The much-to-be-pitied emperor fled to Burma, but was taken back to China by General Wu San-kwei, the one who later, while defending the Great Wall against the Manchus, was to go over to the enemy in order to save his lady from the bandit leader. In his campaign against his own people in south China he came to Yunnan, where the captive emperor was brought before him.

"What do you have to say?" asked the general, as the story has it.

"Nothing," replied the last emperor of the Mings. "The only thing I want to know is, why did you rebel against my forefathers, from whom you received so much favor and so many honors?"

Wu San-kwei trembled at these words and ordered the captive emperor strangled at the spot where the stone tablet now stands. It reads: "Here died Emperor Yung-li of the Ming Dynasty for his country."

About ten kilometers from the city is the Black Dragon Pool. Spring water, crystal clear, oozes out from the bottom and overflows into tiny streams. Around it are temples and gigantic moss-grown trees. A scholar and his family lived here toward the end of the Ming Dynasty. When news of the emperor's death and the consequent downfall of the dynasty reached him, he plunged into the pool and committed suicide. His family and servants followed suit. The whole family died for their country by suicide and were all buried there. This is difficult for the Western mind to understand, but Chinese philosophy holds that if you cannot do anything else to save your country, death is the only way to redeem the debt of your conscience. By this philosophy the Chinese soldiers laid down their lives during this war willingly by hundreds of thousands in a battle often of simple flesh and blood against the enemy's steel and fire.

九江、安庆、南京而漂到吴淞江口呢？说不定还会有渔人捡起藏着信件的瓶子而转到浙江我的故乡呢！自然，这只是远适异地的思乡客的一种梦想而已。

纵横的沟渠把湖水引导到附近田野，灌溉了千万亩肥沃的土地。沟渠两旁是平行的堤岸，宽可纵马骋驰；我们可以悠闲地放马畅游，沿着漫长的堤防跑进松香扑鼻的树林，穿越苍翠欲滴的田野。

城里有一个石碑，立碑处据说是明朝最后的一位流亡皇帝被缢身死的故址。石碑立在山坡上，似乎无限哀怨地凝视着路过的行人。这可怜的皇帝曾经逃到缅甸，结果却被叛将吴三桂劫持押回中国。吴三桂原来奉命防守长城抗御清兵，据传说他是为了从闯王李自成手中援救陈圆圆，终于倒戈降清。他为了镇压西南的反抗被派到云南，已经成为他阶下囚的永历帝被带到他的面前受审。

"你还有什么话要说没有？"据说吴三桂这样问。

"没有，"明代的末朝皇帝回答说，"唯一我想知道的事是你为什么背叛我的祖上？你受明室的恩泽不能不算深厚吧？"

吴三桂闻言之下，真是心惊胆战，他马上下令绞死这位皇帝。后人在那里立了纪念碑，上刻："明永历帝殉国处。"

离城约十公里处有个黑龙潭。春天里，澄澈的潭水从潭底徐徐渗出，流入小溪浅涧。黑龙潭周围还有许多古寺和长满青苔的大树。明朝末年曾有一位学者和他的家人住在这里。崇祯帝殉国和明朝灭亡的消息传来以后，他就投身潭中自杀了。他的家属和仆人也都跟着跳入潭中，全家人都以身殉国，后来一齐葬在黑龙潭岸旁。西洋人是很难了解这件事的，但是根据中国的哲学，如果你别无办法拯救国家，那末避免良心谴责的唯一方法就是以死殉国。抗战期间，中国军人以血肉之躯抵抗敌人的弹雨火海，视死如归；他们的精神武装就是这种人生哲学。

Our more or less chronological story is here ended for the time being. The following chapters will discuss some of the problems of Chinese civilization and culture, past, present, and future, and some of the persistent national problems that will present themselves in China in years to come.

From Hongkong in 1842 to Pearl Harbor in 1941 is a period of exactly one century; to tell the story of that period this volume has been written. England was instrumental in blasting China's southern gates open to world commerce. With the flow of opium and Western manufactures came the seeds of Western thought and science, which affected China's view toward life and the universe. She resisted, struggled, and finally absorbed Western culture, as she did Indian culture centuries and centuries before. England was the instrument of Fate that brought China into the community of the world.

The course China took was rather roundabout, like the winding of the Yangtze River. But in direction she remained unchanged—like the Yangtze which moves down over its course of more than two thousand miles to color the Yellow Sea, in spite of its many windings. It flows day and night, month after month, year after year, and will flow in the same way for endless centuries to come. The invincible Yangtze is the symbol of China's national life and culture.

这个多少依年份先后记述的故事到此暂告段落。后面几章将讨论中国文化上的若干问题，包括过去的、现在的和未来的；同时我们将讨论若干始终未能解决的全国性问题，这些问题在未来的年月里也将继续存在。

　　从一八四二年香港割让到一九四一年珍珠港事变，恰恰是一世纪。《西潮》所讲的故事，主要就是这一段时期内的事情。英国人用大炮轰开了中国南方的门户，开始向中国输入鸦片和洋货，但同时也带来了西方的思想和科学的种籽，终于转变了中国人对人生和宇宙的看法。中国曾经抵抗、挣扎，但是最后还是吸收了西方文化，与一千几百年前吸收印度文化的过程如出一辙。英国是命运之神的工具，她带领中国踏入国际社会。

　　中国所走的路途相当迂回，正像曲折的长江，但是她前进的方向却始终未变，正像向东奔流的长江，虽然中途迂回曲折，但是终于经历二千多哩流入黄海。它日以继夜、经年累月地向东奔流，在未来的无穷岁月中也将同样地奔腾前进。不屈不挠的长江就是中国生活和文化的象征。

PART SEVEN

第七部　现代世界中的中国

CHINA IN THE MODERN WORLD

CHAPTER 32   CHINA AND JAPAN—A COMPARISON

Before the coming of Admiral Perry Japan was an offshoot of Chinese civilization, pure and simple. After that time she became a blend of offshoots of both Chinese and Western civilizations. Unless one understands both China and the West he is not in a position to understand Japan.

Yet there is something more. Offshoots may be similar to their main roots, but they are not identical. To render judgment upon things similar as if they were the same may lead miles away from the truth. Moreover, the blending of two civilizations may change the character of the contributing originals.

The offshoots of Chinese civilization in Japan were of the Tang era (618-905). While many of the precious elements of Tang culture had been worn away in China through centuries of barbaric invasion, they were preserved in Japan. Dancing, music, the arts, ways of living, the pronunciation of Chinese words and China's martial spirit, all of Tang origin, found living embodiment in the Island Empire of the Rising—or hereafter the Setting—Sun. If you want to know something about the Tang civilization, go to Japan. Upon a foundation of Tang culture Japan made herself great by the absorption of Western science.

However, an offshoot is but an offshoot; it has to receive nourishment from the roots of the mother tree. As soon as the mother tree in China withered, the offshoot had to depend for nourishment on the local soil of Japan. Now, Japan had every nourishment in her soil to nurse the Tang offshoots to grow, save one—originality. In this respect she failed miserably, and for lack of this one element Japan remained a dwarf tree.

After Perry's arrival she began to tap the flow of Western civilization to fertilize her land. The tree did shoot up heavenward after receiving new nourishment from this source. But again she failed in respect of that most valuable element of Western civilization—originality.

叁贰 中国与日本——谈敌我之短长

　　日本在培利上将抵达以前，只是中国大陆文化的一支而且是很单纯的一支。自从这位海军上将来过以后，日本就变为中西文化的混合体了。除非你能同时了解中国和西方，否则你就无法了解日本。

　　但是单单了解日本的中西两种文化的来源是不够的。分支可能与它们的主体相似，但是并不完全相同。把相似的东西看成完全相同而遽下断语，很可能差以毫厘而谬以千里。同时，两种文化的混合，还可能使原来文化变质。

　　中国大陆文化在日本的支流导源于唐朝（六一八——九〇五年）。唐代文化中许多可贵的成份，其中包括从西域输入的印度文化与从伊兰民族间接输入的希腊文化，在中国因千余年来历经异族侵略，已逐渐衰落，但在日本却被保留下来了。唐代的舞蹈、音乐、美术、习俗、语音和尚武精神，都还留在日本。如果你想了解一点唐代文化，你最好还是到日本去一趟。日本以唐代文化为基础，其中包括儒家思想并唐代所吸收的佛教文化及其他外来文化。又在南宋时代（日本镰仓时代）输入宋儒朱子之学，盖随禅僧而俱来者。因此造成在日本儒佛一致之思想。寻至明末之际，德川氏本其向来保护禅僧研究儒学之素志，于开府江户（东京古名）时，广招儒者讲学刻书，极一时之盛。并藉新政权之威力，使儒家之学为此后日本兴国之张本，而为日本发展了道德、政治、经济、史学、数学与夫流入民间之教育。日本虽于晋初从朝鲜人王仁得《论语》、《千字文》，而在明末又输入了阳明之学，但经世之学的中心则在朱子之学。到了咸同之间，明治维新，以儒家经世之学与西洋近世社会科学、自然科学相接引，遂在短短数十年里成为史无前例的东西两洋文化的大结合，而致日本于盛强之境。并予文化祖国的中国以极大的鼓励与兴奋。在我幼年时代，我们一辈青年，都奉日本为师，希望日本反哺文化之母鸟而帮助中国复兴。惜乎日本秉国的军阀，知尽忠于己，而不知施恕于人。知义而不知仁，见小而不见大，识近而不识远。致使中国近六十年之历史成为中日关系之惨痛史，终至鹬蚌相争，渔翁得利，真是历史上很大的一幕悲剧。

　　我们此后应把中国文化广称为大陆文化，作为中国、日本、韩国、越南共有之文化，亦犹希罗文化（希腊罗马合流之文化）之为欧美各国共同之文化。若在文化方面抱狭义之国家主义，则反将文化之价值减低了。

　　实际言之，唐代文化所包含外来因素既广且多，在当时已成为国际文化，因其来甚渐，故国人不自觉耳。日本于吸收唐代文化时，亦于不知不觉中吸收了当时的国际文化，此亦日本之大幸也。

She copied. She copied the Tangs in her civilization. She copied England in building up her navy. She copied Germany in training her army. She copied America in developing her industry. She copied the nineteenth-century Western anachronism of building a colonial empire—a bit too late. She copied Germany's blitzkrieg by hitting at Pearl Harbor—a bit too far. Japan is a wonderful copy which is almost as good as the original but falls short in reproducing the spirit behind it, something rather elusive. Her copybook is closed now, I hope, forever. She grew on copying, became strong on copying, and I hope will not commit hara-kiri on copying.

I admire Japan for her genius of exact aping—something China was unable to do, for she was too clumsy for that. But China made up for it by the possession of originality. She created and created until her energy was sapped by centuries of barbarian invasion, famine, and disease after the downfall of the Tangs.

In parallel fashion, America is an offshoot of European civilization. But here the case is different, for the early colonist from England brought with him the seeds of a love of freedom, which is an expression of originality in ideas. So America created and created till she became the most highly industrialized nation in the world: the most materialistic and at the same time the most idealistic and humanitarian. In the combination of these great opposing elements into one unity lies the greatness of America.

The martial spirit of Japan, of which the Japanese are very proud, is embodied in Bushido, the way of chivalry, which she incorporates into what she calls vaguely Yamato, the "spirit of Japan." Bushido as revealed in peace is an intense loyalty to one's country; in war it means to fight to the last man. Japan has forgotten that what she calls Bushido is nothing more than the martial spirit of ancient China. The very word shows the Tang origin. The modern Chinese pronunciation is Wu-shi-tao—in Cantonese, Mu-shi-do, very similar to Tang pronunciation, whence the Japanese Bu-shi-do.

With strict discipline and efficient organization, and with a thorough application of modern science, Bushido became a mighty weapon of war with which Japan won victory in the Sino-Japanese and Russo-Japanese Wars and ultimately hoped to conquer China and the world. Out of it grew a will to power; upon this foundation she built up a military empire which recognized nothing but power.

The secret of the phenomenal success of Japan in world power lies in reforms along Western lines made by hereditary ruling classes nurtured in the martial spirit, with a strong aptitude for copying and an intense loyalty to leaders and to their native land. They had at hand a people whose supreme virtue is to follow their leaders and obey orders. So the reforms of Japan since the beginning of the Meiji period have moved in a constant and unchanging direction.

日本善于效法。她效法唐宋的文化而定立国之基础；她效法英国建立海军；效法德国训练陆军；效法美国发展工业。她效法十九世纪的西方建立殖民帝国——只可惜晚了一步。她效法德国闪电战术而发动珍珠港的突击——只可惜太远了一点。

我很钦佩日本的善于模仿，这是中国所做不到的，因为她在这方面似乎有点笨脚。但中国创造能力弥补了这一缺憾，她创造又创造，一直到唐代衰亡。此后千余年历经异族侵略、饥馑、疾病等灾祸，终至精疲力竭。

美国的情形和日本很相似，美国文化是欧洲文化的一支，所不同的是从英国来的早期殖民者是带爱好自由的种籽而俱来的。因此美国创造又创造，直到她成为世界上最工业化的国家，同时也是最重理想和人道的国家。美国的伟大就在于这两种矛盾因素的溶而为一。

日本在国际舞台上的空前成就，应该完全归功于依循西方路线所进行的改革。这些改革是在世袭的统治阶级领导下完成的。他们孕育于尚武精神之中，效法他国并使之适应本国，对于领袖和祖国更是精忠不贰。他们统治下的老百姓，最大的美德就是拥护领袖，服从命令。因此从明治初年开始的日本改革运动，始终是坚定不移地朝着固定目标前进。

Reforms in China, on the other hand, have to start from the bottom. There have been no hereditary ruling classes, no aristocracy but the aristocracy of learning. The vast country has to be whipped into unity of purpose by learned leaders from among the common people. Thus the process is necessarily slow and follows a zigzag way. Political leaders such as Sun Yat-sen and intellectual leaders such as Chang Pin-ling, Liang Chi-chao, and Tsai Yuan-pei have all been scholarly men drawn from ordinary backgrounds. From the common people they came and to the common people they went with their great gifts of social and intellectual vision.

Modern Japan has been built up by ruling classes, modern China by the common people. It is therefore much easier to be a leader in Japan, where a leader dictates to the people; in China he has to educate and really lead them—a much more difficult art, which requires a good deal of resourcefulness and originality.

China was comparatively slow in making reforms, but once she made up her mind to it she always tried to find their deeper meaning. In the course of the last hundred years, as we have seen, she began by making cannon balls, from which she was led to political reforms, thence to social reforms and to the introduction of ideas from the West. She wanted to strike at the core of everything. She penetrated deeper and deeper to the heart of Western civilization. She recast her old beliefs and constructed new ones until they became part and parcel of her life. She is a scholar, a moral philosopher, an artist. Her civilization and culture have grown out of her life and she could not be satisfied with Western ideas until they were thoroughly assimilated into that life. In contrast to Japan, therefore, China's thought is modern but her social and industrial structure still lags behind. This is something inherent in the philosopher, the dreamer.

China is broad-minded and democratic and possesses originality but she lacks organization, discipline, and the martial spirit. She is a country of scholars, where learning is most honored and culture most treasured. Yet the military might to defend herself within her own boundaries is something that China has yet to achieve. In China's strong points her weaknesses lie.

So it is with Japan. The Japanese is a warrior and an efficient administrator. The adopted Western civilization has been but a military superstructure which made Japan a militarily potent nation but did not

回头看看我们自己：中国的改革却必须从基层开始，也就是由下而上的。我们没有世袭的统治阶层，除了相当于贵族的士大夫阶级之外，也没有贵族阶级，要使这辽阔的国度里的人民万众一心，必须仰仗老百姓之间的学者领袖来驱策督导。因此改革的过程必然很缓慢，而且迂回曲折。政治领袖像孙中山先生，学者领袖像章太炎、梁任公、蔡子民诸先生，都是来自民间的学者。他们来自民间，又带着能根据他们的社会理想和知识上的远见而深入民间。

现代日本是统治阶级建立起来的，现代中国系平民百姓所缔造。因此，在日本当一个领袖要容易得多，他可以任意独裁，他要人民做什么，人民就会做什么；在中国当一个领袖的却必须教育人民，而且真正地领导人民——这是一种远为困难的才能，也必须具备超人的才智创造能力。

中国在采取改革措施方面每较迟缓，但是她一旦决心改革，她总希望能够做得比较彻底。在过去的一百年中，她从制造炮弹着手，进而从事政治改革、社会改革，乃至介绍西方思想。她扬弃了旧的信仰，另行建立新的，直至这些信仰成为她生活中不可分的一部分为止。她是一位学者，一位道德哲学家，也是一位艺术家。她的文化是从她的生活发展而来的，她不会轻易满足于西方的思想观念，除非她能够把这些观念彻底同化而纳之于她的生活之中。因此与日本比起来，中国的思想是现代化的，但是她的社会和工业建设却仍旧落在日本之后。这是这位哲学家兼梦想家的天性使然。

中国胸襟宽大，生活民主，而且能自力创造，但是她缺乏组织、纪律和尚武精神。她是学者之国，最受尊敬的是学问，最受珍视的是文化。但是保卫国土的武力则尚待建立。中国的优点正是她的弱点所在。

日本的情形也是优劣互见，日本人是位斗士，也是位很干练的行政人员。日本所吸收的西方文明只是军事方面的上层结构，并未

touch the deeper life and thought of the people. While her structure is modern, her spirit and ideas are medieval. This should not surprise the reader, since the feudal system actually existed in Japan until only yesterday—the beginning of the Meiji period. Its abolition took place almost simultaneously with the introduction of Western civilization, while China abolished feudalism before the Christian era.

By elevating the martial spirit to the highest plane which it is possible to maintain by strict discipline, Japan has sacrificed the creative spirit which, in the long run, is the heart of a culture and the sure foundation of a nation. The creative spirit is something one cannot ape. The more one relies on imitation, the more one is apt to lose his creativeness. The more strict the discipline for war required of a people, the more that people will lose the creative spirit.

In the assimilation of Chinese culture, as with the Western, Japan was only partially successful. For example, of the two important moral precepts which are the guiding principles of life in China—loyalty and considerateness—Japan learned loyalty, an indispensable virtue in a feudal state or a militaristic nation, but failed to understand considerateness, which is the virtue of the scholar. She stuck to her own ideas stubbornly or faithfully but refused to consider other people's viewpoints. The narrow-mindedness of the Japanese, of which even they themselves are conscious, deprived them of the leadership necessary for a continental colonial empire. They had ambition and military might but no statesmanship. The Japanese see things very clearly within certain limits but are blind to major cultural movements of the world. They are bigoted, intolerant, and inflexible under the cover of extreme courtesy.

On the other hand, the two virtues went hand in hand in China. She is faithful and at the same time considerate. China does not feel that faithfulness to her own ideas precludes the existence of other points of view. She always tries to imagine herself in the position of others. That is considerateness, of which Japan was not capable. So she failed to understand China.

Japan has acted like a strong little boy who tries to take a ram by the horns. It snorts, jumps, arches its back, and butts at him until he is forced to let go or is laid flat on his back. Then he wonders why the creature should act that way. Poor boy! Think what you would do if someone took you by the ear—try to see yourself in another's position—and you will understand China.

触及人民较深一层的生活和思想，她的上层结构固然现代化了，她的精神和观念却仍然是中世纪的。对这种情形，读者自然不会感到惊奇，因为封建制度废除的时间甚短，故封建精神在明治时代仍然存在，中国则在西历纪元以前就已经废除了。

日本对同化中国文化和西方文化都只有部分的成功。例如日本对忠和恕这两个重要的道德观念只学到忠，却无法了解恕。这或许受政治与地理环境之影响而使然，然而日本人之不能以恕道待人，却是事实。忠和恕是中国生活的两大指导原则，忠在封建国家或黩武国家是必不可少的品德，恕则是学者的美德。日本一向坚执己见，不肯考虑别人的观点。日本人胸襟狭窄，连他们自己都有此自觉，这种褊狭的心理使他们无法具备建立洲际殖民帝国所必需的领导能力。他们有野心，有武力，但是缺乏政治家风度。所以他们藉武力而建立的"东亚共荣圈"，只如空中楼阁，顷刻幻灭。忠和恕在中国却是携手同行的。她不但忠贞，而且处处为人设想。中国并不觉得忠于她自己的思想观念就应该排斥他人的观点。她常常设身处地考虑别人的观点，这就是所谓恕。日本人对恕的观念很薄弱，所以不克了解中国。

日本的行为很像一个身体健壮的顽童。他抓住了公羊的两只角不许它动，公羊急得乱叫乱跳，用角来撞他，结果他不是被迫放手，就是被撞倒地上。他想不通这只公羊为什么这样不听话。可怜的孩子！他应该想想如果有人抓住他的两只耳朵，他的反应又如何？他应该设身处地想一想，这样他就会了解中国了。

Another important factor that has made the Japanese a war-loving race is the belief that Japan is a divine country, born of gods and living and conquering by divine will. This is not easily understood either by the West or by the Chinese. But it is a fact that the Japanese believe it reverently. The Chinese believe in gods, but they take them as the guardians of morals, not of war. For the Chinese the gods have nothing to do with the rise or downfall of an empire. But to the Japanese the rise of Japan was the will of the gods.

From time immemorial the ruling classes of Japan have believed that in war the gods are always on the side of Dai Nippon. When the Yuans or Mongols failed to conquer her, they thought the gods had protected her with their divine power. The typhoon that destroyed Kublai Khan's Mongol fleet was an act of the gods. The reigning dynasty of the Mikado, the Japanese have believed up to now, is of divine origin and its emperors the direct descendants of gods.

A Chinese graduate of Tokyo Imperial University, later a professor in a Chinese university, has done an illuminating piece of historical research to show how Japanese imperialism grew out of this religious-patriotic fervor. Expressions of it in the everyday life of the soldier are not lacking. During the war Japanese soldiers almost all carried Buddhist or Shinto charms for protection in battle. I saw many such charms brought back from battlegrounds by Chinese soldiers, who finally came to regard them as an indispensable part of enemy military equipment and paid no more attention to them, except to joke about them occasionally.

After one battle between the American Air Force and the Japanese invaders I acted as guide to a party of American officers and soldiers who drove in jeeps over miles of rugged mountain paths to a crashed Japanese bomber. In the pockets and on the bodies of the dead pilots we found the usual Buddhist and Shinto charms; smeared with blood and riddled with bullets. An American captain pulled a cloth charm from the dead pilot and asked me what it was. I told him.

"What's the use of it?" asked the captain.

"For divine protection," I replied.

"No protection, though—" he turned over the cloth and tried to make out the indecipherable signs on it, "—you get me?" And he threw it on

　　使日本人变为好战民族的另一重要因素，是他们的一种错误信念，他们认为日本是个神圣的国家，系神所缔造，而且应该根据神的意志行事，并且征服世界。这种心理是由军阀御用的历史家歪曲史实所造成的。为西洋人或中国人所不易了解，但是日本人却的确如此深信不疑。中国人也相信神佛，但是他们把神佛当作道德的监护者，而不是战争的呵护者。日本人却认为日本称霸是神的意旨。

　　从悠远的年代以来，日本的统治阶级一直相信神佛在战时总是站在大日本这一边的。元朝不克征服她时，他们就认为那是神佛以无边的法力保护了她。他们认为吹毁忽必烈汗蒙古舰队的台风就是神佛的意旨。我修改本稿时，已在战后十多年了，还在日本箱根遇见一位老尼。她说人们应该信佛，日本打败蒙古人，就靠佛的法力的。日本人一直相信历代天皇都是神的嫡亲后裔。直到战后，日本历史家得到言论自由，才用科学方法，把那些凝结在教科书里的神话，一口气吹散了。

　　中国某大学的一位教授，原是东京帝大的毕业生，他曾作过一件发人深省的历史研究工作，说明了这种宗教性的爱国热狂如何发展为日本帝国主义。这种宗教性的爱国热狂表现于军人日常生活者更是屡见不鲜。中日战争期间，几乎所有日本士兵身上都带着佛教或神道的护身符。我曾经见过许多由中国士兵从战场捡回来的这种护身符。中国士兵因为见得多了，就把这些护身符看作敌人装备中必备的一部分，除了偶而拿它们开开玩笑之外，并不拿它们当回事。

　　其次美国空军与日本入侵飞机发生空战之后，我曾经权充向导，领了一群美国官兵，乘吉普车经过好几里崎岖的山路，去看一架被击落坠毁的日本轰炸机残骸。我们从飞行员的尸身上和口袋里发现常见的佛教和神道的护身符，符上满是血迹，且已为枪弹所洞穿。一位美军上尉从日本飞行员尸体上捡出一块布符，问我那是什么。我告诉他那是符。

　　"那是做什么用的？"上尉问道。

　　"求神佛保佑。"我回答说。

　　"不过，佛好像并没有保佑他——"他翻过布符，想看看上面无法辨认的符号究竟说些什么，说了一声"我真不懂"，接着随手把布符

the ground casually and forgot about it. Like this American officer, the Chinese had come to dismiss lightly these tokens of invulnerability. So it is with the world.

On the day of that aerial battle I saw seven enemy bombers spinning down from the skies in white smoke. The other search parties brought back from the wrecked planes many similar talismans, besides cartridges, maps, and scientific charts. A curious combination of medieval superstition with modern science. But to the Japanese it is no superstition; there is a living divine force which spurs them on to fight for their country, protected by the gods. The charms are but the symbol of that divine power.

After the fall of Hongkong a Chinese couple—a Mr. and Mrs. Huang whom I know well and who understand the psychology of the Japanese—presented an image of Buddha to a Japanese soldier who entered their house. Crossing the harbor to Kowloon the little boat he took capsized and all on board were drowned but himself. He came back to them to express his gratitude, for he believed that the image had saved his life. But to the Chinese way of thinking the image had protected the couple from being molested by the enemy, while the escape from drowning was mere luck.

The world does not know much about Japanese religious fanaticism in war because the Japanese themselves have not said much about it in their propaganda. While in China modern science has sapped the old beliefs and is a disintegrating factor in relation to them, in Japan it became merely a powerful weapon of the gods to weld the country together in a war of aggression. This psychological background of intense religious patriotism has made the Japanese warlords unamenable to reason, the Japanese soldier a hard nut to crack, and Japan herself a menace to the world; such is the result of fanaticism combined with modern science.

To have such a fanatical neighbor would be a headache to any country. And Japan has been much more than a headache to China during the last fifty long, troubled years. Only utter defeat and unconditional surrender could make Japan come to her senses. The inevitable fate awaited her, and we must now hope that it will have its bitter but salutary consequence.

When the gods of the Allied nations have fulfilled their mission, Japan—as I can imagine—may be a picturesque and peaceful country, with enchanting mountain scenery, pretty gardens wreathed in *sakura* blossoms, attractive pavilions with ladies in beautiful kimonos; and an industrious, courteous, and docile people, in whose ears will ring no voices of gods urging them onward to war and to conquest.

Then, and not until then, will peace reign in Japan, in China, in the Far East, and in the world.

往地上一丢，就立刻把它忘了。中国人也像这位美国军官一样，对于这种刀枪不入的表征始终一笑置之。世界各地人士也是如此。

那次空战时，我曾经看到七架敌机冒着白烟回旋下坠。其他的搜索队也从敌机残骸中捡回许多类似的符箓，以及弹药、地图和科学图表。这是中世纪迷信和现代科学一种奇怪的混合，但是日本人绝不以为那是迷信；一种存在于冥冥之中的神圣力量驱策着他们为国家奋斗，神佛则随时随地在呵护他们，护符只是那种神圣力量的象征而已。

香港陷落以后，有一对我很熟识的黄氏夫妇住在香港，他们很了解日本人的心理，当一位日本士兵进他们房子盘查时，他们就送了一尊佛像给他。这位日本兵由香港赴九龙时，所乘小船不意覆没，船上乘客除他之外全体没顶。他后来回来向黄氏夫妇道谢，因为他相信是那尊佛像救了他的命。但是按照中国人的想法，他之没有被淹死，不过是运气而已。

世界人士对于日本人在战时的宗教狂热所知不多，因为日本人自己在他们的宣传中很少提到它。但是在中国，现代科学却已削弱了旧的信仰，而且成为使旧信仰解体的一个因素。在日本，现代科学反而成为神的一种有力武器，使日本在侵略战争中团结一致。这种由强烈的宗教性爱国心所形成的心理背景，终使日本军阀无可理喻，使日本兵难于制服，使日本本身成为世界的一个威胁；这就是宗教狂热与现代科学结合的结果。

任何国家有这一位疯狂的邻居都会头痛。在过去六十年的动乱时代里，日本又岂仅使我国头痛而已！

讲到这里，我们不得不责备从明治以来至战事结束这一时代之日本历史家，他们仰军阀鼻息，无古太史之风。其中虽偶有若干史家，敢批军阀逆鳞，但在环境逼迫之下，亦属孤掌难鸣，遂使日本历史成为神权迷信军权崇拜之护符。我就在碰见那老尼的同一天，在箱根的一家理发店理发。店主自称其祖若父，曾在封建时代为将军武士们束发整容。幼时曾听人们说，天皇的祖宗是中国人，从中国来的，这些话现在大家敢说了。以前没有人敢说，说了要杀头的。可见这些天皇非神说，早在武士阶级及民间流传。他还有几句有趣的话，我们可以在此作一插曲。他好蓄古钱，在他的小小搜集里，倒点缀了宋元明清四朝的铜钱，及相当时代的日本钱，他说日本钱是用日本铜在中国铸的。最有趣味的是，把大正昭和两代的硬币排列成行。中日战争开始以后，硬币步步缩小，战事愈久，钱缩得愈小，在最后一两年间，缩小了几等于鹅眼。他很幽默的指着说，这是代表"东亚共荣圈"的。从民间流传的关于天皇源流故事看来，可以推想到日本历史虽受军阀之统制，而民间仍保存着乃祖若宗世代相传之口史，为军阀所不能毁灭者。

战后因思想言论自由，近年来新出版的日本史是值得我们一读的。昔韩宣子适鲁，见易象与鲁春秋，曰周礼尽在鲁矣。读日本最近出版之日本历史并各种学术的书籍，几乎使我与宣子有同样的感叹！

六七十年来，我国与日本所定的国策，同为富国强兵。日本所走的路线为资本主义与军国主义。用资本主义所产生的财富来养兵，军阀与财阀联合操纵军政大权。他们的权力超越一切党派与学派。军国主义与资本主义的日本，一战而胜中国，再战而胜帝俄，三战横冲直撞而轰炸到珍珠港。

我国为何想富国而国不富，想强兵而兵不强呢？

第一，内政问题。日本倒幕尊皇，政权统一已数十年。我国初则保皇革命，国是未定。继则军阀割据，全国扰攘。等到国民革命军统一全国的时候，内则战乱频仍，外则日本侵略，内忧外患接踵而起。那里还谈得到富国强兵呢？

第二，经济思想问题。我国儒家"不患寡而患不均"的经济思想，先天上已有不赞成资本主义的色彩，数十年来一般士大夫复颇有仰慕王安石统制经济之倾向，故对西洋资本主义，虽不一定反对，却不热心拥护。这个事实，是谁也不能否定的。只以此而论，就可知道建设一个资本主义的社会是怎样的不容易了。

第三，门户开放问题。中国明清两代均采锁国主义。日本在德川时代亦采锁国主义。十九世纪之资本主义迫开了两国之门。在中国称之为通商，日本称之为开国。然日本之开国发之于统一之政府，故全国一致而收实效。中国则此开彼闭，前迎后拒，步骤极不一致。故开国之实效未显，而瓜分之祸兆已见。

以上对于中国与日本的比较，和对日本之批评，大部分是抗战期间我在重庆所想到而记下来的。当全国被日军蹂躏，千千万万人民在日军铁蹄下牺牲生命财产的期间，我这记录似乎相当客观和公平。这是出于儒家忠恕平衡的传统观念，而日本却缺少一个恕字。对日和约，我国主张维持日本皇室，放弃赔款要求，遣送全体俘虏返国，凡此种种，虽出于政治远见，根本思想还是出于恕道。我国人民知道"不念旧恶"为维持和平的要道，所以这种和约，为全国人民所拥护。

停战以后，我视察了好多日本俘虏营（湘西、汉口、南京等址）；我未曾看见当地民众对日俘有嘲笑或侮辱的举动，使我感觉到中国人民度量的宽宏。

日本战败后十余年，其国内思想颇有变动，有些地方和我们在战前所见和战时所论的颇有不同。如民主主义之抬头，思想和言论之充分自由，神道迷信之渐趋薄弱，历史之重史实而放弃传统的虚伪，工业化之加速与产品的进步，学术研究之加速的发达。凡此种种，影响日本本身之将来与东亚之局势者必甚大。

东欧之西德与远东之日本，已居冷战中重要地位。西德则站在西方民主阵线而为其重要的一环。日本则表面似倾向西方，而其内心则犹站在三岔路中，游移未定。亲西方乎？中立乎？抑或倾向共产主义集团乎？现在日本各种不同之政见，归纳起来，不外乎此三点。这是日本的内心烦恼，亦是她本身的课题，而亦为西方民主集团的课题。

（注）本章【中文】全文经宋越伦先生之口译，得嘉治隆一先生之指教，而关于日本历史方面指正尤多，特此志谢，但其文责仍由作者负之。

CHAPTER 33 CHARACTERISTICS OF CHINESE CULTURE

East and West are different because their cultures are different. Yet you will find similarities in both. These parallels, no matter how close, will not make two cultures alike; the peculiar characteristics of each still render one different from the other. In the West varying culture traits make the Germans different from the English and the French from the Dutch. Yet there are characteristics common to all—common ties which hold the Western nations together culturally under the loose name of "Western culture." These again differ from the Eastern nations. Similarities or contrasts of culture, therefore, are not to be judged by outward parallels but by the fundamental character of each.

In this chapter we will examine the characteristics of Chinese culture under three headings: (1) the absorbing power of Chinese civilization, (2) morals and intellect, and (3) the practical wisdom of the Chinese people.

1. The Absorbing Power of Chinese Civilization

Some forty years ago, when I was still in school, we were constantly told by foreigners and progressive Chinese alike that China was like a solid rock which absorbs little or nothing. That is to say, Chinese civilization was stagnant and petrified and China was incurably conservative. She loved and lived by her own ways. Nothing could effect a change in John the Chinaman.

This appeared to be all right but proved all wrong. From the opening of the treaty ports until after the Sino-Japanese War in 1894 China appeared to resist Western influence. However, during previous centuries she had absorbed many of the outlandish things which from time to time made inroads upon her life.

In music, the so-called "national" Chinese music of the present day is played on instruments mostly of foreign origin. Forms of the fiddle, flute, and harp were introduced from Turkestan[1] centuries ago. We also kept the ancient Chinese harp, but only a few understand its music and still fewer can play it.

Various foods have been introduced to the Chinese dinner table from foreign lands: watermelons, cucumbers, grapes, and peppers

叁叁 敌机轰炸中谈中国文化

东方与西方不同，因为它们的文化不同。但是你仍旧可以找出东西文化之间的相似之点。无论两种文化如何相似，不可能完全相同，每一文化的特点也必有异于他种文化。就西方而论，不同的文化特征使德国人异于英国人，同时也使法国人不同于荷兰人。但是他们之间仍有共通的特征，这些特征使西方国家在文化上结为一体，泛称"西方文化"。这些特征又使他们与东方各国显出不同。因此，文化上的异同，不应该由表面上的类似之点来判断，而应该由各别的基本特征来论定。

在这一章里，我们将从三方面来讨论中国文化的特征：（一）中国文化之吸收力。（二）道德与理智。（三）中国人的人情。

（一）中国文化之吸收力

大约五十年前，当我还在学校念书的时候，外国人和前进的中国人都常常说，中国很像一块绝少吸收能力，甚至毫无吸收能力的岩石，那也就是说中国文化已经停滞不前，而且成为化石，因此中国已经变得无可救药地保守。她一直我行我素，谁也不能使这位"支那人"改变分毫。

这种说法表面上似乎言之成理，但是结果却证明完全错误。从五口通商开始，至一八九四年中日战争为止，中国似乎一直在抗拒西方影响。但是在以前的几百年内，她曾经吸收了许多先后侵入她生活之中的外来东西。

在音乐方面，现在所谓的"国乐"，实际上多半是用起源于外国的乐器来弹奏的。胡琴、笛和七弦琴，都是几百年前从土耳其斯坦传入的。我们现在仍旧保留着中国的古琴，但是只有极少数人能够欣赏，至于能弹古琴的人就更少了。

从外国介绍到中国的食品更不计其数：西瓜、黄瓜、葡萄和

came hundreds of years ago; sweet potatoes, peanuts, and Indian corn have appeared in recent centuries. In late decades the Irish potato, tomato, cauliflower, cabbage, and lettuce have found their way into Chinese cooking. Tenderloin steaks of the West, chopped very fine and served with bean sauce, have kept delightful company with Chinese dishes. Tomato soup with tender shrimp meat and hot fried rice hissing euphoniously in it was an innovation. Dinner in China is sometimes topped off with ice cream, American coffee, and Sunkist oranges, together with fruits of native production. Oranges grew originally in Chinese soil, traveled to America, received their education in the Luther Burbank school of California, and returned to their native land with a new title—something like the B.A. or Ph.D. brought back by Chinese students from American universities. Chinese oranges also went to Germany many, many years ago, where they turned into apples—for the Germans called orange *apfelsine*, Chinese apple.

Spiritual or intellectual nourishment from any quarter that was worth the trouble of absorbing China was always ready to welcome. During the Ming Dynasty the Jesuits brought to China astronomy, mathematics, and the Bible. An Imperial minister was converted and his residence in the Siccawei district of Shanghai was made a center of Catholic activities. From the Jesuits the Chinese learned Western astronomy and some became Christians because of it. The Siccawei Observatory has been a guiding star for shipping along that coast ever since the opening of the treaty ports.

Huang Chung-hsi, a great Ming scholar living during the end of the Ming and the beginning of the Ching (Manchu) Dynasty, was one of the admirers of Western astronomy brought by the Jesuits. He said: "Learning has been preserved in foreign lands while China has lost it owing to the lack of proper care." He once told a friend that "so far as astronomy is concerned, we are only babies in comparison with the Western scholar." Which shows how open-minded great Chinese scholars were.

The fact is that China has endured many vicissitudes of fortune in the course of her centuries because of her great capacity for absorption. No civilization in the world could sustain itself without taking in alien elements from time to time in one way or another. I think it needs no historian to prove that point. The interdependence and mutual influences of Western civilizations are so obvious as to require no argument. But the interaction of Eastern and Western civilizations is less apparent.

胡椒是好几百年前传入中国的；甘薯、落花生、玉蜀黍则是最近几百年传入的；在最近的几十年中，洋山芋、番茄、花菜、白菜和堇菜也传入中国了。切成小块，用酱油红烧的西方牛排，也已经变为一道中国菜。锅巴虾仁加番茄汁更是一种新花样。中菜筵席有时也要加上冰淇淋、咖啡和金山橙子。柑橘原是中国的土产，后来出洋赴美，在加利福尼亚经过园艺试验家褒朋克改良后，带着新的头衔又回到了本乡，与中国留学生从美国大学带着硕士、博士的头衔学成归国的情形差不多。中国柑橘还在很久很久以前传到德国，想不到柑橘到了德国却变成了苹果，因为德国人把柑橘叫做"中国苹果"。

凡是值得吸收的精神食粮或知识养分，不论来自何方，中国总是随时准备欢迎的。明朝时，耶稣会教士把天文、数学和圣经传到中国。大学士徐光启，不但从他们学习天算，而且还信仰了天主，把他在上海徐家汇的住宅作为天主教活动中心，我们从耶稣会教士学到西方的天文学，有些人因此而成为天主教徒。五口通商以后，徐家汇天文台一直是沿海航行的指针。

明末清初有位学者黄梨洲，他非常佩服耶稣会教士传入的天文学。他曾说过这样一句话，中国有许多学问因自己没有好好地保存，所以有不少已经流到外国去了。他有一次告诉一位朋友说："就天文学而论，我们与西方学者比起来，实在幼稚得很。"可见中国学者是如何虚怀若谷！

事实上正因为她有伟大的吸收能力，中国才能在几千年的历史过程中历经沧桑而屹立不坠。世界上没有任何文化能够不随时吸收外国因素而可维系不坠。我想这是不必历史家来证明的。西方各国文化间的相互依存关系和相互影响，彰彰在人耳目，无庸争辩。但是东方文化与西方文化间的相互作用却比较不太明显。剑桥大学的

I have been told by Professor Joseph Needham of Cambridge that the expanding properties of gunpowder influenced the discovery of steam power, and that the idea of good in human nature, of the Confucian school, influenced the Encyclopedists in France. A number of things have trickled from time to time into the West from the East. But I would like to leave it to the West to tell us.

We did not absorb more than music, foodstuffs, and things of similar nature through our western and northern frontiers by land because there was not much more to absorb. The races in those regions had little spiritual or mental food to offer. For the latter we turned to India. In the field of arts Chinese painting and architecture were influenced by Buddhism; in Chinese philosophy Buddhist thought played a very important part, and it even affected the style and vocabulary of Chinese literature.

Centuries before the Jesuits the Chinese had assimilated the moral aspects of Buddhism, but they left the system of other-worldly philosophy alone. After centuries of sojourning in China, with tens of thousands of Buddhist temples and monasteries occupying the best sites on mountains as well as in cities, its basic philosophy and religion still remain foreign to the Chinese mind. The scholars befriend or tolerate it and the common people worship it as one of the religions in China. Nevertheless it remains foreign. To the practical-minded Chinese its metaphysical system is not palatable. It exists in China because there are moral teachings in it and in time of distress one could find moral refuge in it. The Chinese only wanted to absorb foreign elements into their own system of thought, to be enriched by them; they would not surrender their own system to an alien one.

Out of their virtue of tolerance the Chinese had an ingenious way of dealing with any system they could not absorb into their own. They would take part of it and leave the rest to co-exist with the indigenous products. Thus a portion of her teeming millions would take in the imported system and become Buddhists, Mohammedans, or Christians, and all lived side by side in a good, neighborly way.

尼邓教授曾告诉我，火药的膨胀性导致蒸汽机的发明，而儒家的性善学说则影响了法国大光明时代学派的思想。许多东西曾经悄无声息地从东方流传到西方。至于这些东西究竟是什么，我想还是让西洋人自己来告诉我们罢。

但是我们除了音乐、食物之类以外，并没有经由西面和北面陆上边界吸收其他的东西。这些区域里的民族，所能提供的精神食粮事实上很少，因此我们转而求诸印度。在艺术方面，我国的绘画和建筑都有佛教的影响，佛教思想在中国哲学方面更占着重要的地位，佛教经典甚至影响了中国文学的风格和辞藻。

在耶稣会教士到达中国之前好几百年，中国人已经吸收了佛教的道德观念，但是对佛教的超世哲学却未加理睬。佛教传入中国虽已有千百年的历史，而且千千万万的佛教寺庙也占据着城市和山区的最好位置，但是佛教的基本哲学和宗教在中国人的思想里仍然是陌生的。学者们对佛教保持友善或容忍的态度，一般老百姓把它当作中国的诸多宗教之一来崇拜。但是它始终还是外国的东西。在重实用的中国人看来，佛教的超知识主义并无可用。超知识主义所以能在中国存在，是因为它含有道德教训，同时遇到苦难的时候，可以作精神上的避风港。中国人只想把外国因素吸收进来充实自己的思想体系；但是他们绝不肯放弃自己的思想体系而完全向外国投降。

中国人凭藉容忍的美德，对于无法吸收的任何思想体系都有巧妙的应付办法。他们先吸收一部分，让余留的部分与本国产物和平共存。因此亿万人口中的一部分就接纳了外国的思想文化，成为佛教徒、回教徒，或基督教徒，大家和睦相处，互不干扰。

中国历史上最有趣味的两件事，一件是关于道家思想的。我们把它劈成两半。一半为老庄哲学，以此立身，为任自然而无为；以此治国，为无为而治。另一半成为道教，起于东汉张道陵之五斗米道。流入特殊社会而成帮会，二千年来，揭竿而起，改朝换代，都是与帮会有关系的。流入通俗社会则成道教。既拜神也拜佛，台湾之"拜拜"即此。通俗所迷信之阎罗王，本为印度婆罗门教冥府之司狱吏，由佛教于无意中传来中国而入了道教。至轮回之说，入了道教而亦忘其来源矣。

第二件是把佛教也劈成两半。宗教部分入了道教，哲学部分则合道家而入了儒家。老子之无为主义，凑合了佛家之无为主义，使佛学在中国思想系统里生了根。故宋儒常把老佛并称。

自宋以来之儒家，可以说没有不涉猎道家哲学与佛学的。儒家之洒脱思想，实因受其影响而来。

中国之学人，以儒立身，以道处世，近年以来加上了一项以科学处事。美国本年六月份《幸福》杂志，以幽默的口气，谓台湾有人对美国人说，台湾的建设靠三子。一孔子，二老子，三鬼子。问什么叫鬼子，则笑谓洋鬼子。

But to go back to the introduction of Western civilization during the last half century. In the matter of clothing the process of westernization in the past thirty years has been still more striking. Felt or straw hats have taken the place of old types of headgear; cut hair has banished the "Chinaman's queue" as you have seen it in old pictures. Women wear bobbed hair with permanent waves. Short skirts and silk and nylon stockings have given Chinese women a chance to show their pretty and well-developed legs. As regards their feet, they have indeed gone through a revolution. Western shoes have relieved the agelong agonies of foot-binding, with subsequent improvement in their bodily health. Healthy mothers bring forth healthy children—the effect upon the coming generation has been remarkable. Our children are not only healthier as compared with children of days gone by, but more active—quicker in movement and keener in mind.

In social affairs both sexes intermingle more freely in contrast with the old customs of segregation. In civil law marriages no longer have to be arranged by parents; young men and women have the right to find their lovers and choose their own mates. Coeducational institutions are rather the rule than the exception.

As regards dwellings the old superstition of *feng-shui* that affected the choice of sites for buildings has given way to modern theories of architecture. While the old artistic styles are still preserved for their beauty and grandeur in some cases, air, light, convenience, comfort, and hygienic conditions are first considerations. Flush toilets, baths, and a steam heating system are installed in modern houses. Stiff-backed chairs and hard beds have given way to sofas and spring mattresses.

Chinese food is rich in its variety because it is always ready to absorb alien elements. Western food is comparatively simple because it is, I think, not so ready to take in foreign materials. Tea was indeed introduced into Europe from China centuries ago. Spices were introduced from the East, and in search for a shorter trade route to India Columbus happened upon America. Worcestershire sauce, I am told, was developed from Chinese bean sauce. Aside from these, Western food has remained untouched by Eastern influences. Chop suey houses are found by the hundreds in America and Americans are quite fond of chop suey but know few other Chinese dishes.

现在让我们再回头看一看过去五十年间西方文化传入中国的情形。在衣着方面过去三十年间西化的趋势最为显著。呢帽和草帽已经取代旧式的帽子和头巾；昔日电影中所看到的辫子已失去了踪迹。女人都已烫了头发，短裙、丝袜和尼龙袜已使中国妇女有机会显示她们的玉腿。女人的足更已经历一次重大的革命，西式鞋子使她们放弃了几千年来的缠足恶习，结果使她们的健康大为改善。健康的母亲生育健康的子女，天足运动对于下一代的影响至为明显。现代的儿童不但比从前的儿童健康，而且远较活泼，不但行动比较迅速，心智也远较敏锐。

在社交方面，男女可以自由交际，与过去授受不亲的习俗适成强烈的对照。民法中规定，婚姻不必再由父母安排；青年男女成年以后，有权自行选择对象。男女同校已经成为通例，男女分校倒成了例外。

在住的方面，一向左右屋基选择的风水迷信已经渐为现代的建筑理论所替代。在若干实例中，古代的艺术风格固然因其华丽或雄伟而保留了下来，但是大家首先考虑的还是阳光、空气、便利、舒适、卫生等要件。现代房屋已经装置抽水马桶、洋瓷浴盆和暖气设备。硬背椅子和硬板床已经渐为沙发及弹簧床垫所取代。

中国菜肴花样繁多，因为我们随时愿意吸收外国成分。西菜比较简单，我想主要是因为不大愿意采用外国材料的缘故。不错，茶是好几世纪以前从中国传入欧洲的。香料也是由东方传去。哥伦布就是为了找寻到印度的通商捷径而无意中发现新大陆的。有人告诉我，渥斯特郡辣酱油也是从中国酱油发展而来的。但是除此以外，西菜始终很少受东方的影响。美国的"杂碎"店固然数以万计，而且美国人也很喜欢"杂碎"，但是除此以外，他们就很少知道别的中国菜了。

On the other hand, China keeps on absorbing more and more alien elements, sometimes sensibly and at other times rather indiscriminately—not only food but clothing, shelter, ideas, social customs, and so forth. In most cases the process of absorption is through unconscious rather than conscious action. It is something like the absorption of nutriment from the soil by the roots of a tree: they absorb and cannot do otherwise. It is the nature of a growing tree to absorb, or it would cease to grow.

The introduction and absorption of alien civilization from China's western frontiers were accomplished in the course of many, many centuries, during which foreign elements came into the country only in trickles. Therefore she took them in gradually and slowly digested them. It was for the most part an unconscious process; it did not change the main course of Chinese civilization, but was something like the attraction of a magnet for iron particles. They cluster around it, but the magnet does not change its position.

Western civilization, on the other hand, came to China's eastern frontiers by sea in torrents, in all its fierceness, speed, and magnitude, and in the short span of some fifty years. To try to absorb Western civilization—with all that the French and industrial revolutions had contributed to it—was like gobbling up many days' food supply at one meal. Naturally China suffered some discomfort—not to say unbearable stomachache. Thus Western civilization at one time became so distasteful to China that she feared it, cursed, kicked the table over, and turned from it in despair, only to find more food being pressed on her. The reaction against Western civilization was a reaction against food after a stomachache through much overeating. The abortive reforms of 1898 were but a case of overeating. The Boxer Rebellion of 1900 was a violent case of acute and complicated indigestion. China was forced on the operating table, to be operated on by Western doctors—the allied armies of eight nations. For that she had a handsome bill to pay—450,000,000 taels—and in the operation almost lost her life.

The doctrine of Chang Chi-tung that "Chinese culture is fundamental and Western civilization is supplementary" is no more than to say that a sound stomach is more important to health than the foods it is to take. So China tried to move cautiously, measuring her steps instead of lengthening them. But the tides of Western civilization would not wait for her. They lashed her eastern shores, overflowed into the rich Pearl and

中国却一直不断地在吸收外国东西，有时候经过审慎选择，有时候则不分皂白，乱学一气——不但食物方面如此，就是衣着、建筑、思想、风俗习惯等等也是如此。吸收的过程多半是不自觉的，很像一棵树通过树根从土壤吸收养分。吸收养分是成长中树木的本能，否则它就不会再长大。

中国由新疆输入外国文化并加吸收的过程很缓慢，千余年来只点点滴滴地传入了少许外国东西。因此她是逐步接受这些东西，有时间慢慢加以消化。大体上这是一种不自觉的过程，因此并未改变中国文化的主流，很像磁石吸收铁屑。铁屑聚集在磁石上，但是磁石的位置并未改变。

由华东沿海输入的西方文化，却是如潮涌至，奔腾澎湃，声势慑人；而且是在短短五十年之内涌到的。西方文化在法国革命和工业革命之后正是盛极一时，要想吸收这种文化，真像一顿饭要吃下好几天的食物。如果说中国还不至于胀得胃痛难熬，至少已有点感觉不舒服。因此中国一度非常讨厌西方文化，她惧怕它，诅咒它，甚至踢翻饭桌，懊丧万分地离席而去，结果发现饭菜仍从四面八方向她塞过来。中国对西方文化的反感，正像一个人吃得过饱而闹胃痛以后对食物的反感。一八九八年的康梁维新运动，只是吃得过量的毛病；一九〇〇年的"义和团之乱"，则是一次严重而复杂的消化不良症，结果中国硬被拖上手术台，由西医来开刀，这些西医就是八国联军。这次医药费相当可观，共计四亿五千万两银子，而且她几乎在这次手术中丧命。

张之洞"中学为体，西学为用"的主张，事实上也不过是说：健全的胃比它所接受的食物对健康更重要。因此中国很想稳步前进，不敢放步飞奔。但是西方文化的潮流却不肯等她。西潮冲激着她的东海岸，泛滥了富庶的珠江流域和长江流域，并且很快

Yangtze Valleys, and rapidly extended to the Yellow River Valley. She had to go on taking more imported food in spite of her recent serious upset.

By 1902 the students, who had the best appetites, caught up with the spirit of the times, and revolution—against established authorities, educational, political, and moral, as well as intellectual—became the catchword of the rising generation. Burdened with a legacy of the past which seemed to them at the time no more than the dead hand of a bygone civilization, the receptive mind of youth took so enthusiastically to Western ideas as to offset the influences of tradition.

Soon after the opening of the five treaty ports, China had established arsenals, dockyards, machine shops, schools of foreign languages; had translated books on elementary sciences and sent students to study in America. Being defeated in various wars of self-defense against Western Powers, she started to build a navy. A small navy was built, indeed, only to be destroyed by Japan in 1894. Japan could not endure to have China have a navy.

Failing this, China went a step further by taking up the reform of government, army, and education. The Inertial government at Peking began to prepare for the adoption of a Western constitutional form of government; it established new systems of education, organized modern armies and police, and sent large numbers of students to study abroad. This may be regarded as the first conscious effort in history to absorb a foreign civilization on a large scale, and it had far-reaching consequences in China's national life.

The reforms in education were the most important, because they were the best planned, with most foresight, and dealt directly with the rising generation whose minds were least fettered by traditional ideas. Later, when the students of one school generation grew up and came into power, they adopted more Western ways and consequently those of the succeeding generation were in a better position to absorb more new ideas. When these came to power in their turn, they went still further in westernization and more new measures were introduced into the government, army, and schools. Thus each new generation was more modernized than the previous one.

The 1919 student movement in Peking, the emphasis upon science and modern democratic ideas by professors of the National University there, and the literary revolution sponsored by Professor Hu Shih, were

弥漫到黄河流域。虽然她最近闹了一场严重的胃病，她也不得不再吃一点比较重要的食物。

到了一九〇二年，胃口最佳的学生已为时代精神所沾染，革命成为新生的一代的口头禅。他们革命的对象包括教育上的、政治上的、道德上的，以及知识上的各种传统观念和制度，过去遗留下来的一切，在这班青年人看起来不过是旧日文化的骸骨，毫无值得迷恋之处。他们如饥如渴地追求西方观念，想藉此抵消传统的各种影响。

五口通商后不久，中国即已建立兵工厂、码头、机器厂和外语学校，翻译了基本科学的书籍，而且派学生留学美国。因为她在抵抗西方列强的保卫战中屡遭败北，于是决定先行建立一支海军。一支小型的海军倒是真的建立起来了，结果却在一八九四年被日本所毁灭。日本是无法容忍中国有海军的。

海军既然建不成，中国就进一步进行政治、陆军和教育上的改革。北京的满清政府开始准备采取西方的立宪政制；它建立了新的教育制度，组织了现代化的军队和警察，并且派遣了大批学生出洋留学。这可算是中国文化有史以来首次自觉地大规模吸收外国文明，其结果对往后国民生活发生了非常深远的影响。

最重要的是教育上的改革，因为这些改革的计划最完善，眼光最远大，而且是针对新兴一代而发的，传统观念对这班年轻人的影响最小。后来这班年龄相若的学生逐渐成长而在政府中掌握大权，他们又采取了更多的西洋方法，使较年轻的一代有更佳的机会吸收新的观念思想。这年轻的一代接着握权以后，他们又进一步从事西化工作，更多的新措施也随之介绍到政府、军队和学校等部门。因此新兴的每一代都比前一代更现代化。

民国八年（一九一九年）北京的学生运动，北大教授所强调的科学和现代民主观念，以及胡适教授所提倡的文学革命，只是自觉地

the beginnings of conscious effort to absorb Western thought, hitherto limited mainly to the industrial and political spheres. This effort came nearer to the heart of Chinese culture and with it a new leaf was turned in the cultural history of China. For by this means China has been trying to catch up with the advancing tides of the world. Chinese civilization, with compass pointing to the West, has gradually shifted its course to meet the main currents of Western civilization, and in the next fifty years, while still retaining its own characteristics, it will flow in the common channels of the coming civilization of the world.

So far China has already received much benefit from westernization. The freedom of women to be on equal terms with men in social activities, to marry and remarry, and to have their feet unbound has been gained through the influence of Western respect for women. Western medicine has prevented plagues which wrought yearly havoc among the teeming millions. Painless operations have relieved the suffering of thousands of people. Machinery and inventions have improved means of production and contributed much to the enjoyment of life. And it goes without saying that modern weapons of war have also helped people to kill more, and to be killed. Modern science has widened the scope of knowledge; scientific methods have been carried into the study of Chinese history, philosophy, and literature. Above all, the old superstitions in which people used to live are giving way to the enlightenment of scientific truths. The greater our capacity to absorb Western ideas, the more our civilization will be enriched. Poverty and disease, twin curses of Chinese national life, will gradually disappear in proportion to the extent and thoroughness of China's modernization. To me, in this respect, modernization and westernization seem inseparable, if not identical, since the process of modernization began in the West and has gone forward without interruption. So China cannot get one without getting the other.

In a way, modernization has been as much imposed upon the West as westernization upon China. Wherever the spearhead of modern invention passes through, it changes the means of production, creates problems of distribution and control, and thus gives rise to new problems. Men must adjust themselves to changing conditions; the constant changes of environment and adjustments of man to them impose a progress on him. Imagine yourself looking down on Europe after the French Revolution; you would see that there had not been much visible change on the surface

致力吸收西方思想的开端，这种努力在过去只限于工业和政治方面。这次自觉的努力比较更接近中国文化的中心，同时中国文化史也随之转入新页。因为中国正想藉此追上世界潮流。中国文化把罗盘指向西方以后，逐渐调整航线，以期适应西方文化的主流。在今后五十年内，它在保持本身特点的同时，亦必将驶进世界未来文化共同的航道而前进。

到目前为止，中国已经从西化运动中获得很多好处。妇女与男子享受同等的社会地位，享受结婚和再嫁的自由，并且解放缠足，这就是受到西方尊重妇女的影响而来的。西方医药也已阻遏了猖獗的时疫，麻醉药的应用已使千万病人在施行手术时免除痛苦。机器和发明已经改进了生产技术，对于人民的生活提供了重大的贡献。现代作战武器增加了杀伤的能力，因而也招致了更大的生命损失。现代科学已经拓宽了知识范围；中国的历史、哲学和文学的研究工作已采用了科学方法。大家一向信守不疑的迷信，也因科学真理的启示而渐渐失势。我们吸收西方思想的能力愈强，我国的文化亦将愈见丰富。中国的现代化工作愈广泛彻底，则与中国国民生活结着不解缘的贫困和疾病两大祸患亦将随之逐渐消灭。在这一方面，我认为现代化运动和西化运动，即使并非完全相同，也是不可分的，因为现代化运动肇始于西化，而且已经毫无间断地向前迈进。中国无法取此而舍彼。

西方被迫现代化，多少有点像中国之被迫西化。现代发明浪潮所经之处，随即改变了生产的方式，招致分配和控制的问题，并进而引起其他新的问题。人类必须适应日新月异的环境，进步就是由环境的不断改变和人类适应新的环境产生的。你不妨看一看法国革命以后的欧洲情形，你或许会发现自从罗马帝国以来，欧洲大陆在

of that continent since the Roman Empire. But if you took another look half a century after the industrial revolution the changes would be quite noticeable. After still another half century you would find networks of railways covering the surface of all Europe and America, too, with trains crawling on them like thousands of centipedes. Here and there factories with chimneys sticking up would cluster in the large industrial centers like fantastic beehives. Steamboats carrying manufactured goods would be shuttling in and out of harbors, ready to bear the finished products of the factories to all the corners of the earth.

These same steamboats half a century ago brought to China the lucifer matches, clocks, kerosene lamps, toys, and other useful and ingenious foreign articles that I played with in childhood in that tranquil village. The innocent and unconscious absorption of these curious things was the beginning of the great change that was to bring China in line with the trend toward modernization—with all its accompanying sufferings, turmoils, and perils, and with the rapid disappearance of the pleasant, tranquil life of old China.

Heretofore the absorption of foreign elements, conscious or unconscious, had enriched the life of the people and led to no complications. With the absorption of modern Western manufactures and systems or ideas, trouble began to spring up. Like the modern sulfa drugs, they cure diseases but sometimes cause serious reactions, which may prove fatal. To absorb Western civilization with less violence of reaction is the problem China has yet to face. It calls for experiment and scientific research, which again are western products—machine tools to make all modern machinery, mental, social, or industrial.

2. Morals and Intellect

When for the first time I read the Greek philosophers in the ethics class in California I began to feel, as I have said before, that Chinese thinkers in ancient times were enclosed in an atmosphere of morals, while the Greeks possessed the quality of all-piercing intellect. As I read more books on Greek life and culture it became more clear and convincing to me that some such striking contrast did exist between ancient Chinese and Greek thought, and that among other causes this was probably the main one for the divergence in development of Eastern and Western

表面上几无多大改变。但是你如果再仔细看看工业革命以后五十年来的欧洲情形，你一定会发现许多显著的变化。再隔五十年之后，你又会发现整个欧洲大陆和美洲都已经遍布了铁路网，一列列的火车则像千万条蜈蚣爬行在铁路上。烟囱高耸入云的工厂像蜂房一样集中在工业大城里。装载工业成品的轮船在港口穿梭进出，准备把工厂产品运送到世界的每一角落。

半世纪以前，这些轮船曾经把自来火、时辰钟、洋油灯、玩具，以及其他实用和巧妙的外国货带到中国。我童年时代在安宁的乡村里就曾经玩过这些洋货。我们天真而不自觉地吸收这些新鲜的玩艺儿，实际上正是一次大转变的开端，这次转变结果使中国步上现代化之途，同时也经历了相伴而生的苦难、扰攘、危险，以及旧中国恬静生活的迅速消逝。

中国在此以前所吸收的外国东西，不论是自觉的或是不自觉的，都曾使人民生活更见充实丰富，而且并未导致任何纷扰。但是自从西方工业制品和思想制度传入以后，麻烦就来了。正像现代的磺胺药品，它们固然可以治病，但是有时候也会引起严重的副作用，甚至致人于死。中国所面临的问题就是如何吸收西方文化而避免严重的副作用。此项工作有赖于实验与科学研究，因为实验和科学研究是推动心理、社会、工业各项建设的基本工具。不过这些工具仍然是西方的产物。

（二）道德与理智

我在加州大学伦理学班上初次读到希腊哲学家的著作时，我开始觉得中国古代思想家始终囿于道德范围之内，希腊哲学家则有敏锐深刻的理智。后来我读了更多有关希腊生活和文化的书籍以后，更使我深信古代中国思想和古希腊思想之间，的确存在着这种鲜明的对照，同时我相信就是东西文化分道扬镳的主要原因。

civilizations. Perhaps this assertion will seem rather too sweeping, but as my experience grew with the years I could not see it otherwise, and I still believe it to be so.

After my return from abroad I constantly tried to drive home to the minds of my people the importance of the development of intellect. The names of Socrates, Plato, and Aristotle appeared in my lectures and writings so often that I was caricatured by tabloid papers in Shanghai as "a man with mouthfuls of Plato and Aristotle." Seeing that I was not carrying the public with me, I gave it up as a bad job and changed my tactics to preaching the study of natural science. Instead of leading people to the source of the current I reversed the process by letting them see the current first. Naturally they would go back to the sources later on.

My compatriots, children of ages of practical sense, had rebuked me for forgetting the true nature of my own people.

A prominent Chinese scientist once was asked why China has not developed natural science. He offered four reasons: First, the belief of Chinese scholars in Yin, the negative, and Yang, the positive, as complementary principles of the universe. Second, the belief in the Five Elements—metal, wood, water, fire, and earth—as the constituents of the universe, and the application of this analysis of the material world around us to human life, even to medicine. Third, the Chinese rule-of-thumb ways, which are an enemy to accurate calculations. Fourth, the aversion of scholars to using their hands or doing manual work.

All these may be obstacles to the growth of natural science; but quite aside from them I do not believe that natural science would have grown up. It could not, for our attention was not directed along that line.

My people are most interested in things practical—something useful to them. I often noticed in America that when people were shown something they were apt to say, "That's interesting." The response from my own people in like case would be, "What is the use of it?" This shows the truth of the common Chinese saying that the virtuous see virtue while the wise see wisdom in the things they come in contact with. A difference in mental attitude produces different manifestations of interest. The use of a thing interests my people more than the thing itself.

Chinese thinkers see all things in their relation to man, to moral applications, to artistic or poetic sense, or to practical use. The scientific

这种说法也许过于武断，但是据我后来的经验来说，我并未发现有予以修正的必要，而且我至今仍如此深信不疑。

我从美国留学回来以后，曾不断努力使国人了解发展理智的重要，无论是上课或写作，我总是经常提到苏格拉底、柏拉图和亚里士多德等名字，以致若干上海小报讥讽我是"满口柏拉图、亚里士多德的人"。我发现并没有多少人听我这一套，结果只好自认失败而放弃了这项工作，同时改变策略转而鼓吹自然科学的研究。事实上这是一种先后倒置的办法，我不再坚持让大家先去看看源头，反而引大家先去看看水流。他们看到水流以后，自然而然会探本穷源。

有人曾经请教一位著名的中国科学家，为什么中国未曾发展自然科学。他提出四个理由：第一，中国学者相信阴阳是宇宙中相辅相成的两大原则。第二，他们相信金、木、水、火、土，五行是构成宇宙的五大要素，并把这种对物质世界的分析应用到人类生活以及医药方面。第三，中国人的粗枝大叶，不求甚解。这是精确计算的大敌。第四，中国学者不肯用手，鄙夷体力劳动。

这些很可能都是自然科学发展的障碍，但是即使没有这些障碍，我也不相信自然科学就能发展起来，因为我们根本就没有注意到这方面的工作。

我们中国人最感兴趣的是实用东西。我在美国时常常发现，如果有人拿东西给美国人看，他们多半会说："这很有趣呀！"碰到同样情形时，中国人的反应却多半是："这有什么用处？"这真是中国俗语所谓智者见智，仁者见仁。心理状态的不同，所表现的兴趣也就不同了。我们中国对一种东西的用途，比对这种东西的本身更感兴趣。

中国思想对一切事物的观察都以这些事物对人的关系为基础，看它们有无道德上的应用价值，有无艺术价值，是否富于诗意，

thought of ancient Greece found its origin in Egypt and Babylon. Babylonian astronomy and Egyptian geometry, like astronomy and mathematics in China, aimed at practical applications. But the intellectual quality of the Hellenic genius was to seek the *general truth* in these sciences by generalizing and formulating their principles, a process which paved the way for the discovery of natural law.

For the Greeks there were two worlds: the world of the senses and the world of reason. The senses deceive us; therefore the philosopher should not trust his sense impressions but develop his reason. It was not for its practical use that Plato insisted upon the study of geometry, but in order to develop the faculty of abstraction and train the mind to correct and vigorous thinking. Applying these powers to ethics and politics, Plato laid the foundation of Western social philosophy, and by their application in studying the reality of concrete things Aristotle laid the foundation of physical science.

For Aristotle trusted reality as seen through the senses. His was a great systematizing intellect which has left its imprint on nearly every branch of knowledge. For him, to know properly involved a correct use of the senses as well as of the reason; the advance of science depends upon development of both speculation and observation. From applied mathematics Aristotle deduced certain general laws, the study and exploration of which provided a form of mental gymnastics through which he disciplined a powerful and penetrating intellect. And by means of the same well-exercised intellect and right use of the senses, he created a system of knowledge which has been the foundation of modern science. Logic and the theory of knowledge were outgrowths of these same intellectual exercises which systematized Western thought.

Chinese thought is centered upon the development of human relations. We are interested in natural laws only so far as they are capable of serving as guides for human conduct. The *Great Learning*, one of the Confucian classics, taught us a system of knowledge to which I have alluded in an earlier chapter. It starts with the search for truths in things, from which we gain our knowledge. Knowledge is the power by which the mind is developed.

So far the story is intellectual. But as it goes on the shading of moral sense begins to grow. Mental development is for personal culture, which

是否切合实用。古希腊的科学思想源于埃及与巴比伦。巴比伦的天文学和埃及的几何学，和中国天文数学一样，都以实际应用为目的。但是希腊学者具有重理知的特性，他们概括并简化各种科学原则，希望由此求出这些科学的通理。这种追求通理的过程为天然律的发现铺平了道路。

对希腊人而言，一共有两个世界：即官觉世界与理性世界。官觉有时会弄玄虚；所以哲学家不能信赖他的官觉的印象，而必须发展他的理性。柏拉图坚主研究几何学，并不是为了几何学的实际用途，而是想发展思想的抽象力，并训练心智使之能正确而活泼地思考。柏拉图把思想的抽象力和正确的思考能力应用在伦理与政治上，结果奠定了西方社会哲学的基础；亚里士多德把它们应用在研究具体事物的真实性上，结果奠定了物质科学的基础。

亚里士多德相信由官觉所得知识的真实性。他并有惊人的分析的理智力，他的这种理智力几乎在任何学问上都留有痕迹。他认为正确的知识不但需要正确地运用理性，同时也牵涉到官觉的正确运用；科学的进步则同时仰赖推理能力和观察能力的发展。亚里士多德从应用数学演绎出若干通则，研究与探讨这些原则是一种心智的锻炼，他便由此训练出一种有力而深刻的理智力。凭着这种训练有素的理智力以及官觉的正确运用，他创造了一套成为现代化科学基础的知识系统。使西方思想系统化的逻辑和知识理论也同是这种理智锻炼的产物。

中国思想集中于伦理关系的发展上。我们之对天然律发生兴趣，只是因为它们有时可以作为行为的准则。《四书》之一的《大学》曾经提出一套知识系统，告诉我们应该先从格物着手，然后才能致知。知识是心智发展的动力。

到此为止，我们所谈的还是属于知识方面的。讨论再进一步以后，道德的意味就加强了。心智发展是修身的一部分，修身

in turn will serve as the foundation for a well-ordered family life. The latter is the foundation of a well-governed state, which in turn will serve as a step toward international peace. From the rudiments of knowledge down to international peace this forms a complete scheme of practical moral idealism. To the Chinese, world peace is not something to be dreamed about but a practical moral scheme. For national prosperity is invariably bound up with peace between nations. A type of knowledge which does not lead to this end is but secondary or trifling.

For such an attitude toward learning, to ascertain whether the earth goes round the sun or the sun round the earth is but trivial.

Or again, what is the use of bothering with the expansion of water in a boiling kettle, as Watt did if we are to believe the story? The Chinese would be more interested in the hissing sound, which suggests making tea in preparation for guests. It is poetic.

The drop of an apple to the ground is only natural. The Chinese would moralize it. They would say that when a thing is ripe, it drops. When you do things in a proper way they come to their natural conclusion. There is no use in puzzling about it. Should the apples in your garden shoot up to the sky, it would set the Chinese to fearing that some great calamity might fall upon the people; as would the appearance of a comet, or some other perversion of the familiar order of things. It would take a Newton to think along the line of the attraction of the earth.

Thus with my own effort to preach. What is the use to China of those figures of Greek antiquity or their teachings? In my people's eyes natural science is useful only because practical uses come out of it. The Greek philosophers are remote even from modern natural sciences. What earthly use is there in them? The Chinese are in sympathy with the usefulness of science but recoil from the idea of science for science' sake. "Learning is for the sake of its use," is an accepted dictum among Chinese scholars.

With such a mental attitude it is small wonder that China has not developed pure science, an elaboration of intellectual interest rather than of practical considerations. We built the Great Wall and the Grand Canal and developed a system of irrigation; the grandeur of our architectural design, our palaces and temples, has inspired world-wide admiration. These works are among the greatest engineering feats the world has ever

则是齐家的基础。齐家而后方能治国，国治而后方能平天下。从格物致知到平天下恰恰形成一个完整的、非常实际的、道德上的理想体系。在中国人看起来，世界和平绝非梦想，而是实际的道德体系。因为国家的安定必然是与国际和平密切关联的。离开此目标的任何知识都是次要的或无关痛痒的。

在这种学问态度之下，查问地球究竟绕日而行，抑或太阳绕地球而运行，原是无关痛痒的事。

再说，我们何苦为沸水的膨胀而伤脑筋？瓦特实在太傻了！我们中国人倒是对沸水的嘶嘶声更感兴趣，因为这种声音可以使我们联想到煮茗待客的情调。那该多么富于诗意！

苹果落地是自然的道理，中国人可以在这件事情上找出道德意义。他们会说，一样东西成熟了自然就掉下来。因此，你如果好好地做一件事情，自然就会得到应有的结果，为此多伤脑筋毫无好处。如果你家花园里的苹果不是往地下落，而是往天上飞，那倒可能使中国人惴惴不安，认为老百姓即将遭逢劫难。彗星出现，或者其他习见情形失常，中国人就是如此解释的。只有牛顿这种人才会从苹果落地想到地心吸力上面去。

我一度鼓吹发展理智，结果徒劳无功，原因不言而喻。这些古希腊人物和他们的学说对中国有什么用？在我们中国人的眼光里，自然科学的价值只是因为它们能够产生实际的用途。希腊哲学家离现代自然科学太远了，他们还有些什么实际用途？我们中国人对科学的用途是欣赏的，但是对为科学而科学的观念却不愿领教。中国学者的座右铭就是"学以致用"。

在这样的心理状态之下，中国未能发展纯粹科学是毫不足奇的，因为纯粹科学是知识兴趣的表现，而非实际应用的产物。我们曾经建造长城和运河，也曾建设伟大的水利工程；我国建筑式样的宏丽，我们的宫殿和庙宇，都曾获得举世人士的激赏。这些工程足与世界上

known. But they were not developed from a foundation of pure science and therefore, however remarkable they were, no further development was possible until modern engineering came to the rescue. For without pure science the applied science of modern engineering could not attain its present high plane. The discovery of the compass and gunpowder by the Chinese has served useful purposes in the world. But it was a Western mind that observed the principle of explosive expansion in gunpowder and applied it to boiling water, thus making possible the discovery of steam power.

In China discoveries stopped at their immediate practical use. We did not, like the Greeks, try to venture into generalization; nor, like modern Europeans, did we try to get universal laws from particular discoveries—a trait inherited from the Hellenic world in its improved form. Once the useful purposes of an invention were served, we stopped there; therefore Chinese science traveled unaided and without the guiding light of scientific thought. The development of science in China was arrested because we were too practical-minded.

I do not mean to say that the Chinese do not think logically. But their minds were not aided by systematic mental gymnastics. This defect has been reflected in Chinese philosophy, political and social organization, and daily life. It has become more glaring as the rest of the world came to live under the light of modern science in an industrialized society.

Besides being practical, our people are imbued with a sound moral sense. It may also be said that because we are moral we are practical. For morals refer to conduct, which is necessarily judged by practical results. There will be no such fanciful ideas or speculation about conduct as the Greeks had with physics and metaphysics.

At times we may venture beyond that practical moral way of thinking, but the antennae of our minds recoil as soon as we feel we are getting away from the sphere of human relations, and stop right there. A Sung philosopher of the twelfth century once stepped over the moral bounds by speculating on the formation of mountain ranges and on the finding of seashells on the tops of mountains. He observed that the waves of the mountain ranges indicated the fluidity of the mountains many thousands of years earlier, while the shells bore witness to the fact that

最伟大的工程成就相提并论。但是它们并不是纯粹科学的基础上发展而来的。因此它们无论如何伟大，也没有进一步发展的可能，直到现代工程技术输入以后，才见转机。如果没有纯粹科学，现代工程科学根本无法达到目前的巅峰状态。中国人所发明的指南针和火药曾使全世界普受其利，但是发现火药爆炸的膨胀原理，把这原理应用于沸水，并进而发明蒸汽机的，结果还是西洋人。

在中国，发明通常止于直接的实际用途。我们不像希腊人那样肯在原理原则上探讨；也不像现代欧洲人那样设法从个别的发现中归纳出普遍的定律。现代欧洲人的这种习性是从古希腊继承而来的，不过较诸希腊时代更进步而已。中国人一旦达到一件新发明的实用目的，就会马上止步不前；因此中国科学的发展是孤立无援的，也没有科学思想足为导向的明灯。科学发展在中国停滞不进，就是因为我们太重实际。

我并不是说中国人不根据逻辑思考，而是说他们的思想没有受到精密的系统的训练。这缺点已经反映在中国哲学、政治组织、社会组织，以及日常生活之中。世界其余各地的人民普遍享受现代科学的光明和工业社会的福利以后，这种缺点在中国已经更见显著。

除了重实际之外，我们中国人还充满着强烈的道德观念。也可以说正因为我们注重道德，我们才重实际。因为道德系指行为而言，行为则必然要凭实际结果来判断。希腊人在物理学和形而上学方面曾有离奇的幻想和推测，但是我们对行为却不可能有同样的幻想和推测。

有时候我们也可能闯出重实际、重道德的思想常规，但是我们一旦发觉离开伦理范围太远时，我们马上就会收回心灵的触角。宋代的朱子就曾有一次超越道德的范围。他从山顶上发现的贝壳而推断到山脉的成因。他认为山势的起伏显示千万年以前的山脉一定是一种流体，山顶上的贝壳正可以说明，目前的山峰一度曾是深渊之底。

their peaks must once have been at the bottom of the sea. But when and how the fluid suddenly coagulated into mountains, and how the bottom of the sea was raised to such a height, he had no means of discovering. There he stopped, fearing shipwreck if he should venture too far. There have been similar instances of observing nature both before and after this philosopher, but Chinese thinkers were always scrupulous, in their mental excursions, not to drift too far away from the camp of human relations.

That the Chinese are not a nonintellectual people needs no proof as it is so evident; but their intellect was exercised within the sphere of morals and practical uses. Thus they set limits to their own intellectual activities. Like silkworms, they wove their moral cocoons with threads drawn from their own minds, as it were, to encase themselves. And they loved their encasement and felt comfortable in it. Chinese life is a life of contentedness. Stability is aimed at in Chinese philosophy. Progress? No—it will create discontent, which will destroy stability. The Chinese is contented with his immediate world and has never wanted to speculate far and deep in nature. China has not produced natural science because she did not want it.

The Greeks were quite a different sort of people. Aristotle's mind ventured high up into the heavens, low down beneath the earth, and far away beyond the corners of the land. The universe was material for the exercise of Greek intellect. To the Greeks the mere use of the intellect was a pleasure. They did not care much about whether it was practical or had anything to do with morals or human relations. "What do I get by learning these things?" asked a pupil of Euclid. "Give him sixpence, since he must make gain out of what he learns," said Euclid to his servant, as the story runs. Even with morals they developed a system of ethics, looking into the validity of moral laws through intellectual inquiry, and this was how Socrates got into trouble, being accused of poisoning the souls of young people with dangerous questionings.

Out of Greek ideas about nature and love of intellectual exercise in systematic thinking—flowing intermittently through the Renaissance, the Reformation, and the French Revolution and receiving great impetus from the industrial revolution, through which it gradually improved its instruments and technique—natural science has grown to its modern stage. The practical considerations of science were never neglected in

至于这种流体何时凝结为山脉，如何凝结为山脉，以及海底如何突出水面而成高峰等等问题，他却无法解答了。他的推断也就到此为止，深恐冒险前进要栽筋斗。在朱子之前以及朱子之后都曾有过同样的观察自然的例子，但是中国思想家在理论方面的探讨一向是谨慎的，惟恐远离伦理关系的范围。

中国人当然不是缺乏理智的民族；但是他们的理智活动却局限于道德与实用的范围。他们像蚕一样作茧自缚，自立智识活动的界限。他们深爱他们的道德之茧，而且安居不出。中国人的生活就是一种乐天知命的生活。中国哲学的目标是安定。求进步？算了吧——进步势将招致对现状的不满，不满现状则会破坏安定，中国人很满意现实世界，从来不想对大自然作深入的探讨。中国未曾发展自然科学，只是因为她根本无意于此。

希腊人却大不相同。亚里士多德的思想可以上天入地，无远弗届。整个宇宙都是希腊理智活动的范围。希腊人觉得运用理智，本身就是一种快乐。他们不管它是否切合实际，也不管它与道德伦理有没有关系。据说古希腊数学家欧几里得的一位学生曾经这样问过老师："我学这些东西能得到些什么呢？"欧几里得吩咐他的仆人说："既然他一定要从所学的里面得到些东西，你就给他六个铜板让他走吧。"希腊人甚至对道德也发展了一套伦理学，以理智的研究来检讨道德的正确性。苏格拉底就是因此而招致了麻烦，被控以危险的研究毒害青年的心灵。

自然科学之能发展到目前的阶段，首先归功于希腊人对大自然的观念以及对有系统的智力训练的爱好，中间经过文艺复兴、宗教革命、法国革命，后来又受到工业革命的大刺激。工业革命使工具和技术逐渐改进。西欧在自然科学的后期发展中，从未忽视科学的

its later development in Europe. Frequent inventions and discoveries gave further impetus to scientific research. Scientific generalizations and applied science marched shoulder to shoulder. So the influences of pure and applied science react one upon another to their mutual benefit.

When modern science began to trickle into China after the opening of the commercial ports, it was its practical value that attracted the attention of the Chinese scholars. They built arsenals and dockyards. Incidentally they translated books on elementary science. They were not interested in whether the sun goes round the earth or vice versa; it was immaterial to them, since the alternatives had no practical consequence in their relation to man. More than a century earlier, when the Jesuits brought mathematics and astronomy to the court of the Ming emperors, scholars were interested because these sciences would mend the deficiencies then found to exist in the Chinese calendar. For the calendar is indispensable not only for reckoning days, months, and years but also for sowing and harvesting.

Around the beginning of the twentieth century the theory of evolution was brought into China. Chinese scholars at once saw the practical moral significance of it. With the application of a natural law of "struggle for existence," "natural selection," and "survival of the fittest," they came to the conclusion that nations in the world were struggling for existence, and through natural selection only the fittest would survive. Would China be the fittest and would she survive? She must struggle— struggle for existence. As to the validity of the theory, they had no particular interest and no scientific background to start an investigation, anyhow. Right away they threw a moral cushion over the intellectual undertaking of Darwin. At once they moralized it by saying, "The flesh of the weak is the food of the strong." Being a weak nation, China had to worry about her flesh. Countrymen, arise! It is your duty to your country to look out for the "cannibal" nations around us!

Another phase of the theory of evolution was taken up in its application to history. History goes round in a circle, the Chinese scholars believed. Under the influence of Darwinism they recast their old belief into a new faith that history forges ahead, or else recedes, or remains stationary. This change in the conception of history exercised a paramount influence upon the minds of Chinese scholars in regard to progress.

实际用途。不断的发现和发明更进一步刺激了科学研究。理论科学和应用科学齐头并进，而相辅相成。

五口通商以后，现代科学开始涓涓滴滴地流传到中国时，引起中国学者注意的还是科学的实用价值。他们建立了兵工厂和轮船码头。他们附带翻译了基本科学的书籍。究竟是太阳绕地球运行或者是地球绕太阳运行，他们仍未感觉兴趣。在他们看起来，那是无足轻重的，因为无论谁绕谁转，对人都没有实际的影响。三百多年前耶稣会教士把天文数学传到中国时，学者们马上发生兴趣，因为这些科学可以纠正当时中国日历上的许多错误。不但计算日子、月份、年份缺不得日历，就是播种收获，日历也是不可或缺的。

二十世纪初叶，进化论传入中国。我国学者马上发现它的实用的道德价值。应用"物竞天择，适者生存"这项天然律，他们得到一项结论，知道世界各国正在互相竞争以求生存，而且经过天择之后只有适者才能生存。中国会不会是适者？她会不会生存呢？她必须竞争，为生存而竞争！进化论如需证据，只要看街头大狗和小狗打架，小狗会被大狗咬死，小虫碰到大虫，小虫会被大虫吃掉的事实。俗语说："大虫吃小虫，小虫吃眯眯虫。"这已经足够证明"物竞天择，适者生存"的正确性了，又何必向达尔文讨证据呢？他们就这样轻易地为达尔文的科学研究披上了一件道德的外衣。下面就是他们道德化的结果，他们说："弱肉强食。"中国既然是弱国，那就得当心被虎视眈眈的列强吃掉才行。

进化论的另一面则被应用于历史上，照中国过去学者的历史观，世运是循环的。受了达尔文学说影响以后，他们相信世运是依直线进行的，不进则退，或者停住不动。这种历史观的转变，对中国学者有关进步这一观念产生了重大的影响。

The conceptions of Yin and Yang and the Five Elements undoubtedly grew out of naïve observations of nature. They were good enough for rationalizing the conduct of nature and man. No minute calculations were necessary, much less the use of the hands. I presume that if Chinese scholars were interested in manual work, they would apply it to making useful or beautiful objects of art rather than to experiments in the scientific laboratory. People would still think and do only along the lines where their interests lay. The magnetic needle will only point in the direction of the magnetic pole.

Such an attitude of mind is of course no fertile soil for pure science. However, slowly but steadily China is modifying her attitude—from applied science she has been led to pure science, from pure science to new ways of thinking, and finally to actual modification of her attitude of mind. We have opened windows in the walls of our moral universe and looked into the gardens of a new intellectual universe where the fruits of science and invention abound.

This modification of mental attitude has set a new value upon nature—nature as the pure scientist sees it and not only as the moralist or poet sees it. The universe to the modern Chinese is not only a moral one as the ancient Chinese saw it but also an intellectual one as the Greeks saw it.

The moralist studies nature with a view to finding its laws for the benefit of human relations. The scientist studies it with a view to finding its natural laws for intellectual interest—knowledge for the sake of knowledge. China's absorption of modern science has penetrated through these moral bounds of her universe and the minds of the modern Chinese are reaching further and further out to search for truths. Their thinking has been becoming more adventurous, like a ship sailing in unknown seas, exploring for hidden treasures. In other aspects this intellectual release has caused the minds of the younger generation to adopt a critical attitude toward traditional ideas—make critical inquiries into morals, government, and social customs—with far-reaching consequences. While men of the older generation have been very much alarmed at the possible destruction of their tranquil moral abodes and have lamented the passing of the good old days, the younger generation has busied itself in building a new intellectual edifice.

All that, I think, is one of the most valuable contributions that the West has made to China.

阴阳和五行等观念显然是从直接观察大自然得来，拿这些观念来理性化宇宙的变幻和人类的行为已经绰有余裕。我们不必作精密的计算，更不必动手。我猜想，中国学者如果有兴趣从事体力劳动，他们宁愿去制作实用的东西，或者美丽的艺术品，而不愿在科学实验室里从事试验。大家仍旧只根据自己的兴趣去思想，去行动。磁针永远是指向磁极的。

这样的心理状态自然不是纯粹科学的园地。不过中国已在慢慢地、不断地改变她的态度，她已经从运用科学进而研究纯粹科学，从纯粹科学进而接触到新的思想方法，最后终于切实修正了她的心理状态。我们已经在道德宇宙的墙上开了一扇窗子，凭窗可以眺望长满科学与发明果实的理智的宇宙。

这种心理状态的改变已经使大自然有了新的价值，从此以后，大自然不再仅仅是道德家或诗人心目中的大自然，而且是纯粹科学家心目中的大自然。对现代中国人而言，宇宙不仅是我国先贤圣哲心目中的道德宇宙，而且是古希腊人心目中的理智宇宙。

道德家观察大自然的目的在于发现有利伦理道德的自然法则。科学家观察大自然则是为了发现自然法则，满足知识上的兴趣，也就是为知识而求知识。中国所吸收的现代科学已经穿越她那道德宇宙的藩篱，近代中国学人正深入各处探求真理。他们的思想愈来愈大胆，像一只小舟在浩瀚的海洋上扬帆前进搜寻秘密的宝藏。这种知识上的解放已经使年轻的一代对某些传统观念采取了批评的态度，对道德、政治和社会习俗予以严厉的检讨，其影响至为深远。年纪较大的一代忧虑宁静的道德乐园将被毁灭，惋叹太平盛世渐成过去，年轻的一代则为建筑新的知识之宫而竟日忙碌。

我想这就是西方对中国的最大贡献。

Inversely, as the Greeks found with the Babylonian and Egyptian sciences, a study of Chinese sciences may yield profitable contributions to the modern scientific world. A modest beginning made in recent years in the scientific study of Chinese architecture, medicine, and economic botany has yielded fruitful results.

Civilizations are built around different systems of the universe as men conceive it. The Chinese conceived a moral universe, around which they built their civilization. The Greeks conceived an intellectual universe, around which they built theirs. European morals as they are today have been drawn from Christianity—a moral universe as revealed through God. On the other hand, the Chinese moral universe is as revealed through nature's ways. The Christians have endeavored to build a kingdom of heaven on earth, while the Chinese were content with trying to build a kingdom of peace and stability.

Chinese morals are derived from nature; Christian morals from divine power; for the Chinese the gods are but part of nature, while to Christians nature is but the creation of God. On these grounds it is plain that the conflicts between Christian dogma and science were bound to be very serious, as Western history has proven in abundance; while the conflicts between science and Chinese moral precepts would be mild since both started from the same ground—nature—only traveling in different directions.

It has been said that Christian thought is heavenly or godly, Chinese thought is worldly, and Greek thought unworldly. It is this unworldly thought that has led men to the discovery of the natural laws which are the foundation of modern science and hence of modern invention. The unworldly thought in the applications of science has brought prosperity to the world, if not peace and stability.

The development of European civilization, as I see it, is a struggle at various times between the Christian moral universe and the Greek intellectual universe. The Renaissance, the Reformation, and the French Revolution were but the bursting out of a submerged intellectual universe under the domination of a moral one—these various movements were only different phases of the same current. Finally came the industrial revolution in which the same intellectual universe, continuously developing through centuries, came to the surface in an overwhelming

在相反的一方面，把中国的学问加以整理研究，也可能对现代科学世界提供重大的贡献，希腊人研究巴比伦和埃及科学的结果就是如此。近年来对中国建筑、医学和实用植物学的初步科学研究已经有了可喜的成绩。

世界各国的文化奠基于不同的宇宙观。中国人所想的是一个道德的宇宙，并以此为基础而发展了他们的文化。希腊人所想的是一个理智的宇宙，也以此为基础发展了他们的文化。今日欧洲人的道德观念导源于基督教教义——一个上帝所启示的道德的宇宙。但中国人的道德宇宙是自然法则所启示的。基督徒努力想在地球上建立一个天国，中国人却只想建立一个和平安定的王国。

中国道德观念本诸自然，基督的道德观念则本诸神权；在中国人看起来，神只是大自然的一部分，在基督徒看起来，大自然却是上帝所创造的。由此可见基督教教条与科学之间的矛盾必然是很严重的，西方历史已经一再证明如此；科学与中国的道德观念之间的矛盾却比较缓和，因为二者的出发点都是大自然，所不同的只是发展的方向。

有人说过，基督教思想是天国的或神国的，中国思想是为人世的，希腊思想是不为人世的，换言之，即越出人世以外的。引导人类发现自然法则的就是这种超越人世的思想。自然法则是现代科学的基础。有了现代科学，然后才有现代发明。这种不为人世的思想在科学上应用的结果，如果说未为世界带来和平与安定，至少也已为世界带来繁荣。

据我个人的看法，欧洲文化的发展过程就是基督教的道德宇宙与希腊的理智宇宙之间的一部斗争史。文艺复兴、宗教革命和法国革命，都不过是长久淹没在道德宇宙下的理智宇宙的重现而已，这些运动事实上只是同一潮流中的不同阶段。最后工业革命爆发，理智宇宙经过

torrent and swept aside everything in its way. Its spearhead had already taken China unawares before and during the time of my childhood; it pierced our moral universe, burst out later to destroy the stability of Chinese life, and thus furnished the materials for the writing of this volume.

One universe cannot be expected to produce the fruits of another. The fruits of the tree of science ripen in intellectual gardens alone— within the system of Christian dogma or that of Chinese moral precepts no science could have been produced.

Though, indeed, we find much scientific thought in Mencius[2] in ancient times, this is a nonessential part of his philosophical system. Such thoughts are but satellites to a planet; his system is fundamentally moral.

For science grows out of man's whole being, a burning desire for unworldly truths; a fearless, ever-searching intellect with unbiased spirit continuously reaching out for truth, and an indomitable vigor of mind and body; in other words, it grows out of the very soul of man in his intellectual world. No mere side interests or occasional excursions of the mind into nature, or lukewarm desire to understand it, could ever crown man with the glorious garland of science.

In China, under the influence of modern science, there is growing up a new moral edifice stripped of superstition and false analogies to nature; tested through intellectual inquiry and supported by findings of social science based upon methods adapted from physical research to the investigation of society.

On the other hand we must not forget that the old Chinese moral edifice, built up through centuries of vicarious experience and generations of continuous effort, by such various means as the Confucian classics, literature in general, the graphic arts, music, the family, theatre, gods, temples, even toys—this moral structure has made Chinese people trustworthy, their society stable, and their civilization enduring. Such moral precepts as loyalty, honesty, love of parents, truthfulness, benevolence, righteousness, moderation, and broad-mindedness have contributed much toward the moral emotional make-up of the Chinese people. Intellectual honesty that grows out of modern science will reinforce these virtues that have grown out of ages of moral teaching.

几百年的不断发展，终于涌出水面，奔腾澎湃，横扫全球。工业革命狂潮的前锋，在我童年时代前后已经突然冲到中国；它冲破了我们的道德宇宙，破坏了我们的安定生活；《西潮》所讲的正是这些故事。

道德宇宙不可能产生理智宇宙的果实，理智宇宙也不可能产生道德宇宙的果实。科学之果只能在理智之园成长，在基督教教条或中国的道德观念之下，不可能产生任何科学。

不错，我们发现古时的墨子也有过科学思想，但是那只是他哲学体系中无关紧要的一部分，这些科学思想只是行星的卫星，墨子的哲学体系基本上仍旧是属于道德方面的。

科学的发展有赖于人们全力以赴，需要对超越人世以外的真理持有梦寐以求的热忱；并且有赖于不屈不挠、无休无止的思维和不偏不倚的精神去探索真理；无论身心，均须不辞劳瘁，愈挫愈奋。换一句话说，科学是人的整个灵魂从事知识活动的结果。仅凭玩票的态度，或者偶而探讨大自然的奥秘，或者意态阑珊，不求甚解，绝不可能使人类荣获科学的桂冠。

在现代科学影响之下，中国正在建立起一个新的道德体系。扬弃了迷信和那些对大自然似是而非的推断，经过理智探究的考验，并受到社会科学结论的支持，这些结论是根据对社会的实地调查而获得的。

在另一方面，我们绝不可忘记中国旧的道德体系，这个旧体系是经过千百年长期的经验和历代不断的努力而建立起来的，建立过程中所运用的方法或工具包括四书五经、一般文学、雕刻、音乐、家庭、戏剧、神佛、庙宇，甚至玩具，这个道德体系曾使中国人诚实可靠，使中国社会安定平静，并使中国文化历久不衰。道德观念如忠、孝、仁、义、诚、信、中庸、谦冲、诚实等等都曾对中国人的心情个性有过重大贡献。现代科学所导致的知识上的忠实态度，自将使几千年来道德教训所产生的这些美德，更为发扬光大。

Side by side with the new moral universe, a new intellectual edifice will be raised to house the achievements of the creative genius of young China. On the stem of the Confucian system of knowledge, which starts with the investigation of things, or nature, and leads to human relationships, we shall graft the Western system of scientific knowledge, which starts with the same investigation of things or nature but leads the other way round to their interrelationships.

As in the West, the moral universe will co-exist in China with the intellectual, one for stability and the other for progress. Can we strike the happy mean?

3. The Practical Wisdom of the Chinese People

Learning is for the sake of its use. What is this use? It comes under two main principles. First, whatever has to do with the elevation of moral sentiments in the masses and with the cultivation of right moral attitudes in the individual. Second, whatever will contribute to national prosperity and the people's livelihood. These principles are the summary of ages of teachings from the sages and scholars. Whatever they say and teach has come eventually to these. Scholars learned them and diffused their learning to the common people. The common people, under this influence, through ages of accumulated effort have gradually and unconsciously developed a mentality, as the reader will readily see, of common sense and practical wisdom. They have kept on asking what is the use of this or that in the light of these same principles.

When trains and steamboats came to China, people were ready to ride on them because they went much faster. They used kerosene oil because it gave more light. Telephone and telegraph facilities transmit messages without the necessary delay of mail or foot—or even house— messengers. Clocks and watches give exact time without looking at the sun. People bought Western manufactures because they served useful purposes in daily life.

When missionaries came they established schools and hospitals. What wonderful people they are, said the Chinese: they heal the sick and educate the children of the poor. When the Chinese assembled to listen to the preaching of the gospel, the eyes of a number of them were usually directed toward the hospitals or the schools. Through the leaves of the

一片新的知识园地将与新的道德观念同时建立起来，以供新中国富于创造能力天才的发展。我们将在儒家知识系统的本干上移接西方的科学知识。儒家的知识系统从探究事物或大自然出发，而以人与人的关系为归趋；西方的科学知识系统也同样从探究事物或大自然出发，但以事物本身之间的相互关系为归趋，发展的方向稍有不同。

道德宇宙与理智宇宙将和在西方一样在中国平行并存，一个保持安定，一个促成进步。问题在于我们是否能觅得中庸之道。

（三）中国人的人情

我们说，学以致用，那末所谓"用"又是什么呢？这里有两大原则：第一是有益于世道人心，第二是有益于国计民生。这是为世俗所熟知的，亦即《左传》里所说的"正德利用厚生"。这两大原则是先贤圣哲几千年来训诲的总结，他们所说所论，最后总是归结到这两点。学者们从先贤学到这些原则，然后又把所学传播给老百姓。老百姓在这种影响之下已逐渐而不自觉地形成一种重常识与重人情的心理。他们根据上述两大原则，随时要问这样东西有什么用，那样东西有什么用。

轮船火车传到中国时，大家都很愿意搭乘，因为它们走得比较快。他们采用洋油灯，因为洋油灯比较亮。电话电报使消息传递更为便利，而且不像邮寄或者专差送递那样迟缓。有了钟表以后，可以不必看太阳就知道正确的时刻。大家购买西方货品，因为它们能够满足日常生活中的实际需要。

传教士到了中国以后，到处设立学校和医院。中国人异口同声地说：这些人真了不起啊，他们为患病者诊疗，又使贫穷的子弟受教育。当中国人上礼拜堂听福音时，许多人的眼睛却

Holy Bible they peeped at the useful things of Western manufacture the preacher had brought to China from his homeland. My father made friends with a local missionary because he repaired our water pumps and gave us cough drops and quinine powder. He was honest and friendly in dealing with his neighbors. The last is important because the Chinese are both practical and moral. What about the religion they taught us? Oh—that is a good religion. It teaches people to be good. What about their God? Oh, yes. Their God? He is a good God. Put him in our temples beside many other good gods. We'll worship him, burn candles and incense before him. But He will not sit in your temples beside your idols. Well, we'll make an idol for him. No, that can't be done. He is omnipotent and omnipresent. God is in you, not in the idol. Yes, yes. When he is not in me, maybe he likes to be in an idol. No, He is in heaven. Yes, I know he is, as all the other gods are. Maybe he wants to take a trip down to earth and use the temples as his hotels. Then we can worship him there. No, He is the only God—when you worship Him you cannot worship other gods.

Then our people would hesitate and say, you worship yours; we will worship ours. "There it is if you believe it so; it is not there if you do not believe it." Herein lies China's wisdom of religious toleration.

Modern legal sense as the West understands it is not developed in China. Avoid the courts if you can. Let us settle our disputes without going to law. Let's compromise. Let's have a cup of tea and sip together with friends and talk things over. It is much less expensive, much less troublesome, and much fairer. What is the use of going to law? You often see stone tablets on the highways near a hsien capital bearing these bold letters: "DO NOT GO TO LAW."

This may be the reason for the nonlegal-mindedness of the Chinese. But as modern industry and commerce grow, society will grow in complexity, and laws for governing the complicated social relations will be necessary. When laws become a necessity, the practical wisdom of the Chinese will see to it that we are more legal-minded. But would it not lessen the burdens of the courts if people should settle their cases by sipping a cup of tea?

瞅在医院和学校上面。他们的手里虽然拿着《圣经》，眼睛却偷偷地瞅着牧师从西方故乡带来的实用货品。我父亲与当地的一位牧师交了朋友，因为这位牧师替我们修好了抽水机，并且还送给我们咳嗽糖和金鸡纳霜。他非常诚实，而且对邻居很客气。最后一点非常重要，因为中国人不但实际，而且最重道德。那末，他们所宣扬的宗教怎么样？哦，那是一个好宗教，它是劝人为善的。那末，他们的上帝呢？哦，当然，当然。你说他们的上帝吗？他是个好上帝呀。我们要把它与其他好神佛一齐供奉在庙宇里。我们应崇拜它，在它的面前点起香烛。但是它不肯与你们的偶像并供在庙宇里又怎么办呢？那末，我们就给它也塑个偶像吧！不行，那怎么可以？它是无所不能，无所不在的。上帝就在你身上，而不是在偶像上。哦，是的，是的。不过它不在我身上时，也许喜欢托身在偶像上呢。不，它住在天堂。是，是，我知道，其它神佛不也都是住在天上吗？不过，他也许愿意到下界来玩玩，拿庙宇作旅馆暂住，那时候我们就可以在庙宇里祭拜它了。不行，它是独一无二的神——你崇拜它，就不能崇拜其他的神佛。

这可使中国人颇费踌躇了。最后他们说，好吧，你们崇拜你们的上帝，我们还是崇拜我们的神佛算了。"信者有，不信者无。"中国对宗教的包容并蓄，其故在此。

西方人所了解的现代法律观念在中国尚未充分发展。中国人以为最好是不打官司。不必诉诸法律就能解决纠纷不是很好吗？还是妥协算了！让我们喝杯茶，请朋友评个理，事情不就完了？这样可以不必费那么多钱，不必那么麻烦，而且也公平得多。打官司有什么用？你常常可以在县城附近的大路旁边看到一些石碑，上面刻着"莫打官司"四个大字。

这或许就是中国人不重法律的原因。但是现代工商业发达以后，社会也跟着变得复杂了，处理复杂的社会关系的法律也成为必需的东西，法律成为必需时，通达人情的中国人自将设法发展法律观念。但是，如果能凭饮杯茶，评个理就解决事端，法院的负担不是可以减轻了吗？

Do not do unto others what you would not have others do unto you. Critics say this is negative, while "Do unto others what you would have others do unto you" is positive. Yes, that is true. But the Chinese prefer the negative, from practical sense. You may like onions, so you try to force them upon others. That is positive. Onions may taste good to me, but others may not have the same feeling; they may fear them as ladies do rats. If you were not a lover of this obnoxious vegetable, would you like others to impose it upon you? No, of course not. Then why should you impose it upon others? It's negative, but it's more sensible. For the positive way, if you persist, will lead to trouble, while the negative way will avoid it.

Love your friend, be fair to your enemy. Of course it is a higher ideal to love your enemy. But how many in all history have ever loved their enemy? It looks like hitching your wagon to a star—it is something unattainable. It is practical idealism to be fair to your enemy. So the Chinese prefer it to pure idealism.

Is there any use in music? Yes, it is very useful. It can bring the feelings of an individual to harmony. It can raise the morals of a people to a higher level.

Is there any use in the arts? Yes, they are very useful. They will cultivate the finer sense of the people and thus raise their morals to a higher level. Landscape gardening, splendid palaces and temples, landscape painting, literature, poetry, calligraphy, porcelains, bronzes, skillful carvings, and the like all cultivate this finer sense in man.

Why must a man be honest? Because if you are dishonest and untrustworthy people will not believe and trust you. Then you will fail in business and in dealing with other people. Dishonesty simply does not pay. Not only is honesty a virtue, but its practical results are invaluable to human relations.

The Chinese love humor. Why? Because you can say things without offending people; besides, you can get a lot of innocent pleasure from it.

You can get along with people better by innocent and amusing suggestions. Humor makes company more congenial and life more enjoyable.

Perseverance is one of the great virtues necessary to success. If you keep on filing and filing, you will break the steel. If you keep on grinding and grinding, you will shape the precious stone.

己所不欲，勿施于人。批评家说这是消极的，"己之所欲，施之于人"才算积极。不错，这说法很正确。但是中国人基于实际的考虑，还是宁愿采取消极的作风。你也许喜欢大蒜，于是你就想强迫别人也吃大蒜，那是积极的作法。我也许觉得大蒜味道好，别人却未必有同样的感觉；他们也许像太太小姐怕老鼠一样怕大蒜。如果你不爱好臭味冲天的大蒜，难道你会高兴别人硬塞给你吃吗？不，当然不。那末，你又何必硬塞给别人呢？这是消极的，可是很聪明。因为坚持积极的办法很可能惹出麻烦，消极的作风则可避免麻烦。

以直报怨，以德报德。自然，更高的理想应该是爱敌如己。但是历史上究竟有多少人能爱敌如己呢？这似乎要把你的马车赶上天边的一颗星星，事实上，那是达不到的。以直报怨则是比较实际的想法。所以中国人宁舍理想而求实际。

音乐有没有用处？当然很有用。它可以陶冶性情，可以移风易俗。

艺术有没有用处？当然很有用。艺术可以培养人民的高尚情操，有益于世道人心。花卉草木、宫殿庙宇、山水名画、诗词歌赋、陶瓷钟鼎、雕塑篆刻等等都足以启发人的高尚情操。

一个人为什么必须诚实呢？因为你如果不诚实，不可靠，人们就不会相信你，你在事业上和社交上也会因此失败，不诚实是不合算的。诚实不但是美德，它的实际效果对人与人之间的关系也有很大的价值。

中国人爱好幽默。为什么？因为幽默的话不会得罪人；而且你可从幽默中觅得无限的乐趣。你如果常常提些无伤大雅而有趣的建议，你一定可以与大家处得更好。幽默使朋友聚晤更觉融洽，使人生更富乐趣。

有恒为成功之本。只要有恒心，铁杵磨成针。

In the scenic Western Hills of Peking, one summer afternoon, Professor John Dewey, Dr. Hu Shih, and I watched a Sisyphus beetle pushing a tiny mud ball up the slope. It pushed first with forelegs, then with hind legs, and then with its side legs. The ball rolled up and up until some mishap occurred which set it rolling down to where it started with the diminutive Sisyphus riding on it. He repeated the process but met with the same failure. Again and again he tried. We admire his perseverance, said both Hu Shih and I. Yes, but his lack of intelligence is regrettable, said John Dewey. Thus the virtuous see virtue; the wise see wisdom. There are different aspects in the same thing. The eminent philosopher is truly a loyal son of the West, while his disciples are truly loyal sons of the East. The West pitied Mr. Sisyphus' lack of head, while the East admired his heart.

The Chinese people are contented with their lot. If a Chinese lives on a frugal diet, takes a humble house, and has enough clothes to keep warm, he feels satisfied. This attitude toward a simple way of living keeps China's millions contented and happy, but it precludes progress as the West understands it. Unless China is industrialized, she cannot lift the people to any level of material prosperity. Perhaps for years to come her countless people will have to be content with their lot.

The Chinese people are devoted to nature, not in the sense of finding the natural laws but in the sense of cultivating the poetic, artistic, or moral sense of lovers of nature. To be under pine trees steeped in the moon and listen to streams flowing gently over the rocks gives one a placid mind and a tranquil heart. To see spring flowers in bloom makes one feel the universe filled with the spirit of growth; to observe autumn leaves falling serves as a warning of the approach of declining days.

From nature the Chinese learns the sublime nature of man. In Peking there is the Altar of Heaven, built of white marble somewhat like a great theatre, but terraced upward toward the center, which is raised higher than the surrounding terraces. At this altar the emperors of the past worshiped heaven. On one clear moonlit autumn night, when the sky was blue without a speck of cloud upon it, the full moon shone directly upon my head and the marble terraces were flooded with silver light overflowing into the vast space around me. I stood at the center of the altar and all of a sudden felt as if heaven, earth, and myself merged into one vastness.

有一个夏天下午，杜威教授、胡适之先生和我三个人在北平西山看到一只屎蜣螂正在推着一个小小的泥团上山坡。它先用前腿来推，然后又用后腿，接着又改用边腿。泥团一点一点往上滚，后来不知怎么一来，泥团忽然滚回原地，屎蜣螂则紧攀在泥团上翻滚下坡。它又从头做起，重新推着泥团上坡，但结果仍旧遭遇同样的挫败。它一次接一次地尝试，但是一次接一次地失败。适之先生和我都说，它的恒心毅力实在可佩。杜威教授却说，它的毅力固然可嘉，它的愚蠢却实在可怜。这真是智者见智，仁者见仁。同一东西却有不同的两面。这位杰出的哲学家是道地的西方子弟，他的两位学生却是道地的东方子弟。西方惋叹屎蜣螂之缺乏智慧，东方则赞赏它之富于毅力。

中国人多半乐天知命。中国人如有粗茶淡饭足以果腹，有简陋的房屋足以安身，有足够的衣服可以御寒，他就心满意足了。这种安于俭朴生活的态度使中国亿万人民满足而快乐，但是阻滞了中国的进步。除非中国能够工业化，她无法使人民达到高度的物质繁荣。或许在今后的一段长时间内，她的亿万人民仍须安贫乐道。

中国人深爱大自然，这不是指探求自然法则方面的努力，而是指培养自然爱好者的诗意、美感或道德意识。月下徘徊，松下闲坐，静听溪水细语低吟，可以使人心神舒坦。观春花之怒放感觉宇宙充满了蓬勃的精神；见落叶之飘零则感觉衰景的凄凉。

中国人从大自然领悟到了人性的崇高。北京有一个天坛，是用白色大理石建造的，这个天坛就是昔日皇帝祭天之所。一个秋天的夜晚，万里无云，皓月当空，银色的月光倾泻在大理石的台阶上，同时也弥漫了我四周的广大空间。我站在天坛的中央，忽然之间我觉得自己已与天地融而为一。

This experience of sudden sublimation made me understand why the Chinese regard heaven, earth, and man as one and inseparable. By believing in their unity the Chinese elevate man from the pettiness of daily life to the higher plane of sublime spirit. The vastness of space, the brilliance of the sun, the placidity of the moon, the multitude of stars, the luxuriant growth of plants, the rotation of the seasons, the timely rains that nourish the crops, the winding rivers that irrigate the fields, the dashing tides that reveal the power of nature, the high mountains that touch the sky—each and all furnish rich materials in cultivating man's sublime spirit. Of nature man is born; to nature man owes his life; from nature he learns his ways of good living. Nature and man are one and inseparable.

Nature is so good, so kind, so sincere, and so generous that man in his own very nature—which is but part and parcel of greater nature—must be good, kind, sincere, and generous. Here comes the belief of the Chinese that human nature is all-good. Evils grow only out of the perversion of good. This is why great Chinese teachers and statesmen always trust the good that is in man. Great statesmen like Dr. Sun Yat-sen and great teachers like Dr. Tsai Yuan-pei always take any Tom, Dick, or Harry for a good man until he proves the contrary. And they are always ready to forgive and forget. Herein lies their greatness and broad-mindedness. It is proverbial that a statesman's mind is so broad that you could row a boat in it, while a scholar's heart is as resonant as a hollow in mountain regions that echoes with every vibration of sound.

Nature is China's national teacher. Upon nature she built her moral universe, and thus her culture and civilization. Since Chinese civilization furnishes only inadequate means to control nature, she follows nature. Here lie the differences between East and West. It is the duty of the moralists and poets to follow nature; it is the duty of the scientist to control it. Under the influence of Western civilization the younger generation is changing—changing from a poetic and moral appreciation to a scientific study of nature. Hereafter China will understand nature not only through feelings and empirical observation but through the intellect and scientific research. China will know nature more intimately and control it more effectively to bring prosperity to the nation and better the livelihood of the people.

　　这次突然升华的经验使我了解中国人为什么把天、地、人视为不可分的一体。他们因相信天、地、人三位一体，使日常生活中藐不足道的人升入庄严崇高的精神境界。茫无边际的空间、灿烂的太阳、澄明的月亮、浩繁的星辰、葱翠的树木、时序的代谢、滋润五谷的甘霖时雨、灌溉田地的江河溪涧、奔腾澎湃的海浪江潮、高接云霄的重峦叠嶂，这一切的一切，都培养了人的崇高精神。人生于自然，亦养于自然；他从大自然学到好好做人的道德。自然与人是二而为一的。

　　大自然这样善良、仁慈、诚挚，而且慷慨，人既然是大自然不可分的一部分，人的本性必然也是善良、仁慈、诚挚，而且慷慨的。中国人的性善的信念就是由此而来。邪恶只是善良的本性堕落的结果。中国伟大的教育家和政治家始终信赖人的善良本性，就是这个缘故。伟大政治家如孙中山先生，伟大教育家如蔡子民先生，把任何人都看成好人，不管他是张三、李四，除非张三或李四确实证明是邪恶的。他们随时准备饶恕别人的过错，忘记别人的罪愆。他们的伟大和开明就在这里。所以我国俗语说："宰相腹内可撑船"，又用虚怀若谷来形容学者的气度。

　　大自然是中国的国师。她的道德观念和她的一切文物都建筑于大自然之上。中国文化既不足以控制自然，她只好追随自然。中西之不同亦即在此。道德家和诗人的责任是追随自然；科学家的责任则是控制自然。中国年轻一代在西方文明影响之下，已开始转变——从诗意的道德的自然欣赏转变到科学的自然研究。中国此后将不单凭感觉和常识的观察来了解自然，而且要凭理智的与科学的探讨来了解自然。中国将会更真切地认识自然，更有效地控制自然，使国家臻于富强，使人民改善生活。

At the same time, science will not destroy the sense of beauty in nature as some people think it may. As I write I look out through the windows and see in the gardens the old pine trees and bamboo groves, flesh after a rain, and over the bamboo trees I see the Yangtze River gracefully winding its tranquil way past the hilly city of Chungking. The sense of the beauty of nature gives me peacefulness of mind and tranquility of heart. But if I think of the plants botanically, I see in them the growth of the cells and the circulation of the sap, which does not lessen my sense of beauty at all. If I look at the river geologically, I see through its silt-carrying waters to its bed, which millions and millions of years ago may have been just dry land or even the bottom of a rough sea. Thinking in this way, the beauty of the gentle Yangtze remains in my mind just the same or even with richer associations. That a knowledge of the working of their cells should destroy one's sense of the beauty of pine trees or bamboo groves is unthinkable. It makes me feel that nature is even more wonderful and beautiful with a scientific outlook.

From love of the beauty in nature and a feeling of her irresistible force, a strong fatalism grew up in the minds of the Chinese people. In spite of all human efforts, nature will stick to its invariable course. Thus flood and drought are beyond human power to control, and people have learned to submit to Fate. Since it is Fate, they may just as well take it good-naturedly. What is the use of making much fuss over Fate? This is why one finds many a toiler in China with a smiling face. Misery is a fate—why not take it in good humor?

Here is one secret of why the Chinese people have had so great a capacity to stand hardship and suffering during the years of war. Do your best, perform your duty, and let Fate take care of the rest. "Enjoy Nature's way and be contented with your lot." The placid autumn moon, the tender June breeze, spring blossoms, winter snows, all are in store for your enjoyment, rich and poor alike.

有人以为科学会破坏自然的美感，其实未必如此。我现在一面握笔属稿，一面抬头眺望窗外，欣赏着花园中在雨后显得特别清新的松树和竹丛。在竹丛的外边，我还可以看到长江平静徐缓地在重庆山城旁边流过。大自然的美感使我心旷神怡。但是我如果以植物学观点来观察树木，我会想到它们细胞的生长，树液的循环，但是这种想法并不至于破坏我的美感。如果我以地理学的观点来看长江，我可能想到挟带污泥的江水之下的河床，亿万年之前，这河床或许只是一块干燥的陆地，也可能是深海之底。这些思想虽然在我脑海掠过，但是长江优美的印象却始终保留在我心里，甚至使我产生更丰富的联想。如果说对于细胞作用的知识足以破坏一个人对松树或竹丛的美感，那是不可想像的。我觉得科学的了解只有使大自然显得更奇妙、更美丽。

中国人因为热爱大自然的美丽，同时感觉大自然力量之不可抗拒，心里慢慢就形成了一种强烈的宿命论。无论人类如何努力，大自然不会改变它的途径。因此，洪水和旱灾都不是人力所能控制的，人们不得不听任命运的摆布。既然命中注定如此，他们也就不妨把它看得轻松点。天命不可违，何必庸人自扰？我们发现中国的许多苦力也笑容满面，原因在此。苦难是命中注定的，何不逆来顺受？

抗战期间，中国人民表现了无比的忍受艰难困苦的能力，秘密就在此。尽力而为之，其余的听天由命就是了。你最好乐天知命。秋天的明月、六月的微风、春天的花朵、冬天的白雪，一切等待你去欣赏，不论你是贫是富。

CHAPTER 34   MODERN CIVILIZATION

Modern civilization originated in Europe; American civilization is but its offspring. Chinese civilization, which developed from its own sources and is of a very high order, is regarded as ancient—China began to be modernized only with the influx of modern influences from Europe and America. In the last fifty years she has been going through the metamorphosis of coming up to date, with its accompanying agonies. She has been forced into the modern world step by step, by the tides of westernization, as we have seen in these pages.

"Modern civilization" is an ambiguous term. It yields various impressions. It may mean more and better weapons of war for men to massacre each other with, until it destroys them all. It may mean better means of production, to support more millions in comfort and luxury and create a higher standard of living. Or the term may be used for the science and invention that have made both modern warfare and a high standard of living possible. It may represent the mentality which searches for objective truths in order to enable man to control nature. It may refer to better communication, and better organization in mobilizing resources and wealth. It may signify democracy to the democratic countries or totalitarianism to totalitarian nations.

Part or all of these may be called modern civilization—as to what is most essential or most truly typical no two people seem to agree. Then what has China been doing during these fifty troubled years? She has trodden in the dark. Sometimes she has seemed to be walking into a trap, as a fly will, by licking the sweetness that leads it along the path of doom. At other times she seems to have been cornered by a group of armed gangsters who forced her into submission. This she resented, and afterward tried to get weapons to defend herself. All in all, she has struggled and muddled and finally began to see light in what is called Western civilization, with its good as well as evil, blessings as well as curses.

What are the goods and blessings she should try to absorb, what evils reject? Here, too, there seems to be no agreement, whether among individuals or groups. The evils she has taken in may later prove to be laden with blessings. Thus from the evil of opium, forced upon China by superior weapons of war, she got the seeds of modern science. The goods

叁肆 二次大战期间看现代文化

现代文化肇始于欧洲；美国文化不过是欧洲文化的一支而已。中国文化是中华民族自己发展出来的，历史悠久，而且品级很高。现代思潮从欧美涌到后，中国才开始现代化。在过去五十年内，她已经逐渐蜕变而追上时代潮流，在蜕变过程中曾经遭受许多无可避免的苦难。中国已经身不由主地被西潮冲到现代世界之中了。

"现代文化"是个笼统的名词。它可以给人许多不同的印象。它可以指更多更优良的作战武器，使人类互相残杀，直至大家死光为止。它也可以指更优越的生产方法，使更多的人能够享受安适和奢华，达到更高的生活水准。现代文化也可以指同时促成现代战争和高级生活水准的科学和发明。它可以代表人类追求客观真理，控制自然的欲望，也可以指动员资源和财富的交通建设和组织制度。对民主国家而言，它可以代表民主政治，对极权国家而言，它又可以代表极权政治。

这一切的一切，或者其中的任何一项，都可以叫现代文化——至于究竟什么最重要，或者什么最标准，似乎没有任何两个人的意见会完全相同。那末，在过去多灾多难的五十年中，中国究竟在做些什么呢？她可以说一直在黑暗中摸索，有时候，她似乎已掉进陷阱，正像一只苍蝇被蜜糖引诱到灭亡之路。有时候，她又似乎是被一群武装强盗所包围，非逼她屈服不可。她自然不甘屈服，于是就设法弄到武器来自卫。总而言之，她一直在挣扎，在暗中摸索，最后发现了"西方文化"的亮光，这亮光里有善也有恶，有祸也有福。

哪些是她应该努力吸收的善因，哪些又是她必须拒斥的祸根呢？这问题似乎没有一致的结论，个人之间与团体之间都是如此。她所遭遇的祸患，也可能在后来证明竟是福祉。鸦片是列强用枪炮硬加到她身上的祸害，但是她却因此而获得现代科学的种子。

she has adopted may prove to be accompanied by unsuspected evils. For example, by relying too much on system and organization we forgot the virtues of individual integrity and responsibility. There are cases where new systems and organizations have failed in their work for lack of due emphasis upon these qualities.

The standard of living was raised for the few who lived upon the exploitation of many. Thus automobiles were imported and used without making an effort to manufacture them. It takes thousands of farmers, each raising hundreds of bushels of rice, to produce the means of exchange for one imported car. Modern conveniences in modern towns, such as electric lights, radios, flush toilets, and other comforts, must be paid for by the sweat of millions of tillers of the land. In lifting our standard of living we are impoverishing the country by an unfavorable trade balance. Yet the standard of living must be raised, and accompanying evils must be remedied by scientific agriculture, farm machinery, and an irrigation system for increased productivity.

These again will give rise to new problems. We have suffered much from modern civilization, yet we still need more of it. If we take too much at a time we vomit it forth again violently as in the case of the Boxer uprising of 1900; if we take too little it is ineffective. This seems to be how modern civilization goes in China. Yet China must muddle along with the world, willy-nilly.

In the West, during the last hundred years, one invention has led to another, one idea to another, one step in progress to another, one prosperity to another, and one war to another. Only peace did not lead to another peace, but to war. This is how the world has forged ahead in the name of modern civilization. Must China fall in line with the rest of the world?

If there should be another war, as the world so much fears, it seems probable that it will start again, like the first World War, in eastern and middle Europe; or like the recent cataclysm, in the Chinese Three Eastern

Provinces, known as Manchuria. The people of middle Europe want lebensraum elsewhere, while as to Manchuria, outside peoples want to find their lebensraum there. The former, being a densely populated area, tends to spill its troubles, while the latter—a vast vacuum—sucks trouble in.

在另一方面，她接纳的福祉在后来却又可能夹带着意想不到的祸患。例如我们因为过分相信制度和组织，竟然忘记了人格和责任感的重要。因缺乏对这些品德的强调而使新制度、新组织无法收效的例子已经屡见不鲜。

少数以剥削他人为生的人，生活水准确是提高了。汽车进口了，但是他们从来不设法自己制造。事实上要靠成千的农夫，每人生产几百担谷子，才能够赚换一辆进口汽车的外汇。现代都市里的电灯、无线电、抽水马桶等等现代物质享受，也必须千千万万农夫的血汗来偿付。我们以入超来提高生活水准，结果使国家愈来愈贫困。但是生活水准是必须提高的，因此而产生的祸害只有靠增加生产来补救。为了增加生产，我们必须利用科学耕种、农业机械和水利系统。

这种工作势将引起其他新的问题。我们吃足了现代文化的苦头，然而我们又必须接受更多的现代文化。我们如果一次吃得太多，结果就会完全吐出来。一九〇〇年的义和团之乱就是一个例子；如果我们吃得太少，却又不够营养。现代文化在中国所产生的影响就是这样。无论如何，中国还是不得不跟着世界各国摸索前进。

西方在过去一百年中，每一发明总是导致另一发明，一种思想必定引发另一种思想，一次进步之后接着必有另一次进步，一次繁荣必定导致另一次繁荣，一次战争之后必有另一次战争。惟有和平不会导致和平，继和平而来的必是战争。这就是这个世界在现代文化下前进的情形。中国是否必须追随世界其余各国亦步亦趋呢？

大家都在担忧发生第三次世界大战，如果另一次大战争真地发生的话，很可能仍像第一次大战一样爆发于东欧和中欧，也可能像第二次大战一样爆发于中国的东三省。中欧的人民想在别处找个生存空间，至于中国的东北，则是别国人民想在那里找生存空间。中欧是个人口稠密的区域，境内的纷扰很容易蔓延到其他区域；东三省

Either is a potential source of war, in which, if it comes, the whole world must again be involved, to its incalculable disaster.

In safeguarding the powder magazines of the East, responsibility will inevitably rest upon the shoulders of China. Therefore the political, social, economic, and industrial development of China during the next twenty or thirty years will have a determining effect upon the peace situation of the world. A strong and prosperous China, co-operating with the major Powers of the West, could eliminate the danger to a very great extent if not entirely. It is to the mutual interest of the Allied Powers and of world peace in general that the Western Powers should co-operate with China, say for a period of fifty years, in the development of her natural resources; and for the coming twenty years, perhaps, in the work of her economic and social rehabilitation.

Before Western influence made inroads into China, her troubles for many centuries had come solely from Manchuria and the neighboring region known as Mongolia. When Japan became a world Power after the Sino-Japanese War, she contended with Tsarist Russia for control over that vast territory, a conflict which culminated in the Russo-Japanese War. Japan's scheme to use that part of China as a steppingstone to control of the whole country led to the Mukden Incident. If history since the downfall of the Tangs has taught us anything, we may be reasonably sure that the Three Eastern Provinces will still be a trouble center for China and a cause of worry to the world until China herself is strong and prosperous and the vast vacuum of Manchuria is filled.

In building up a modern democracy and industries China needs time and favorable conditions for experiment. These conditions are peace and security. Internal peace depends upon unification of the country. Security depends upon international understanding. China will have security only when Manchuria becomes a center of peace.

We shall have to start anew in creating our future by making that vast territory a focus of peace instead of war. In that important work I hope the world—especially America, Britain, and Soviet Russia—will co-operate with China. With their co-operation the task must be crowned by complete success, a blessing for China in particular and for the world generally.

则是辽阔的真空地带，很容易招惹外来的纷扰。二者都可能是战争的导火线，战争如果真地发生，势将再度牵涉整个世界，未来浩劫实不堪设想。

确保东方导火线不着火的责任，自然要落在中国的肩膀上。因此今后二三十年间，中国在政治、社会、经济和工业各方面的发展，对于世界和平自将发生决定性的影响。一个强盛兴旺的中国与西方列强合作之下，即使不能完全消弭战争的危机，至少也可以使战争危机大为减低。西方列强如能与中国合作，不但同盟国家均蒙其利，即对整个世界的和平亦大有裨益。西方国家在今后五六十年内至少应该协助中国发展天然资源，在今后二十年内尤其需要协助中国进行经济复员和社会重建的工作。

在西方潮流侵入中国以前，几百年来的祸患可说完全导源于满洲和蒙古。甲午中日战争之后，日本一跃而为世界强国，遂即与帝俄抢夺满洲的控制权，终至触发日俄之战。日本处心积虑，想利用东三省作为征服全中国的跳板，结果发生九·一八事变。如果唐朝灭亡以后的历史发展能够给我们一点教训的话，我们就很有理由相信，东三省今后仍系中国的乱源，除非中国成为强大富足的国家，并且填补好满洲的真空状态。

在建立现代民主政治和工业的工作上，中国需要时间和有利的条件从事试验。这些条件就是和平和安全。国内和平有赖于国家的统一。国家安全则有赖于国际间的了解。只有在东北成为和平中心时，中国才有安全可言。

我们必须从头做起，设法把广大的东北领土从战乱之源转化为和平的重镇。在这件艰巨的工作上，我希望全世界——尤其是美国、英国和苏俄——能够与中国合作。如果她们肯合作，这件工作自然会成功，那不但是中国之福，也是全世界之福。

In 1921 I was elected an unofficial observer to the Washington Conference by the Chamber of Commerce and educational associations in Shanghai, and supported by Dr. Sun Yat-sen's Nationalist government in Canton. In the following year, 1922, I went to Europe for a visit to the source of modern civilization. It was very soon after the first World War. One could see that every country in Europe was busy planning postwar rehabilitation and the major victorious Powers were occupied in trying to make peace more enduring. But no one seemed to realize then that they were all helping to sow the seeds of a next war.

France was tired and longed for a permanent peace. Her eyes looked over the Rhine, whence came the danger to her national existence. Her defensive mood was later embodied in the Maginot Line, which she thought would make her immune to German attack. Like the first emperor of the Chin Dynasty (246-207 B.C.)[1] who built the Great Wall to defend China from the attack of the Tartars, France built the Maginot Line. And as trouble for the empire of the Chins came not from outside but from inside the Great Wall, so it was with the French Republic and her "impregnable" barrier.

England was busy with the economic reconstruction of Europe and endeavoring to maintain the balance of power on the Continent. Germany, defeated, was licking her wounds. Tsarist Russia was utterly ruined and a new political experiment was under way in that gigantic Republic of Soviet Russia. Such was the political aspect of Europe after World War I.

America, unwilling to pull European chestnuts out of the fire, had withdrawn from that much-troubled continent and summoned the Washington Conference, at which the Nine-Power Treaty was penned, the Anglo-Japanese Alliance superseded, and the Shantung question settled; this, to save Japan's face, was negotiated outside the conference. The Twenty-One Demands, superseded by the new treaty, were thus unostentatiously sent to the grave. Tsingtao, a seaport in the peninsula of

Shantung, had been awarded to Japan at Versailles and the complications which grew out of the award were known as the Shantung question. Indignation at this move gave rise in China to the student movement which had such far-reaching repercussions in Sino-Japanese relations, as well as in political and cultural developments in China, during the following twenty years. In America it troubled public men who had sympathy for China and became a knotty political problem. Both the

民国十年（一九二一年），我承上海市商会及各教育团体的推选，并受广州中山先生所领导的国民党政府的支持，曾以非官方观察员身份列席华盛顿会议。翌年我又到欧洲访问现代文化的发祥地。那时刚是第一次世界大战结束后不久，欧洲各国正忙于战后复员，主要的战胜国则忙于确保永久和平。但是当时似乎没有一个国家意识到，实际上他们正在帮着散布下一次大战的种籽。

法国已经精疲力竭，渴望能有永久和平。她目不转睛地监视着莱茵河彼岸，因为威胁她国家生存的危机就是从那里来的。法国的防御心理后来表现在马奇诺防线上，她认为有了这道防线，就可以高枕无忧，不至于再受德国攻击了。秦始皇（公元前二四六——前二〇七年）筑长城以御鞑靼，法国则筑马奇诺防线以抵御德国的侵略。但是中国的祸患结果并非来自长城以外，而是发于长城之内，法国及其"固若金汤"的防线，命运亦复如是。

英国忙于欧洲的经济复兴，并在设法维持欧陆的均势。战败的德国正在休养将息。帝俄已经覆亡。一种新的政治实验正在地广人众的苏俄进行。这就是第一次世界大战后的欧洲政治情势。

美国因为不愿卷入欧洲纷扰的漩涡，已经从多事的欧陆撤退而召开华盛顿会议；九国公约就是在这次会议中签订的。此项公约取代了英日同盟，所谓山东问题，经过会外磋商后，亦告解决，日本对华的二十一条要求终于静悄悄地被放进坟墓。巴黎和会中曾决定把青岛赠送给日本，所谓山东问题就是因此而起的。中国人民对巴黎和会的愤慨终于触发了学生运动，在中日关系上发生了深远的影响，同时在此后二十年间，对中国政治和文化上的发展也有莫大的影响。巴黎和会的决定使同情中国的美国政界人士也大伤脑筋，终至演化为棘手的政治问题。共和党和民主党

Republican and Democratic parties more or less committed themselves to right the wrongs done to China by the ill-fated Versailles Treaty; thus while America withdrew her fingers from Europe she dipped them deep into Pacific waters. The result, twenty years later, was Pearl Harbor.

Without the active participation of America in the League of Nations of which she was the author; with a defensive psychology on the part of France, whose only desire was to avoid trouble; and with Britain's main interest focused on maintaining the balance of power on the Continent, the League became toothless. It barked a lot but never meant to bite. Yet any problem that member nations could not handle among themselves was handed over to the League. So it became a dumping ground for international difficulties. When China was unable to meet her difficulties vis-à-vis Manchurian problems she, too, dumped them on the League, of which Japan was a member. In the ease of the Mukden Incident France was not interested. Britain was concerned only so far as the balance of power in the Far East was involved, but she was afraid of being drawn in. The League, therefore, had scarcely even the nerve to bark at Japan. Its few mild yelps might indeed be construed as connivance.

The League, however, made an invaluable contribution to our experience. Learning from its failures, the world may profit in planning the coming peace. Born of American idealism, it died of conflicting interests and the ambitions of member nations, especially the major Powers.

So matters developed in the course of some twenty years after the Versailles Treaty. The seeds of war sown at Versailles grew in every corner of the world like weeds, which eventually caught fire and set the whole world aflame.

But politics are but a passing show destined soon to vanish into history. What will always remain is the fundamental problem of culture. It is undeniable that Europe has produced modern science and organized democracy, which have brought to mankind more blessings than evils.

Germany appeared to me a country of telescopes, microscopes, and test tubes; her inventions and discoveries multiplied by leaps and bounds. In Shanghai foreign manufactures of superlative quality became known as *Jahming huo*—"German goods." The Germans were masters of material things but fell short in human relations. This, as I see it, is why they often got into trouble in dealing with other nations. Their sight was

都以打抱不平自任，承诺为中国伸雪因凡尔赛和约而遭受的冤抑。因此，美国固然从欧洲脱身，却又卷入了太平洋的漩涡。二十年后的珍珠港事变即种因于此。

美国虽然是国际联盟的倡导者，结果却并未参加国联的实际活动；法国唯一的愿望是避免纠纷，防御心理弥漫全国；英国的注意力集中在维持欧陆均势上面；结果国际联盟形同虚设。它只会啍啍狂吠却从来不会咬人。但是会员本身无法解决的问题，还是一古脑儿往国际联盟推，结果国联就成了国际难题的垃圾堆。中国无法应付东北问题的困难时，也把这些难题推到国联身上，因为日本是国联的会员国。法国对沈阳事变 [2] 漠不关心，英国所关切的只是欧洲大陆的均势，惟恐卷入远东纠纷，因此国联连向日本吠几声的胆量都没有。结果只懒洋洋地打了几个呵欠，如果说那是默认既成事实，未始不可。

国联虽然一事无成，却是一个很有价值的教训。世界人士可以从它的失败中，学习如何策划未来的和平。国联诞生于美国之理想，结果因会员国间利益之冲突，以及列强间的野心而夭折。

凡尔赛和约订立后约二十年间，世局演变大致如此。由凡尔赛和约播下的战争种籽在世界每一角落里像野草一样蔓生滋长，这些野草终于着火燃烧，火势遍及全球。

但是政治究竟只是过眼云烟，转瞬即成历史陈迹。恒久存在的根本问题是文化。我们无法否认欧洲已经发展了现代科学和民主制度，为人类带来了许多幸福。

在我看起来，德国是个遍地是望远镜、显微镜和试验管的国家。她的发明日新月异，突飞猛进。上海人甚至把高级舶来品统称为"茄门货"（德国货）。德国人在物质发明上的确称得起能手，但是在人事关系上却碌碌无能。我想，这或许就是他们无法与其他国家

focused through the microscope or the telescope, which concentrated their view either too near or too far to perceive human behavior or feelings. They could not very well put international relations or human feelings into a test tube to observe their reactions. In the broader realm of human activities the Germans often failed to grasp the essentials or shortcomings of human nature. They had highly developed special senses in which other nations did not excel, but they were short of common sense. Their special endowments gave them the scientific thoroughness which has made so many special contributions to the world, and their lack of common sense brought misery alike to their own country and to others.

The British were just the opposite. They were a nation of common sense and masters of human relations. Their views on world affairs and policies relative to them were flexible and adaptable. They never let the cord stretch to the point of breaking. If a stronger force pulled at the other end of the rope, the British would loosen it a little to save it from snapping. If the other side was weaker they would keep on drawing the cord to themselves until it slipped from their opponents' hands. But the British would never let go their end of the rope—they would stick to the last, irrespective of consequences. In relations with other countries and in colonial policies this trait of the British people was seen everywhere.

Hand in hand with flexibility and adaptability went such other British traits as tolerance, moderation, considerateness, fair play, and an attitude of compromise. They never went to extremes in their views, and were always trying to understand other people's view in order either to bring themselves to it or to bring others to their own. They loved freedom of speech and thought, disliked hard and fast rules which might prove unadjustable to varying conditions.

The British are reserved to the point of brutal coolness, a trait disliked by other peoples and often the cause of suspicion. It has lost the British many a friend among other nations. But when you know them better, or rather when they know you better, you want to make friends with them.

Some or all of these traits together made English democracy possible. For democracy is not something abstract, something that has dropped from the sky. It consists of the best traits there are in the people who have succeeded in it. If you run through the constitutional history of England, you will find that intolerance, persecutions, corruption, and cruelties fill

和睦相处的原因。他们透过望远镜或显微镜看人，目光焦点不是太远就是太近，因而无法了解人类的行为和情感。他们不可能把国际关系或人类情绪放到试管里去观察它们的反应。在人类活动的广大领域里，德国人常常抓不到人性的要点或缺点。他们已经发展了其他民族望尘莫及的特殊才智，但是欠缺常识。他们的特长使他们在科学上穷根究底，对世界提供了许多特殊的贡献；但是他们在常识方面的欠缺，却使德国和其他国家同受其害。

英国人刚刚与德国人相反。他们是个常识丰富的民族，也是应付人事关系的能手。他们对国际事务的看法以及有关的政策富于弹性和适应性。他们从来不让绳子拉紧到要断的程度。如果拉着绳子另一端的力量比较强，英国人就会放松一点免得绳子拉断。如果拉着另一端的力量比较弱，英国人就会得寸进尺地把绳子拉过来，直至人家脱手为止。但是他们绝不会放弃自己拿着的这一端——他们会坚持到底，不顾后果。在国际关系和殖民政策上，英国人的这种特性随处可见。

英国人的特性中，除了弹性和适应性之外，同时还有容忍、中庸、体谅、公平以及妥协的精神。他们的见解从来不走极端，而且始终在努力了解别人的观点，希望自己能因此迁就别人，或者使别人来接受他们自己的观点。他们爱好言论自由和思想自由，憎恶无法适应不同情况的刻板规律。

英国的拘谨矜持几乎到了冷酷的程度，这是英国人最受其他民族讨厌的一种特性，而且常常因此引起猜疑误会。这种特性使英国人丧失了许多朋友。但是当你对他们有较深的认识时，或者说当他们对你了解较深时，你就会愿意与他们交朋友了。

这许多特性凑合在一起时，英国的民主政治才成为可能。因为民主不是抽象的东西，也不是天上掉下来的，民主政治包含着民主先进国家的所有特长。翻开英国的宪政史，你会发现其中充满了偏执、

its pages. Quite a number of lives, including that of a king, have been sacrificed to democracy. The experience of English democracy is worth our serious study.

One fact, however, we must bear in mind: that English democracy grew fast after the unification of the United Kingdom, and American democracy, too, developed by leaps and bounds only after the Civil War. History teaches us that unification and security must go hand in hand to make an organized democracy. For England was lucky in that her islands were small and protected by the sea. In the old days invasion was not easy. So the English enjoyed security and therefore had plenty of time for trial and error. Their national existence was not endangered by foreign invasion during the period of incubation and experiment.

A similar situation existed in America. The North American Continent is itself a gigantic island, the seas around it preventing any formidable invasion. The early colonists from England brought with them seeds of the love of freedom which grew into a great tree of liberty, sheltered from the ax of foreign invaders. In the course of a century or so the democracy of America took firm root. Not only was experiment freely made in human relations but also in things material, by which I mean scientific research. While American democracy grew out of the English model, American science owed a great debt to the Germans.

The American system of higher education is a combination of the English college and the German university; the American academic dress is, so to speak, an English gown with a German cap. In the American colleges boys and girls lived in a spirit of comradeship and free association and secured a liberal foundation of learning. Knowledge was not strictly regimented; human relationships were learned through free mingling of the strident body; the sight of the younger generation was not simply narrowed into telescopes, microscopes, or test tubes; a general culture was furnished to all those who cared to absorb it.

In the university proper, or the graduate school, American students were taught methods of research, German thoroughness was admired and encouraged, but its full realization had yet to be achieved at the time of my college days. During the First World War the five colors of the former Chinese flag—red, yellow, blue, white, and black were reduced to two: black and white. The reason was that German dyes were no longer available in China on account of the war. An American chemist in New

迫害、腐败和残忍的史实。许多生命，包括一位君主，曾经为民主牺牲。英国实行民主的经验的确值得我们好好研究。

不过，我们必须记住一项事实：英国的民主政治在联合王国达成统一之后才迅速发展，美国民主政治也是在南北战争之后才突飞猛进。历史告诉我们：只有统一与安全同时并进时，有组织的民主政治才能实现。英国幸而是小岛组成的王国，四围有海洋保护着。在古代，外国侵入英国是不容易的，因此英国人得以永久安全，有足够的时间从事民主实验。在民主的孕育和实验期间，英国的生存始终未受外来侵略的威胁。

美国的情形也很相似。北美大陆本身就是一个大岛，周围的海洋使它不受外来的侵略。从英国来的早期殖民者带来爱好自由的种籽，这些种籽遂即滋长为自由大树，海洋则保护了这些大树，免受外来侵略者的斧斤之扰。经过约一百年的发荣滋长，美国的民主已经根深蒂固，不但人事方面普遍进行实验，即在物质方面也是如此，换一句话说，科学研究之风已吹遍美洲的每一角落。美国的民主固然由英国模型发展而来，美国的科学却受德国之惠不浅。

美国的高等教育制度是英国学院和德国大学的混合体；打个比喻，美国的学术服装是由一件英国袍子和一顶德国帽子凑合而成的。美国大学里男女学生的友好相处与交际自由，建立了自由研究的基础。知识不受严格的管制；人与人的关系是经由学生团体的自由接触而学到的；年轻一代的目光并未受到望远镜、显微镜或试验管的局限；凡是有兴趣的人都可以接受一种普遍文化的陶冶。

在大学部和研究院里，美国学生普遍接受研究方法的训练。德国学者的彻底精神普受赞许与提倡，但是这种彻底精神直到我进大学的时代才充分发挥。第一次世界大战期间，中国旧国旗中的红黄蓝白黑五色一度只剩下黑白两色。理由是德国颜料因战事关系已无法再输入中国。纽约一位美国化学家告诉我，在德国，通常是

York told me that in Germany several specialists worked on one color, whereas in America one chemist dealt with many colors. This was some twenty years ago. Conditions have changed by now, since Americans have acquired so much of the German thoroughness during the last two or three decades.

Thus on the American side of the water English democracy and German science have gone hand in hand. With her rich natural resources, her power of organization and love of great projects, America may now easily be ranked as first of the democracies of the world. Just the other day at a party in the American Embassy in Chungking, a British diplomat remarked to me that "England is Americanized, Russia is Americanized, and China is Americanized."

"In what way is England Americanized?" I asked.

"Hollywood, for example," was the reply.

"Russia—in the sense of great industries?"

"Yes."

Meanwhile flashes of pictures passed rapidly through my mind, in which I saw that Chinese political and educational systems, social changes, and industrial developments were richly tinged with Americanization. At the same time I was not unaware of the fact that China colors all the sea that washes her shores.

Pointing at the six rows of eight stars each on the American flag, the same diplomat turned to a high-ranking American military officer standing by and asked with a touch of humor, "What are you going to do when you add one state more?"

"Well, we'll make it seven rows of seven, but what new state do you have in mind?"

"England," replied the diplomat. We all laughed. It was only a joke, but in jokes one may see the temper of the times.

In days of old, when the West fought for colonial empire in the East, all the important Western Powers except America at various times wronged China. Even Portugal bit off a tiny piece of land called Macao, in the province of Kwangtung. The only thing America got from China was extraterritoriality, but what she has done for China is far more and will be remembered for generations to come. As everybody knows this, I need not elaborate here. Now both America and Britain have abolished

好几位专家共同研究一种颜料，在美国却是一位化学家同时研究好几种颜料。这是二十多年前的事了，目前的情况已经有了改变，因为在过去二三十年间，美国人民已经深获德国彻底精神的诀窍。

英国民主和德国精神在美国携手并进，相得益彰。美国以其丰富的天然资源，强大的组织能力，以及对大规模建设的热诚，已经一跃而登民主国家的首座。有一天，重庆的美国大使馆举行酒会，会中一位英国外交官对我说："英国美国化了，俄国美国化了，中国也美国化了。"

"英国在哪一方面美国化了呢？"我问道。

"好莱坞电影就是一个例子。"他回答说。

"那末俄国呢——你是不是指大工业？"

"是的。"

这使我联想到中国的政治制度、教育制度、社会改革和工业发展，这一切都带着浓厚的美国色彩。但是我并没有忘记：中国也已使冲激着她海岸的汪洋染上了她自己的色彩。

这位英国外交官用手指着缀有四十八颗星星的美国国旗，带点幽默地转身问站在他身边的一位美国高级将领说："这上面是六行星星，每行八颗。如果你们增加一个新的州时，你们预备怎么安排？"

"呃，我想它们排成七行，每行七颗星就成了。但是你问这个干什么？你心里所想的是哪一个新的州？"

"英格兰。"这位外交官回答说。我们大家都笑了。这当然只是一个笑话，但是从笑话里，我们可以看出时代的潮流。

昔日西方在东方争取殖民地时，西方列强除了美国之外都曾或先或后地侵略过中国。甚至连葡萄牙也从广东省咬走一小块土地——澳门。美国取自中国的唯一东西是治外法权，但是美国所施于中国者实远较其所取者为多。这些人人皆知的事实，用不到我浪费笔墨。现在美国与英国都已放弃了在华的治外法权，英国虽然

that system and Britain has returned all the settlements, which were an anachronism—though Hongkong remains in British hands. In spite of terrible wars all over the world, much encouraging light has shone through the international clouds. Let us hope that, with victory achieved, it may grow into brilliant sunshine in a cloudless sky.

America has definitely joined the coming international peace organization. She has fought the war. She is to fight for an enduring peace. A new epoch in history is in the making. The combined resources of America, Britain, Soviet Russia, and China are so great that if they desire peace, with an effective world organization backed up by an international defense force to enforce it, peace will indeed be enduring.

For China's part, she will have to redouble her effort of reconstruction and regeneration for the coming twenty or probably thirty years. This will be a critical period for China. Success depends upon foresight and leadership, and the extent to which our Allies will co-operate. The extent to which co-operation is given will also depend upon our political developments and how sound a policy we adopt regarding international investments. Our difficulties are enhanced by the devastations of war and wanton destruction in all the once-prosperous provinces where the heel of the enemy has trodden.

On the other hand, China has a double duty to perform. First, it is her duty to herself to become strong and prosperous. Second, it is her duty to the world to help make world peace secure. In the political philosophy of the Confucian school, peace for the world is the ultimate aim. On the basis of the Confucian philosophy Dr. Sun Yat-sen aimed at world peace in his Three Principles of the People.

If we can bridge over this critical period of twenty or thirty years the momentum thus gathered will carry reforms and reconstruction forward, ever increasing and ever widening, into a glorious future in which China will be in a position to help the world in assuring a more permanent peace.

From the West China has still much to learn. Ever since the downfall of the great dynasty of the Tangs she has been overrun from time to time by peoples from the immense outlying territories of Asia. The decline of Chinese civilization after the fall of that dynasty was due to the invasion of barbarians who at intermittent periods devastated the country and turned it into a stretch of ruins. The successive invasions, together with famine, disease, and internal dissensions, sapped the energy of the Chinese people and thus weakened their creative power. When Western influence began to come into China, therefore, she met it with her civilization at the lowest ebb.

仍旧保持香港，却已交还了所有的租界。全世界虽然历经战争惨祸，国际乌云之中已经透露出一线曙光了。希望这一线曙光，在大战胜利之后，能够渐渐扩大而成为光芒万丈的霁日。

美国已经决意参加未来的国际和平组织，她已经英勇地参加战斗，为永久和平而战斗。历史上的一个新时代正在形成中。中、美、英、苏俄如能合力谋求和平，再由一个有效的世界组织来维护和平，永久和平并非不可能的。

就中国而论，在未来二十年或者三十年里，她尤须加倍努力，从事建设和复兴。今后二三十年将是中国的兴衰关头。我们的努力能否成功，要看我们有无远大眼光，有无领导人才，以及盟国与我们合作的程度而定。盟国与我们合作的程度，又要看我们国内的政治发展以及我们对国际投资所采取的政策而定。战争的破坏，敌骑的蹂躏，更使我们的复兴工作倍形困难。

在另一方面，中国必须完成双重的任务。第一是使她自己富强。第二是协力确保世界和平。在儒家的政治哲学里，世界和平是最终的目的。中山先生根据儒家哲学，也把世界和平定为他的三民主义的目标。

我们如果能够度过这二三十年的难关，自然就可以驾轻就熟，继续进行更远大的改革和建设，为中国创造辉煌的将来，到那时候，中国自然就有资格协助世界确保永久的和平了。

有许多地方，中国仍得向西方学习。自从唐朝覆亡以后，中国曾经一再被来自附近亚洲地区的异族所征服。唐亡以后中国文化的衰退，就是蛮夷戎狄不断蹂躏中国的结果。异族一再入寇中原，加上饥馑、疾病和内乱，终使中国元气衰竭，人民创造能力大为削弱。西方影响开始侵入中国时，正是中国文化陷于最低潮的时候。

People in China now talk of the Tang civilization as if in hopes of restoring the glories of that era. It is a good thing, so far as we can, to draw inspiration from the Tangs and be stimulated by their more humanistic civilization as contrasted with the ascetic type of the later Sungs. In Tang paintings we admire the strong physique of the people. Music, dancing, poetry, painting, and calligraphy were developed to a very high level, which finds no equal in later days.

But for China to go back to this brilliant period of her history is next to impossible. For centuries we have tried to recover our past glories, yet our civilization slid progressively downward in steady decline. For conditions had changed. The fertile soil in which the Tang civilization grew had been washed away by the tides of long years of devastation. If, however, we can get rid of the cause of the Tang downfall by learning from such modern Tangs as America and other countries where arts, science, political and military organization, health and wealth, are on a very high plane, we shall then perhaps find the glories of the Tangs redescending upon us.

In making the peace China's part will be by no means small. Throughout her history she has had many wars. But they have been wars more in the nature of internal revolution than external aggression—internal conflicts generally caused by the rebellion of oppressed farmers and suffering people against a rotten officialdom. Even her external wars have been more defensive than offensive in nature. China has been oppressed much more than oppressing. Ever since the time of the first emperor of the Chin Dynasty who built the Great Wall—symbol of a defensive mentality—China has wished to be let alone.

Confucius' teaching of proper human relations and world peace, and the democratic ideas of Mencius, will fit China to be a modern democratic state which wishes to do no wrong to other peoples. What China must emphasize after the war is modern science with its applications to means of production; and democracy in its organized form, with emphasis upon unification of the country. Science and democracy, twin instruments of a progressive modern state, is the key to power, prosperity, and a more lasting peace.

With the practical wisdom of her people, in its special emphasis on human relations and democratic ways of living and thinking, China has the solid foundation for a modern democracy. As we have seen,

现在我们中国人一提到唐朝文化，不禁眉飞色舞，心向往之，满望能恢复旧日的光荣。唐朝的文化比起后来宋朝禁欲主义的文化要近人情得多。如果我们能从唐朝文化得到些灵感与鼓舞，也未始不是一件好事。从唐人的绘画里，我们深深赞叹唐人体格的强健。唐朝的音乐、舞蹈、诗歌、绘画和书法都有登峰造极的成就，后代少能望其项背。

但中国要想回到历史上的这个辉煌时代是不可能的。千百年来我们一直在努力恢复过去的光荣，但是我们的文化却始终在走下坡。因为环境已经改变了。唐代文化赖以滋长的肥沃土壤，已经被历代祸乱的浪潮冲刷殆尽，但是我们如果能避免重蹈唐代灭亡的覆辙，转向在艺术、科学、军事、政治、卫生、财富各方面均有高度成就的现代文明国家如美国等学习，我们或许会发现唐代的光荣将有重临的一日。在维护和平的工作上，中国的职责将是相当重大的。中国的历史上曾经有过不少次的战争，但是这些战争多半属于国内革命的性质。对外的比较少，国内战争多半是被压迫的农民和苦难人民反抗腐败的政府所引起。至于对外战争，性质上也是防御多于攻击。中国受外国侵略者多，侵略外国者少，从筑万里长城的秦始皇开始，中国就一直希望能闭关自守，长城本身就是防御心理的象征。

孔子的忠孝、仁爱、信义、和平的教训和孟子的民主观念，都使中国适于做一个不愿欺凌其他民族的现代民主国家。中国在战后必须强调的是现代科学和民主政治；科学方面应注重生产方法的应用，民主方面应强调国家的统一。科学和民主是现代进步国家的孪生工具，也是达成强盛、繁荣和持久和平的关键。

中国人民深通人情，特别注重待人接物的修养，生活思想习于民主，这一切都使中国具备现代民主国家的坚强基础。我们在前面

her democracy is loosely organized. Her intense love of individual liberty has not kept step with modern social consciousness. Strong family ties have been partly responsible for retarding the organization of individuals into a broader society. But these ties are rapidly loosening; modern institutions have appeared in the larger cities, and further industrialization will mean a further loosening of family bonds and socialization of individuals.

In the field of knowledge China's way of looking at things has given her a practical wisdom but made her neglect the importance of generalization and abstraction. Her love of nature in poetic, artistic, and moral ways has given her breadth of mind, as exemplified by great scholars and statesmen, and a harmony of feeling, as revealed in the arts and in conduct; it has not extended to the investigation of natural laws, which are the indispensable weapon of man in controlling nature. With the assimilating power of Chinese civilization, the Western contribution of science will be absorbed in due course of time, and with the rich natural resources of the country and high intelligence of her people, the integration of science into her life will open up wonderful opportunities in the future. Chinese morals and arts will prosper in the material wealth thus developed, while Chinese thought and the rich store of literature and philosophy will tend to be clarified and systematized by modern logical and scientific ways of thinking.

On this new basis of initial peace and prosperity, China will be in a position to build up a new defense force to preserve and sustain peace. No country would be a worthy partner for peace that was not a worthy partner for war. The attention of the world has already been drawn to China by the contribution she has made to the world in a war of resistance for eight long years, in spite of weaknesses and shortcomings in some aspects of her national life during the war.

Modern science, with special reference to inventions and industry, will fuse with China's rich treasures of art and sound morals. A new civilization is in the making; perhaps it, too, can contribute to the world's progress.

已经提到，中国的民主社会组织相当松泛。中国人对于个人自由的强烈爱好并未能与现代社会意识齐头并进。强烈的家族观念已经阻滞了使个人结合为广大团体的过程。不过这种褊狭的观念正在迅速衰退；现代社团已经在大城市里相继出现；进一步工业化之后，家族关系自将愈来愈松弛，个人社会化的程度也将愈来愈深。

在知识方面，中国人看待事物的态度使他深通人情，但是也使他忽视概括与抽象的重要。他以诗人、艺术家和道德家的心情热爱自然，因而胸怀宽大，心平气和。但是这种对自然的爱好尚未推展到对自然法则的研究，人类要控制自然，必须靠这些法则作武器。以中国文化同化能力之强，她必定能慢慢地吸收西方在科学上的贡献；以中国天然资源之富，人民智慧之高，科学的发展将使她前途呈现无限光明。物质文明发展之后，她的道德和艺术更将发扬光大；她的文学和哲学也将在现代逻辑方法和科学思想影响下更见突出而有系统。

在这个初步的和平与繁荣的新基础上，中国将可建立新的防卫力量来维护和平。只有战斗中的伙伴才有资格成为和平时期的伙伴。中国八年抗战对世界和平的贡献，已使举世人士刮目相看。

现代科学，特别是发明和工业上的成就，将与中国的艺术宝藏和完美道德交织交融。一种新的文化正在形成，这种新文化对世界进步一定会提供重大的贡献。

注释

序

[1] 此处所称 the cession of Hongkong in 1842（1842 年割让香港），指 1840 年第一次鸦片战争后，英国强迫清政府于 1842 年签订《南京条约》，割让香港岛。1856 年第二次鸦片战争后，清政府被迫于 1860 年签订《北京条约》，割让九龙半岛。1894 年中日甲午战争后，英国逼迫清政府于 1898 年签订《展拓香港界址专条》，强租新界，租期 99 年，至 1997 年 6 月 30 日结束。

前言：边城昆明

[1] Burma：缅甸在英国殖民统治时期的旧称，现官方名称为 Myanmar。

第一章

[1] 唐朝（618—907）。

[2] 明朝（1368—1644）。

[3] 参见序注 1。

[4] Amoy：15—16 世纪葡萄牙殖民主义者对厦门的称呼。

[5] Formosa：16 世纪葡萄牙殖民主义者对台湾的称呼。

第二章

[1] Indo-China：法属印度支那，源自法文"Indochine"，通常指曾经是法国殖民地的亚洲东南部地区，包括今日的越南、柬埔寨、老挝三国。在本书中亦特指越南。

[2] An uprising which started in the south in 1851, capitalizing peasant discontent, and swept over most of the country until crushed with foreign help several years later.（作者原注）

[3] foreign dynasties：指蒙古族和满族分别建立的元朝和清朝。

[4] 本书中的"纪元"指公元纪年，与"公元"混用。

[5] Manchu Dynasty：清朝（Qing Dynasty）。

第三章

[1] 英文原文如此，疑以中文（十二月二十一）为准。

[2] One of the formal titles of the Emperor.（作者原注）

3   That is, the hair was trimmed across the front of the head, and the long queue worn behind.
    （作者原注）

第五章

1   甲午海战发生在黄海海域。

2   古越国确切纪年说法不一。此处疑作者采纳《史记》的说法："史载夏少康封庶子无
    余于会稽，以奉守禹祀，号於越"（约公元前 2068 年）；周显王三十六年（公元前
    333 年），"楚威王兴兵败越，杀越王无彊"，"而越以此散"。

3   南宋（1127—1279）。

4   英文原文如此，疑以中文（八个县）为准。

5   此处应为"戊戌变法"，亦称"百日维新"。"戊戌政变"是指以慈禧太后为首的守
    旧派势力向以光绪帝为首的维新派势力发动的政变。

第六章

1   1885 年，中法签订《中法新约》（即《中法会订越南条约》），中国正式放弃对越南
    的宗主权。

2   此处特指 Han Chinese。

3   此处 China（即汉语中的"中国"一词）指中国古代与蒙古、满等少数民族政权并
    立的汉族政权；Chinese 可特指汉族、汉人。"中国"的这一用法在古代汉语中十分
    常见，指"我国中原地区或在中原地区华夏族建立的政权"。例如，《史记·孝武本
    纪》："天下名山八，而三在蛮夷，五在中国。"又如，《汉书·匈奴传下》："[伊黑居
    次] 云常欲与中国和亲。"后文亦有表示此含义的 China 和"中国"，请参考此注。

第七章

1   Manchuria：满洲，旧指中国东北一带。

第十章

1   Tsai Hsun：溥仪父应为醇亲王载沣（Tsai Feng）。此处应为作者笔误。

2   Dutch East Indies：荷属东印度，指荷兰殖民统治下的印度尼西亚。

第十一章

1   关于日俄战争对当时中国的影响，可以参见雷颐《百年前国人的日俄战争观》："此
    前十年的甲午战争使一些先进者感到中国的富强在于维新，但有此认识者毕竟少而
    又少，而此时的日俄战争再次给国人以强烈刺激，促人猛醒，社会舆论和观念发生了
    相当大的变化，越来越多的人相信立宪可以富国强兵、可以救亡图存，甚至某些原

先反对立宪的守旧人物也转而倾向支持立宪。这样，原本影响不大、只是少数人的立宪活动因此影响大增，迅速高涨，对全国性立宪运动的形成起了有力的推动作用。"

第十五章

1. 此处应为作者笔误。当时陆宗舆任币制局总裁（1913—1916 年任驻日公使），章宗祥任驻日公使。

2. Chinese Eastern Railway：中东铁路，系沙俄根据从中国所获之特权于 19 世纪末至 20 世纪初在中国东北地区修建的一条连接俄国西伯利亚和海参崴（符拉迪沃斯托克）的"丁"字形宽轨铁路，最初称"东清铁路"、"中国东省铁路"，后来又称"满洲铁路"、"中国长春铁路"等等。1905 年 9 月，根据沙俄与日本签订的《朴茨茅斯和约》，该铁路的长春至旅顺口的支线让给日本，称为"南满铁路"。1931 年九一八事变后，日本侵占中国东北并于次年建立伪满洲国。此后，中东铁路实际上由日伪与苏联共管。1933 年，中东铁路改称"北满铁路"。1945 年 8 月，根据中苏有关协定，北满铁路和南满铁路合并，改称"中国长春铁路"，简称"中长铁路"。1952 年 12 月，中长铁路移交给中国。

第十九章

1. 英文部分所附数字与实际有出入，以中文部分为准。

第二十章

1. South Manchurian Railway：参见第十五章注 2。

2. 此处指福建事变：1933 年 11 月 20 日，李济深、蔡廷锴、蒋光鼐等人以国民党第十九路军为主力，在福建福州发动的抗日反蒋事件。作者所称的"抗战前一年"疑为误记。

3. 此处关于南京国民政府修建铁路和电报线路的数字，中英文版有出入，以英文版记述较为准确（参见李新总主编《中华民国史·第八卷》，中华书局，2011）。

第二十二章

1. colonization：殖民，拓殖。在此语境中指将汉民族的居民、住民等送往偏远地区长期居住，建立商业或永久定居点。

2. 异族：相较于汉族而言的少数民族。此处的"异族入侵"实指边疆的少数民族进入中原。其中，蒙古族、满族进入中原之后建立了全国性政权。

第二十三章

1. 定都北京的应为元世祖忽必烈，成吉思汗之孙。

² 光绪去世于 1908 年 11 月 14 日。此处应为作者笔误。

³ 商朝（公元前 1600—前 1046）。

第二十五章

¹ China proper：中国本部，指中国历史上以汉文化为主导、汉族占人口绝大多数的地区，一般不包括东北、新疆、蒙古、青海、西藏等地区。此英文名词为当时的传统用法，今日主要用于历史或地理研究。

² China：参见第六章注 3。

³ Dairen：大连（Dalian）旧译。

⁴ Port Arthur：西方对旅顺（Lüshun）的称谓。

⁵ 此处疑原文有误。1161 年，金朝皇帝完颜亮（1122—1161）强征各族人民，大举南侵攻宋，在南宋境内作战时被部将杀死。据说他曾即兴题诗称："万里车书一混同，江南岂有别疆封？提兵百万西湖上，立马吴山第一峰。"（《鹤林玉露》卷一）

⁶ 此处疑原文有误。1276 年，元军攻占南宋都城。1279 年，南宋彻底灭亡。

⁷ 汉城：2005 年起中文译名作"首尔"。

第二十八章

¹ 张高峰，即张鼓峰。1938 年日、苏两国在此发生军事冲突，史称张鼓峰事件。

第二十九章

¹ Annam：安南，越南（Vietnam）的旧称。

第三十一章

¹ 中国国民党和中国共产党领导的抗日军队，分别担负着正面战场和敌后战场的作战任务，形成了共同抗击日本侵略者的战略态势。以国民党军队为主体的正面战场，组织了一系列大仗，特别是全国抗战初期的淞沪、忻口、徐州、武汉等战役，给日军以沉重打击。

² 此处与事实不符。长江注入东海，而非黄海（长江口北岸的启东角与韩国济州岛西南角的连线是黄海和东海的分界线）。

第三十三章

¹ Turkestan：土耳其斯坦。现习惯称突厥斯坦，一般指里海以东的广大中亚地区。

² 此处疑原文有误，疑应作 Micius（墨子）。

第三十四章

[1] 秦始皇（公元前 246 年—前 210 年在位）。

[2] 沈阳事变，即九一八事变。

编后记

　　蒋梦麟的著作《西潮》诞生于上世纪 40 年代，初以英文写就，1947 年以 *Tides from the West: A Chinese Autobiography* 为名由耶鲁大学出版社出版。《西潮》丹麦文译本于 1949 年出版。作者于上个世纪 50 年代将此书译为中文，同时在原英文版基础上对内容有所增订。中文版于 1958 年完成，同年开始在台湾《中华日报》刊载，第二年由台湾中华日报社出版。

　　《西潮》英文版写于抗日战争期间（中文版增订于十余年之后），因此作品无可避免地带有其所处时代的背景与印记。举例来说，当时对一些地名、译名、朝代称谓、民族关系、世界政治等的表述与当前的通行用法不尽一致，亦有部分词语已不再使用，因而不为读者所熟悉。中文版和英文版的写作时间间隔较长，因此文中两种语言并非严格对照，也存在一些数据上的出入。此外，因当时条件所限，书中也存在个别事实性错误。对于上述几类情况，本版尽可能保留作品原貌，适当作注说明于书后，供读者参阅。除保留原作英文注释外，其余中文注释为编者所加。特此说明。

2012 年 6 月